The genius of Christianity ; or, The spirit and beauty of the Christian religion

François-René Chateaubriand,
Charles 1807-1878 White

Bergen, ... Kev. 6. 93.

THE

Genius of Christianity;

OR THE

Spirit and Beauty of the Christian Religion.

BY

VISCOUNT DE CHATEAUBRIAND,

Author of "Travels in Greece and Palestine," "The Martyrs," "Atala," etc. etc.

A New and Complete Translation from the French.

WITH A

Preface, Biographical Notice of the Author, and Critical and Explanatory Notes.

BY CHARLES I. WHITE, D.D.

ELEVENTH REVISED EDITION.

BALTIMORE:
PUBLISHED BY JOHN MURPHY & CO.
PHILADELPHIA......J. B. LIPPINCOTT & CO.
1875.

PREFACE.

In 1798, while the author of this work was residing in London, exiled from France by the horrors of the Revolution, and gaining a subsistence by the productions of his pen, which were tinctured with the skepticism and infidelity of the times, he was informed of the death of his venerable mother, whose last days had been embittered by the recollection of his errors, and who had left him, in her dying moments, a solemn admonition to retrace his steps. The thought of having saddened the old age of that tender and religious parent who had borne him in her womb, overwhelmed him with confusion; the tears gushed from his eyes, and the Christian sentiments in which he had been educated returned under the impulses of a generous and affectionate heart: "*I wept and I believed.*" But the trouble which harassed his mind did not entirely vanish, until he had formed the plan of redeeming his first publications by the consecration of his splendid abilities to the honor of religion. Such was the origin of the *Genius of Christianity*, in the composition of which he labored with "all the ardor of a son who was erecting a mausoleum to his mother."*

* *Mémoires d' Outre-Tombe*, vol. i.

When this work made its appearance, in 1802, infidelity was the order of the day in France. That beautiful country, whose people had once held so prominent a rank among the Catholic nations of Europe, presented but a vast scene of ruins, the fatal consequences of that systematic war which impious sophists had waged against religion during the latter half of the eighteenth century. The Revolution had swept away in its desolating course all the landmarks of the ancient society. Churches and altars had been overthrown; the priests of God had been massacred, or driven into exile; asylums of virtue and learning had been profaned and laid waste; every thing august and sacred had disappeared. In the political and social sphere the same terrific destruction was witnessed. After a succession of convulsions, which had overthrown the Bourbon dynasty, and during which the passions of men had rioted amid the wildest anarchy and the most savage acts of bloodshed, the chief authority became vested in a consul whose mission was to re-establish social order, and whose efforts in that direction were gladly welcomed by the nation, grown weary and sick, as it were, of the dreadful calamities that had come upon them. It was an auspicious moment for the fearless champion of Christianity, to herald the claims of that religion whose doctrines constitute the only safe guide of the governing and the governed. But, among a people who to a great extent had conceived a profound antipathy to the theory and practice of religion, by the artful and persevering efforts of an infidel philosophy to render the Christian name an object of derision and contempt, a new method of argument was necessary to obtain even a hearing in the case, much more to bring back the popular mind to a due veneration for the Church and her teachings. It would have been useless, when the great principles of religious belief were disregarded, when the authority of ages was set at naught, to undertake the vindication of Christianity by the exhibition of those external evidences which demonstrate its divine origin. Men had become deluded with the idea that the Christian religion had been a serious obstacle in the way of human progress; that, having been invented in a barbarous age, its dogmas were absurd and its ceremonies ridiculous; that it tended to enslave the mind, opposed the arts and sciences, and was in general hostile to the liberty of man and the advancement of civilization. It was necessary, therefore, in order to refute these errors, to exhibit the intrinsic excellence and beauty of the Christian religion, to show its analogy with the dictates of natural reason, its admirable correspondence with the instincts of the human heart, its ennobling influence upon literature and the arts, its beneficent effects upon society, its wonderful achievements for the civilization and happiness of nations, its infinite superiority over all other systems, in elevating the character, improving the condition, and answering the wants of man, under all the circumstances of life; in a word, to show, according to the design of our author, *not that the Christian religion is excellent because it comes from God, but that it comes from God because it is excellent.*

For this purpose, he passes in review the principal

nysteries and tenets of Christianity, draws a compa-ison between Christian and pagan literature, displays he advantages which painting, sculpture, and the ther arts, have derived from religious inspiration, its ccordance with the scenes of nature and the senti-nents of the heart, describes the wonders of mis-ionary enterprise, the extensive services of the mo-astic orders, and concludes with a general survey of he immense blessings conferred upon mankind by he Christian Church. In displaying this magnificent icture to the contemplation of the reader, the author mploys all the resources of ancient and modern earning, the information derived from extensive ravel and a profound study of human nature, and hose ornaments of style which the loftiest poetry and he most glowing fancy can place at his command. n turn the philosopher, the historian, the traveller, nd the poet, he adopts every means of promoting the reat end in view,—to enamor the heart of man with he charms of religion, and to prove that she is emi-ently the source of all that is "lovely and of good re-ort," of all that is beautiful and sublime. Among all he works of Chateaubriand, none, perhaps, is so re-narkable as this for that combination of impressive loquence, descriptive power, and pathetic sentiment, hich imparts such a fascination to his style, and hich caused Napoleon I. to observe, that it was "not he style of Racine, but of a prophet; that nature had iven him the sacred flame, and it breathed in all his vorks."

The publication of such a work at such a time could iot but enlist against it a powerful opposition among the advocates of infidelity; but its superior excellence and brilliant character obtained an easy triumph over the critics who had attempted to crush its influence. In two years it had passed through seven editions; and such was the popularity it acquired, that it was translated into the Italian, German, and Russian languages. In France, the friends of religion hailed it as the olive branch of peace and hope—a messenger of heaven, sent forth to solace the general affliction, to heal the wounds of so many desolate hearts, after the frightful deluge of impiety which had laid waste that unfortunate country. On the other hand, the wavering in faith, and even they who had been perverted by the sophistry of the times, were drawn to a profitable investigation of religion, by the new and irresistible charms that had been thrown around it. It cannot be denied that the *Genius of Christianity* exerted a most powerful and beneficial influence in Europe for the good of religion and the improvement of literature. The eloquent Balmes has well said: "The mysterious hand which governs the universe seems to hold in reserve, for every great crisis of society, an extraordinary man. . . . . Atheism was bathing France in a sea of tears and blood. An unknown man silently traverses the ocean, ... returns to his native soil." . . . . He finds there "the ruins and ashes of ancient temples devoured by the flames or destroyed by violence; the remains of a multitude of innocent victims, buried in the graves which formerly afforded an asylum to persecuted Christians. He observes, however, that something is in agitation: he sees that religion is about to redescend upon France, like consolation upon the unfortunate, or the breath of life upon a corpse. From that moment he hears on all sides a concert of celestial harmony; the inspirations of meditation and solitude revive and ferment in his great soul; transported out of himself, and ravished into ecstasy, he sings with a tongue of fire the glories of religion, he reveals the delicacy and beauty of the relations between religion and nature, and in surpassing language he points out to astonished men the mysterious golden chain which connects the heavens and the earth. That man was Chateaubriand."*

The eloquent work here referred to must, we may easily conceive, be productive of good in any age and in any country. Although the peculiar circumstances that prompted its execution and proved so favorable to its first success have passed away, the vast amount of useful information which it embodies will always be consulted with pleasure and advantage by the scholar and the general reader; while the "vestrure of beauty and holiness" which it has thrown round the Church cannot fail to be extensively instrumental in awakening a respectful attention to her indisputable claims. One of the saddest evils of our age and country is the spirit of indifferentism which infects all classes of society; and the question, among a vast number, is not what system of Christianity is true, but whether it is worth their while to make any system the subject of their serious inquiry. Such minds, wholly absorbed by the considerations of this world, would recoil from a doctrinal or theological essay with almost the same aversion as would be excited by the most nauseous medicine. But deck religious truth in the garb of fancy, attended by the muses, and dispensing blessings on every side, and the most apathetic soul will be arrested by the beauteous spectacle, as the child is attracted and won by the maternal smile. Among unbelievers and sectarians of different complexions, who discard all mysteries, who consult only their reason and feelings as the source and rule of religious belief, who look upon Catholicism as something *effete*, and unsuited to the enlightenment of the age, this work will be read with the most beneficial results. It will warm into something living, consistent, and intelligible, the cold and dreamy speculations of the rationalist; it will indicate the grand fountain-head whence flow in all their fervor and efficiency those noble sentiments which for the modern philosopher and philanthropist have but a theoretical existence. It will hold up to view the inexhaustible resources of Catholicism, in meeting all the exigencies of society, all the wants of man, and triumphantly vindicate her undoubted claims to superiority over all other systems in advancing the work of true civilization.

It was to establish this truth that Balmes composed his splendid work on the *Comparative Influence of Protestantism and Catholicity*, and Digby described the *Ages of Faith*, and the *Compitum*, or *Meeting of the Ways*. These productions are of a kindred class with the *Genius of Christianity*, and the former embraces to a certain extent the same range of subject, having in view to display the internal evidences of Catholicity, as derived from its beneficial influence upon European civilization. But Chateaubriand was the first to enter the field against the enemies of religion, clad in that effective armor which is peculiarly adapted to the circumstances of modern times. Without pretending in the least to question the necessity or detract from the advantages of theological discussion, we are firmly convinced that the mode of argument adopted by our author is, in general, and independently of the practical character of the age in which we live, the most effectual means of obtaining for the Church that favorable consideration which will result in the recognition of her divine institution. "The foolish man hath said in his heart, there is no God."* The disorder of the heart, arising partly from passion, partly from prejudice, shuts out from the mind the light of truth. Hence, whoever wins the heart to an admiration of the salutary influences which that truth has exerted in every age for the happiness of man, will have gained an essential point, and will find little difficulty in convincing the understanding, or securing a profitable attention to the grave expositions of the theologian and the controversialist.

Such were the considerations that led to the present translation of the *Genius of Christianity*. The work was presented in an English dress for the first time in England; and the same edition, reprinted in this country in 1815, would have been republished now, if it had not been discovered that the translator had taken unwarrantable liberties with the original, omitting innumerable passages and sometimes whole chapters, excluding sentences and paragraphs of the highest importance, those particularly which gave to the author's argument its peculiar force in favor of Catholicism. Such, in fact, was the number and nature of these omissions, that, with the introduction of occasional notes, they detracted, in a great measure, from the author's purpose, and gave to a latitudinarian Christianity an undue eminence, which he never contemplated. With these important exceptions, and various inaccuracies in rendering the text, the translation of Mr. Shoberl has considerable merit. In preparing the present edition of the work, we have furnished the entire matter of the original production, with the exception of two or three notes in the Appendix, which have been condensed, as being equally acceptable to the reader in that form. Nearly one hundred pages have been supplied which were never before presented to the public in English. In rendering the text, we have examined and compared different French editions; but there is little variation between that of 1854 and its predecessors. Where the sense of the author appeared obscure or erroneous, we have introduced critical and explanatory notes. Those marked S and K have been retained from Mr. Shoberl's translation; those marked T were prepared for this edition. In offering this translation to the public, we take pleasure in stating that we have made a free use of that to which we have alluded, especially in the latter portion of the work. We have also consulted the translation by the Rev. E. O'Donnel, which was issued in Paris in 1854. In that edition, however, nearly one-half of the original production has been omitted, and the order of the contents has been entirely changed.

In conclusion, we present this work to the public with the hope that it may render the name of its illustrious author more extensively known among us, and may awaken a more general interest in the study of that religion which, as Montesquieu observes, "while it seems only to have in view the felicity of the other life, constitutes the happiness of this."

THE TRANSLATOR.

Pikesville, Md. April, 1856.

CONTENTS.

PART I.

DOGMAS AND TENETS.

BOOK I.

MYSTERIES AND SACRAMENTS.

BOOK II.

VIRTUES AND MORAL LAWS.

BOOK III.

THE TRUTHS OF THE SCRIPTURES—THE FALL OF MAN.

BOOK IV.

CONTINUATION OF THE TRUTHS OF SCRIPTURE—OBJECTIONS AGAINST THE SYSTEM OF MOSES.

BOOK V.

THE EXISTENCE OF GOD DEMONSTRATED BY THE WONDERS OF NATURE.

BOOK VI.

THE IMMORTALITY OF THE SOUL PROVED BY THE MORAL LAW AND THE FEELINGS.

PART II.

THE POETIC OF CHRISTIANITY.

BOOK I.

GENERAL SURVEY OF CHRISTIAN EPIC POEMS.

BOOK II.

OF POETRY CONSIDERED IN ITS RELATIONS TO MAN.

Characters.

BOOK III.

OF POETRY CONSIDERED IN ITS RELATIONS TO MAN—THE SUBJECT CONTINUED.

The Passions.

BOOK IV.

OF THE MARVELLOUS; OR, OF POETRY IN ITS RELATIONS TO SUPERNATURAL BEINGS.

BOOK V.

THE BIBLE AND HOMER.

PART III.

THE FINE ARTS AND LITERATURE.

BOOK I.

THE FINE ARTS.

BOOK II.

PHILOSOPHY.

BOOK III.

HISTORY.

BOOK IV.

ELOQUENCE.

BOOK V.

THE HARMONIES OF THE CHRISTIAN RELIGION WITH THE SCENES OF NATURE AND THE PASSIONS OF THE HUMAN HEART.

PART IV.

WORSHIP.

BOOK I.

CHURCHES, ORNAMENTS, SINGING, PRAYERS, ETC.

BOOK II.

TOMBS.

BOOK III.

GENERAL VIEW OF THE CLERGY.

BOOK IV.

MISSIONS.

BOOK V.

MILITARY ORDERS OR CHIVALRY.

BOOK VI.

SERVICES RENDERED TO MANKIND BY THE CLERGY AND BY THE CHRISTIAN RELIGION IN GENERAL.

NOTICE

OF THE

VISCOUNT DE CHATEAUBRIAND.*

René Francis Augustus, Viscount de Chateaubriand, was born at Saint-Malo, in France, on the 4th of September, 1768. His family, on the paternal side, one of the most ancient in Brittany, descended in a direct line, by the barons of Chateaubriand, from Thierri, grandson of Alain III., who was the sovereign of the Armorican peninsula. Having commenced his classical studies at the college of Dol, he continued them at Rennes, where he had Moreau for a rival, and completed them at Dinan in the company of Broussais. Of a proud disposition, and sensitive to a reprimand, young Chateaubriand distinguished himself by a very precocious intellect and an extraordinary memory. His father, having destined him for the naval profession, sent him to Brest for the purpose of passing an examination; but having remained some time without receiving his commission, he returned to Combourg, and manifested some inclination for the ecclesiastical state. Diverted, however, from this project by the reading of pernicious books, he

* Compiled chiefly from an article in Feller's *Dictionnaire Historique.*

exchanged his sentiments of piety for those of infidelity, and in his solitary situation, with the passions for his guides, he became the sport of the most extravagant fancies. Weary of life, he had even to struggle against the temptation of committing suicide; but he was relieved from these sombre thoughts by the influence of his eldest brother, the Count of Combourg, who obtained for him a lieutenancy in the regiment of Navarre. After the death of his father, in 1786, he left his military post at Cambrai, to look after his inheritance, and settled with his family at Paris. Through the means of his brother, who had married Mademoiselle de Rosambo, grand-daughter of Malesherbes, he was introduced into society and presented at court, which obtained for him at once the rank of a captain of cavalry. It was designed to place him in the order of Malta; but Chateaubriand now began to evince his literary predilections. He cultivated the society of Ginguené, Lebrun, Champfort, Delisle de Salles, and was much gratified in having been permitted, through them, to publish in the *Almanach des Muses* a poem which he had composed in the forest of Combourg. In 1789 he attended the session of the States of Brittany, and took the sword in order to repulse the mob that besieged the hall of assembly. On his return to Paris, after the opening of the States-general, he witnessed the first scenes of the revolution, and in 1790 he quit the service on the occasion of a revolt that had taken place in the regiment of Navarre. Alarmed by the popular excesses, and having a great desire to travel, he embarked in January, 1791, for the United States of America. He hoped, with the advice and support of Malesherbes, to discover a north-west passage to the Polar Sea, which Hearn had already descried in 1772. A few days after his arrival at Baltimore, he proceeded to Philadelphia, and having a letter of introduction to General Washington from Colonel Armand, (Marquis de la Rouërie,) who had served in the war of American Independence, he lost no time in calling on the President. Washington received him with great kindness and with his usual simplicity of manners. On the following day, Chateaubriand had the honor of dining with the President, whom he never saw afterward, but whose character left an indelible impression upon his mind. "There is a virtue," he says, "in the look of a great man."* On leaving Philadelphia, he visited New York, Boston, and the other principal cities of the Union, where he was surprised to find in the manners of the people the cast of modern times, instead of that ancient character which he had pictured to himself. From the haunts of civilized life he turned to those wild regions which were then chiefly inhabited by the untutored savage, and as he travelled from forest to forest, from tribe to tribe, his poetical mind feasted upon the grandeur and beauty of that virginal nature which presented itself to his contemplation. At the falls of Niagara he was twice in the most imminent danger of losing his life, by his enthusiastic desire to enjoy the most impressive view of the wonderful cataract.

While thus setting to profit his opportunities of ob-

* *Mémoires d' Outre-Tombe.*

servation in the new world, Chateaubriand learned from the public prints the flight and capture of Louis XVI., and the progress of the French emigration. He at once resolved upon returning to his native country. After a narrow escape from shipwreck, he arrived at Havre in the beginning of 1792, whence he proceeded to St. Malo, where he had the happiness of again embracing his mother. Here also he formed a matrimonial alliance with Mademoiselle de Lavigne, a lady of distinction. A few months after, in company with his brother, he set out for Germany with a view to join the army of French nobles who had rallied in defence of their country. At the siege of Thionville, his life was saved by the manuscript of *Atala*, a literary production which he carried about him, and which turned a shot from the enemy. He was, however, severely wounded in the thigh on the same occasion, and, to add to his misfortunes, he was attacked with the small-pox. In this suffering condition he undertook a journey of six hundred miles on foot, and was more than once reduced to the very verge of the grave by the pressure of disease and the extraordinary privations he was compelled to undergo. One evening he stretched himself to rest in a ditch, from which he never expected to rise. In this situation he was discovered by a party attached to the Prince of Ligne, who threw him into a wagon and carried him to the walls of Namur. As he made his way through that city, crawling on his knees and hands, he excited the compassion of some good women of the place, who afforded him what assistance they could. Having at length reached Brussels, he was there recognised by his brother, who happened to meet him, and from whom he received every aid and attention. Though far from having recovered his strength, he left this place for Ostend, where he embarked in a fisherman's boat for the Isle of Jersey. Here he met with a portion of his family who had emigrated from France, and among whom he received the attentions which his suffering condition demanded. He soon after repaired to London, where he lived for some time in a state of poverty. Too haughty to apply for assistance to the British government, he relied altogether upon his own efforts for the means of subsistence. He spent the day in translating, and the night in composing his Essay on Revolutions. But this incessant labor soon undermined his health, and there being moreover little to do in the way of translating, the unfortunate exile experienced for some days the cravings of hunger. Happily, at this juncture, his services were requested by a body of learned men who, under the direction of the pastor of Beccles, were preparing a history of the county of Suffolk. His part of the labor consisted in explaining some French manuscripts of the twelfth century, the knowledge of which was necessary to the authors of the enterprise.

On his return to London, Chateaubriand completed his *Essai sur les Révolutions*, which was published in 1797. This work produced quite a sensation, won for him the commendations and sympathy of the French nobility then in England, and placed him in relation with Montlosier, Delille and Fontanes. He was sorely tried, however, by the afflictions of his family. He had received the distressing intelligence that his brother and sister-in-law, with his friend Malesherbes, had been guillotined by the revolutionary harpies, and that his wife and sister had been imprisoned at Rennes, and his aged mother at Paris. This pious lady, after having suffered a long confinement, died in 1798, with a prayer on her lips for the conversion of her son. Young Chateaubriand was not insensible to this prayer of his venerated parent. "She charged one of my sisters," he writes, "to recall me to a sense of that religion in which I had been educated, and my sister made known to me her wish. When the letter reached me beyond the water, my sister also had departed this life, having succumbed under the effects of her imprisonment. Those two voices coming up from the grave, and that death which had now become the interpreter of death, struck me with peculiar force. I became a Christian. I did not yield to any great supernatural light: my conviction came from the heart. I wept, and I believed." His ideas having thus undergone a serious change, he resolved to consecrate to religion the pen which had given expression to the skepticism of the times, and he planned at once the immortal work, *Le Génie du Christianisme.*

As soon as Buonaparte had been appointed First Consul, Chateaubriand returned to France under an assumed name, associated himself with Fontanes in the editorship of the *Mercure*, and in 1801 published his *Atala*. This romance, attacked by some, but enthusiastically received by the greater number, was eminently successful, and added to the circle of the author's friends many illustrious names. Madame Bacciocl [illegible] Buonaparte became his protectors, while he was brought into intercourse with Joubert, de Bonald, La Harpe, Chênedollé, Mesdames Récamier and de Beaumont. His design, in the publication of *Atala*, was to introduce himself to the public, and to prepare the way for the *Géne du Christianisme*, which appeared in 1802. No sooner was it issued from the press, than the disciples of Voltaire stamped it as the offspring of superstition, and pamphleteers and journalists united in visiting the author and his work with proud contempt; but the friends of religion and of poetry applauded the intentions and admired the talents of the writer.

Buonaparte, who was at this time busy with the *concordat*, was desirous of seeing the man who so ably seconded his views; and, with the hope of attaching him to his fortune, appointed him first secretary of Cardinal Fesch, then ambassador to the Court of Rome. When the new diplomatist was presented to Pius VII., this venerable pontiff was reading the *Génie du Christianisme*. The honors of the French embassy had no great attractions for our author. Averse to being an instrument of the tortuous policy which it began to display, he resigned his post and returned to Paris. Napoleon, sensible of his eminent abilities, sought rather to conquer than to crush his independent spirit, and appointed him minister plenipotentiary to the Valais. He received this commission the day before the Duke d'Enghien, who had been seized on foreign territory, in contempt of the law of nations, was shot in the ditch of Vincennes. That very evening, while fear or astonishment still pervaded the minds of all, Chateaubriand sent in his resignation.

Napoleon could not but feel the censure implied in this bold protestation, which was the more meritorious as it was the only expression of fearless opposition to his proscriptive measure. He did not, however, betray his displeasure, nor did he disturb the courageous writer in whom he began to detect an enemy; on the contrary, in order to draw him into his service, he made him every offer that could flatter his interest or ambition. The refusal of Chateaubriand to accept any post under the consular *régime* made him obnoxious to Napoleon, who gratified his resentment by crippling the literary resources of his political adversary.

Under these circumstances, he paid a visit to Madame de Stael, who had become his friend by a community of sentiment and misfortune, and who was living in exile at Coppet. The following year—1806—he executed his design of a pilgrimage to the Holy Land. Revisiting Italy, he embarked for Greece, spent some time among the ruins of Sparta and the monuments of Athens, passed over to Smyrna, thence to the island of Cyprus, and at length reached Jerusalem. Here, having venerated the relics of the noble crusaders, and especially that tomb "which alone will have nothing to send forth at the end of time," he sailed for Egypt, explored the fields of Carthage, passed over to Spain, and amid the ruins of the Alhambra wrote *Le dernier des Abencerages*. On his return to France, in May, 1807, he published in the *Mercure*, which partly belonged to him, an article which greatly incensed the government against him. The emperor spoke of having him executed on the steps of [illegible] T[illegible]; but, after having issued the order to arrest him, he was satisfied with depriving him of his interest in the *Mercury*. Chateaubriand now retired to his possessions near Aulnay, where he wrote his *Itinéraire*, *Moïse*, and *Les Martyrs*. When the first-mentioned work was about to appear, in 1811, the author was notified by the government that the publication would not be permitted, unless he would introduce into its pages a eulogy of the emperor. Chateaubriand refused to submit to such a condition; but having been informed that his publisher would suffer materially by the suppression of the work, he was induced by this consideration, to do, in some measure, what neither fear nor personal interest could extort from him. In complying with the requisition of the authorities, he alluded in truthful language to the exploits of the French armies, and to the fame of their general who had so often led them on to victory; but he carefully abstained from signalizing the acts of a government whose policy was so much at variance with the principles which he professed.

Buonaparte had still some hope of gaining over the independent and fearless writer. When a vacancy had occurred in the French Academy by the death of Chénier, the situation was offered to Chateaubriand, who was also selected by the emperor for the general superintendence of the imperial libraries, with a salary equal to that of a first-class embassy. Custom, however, required that the member-elect should pronounce the eulogy of his predecessor; but in this instance the independence of Chateaubriand gave sufficient reason to think that, instead of heralding the merit of Chénier, who had participated in the judicial murder of

Louis XVI., he would denounce in unmeasured terms the crimes of the French Revolution. His inaugural address having been submitted, according to custom, to a committee of inspection, they decided that it could not be delivered by the author. The emperor, moreover, having obtained some knowledge of its contents, which formed an eloquent protest against the revolutionary doctrines and the despotic tendencies of the existing government, he was exasperated against the writer, and in his excitement he paced his room to and fro, striking his forehead, and exclaiming—"Am I, then, nothing more than a usurper? Ah, poor France! how much do you still need an instructor!" The admission of Chateaubriand to the Academy was indefinitely postponed.

But the star of Buonaparte had now begun to wane. The allied armies having entered France, Chateaubriand openly declared himself in favor of the ancient dynasty. His sentiments were unequivocally expressed in a pamphlet, which he published in 1814, under the title of *Buonaparte et les Bourbons*, and which Louis XVIII. acknowledged to have been worth to him an army. Upon the restoration of this monarch to the throne, Chateaubriand was appointed ambassador to Sweden; but he had not yet taken his departure, when it was announced that Buonaparte had again appeared on the soil of France. Our author advised the king to await his rival in Paris; but this suggestion was not followed. Louis XVIII. proceeded to Gand, where Chateaubriand was a member of his council, in the capacity of Minister of the Interior, and drew up an able rep[illegible]tion of France, which was considered as a political manifesto. After the second restoration of the Bourbons, he declined a portfolio in connection with Fouché and Talleyrand. Called to a seat in the House of Peers, he attracted considerable attention by some of his speeches. Not less a friend of the Bourbons than of the liberties guaranteed by the charter, he endeavored to conciliate the rights of the throne with those of the nation; and he beheld with indignation men who had been too prominent during the revolutionary period, admitted to the royal councils and to various offices of the administration. Under the influence of these sentiments he published, in 1816, a pamphlet entitled *La Monarchie selon la Charte,* which was an able and popular defence of constitutional government; but by the order of de Cazes, president of the council, the work was suppressed, and its author, although acquitted before the tribunals, was no longer numbered among the ministers of state. Deprived of his station and of his income, Chateaubriand was compelled to dispose of his library as a means of subsistence. At the same time, he established the *Conservateur,* a periodical opposed to the *Minerve,* the ministerial organ, and, in conjunction with the Duc de Montmorency and others, he carried on a vigorous war against the favorite of the crown. The cabinet of de Cazes could not withstand such an antagonist; the daily assaults of the *Conservateur* made it waver, and the assassination of the Duke of Berry completed its downfall. On the accession of M. de Villele to power, Chateaubriand accepted the mission to Berlin. While he occupied this post, he won the attachment of the royal family, the confidence of the

Prussian ministers, and the intimate friendship of the Duchess of Cumberland. In 1822, he succeeded M. de Cazes as the representative of France at the court of St. James, and soon afterward crossed the Alps as a delegate to the Congress of Verona. Having distinguished himself in this assembly by eloquently pleading the cause of Greece, and defending the interests of his own country in relation to the Spanish war, he returned to France and became Minister of Foreign Affairs. While he held this station, he succeeded in effecting the intervention of his government in behalf of Ferdinand VII., notwithstanding the opposition of M. de Villele. He could not, however, maintain his position long, with the antipathies of the king and the jealousy of his prime minister against him. He accordingly retired from the cabinet in 1824, and reentered the ranks of the liberal opposition, of which he soon became the leader. The contributions of his pen to the columns of the *Journal des Débats* allowed not a moment's truce to the ministry. He assailed all the measures of the cabinet; the reduction of rents, the rights of primogeniture, the law of sacrilege, the dissolution of the national guard, all were denounced by him with a vigor and constancy which accomplished the fall of M. de Villele.

Such was the state of things when Louis XVIII. was summoned from life; and Chateaubriand, carefully distinguishing the cause of the dynasty from that of its ministers, who, according to him, were unworthy of their position, published a pamphlet entitled *Le roi est mort, vive le roi!* which was a new proof of his devotedne[illegible] Bourbons. After the inauguration of Charles X. and the formation of the Martignac cabinet, he accepted a mission to Rome, after having declined the offer of a ministerial position. Upon the accession, however, of Prince Polignac to the office of Foreign Affairs, he immediately sent in his resignation, and used his influence against the administration. The events which soon followed justified his political views. The fatal ordinances of the government, in July, 1830, against the liberty of the press and the right of suffrage, precipitated a revolution, which resulted in the exile of the *elder branch of the Bourbons.* In this crisis, Chateaubriand made an eloquent protest, in the House of Peers, against the change of dynasty, and advocated with all his ability the recognition of the Duke of Bordeaux and the appointment of a regent during his minority; but his efforts were fruitless, and the Duke of Orleans rose to power, under the name of Louis Philippe.

Unwilling to pledge himself to this new state of things, he relinquished his dignity of peer of the realm, with his public honors and pensions, and retired poor into private life. The following year, however, he was roused from his political slumbers, and he published a pamphlet on the *Nouvelle Restauration*, and, in 1832, a *Mémoire sur la Captivité de Madame la Duchesse de Berry*, whom he had visited in her prison; and in 1833 appeared another work, entitled *Conclusions.* This last production was seized by the government, and the author was arraigned before the tribunals, but was acquitted by the jury. After a visit to Italy and the south of France, Chateaubriand paid his respects to the family of Charles X., at Prague. On his return to Paris, he took no part in public affairs, and left his domestic privacy only to visit the Abbaye-aux-Bois, where Madame Recamier assembled in her mansion the flower of the old French society. During the remainder of his life, he was occupied in the study of English literature, in writing the *Life of the Abbé de Rancé*, and preparing his *Mémoires d'Outre-Tombe.* The political revolution of February, 1848, which hurled Louis Philippe from the throne, did not surprise him, because he had predicted it in 1830. Drawing near to his end when the insurrection of June broke forth at Paris, he spoke with admiration of the heroic death of the archbishop, and, having received the last rites of religion with great sentiments of piety, he expired on the 4th of July, 1848. His remains were conveyed to St. Malo, his native city, and, in compliance with his own request, were deposited in a tomb which the civil authority had prepared for him under a rock projecting into the sea. M. Ampere, in the name of the French Academy, delivered an address on the spot, and the Duke de Noailles, who succeeded him in that illustrious society, pronounced his eulogy at a public session held on the 6th of December, 1849.

Chateaubriand had rather a haughty bearing, and spoke little. He was fond of praise, and bestowed it liberally upon others. With republican tastes, he defended and served the monarchical system as the established order, and was devoted to the Bourbon dynasty as a matter of honor. His political sentiments never changed, and he never ceased to be the advocate of enlightened liberty. His religious views once formed, [illegible] by his writings, and honored them in the practice of his life. His disinterestedness was equal to his genius, and his beneficence was continually seconded by that of his wife. They were the founders of the asylum *Marie Thérèse* at Paris, a home for clergymen who are disabled by infirmity.

The works of Chateaubriand are: *Essai Historique, Politique, et Moral, sur les Révolutions Anciennes et Modernes, considerées dans leur rapport avec la Révolution Française.* Londres, 1797, in 8vo, tome i. In this work, the author, in his attempts to assimilate the events and personages of the French Revolution to those of antiquity, displays more imagination than reflection. The style as well as the substance of the volume betrays the youth and inexperience of the writer. He completed this *Essai* in 1814, observing that his political views had suffered no change. This was in fact true, as he espoused in his work the principles of constitutional monarchy, to which he had always adhered. To the honor of the author, he did not assert the same irreligious sentiments that had appeared in the *Essai.* These he nobly retracted in a series of notes which he added to the work, without deeming it necessary to expunge the objectionable passages from the context.

Atala, ou les Amours de deux Sauvages dans le Désert. Paris, 1801, in 18mo. This little romance has been translated into several languages, and derives a singular charm from the vivid descriptions and impassioned sentiments which it contains. Religion, however, has justly censured the too voluptuous character of certain passages, which are unfit for the youthful eye.

Le Génie du Christianisme; or, *The Genius of Christianity.* Paris, 1802, 3 vols. 8vo. Of all the works of Chateaubriand, this had the happiest influence upon his age and country. Voltaire and his school had too well succeeded in representing the dogmas of Christianity as absurd, its ceremonial ridiculous, and its influence hostile to the progress of knowledge. But Chateaubriand, by the magic power of his pen, produced a revolution in public sentiment. Addressing himself chiefly to the imagination and the heart, he compares the poets, philosophers, historians, orators, and artists of modern times with those of pagan antiquity, and shows how religion dignifies and improves all that breathes its hallowed inspiration. The inaccuracies of thought and expression which appeared in the first edition, were corrected in the subsequent issues of the work.

René, an episode of the *Génie du Christianisme.* Paris, 1807, in 12mo. In this fiction the writer depicts the advantages of religious seclusion, by showing the wretchedness of solitude where God is not the sustaining thought in the soul of man.

Les Martyrs; ou, Le Triomphe de la Religion Chrétienne. Paris, 1810, 3 vols. in 8vo. The subject and characters of this work are borrowed from antiquity, sacred and profane. The author proves what he advances in his *Genius of Christianity*—that religion, far more than mythology, ministers to poetic inspiration. The expiring civilization of paganism, Christianity emerging from the catacombs, the manners of the first Christians and those of the barbarous tribes of Germany, furnish t[illegible] and interesting theme, which he presents with all the attractions of the most cultivated style.

Itinéraire de Paris à Jerusalem, et de Jerusalem à Paris, &c. Paris, 1811, 3 vols. in 8vo. This work—one of the most interesting from the pen of the illustrious author—is characterized by beauty and fidelity of description, grand and poetic allusions, a happy choice of anecdote, sound erudition, and a perfect acquaintance with antiquity. With the publication of his travels in the East, Chateaubriand considered his literary life brought to a close, as he soon after entered the career of politics, which continued until the downfall of Charles X. in 1830.

During that period he published a large number of works, relating chiefly to the political questions of the day. The more important are those entitled *De Buonaparte, des Bourbons, &c.*, 1814; *Réflexions Politiques*, 1814; *Mélanges de Politique*, 1816; *De la Monarchie selon la Charte*, 1816. This treatise may be considered as the political programme of the author, and is divided into two parts. In the first he exposes the principles of representative government, the liberty of thought and of the press, &c.; and in the second he urges the necessity of guarding against revolutionary license, and points out the rights of the clergy and the popular system of public instruction. In his *Études Historiques*, 2 vols. 8vo, 1826, he lays down three kinds of truth as forming the basis of all social order:—religious truth, which is found only in the Christian faith; philosophical truth, or the freedom of the human mind in its efforts to discover and perfect intellectual, moral, and physical science; political truth, or the union of order with liberty. From the alliance, separation, or collision of these three principles, all the facts of history have emanated. The world's inhabitants he divides into three classes: pagans, Christians, and barbarians; and shows how, in the first centuries of our era, they existed together in a confused way, afterward commingled in the medieval age, and finally constituted the society which now covers a vast portion of the globe. During the same year (1826) the author published his *Natchez*, 2 vols. 8vo, containing his recollections of America, and *Aventures du dernier des Abencerages*, in 8vo,—a romance not less charming than his *Atala*, and free from the objectionable character of that publication. The works that came from the author's pen after his retirement into private life, are, besides those mentioned above, *Essai sur la Litérature Anglaise*, &c., 2 vols. 8vo; *Le Paradis Perdu de Milton: traduction nouvelle*, 2 vols. 8vo, 1836; *Le Congrés de Verone*, 2 vols. 8vo, 1838; *Vie de l'Abbé de Rancé*, in 8vo, 1844,—rather a picture of the manners of the French court in the seventeenth century than a life of the distinguished Trappist. But the pen of the immortal writer still displays the vigorous and glowing style of his earlier productions, though certain passages criticized by the religious press show that it is not unexceptionable.

The *Mémoires d'Outre-Tombe*, a posthumous work of the author, was published at Paris in ten, and has been reprinted in this country in five volumes. Chateaubriand here sketches with a bold hand the picture of his whole life; a mixture of reverie and action, of misfortune and contest, of glory and humiliation. We see gro[illegible] the prominent events of contemporaneous history, which he explains and clears up. A remarkable variety exists in the subject-matter and in the tone of this work. The gayest and most magnificent descriptions of nature often appear side by side with the keenest satire upon society, and the loftiest considerations of philosophy and morals are blended with the most simple narrative. The vanity of human things appears here with striking effect, and the sadness which they inspire becomes still more impressive under the touches of that impassioned eloquence which describes them. At times we discover in the writer the ingenious wit, and the clear, expressive, and eminently French prose, of Voltaire. These *Mémoires*, however, are not faultless. The first part, in which he portrays the dreamy aspirations of his youth, may prove dangerous to the incautious reader. Critics charge the author with an affectation of false simplicity, with the abuse of neology, and with a puerile vanity in speaking either in his own praise or otherwise. They pretend, also, that the work is overwrought, contains contradictions, and betrays sometimes in the same page the changing impressions of the author.

But, whatever the defects of Chateaubriand's style, he is universally allowed by the French of all parties to be their first writer. "He is also," says Alison, "a profound scholar and an enlightened thinker. His knowledge of history and classical literature is equalled only by his intimate acquaintance with the early annals of the Church and the fathers of the Catholic faith; while in his speeches delivered in the Chamber of Peers since the Restoration, will be found not only the most eloquent, but the most complete and satisfactory, dissertations on the political state of France during that period which are anywhere to be met with. . . . . Few are aware that he is, without one single exception, the most eloquent writer of the present age; that, independent of politics, he has produced many works on morals, religion, and history, destined for lasting endurance; that his writings combine the strongest love of rational freedom with the warmest inspiration of Christian devotion; that he is, as it were, the link between the feudal and the revolutionary ages, retaining from the former its generous and elevated feeling, and inhaling from the latter its acute and fearless investigation. The last pilgrim, with devout feelings, to the holy sepulchre, he was the first supporter of constitutional freedom in France, discarding thus from former times their bigoted fury, and from modern their infidel spirit, blending all that was noble in the ardor of the Crusades with all that is generous in the enthusiasm of freedom."*

* *Essays*, Art. Chateaubriand.

THE

GENIUS OF CHRISTIANITY

Part the First.

DOGMAS AND TENETS.

BOOK I.

MYSTERIES AND SACRAMENTS.

CHAPTER I.

INTRODUCTION.

EVER since Christianity was first published to the world, it has been continually assailed by three kinds of enemies—heretics, sophists, and those apparently frivolous characters who destroy every thing with the shafts of ridicule. Numerous apologists have given victorious answers to subtleties and falsehoods, but they have not been so successful against derision. St. Ignatius of Antioch,[1] St. Irenæus, Bishop of Lyons,[2] Tertullian, in his *Prescriptions*,[3] which Bossuet calls *divine*, combated the inno-

---

[1] *Ignat. Epist. ad Smyrn.* He was a disciple of St. John, and Bishop of Antioch about A.D. 70.

[2] *In Hæreses*, Lib. vi. He was a disciple of St. Polycarp, who was taught Christianity by St. John.

[3] *Tertullian* gave the name of *Prescriptions* to the excellent work he wrote against heretics, and the great argument of which is founded on the antiquity

vators of their time, whose extravagant expositions corrupted the simplicity of the faith.

Calumny was first repulsed by Quadratus and Aristides, philosophers of Athens. We know, however, nothing of their apologies for Christianity, except a fragment of the former, which Eusebius has preserved.[1] Both he and St. Jerome speak of the work of Aristides as a master-piece of eloquence.

The Pagans accused the first Christians of atheism, incest, and certain abominable feasts, at which they were said to partake of the flesh of a new-born infant. After Quadratus and Aristides, St. Justin pleaded the cause of the Christians. His style is unadorned, and the circumstances attending his martyrdom prove that he shed his blood for religion with the same sincerity with which he had written in its defence.[2] Athenagoras has shown more address in his apology, but he has neither the originality of Justin nor the impetuosity of the author of the *Apologetic*.[3] Tertullian is the unrefined Bossuet of Africa. St. Theophilus, in his three books addressed to his friend Autolychus, displays imagination and learning;[4] and the Octavius of Minucius Felix exhibits the pleasing picture of a Christian and two idolaters conversing on religion and the nature of God, during a walk along the sea-shore.[5]

---

and authority of the Church. It will always be an unanswerable refutation of all innovators that they came too late; that the Church was already in possession; and, consequently, that her teaching constitutes the last appeal. Tertullian lived in the third century. T.

[1] This curious fragment carries us up to the time of our Saviour himself; for Quadratus says, "None can doubt the truth of our Lord's miracles, because the persons healed and raised from the dead had been seen long after their cure; so that many were yet living in our own time." *Euseb. Eccles. Hist.* lib. iv. K.

[2] Justin, surnamed the Martyr, was a Platonic philosopher before his conversion. He wrote two Defences of the Christians in the Greek language, during a violent persecution in the reign of Antoninus, the successor of Adrian. He suffered martyrdom A.D. 167. K.

[3] Athenagoras was a Greek philosopher of eminence, and flourished in the second century. He wrote not only an apology, but a treatise on the resurrection, both of which display talents and learning. K.

[4] St. Theophilus was Bishop of Antioch, and one of the most learned fathers of the Church at that period. T.

[5] He [illegible] of Antioch, and wrote in [illegible] apologists, by the Abbé de [illegible]

Arnobius, the rhetorician,[1] Lactantius,[2] Eusebius,[3] and St. Cyprian,[4] also defended Christianity; but their efforts were not so much directed to the display of its beauty, as to the exposure of the absurdities of idolatry.

Origen combated the sophists, and seems to have had the advantage over Celsus, his antagonist, in learning, argument and style. The Greek of Origen is remarkably smooth; it is, however, interspersed with Hebrew and other foreign idioms, which is frequently the case with writers who are masters of various languages.[5]

During the reign of the emperor Julian[6] commenced a persecution, perhaps more dangerous than violence itself, which consisted in loading the Christians with disgrace and contempt. Julian began his hostility by plundering the churches; he then forbade the faithful to teach or to study the liberal arts and sciences.[7] Sensible, however, of the important advantages of the institutions of Christianity, the emperor determined to establish hospitals and monasteries, and, after the example of the gospel system, to combine morality with religion; he ordered a kind of sermons to be delivered in the Pagan temples.

---

[1] He was an Arian, and flourished in the third century. In an elaborate work *against the Gentiles,* he defends the Christians with ability. K.

[2] He was a scholar of Arnobius. He completely exposed the absurdity of the Pagan superstitions. So eminent were his talents and learning, that Constantine the Great, the first Christian emperor, entrusted the education of his son Crispus to his care. Such is the elegance of his Latin style, that he is called the *Christian Cicero.* K.

[3] He was Bishop of Cæsarea, and flourished in the fourth century. He is a Greek writer of profound and various learning. So copious and highly valuable are his works, that he is styled the *Father* of Ecclesiastical History. Constantine the Great honored him with his esteem and confidence: but he was unfortunately tinctured with Arianism. T.

[4] He was Bishop of Carthage in the third century, a Latin writer of great eloquence, and a martyr for the faith.

[5] Origen flourished in the third century. He was a priest of Alexandria. His voluminous works, written in Greek, prove his piety, active zeal, great abilities, and extensive learning. K.

[6] Julian flourished at the close of the fourth century. He became an apostate from Christianity, partly on account of his aversion to the family of Constantine, who had put several of his relatives to death, and partly on account of the seductive artifices of the Platonic philosophers, who abused his credulity and flattered his ambition. K.

[7] *Socr.* iii. ch. 12.

The sophists, by whom Julian was surrounded, assailed the Christian religion with the utmost violence. The emperor himself did not disdain to combat those whom he styled contemptible *Galileans*. The work which he wrote has not reached us; but St. Cyril, Patriarch of Alexandria, quotes several passages of it in his refutation, which has been preserved. When Julian is serious, St. Cyril proves too strong for him; but when the Emperor has recourse to irony, the Patriarch loses his advantage. Julian's style is witty and animated; Cyril is sometimes passionate, obscure, and confused. From the time of Julian to that of Luther, the Church, flourishing in full vigor, had no occasion for apologists; but when the western schism took place, with new enemies arose new defenders. It cannot be denied that at first the Protestants had the superiority, at least in regard to forms, as Montesquieu has remarked. Erasmus himself was weak when opposed to Luther, and Theodore Beza had a captivating manner of writing, in which his opponents were too often deficient.

When Bossuet at length entered the lists, the victory remained not long undecided; the hydra of heresy was once more overthrown. His *Exposition de la Doctrine Catholique* and *Histoire des Variations*, are two master-pieces, which will descend to posterity.

It is natural for schism to lead to infidelity, and for heresy to engender atheism. Bayle and Spinosa arose after Calvin, and they found in Clarke and Leibnitz men of sufficient talents to refute their sophistry. Abbadie wrote an apology for religion, remarkable for method and sound argument. Unfortunately his style is feeble, though his ideas are not destitute of brilliancy. "If the ancient philosophers," observes Abbadie, "adored the Virtues, their worship was only a beautiful species of idolatry."

While the Church was yet enjoying her triumph, Voltaire renewed the persecution of Julian. He possessed the baneful art of making infidelity fashionable among a capricious but amiable people. Every species of self-love was pressed into this insensate league. Religion was attacked with every kind of weapon, from the pamphlet to the folio, from the epigram to the sophism. No sooner did a religious book appear than the author was ove[illegible] while works which Voltaire was the first [illegible] friends were extolled to the skies.

Such was his superiority over his disciples, that sometimes he could not forbear diverting himself with their irreligious enthusiasm. Meanwhile the destructive system continued to spread throughout France. It was first adopted in those provincial academies, each of which was a focus of bad taste and faction. Women of fashion and grave philosophers alike read lectures on infidelity. It was at length concluded that Christianity was no better than a barbarous system, and that its fall could not happen too soon for the liberty of mankind, the promotion of knowledge, the improvement of the arts, and the general comfort of life.

To say nothing of the abyss into which we were plunged by this aversion to the religion of the gospel, its immediate consequence was a return, more affected than sincere, to that mythology of Greece and Rome to which all the wonders of antiquity were ascribed.[1] People were not ashamed to regret that worship which had transformed mankind into a herd of madmen, monsters of indecency, or ferocious beasts. This could not fail to inspire contempt for the writers of the age of Louis XIV., who, however, had reached the high perfection which distinguished them, only by being religious. If no one ventured to oppose them face to face, on account of their firmly-established reputation, they were, nevertheless, attacked in a thousand indirect ways. It was asserted that they were unbelievers *in their hearts;* or, at least, that they would have been much greater characters had they lived *in our times.* Every author blessed his good fortune for having been born in the glorious age of the Diderots and d'Alemberts, in that age when all the attainments of the human mind were ranged in alphabetical order in the *Encyclopedie,* that Babel of the sciences and of reason.[2]

Men distinguished for their intelligence and learning endeavored to check this torrent; but their resistance was vain. Their voice was lost in the clamors of the crowd, and their victory was unknown to the frivolous people who directed public opinion in France, and upon whom, for that reason, it was highly necessary to make an impression.[3]

---

[1] The age of Louis XIV., though it knew and admired antiquity more than we, was a Christian age.

[2] See note A at the end of the volume.

[3] The *Lettres de quelques Juifs Portugais* had a momentary success, but it

Thus, the fatality which had given a triumph to the sophists during the reign of Julian, made them victorious in our times. The defenders of the Christians fell into an error which had before undone them: they did not perceive that the question was no longer to discuss this or that particular tenet since the very foundation on which these tenets were built was rejected by their opponents. By starting from the mission of Jesus Christ, and descending from one consequence to another, they established the truths of faith on a solid basis; but this mode of reasoning, which might have suited the seventeenth century extremely well, when the groundwork was not contested, proved of no use in our days. It was necessary to pursue a contrary method, and to ascend from the effect to the cause; not to prove that *the Christian religion is excellent because it comes from God, but that it comes from God because it is excellent.*

They likewise committed another error in attaching importance to the serious refutation of the sophists; a class of men whom it is utterly impossible to convince, because they are always in the wrong. They overlooked the fact that these people are never in earnest in their pretended search after truth, that they esteem none but themselves; that they are not even attached to their own system, except for the sake of the noise which it makes, and are ever ready to forsake it on the first change of public opinion.

For not having made this remark, much time and trouble were thrown away by those who undertook the vindication of Christianity. Their object should have been to reconcile to religion, not the sophists, but those whom they were leading astray. They had been seduced by being told that Christianity was the offspring of barbarism, an enemy of the arts and sciences, of reason and refinement; a religion whose only tendency was to encourage bloodshed, to enslave mankind, to diminish their happiness, and to retard the progress of the human understanding.

It was, therefore, necessary to prove that, on the contrary, the Christian religion, of all the religions that ever existed, is the most humane, the most favorable to liberty and to the arts and

---

was [illegible] ...thering over France.

sciences; that the modern world is indebted to it for every improvement, from agriculture to the abstract sciences—from the hospitals for the reception of the unfortunate to the temples reared by the Michael Angelos and embellished by the Raphaels. It was necessary to prove that nothing is more divine than its morality—nothing more lovely and more sublime than its tenets, its doctrine, and its worship; that it encourages genius, corrects the taste, develops the virtuous passions, imparts energy to the ideas, presents noble images to the writer, and perfect models to the artist; that there is no disgrace in being believers with Newton and Bossuet, with Pascal and Racine. In a word, it was necessary to summon all the charms of the imagination, and all the interests of the heart, to the assistance of that religion against which they had been set in array.

The reader may now have a clear view of the object of our work. All other kinds of apologies are exhausted, and perhaps they would be useless at the present day. Who would now sit down to read a work professedly theological? Possibly a few sincere Christians who are already convinced. But, it may be asked, may there not be some danger in considering religion in a merely human point of view? Why so? Does our religion shrink from the light? Surely one great proof of its divine origin is, that it will bear the test of the fullest and severest scrutiny of reason. Would you have us always open to the reproach of enveloping our tenets in sacred obscurity, lest their falsehood should be detected? Will Christianity be the less true for appearing the more beautiful? Let us banish our weak apprehensions; let us not, by an excess of religion, leave religion to perish. We no longer live in those times when you might say, "Believe without inquiring." People *will* inquire in spite of us; and our timid silence, in heightening the triumph of the infidel, will diminish the number of believers.

It is time that the world should know to what all those charges of absurdity, vulgarity, and meanness, that are daily alleged against Christianity, may be reduced. It is time to demonstrate, that, instead of debasing the ideas, it encourages the soul to take the most daring flights, and is capable of enchanting the imagination as divinely as the deities of Homer and Virgil. Our arguments will at least have this advantage, that they will be intelligible to the world at large, and will require nothing but common sense to determine their weight and strength. In works of this kind authors neglect, perhaps rather too much, to speak the language of their readers. It is necessary to be a scholar with a scholar, and a poet with a poet. The Almighty does not forbid us to tread the flowery path, if it serves to lead the wanderer once more to him; nor is it always by the steep and rugged mountain that the lost sheep finds its way back to the fold.

We think that this mode of considering Christianity displays associations of ideas which are but imperfectly known. Sublime in the antiquity of its recollections, which go back to the creation of the world, ineffable in its mysteries, adorable in its sacraments, interesting in its history, celestial in its morality, rich and attractive in its ceremonial, it is fraught with every species of beauty. Would you follow it in poetry? Tasso, Milton, Corneille, Racine, Voltaire, will depict to you its miraculous effects. In the belles-lettres, in eloquence, history, and philosophy, what have not Bossuet, Fénélon, Massillon, Bourdaloue, Bacon, Pascal, Euler, Newton, Leibnitz, produced by its divine inspiration! In the arts, what master-pieces! If you examine it in its worship, what ideas are suggested by its antique Gothic churches, its admirable prayers, its impressive ceremonies! Among its clergy, behold all those scholars who have handed down to you the languages and the works of Greece and Rome; all those anchorets of Thebais; all those asylums for the unfortunate; all those missionaries to China, to Canada, to Paraguay; not forgetting the military orders whence chivalry derived its origin. Every thing has been engaged in our cause—the manners of our ancestors, the pictures of days of yore, poetry, even romances themselves. We have called smiles from the cradle, and tears from the tomb. Sometimes, with the Maronite monk, we dwell on the summits of Carmel and Lebanon; at others we watch with the Daughter of Charity at the bedside of the sick. Here two American lovers summon us into the recesses of their deserts;[1] there we listen to the sighs of the virgin in the solitude

[1] The author alludes to the very beautiful and pathetic tale of *Atala*, or *The Lov*[illegible] *De*[illegible], which was at first [illegible]ntroduced into the [illegible] and detached from it. T.

of the cloister. Homer takes his place by Milton, and Virgil beside Tasso; the ruins of Athens and of Memphis form contrasts with the ruins of Christian monuments, and the tombs of Ossian with our rural churchyards. At St. Dennis we visit the ashes of kings; and when our subject requires us to treat of the existence of God, we seek our proofs in the wonders of Nature alone. In short, we endeavor to strike the heart of the infidel in every possible way; but we dare not flatter ourselves that we possess the miraculous rod of religion which caused living streams to burst from the flinty rock.

Four parts, each divided into six books, compose the whole of our work. The *first* treats of dogma and doctrine. The *second* and *third* comprehend the poetic of Christianity, or its connection with poetry, literature, and the arts. The *fourth* embraces its worship,—that is to say, whatever relates to the ceremonies of the Church, and to the clergy, both secular and regular.

We have frequently compared the precepts, doctrines, and worship of other religions with those of Christianity; and, to gratify all classes of readers, we have also occasionally touched upon the historical and mystical part of the subject. Having thus stated the general plan of the work, we shall now enter upon that portion of it which treats of *Dogma and Doctrine*, and, as a preliminary step to the consideration of the Christian mysteries, we shall institute an inquiry into the nature of mysterious things in general

---

CHAPTER II.

OF THE NATURE OF MYSTERIES.

THERE is nothing beautiful, pleasing, or grand in life, but that which is more or less mysterious. The most wonderful sentiments are those which produce impressions difficult to be explained. Modesty, chaste love, virtuous friendship, are full of secrets. It would seem that half a word is sufficient for the mutual understanding of hearts that love, and that they are, as it were, disclosed to each other's view. Is not innocence, also, which is nothing but a holy ignorance, the most ineffable of mysteries? If infancy is so happy, it is owing to the absence of knowledge; and if old age is so wretched, it is because it knows every thing; but, fortunately for the latter, when the mysteries of life are at an end, those of death commence.

What we say here of the sentiments may be said also of the virtues: the most angelic are those which, emanating immediately from God, such as charity, studiously conceal themselves, like their source, from mortal view.

If we pass to the qualities of the mind, we shall find that the pleasures of the understanding are in like manner secrets. Mystery is of a nature so divine, that the early inhabitants of Asia conversed only by symbols. What science do we continually apply, if not that which always leaves something to be conjectured, and which sets before our eyes an unbounded prospect? If we wander in the desert, a kind of instinct impels us to avoid the plains, where we can embrace every object at a single glance; we repair to those forests, the cradle of religion,—those forests whose shades, whose sounds, and whose silence, are full of wonders,—those solitudes, where the first fathers of the Church were fed by the raven and the bee, and where those holy men tasted such inexpressible delights, as to exclaim, "Enough, O Lord! I will be overpowered if thou dost not moderate thy divine communications." We do not pause at the foot of a modern monument; but if, in a desert island, in the midst of the wide ocean, we come all at once to a statue of bronze, whose extended arm points to the regions of the setting sun, and whose base, covered with hieroglyphics, attests the united ravages of the billows and of time, what a fertile source of meditation is here opened to the traveller! There is nothing in the universe but what is hidden, but what is unknown. Is not man himself an inexplicable mystery? Whence proceeds that flash of lightning which we call existence, and in what night is it about to be extinguished? The Almighty has stationed Birth and Death, under the form of veiled phantoms, at the two extremities of our career; the one produces the incomprehensible moment of life, which the other uses every exertion to destroy.

Considering then the natural propensity of man to the mysterious, i[illegible] that the religions of all nations should have had their impenetrable secrets. The Selli studied the miraculous words of the doves of Dodona;[1] India, Persia, Ethiopia, Scythia, the Gauls, the Scandinavians, had their caverns, their holy mountains, their sacred oaks, where the Brahmins, the Magi, the Gymnosophists, or the Druids, proclaimed the inexplicable oracle of the gods.

Heaven forbid that we should have any intention to compare these mysteries with those of the true religion, or the inscrutable decrees of the Sovereign of the Universe with the changing ambiguities of gods, "the work of human hands."[2] We merely wished to remark that there is no religion without *mysteries;* these, with *sacrifices,* constitute the essential part of worship. God himself is the great secret of Nature. The Divinity was represented veiled in Egypt, and the sphinx was seated upon the threshold of the temples.[3]

CHAPTER III.

OF THE CHRISTIAN MYSTERIES.

The Trinity.

We perceive at the first glance, that, in regard to mysteries, the Christian religion has a great advantage over the religions of antiquity. The mysteries of the latter bore no relation to man, and afforded, at the utmost, but a subject of reflection to the philosopher or of song to the poet. Our mysteries, on the con-

[1] They were an ancient people of Epirus, and lived near Dodona. At that place there was a celebrated temple of Jupiter. The oracles were said to be delivered from it by doves endowed with a human voice. Herodotus relates that a priestess was brought hither from Egypt by the Phœnicians; so the story of the doves might arise from the ambiguity of the Greek term Πελεια, which signifies a dove, in the general language, but in the dialect of Epirus it means an aged woman. K.

[2] Wisdom, ch. xiii. v. 10.

[3] The Sphinx, a monstrous creature of Egyptian invention, was the just emblem of mystery, as, according to the Grecian mythology, she not only infested Bœotia with her depredations, but perplexed its inhabitants, not famed for their acuteness, with her enigmas. K.

trary, speak directly to the heart; they comprehend the secrets of our existence. The question here is not about a futile arrangement of numbers, but concerning the salvation and felicity of the human race. Is it possible for man, whom daily experience so fully convinces of his ignorance and frailty, to reject the mysteries of Jesus Christ? They are the mysteries of the unfortunate!

The Trinity, which is the first mystery presented by the Christian faith, opens an immense field for philosophic study, whether we consider it in the attributes of God, or examine the vestiges of this dogma, which was formerly diffused throughout the East. It is a pitiful mode of reasoning to reject whatever we cannot comprehend. It would be easy to prove, beginning even with the most simple things in life, that we know absolutely nothing; shall we, then, pretend to penetrate into the depths of divine Wisdom?

The Trinity was probably known to the Egyptians. The Greek inscription on the great obelisk in the *Circus Major*, at Rome, was to this effect:—

Μέγας Θεὸς, The Mighty God; Θεογένητος, the Begotten of God; Παμφεγγής, the All-Resplendent, (Apollo, the Spirit.)

Heraclides of Pontus, and Porphyry, record a celebrated oracle of Serapis:—

> *Πρῶτα Θεὸς, μετέπειτα λόγος και πνεῦμα σὺν αὐτοῖς.*
> *Σύμφυτα δὴ τρία πάντα, καὶ εἰς ἓν ἰόντα.*

"*In the beginning was God, then the Word and the Spirit; all three produced together, and uniting in one.*"

The Magi had a sort of Trinity, in their Metris, Oromasis, and Araminis; or Mitra, Oramases, and Arimane.

Plato seems to allude to this incomprehensible dogma in several of his works. "Not only is it alleged," says Dacier, "that he had a knowledge of the *Word*, the eternal Son of God, but it is also asserted that he was acquainted with the Holy Ghost, and thus had some idea of the Most Holy Trinity; for he writes as follows to the younger Dionysius:—

"'I must give Archedemus an explanation respecting what is infinitely more important and more divine, and what you are extremely [illegible] for the express[illegible] you are of opi nion that I have not sufficiently explained what I think of the nature of the first principle. I am obliged to write to you in enigmas, that, if my letter should be intercepted either by land or sea, those who read may not be able to understand it. All things are around their king; they exist for him, and he alone is the cause of good things—second for such as are second, and third for those that are third.'[1]

"In the *Epinomis*, and elsewhere, he lays down as principles the first good, the word or the understanding, and the soul. The first good is God; the word, or the understanding, is the Son of this first good, by whom he was begotten like to himself; and the soul, which is the middle term between the Father and the Son, is the Holy Ghost."[2]

Plato had borrowed this doctrine of the Trinity from Timæus, the Locrian, who had received it from the Italian school. Marsilius Ficinus, in one of his remarks on Plato, shows, after Jamblichus, Porphyry, Plato, and Maximus of Tyre, that the Pythagoreans were acquainted with the excellence of the number Three. Pythagoras intimates it in these words: *Προτίμα τὸ σχῆμα, καὶ βῆμα καὶ Τριώβολον;* "Honor chiefly the habit, the judgment-seat, and the triobolus," (three oboli.)

The doctrine of the Trinity is known in the East Indies and in Thibet. "On this subject," says Father Calamette, "the most remarkable and surprising thing that I have met with is a passage in one of their books entitled Lamaastambam. It begins thus: 'The Lord, the good, the great God, in his mouth is the Word.' The term which they employ personifies the Word. It then treats of the Holy Ghost under the appellation of the *Wind, or Perfect Spirit,* and concludes with the Creation, which it attributes to one single God."[3]

"What I have learned," observes the same missionary in another place, "respecting the religion of Thibet, is as follows: They call God *Konciosa*, and seem to have some idea of the adorable Trinity, for sometimes they term him *Koncikocick*, the one God,

---

[1] This passage of Plato, which the author could not verify, from its having been incorrectly quoted by Dacier, may be found in Plato Serrani, tome i. p. 312, letter the second to Dionysius. The letter is supposed to be genuine. K.

[2] *Œuvres de Platon, trad. par Dacier*, tome i. p. 194

[3] *Lettres édif.*, tome xiv. p. 9.

and at others *Koncioksum,* which is equivalent to the Triune God. They make use of a kind of chaplet, over which they pronounce the words, *om, ha, hum.* When you ask what these mean, they reply that the first signifies intelligence, or arm, that is to say, power; that the second is the word; that the third is the heart, or love; and that these three words together signify God."[1]

The English missionaries to Otaheite have found some notion of the Trinity among the natives of that island.[2]

Nature herself seems to furnish a kind of physical proof of the Trinity, which is the archetype of the universe, or, if you wish, its divine frame-work. May not the external and material world bear some impress of that invisible and spiritual arch which sustains it, according to Plato's idea, who represented corporeal things as the shadows of the thoughts of God? The number *Three* is the term by excellence in nature. It is not a product itself, but it produces all other fractions, which led Pythagoras to call it the motherless number.[3]

Some obscure tradition of the Trinity may be discovered even in the fables of polytheism. The Graces took it for their number; it existed in Tartarus both for the life and death of man and for the infliction of celestial vengeance; finally, three brother gods[4] possessed among them the complete dominion of the universe.

The philosophers divided the *moral* man into three parts; and the Fathers imagined that they discovered the image of the spiritual Trinity in the human soul.

---

[1] *Lettres edif.,* tom. xii. p. 437.

[2] "The three deities which they hold supreme are—
1. Tane, te Medooa, the Father.
2. Oromattow, God in the Son.
3. Taroa, the Bird, the Spirit."
Appendix to the Missionary Voyage, p. 333. K.

[3] Hier., *Comm. in Pyth.* The 3, a simple number itself, is the only one composed of simples, and that gives a simple number when decomposed. We can form no complex number, the 2 excepted, without the 3. The formations of the 3 are beautiful, and embrace that powerful unity which is the first link in the chain of numbers, and is everywhere exhibited in the universe. The ancients very frequently applied numbers in a metaphysical sense, and we should not be too hasty in condemning it as folly in Pythagoras, Plato, and the Egyptian p[illegible] [illegible]d this science.

[4] That is, [illegible] K.

"If we impose silence on our senses," says the great Bossuet, "and retire for a short time into the recesses of our soul, that is to say, into that part where the voice of truth is heard, we shall there perceive a sort of image of the Trinity whom we adore. Thought, which we feel produced as the offspring of our mind, as the son of our understanding, gives us some idea of the Son of God, conceived from all eternity in the intelligence of the celestial Father. For this reason this Son of God assumes the name of the Word, to intimate that he is produced in the bosom of the Father, not as bodies are generated, but as the inward voice that is heard within our souls there arises when we contemplate truth.

"But the fecundity of the mind does not stop at this inward voice, this intellectual thought, this image of the truth that is formed within us. We love both this inward voice and the intelligence which gives it birth; and while we love them, we feel within us something which is not less precious to us than intelligence and thought, which is the fruit of both, which unites them and unites with them, and forms with them but one and the same existence.

"Thus, as far as there can be any resemblance between God and man, is produced in God the eternal Love which springs from the Father who thinks, and from the Son who is his thought, to constitute with him and his thought one and the same nature, equally happy and equally perfect."[1]

What a beautiful commentary is this on that passage of Genesis: "*Let us make man!*"

Tertullian, in his *Apology*, thus expresses himself on this great mystery of our religion: "God created the world by his *word*, his *reason*, and his *power*. You philosophers admit that the *Logos*, the word and reason, is the Creator of the universe. The Christians merely add that the proper substance of the *word* and *reason*—that substance by which God produced all things—is *spirit;* that this word must have been pronounced by God; that having been pronounced, it was generated by him; that consequently it is the *Son* of God, and *God* by reason of the unity of substance. If the sun shoots forth a ray, its substance is not

---

[1] Bossuet, *Hist. Univ.*, sec. i. p. 248.

separated, but extended. Thus the Word is *spirit* of a spirit, and *God* of God, like a light kindled at another light. Thus, whatever proceeds from God is *God*, and the two, with their spirit, form but one, differing in properties, not in number; in order, not in nature: the Son having sprung from his principle without being separated from it. Now this ray of the Divinity descended into the womb of a virgin, invested itself with flesh, and became man united with God. This flesh, supported by the spirit, was nourished; it grew, spoke, taught, acted; it was Christ."

This proof of the Trinity may be comprehended by persons of the simplest capacity. It must be recollected that Tertullian was addressing men who persecuted Christ, and whom nothing would have more highly gratified than the means of attacking the doctrine, and even the persons, of his defenders. We shall pursue these proofs no farther, but leave them to those who have studied the principles of the Italic sect of philosophers and the higher department of Christian theology.

As to the images that bring under our feeble senses the most sublime mystery of religion, it is difficult to conceive how the awful triangular fire, resting on a cloud, is unbecoming the dignity of poetry. Is Christianity less impressive than the heathen mythology, when it represents to us the Father under the form of an old man, the majestic ancestor of ages, or as a brilliant effusion of light? Is there not something wonderful in the contemplation of the Holy Spirit, the sublime Spirit of Jehovah, under the emblem of gentleness, love, and innocence? Doth God decree the propagation of his word? The Spirit, then, ceases to be that Dove which overshadowed mankind with the wings of peace; he becomes a visible word, a tongue of fire, which speaks all the languages of the earth, and whose eloquence creates or overthrows empires.

To delineate the divine Son, we need only borrow the words of the apostle who beheld him in his glorified state. He was seated on a throne, says St. John in the Apocalypse; his face shone like the sun in his strength, and his feet like fine brass melted in a furnace. His eyes were as a flame of fire, and out of his [illegible] two-edged sword. In his right hand he held [illegible] stars [illegible] in his left a book sealed with seven seals: his voice was as the sound of many waters. The seven spirits of God burned before him, like seven lamps; and he went forth from his throne attended by lightnings, and voices, and thunders.

CHAPTER IV.

OF THE REDEMPTION.

As the Trinity comprehends secrets of the metaphysical kind, so the redemption contains the wonders of man, and the inexplicable history of his destination and his heart. Were we to pause a little in our meditations, with what profound astonishment would we contemplate those two great mysteries, which conceal in their shades the primary intentions of God and the system of the universe! The Trinity, too stupendous for our feeble comprehension, confounds our thoughts, and we shrink back overpowered by its glory. But the affecting mystery of the redemption, in filling our eyes with tears, prevents them from being too much dazzled, and allows us to fix them at least for a moment upon the cross.

We behold, in the first place, springing from this mystery, the doctrine of original sin, which explains the whole nature of man. Unless we admit this truth, known by tradition to all nations, we become involved in impenetrable darkness. Without original sin, how shall we account for the vicious propensity of our nature continually combated by a secret voice which whispers that we were formed for virtue? Without a primitive fall, how shall we explain the aptitude of man for affliction—that sweat which fertilizes the rugged soil; the tears, the sorrows, the misfortunes of the righteous; the triumphs, the unpunished success, of the wicked? It was because they were unacquainted with this degeneracy, that the philosophers of antiquity fell into such strange errors, and invented the notion of reminiscence. To be convinced of the fatal truth whence springs the mystery of redemption, we need no other proof than the malediction pronounced against Eve,—a malediction which is daily accomplished before our eyes. How significant are the pangs, and at the same time the joys, of a mother! What mysterious intimations of man and his twofold destiny, predicted at once by the pains and pleasures of child-birth! We cannot mistake the views of the Most High, when we behold the two great ends of man in the labor of his mother; and we are compelled to recognise a God even in a malediction.

After all, we daily see the son punished for the father, and the crime of a villain recoiling upon a virtuous descendant, which proves but too clearly the doctrine of original sin. But a God of clemency and indulgence, knowing that we should all have perished in consequence of this fall, has interposed to save us. Frail and guilty mortals as we all are, let us ask, not our understandings, but our hearts, how a God could die for man. If this perfect model of a dutiful son, if this pattern of faithful friends, if that agony in Gethsemane, that bitter cup, that bloody sweat, that tenderness of soul, that sublimity of mind, that cross, that veil rent in twain, that rock cleft asunder, that darkness of nature—in a word, if that God, expiring at length for sinners, can neither enrapture our heart nor inflame our understanding, it is greatly to be feared that our works will never exhibit, like those of the poet, the "brilliant wonders" which attract a high and just admiration.

"Images," it may perhaps be urged, "are not reasons; and we live in an enlightened age, which admits nothing without proof."

That we live in an enlightened age has been doubted by some; but we would not be surprised if we were met with the foregoing objection. When Christianity was attacked by serious arguments, they were answered by an Origen, a Clark, a Bossuet. Closely pressed by these formidable champions, their adversaries endeavored to extricate themselves by reproaching religion with those very metaphysical disputes in which they would involve us. They alleged, like Arius, Celsus, and Porphyry, that Christianity is but a tissue of subtleties, offering nothing to the imagination and the heart, and adopted only by *madmen* and *simpletons*. But if any one comes forward, and in reply to these reproaches endeavors [illegible] the gospel is the religion of the sou[illegible] immediately exclaim,

"Well, and what does that prove, except that you are more or less skilful in drawing a picture?" Thus, when you attempt to work upon the feelings, they require axioms and corollaries. If, on the other hand, you begin to reason, they then want nothing but sentiments and images. It is difficult to close with such versatile enemies, who are never to be found at the post where they challenge you to fight them. We shall hazard a few words on the subject of the redemption, to show that the theology of the Christian religion is not so absurd as some have affected to consider it.

A universal tradition teaches us that man was created in a more perfect state than that in which he at present exists, and that there has been a fall. This tradition is confirmed by the opinion of philosophers in every age and country, who have never been able to reconcile their ideas on the subject of moral man, without supposing a primitive state of perfection, from which human nature afterward fell by its own fault.

If man was created, he was created for some end: now, having been created perfect, the end for which he was destined could not be otherwise than perfect.

But has the final cause of man been changed by his fall? No; since man has not been created anew, nor the human race exterminated to make room for another.

Man, therefore, though he has become mortal and imperfect through his disobedience, is still destined to an immortal and perfect end. But how shall he attain this end in his present state of imperfection? This he can no longer accomplish by his own energy, for the same reason that a sick man is incapable of raising himself to that elevation of ideas which is attainable by a person in health. There is, therefore, a disproportion between the power, and the weight to be raised by that power; here we already perceive the necessity of succor, or of a redemption.

"This kind of reasoning," it may be said, "will apply to the first man; but as for us, we are capable of attaining the ends of our existence. What injustice and absurdity, to imagine that we should all be punished for the fault of our first parent!" Without undertaking to decide in this place whether God is right or wrong in making us sureties for one another, all that we know, and all that it is necessary for us to know at present, is, that such a law exists. We know that the innocent son universally suffers the punishment due to the guilty father; that this law is so interwoven in the principles of things as to hold good even in the physical order of the universe. When an infant comes into the world diseased from head to foot from its father's excesses, why do you not complain of the injustice of nature? What has this little innocent done, that it should endure the punishment of another's vices? Well, the diseases of the soul are perpetuated like those of the body, and man is punished in his remotest posterity for the fault which introduced into his nature the first leaven of sin.

The fall, then, being attested by general tradition, and by the transmission or generation of evil, both moral and physical, and, on the other hand, the ends for which man was designed being now as perfect as before his disobedience, notwithstanding his own degeneracy, it follows that a redemption, or any expedient whatever to enable man to fulfil those ends, is a natural consequence of the state into which human nature has fallen.

The necessity of redemption being once admitted, let us seek the order in which it may be found. This order may be considered either in man, or above man.

1. In man. The supposition of a redemption implies that the price must be at least equivalent to the thing to be redeemed. Now, how is it to be imagined that imperfect and mortal man could have offered himself, in order to regain a perfect and immortal end? How could man, partaking himself of the primeval sin, have made satisfaction as well for the portion of guilt which belonged to himself, as for that which attached to the rest of the human family? Would not such self-devotion have required a love and virtue superior to his nature? Heaven seems purposely to have suffered four thousand years to elapse from the fall to the redemption, to allow men time to judge, of themselves, how very inadequate their degraded virtues were for such a sacrifice.

We have no alternative, then, but the second supposition, namely, that the redemption could have proceeded only from a being superior to man. Let us examine if it could have been accompl[illegible] f th[illegible]termediate beings between him and God.

It was a beautiful idea of Milton[1] to represent the Almighty announcing the fall to the astonished heavens, and asking if any of the celestial powers was willing to devote himself for the salvation of mankind. All the divine hierarchy was mute; and among so many seraphim, thrones, dominations, angels, and archangels, none had the courage to make so great a sacrifice. Nothing can be more strictly true in theology than this idea of the poet's. What, indeed, could have inspired the angels with that unbounded love for man which the mystery of the cross supposes? Moreover, how could the most exalted of created spirits have possessed strength sufficient for the stupendous task? No angelic substance could, from the weakness of its nature, have taken upon itself those sufferings which, in the language of Massillon, accumulated upon the head of Christ all the physical torments that might be supposed to attend the punishment of all the sins committed since the beginning of time, and all the moral anguish, all the remorse, which sinners must have experienced for crimes committed. If the Son of Man himself found the cup bitter, how could an angel have raised it to his lips? Oh, no; he never could have drunk it to the dregs, and the sacrifice could not have been consummated.

We could not, then, have any other redeemer than one of the three persons existing from all eternity; and among these three persons of the Godhead, it is obvious that the Son alone, from his very nature, was to accomplish the great work of salvation. Love which binds together all the parts of the universe, the

---

[1] Say, heavenly powers, where shall we find such love
Which of you will be mortal to redeem
Man's mortal crime? and just, th' unjust to save?
Dwells in all heaven charity so dear?
He ask'd, but all the heavenly choir stood mute,
And silence was in heaven: on man's behalf
Patron or intercessor none appear'd;
Much less that durst upon his own head draw
The deadly forfeiture, and ransom set.
And now without redemption all mankind
Must have been lost, adjudged to death and hell,
By doom severe, had not the Son of God,
In whom the fulness dwells of love divine,
His dearest mediation thus renew'd.

PARADISE LOST, b. iii., l. 213. K.

Mean which unites the extremes, Vivifying Principle of nature, he alone was capable of reconciling God with man. This second Adam came;—man according to the flesh, by his birth of Mary; a man of sanctity by his gospel; a man divine by his union with the Godhead. He was born of a virgin, that he might be free from original sin and a victim without spot and without blemish. He received life in a stable, in the lowest of human conditions, because we had fallen through pride. Here commences the depth of the mystery; man feels an awful emotion, and the scene closes.

Thus, the end for which we were destined before the disobedience of our first parents is still pointed out to us, but the way to secure it is no longer the same. Adam, in a state of innocence, would have reached it by flowery paths: Adam, in his fallen condition, must cross precipices to attain it. Nature has undergone a change since the fall of our first parents, and redemption was designed, not to produce a new creation, but to purchase final salvation for the old. Every thing, therefore, has remained degenerate with man; and this sovereign of the universe, who, created immortal, was destined to be exalted, without any change of existence, to the felicity of the celestial powers, cannot now enjoy the presence of God till, in the language of St. Chrysostom, he has passed through the *deserts of the tomb*. His soul has been rescued from final destruction by the redemption; but his body, combining with the frailty natural to matter the weakness consequent on sin, undergoes the primitive sentence in its utmost extent: he falls, he sinks, he passes into dissolution. Thus God, after the fall of our first parents, yielding to the entreaties of his Son, and unwilling to destroy the whole of his work, invented death, as a demi-annihilation, to fill the sinner with horror of that complete dissolution to which, but for the wonders of celestial love, he would have been inevitably doomed.

We venture to presume, that, if there be any thing clear in metaphysics, it is this chain of reasoning. There is here no wresting of words; there are no divisions and subdivisions, no obscure or barbarous terms. Christianity is not made up of such things as the sarcasms of infidelity would fain have us imagine. To the poor in spirit the gospel has been preached, and by the poor in [illegible] has been heard: it is the plainest book that exists. [illegible] has not its seat in the head, but in the heart; it teaches not the art of disputation, but the way to lead a virtuous life. Nevertheless, it is not without its secrets. What is truly ineffable in the Scripture is the continual mixture of the profoundest mysteries and the utmost simplicity—characters whence spring the pathetic and the sublime. We should no longer be surprised, then, that the work of Jesus Christ speaks so eloquently. Such, moreover, are the truths of our religion, notwithstanding their freedom from scientific parade, that the admission of one single point immediately compels you to admit all the rest. Nay, more: if you hope to escape by denying the principle,—as, for instance, original sin,—you will soon, driven from consequence to consequence, be obliged to precipitate yourself into the abyss of atheism. The moment you acknowledge a God, the Christian religion presents itself, in spite of you, with all its doctrines, as Clarke and Pascal have observed. This, in our opinion, is one of the strongest evidences in favor of Christianity.

In short, we must not be astonished if he who causes millions of worlds to roll without confusion over our heads, has infused such harmony into the principles of a religion instituted by himself; we need not be astonished at his making the charms and the glories of its mysteries revolve in the circle of the most convincing logic, as he commands those planets to revolve in their orbits to bring us flowers and storms in their respective seasons. We can scarcely conceive the reason of the aversion shown by the present age for Christianity. If it be true, as some philosophers have thought, that some religion or other is necessary for mankind, what system would you adopt instead of the faith of our forefathers? Long shall we remember the days when men of blood pretended to erect altars to the *Virtues*, on the ruins of Christianity.[1] With one hand they reared scaffolds; with the other, on the fronts of our temples they inscribed *Eternity* to God and *Death* to man; and those temples, where once was found that God who is acknowledged by the whole universe, and where devotion to Mary consoled so many afflicted hearts,—those temples were dedicated to *Truth*, which no man knows, and to *Reason*, which never dried a tear.

[1] The author alludes to the disastrous tyranny exercised by Robespierre over the deluded French people. K.

CHAPTER V.

OF THE INCARNATION.

THE Incarnation exhibits to us the Sovereign of Heaven among shepherds; him who hurls the thunderbolt, wrapped in swaddling-clothes; him whom the heavens cannot contain, confined in the womb of a virgin. Oh, how antiquity would have expatiated in praise of this wonder! What pictures would a Homer or a Virgil have left us of the Son of God in a manger, of the songs of the shepherds, of the Magi conducted by a star, of the angels descending in the desert, of a virgin mother adoring her new-born infant, and of all this mixture of innocence, enchantment, and grandeur!

Setting aside what is direct and sacred in our mysteries, we would still discover under their veils the most beautiful truths in nature. These secrets of heaven, apart from their mystical character, are perhaps the prototype of the moral and physical laws of the world. The hypothesis is well worthy the glory of God, and would enable us to discern why he has been pleased to manifest himself in these mysteries rather than in any other mode. Jesus Christ, for instance, (or the moral world,) in taking our nature upon him, teaches us the prodigy of the physical creation, and represents the universe framed in the bosom of celestial love. The parables and the figures of this mystery then become engraved upon every object around us. Strength, in fact, universally proceeds from grace; the river issues from the spring; the lion is first nourished with milk like that which is sucked by the lamb; and lastly, among mankind, the Almighty has promised ineffable glory to those who practise the humblest virtues.

They who see nothing in the chaste Queen of angels but an obscure mystery are much to be pitied. What touching thoughts are suggested by that mortal woman, become the immortal mother of a Saviour-God! What might not be said of Mary, who is at once a virgin and a mother, the two most glorious characters [illegible] ...uthful daughter of ancient Israel, who presents herself for the relief of human suffering, and sacrifices a son for the salvation of her paternal race! This tender mediatrix between us and the Eternal, with a heart full of compassion for our miseries, forces us to confide in her maternal aid, and disarms the vengeance of Heaven. What an enchanting dogma, that allays the terror of a God by causing beauty to intervene between our nothingness and his Infinite Majesty!

The anthems of the Church represent the Blessed Mary seated upon a pure-white throne, more dazzling than the snow. We there behold her arrayed in splendor, as a mystical rose, or as the morning-star, harbinger of the Sun of grace: the brightest angels wait upon her, while celestial harps and voices form a ravishing concert around her. In that daughter of humanity we behold the refuge of sinners, the comforter of the afflicted, who, all good, all compassionate, all indulgent, averts from us the anger of the Lord.

Mary is the refuge of innocence, of weakness, and of misfortune. The faithful clients that crowd our churches to lay their homage at her feet are poor mariners who have escaped shipwreck under her protection, aged soldiers whom she has saved from death in the fierce hour of battle, young women whose bitter griefs she has assuaged. The mother carries her babe before her image, and this little one, though it knows not as yet the God of Heaven, already knows that divine mother who holds an infant in her arms.

CHAPTER VI.

OF THE SACRAMENTS.

Baptism.

If the mysteries overwhelm the mind by their greatness, we experience a different kind of astonishment, but perhaps not less profound, when we contemplate the sacraments of the Church. The whole knowledge of man, in his civil and moral relations, is implied in these institutions.

Baptism is the first of the sacraments which religion confers upon man, and, in the language of the apostle, *clothes him with Jesus Christ.* This sacred rite reminds us of the corruption in which we were born, of the pangs that gave us birth, of the tribulations which await us in this world. It teaches us that our sins will recoil upon our children, and that we are all sureties for each other—an awful lesson, which alone would suffice, if duly pondered, to establish the empire of virtue among men.

Behold the new convert standing amid the waves of Jordan! the hermit of the rock pours the lustral water upon his head; while the patriarchal river, the camels on its banks, the temple of Jerusalem, and the cedars of Libanus, seem to be arrested by the solemn rite. Or, rather, behold the infant child before the sacred font! A joyous family surround him; in his behalf they renounce sin, and give him the name of his grandfather, which is thus renewed by love from generation to generation. Already the father hastens to take the child in his arms, and to carry it home to his impatient wife, who is counting under her curtains each sound of the baptismal bell. The relatives assemble; tears of tenderness and of religion bedew every eye; the new name of the pretty infant, the ancient appellative of its ancestor, passes from mouth to mouth; and every one, mingling the recollections of the past with present joys, discovers the fancied resemblance of the good old man in the child that revives his memory. Such are the scenes exhibited by the sacrament of baptism; but Religion, ever moral and ever serious, even when the most cheerful smile irradiates her countenance, shows us also the son of a king, in his purple mantle, renouncing the pomps of Satan at the same font where the poor man's child appears in tatters, to abjure those vanities of the world which it will never know.[1]

We find in St. Ambrose a curious description of the manner in which the sacrament of baptism was administered in the first ages of the Church.[2] Holy Saturday was the day appointed for the ceremony. It commenced with touching the nostrils and

---

[1] That is, the outward pomp of this world; but the poor as well as the rich must renounce all inordinate aspiration after the vain show of this world. T.

[2] Ambr., *de Myst.* Tertullian, Origen, St. Jerome, and St. Augustin, speak less in detail of this ceremony than St. Ambrose. The triple immersion and the touch [illegible] here, are mentioned in the six books on [illegible] attributed to this father.

opening the ears of the catechumen, t e person officiating at the same time pronouncing the word *ephpheta*, which signifies, *be opened*. He was then conducted into the holy of holies. In the presence of the deacon, the priest, and the bishop, he renounced the works of the devil. He turned toward the west, the image of darkness, to abjure the world; and toward the east, the emblem of light, to denote his alliance with Jesus Christ. The bishop then blessed the water, which, according to St. Ambrose, indicated all the mysteries of the Scripture,—the Creation, the Deluge, the Passage of the Red Sea, the Cloud, the Waters of Mara, Naaman, and the Pool of Bethsaida. The water having been consecrated by the sign of the cross, the catechumen was immersed in it three times, in honor of the Trinity, and to teach him that three things bear witness in baptism—water, blood, and the Holy Spirit. On leaving the holy of holies, the bishop anointed the head of the regenerated man, to signify that he was now consecrated as one of the chosen race and priestly nation of the Lord. His feet were then washed, and he was dressed in white garments, as a type of innocence, after which he received, by the sacrament of confirmation, the spirit of divine fear, of wisdom and intelligence, of counsel and strength, of knowledge and piety. The bishop then pronounced, with a loud voice, the words of the apostle, "God the Father hath marked thee with his seal. Jesus Christ our Lord hath confirmed thee, and given to thy heart the earnest of the Holy Ghost." The new Christian then proceeded to the altar to receive the bread of angels, saying, "I will go to the altar of the Lord, of God who rejoices my youth." At the sight of the altar, covered with vessels of gold and silver, with lights, flowers, and silks, the new convert exclaimed, with the prophet, "Thou hast spread a table for me; it is the Lord who feeds me; I shall know no want, for he hath placed me in an abundant pasture." The ceremony concluded with the celebration of the mass. How august must have been the solemnity, at which an Ambrose gave to the innocent poor that place at the table of the Lord which he refused to a guilty emperor![1]

[1] Theodosius, by whose command great numbers of the inhabitants of Thessalonica were put to death for an insurrection. For this sanguinary deed, St. Ambrose, then bishop of Milan, refused to admit him into the Church until he

If there be not, in this first act of the life of a Christian, a divine combination of theology and morality, of mystery and simplicity, never will there be in religion any thing divine.

But, considered in a higher relation, and as a type of the mystery of our redemption, baptism is a bath which restores to the soul its primeval vigor. We cannot recall to mind without deep regret the beauty of those ancient times, when the forests were not silent enough, nor the caverns sufficiently solitary, for the believers who repaired thither to meditate on the mysteries of religion. Those primitive Christians, witnesses of the renovation of the world, were occupied with thoughts of a very different kind from those which now bend us down to the earth,—us Christians who have grown old in years, but not in faith. In those times, wisdom had her seat amid rocks and in the lion's den, and kings went forth to consult the anchorite of the mountain. Days too soon passed away! There is no longer a St. John in the desert, nor will there be poured out again upon the new convert those waters of the Jordan which carried off all his stains to the bosom of the ocean.

Baptism is followed by confession; and the Church, with a prudence peculiar to her, has fixed the time for the reception of this sacrament at the age when a person becomes capable of sin, which is that of seven years.

All men, not excepting philosophers themselves, whatever may have been their opinions on other subjects, have considered the sacrament of penance as one of the strongest barriers against vice, and as a master-piece of wisdom. "How many restitutions and reparations," says Rousseau, "does not confession produce among Catholics!"[1] According to Voltaire, "confession is a most excellent expedient, a bridle to guilt, invented in the remotest antiquity: it was practised at the celebration of all the ancient mysteries. We have imitated and sanctified this wise custom, which has a great influence in prevailing on hearts burning with resentment to forgive one another."[2]

had performed a canonical penance. The emperor having remonstrated, and cited the example of King David, who had committed murder and adultery, the Saint answered, "As you have imitated him in his crime, imitate him in his penance." [illegible] Theodosius humbly submitted. T.

[1] *Æmi*[illegible]

[2] *Quest*[illegible] under the head *Curé de Campagne*, sect. ii.

Without this salutary institution, the sinner would sink into despair. Into what bosom could he unburden his heart? Into that of a friend? Ah! who can rely upon the friendship of men? Will he make the desert his confidant? The desert would incessantly reverberate in the guilty ear the sound of those trumpets which Nero fancied he heard around the tomb of his mother.[1] When nature and our fellow-creatures show no mercy, how delightful is it to find the Almighty ready to forgive! To the Christian religion alone belongs the merit of having made two sisters of Innocence and Repentance.

CHAPTER VII.

OF THE HOLY COMMUNION.

At the age of twelve years, and in the gay season of spring, the youth is admitted for the first time to a union with his God. After having wept with the mountains of Sion over the death of the world's Redeemer, after having commemorated the darkness which covered the earth on that tragic occasion, Christendom throws aside her mourning; the bells commence their merry peals, the images of the saints are unveiled, and the domes of the churches re-echo with the song of joy—with the ancient alleluia of Abraham and of Jacob. Tender virgins clothed in white, and boys bedecked with foliage, march along a path strewed with the first flowers of the year, and advance toward the temple of religion, chanting new canticles, and followed by their overjoyed parents. Soon the heavenly victim descends upon the altar for the refreshment of those youthful hearts. The bread of angels is laid upon the tongue as yet unsullied by falsehood, while the priest partakes, under the species of wine, of the blood of the immaculate Lamb.

In this solemn ceremony, God perpetuates the memory of a bloody sacrifice by the most peaceful symbols. With the immeasurable heights of these mysteries are blended the recollections

[1] Tacit., Hist.

of the most pleasing scenes. Nature seems to revive with her Creator, and the angel of spring opens for her the doors of the tomb, like the spirit of light who rolled away the stone from the glorious sepulchre. The age of the tender communicants and that of the infant year mingle their youth, their harmonies, and their innocence. The bread and wine announce the approaching maturity of the products of the fields, and bring before us a picture of agricultural life. In fine, God descends into the souls of these young believers to bring forth his chosen fruits, as he descends at this season into the bosom of the earth to make it produce its flowers and its riches.

But, you will ask, what signifies that mystic communion, in which *reason* submits to an *absurdity*, without any advantage to the moral man? To this objection I will first give a general answer, which will apply to all Christian rites: that they exert the highest moral influence, because they were practised by our fathers, because our mothers were Christians over our cradle, and because the chants of religion were heard around the coffins of our ancestors and breathed a prayer of peace over their ashes.

Supposing, however, that the Holy Communion were but a puerile ceremony, those persons must be extremely blind who cannot perceive that a solemnity, which must be preceded by a confession of one's whole life, and can take place only after a long series of virtuous actions, is, from its nature, highly favorable to morality. It is so to such a degree, that, were a man to partake worthily but once a month of the sacrament of the Eucharist, that man must of necessity be the most virtuous person upon earth Transfer this reasoning from the individual to society in general, from one person to a whole nation, and you will find that the Holy Communion constitutes a complete system of legislation.

"Here then are people," says Voltaire, an authority which will not be suspected, "who partake of the communion amid an august ceremony, by the light of a hundred tapers, after solemn music which has enchanted their senses, at the foot of an altar resplendent with gold. The imagination is subdued and the soul powerfully affected. We scarcely breathe; we forget all earthly considerations: we are united with God and he is incorporated with us. [illegible], who could, after this, be guilty of a single crime or only conceive the idea of one? It would indeed be impossible to devise a mystery capable of keeping men more effectually within the bounds of virtue."[1]

The Eucharist was instituted at the last supper of Christ with his disciples; and we call to our aid the pencil of the artist, to express the beauty of the picture in which he is represented pronouncing the words, *This is my body.* Four things here require attention.

First, In the *material* bread and wine we behold the consecration of the food of man, which comes from God, and which we receive from his bounty. Were there nothing more in the Communion than this offering of the productions of the earth to him who dispenses them, that alone would qualify it to be compared with the most excellent religious customs of Greece.

Secondly, The Eucharist reminds us of the Passover of the Israelites, which carries us back to the time of the Pharaohs; it announces the abolition of bloody sacrifices; it represents also the calling of Abraham, and the first covenant between God and man. Every thing grand in antiquity, in history, in legislation, in the sacred types, is therefore comprised in the communion of the Christian.

Thirdly, The Eucharist announces the reunion of mankind into one great family. It inculcates the cessation of enmities, natural equality, and the commencement of a new law, which will make no distinction of Jew or Gentile, but invites all the children of Adam to sit down at the same table.

Fourthly, The great wonder of the Holy Eucharist is the real presence of Christ under the consecrated species. Here the soul must transport itself for a moment to that intellectual world which was open to man before the fall

When the Almighty had created him to his likeness, and animated him with the breath of life, he made a covenant with him. Adam and his Creator conversed together in the solitude of the garden. The covenant was necessarily broken by the disobedience of the father of men. The Almighty could no longer communicate with death, or spirituality with matter. Now, between two things of different properties there cannot be a point

[1] *Questions sur l'Encyclopedie*, tome iv. Were we to express ourselves as forcibly as Voltaire here does, we would be looked upon as a fanatic.

of contact except by means of something intermediate. The first effort which divine love made to draw us nearer to itself, was in the calling of Abraham and the institution of sacrifices—types announcing to the world the coming of the Messiah. The Saviour, when he restored us to the ends of our creation, as we have observed on the subject of the redemption, reinstated us in our privileges, and the highest of those privileges undoubtedly was to communicate with our Maker. But this communication could no longer take place immediately, as in the terrestrial paradise: in the first place, because our origin remained polluted; and in the second, because the body, now an heir of death, is too weak to survive a direct communication with God. A medium was therefore required, and this medium the Son has furnished. He hath given himself to man in the Eucharist; he hath become the sublime way by which we are again united with Him from whom our souls have emanated.

But if the Son had remained in his primitive essence, it is evident that the same separation would have continued to exist here below between God and man; since there can be no union between purity and guilt, between an eternal reality and the dream of human life. But the Word condescended to assume our nature and to become like us. On the one hand he is united to his Father by his spirituality, and on the other, to our flesh by his humanity He is therefore the required medium of approximation between the guilty child and the compassionate Father. Represented by the symbol of bread, he is a sensible object to the corporeal eye, while he continues an intellectual object to the eye of the soul; and if he has chosen bread for this purpose, it is because the material which composes it is a noble and pure emblem of the divine nourishment.

If this sublime and mysterious theology, a few outlines only of which we are attempting to trace, should displease any of our readers, let them but remark how luminous are our metaphysics when compared with the system of Pythagoras, Plato, Timæus. Aristotle, and Epicurus. Here they meet with none of those abstract ideas for which it is necessary to create a language unintelligible to the mass of mankind

To sum up what we have said on this subject. we see, in the first place that the Holy Communion displays a beautiful ceremonial; that it inculcates morality, because purity of heart is essential in those who partake of it; that it is an offering of the produce of the earth to the Creator, and that it commemorates the sublime and affecting history of the Son of man. Combined with the recollection of the Passover and of the first covenant, it is lost in the remoteness of time; it reproduces the earliest ideas of man, in his religious and political character, and denotes the original equality of the human race. Finally, it comprises the mystical history of the family of Adam, their fall, their restoration, and their reunion with God.

CHAPTER VIII.

CONFIRMATION, HOLY ORDERS, AND MATRIMONY.

Celibacy considered under its Moral Aspect.

In considering the period of life which religion has fixed for the nuptials of man and his Creator, we find a subject of perpetual wonder. At the time when the fire of the passions is about to be kindled in the heart, and the mind is sufficiently capable of knowing God, he becomes the ruling spirit of the youth, pervading all the faculties of his soul in its now restless and expanded state. But dangers multiply as he advances; a stranger cast without experience upon the perilous ways of the world, he has need of additional helps. At this crisis religion does not forget her child: she has her reinforcements in reserve. Confirmation will support his trembling steps, like the staff in the hands of the traveller, or like those sceptres which passed from race to race among the royal families of antiquity, and on which Evander and Nestor, pastors of men, reclined while judging their people. Let it be observed that all the morality of life is implied in the sacrament of Confirmation; because whoever has the courage to confess God will necessarily practise virtue, as the commission of crime is nothing but the denial of the Creator.

The same wise spirit has been displayed in placing the sacraments of Holy Orders and Matrimony immediately after that of Confirmation. The child has now become a man, and religion, that watched over him with tender solicitude in the state of nature, will not abandon him in the social sphere. How profound are the views of the Christian legislator! He has established only two social sacraments, if we may be allowed this expression, because, in reality, there are but two states in life—celibacy and marriage. Thus, without regard to the civil distinctions invented by our short-sighted reason, Jesus Christ divided society into two classes, and decreed for them, not political, but moral laws, acting in this respect in accordance with all antiquity. The old sages of the East, who have acquired such a wide-spread fame, did not call men together at random to hatch utopian constitutions. They were venerable solitaries, who had travelled much, and who celebrated with the lyre the remembrance of the gods. Laden with the rich treasure of information derived from their intercourse with foreign nations, and still richer by the virtues which they practised, those excellent men appeared before the multitude with the lute in hand, their hoary locks encircled with a golden crown, and, seating themselves under the shade of the plane-tree, they delivered their lessons to an enchanted crowd. What were the institutions of an Amphion, a Cadmus, an Orpheus? They consisted in delightful music called *law*, in the dance, the hymn, the consecrated tree; they were exhibited in youth under the guidance of old age, in matrimonial faith plighted near a grave. Religion and God were everywhere. Such are the scenes which Christianity also exhibits, but with much stronger claims to our admiration.

Principles, however, are always a subject of disagreement among men, and the wisest institutions have met with opposition. Thus, in modern times, the vow of celibacy which accompanies the reception of Holy Orders has been denounced in no measured terms. Some, availing themselves of every means of assailing religion, have imagined that they placed her in opposition to herself by contrasting her present discipline with the ancient practice of the Church, which, according to them, permitted the marriag [illegible] content with making the cha [illegible] their raillery. Let us examine, first, the views of those who have assailed it with seriousness and on the ground of morality.

By the seventh canon of the second Council of Lateran,[1] held in 1139, the celibacy of the clergy was definitely established, in accordance with the regulations of previous synods, as those of Lateran in 1123, Troslé in 909, Tribur in 895, Toledo in 633, and Chalcedon in 451[2] Baronius shows that clerical celibacy was in force generally from the sixth century[3] The first Council of Tours excommunicated any priest, deacon, or sub-deacon, who returned to his wife after the reception of Holy Orders From the time of St. Paul, virginity was considered the more perfect state for a Christian.

But, were we to admit that marriage was allowed among the clergy in the early ages of the Church, which cannot be shown either from history or from ecclesiastical legislation, it would not follow that it would be expedient at the present day. Such an innovation would be at variance with the manners of our times, and, moreover, would lead to the total subversion of ecclesiastical discipline.

In the primitive days of religion, a period of combats and triumphs, the followers of Christianity, comparatively few in number and adorned with every virtue, lived fraternally together, and shared the same joys and the same tribulations at the table of the Lord. We may conceive, therefore, that a minister of religion might, strictly speaking, have been permitted to have a family amid this perfect society, which was already the domestic circle for him. His own children, forming a part of his flock, would not have diverted him from the attentions due to the remainder of his charge, nor would they have exposed him to betray the confidence of the sinner, since in those days there were no crimes to be concealed, the confession of them being made publicly in those *basilics of the dead* where the faithful assembled to pray over the ashes of the martyrs. The Christians of that age had received from heaven a spirit which we have lost. They

[1] This was the tenth general council, at which one thousand bishops were present. T.

[2] The fourth general council, numbering between five and six hundred bishops. T.

[3] Baron., *An.* 58, No. 18.

formed not so much a popular assembly as a *community* of Levites and religious women. Baptism had made them all priests and confessors of Jesus Christ.

St. Justin the philosopher, in his first *Apology*, has given us an admirable description of the Christian life in those times. "We are accused," he says, "of disturbing the tranquillity of the state, while we are taught by one of the principal articles of our faith that nothing is hidden to the eye of God, and that he will one day take a strict account of our good and evil deeds. But, O powerful Emperor, the very punishments which you have decreed against us only tend to confirm us in our religion, because all this persecution was predicted by our Master, the son of the sovereign God, Father and Lord of the universe.

"On Sunday, those who reside in the town and country meet together. The Scriptures are read, after which one of the ancients[1] exhorts the people to imitate the beautiful examples that have been placed before them. The assembly then rises; prayer is again offered up, and water, bread, and wine being presented, the officiating minister gives thanks, the others answering *Amen*. A portion of the consecrated elements is now distributed, and the rest is conveyed by the deacons to those who are absent. A collection is taken; the rich giving according to their disposition. These alms are placed in the hands of the minister, for the assistance of widows, orphans, sick persons, prisoners, poor people, strangers; in short, all who are in need, and the care of whom devolves especially upon the minister. We assemble on Sunday, because on that day God created the world, and the same day his Son arose to life again, to confirm his disciples in the doctrine which we have exposed to you.

"If you find this doctrine good, show your respect for it; if not, reject it. But do not condemn to punishment those who commit no crime; for we declare to you that, if you continue to act unjustly, you will not escape the judgment of God. For the rest, whatever be our faith, we desire only that the will of God be done. We might have claimed your favorable regard in con-

[1] That is, a priest. In the first ages, the word πρεσβύτερος or ancient was very frequently [illegible] to signify a bishop or priest, set apart by ordination for the ministry [illegible] designate the priestly

sequence of the letter of your father, Cæsar Adrian, of illustrious and glorious memory; but we have preferred to rely solely upon the justice of our cause."[1]

The Apology of Justin was well calculated to take the world by surprise; for it proclaimed a golden age in the midst of a corrupt generation, and pointed out a new people in the catacombs of an ancient empire. The Christian life must have appeared the more admirable in the public eye, as such perfection had never before been known, harmonizing with nature and the laws, and on the other hand forming a remarkable contrast with the rest of society. It is also invested with an interest which is not to be found in the fabulous excellence of antiquity, because the latter is always depicted in a state of happiness, while the former presents itself through the charms of adversity. It is not amid the foliage of the woods or at the side of the fountain that virtue exerts her greatest power, but under the shade of the prison-wall or amid rivers of blood and tears. How divine does religion appear to us when, in the recess of the catacomb or in the silent darkness of the tomb, we behold a pastor who is surrounded by danger, celebrating, by the feeble glare of his lamp and in presence of his little flock, the mysteries of a persecuted God!

We have deemed it necessary to establish incontestably this high moral character of the first Christians, in order to show that, if the marriage of the clergy was considered unbecoming in that age of purity, it would be altogether impossible to introduce it at the present day. When the number of Christians increased, and morality was weakened with the diffusion of mankind, how could the priest devote himself at the same time to his family and to the Church? How could he have continued chaste with a spouse who had ceased to be so? If our opponents object the practice of Protestant countries, we will observe that it has been necessary in those countries to abolish a great portion of the external worship of religion; that a Protestant minister appears in the church scarcely two or three times a week; that almost all spiritual relations have ceased between him and his flock, and that very often he is a mere man of the world.[2] As to certain Puri-

[1] Justin, *Apolog.*, edit. Marc., fol. 1742. See note B.

[2] "It was no trivial misfortune," says Dr. King, "for the cause of Christianity in England, that at the period of our separation from popery the clergy were

tanical sects that affect an evangelical simplicity, and wish to have a religion without a worship, we hope that they will be passed over in silence. Finally, in those countries where the marriage of the clergy is allowed, the confession of sin, which is the most admirable of moral institutions, has been, and must necessarily have been, discontinued. It cannot be supposed that the Christian would confide the secrets of his heart to a man who has already made a woman the depositary of his own; and he would, with reason, fear to make a confidant of him who has proved faithless to God, and has repudiated the Creator to espouse the creature.

We will now answer the objection drawn from the general law of population. It seems to us that one of the first natural laws that required abrogation at the commencement of the Christian era, was that which encouraged population beyond a certain limit. The age of Jesus Christ was not that of Abraham. The latter appeared at a time when innocence prevailed and the earth was but sparsely inhabited. Jesus Christ, on the contrary, came into the midst of a world that was corrupt and thickly settled. Continence, therefore, may be allowed to woman. The second Eve, in curing the evils that had fallen upon the first, has brought down virginity from heaven, to give us an idea of the purity and joy which preceded the primeval pangs of maternity.

The Legislator of the Christian world was born of a virgin, and died a virgin. Did he not wish thereby to teach us, in a political and natural point of view, that the earth had received its complement of inhabitants, and that the ratio of generation,

---

allowed to marry; for, as might have been foreseen, our ecclesiastics since that time have occupied themselves solely with their wives and their children. The dignitaries of the Church could easily provide for their families with the aid of their large revenues; but the inferior clergy, unable with their slender incomes to establish their children in the world, soon spread over the kingdom swarms of mendicants. . . . . . . As a member of the republic of letters, I have often desired the re-enactment of the canons that prohibited marriage among the clergy. To episcopal celibacy we are indebted for all the magnificent grants that distinguish our two universities: but since the period of the Reformation those two seats of learning have had few benefactors among the members of the hierarchy. If the rich donations of Laud and Sheldon have an eternal claim to our gratitude, it must be remembered that these two prelates were never married," [illegible] &c. Edinburgh Review, July, 1819. T.

far from being extended, should be restricted? In support of this opinion, we may remark that states never perish from a want, but from an excess, of population. The barbarians of the North spread devastation over the globe when their forests became overcrowded; and Switzerland has been compelled to transfer a portion of her industrious inhabitants to other countries, as she pours forth her abundant streams to render them productive. Though the number of laborers has been greatly diminished in France, the cultivation of the soil was never more flourishing than at the present time. Alas! we resemble a swarm of insects buzzing around a cup of wormwood into which a few drops of honey have accidentally fallen; we devour each other as soon as our numbers begin to crowd the spot that we occupy! By a still greater misfortune, the more we increase, the more land we require to satisfy our wants; and as this space is always diminishing, while the passions are extending their sway, the most frightful revolutions must, sooner or later, be the consequence.[1]

Theories, however, have little weight in the presence of facts. Europe is far from being a desert, though the Catholic clergy within her borders have taken the vow of celibacy. Even monasteries are favorable to society, by the good management of the religious, who distribute their commodities at home, and thus afford abundant relief to the poor. Where but in the neighborhood of some rich abbey, did we once behold in France the comfortably dressed husbandman, and laboring people whose joyful countenances betokened their happy condition? Large possessions always produce this effect in the hands of wise and resident proprietors; and such precisely was the character of our monastic domains. But this subject would lead us too far. We shall return to it in treating of the religious orders. We will remark, however, that the clergy have been favorable to the increase of population, by preaching concord and union between man and wife, checking the progress of libertinism, and visiting with the denunciations of the Church the crimes which the people of the cities directed to the diminution of children.

There can be no doubt that every great nation has need of men who, separated from the rest of mankind, invested with some

[1] Note C.

august character, and free from the encumbrances of wife, children, and other worldly affairs, may labor effectually for the advancement of knowledge, the improvement of morals, and the relief of human suffering. What wonders have not our priests and religious accomplished in these three respects for the good of society? But place them in charge of a family: would not the learning and charity which they have consecrated to their country be turned to the profit of their relatives? Happy, indeed, if by this change their virtue were not transformed into vice!

Having disposed of the objections which moralists urge against clerical celibacy, we shall endeavor to answer those of the poets; but for this purpose it will be necessary to employ other arguments, to adduce other authorities, and to write in a different style.

CHAPTER IX.

THE SAME SUBJECT CONTINUED—HOLY ORDERS.

Most of the sages of antiquity led a life of celibacy; and the Gymnosophists, the Brahmins, and the Druids, held chastity in the highest honor. Even among savage tribes it is invested with a heavenly character; because in all ages and countries there has prevailed but one opinion respecting the excellence of virginity. Among the ancients, priests and priestesses, who were supposed to commune intimately with heaven, were obliged to live as solitaries, and the least violation of their vows was visited with a signal punishment. They offered in sacrifice only the heifer that had never been a mother. The loftiest and most attractive characters in mythology were virgins. Such were Venus, Urania, and Minerva, goddesses of genius and wisdom, and Friendship, who was represented as a young maiden. Virginity herself was personified as the moon, and paraded her mysterious modesty amid the refreshing atmosphere of night.

Virginity is not less amiable, considered in its various other relations. In the three departments of nature, it is the source of grace and the perfection of beauty. The poets whom we are now seeking to convince will readily admit what we say. Do they not themselves introduce everywhere the idea of virginity, as lending a charm to their descriptions and representations? Do they not find it in the forest-scene, in the vernal rose, in the winter's snow? and do they not thus station it at the two extremities of life—on the lips of childhood and the gray locks of aged man? Do they not also blend it with the mysteries of the tomb, telling us of antiquity that consecrated to the manes seedless trees, because death is barren, or because in the next life there is no distinction of sex, and the soul is an immortal virgin? Finally, do they not tell us that the irrational animals which approach the nearest to human intelligence are those devoted to chastity? Do we not seem, in fact, to recognise in the bee-hive the model of those monasteries, where vestals are busily engaged in extracting a celestial honey from the flowers of virtue?

In the fine arts, virginity is again the charm, and the Muses owe to it their perpetual youth. But it displays its excellence chiefly in man. St. Ambrose has composed three treatises on virginity, in which he has scattered with a profuse hand the ornaments of style,—his object, as he informs us, being to gain the attention of virgins by the sweetness of his words.[1] He terms virginity *an exemption from every stain*, and shows that the tranquillity which attends it is far superior to the cares of matrimonial life. He addresses the virgin in these words: "The modesty which tinges your cheeks renders you exceedingly beautiful. Retired far from the sight of men, like the rose in some solitary spot, your charms form not the subject of their false surmises. Nevertheless, you are still a competitor for the prize of beauty; not that indeed which falls under the eye, but the beauty of virtue—that beauty which no sickness can disfigure, no age can diminish, and not death itself can take away. God alone is the umpire in this rivalry of virgins, because he loves the beautiful soul, even in a body that is deformed. . . . .
A virgin is the gift of heaven and the joy of her family. She exercises under the paternal roof the priesthood of chastity; she is a victim daily immolated for her mother at the altar of filial piety."[2]

[1] De Virgin., lib. ii. ch. 1.

[2] Ibid., lib. i. ch. 5.

In man, virginity assumes the character of sublimity. When, in the fierce rebellion of the passions, it resists the invitation to evil, it becomes a celestial virtue. "A chaste heart," says St. Bernard, "is by virtue what an angel is by nature. There is more felicity in the purity of the angel, but there is more courage in that of the man." In the religious, virginity transforms itself into humanity: witness the fathers of the Redemption and the orders of Hospitallers, consecrated to the relief of human misery. The learned man it inspires with the love of study; the hermit with that of contemplation: in all it is a powerful principle, whose beneficial influence is always felt in the labors of the mind, and hence it is the most excellent quality of life, since it imparts fresh vigor to the soul, which is the nobler part of our nature.

But if chastity is necessary in any state, it is chiefly so in the service of the divinity. "God," as Plato observes, "is the true standard of things, and we should make every effort to resemble him." He who ministers at his altar is more strictly obliged to this than others. "The question here," says St. Chrysostom, "is not the government of an empire or the command of an army, but the performance of functions that require an angelic virtue. The soul of the priest should be purer than the rays of the sun." "The Christian minister," adds St. Jerome, "is the interpreter between God and man." The priest, therefore, must be a divine personage. An air of holiness and mystery should surround him. Retired within the sacred gloom of the temple, let him be heard without being perceived by those without. Let his voice, solemn, grave, and religious, announce the prophetic word or chant the hymn of peace in the holy recesses of the tabernacle. Let his visits among men be transient; and if he appear amid the bustle of the world, let it be only to render a service to the unhappy."

It is on these conditions that the priest will enjoy the respect and confidence of his people. But he will soon forfeit both if he be seen in the halls of the rich, if he be encumbered with a wife, if he be too familiar in society, if he betray faults which are condemned in the world, or if he lead those around him to suspect for a moment that he is a man like other men.

Chastity in old age is something superhuman. Priam, ancient as mou[illegible] Gargarus, surrounded in his pal[illegible] presents a noble type of paternity;

but Plato without wife and children, seated on the steps of a temple at the extremity of a cape lashed by the waves, and there lecturing to his disciples on the existence of God, exhibits a far more elevated character. He belongs not to the earth; he seems to be one of those spirits or higher intelligences of whom he speaks in his writings.

Thus, virginity, ascending from the last link in the chain of beings up to man, soon passes from man to the angels, and from the angels to God, in whom it is absorbed. God reigns in a glory unique, inimitable in the eternal firmament, as the sun, his image, shines with unequalled splendor in the visible heavens.

We may conclude, that poets and men even of the most refined taste can make no reasonable objection to the celibacy of the priesthood, since virginity is among the cherished recollections of the past, is one of the charms of friendship, is associated with the solemn thought of the tomb, with the innocence of childhood, with the enchantment of youth, with the charity of the religious, with the sanctity of the priest and of old age, and with the divinity in the angels and in God himself.

CHAPTER X.

SAME SUBJECT CONTINUED—MATRIMONY.

EUROPE owes also to Christianity the few good laws which it possesses. There is not, perhaps, a single contingency in civil affairs for which provision has not been made by the canon law, the fruit of the experience of fifteen centuries and of the genius of the Innocents and the Gregories. The wisest emperors and kings, as Charlemagne and Alfred the Great, were of opinion that they could not do better than to introduce into the civil code a part of this ecclesiastical code, which contains the essence of the Levitical law, the gospel, and the Roman jurisprudence. What an edifice is the Church of Christ! How vast! how wonderful!

In elevating marriage to the dignity of a sacrament, Jesus

Christ has shown us, in the first place, the great symbol of his union with the Church. When we consider that matrimony is the axis on which the whole social economy revolves. can we suppose it to be ever sufficiently sacred, or too highly admire the wisdom of him who has stamped it with the seal of religion?

The Church has made every provision for so important a step in life. She has determined the degrees of relationship within which matrimony is allowable. The canon law,[1] which determines the degree of consanguinity by the number of generations from the parent stock, has forbidden marriage within the fourth generation; while the civil law, following a double mode of computation, formerly prohibited it only within the second degree. Such was the Arcadian law, as inserted in the Institutes of Justinian.[2] But the Church, with her accustomed wisdom, has been governed in this by the gradual improvement of popular manners.[3] In the first ages of Christianity, marriage was forbidden within the seventh degree of consanguinity; and some Councils, as that of Toledo in the sixth century, prohibited without exception all alliances between members of the same family.[4]

The spirit that dictated these laws is worthy of the pure religion which we profess. The pagan world was far from imitating this chastity of the Christian people. At Rome, marriage was permitted between cousins-german; and Claudius, in order to marry Agrippina, enacted a law which allowed an uncle to form an alliance with his niece.[5] By the laws of Solon, a brother could marry his sister by the mother's side.[6]

---

[1] Concil. Lat., an. 1205 [2] De Nupt., tit. 10

[3] Concil. Duziac., an. 814. The canon law was necessarily modified according to the manners of the different nations—Goths, Vandals, English, Franks, Burgundians—who entered successively into the Church.

[4] Can. 5.

[5] Suet., in *Claud.* It should be observed that this law did not become general, as we learn from the *Fragments* of Ulpian, tit. 5 and 6, and that it was repealed by the code of Theodosius, as well as that relating to cousins-german. In the Christian Church the pope has the power to dispense from the canon law, according to circumstances: a very wise provision, since no law can be so universally applicable as to comprehend every case. As to the regulation under the Old Testament regarding marriage between brothers and sisters, it belonged to the general law of population, which, as we have observed, was abolished at the comi[illegible] men had received their complement.

[6] Plut., in *Sol.*

The Church, however, did not confine her precautions to the above-mentioned legislation. For some time she followed the Levitical law in regard to those who were related by affinity; but subsequently she numbered among the nullifying impediments of marriage, all the degrees of affinity corresponding to the degrees of consanguinity within which marriage is prohibited.[1] She also provided for a case which had escaped the notice of all previous jurisprudence—that of a man guilty of illicit intercourse with a woman. According to the discipline of the Church, this man cannot marry any woman who is related within the second degree to the object of his unlawful love.[2] This law, which had existed to a certain extent in the early ages of Christianity,[3] became a settled point by a decree of the Council of Trent, and was considered so wise an enactment that the French code, though it rejected the Council as a whole, willingly adopted this particular canon.

The numerous impediments to marriage between relatives which the Church has established, besides being founded on moral and spiritual considerations, have a beneficial tendency in a political point of view, by encouraging the division of property, and preventing all the wealth of a state from accumulating, in a long series of years, in the hands of a few individuals.

The Church has retained the ceremony of betrothing, which may be traced to a remote antiquity. We are informed by Aulus Gellius that it was known among the people of Latium:[4] it was adopted by the Romans,[5] and was customary among the Greeks. It was honored under the old covenant; and in the new, Joseph was betrothed to Mary. The intention of this custom is to allow the bride and bridegroom time to become acquainted with each other previously to their union.[6]

In our rural hamlets, the ceremony of betrothing was still witnessed with its ancient graces.[7] On a beautiful morning in the month of August, a young peasant repaired to the farm-house of

[1] Conc. Lat. [2] Ibid., ch. 4, sess. 24. [3] Conc. Anc., cap. ult., an. 304. [4] Noct. Att., lib. iv. cap. 4. [5] Lib. ii. ff. de Spons.

[6] St. Augustine, speaking of this usage, says that the bride is not given to her lord immediately after the betrothing, "lest he be inclined to think less of one who has not been the object of his prolonged aspirations."

[7] The author uses the past tense, alluding to customs before the French Revolution. T.

his future father-in-law, to join his intended bride. Two musicians, reminding you of the minstrels of old, led the way, playing tunes of the days of chivalry, or the hymns of pilgrims. Departed ages, issuing from their Gothic tombs, seemed to accompany the village youth with their ancient manners and their ancient recollections. The priest pronounced the accustomed benediction over the bride, who deposited upon the altar a distaff adorned with ribbons. The company then returned to the farm-house; the lord and lady of the manor, the clergyman of the parish, and the village justice, placed themselves, with the young couple, the husbandmen and the matrons, round a table, upon which were served up the Eumœan boar and the fatted calf of the patriarchs. The festivities concluded with a dance in the neighboring barn; the daughter of the lord of the manor took the bridegroom for her partner, while the spectators were seated upon the newly-harvested sheaves, forcibly reminded of the daughters of Jethro, the reapers of Booz, and the nuptials of Jacob and Rachel.

The betrothing is followed by the publication of the bans. This excellent custom, unknown to antiquity, is altogether of ecclesiastical institution. It dates from a period anterior to the fourteenth century, as it is mentioned in a decretal of Innocent III., who enacted it as a general law at the Council of Lateran. It was renewed by the Tridentine Synod, and has since been established in France. The design of this practice is to prevent clandestine unions, and to discover the impediments to marriage that may exist between the contracting parties.

But at length the Christian marriage approaches. It comes attended by a very different ceremonial from that which accompanied the betrothing. Its pace is grave and solemn; its rites are silent and august. Man is apprised that he now enters upon a new career. The words of the nuptial blessing—words which God himself pronounced over the first couple in the world—fill the husband with profound awe, while they announce to him that he is performing the most important act of life; that, like Adam, he is about to become the head of a family, and to take upon himself the whole burden of humanity. The wife receives a caution equally impressive. The image of pleasure vanishes before that of her duties. A voice seems to issue from the altar, and to address her in these words: "Knowest thou, O Eve, what thou art doing? Knowest thou that there is no longer any liberty for thee but that of the tomb? Knowest thou what it is to bear in thy mortal womb an immortal being, formed in the image of God?"

Among the ancients, the hymeneal rites were a ceremony replete with licentiousness and clamorous mirth, which suggested none of the serious reflections that marriage inspires. Christianity alone has restored its dignity.

Religion also, discovering before philosophy the proportion in which the two sexes are born, first decreed that a man should have but one wife, and that their union should be indissoluble till death. Divorce is unknown in the Catholic Church, except among some minor nations of Illyria, who were formerly subject to the Venetian government, and who follow the Greek rite.[1] If the passions of men have revolted against this law,—if they have not perceived the confusion which divorce introduces into the family, by disturbing the order of succession, by alienating the paternal affections, by corrupting the heart and converting marriage into a civil prostitution,—we cannot hope that the few words which we have to offer will produce any effect. Without entering deeply into the subject, we shall merely observe, that if by divorce you think to promote the happiness of the married couple, (and this is now the main argument,) you lie under a strange mistake. That man who has not been the comfort of a first wife,—who could not attach himself to the virginal heart and first maternity of his lawful spouse,—who has not been able to bend his passions to the domestic yoke, or to confine his heart to the nuptial couch,—that man will never confer felicity on a second wife. Neither will he himself be a gainer by the exchange. What he takes for differences of temper between himself and the wife to whom he is

---

[1] By a departure from the tradition and practice of the Church, and a preference for the concessions of the civil code, it had become the custom in these countries not only to allow divorce *a mensa et thoro* in cases of adultery, but also to permit the parties to marry again. The Council of Trent was on the point of condemning those who hold that marriage is dissolved *quoad vinculum* by the crime of adultery; but, for reasons of expediency, the canon on this subject was so framed as not to stigmatize them with the note of heresy. See Tournely, *De Matr.*, p. 394; Archbp. Kenrick, *Theol. Dogm.*, vol. iv. p. 120; *Biblioth. Sacrée*, tome xvi. art. *Mariage*; Waterworth's *Canons and Decrees of Counc. of Trent*, p. 228, &c. T.

united, is but the impulse of an inconstant disposition and the restlessness of desire. Habit and length of time are more necessary to happiness, and even to love, than may be imagined. A man is not happy in the object of his attachment till he has passed many days, and, above all, many days of adversity, in her company. They ought to be acquainted with the most secret recesses of each other's soul; the mysterious veil with which husband and wife were covered in the primitive Church, must be lifted up in all its folds for them, while to the eye of others it remains impenetrable. What! for the slightest pretence or caprice must I be liable to lose my partner and my children, and renounce the pleasing hope of passing my old age in the bosom of my family? Let me not be told that this apprehension will oblige me to be a better husband. No; we become attached to that good only of which we are certain, and set but little value on a possession of which we are likely to be deprived.

Let us not give to matrimony the wings of lawless love; let us not transform a sacred reality into a fleeting phantom. There is something which will again destroy your happiness in your trancient connections: you will be pursued by remorse. You will be continually comparing one wife with another, her whom you have lost with her whom you have found; and, believe me, the balance will always be in favor of the former. Thus has God formed the heart of man. This disturbance of one sentiment by another will poison all your pleasures. When you fondly caress your new child, you will think of that which you have forsaken. If you press your wife to your heart, your heart will tell you that it is not the bosom of the first. Every thing tends to unity in man. He is not happy if he divides his affections; and like God, in whose image he was created, his soul incessantly seeks to concentrate in one point the past, the present, and the future.

These are the remarks which we had to offer on the sacraments of Holy Orders and Matrimony. As to the images which they suggest to the mind, we deem it unnecessary to present them. Where is the imagination that cannot picture to itself the priest bidding adieu to the joys of life, that he may devote himself to the cause of humanity; or the maiden consecrating herself to the silence of a convent that she may find the silent repose of her heart; or the betrothed couple appearing at the altar of religion, to vow to each other an undying love?

The wife of a Christian is not a mere mortal. She is an extraordinary, a mysterious, an angelic being; she is flesh of her husband's flesh and bone of his bone. By his union with her he only takes back a portion of his substance. His soul, as well as his body, is imperfect without his wife. He possesses strength, she has beauty. He opposes the enemy in arms, he cultivates the soil of his country; but he enters not into domestic details; he has need of a wife to prepare his repast and his bed. He encounters afflictions, and the partner of his nights is there to soothe them; his days are clouded by adversity, but on his couch he meets with a chaste embrace and forgets all his sorrows. Without woman he would be rude, unpolished, solitary. Woman suspends around him the flowers of life, like those honeysuckles of the forest which adorn the trunk of the oak with their perfumed garlands. Finally, the Christian husband and his wife live and die together; together they rear the issue of their union; together they return to dust, and together they again meet beyond the confines of the tomb, to part no more.

CHAPTER XI.

EXTREME UNCTION.

But it is in sight of that tomb, silent vestibule of another world, that Christianity displays all its sublimity. If most of the ancient religions consecrated the ashes of the dead, none ever thought of preparing the soul for that unknown country "from whose bourn no traveller returns"

Come and witness the most interesting spectacle that earth can exhibit. Come and see the faithful Christian expire. He has ceased to be a creature of this world: he no longer belongs to his native country: all connection between him and society is at an end. For him the calculations of time have closed, and he has already begun to date from the great era of eternity. A priest, seated at his pillow, administers consolation. This minister of God cheers the dying man with the bright prospect of immortality; and that sublime scene which all antiquity exhibited but once, in the last moments of its most eminent philosopher, is daily renewed on the humble pallet of the meanest Christian that expires!

At length the decisive moment arrives. A sacrament opened to this just man the gates of the world; a sacrament is about to close them. Religion rocked him in the cradle of life; and now her sweet song and maternal hand will lull him to sleep in the cradle of death. She prepares the baptism of this second birth: but mark, she employs not water; she anoints him with oil, emblem of celestial incorruptibility. The liberating sacrament gradually loosens the Christian's bonds. His soul, nearly set free from the body, is almost visible in his countenance. Already he hears the concerts of the seraphim: already he prepares to speed his flight to those heavenly regions where Hope, the daughter of Virtue and of Death, invites him. Meanwhile, the angel of peace, descending toward this righteous man, touches with a golden sceptre his weary eyes, and closes them deliciously to the light. He dies; yet his last sigh was inaudible. He expires; yet, long after he is no more, his friends keep silent watch around his couch, under the impression that he only slumbers: so gently did this Christian pass from earth.

BOOK II.

VIRTUES AND MORAL LAWS.

CHAPTER I.

VICES AND VIRTUES ACCORDING TO RELIGION.

MOST of the ancient philosophers have marked the distinction between vices and virtues; but how far superior in this respect also is the wisdom of religion to the wisdom of men!

Let us first consider pride alone, which the Church ranks as the principal among the vices. Pride was the sin of Satan, the first sin that polluted this terrestrial globe. Pride is so completely the root of evil, that it is intermingled with all the other infirmities of our nature. It beams in the smile of envy, it bursts forth in the debaucheries of the libertine, it counts the gold of avarice, it sparkles in the eyes of anger, it is the companion of graceful effeminacy.

Pride occasioned the fall of Adam; pride armed Cain against his innocent brother; it was pride that erected Babel and overthrew Babylon. Through pride Athens became involved in the common ruin of Greece; pride destroyed the throne of Cyrus, divided the empire of Alexander, and crushed Rome itself under the weight of the universe.

In the particular circumstances of life, pride produces still more baneful effects. It has the presumption to attack even the Deity himself.

Upon inquiring into the causes of atheism, we are led to this melancholy observation: that most of those who rebel against Heaven imagine that they find something wrong in the constitution of society or the order of nature; excepting, however, the young who are seduced by the world, or writers whose only object is to attract notice. But how happens it that they who are deprived of the inconsiderable advantages which a capricious fortune gives or takes away, have not the sense to seek the remedy of this trifling evil in drawing near to God? He is the great fountainhead of blessing. So truly is he the quintessence itself of beauty, that his name alone, pronounced with love, is sufficient to impart something divine to the man who is the least favored by nature, as has been remarked in the case of Socrates. Let atheism be for those who, not having courage enough to rise superior to the trials of their lot, display in their blasphemies naught but the first vice of man.

If the Church has assigned to pride the first place in the scale of human depravity, she has shown no less wisdom in the classification of the six other capital vices. It must not be supposed that the order of their arrangement is arbitrary: we need only examine it to perceive that religion, with an admirable discrimination, passes from those vices which attack society in general to such as recoil upon the head of the guilty individual alone. Thus, for instance, envy, luxury, avarice and anger, immediately follow pride, because they are vices which suppose a foreign object and exist only in the midst of society; whereas gluttony and idleness, which come last, are solitary and base inclinations, that find in themselves their principal gratification.

In the estimate and classification of the virtues, we behold the same profound knowledge of human nature. Before the coming of Jesus Christ the human soul was a chaos; the Word spoke, and order instantly pervaded the intellectual world, as the same *fiat* had once produced the beautiful arrangement of the physical world: this was the moral creation of the universe. The virtues, like pure fires, ascended into the heavens: some, like brilliant suns, attracted every eye by their glorious radiance; others, more modest luminaries, appeared only under the veil of night, which, however, could not conceal their lustre. From that moment an admirable balance between strength and weakness was established; religion hurled all her thunderbolts at Pride, that vice which feeds upon the virtues: she detected it in the inmost recesses of the heart, she pursued it in all its changes; the sacraments, in holy array, were marshalled against it; and Humility, clothed in sackcloth, her waist begirt with a cord, her feet bare, her head covered with ashes, her downcast eyes swimming in tears, became one of the primary virtues of the believer.

CHAPTER II.

OF FAITH.

And what were the virtues so highly recommended by the sages of Greece? Fortitude, temperance, and prudence. None but Jesus Christ could teach the world that faith, hope and charity, are virtues alike adapted to the ignorance and the wretchedness of man.

It was undoubtedly a stupendous wisdom that pointed out faith to us as the source of all the virtues. There is no power but in conviction. If a train of reasoning is strong, a poem divine, a picture beautiful, it is because the understanding or the eye, to whose judgment they are submitted, is convinced of a certain truth hidden in this reasoning, this poem, this picture. What wonders a small band of troops persuaded of the abilities of their leader is capable of achieving! Thirty-five thousand Greeks follow Alexander to the conquest of the world; Lacedæmon commits her destiny to the hands of Lycurgus, and Lacedæmon becomes the wisest of cities; Babylon believes that she is formed for greatness, and greatness crowns her confidence; an oracle gives the empire of the universe to the Romans, and the Romans obtain the empire of the universe; Columbus alone, among all his contemporaries, persists in believing the existence of a new world, and a new world rises from the bosom of the deep. Friendship, patriotism, love, every noble sentiment, is likewise a species of faith. Because they had faith, a Codrus, a Pylades, a Regulus, an Arria, performed prodigies. For the same reason, they who believe nothing, who treat all the convictions of the soul as illusions, who consider every noble action as insanity, and look with pity upon the warm imagination and tender sensibility of genius—for the same reason such hearts will never achieve any thing great or generous: they have faith only in matter and in death, and they are already insensible as the one, and cold and icy as the other.

In the language of ancient chivalry, to *pledge one's faith* was synonymous with all the prodigies of honor. Roland, Duguesclin, Bayard, were *faithful* knights; and the fields of Roncevaux, of Auray, of Bresse, the descendants of the Moors, of the English, and of the Lombards, still tell what men they were who plighted their faith and homage to their God, their lady, and their country. Shall we mention the martyrs, "who," to use the words of St. Ambrose, "without armies, without legions, vanquished tyrants, assuaged the fury of lions, took from the fire its vehemence and from the sword its edge"?[1] Considered in this point of view, faith is so formidable a power, that if it were applied to evil purposes it would convulse the world. There is nothing that a man who is under the influence of a profound conviction, and who submits his reason implicitly to the direction of another, is not capable of performing. This proves that the most eminent virtues, when separated from God and taken in their merely moral relations, border on the greatest vices. Had philosophers made this observation, they would not have taken so much pains to fix the limits between good and evil. There was no necessity for the Christian lawgiver, like Aristotle, to contrive a scale for the purpose of ingeniously placing a virtue between two vices; he has completely removed the difficulty, by inculcating that virtues are not virtues unless they flow back toward their source—that is to say, toward the Deity.

Of this truth we shall be thoroughly convinced, if we consider faith in reference to human affairs, but a faith which is the offspring of religion. From faith proceed all the virtues of society, since it is true, according to the unanimous acknowledgment of wise men, that the doctrine which commands the belief in a God who will reward and punish is the main pillar both of morals and of civil government.

Finally, if we employ faith for its higher and specific objects,—if we direct it entirely toward the Creator,—if we make it the intellectual eye, by which to discover the wonders of the holy city and the empire of real existence,—if it serve for wings to our soul, to raise us above the calamities of life,—we will admit that the Scriptures have not too highly extolled this virtue, when

[1] [illegible], *de Off.*, c. 35.

they speak of the prodigies which may be performed by its means. Faith, celestial comforter, thou dost more than remove mountains: thou takest away the heavy burdens by which the heart of man is grievously oppressed![1]

CHAPTER III.

OF HOPE AND CHARITY.

HOPE, the second theological virtue, is almost as powerful as faith. Desire is the parent of power; whoever strongly desires is sure to obtain. "Seek," says Jesus Christ, "and ye shall find; knock, and it shall be opened unto you." In the same sense Pythagoras observed that "Power dwelleth with necessity;" for necessity implies privation, and privation is accompanied with desire. Desire or hope is genius. It possesses that energy which produces, and that thirst which is never appeased. Is a man disappointed in his plans? it is because he did not desire with ardor; because he was not animated with that love which sooner or later grasps the object to which it aspires; that love which in the Deity embraces all things and enjoys all, by means of a boundless hope, ever gratified and ever reviving.

There is, however, an essential difference between faith and hope considered as a power. Faith has its focus out of ourselves; it arises from an external object. Hope, on the contrary, springs up within us, and operates externally. The former is instilled into us, the latter is produced by our own desire; the former is obedience, the latter is love. But as faith more readily produces the other virtues, as it flows immediately from God, and is therefore superior to hope, which is only a part of man, the Church necessarily assigned to it the highest rank.

The peculiar characteristic of hope is that which places it in relation with our sorrows. That religion which made a virtue of hope was most assuredly revealed by heaven. This nurse of the unfortunate, taking her station by man like a mother beside her

[1] See note D

suffering child, rocks him in her arms, presses him to her bosom, and refreshes him with a beverage which soothes all his woes. She watches by his solitary pillow; she lulls him to sleep with her magic strains. Is it not surprising to see hope, which is so delightful a companion and seems to be a natural emotion of the soul, transformed for the Christian into a virtue which is an essential part of his duty? Let him do what he will, he is obliged to drink copiously from this enchanted cup, at which thousands of poor creatures would esteem themselves happy to moisten their lips for a single moment. Nay, more, (and this is the most marvellous circumstance of all,) he will be *rewarded for having hoped*, or, in other words, *for having made himself happy*. The Christian, whose life is a continual warfare, is treated by religion in his defeat like those vanquished generals whom the Roman senate received in triumph, for this reason alone, that they had not despaired of the final safety of the commonwealth. But if the ancients ascribed something marvellous to the man who never despaired, what would they have thought of the Christian, who, in his astonishing language, talks not of entertaining hope, but of practising it?

What shall we now say of that charity which is the daughter of Jesus Christ? The proper signification of charity is grace and joy. Religion, aiming at the reformation of the human heart, and wishing to make its affections and feelings subservient to virtue, has invented a *new passion*. In order to express it, she has not employed the word love, which is too common; or the word friendship, which ceases at the tomb; or the word pity, which is too much akin to pride: but she has found the term *caritas*, CHARITY, which embraces all the three, and which at the same time is allied to something celestial. By means of this, she purifies our inclinations and directs them toward the Creator; by this she inculcates that admirable truth, that men ought to love each other in God, who will thus spiritualize their love, divesting it of all earthly alloy and leaving it in its immortal purity. By this she inculcates the stupendous truth that mortals ought to love each other, if I may so express myself, through God, who spiritualizes their love, and separates from it whatever belong [illegible]

But [illegible] Christian virtue, an immediate emanation

from the Almighty and his Word, it is also in close alliance with nature. It is in this continual harmony between heaven and earth, between God and man, that we discover the character of true religion. The moral and political institutions of antiquity are often in contradiction to the sentiments of the human soul. Christianity, on the contrary, ever in unison with the heart, enjoins not solitary and abstract virtues, but such as are derived from our wants and are useful to mankind. It has placed charity as an abundant fountain in the desert of life. "Charity," says the apostle, "is patient, is kind; charity envieth not, dealeth not perversely, is not puffed up, is not ambitious, seeketh not her own, is not provoked to anger, thinketh no evil, rejoiceth not in iniquity, but rejoiceth with the truth; beareth all things, believeth all things, hopeth all things, endureth all things."[1]

CHAPTER IV.

OF THE MORAL LAWS, OR THE TEN COMMANDMENTS.

It is a reflection not a little mortifying to our pride, that all the maxims of human wisdom may be comprehended in a few pages: and even in those pages how many errors may be found! The laws of Minos and Lycurgus have remained standing after the fall of the nations for which they were designed, only as the pyramids of the desert, the immortal palaces of death.

Laws of the Second Zoroaster.

Time, boundless and uncreated, is the creator of all things. The word was his daughter, who gave birth to Orsmus, the good deity, and Arimhan, the god of evil.

Invoke the celestial bull, the father of grass and of man.

The most meritorious work that a man can perform is to cultivate his land with care.

Pray with purity of thought, word, and action.[2]

[1] 1 *Cor.* xiii. [2] *Zend-avesta.*

Teach thy child at the age of five years the distinction between good and evil.[1] Let the ungrateful be punished.[2]

The child who has thrice disobeyed his father shall die.

The law declares the woman who contracts a second marriage to be impure.

The impostor shall be scourged with rods.

Despise the liar.

At the end and the beginning of the year keep a festival of ten days.

Indian Laws.

The universe is Vishnu.

Whatever has been, is he; whatever is, is he; whatever will be, is he.

Let men be equal.

Love virtue for its own sake; renounce the fruit of thy works.

Mortal, be wise, and thou shalt be strong as ten thousand elephants.

The soul is God.

Confess the faults of thy children to the sun and to men, and purify thyself in the waters of the Ganges.[3]

Egyptian Laws.

Cnef, the universal God, is unknown darkness, impenetrable obscurity.

Osiris is the good, and Typhon the evil deity.

Honor thy parents.

Follow the profession of thy father.

Be virtuous; the judges of the lake will, after thy death, pass sentence on thy actions.

Wash thy body twice each day and twice each night.

Live upon little.

Reveal no secrets.[4]

Laws of Minos

Swear not by the Gods.

Young man, examine not the law.

---

[1] Xen [illegible] Plat. [illegible] L [illegible] ii. [2] Xenoph., *Cyrop.*

[3] *Pre* [illegible] *B* [illegible] *Hi* [illegible] *Ind.* *D* [illegible] *Sic.*, *&c.*

[4] Her [illegible] Pl [illegible] *Le* [illegible] Plut., *de Is. et Os.*

The law declares him infamous who has no friend.

The adultress shall be crowned with wool, and sold.

Let your repasts be public, your life frugal, and your dances martial.[1]

[We shall not quote here the laws of Lycurgus, because they are partly but a repetition of those of Minos.]

Laws of Solon.

The son who neglects to bury his father, and he who defends him not, shall die.

The adulterer shall not enter the temples.

The magistrate who is intoxicated shall drink hemlock.

The cowardly soldier shall be punished with death.

It shall be lawful to kill the citizen who remains neutral in civil dissensions.

Let him who wishes to die acquaint the Archon, and die.

He who is guilty of sacrilege shall suffer death.

Wife, be the guide of thy blind husband.

The immoral man shall be disqualified for governing.[2]

Primitive Laws of Rome.

Honor small fortune.

Let men be both husbandmen and soldiers.

Keep wine for the aged.

The husbandman who eats his ox shall be sentenced to die.[3]

Laws of the Gauls, or Druids.

The universe is eternal, the soul immortal.

Honor nature.

Defend thy mother, thy country, the earth

Admit woman into thy councils.

Honor the stranger, and set apart his portion out of thy harvest.

The man who has lost his honor shall be buried in mud.

Erect no temples, and commit the history of the past to thy memory alone.

Man, thou art free; own no property.

---

[1] Arist., *Pol.*; Plat., *de leg.*

[2] Plut., *in Vit. Sol.*; Tit. Liv.

[3] Plut., *in Num.*; Tit. Liv

Honor the aged, and let not the young bear witness against them.

The brave man shall be rewarded after death, and the coward punished.[1]

Laws of Pythagoras.

Honor the immortal Gods as established by the law.

Honor thy parents.

Do that which will not wound thy memory.

Close not thine eyes to sleep, till thou hast thrice examined in thy soul the actions of the day.

Ask thyself: Where have I been? What have I done? What ought I to have done?

Then, after a holy life, when thy body shall return to the elements, thou shalt become immortal and incorruptible; thou shalt no longer be liable to death.[2]

Such is nearly all that has been preserved of the so highly vaunted wisdom of antiquity! Here, God is represented as profound darkness; doubtless from excess of light, like the dimness that obstructs the sight when you endeavor to look at the sun: there, the man who has no friend is declared infamous, a denunciation which includes all the unfortunate: again, suicide is authorized by law: and lastly, some of these sages seem totally to forget the existence of a Supreme Being. Moreover, how many vague, incoherent, commonplace ideas are found in most of these sentences! The sages of the Portico and of the Academy alternately proclaim such contradictory maxims, that we may prove from the same book that its author believed and did not believe in God; that he acknowledged and did not acknowledge a positive virtue; that liberty is the greatest of blessings and despotism the best of governments.

[1] Tacit., *de mor. Germ.*; Strab.; Cæsar, *Com.*; Edda, &c.

[2] To these Tables might be added an extract from Plato's *Republic*, or rather from the twelve books of his laws, which we consider his best work, on account of the exquisite picture of the three old men who converse together on their way to the fountain, and the good sense which pervades this dialogue. But these precepts were not reduced to *practice;* we shall therefore refrain from any notice of them. As to the Koran, all that it contains, either holy or just, is borrowe[illegible] Scriptures: the rest is a Rabbin-

If, amid these conflicting sentiments, we were to discover a code of moral laws, without contradictions, without errors, which would remove all our doubts, and teach us what we ought to think of God and in what relation we really stand with men,—if this code were delivered with a tone of authority and a simplicity of language never before known,—should we not conclude that these laws have emanated from heaven alone? These divine precepts we possess; and what a subject do they present for the meditation of the sage and for the fancy of the poet! Behold Moses as he descends from the burning mountain. In his hands he carries two tables of stone; brilliant rays encircle his brow; his face beams with divine glory; the terrors of Jehovah go before him; in the horizon are seen the mountains of Libanus, crowned with their eternal snows, and their stately cedars disappearing in the clouds. Prostrate at the foot of Sinai, the posterity of Jacob cover their faces, lest they behold God and die. At length the thunders cease, and a voice proclaims:—

Hearken, O Israel, unto me, Jehovah, *thy Gods*,[1] who have brought thee out of the land of Mizraim, out of the house of bondage.

1. Thou shalt have no other Gods before my face.

2. Thou shalt not make any idol with thy hands, nor any image of that which is in the *astonishing waters above*, nor on the earth beneath, nor in the waters under the earth. Thou shalt not bow before the images, and thou shalt not serve them; for I, I am Jehovah, *thy Gods*, the strong God, the jealous God, visiting the iniquity of the fathers, the iniquity of those who hate me,

---

[1] We translate the Decalogue *verbatim* from the Hebrew, on account of the expression *thy Gods*, which is not rendered in any version. (*Elohe* is the plural masculine of *Elohim*, God, Judge; we frequently meet with it thus in the plural in the Bible, while the verb, the pronoun, and the adjective remain in the singular. In *Gen.* i. we read *Elohe bara*, the Gods *created*, (sing.) and it is impossible to understand any other than three persons; for if two had been meant, Elohim would have been in the *dual*. We shall make another remark, not less important, respecting the word *Adamah*, which likewise occurs in the Decalogue. *Adam* signifies *red earth*, and *ah*, the expletive, expresses something *farther, beyond*. God makes use of it in promising long days on the earth AND BEYOND to such children as honor their father and mother. Thus the Trinity and the immortality of the soul are implied in the Decalogue by *Elohe, thy Gods*, or *several divine existents in unity*, Jehovah; and *Adam-ah*. earth and beyond.) See note E.

upon the children to the third and fourth generation, and showing mercy a thousand times to those who love me and who keep my commandments.

3. Thou shalt not take the name of Jehovah, *thy Gods*, in vain; for he will not hold him guiltless who taketh his name in vain.

4. Remember the sabbath day to keep it holy. Six days shalt thou labor and do thy work; but the seventh day of Jehovah, *thy Gods*, thou shalt not do any work, neither thou, nor thy son, nor thy daughter, nor thy man-servant, nor thy maid-servant, nor thy camel, nor thy guest *before thy doors;* for in six days Jehovah made the marvellous waters above,[1] the earth and the sea, and all that is in them, and rested the seventh day: wherefore Jehovah blessed and hallowed it.

5. Honor thy father and thy mother, that thy days may be long on the earth and *beyond* the earth which Jehovah, *thy Gods*, hath given thee.

6. Thou shalt not kill.

7. Thou shalt not commit adultery.

8. Thou shalt not steal.

9. Thou shalt not bear false witness against thy neighbor.

10. Thou shalt not covet thy neighbor's house, nor thy neighbor's wife, nor his man-servant, nor his maid-servant, nor his ox, nor his ass, nor any thing that is thy neighbor's.

Such are the laws which the great Creator has engraved, not only upon the marble of Sinai, but also upon the heart of man. What strikes us, in the first place, is that character of universality which distinguishes this divine code from all human codes that precede it. Here we have the law of all nations, of all climates, of all times. Pythagoras and Zoroaster addressed the Greeks and the Medes; Jehovah speaks to all mankind. In him we recognise that Almighty Father who watches over the universe, and who dispenses alike from his bounteous hand the grain of corn that feeds the insect and the sun that enlightens it.

[1] This translation is far from giving any idea of the magnificence of the original. *Shamajim* is a kind of exclamation of wonder, like the voice of a whole nation, which, on viewing the firmament, would cry out with one accord "*Behold those miraculous waters suspended in the expanse above us!—those orbs of crystal and [illegible]!*" How is it possible to render in our language, in the translation [illegible] this poetical idea conveyed in a word of three syllables?

In the next place, nothing can be more admirable than these moral laws of the Hebrews, for their simplicity and justice. The pagans enjoined upon men to honor the authors of their days: Solon decrees death as the punishment of the wicked son. What does the divine law say on this subject? It promises life to filial piety. This commandment is founded on the very constitution of our nature. God makes a precept of filial love, but he has not enjoined paternal affection. He knew that the son, in whom are centred all the thoughts and hopes of the father, would often be but too fondly cherished by his parent: but he imposed the duty of love upon the son, because he knew the fickleness and the pride of youth.

In the Decalogue, as in the other works of the Almighty, we behold majesty and grace of expression combined with the intrinsic power of divine wisdom. The Brahmin expresses but very imperfectly the three persons of the Deity; the name of Jehovah embraces them in a single word, composed of three tenses of the verb *to be* united by a sublime combination: *havah*, he was; *hovah*, being, or he is; and *je*, which, when placed before the three radical letters of a verb in Hebrew, indicates the future, *he will be*.

Finally, the legislators of antiquity have marked in their codes the epochs of the festivals of nations; but Israel's sabbath or day of rest is the sabbath of God himself. The Hebrew, as well as the Gentile, his heir, in the hours of his humble occupation, has nothing less before his eyes than the successive creation of the universe. Did Greece, though so highly poetical, ever refer the labors of the husbandman or the artisan to those splendid moments in which God created the light, marked out the course of the sun, and animated the heart of man?

Laws of God, how little do you resemble those of human institution! Eternal as the principle whence you emanated, in vain do ages roll away; ye are proof against the lapse of time, against persecution, and against the corruption of nations. This religious legislation, organized in the bosom of political legislations, and nevertheless independent of their fate, is an astonishing prodigy. While forms of government pass away or are newly-modelled, while power is transferred from hand to hand, a few Christians continue, amid the changes of life, to adore the same

God, to submit to the same laws, without thinking themselves released from their ties by revolution, adversity, and example. What religion of antiquity did not lose its moral influence with the loss of its priests and its sacrifices? Where are now the mysteries of Trophonius's cave and the secrets of the Eleusinian Ceres? Did not Apollo fall with Delphi, Baal with Babylon, Serapis with Thebes, Jupiter with the Capitol? It can be said of Christianity alone, that it has often witnessed the destruction of its temples, without being affected by their fall. There were not always edifices erected in honor of Jesus Christ; but every place is a temple for the living God: the receptacle of the dead, the cavern of the mountain, and above all, the heart of the righteous. Jesus Christ had not always altars of porphyry, pulpits of cedar and ivory, and happy ones of this world for his servants: a stone in the desert is sufficient for the celebration of his mysteries, a tree for the proclamation of his laws, and a bed of thorns for the practice of his virtues.

BOOK III.

THE TRUTHS OF THE SCRIPTURES, THE FALL OF MAN.

CHAPTER I.

THE SUPERIORITY OF THE HISTORY OF MOSES OVER ALL OTHER COSMOGONIES.

THERE are truths which no one calls in question, though it is impossible to furnish any direct proofs of them. The rebellion and fall of Lucifer, the creation of the world, the primeval happiness and transgression of man, belong to the number of these truths. It is not to be supposed that an absurd falsehood could have become a universal tradition. Open the books of the second Zoroaster, the dialogues of Plato, and those of Lucian, the moral treatises of Plutarch, the annals of the Chinese, the Bible of the Hebrews, the Edda of the Scandinavians; go among the negroes of Africa, or the learned priests of India;[1] they will all recapitulate the crimes of the evil deity; they will all tell you of the too short period of man's felicity, and the long calamities which followed the loss of his innocence.

Voltaire somewhere asserts that we possess a most wretched *copy* of the different popular traditions respecting the origin of the world, and the physical and moral elements which compose it. Did he prefer, then, the cosmogony of the Egyptians, the great winged egg of the Theban priests?[2] Hear what is related by the most ancient historian after Moses:—

"The principle of the universe was a gloomy and tempestuous atmosphere,—a wind produced by this gloomy atmosphere and a turbulent chaos. This principle was unbounded, and for a long time had neither limit nor form. But when this wind became enamored of its own principles, a mixture was the result, and this mixture was called desire or love.

---

[1] See note F

[2] *Herod.*, lib. ii.; *Diod. Sic.*

"This mixture being complete was the beginning of all things; but the wind knew not his own offspring, the mixture. With the wind, her father, this mixture produced *mud*, and hence sprang all the generations of the universe."[1]

If we pass to the Greek philosophers, we find Thales, the founder of the Ionic sect, asserting water to be the universal principle.[2] Plato contended that the Deity had arranged the world, but had not had the power to create it.[3] God, said he, formed the universe, after the model existing from all eternity in himself.[4] Visible objects are but shadows of the ideas of God, which are the only real substances.[5] God, moreover, infused into all beings a breath of his life, and formed of them a third principle, which is both spirit and matter, and which we call the *soul of the world*.[6]

Aristotle reasoned like Plato respecting the origin of the universe; but he conceived the beautiful system of the chain of beings, and, ascending from action to action, he proved that there must exist somewhere a primary principle of motion.[7]

Zeno maintained that the world was arranged by its own energy; that nature is the system which embraces all things, and consists of two principles, the one active, the other passive, not existing separately, but in combination; that these two principles are subject to a third, which is *fatality;* that God, matter, and fatality, form but one being; that they compose at once the wheels, the springs, the laws, of the machine, and obey as *parts* the laws which they dictate as the *whole*.[8]

According to the philosophy of Epicurus, the universe has existed from all eternity. There are but two things in nature,—matter and space.[9] Bodies are formed by the aggregation of infinitely minute particles of matter or atoms, which have an internal principle of motion, that is, gravity. Their revolution would

---

[1] Sanch., *ap Euseb., Præpar. Evang*, lib. i c. 10.

[2] Cic., *de Nat. Deor.*, lib i n 25.

[3] Tim., p 28; Diog Laert, lib. iii; Plut., *de Gen. Anim.*, p. 78.

[4] Plut, Tim., p. 29 [5] *Id.*, Rep, lib. vii [6] *Id.*, *in Tim.*, p. 34.

[7] Arist., *de Gen An*, lib. ii. c. 3, Met, lib xi c 5; *De Cal*, lib xi. c. 3.

[8] Laert. [illegible] *[illegible]*, c. xiv: Senec, *Consol*, c. xxix.; *Cic. de Nat. Deor.* [illegible]

[9] Lucret, [illegible] Laert [illegible]

be made in a vertical plane, if they did not, in consequence of a particular law, describe an ellipsis in the regions of space.[1]

Epicurus invented this oblique movement for the purpose of avoiding the system of the fatalists, which would be reproduced by the perpendicular motion of the atom. But the hypothesis is absurd; for if the declination of the atom is a law, it is so from necessity; and how can a necessitated cause produce a free effect? But to proceed.

From the fortuitous concourse of these atoms originated the heavens and the earth, the planets and the stars, vegetables, minerals, and animals, including man; and when the productive virtue of the globe was exhausted, the living races were perpetuated by means of generation.[2] The members of the different animals, formed by accident, had no particular destination. The concave ear was not scooped out for the purpose of hearing, nor was the convex eye rounded in order to see; but, as these organs chanced to be adapted to those different uses, the animals employed them mechanically, and in preference to the other senses.[3]

After this statement of the cosmogonies of the philosophers, it would be superfluous to notice those of the poets. Who has not heard of Deucalion and Pyrrha, of the golden and of the iron ages? As to the traditions current among other nations of the earth, we will simply remark that in the East Indies an elephant supports the globe; in Peru, the sun made all things; in Canada, the great hare is the father of the world; in Greenland, man sprang from a shell-fish;[4] lastly, Scandinavia records the birth of Askus and Emla: Odin gives them a soul, Hæner reason, and Lædur blood and beauty.[5]

---

[1] *Loc. cit.*

[2] Lucret., lib. v. et x.; Cic., *de Nat. Deor.*, lib. i. c. 8, 9.

[3] Lucret., lib. iv., v.

[4] See Hesiod; Ovid; Hist. of Hindostan; Herrera, Histor. de las Ind.; Charlevoix, Hist. de la Nouv. Fr.; P. Lafitau, Mœurs des Ind.; Travels in Greenland, by a Missionary.

[5] Askum et Emlam, omni conatu destitutos,
Animam nec possidebant, rationem nec habebant,
Nec sanguinem nec sermonem, nec faciem venustam:
Animam dedit Odinus, rationem dedit Hænerus;
Lædur sanguinem addidit et faciem venustam.

BARTHOLIN, *Ant. Dan.*

In these various cosmogonies we find childish tales on the one hand and philosophical abstractions on the other; and were we obliged to choose between them, it would be better to adopt the former.

In order to distinguish, among a number of paintings, the original from the copy, we must look for that which, in its *ensemble* or in the perfection of its parts, exhibits the genius of the master. Now, this is precisely what we find in the book of Genesis, which is the original of the representations met with in popular traditions. What can be more natural, and at the same time more magnificent,—what more easy of conception, or more consonant with human reason,—than the Creator descending into the realms of ancient night and producing light by the operation of a word? The sun, in an instant, takes his station in the heavens, in the centre of an immense dome of azure; he throws his invisible network over the planets, and detains them about him as his captives; the seas and forests commence their undulations on the globe, and their voices are heard for the first time proclaiming to the universe that marriage in which God himself is the priest, the earth is the nuptial couch, and mankind is the progeny.[1]

CHAPTER II.

THE FALL OF MAN—THE SERPENT—A HEBREW WORD.

WE are again struck with astonishment in contemplating that other truth announced in the Scriptures:—*man dying in consequence of having poisoned himself from the tree of life!*—man lost for having tasted the fruit of knowledge, for having learned

---

[1] The *Asiatic Researches* confirm the truth of the book of Genesis. They divide mythology into three branches, one of which extended throughout India, the second over Greece, and the third among the savages of North America. They also show that this same mythology was derived from a still more ancient tradition, which is that of Moses. Modern travellers in India everywhere fi[illegible] Scripture. The authenticity of these traditio[illegible] contested, has now ceased to be a matter of doubt.

too much of good and evil, for having ceased to resemble the child of the gospel! If we suppose any other prohibition of the Deity, relative to any propensity of the soul whatever, where is the profound wisdom in the command of the Most High? It would seem to be unworthy of the Divinity, and no moral would result from the disobedience of Adam. But observe how the whole history of the world springs from the law imposed on our first parents. God placed knowledge within his reach; he could not refuse it him, since man was created intelligent and free; but he cautioned him that if he was resolved on knowing too much, this knowledge would result in the death of himself and of his posterity. The secret of the political and moral existence of nations, and the profoundest mysteries of the human heart, are comprised in the tradition of this wonderful and fatal tree.

Now let us contemplate the marvellous consequence of this prohibition of infinite wisdom. Man falls, and the demon of pride occasions his fall. But pride borrows the voice of love to seduce him, and it is for the sake of a woman that Adam aspires to an equality with God—a profound illustration of the two principal passions of the heart, vanity and love. Bossuet, in his *Elevations to God,* in which we often perceive the author of the *Funeral Orations,* observes, in treating of the mystery of the serpent, that "the angels conversed with man in such forms as God permitted, and under the figure of animals. Eve therefore was not surprised to hear the serpent speak, any more than she was to see God himself appear under a sensible form." "Why," adds the same writer, "did God cause the proud spirit to appear in that form in preference to any other? Though it is not absolutely necessary for us to know this, yet Scripture intimates the reason, when it observes that the serpent was the most subtle of all animals; that is to say, the one which most aptly represented Satan in his malice, his artifices, and afterward in his punishment."

The present age rejects with disdain whatever savors of the marvellous; but the serpent has frequently been the subject of our observations, and, if we may venture to say it, we seem to recognise in that animal the pernicious spirit and artful malice which are ascribed to it in the Scriptures. Every thing is mysterious, secret, astonishing, in this incomprehensible reptile. His movements differ from those of all other animals. It is impossible to say where his locomotive principle lies, for he has neither fins, nor feet, nor wings; and yet he flits like a shadow, he vanishes as by magic, he reappears and is gone again, like a light azure vapor, or the gleams of a sabre in the dark. Now he curls himself into a circle and projects a tongue of fire; now, standing erect upon the extremity of his tail, he moves along in a perpendicular attitude, as by enchantment. He rolls himself into a ball, rises and falls in a spiral line, gives to his rings the undulations of a wave, twines round the branches of trees, glides under the grass of the meadow, or skims along the surface of water. His colors are not more determinate than his movements. They change with each new point of view, and like his motions, they possess the false splendor and deceitful variety of the seducer.

Still more astonishing in other respects, he knows, like the murderer, how to throw aside his garment stained with blood, lest it should lead to his detection. By a singular faculty, the female can introduce into her body the little monsters to which she has given birth.[1] The serpent passes whole months in sleep. He frequents tombs, inhabits secret retreats, produces poisons which chill, burn, or checquer the body of his victim with the colors with which he is himself marked. In one place, he lifts two menacing heads; in another, he sounds a rattle. He hisses like the mountain eagle, or bellows like a bull. He naturally enters into the moral or religious ideas of men, as if in consequence of the influence which he exercised over their destiny. An object of horror or adoration, they either view him with an implacable hatred, or bow down before his genius. Falsehood appeals to him, prudence calls him to her aid, envy bears him in her bosom, and eloquence on her wand. In hell he arms the scourges of the furies; in heaven eternity is typified by his image.

---

[1] As this part of the description is so very extraordinary, it may appear to want confirmation. "Mr. de Beauvois, as related in the American Philosophical Transactions, declared himself an eye-witness of such a fact as is above stated. He saw a large rattlesnake, which he had disturbed in his walks, open her jaws, and instantly five small ones, which were lying by her, rushed into her mouth. He retired and watched her, and in a quarter of an hour saw her again discharge t[illegible] [illegible] common viper does the same." See *Shaw's General Zoology*, vol. [illegible] p. [illegible]. K.

He possesses, moreover, the art of seducing innocence. His eyes fascinate the birds of the air, and beneath the fern of the crib the ewe gives up to him her milk. But he may himself be charmed by the harmony of sweet sounds, and to subdue him the shepherd needs no other weapon than his pipe.

In the month of July, 1791, we were travelling in Upper Canada with several families of savages belonging to the nation of the Onondagos. One day, while we were encamped in a spacious plain on the bank of the Genesee River, we saw a rattlesnake. There was a Canadian in our party who could play on the flute, and to divert us he advanced toward the serpent with his new species of weapon. On the approach of his enemy, the haughty reptile curls himself into a spiral line, flattens his head, inflates his cheeks, contracts his lips, displays his envenomed fangs and his bloody throat. His double tongue glows like two flames of fire; his eyes are burning coals; his body, swollen with rage, rises and falls like the bellows of a forge; his dilated skin assumes a dull and scaly appearance; and his tail, which sends forth an ominous sound, vibrates with such rapidity as to resemble a light vapor.

The Canadian now begins to play on his flute. The serpent starts with surprise and draws back his head. In proportion as he is struck with the magic sound, his eyes lose their fierceness, the oscillations of his tail diminish, and the noise which it emits grows weaker, and gradually dies away. The spiral folds of the charmed serpent, diverging from the perpendicular, expand, and one after the other sink to the ground in concentric circles. The tints of azure, green, white, and gold, recover their brilliancy on his quivering skin, and, slightly turning his head, he remains motionless in the attitude of attention and pleasure.

At this moment the Canadian advanced a few steps, producing with his flute sweet and simple notes. The reptile immediately lowers his variegated neck, opens a passage with his head through the slender grass, and begins to creep after the musician, halting when he halts, and again following him when he resumes his march. In this way he was led beyond the limits of our camp, attended by a great number of spectators, both savages and Europeans, who could scarcely believe their eyes. After witnessing this wonderful effect of melody, the assembly unanimously decided that the marvellous serpent should be permitted to escape.[1]

To this kind of inference, drawn from the habits of the serpent in favor of the truths of Scripture, we shall add another, deduced from a Hebrew word. Is it not very remarkable, and at the same time extremely philosophical, that, in Hebrew, the generic term for man should signify *fever* or *pain?* The root of *Enosh*, *man*, is the verb *anash*, *to be dangerously ill.* This appellation was not given to our first parent by the Almighty: he called him simply Adam, *red earth* or *slime.* It was not till after the fall that Adam's posterity assumed the name of *Enosh*, or *man*, which was so perfectly adapted to his afflictions, and most eloquently reminded him both of his guilt and its punishment. Perhaps Adam, when he witnessed the pangs of his wife, and took into his arms Cain, his first-born son, lifting him toward heaven, exclaimed, in the acuteness of his feelings, *Enosh*, Oh, anguish! a doleful exclamation that may have led afterward to the designation of the human race.

CHAPTER III.

PRIMITIVE CONSTITUTION OF MAN—NEW PROOF OF ORIGINAL SIN.

WE indicated certain moral evidences of original sin in treating of baptism and the redemption; but a matter of such importance deserves more than a passing notice. "The knot of our condition," says Pascal, "has its twists and folds in this abyss,

---

[1] In India the *Cobra de Capello*, or hooded snake, is carried about as a show in a basket, and so managed as to exhibit when shown a kind of dancing motion, raising itself up on its lower part, and alternately moving its head and body from side to side to the sound of some musical instrument which is played during the time. *Shaw's Zoology*, vol. iii. p. 411.

The *serpentes*, the most formidable of reptiles, as they make a most distinguished figure in natural history, so they are frequently the subject of description with naturalists and poets. But it would be difficult to find, either in Buffon or Shaw, in Virgil, or even in Lucan, who is enamored of the subject, any thing superior to the vivid picture of our author. K.

so that man is more inconceivable without this mystery than this mystery is inconceivable to man."[1]

It appears to us that the order of the universe furnishes a new proof of our primitive degeneracy. If we survey the world around us we shall remark that, by a general, and at the same time a particular law, all the integral parts, all the springs of action, whether internal or external, all the qualities of beings, have a perfect conformity with one another. Thus the heavenly bodies accomplish their revolutions in an admirable unity, and each body, steadily pursuing its course, describes the orbit peculiar to itself. One single globe imparts light and heat. These two qualities are not divided between two spheres; the sun combines them in his orb as God, whose image he is, unites the fertilizing principle with the principle which illumines.

The same law obtains among animals. Their *ideas*, if we may be allowed the expression, invariably accord with their *feelings*, their reason with their passions. Hence it is that they are not susceptible of any increase or diminution of intelligence. The reader may easily pursue this law of conformities in the vegetable and mineral kingdoms.

By what incomprehensible destiny does man alone form an exception to this law, so necessary for the order, the preservation, the peace and the welfare, of beings? As obvious as this harmony of qualities and movements appears in the rest of nature, so striking is their discordance in man. There is a perpetual collision between his understanding and his will, between his reason and his heart. When he attains the highest degree of civilization, he is at the lowest point in the scale of morality; when free, he is barbarous; when refined, he is bound with fetters. Does he excel in the sciences? his imagination expires. Does he become a poet? he loses the faculty of profound thought. His heart gains at the expense of his head, and his head at the expense of his heart. He is impoverished in ideas in proportion as he abounds in feeling; his feelings become more confined in proportion as his ideas are enlarged. Strength renders him cold and harsh, while weakness makes him kind and gracious. A virtue invariably brings him a vice along with it; and a vice,

[1] Pascal's *Thoughts*, chap. iii.

when it leaves him, as invariably deprives him of a virtue. Nations, collectively considered, exhibit the like vicissitudes; they alternately lose and recover the light of wisdom. It might be said that the Genius of man, with a torch in his hand, is incessantly flying around the globe, amid the night that envelops us, appearing to the four quarters of the world like the nocturnal luminary, which, continually on the increase and the wane, at each step diminishes for one country the resplendence which she augments for another.

It is, therefore, highly reasonable to suppose that man, in his primitive constitution, resembled the rest of the creation, and that this constitution consisted in the perfect harmony of the feelings and the faculty of thought, of the imagination and the understanding. Of this we shall perhaps be convinced, if we observe that this union is still necessary in order to enjoy even a shadow of that felicity which we have lost. Thus we are furnished with a clue to original sin by the mere chain of reasoning and the probabilities of analogy; since man, in the state in which we behold him, is not, we may presume, the primitive man. He stands in contradiction to nature; disorderly when all things else are regular; with a double character when every thing around him is simple Mysterious, variable, inexplicable, he is manifestly in the state of a being which some accident has overthrown: he is a palace that has crumbled to pieces, and been rebuilt with its ruins, where you behold some parts of an imposing appearance and others extremely offensive to the eye; magnificent colonnades which lead to nothing; lofty porticos and low ceilings; strong lights and deep shades; in a word, confusion and disorder pervading every quarter, and especially the sanctuary.

Now, if the primitive constitution of man consisted in accordances such as we find established among other beings, nothing more was necessary for the destruction of this order, or any such harmony in general, than to alter the equilibrium of the forces or qualities. In man this precious equilibrium was formed by the faculties of love and thought. Adam was at the same time the most enlightened and the best of men; the most powerful in thought and the most powerful in love. But whatever has been created must necessarily have a progressive course. Instead of waiting for new attainments in *knowledge* to be derived from the revolution of ages, and to be accompanied by an accession of new *feelings*, Adam wanted to know every thing at once. Observe, too, what is very important: man had it in his power to destroy the harmony of his being in two ways, either by wanting to *love* too much, or to *know* too much. He transgressed in the second way; for we are, in fact, far more deeply tinctured with the pride of science than with the pride of love; the latter would have deserved pity rather than punishment, and if Adam had been guilty of desiring to *feel* rather than to *know* too much, man himself might, perhaps, have been able to expiate his transgression, and the Son of God would not have been obliged to undertake so painful a sacrifice. But the case was different. Adam sought to embrace the universe, not with the sentiments of his heart, but with the power of thought, and, advancing to the tree of knowledge, he admitted into his mind a ray of light that overpowered it. The equilibrium was instantaneously destroyed, and confusion took possession of man. Instead of that illumination which he had promised himself, a thick darkness overcast his sight, and his guilt, like a veil, spread out between him and the universe. His whole soul was agitated and in commotion; the passions rose up against the judgment, the judgment strove to annihilate the passions, and in this terrible storm the rock of death witnessed with joy the first of shipwrecks.

Such was the accident that changed the harmonious and immortal constitution of man. From that day all the elements of his being have been scattered, and unable to come together again. The habit—we might almost say the love of the tomb—which matter has contracted destroys every plan of restoration in this world, because our lives are not long enough to confer success upon any efforts we could make to reach primeval perfection.[1]

---

[1] It is in this point that the system of perfectibility is totally defective. Its supporters do not perceive that, if the mind were continually making new acquisitions in knowledge, and the heart in sentiment or the moral virtues, man, in a given time, regaining the point whence he set out, would be, of necessity, immortal; for, every principle of *division* being done away in him, every principle of *death* would likewise cease. The longevity of the patriarchs, and the gift of prophecy among the Hebrews,* must be ascribed to a restoration, more or less complete, of the equilibrium of human nature. Materialists therefore

---

* That is, the natural faculty of predicting. T.

But how could the world have contained so many generations if they had not been subject to death? This is a mere affair of imagination. Are not the means in the hands of God infinite? Who knows if men would have multiplied to that extent which we witness at the present day? Who knows whether the greater number of generations would not have remained in a virgin state,[1] or whether those millions of orbs which revolve over our heads were not reserved for us as delicious retreats, to which we would have been conveyed by attendant angels? To go still farther: it is impossible to calculate the height to which the arts and sciences might have been carried by man in a state of perfection and living forever upon the earth. If at an early period he made himself master of the three elements,—if, in spite of the greatest difficulties, he now disputes with the birds the empire of the air,—what would he not have attempted in his immortal career? The nature of the atmosphere, which at present forms an invincible obstacle to a change of planet, was, perhaps, different before the deluge. Be this as it may, it is not unworthy the power of God and the greatness of man to suppose, that the race of Adam was destined to traverse the regions of space, and to people all those suns which, deprived of their inhabitants by sin, have since been nothing more than resplendent deserts.

---

who support the system of *perfectibility* are inconsistent with themselves, since, in fact, this doctrine, so far from being that of *materialism*, leads to the most mystical *spirituality*.

[1] Such was the opinion of St. John Chrysostom. He supposes that God would have furnished a means of generation which is unknown to us. There stand, he says, before the throne of God, a multitude of angels who were born not by human agency.—*De Virgin.*, lib ii.

BOOK IV.

CONTINUATION OF THE TRUTHS OF SCRIPTURE—OBJECTIONS AGAINST THE SYSTEM OF MOSES.

CHAPTER I.

CHRONOLOGY.

SOME learned men having inferred from the history of man or that of the earth that the world is of higher antiquity than that ascribed to it in the Mosaic account, we have frequent quotations from Sanchoniatho, Porphyry, the Sanscrit books, and other sources, in support of this opinion. But have they who lay so much stress on these authorities always consulted them in their originals?

In the first place, it is rather presumptuous to intimate that Origen, Eusebius, Bossuet, Pascal, Fénélon, Bacon, Newton, Leibnitz, Huet, and many others, were either ignorant or weak men, or wrote in opposition to their real sentiments. They believed in the truth of the Mosaic history, and it cannot be denied that these men possessed learning in comparison with which our imperfect erudition makes a very insignificant figure.

But to begin with chronology: our modern scholars have made a mere sport of removing the insurmountable difficulties which confounded a Scaliger, a Petau, an Usher, a Grotius. They would laugh at our ignorance were we to inquire when the Olympiads commenced? how they agree with the modes of computation by archons, by ephori, by ediles, by consuls, by reigns, by Pythian, Nemæan, and secular games? how all the calendars of nations harmonize together? in what manner we must proceed to make the ancient year of Romulus, consisting of ten months or 354 days, accord with Numa's year of 355, or the Julian year of 365? by what means we shall avoid errors in referring these same years to the common Attic year of 354 days, and to the *embolismic* year of 384?[1]

These, however, are not the only perplexities in respect to years. The ancient Jewish year had but 354 days; sometimes twelve days were added at the end of the year, and sometimes a month of thirty days was introduced after the month Adar, to form a solar year. The modern Jewish year counts twelve months, and takes seven years of thirteen months in the space of nineteen years. The Syriac year also varies, and consists of 365 days. The Turkish or Arabic year has 354 days, and admits eleven intercalary months in twenty-nine years. The Egyptian year is divided into twelve months of thirty days, five days being added to the last. The Persian year, called *Yezdegerdic*, has a similar computation.[2]

Besides these various methods of counting time, all these years have neither the same beginning, nor the same hours, nor the same days, nor the same divisions. The civil year of the Jews (like all those of the Orientals) commences with the new moon of September, and their ecclesiastical year with the new moon of March. The Greeks reckon the first month of their year from the new moon following the summer solstice. The first month of the Persian year corresponds with our June; and the Chinese and Indians begin theirs from the first moon in March. We find, moreover, astronomical and civil months, which are subdivided into lunar and solar, into synodical and periodical; we have months distributed into kalends, ides, decades, weeks; we find days of two kinds, artificial and natural, and commencing, the latter at sunrise, as among the ancient Babylonians, Syrians, and Persians, the former at sunset, as in China, in modern Italy, and of old among the Athenians, the Jews, and the barbarians of the north. The Arabs begin their days at noon; the French, the English, the Germans, the Spaniards, and the Portuguese, at midnight.

---

[1] Embolismic means intercalary, or inserted. As the Greeks reckoned time by the lunar year of 354 days, in order to bring it to the solar year they added a thirteenth lunar month every two or three years.

[2] The other Persian year, called *Gelalean*, which commenced in the year of the world 1089, is the most exact of civil years, as it makes the solstices and the equi[illegible] fal[illegible] pre[illegible] the same days. It is formed by means of an intercalat[illegible] repeated [illegible] seven times in four, and afterward once in five, years.

Lastly, the very hours are not without their perplexities in chronology, being divided into Babylonian, Italian, and astronomical; and were we to be still more particular, we should no longer reckon sixty minutes in a European hour, but one thousand and eighty scruples in that of Chaldæa and Arabia.

Chronology has been termed the torch of history;[1] would to God we had no other to throw a light upon the crimes of men! But what would be our embarrassment if, in pursuing this subject, we entered upon the different periods, eras, or epochs! The Victorian period, which embraces 532 years, is formed by the multiplication of the solar and lunar cycles. The same cycles, multiplied by that of the indiction, produce the 7980 years of the Julian period. The period of Constantinople comprehends an equal number of years with the Julian period, but does not begin at the same epoch. As to eras, they reckon in some places by the year of the creation,[2] in others by olympiads,[3] by the foundation of Rome,[4] by the birth of Christ, by the epoch of Eusebius, by that of the Seleucidæ,[5] of Nabonassar,[6] of the Martyrs.[7] The Turks have their hegira,[8] the Persians their yezdegerdic.[9] The Julian, Gregorian, Iberian,[10] and Actian[11] eras, are also employed in computation. We shall say nothing concerning the Arundelian marbles, the medals and monuments of all sorts, which create additional confusion in chronology. Is there any candid person who will deny, after glancing at these pages, that so many arbitrary modes of calculating time are sufficient to make of history a frightful chaos? The annals of the Jews, by the confession of scientific men themselves, are the only ones whose

---

1 See note G.

2 This epoch is subdivided into the Greek, Jewish, Alexandrian, &c.

3 The Greek historians.

4 The Latin historians.

5 Followed by Josephus, the historian.

6 Followed by Ptolemy and some others.

7 Followed by the first Christians till 532, and in modern times by the Christians of Abyssinia and Egypt.

8 The Orientals do not place it as we do.

9 Thus named after a king of Persia who fell in a battle with the Saracens, in the year 632 of our era.

10 Followed in the councils and on the ancient monuments of Spain.

11 Received its name from the battle of Actium, and was adopted by Ptolemy, Josephus, Eusebius, and Censorius.

chronology is simple, regular, and luminous. Why, then, impelled by an ardent zeal for impiety, should we puzzle ourselves with questions of computation as dry as they are inexplicable, when we possess the surest clue to guide us in history? This is a new evidence in favor of the holy Scriptures.[1]

CHAPTER II.

LOGOGRAPHY AND HISTORICAL FACTS.

After the chronological objections against the Bible, come those which some writers have pretended to deduce from historical facts themselves. They inform us of a tradition among the priests of Thebes, which supposed the kingdom of Egypt to have existed eighteen thousand years; and they cite the list of its dynasties, which is still extant.

Plutarch, who cannot be suspected of Christianity, will furnish us with part of the reply to this objection. "Though their year," says he, speaking of the Egyptians, "comprehended four months, according to some authors, yet at first it consisted of only one, and contained no more than the course of a single moon. In this way, making a year of a single month, the period which has elapsed from their origin appears extremely long, and they are reputed to be the most ancient people, though they settled in their country at a late period."[2] We learn, moreover, from Herodotus,[3] Diodorus Siculus,[4] Justin,[5] Strabo,[6] and Jablonsky,[7] that

---

[1] Sir Isaac Newton applied the principles of astronomy to rectify the errors of chronology. He ascertained that the computations of time in the Old Testament coincided exactly with the revolutions of the heavenly bodies. By the aid of astronomy he corrected the whole disordered state of computing time in the profane writers, and confirmed the accuracy and truth of the Scripture chronology. Neither Cardinal Baronius, in his annals, nor Petavius, nor Scaliger, in his emendations of Eusebius, great as were their labor and diligence, have found their way so well through the labyrinths of chronology, or settled its disputable and intricate points more satisfactorily in their bulky folios, than our auth[illegible] of this short chapter. K.

[2] Plut. [illegible] Diod., lib. i.

[5] Just. [illegible] i. [7] Jablonsk. *Panth. Egypt.*, lib. ii

the Egyptians find a pretended glory in referring their origin to the remotest antiquity, and, as it were, concealing their birth in the obscurity of ages.

The number of their reigns can scarcely be a source of difficulty. It is well known that the Egyptian dynasties are composed of contemporary sovereigns; besides, the same word in the Oriental languages may be read in five or six different ways, and our ignorance has often made five or six persons out of one individual.[1] The same thing has happened in regard to the translation of a single name. The *Athoth* of the Egyptians is translated in Eratosthenes by *Ερμογενης*, which signifies, in Greek, *the learned*, as *Athoth* expresses the same thing in Coptic: but historians have not failed to make two kings of *Athoth* and *Hermes* or *Hermogenes*. But the Athoth of Manetho is again multiplied: in Plato, he is transformed into *Thoth*, and the text of Sanchoniatho proves in fact that this is the primitive name, the letter A being one of those which are retrenched or added at pleasure in the Oriental languages. Thus the name of the man whom Africanus calls *Pachnas*, is rendered by Josephus *Apachnas*. Here, then, we have Thoth, Athoth, Hermes, or Hermogenes, or Mercury, five celebrated men, who occupy together nearly two centuries; and yet these *five* kings were but one *single* Egyptian, who perhaps did not live sixty years.[2]

---

[1] For instance, the monogram of *Fo-hi*, a Chinese divinity, is precisely the same as that of *Menes*, a divinity of Egypt. Moreover, it is well ascertained, that the Oriental characters are only general signs of ideas, which each one renders in his peculiar language, as he would the Arabic figures. Thus, the Italian calls *duodecimo* what the Englishman would express by the word *twelve*, and the Frenchman by the word *douze*.

[2] Some persons, perhaps in other respects enlightened, have accused the Jews of having adulterated the names of history; but they should have known that it was the Greeks, and not the Jews, who were guilty of this alteration, especially in regard to Oriental names. See Boch., *Geog. Sacr.*, &c. Even at the present day, in the East, *Tyre* is called *Asur*, from *Tour* or *Sur*. The Athenians themselves would have pronounced it *Tur* or *Tour;* for the *y* in modern language is *epsilon*, or small *u* of the Greeks. In the same way, *Darius* may be derived from *Assuerus*. Dropping the initial A, according to a preceding remark, we have *Suerus*. But the *delta*, or capital D in Greek, is much like the *sameeh*, or capital S in Hebrew, and the latter was thus changed among the Greeks into the former. By an error in pronunciation, the change was more easily effected: for, as a Frenchman would pronounce the English *th* like *z* or *ds*, or *t*, so the Greek, having no letter like the Hebrew S, was inclined to pro-

What necessity is there, after all, to lay so much stress on logographical disputes, when we need but open the volumes of history to convince ourselves of the modern origin of men? In vain shall we combine with imaginary ages, or conjure up fictitious shades of death; all this will not prevent mankind from being but a creature of yesterday. The names of those who invented the arts are as familiar to us as those of a brother or a grandfather It was Hypsuranius who built huts of reeds, the habitations of primeval innocence; Usoüs first clothed himself with the skins of beasts, and braved the billows on the trunk of a tree;[1] Tubalcain taught men the uses of iron;[2] Noah or Bacchus planted the vine; Cain or Triptolemus fashioned the plough; Agrotes[3] or Ceres reaped the first harvest. History, medicine, geometry, the fine arts, and laws, are not of higher antiquity; and we are indebted for them to Herodotus, Hippocrates, Thales, Homer, Dædalus, and Minos. As to the origin of kings and cities, their history has been transmitted to us by Moses, Plato, Justin, and some others, and we know when and why the various forms of government were established among different nations.[4]

If we are astonished to find such grandeur and magnificence in the early cities of Asia, this difficulty is easily removed by an observation founded on the genius of the Eastern nations. In all ages, it has been the custom of these nations to build immense cities, which, however, afford no evidence respecting their civilization, and consequently their antiquity. The Arabs, who travel over burning sands, where they are quite satisfied to enjoy a little shade under a tent of sheepskins, have erected almost under our eyes gigantic cities, which these citizens of the desert seem to have designed as the enclosures of solitude. The Chinese, also, who have made so little progress in the arts, have the most

nounce it as their D, as the Samech in Hebrew has in fact something of this sound, according to the Masoretic points Hence *Ducrus* for *Suerus*, and by a slight change of vowels, which are not important in etymology, we have *Darius*. They who wish to jest at the expense of religion, morals, the peace of nations, or the general happiness of mankind, should first be well assured that they will not incur, in the attempt, the charge of pitiful ignorance.

[1] Sanch, ap. Eus., *Præparat Evang*, lib i. c. 10.

[2] Gen., iv.

[3] Sanch, *loc cit.*

[4] See [illegible] *Tim.*; Just, lib. ii, *Herod*; Plut, in *Thes*, [illegible] *Lyc* [illegible]

extensive cities on the face of the globe, with walls, gardens, palaces, lakes, and artificial canals, like those of ancient Babylon.[1] Finally, are we not ourselves a striking instance of the rapidity with which nations become civilized? Scarcely twelve centuries ago our ancestors were as barbarous as the Hottentots, and now we surpass Greece in all the refinements of taste, luxury, and the arts.

The general logic of languages cannot furnish any valid argument in favor of the antiquity of mankind. The idioms of the primitive East, far from indicating a very ancient state of society, exhibit on the contrary a close proximity to that of nature. Their mechanism is simple in the highest degree; hyperbole, metaphor, all the poetic figures, incessantly recur; but you will find in them scarcely any words for the expression of metaphysical ideas. It would be impossible to convey with perspicuity in the Hebrew language the theology of the Christian doctrine.[2] Among the Greeks and the modern Arabs alone we meet with compound terms capable of expressing the abstractions of thought. Everybody knows that Aristotle was the first philosopher who invented categories, in which ideas are placed together by a forced arrangement, of whatever class or nature they may be.[3]

Lastly, it is asserted that, before the Egyptians had erected those temples of which such beautiful ruins yet remain, the people already tended their flocks amid ruins left by some unknown nation: a circumstance which would presuppose a very high antiquity.

To decide this question, it is necessary to ascertain precisely

---

[1] See Fath. du Hald., *Hist. de la Ch.*; *Lettr. Edif.*; Macartney's *Emb. to China*, &c.

[2] This may be easily ascertained by reading the Fathers who have written in Syriac, as St. Ephrem, deacon of Edessa.

[3] If languages require so much time for their complete formation, why have the savages of Canada such subtle and such complicated dialects? The verbs of the Huron language have all the inflexions of the Greek verbs. Like the latter, they distinguish by the characteristic, the augment, &c. They have three modes, three genders, three numbers, and, moreover, a certain derangement of letters peculiar to the verbs of the Oriental languages. But, what is still more unaccountable, they have a fourth personal pronoun, which is placed between the second and third person both in the singular and in the plural. There is nothing like this in any of the dead or living languages with which we have the slightest acquaintance.

who were the pastoral tribes, and whence they came. Bruce, the British traveller, who finds every thing in Ethiopia, derives their origin from that country. The Ethiopians, however, so far from being able to send colonies abroad, were themselves at that period a recently-established people. "The Ethiopians," says Eusebius, "rising from the banks of the river Indus, settled near Egypt." Manetho, in his sixth dynasty, calls the shepherds *Phœnician strangers*. Eusebius places their arrival in Egypt during the reign of Amenophis, whence we must draw these two inferences:—1. That Egypt was not then barbarous, since Inachus the Egyptian, about this period, introduced the sciences into Greece; 2. That Egypt was not covered with ruins, since Thebes was then built, and since Amenophis was the father of Sesostris, who raised the glory of the Egyptians to its highest pitch. According to Josephus the historian, it was Thetmosis who compelled the shepherds to abandon altogether the banks of the Nile.[1]

But what new arguments would have been urged against the Scripture, had its adversaries been acquainted with another historical prodigy, which also belongs to the class of ruins,—alas! like every thing connected with the history of mankind! Within these few years, extraordinary monuments have been discovered in North America, on the banks of the Muskingum, the Miami, the Wabash, the Ohio, and particularly the Scioto, where they occupy a space upward of twenty leagues in length. They consist of ramparts of earth, with ditches, slopes, moons, half-moons, and prodigious cones, which serve for sepulchres. It has been asked, what people could have left these remains? But, so far, the question has not been answered.[2] Man is suspended in the present, between the past and the future, as on a rock between two gulfs: behind, before, all around, is darkness; and scarcely

[1] Maneth., *ad. Joseph. et Afric.*; Herod., lib. ii. c. 100; Diod., lib. i.; Ps. xlviii.; Euseb., *Chron.*, lib. i. The invasion of these people, recorded by profane authors, explains a passage in Genesis relative to Jacob and his sons: "That ye may dwell in the land of Gessen, for the Egyptians have all shepherds in abomination." Gen. xlvi. 34. Hence, also, we obtain a clue to the Greek name of the Pharaoh under whom Israel entered Egypt, and that of the second Pharaoh, during whose reign his descendants quitted that country. The Scripture, so f[illegible] profane histories, serves, on the contrary, to prove the [illegible].

[2] See n[illegible]

does he see the few phantoms which, rising up from the bottom of either abyss, float for a moment upon the surface, and then disappear.

Whatever conjectures may be formed respecting these American ruins, though they were accompanied with the visions of a primitive world, or the chimeras of an Atlantis, the civilized nation, whose plough, perhaps, turned up the plains where the Iroquois now pursues the bear, required no longer time for the consummation of its destiny, than that which swallowed up the empires of a Cyrus, an Alexander, and a Cæsar. Fortunate at least is that nation which has not left behind a name in history, and whose possessions have fallen to no other heirs than the deer of the forest and the birds of the air! No one will come into these savage wilds to deny the Creator, and, with scales in his hand, to weigh the dust of departed humanity, with a view to prove the eternal duration of mankind.

For my part, a solitary lover of nature and a simple confessor of the Deity, I once sat on those very ruins. A traveller without renown, I held converse with those relics, like myself, unknown The confused recollections of society, and the vague reveries of the desert, were blended in the recesses of my soul. Night had reached the middle of her course; all was solemn and still—the moon, the woods, and the sepulchres,—save that at long intervals was heard the fall of some tree, which the axe of time laid low, in the depths of the forest. Thus every thing falls, every thing goes to ruin!

We do not conceive ourselves obliged to speak seriously of the four *jogues*, or Indian ages, the first of which lasted three million two hundred thousand years; the second, one million; the third, one million six hundred thousand; while the fourth, which is the present age, will comprehend four hundred thousand years!

If to all these difficulties of chronology, logography, and facts, we add the errors arising from the passions of the historian, or of men who are the partisans of his theories,—if, moreover, we take into account the errors of copyists, and a thousand accidents of time and place,—we shall be compelled to acknowledge that all the reasons drawn from history in favor of the antiquity of the globe, are as unsatisfactory in themselves as their research is useless. Most assuredly, too, it is a poor way of establishing the duration of the world, to make human life the basis of the calculation. Will you pretend to demonstrate the permanence and the reality of things by the rapid succession of momentary shadows? Will you exhibit a heap of rubbish as the evidence of a society without beginning and without end? Does it require many days to produce a pile of ruins? The world would be old indeed were we to number its years by the wrecks which it presents to our view.

CHAPTER III.

ASTRONOMY.

In the history of the firmament are sought the second proofs of the antiquity of the world and the errors of Scripture. Thus, the heavens, which declare the glory of God unto all men, and whose language is heard by all nations,[1] proclaim nothing to the infidel. Happily it is not that the celestial orbs are mute, but the athiest is deaf.

Astronomy owes its origin to shepherds. In the wilds of the primitive creation, the first generations of men beheld their infant families and their numerous flocks sporting around them, and, happy to the very inmost of their souls, no useless foresight disturbed their repose. In the departure of the birds of autumn they remarked not the flight of years, neither did the fall of the leaves apprise them of any thing more than the return of winter. When the neighboring hill was stripped of all its herbage by their flocks, mounting their wagons covered with skins, with their children and their wives, they traversed the forests in quest of some distant river, where the coolness of the shade and the beauty of the wilderness invited them to fix their new habitation.

But they wanted a compass to direct them through those trackless forests, and along those rivers which had never been explored; and they naturally trusted to the guidance of the stars, by whose appearances they steered their course. At once legislators and guides, they [illegible] the shearing of the sheep and the most

---

Ps. xvii

distant migrations; each family followed the course of a constellation; each star shone as the leader of a flock. In proportion as these pastoral people applied to this study, they discovered new laws. In those days God was pleased to unfold the course of the sun to the tenants of the lowly cabin, and fable recorded that Apollo had descended among the shepherds.

Small columns of brick were raised to perpetuate the remembrance of observations. Never had the mightiest empire a more simple history. With the same tool with which he pierced his pipe, by the same altar on which he had sacrificed his firstling kid, the herdsman engraved upon a rock his immortal discoveries. In other places he left similar witnesses of this pastoral astronomy; he exchanged annals with the firmament; and in the same manner as he had inscribed the records of the stars among his flocks, he wrote the records of his flocks among the constellations of the zodiac. The sun retired to rest only in the sheepfolds; the bull announced by his bellowing the passage of the god of day, and the ram awaited his appearance to salute him in the name of his master. In the skies were discovered ears of corn, implements of agriculture, virgins, lambs, nay, even the shepherd's dog: the whole sphere was transformed, as it were, into a spacious rural mansion, inhabited by the Shepherd of men.

These happy days passed away, but mankind retained a confused tradition of them in those accounts of the golden age, in which the reign of the stars was invariably blended with that of the pastoral life. India has still an astronomical and pastoral character, like Egypt of old. With corruption, however, arose property;[1] with property mensuration, the second age of astronomy. But, by a destiny not a little remarkable, the simplest nations were still best acquainted with the system of the heavens; the herdsman of the Ganges fell into errors less gross than the philosopher of Athens: as if the muse of astronomy had retained a secret partiality for the shepherds, the objects of her first attachment.

[1] That is, the rights of property became objects of closer vigilance and more jealous care, as men grew more selfish. The right of property, being a necessary appendage of the social state, cannot be an evil opposed to the divine law, but rather a relation which that law sanctions and commands; so that the violation of the former implies the transgression of the latter. T.

During those protracted calamities which accompanied and succeeded the fall of the Roman empire, the sciences had no other asylum than the sanctuary of that Church which they now so ungratefully profane. Cherished in the silence of the convents, they owed their preservation to those same recluses whom, in our days, they affect to despise. A friar Bacon, a bishop Albert, a cardinal Cusa, resuscitated in their laborious vigils the genius of an Eudoxus, a Timocharis, an Hipparchus, and a Ptolemy. Patronized by the popes, who set an example to kings, the sciences at length spread abroad from those sacred retreats in which religion had gathered them under her protecting wings. Astronomy revived in every quarter. Gregory XIII. corrected the calendar; Copernicus reformed the system of the world; Tycho Brahe, from the top of his tower, renewed the memory of the ancient Babylonian observers; Kepler determined the figure of the planetary orbits. But God humbled again the pride of man by granting to the sports of innocence what he had refused to the investigations of philosophy;—the telescope was discovered by children. Galileo improved the new instrument; when, behold! the paths of immensity were at once shortened, the genius of man brought down the heavens from their elevation, and the stars came to be measured by his hands.

These numerous discoveries were but the forerunners of others still more important; for man had approached too near the sanctuary of nature not to be soon admitted within its precincts. Nothing was now wanted but the proper methods of relieving his mind from the vast calculations which overwhelmed it. Descartes soon ventured to refer to the great Creator the physical laws of our globe; and, by one of those strokes of genius of which only four or five instances are recorded in history, he effected a union between algebra and geometry in the same manner as speech is combined with thought. Newton had only to apply the materials which so many hands had prepared for him, but he did it like a perfect artist, and from the various plans upon which he might have reared the edifice of the spheres, he selected the noblest, the most sublime design—perhaps that of the Deity himself. The understanding at length ascertained the order which the eye admired; the golden balance which Homer and the Scriptures give to the Supreme Arbiter was again put into his hand; the comet submitted; planet attracted planet across the regions of immensity; ocean felt the pressure of two vast bodies floating millions of leagues from its surface; from the sun to the minutest atom all things continued in their places by an admirable equilibrium, and nothing in nature now wanted a counterpoise but the heart of man.

Who could have thought it? At the very time when so many new proofs of the greatness and wisdom of Providence were discovered, there were men who shut their eyes more closely than ever against the light. Not that those immortal geniuses, Copernicus, Tycho Brahe, Kepler, Leibnitz, and Newton, were atheists; but their successors, by an unaccountable fatality, imagined that they held the Deity within their crucibles and telescopes, because they perceived in them some of the elements with which the universal mind had founded the system of worlds. When we recall the terrors of the French revolution, when we consider that to the vanity of science we owe almost all our calamities, is it not enough to make us think that man was on the point of perishing once more, for having a second time raised his hand to the fruit of the tree of knowledge? Let this afford us matter for reflection on the original crime: *the ages of science* have always bordered on the *ages of destruction.*

Truly unfortunate, in our opinion, is the astronomer who can pass his nights in contemplating the stars without beholding inscribed upon them the name of God. What! can he not see in such a variety of figures and characters the letters which compose that divine name? Is not the problem of a Deity solved by the mysterious calculations of so many suns? Does not the brilliant algebra of the heavens suffice to bring to light the great *Unknown?*

The first astronomical objection alleged against the system of Moses is founded on the celestial sphere. "How can the world be so modern?" exclaims the philosopher; "the very composition of the sphere implies millions of years."

It must also be admitted that astronomy was one of the first sciences cultivated by men. Bailly proves that the patriarchs, before the time of Noah, were acquainted with the period of six hundred years, the year of 365 days, 5 hours, 51 minutes, 36 seconds, and likewise that they named the six days of the creation after the planetary order.[1] If the primitive generations were already so conversant with the history of the heavens, is it not highly probable that the ages which have elapsed since the deluge have been more than sufficient to bring the science of astronomy to the state in which we find it at the present day? It is impossible to pronounce with certainty respecting the time necessary for the development of a science. From Copernicus to Newton, astronomy made greater progress in one century than it had previously done in the course of three thousand years. The sciences may be compared to regions diversified with plains and mountains. We proceed with rapid pace over the plain; but when we reach the foot of the mountain a considerable time is lost in exploring its paths and in climbing the summit from which we descend into another plain. It must not then be concluded that astronomy was myriads of centuries in its infancy, because its middle age was protracted during four thousand years: such an idea would contradict all that we know of history and of the progress of the human mind.

The second objection is deduced from the historical epochs, combined with the astronomical observations of nations, and in particular those of the Chaldeans and Indians.

In regard to the former, it is well known that the seven hundred and twenty thousand years of which they boasted are reducible to nineteen hundred and three.[2]

As to the observations of the Indians, those which are founded on incontestable facts date no farther back than the year 3102 before the Christian era. This we admit to be a very high degree of antiquity, but it comes at least within known limits. At this epoch the fourth *jogue* or Indian age commences. Bailly, combining the first three ages and adding them to the fourth, shows that the whole chronology of the Brahmins is comprised in the space of about seventy centuries, which exactly corresponds with the chronology of the Septuagint.[3] He proves to demonstration that the chronicles of the Egyptians, the Chaldeans, the Chinese, the Persians, and the Indians, coincide in a remarkable

[1] Bail., *Hist. de l'Ast. Anc.*

[2] The table of these observations, drawn up at Babylon before the arrival of Alexander, was sent by Callisthenes to Aristotle.

[3] See note I

degree with the epochs of Scripture.[1] We quote Bailly the more willingly, as that philosopher fell a victim to the principles which we have undertaken to refute. When this unfortunate man, in speaking of Hypatia,—a young female astronomer, murdered by the inhabitants of Alexandria,—observed that *the moderns at least spare life, though they show no mercy to reputation*, little did he suspect that he would himself afford a lamentable proof of the fallacy of his assertion, and that in his own person the tragic story of Hypatia would be repeated.

In short, all these endless series of generations and centuries, which are to be met with among different nations, spring from a weakness natural to the human heart. Man feels within himself a principle of immortality, and shrinks as it were with shame from the contemplation of his brief existence. He imagines that by piling tombs upon tombs he will hide from view this capital defect of his nature, and by adding nothing to nothing he will at length produce eternity. But he only betrays himself, and reveals what he is so anxious to conceal; for, the higher the funeral pyramid is reared, the more diminutive seems the living statue that surmounts it; and life appears the more insignificant when the monstrous phantom of death lifts it up in its arms.

CHAPTER IV.

NATURAL HISTORY—THE DELUGE.

ASTRONOMY having been found insufficient to destroy the chronology of Scripture, natural history was summoned to its aid.[2] Some writers speak of certain epochs in which the whole

---

[1] Bail., *Ast. Ind.*, disc. prelim., part ii.

[2] Philosophers have laughed at Joshua, who commanded the sun to stand still. We would scarcely have thought it necessary to inform the present age that the sun, though the centre of our system, is not motionless. Others have excused Joshua by observing that he adopted the popular mode of expression. They might just as well have said that he spoke like Newton. If you wished to stop a watch, you would not break a small wheel, but the main-spring, the suspension of which would instantly arrest the movements of the whole machine.

universe grew young again; others deny the great catastrophes of the globe, such as the universal deluge. "Rain," say they, "is nothing but the vapor of the ocean. Now, all the seas of the globe would not be sufficient to cover the earth to the height mentioned in Scripture." We might reply that this mode of reasoning is at variance with that very knowledge of which men boast so much nowadays, as modern chemistry teaches us that air may be converted into water. Were this the case, what a frightful deluge would be witnessed! But, passing over, as we willingly do, those scientific arguments which explain every thing to the understanding without satisfying the heart, we shall confine ourselves to the remark, that, to submerge the terrestrial portion of the globe, it is sufficient for Ocean to overleap his bounds, carrying with him the waters of the fathomless gulf. Besides, ye presumptuous mortals, have ye penetrated into the *treasures of the hail?*[1] are ye acquainted with all the reservoirs of that abyss whence the Lord will call forth death on the dreadful day of his vengeance?

Whether God, raising the bed of the sea, poured its turbulent waters over the land, or, changing the course of the sun, caused it to rise at the pole, portentous of evil, the fact is certain, that a destructive deluge has laid waste the earth.

On this occasion the human race was nearly annihilated. All national quarrels were at an end, all revolutions ceased. Kings, people, hostile armies, suspended their sanguinary quarrels, and, seized with mortal fear, embraced one another. The temples were crowded with suppliants, who had all their lives, perhaps, denied the Deity; but the Deity denied them in his turn, and it was soon announced that all ocean was rushing in at the gates. In vain mothers fled with their infants to the summits of the mountains; in vain the lover expected to find a refuge for his mistress in the same grot which had witnessed his vows; in vain friends disputed with affrighted beasts the topmost branches of the oak; the bird himself, driven from bough to bough by the rising flood, tired his wings to no purpose over the shoreless plain of waters. The sun, which through sombre clouds shed a lurid light on naught but scenes of death, appeared dull and empurpled; the

[1] Job.

volcanoes, disgorging vast masses of smoke, were extinguished, and one of the four elements, fire, perished together with light.

The world was now covered with horrible shades which sent forth the most terrific cries. Amid the humid darkness, the remnant of living creatures, the tiger and the lamb, the eagle and the dove, the reptile and the insect, man and woman, hastened together to the most elevated rock on the surface of the globe; but Ocean still pursued them, and, raising around them his stupendous and menacing waters, buried the last point of land beneath his stormy wastes.

God, having accomplished his vengeance, commanded the seas to retire within the abyss; but he determined to impress on the globe everlasting traces of his wrath. The relics of the elephant of India were piled up in the regions of Siberia; the shell-fish of the Magellanic shores were fixed in the quarries of France; whole beds of marine substances settled upon the summits of the Alps, of Taurus, and of the Cordilleras; and those mountains themselves were the monuments which God left in the three worlds to commemorate his triumph over the wicked, as a monarch erects a trophy on the field where he has defeated his enemies.

He was not satisfied, however, with these general attestations of his past indignation. Knowing how soon the remembrance of calamity is effaced from the mind of man, he spread memorials of it everywhere around him. The sun had now no other throne in the morning, no other couch at night, than the watery element, in which it seemed to be daily extinguished as at the time of the deluge. Often the clouds of heaven resembled waves heaped upon one another, sandy shores or whitened cliffs. On land, the rocks discharged torrents of water. The light of the moon and the white vapors of evening at times gave to the valleys the appearance of being covered with a sheet of water. In the most arid situations grew trees, whose bending branches hung heavily toward the earth, as if they had just risen from the bosom of the waves. Twice a day the sea was commanded to rise again in its bed, and to invade its deep resounding shores. The caverns of the mountains retained a hollow and mournful sound. The summits of the solitary woods presented an image of the rolling billows, and the ocean seemed to have left the roar of its waters in the recesses of the forest.

CHAPTER V.

YOUTH AND OLD AGE OF THE EARTH.

We now come to the third objection relative to the modern origin of the globe "The earth," it is said, "is an aged nurse, who betrays her antiquity in every thing Examine her fossils, her marbles, her granites, her lavas, and you will discover in them a series of innumerable years, marked by circles, strata, or branches, as the age of a serpent is determined by his rattles, that of a horse by his teeth, or that of a stag by his antlers."[1]

This difficulty has been solved a hundred times by the following answer: *God might have created, and doubtless did create, the world with all the marks of antiquity and completeness which it now exhibits.*

What, in fact, can be more probable than that the Author of nature originally produced both venerable forests and young plantations, and that the animals were created, some full of days, others adorned with the graces of infancy? The oaks, on springing from the fruitful soil, doubtless bore at once the aged crows and the new progeny of doves. Worm, chrysalis, and butterfly—the insect crawled upon the grass, suspended its golden egg in the forest, or fluttered aloft in the air. The bee, though she had lived but a morning, already gathered her ambrosia from generations of flowers. We may imagine that the ewe was not without her lamb, nor the linnet without her young; and that the flowering shrubs concealed among their buds nightingales, astonished at the warbling notes in which they expressed the tenderness of their first enjoyments.

If the world had not been at the same time young and old, the grand, the serious, the moral, would have been banished from the face of nature; for these are ideas essentially inherent in antique objects. Every scene would have lost its wonders. The rock in ruins would no longer have overhung the abyss with its pendent herbage. The forests, stripped of their accidents, would

[1] See note K.

no longer have exhibited the pleasing irregularity of trees curved in every direction, and of trunks bending over the currents of rivers. The inspired thoughts, the venerable sounds, the magic voices, the sacred awe of the forests, would have been wanting, together with the darksome bowers which serve for their retreats; and the solitudes of earth and heaven would have remained bare and unattractive without those columns of oaks which join them together. We may well suppose, that the very day the ocean poured its first waves upon the shores, they dashed against rocks already worn, over strands covered with fragments of shell-fish, and around barren capes which protected the sinking coasts against the ravages of the waters.

Without this original antiquity, there would have been neither beauty nor magnificence in the work of the Almighty; and, what could not possibly be the case, nature, in a state of innocence, would have been less charming than she is in her present degenerate condition. A general infancy of plants, of animals, of elements, would have spread an air of dulness and languor throughout the world, and stripped it of all poetical inspiration. But God was not so unskilful a designer of the groves of Eden as infidels pretend. Man, the lord of the earth, was ushered into life with the maturity of thirty years, that the majesty of his being might accord with the antique grandeur of his new empire; and in like manner his partner, doubtless, shone in all the blooming graces of female beauty when she was formed from Adam, that she might be in unison with the flowers and the birds, with innocence and love, and with all the youthful part of the universe.

BOOK V.

THE EXISTENCE OF GOD DEMONSTRATED BY THE WORKS OF NATURE.

CHAPTER I.

OBJECT OF THIS BOOK.

ONE of the principal doctrines of Christianity yet remains to be examined; that is, *the state of rewards and punishments in another life*. But we cannot enter upon this important subject without first speaking of the two pillars which support the edifice of all the religions in the world—*the existence of God, and the immortality of the soul.*

These topics are, moreover, suggested by the natural development of our subject; since it is only after having followed Faith here below that we can accompany her to those heavenly mansions to which she speeds her flight on leaving the earth. Adhering scrupulously to our plan, we shall banish all abstract ideas from our proofs of the existence of God and the immortality of the soul, and shall employ only such arguments as may be derived from poetical and sentimental considerations, or, in other words, from the wonders of nature and the moral feelings. Plato and Cicero among the ancients, Clarke and Leibnitz among the moderns, have metaphysically, and almost mathematically, demonstrated the existence of a Supreme Being,[1] while the brightest geniuses in every age have admitted this consoling dogma. If it is rejected by certain sophists, God can exist just as well without their suffrage. Death alone, to which atheists would reduce all things, stands in need of defenders to vindicate its rights, since it has but little reality for man. Let us leave it, then, its deplorable partisans, who are not even agreed among themselves; for if they who believe in Providence concur in the principal points of their doctrine, they, on the contrary, who deny the Creator, are involved

[1] See note L.

in everlasting disputes concerning the basis of their nothingness. They have before them an abyss. To fill it up, they want only the foundation-stone, but they are at a loss where to procure it. Such, moreover, is the essential character of error, that when this error is not our own it instantly shocks and disgusts us; hence the interminable quarrels among atheists.

CHAPTER II.

A GENERAL SURVEY OF THE UNIVERSE.

THERE is a God. The plants of the valley and the cedars of the mountain bless his name; the insect hums his praise; the elephant salutes him with the rising day; the bird glorifies him among the foliage; the lightning bespeaks his power, and the ocean declares his immensity. Man alone has said, "There is no God."

Has he then in adversity never raised his eyes toward heaven? has he in prosperity never cast them on the earth? Is Nature so far from him that he has not been able to contemplate its wonders; or does he consider them as the mere result of fortuitous causes? But how could chance have compelled crude and stubborn materials to arrange themselves in such exquisite order?

It might be asserted that man is the *idea of God displayed*, and the universe *his imagination made manifest*. They who have admitted the beauty of nature as a proof of a supreme intelligence, ought to have pointed out a truth which greatly enlarges the sphere of wonders. It is this: motion and rest, darkness and light, the seasons, the revolutions of the heavenly bodies, which give variety to the decorations of the world, are successive only in appearance, and permanent in reality. The scene that fades upon our view is painted in brilliant colors for another people; it is not the spectacle that is changed, but the spectator. Thus God has combined in his work absolute duration and progressive duration. The first is placed in time; the second in space; by means of the former, the beauties of the universe are one, infinite, and invariable; by means of the latter, they are multiplied, finite, and perpetually renewed. Without the one, there would be no grandeur in the creation; without the other, it would exhibit nothing but dull uniformity.

Here time appears to us in a new point of view; the smallest of its fractions becomes a complete whole, which comprehends all things, and in which all things transpire, from the death of an insect to the birth of a world; each minute is in itself a little eternity. Combine, then, at the same moment, in imagination, the most beautiful incidents of nature; represent to yourself at once all the hours of the day and all the seasons of the year, a spring morning and an autumnal morning, a night spangled with stars and a night overcast with clouds, meadows enamelled with flowers, forests stripped by the frosts, and fields glowing with their golden harvests; you will then have a just idea of the prospect of the universe. While you are gazing with admiration upon the sun sinking beneath the western arch, another beholds it emerging from the regions of Aurora. By what inconceivable magic does it come, that this aged luminary, which retires to rest, as if weary and heated, in the dusky arms of night, is at the very same moment that youthful orb which awakes bathed in dew, and sparkling through the gray curtains of the dawn? Every moment of the day the sun is rising, glowing at his zenith, and setting on the world; or rather our senses deceive us, and there is no real sunrise, noon, or sunset. The whole is reduced to a fixed point, from which the orb of day emits, at one and the same time, three lights from one single substance. This triple splendor is perhaps the most beautiful incident in nature; for, while it affords an idea of the perpetual magnificence and omnipresence of God, it exhibits a most striking image of his glorious Trinity.

We cannot conceive what a scene of confusion nature would present if it were abandoned to the sole movements of matter. The clouds, obedient to the laws of gravity, would fall perpendicularly upon the earth, or ascend in pyramids into the air; a moment afterward the atmosphere would be too dense or too rarefied for the organs of respiration. The moon, either too near or too distant, would at one time be invisible, at another would appear bloody and covered with enormous spots, or would alone fill the whole celestial concave with her disproportionate orb.

Seized, as it were, with a strange kind of madness, she would pass from one eclipse to another, or, rolling from side to side, would exhibit that portion of her surface which earth has never yet beheld. The stars would appear to be under the influence of the same capricious power; and nothing would be seen but a succession of tremendous conjunctions. One of the summer signs would be speedily overtaken by one of the signs of winter; the Cow-herd would lead the Pleiades, and the Lion would roar in Aquarius; here the stars would dart along with the rapidity of lightning, there they would be suspended motionless; sometimes, crowding together in groups, they would form a new galaxy; at others, disappearing all at once, and, to use the expression of Tertullian, rending the curtain of the universe, they would expose to view the abysses of eternity.

No such appearances, however, will strike terror into the breast of man, until the day when the Almighty will drop the reins of the world, employing for its destruction no other means than to leave it to itself.

CHAPTER III.

ORGANIZATION OF ANIMALS AND OF PLANTS.

PASSING from general to particular considerations, let us examine whether the different parts of the universe exhibit the same wisdom that is so plainly expressed in the whole. We shall here avail ourselves of the testimony of a class of men, benefactors alike of science and of humanity: we mean the professors of the medical art.

Doctor Nieuwentyt, in his *Treatise on the Existence of God*,[1] has undertaken to demonstrate the reality of final causes. Without following him through all his observations, we shall content ourselves with adducing a few of them.

[1] In all the passages here quoted from the treatise of Nieuwentyt, we have taken the liberty of altering the language and giving a higher coloring to his subject. The doctor is learned, intelligent, and judicious, but dry. We have also added some observations of our own.

In treating of the four elements, which he considers in their harmonies with man and the creation in general, he shows, in respect to air, how our bodies are marvellously preserved beneath an atmospheric column, equal in its pressure to a weight of twenty thousand pounds. He proves that the change of one single quality, either as to rarefaction or density, in the element we breathe, would be sufficient to destroy every living creature. It is the air that causes the smoke to ascend; it is the air that retains liquids in vessels; by its agitation it purifies the heavens, and wafts to the continents the clouds of the ocean.

He then demonstrates, by a multitude of experiments, the necessity of water. Who can behold, without astonishment, the wonderful quality of this element, by which it ascends, contrary to all the laws of gravity, in an element lighter than itself, in order to supply us with rain and dew? He considers the arrangement of mountains, so as to give a circulation to rivers; the topography of these mountains in islands and on the main land; the outlets of gulfs, bays, and mediterranean waters; the innumerable advantages of seas: nothing escapes the attention of this good and learned man. In the same manner he unfolds the excellence of the earth as an element, and its admirable laws as a planet. He likewise describes the utility of fire, and the extensive aid it has afforded in the various departments of human industry.[1]

When he passes to animals, he observes that those which we call domestic come into the world with precisely that degree of instinct which is necessary in order to tame them, while others that are unserviceable to man never lose their natural wildness. Can it be chance that inspires the gentle and useful animals with the disposition to live together in our fields, and prompts ferocious beasts to roam by themselves in unfrequented places? Why should not flocks of tigers be led by the sound of the shepherd's fife? Why should not a colony of lions be seen frisking in our parks, among the wild thyme and the dew, like the little animals celebrated by La Fontaine? Those ferocious beasts could never be employed for any other purpose than to draw the car of some

[1] Modern physics may correct some errors in this part of his work; but the progress of that science, so far from conflicting with the doctrine of final causes, furnishes new proofs of the bounty of Providence.

triumphant warrior, as cruel as themselves, or to devour Christians in an amphitheatre.[1] Alas! tigers are never civilized among men, but men oftentimes assume the savage disposition of the tiger!

The observations of Nieuwentyt on the qualities of birds are not less interesting. Their wings, convex above and concave underneath, are oars perfectly adapted to the element they are designed to cleave. The wren, that delights in hedges of thorn and arbutus, which to her are extensive deserts, is provided with a double eyelid, to preserve its sight from every kind of injury. But how admirable are the contrivances of nature! this eyelid is transparent, and the little songstress of the cottage can drop this wonderful veil without being deprived of sight. Providence kindly ordained that she should not lose her way when conveying the drop of water or the grain of millet to her nest, and that her little family beneath the bush should not pine at her absence.

And what ingenious springs move the feet of birds? It is not by a play of the muscles which their immediate will determines, that they hold themselves firm on a branch: their feet are so constructed, that, when they are pressed in the centre or at the heel, the toes naturally grasp the object which presses against them.[2] From this mechanism it follows that the claws of a bird adhere more or less firmly to the object on which it alights, as the motion of that object is more or less rapid; for, in the waving of the branch, either the branch presses against the foot or the foot against the branch, and in either case there results a more forcible contraction of the claws. When in the winter season, at the approach of night, we see ravens perched on the leafless summit of the oak, we imagine that it is only by continual watchfulness and attention, and with incredible fatigue, they can maintain their position amid the howling tempest and the obscurity of night. The truth, however, is, that unconscious of danger, and defying the storm, they sleep amid the war of winds. Boreas himself fixes them to the branch from which we every moment expect to see them hurled; and, like the veteran mariner whose hammock is

[1] The reader is acquainted with the cry of the Roman populace: "Away with the Christians to the lions!" See Tertullian's *Apology*.

[2] The truth of this observation may be ascertained by an experiment on the foot of a dead bird.

slung to the masts of a vessel, the more they are rocked by the hurricane the more profound are their slumbers.

With respect to the organization of fishes, their very existence in the watery element, and the relative change in their weight, which enables them to float in water of greater or less gravity, and to descend from the surface to the lowest depths of the abyss, are perpetual wonders. The fish is a real hydrostatic machine, displaying a thousand phenomena by means of a small bladder which it empties or replenishes with air at pleasure.

The flowering of plants, and the use of the leaves and roots, are also prodigies which afford Nieuwentyt a curious subject of investigation He makes this striking observation: that the seeds of plants are so disposed by their figure and weight as to fall invariably upon the ground in the position which is favorable to germination.

Now if all things were the production of *chance*, would not some change be occasionally witnessed in the final causes? Why should there not be fishes without the air-bladder, which gives them the faculty of floating? And why would not the eaglet, that as yet has no need of weapons, have its shell broken by the bill of a dove? But, strange to relate, there is never any mistake or accident of this sort in *blind* nature! In whatever way you throw the dice, they always turn up the same numbers. This is a strange *fortune*, and we strongly suspect that before it drew the world from the urn of eternity it had already secretly arranged the *lot* of every thing.

But, are there not monsters in nature, and do they not afford instances of a departure from the final cause? True; but take notice that these beings inspire us with horror, so powerful is the instinct of the Deity in man—so easily is he shocked when he does not perceive in an object the impress of his Supreme Intelligence! Some have pretended to derive from these irregularities an objection against Providence; but we consider them, on the contrary, as a manifest confirmation of that very Providence In our opinion, God has permitted this distortion of matter expressly for the purpose of teaching us what the creation would be *without Him*. It is the shadow that gives greater effect to the light—a specimen of those laws of chance which, according to atheists, brought forth the universe.

CHAPTER IV.

INSTINCTS OF ANIMALS.

HAVING discovered in the organization of beings a regular plan, which cannot possibly be ascribed to chance, and which presupposes a directing mind, we will pass to the examination of other final causes, which are neither less prolific nor less wonderful than the preceding. Here we shall present the result of our own investigations, of a study which we would never have interrupted had not Providence called us to other occupations. We were desirous, if possible, of producing a *Religious Natural History*, in opposition to all those modern scientific works in which mere *matter* is considered. That we might not be contemptuously reproached with ignorance, we resolved to travel, and to see every object with our own eyes. We shall, therefore, introduce some of our observations on the different instincts of animals and of plants,—on their habits, migrations, and loves. The field of nature cannot be exhausted. We always find there a new harvest. It is not in a menagerie, where the secrets of God are kept encaged, that we acquire a knowledge of the divine wisdom. To become deeply impressed with its existence, we must contemplate it in the deserts. How can a man return an infidel from the regions of solitude? Wo to the traveller who, after making the circuit of the globe, would come back an atheist to the paternal roof! Was it possible for us, when we penetrated at midnight into the solitary vale inhabited by beavers and overshadowed by the fir-tree, and where reigned a profound silence under the mild glare of the moon, as peaceful as the people whose labors it illumined—was it possible for us not to discover in this valley some trace of a divine Intelligence? Who, then, placed the square and the level in the eye of that animal which has the sagacity to construct a dam, shelving toward the water and perpendicular on the opposite side? What philosopher taught this singular engineer the laws of hydraulics, and made him so expert with his incisive teeth and his flattened tail? Reaumur never foretold the vicissitudes of the seasons with the accuracy of this same beaver, whose stores, more or less copious, indicate in the month of June the longer or shorter duration of the ices of January. Alas! by questioning the divine Omnipotence, men have struck with sterility all the works of the Almighty. Atheism has extinguished with its icy breath the fire of nature which it undertook to kindle. In breathing upon creation, it has enveloped it in its own characteristic darkness.

There are other facts connected with animal instinct, which, though more common, and falling daily under our observation, are not the less wonderful. The hen, for instance, which is so timid, assumes the courage of a lion when it is question of defending her young. How interesting to behold her solicitude and excitement when, deceived by the treasures of another nest, little strangers escape from her, and hasten to sport in the neighboring lake! The terrified mother runs round the brink, claps her wings, calls back her imprudent brood, sometimes entreating with tenderness, sometimes clucking with authority. She walks hastily on, then pauses, turns her head with anxiety, and is not pacified till she has collected beneath her wings her weakly and dripping family, which will soon give her fresh cause of alarm.

Among the various instincts which the Master of life has dispensed throughout the animal world, one of the most extraordinary is that which leads the fishes from the icy regions of the pole to a milder latitude, which they find without losing their way over the vast desert of the ocean, and appear punctually in the river where their union is to be celebrated. Spring, directed by the Sovereign of the seas, prepares on our shores the nuptial pomp. She crowns the willows with verdure; she covers the grottos with moss, and expands on the surface of the waves the foliage of the water-lily, to serve as curtains to these beds of crystal. Scarcely are these preparations completed, when the scaly tribes make their appearance. These foreign navigators animate all our shores. Some, like light bubbles of air, ascend perpendicularly from the bosom of the deep; others gently balance themselves on the waves, or diverge from one common centre, like innumerable stripes of gold. These dart their gliding forms obliquely through the azure fluid; those sleep in a sunbeam which penetrates the silvery gauze of the billows. Perpetually wandering to and fro, they swim, they dive, they turn round, they form into squadrons, they separate and again unite; and the inhabitant of the seas, endued with the breath of life, follows with a bound the fiery track left for him by his beloved in the waves.

CHAPTER V.

SONG OF BIRDS—IT IS MADE FOR MAN—LAWS RELATIVE TO THE CRY OF ANIMALS.

NATURE has her seasons of festivity, for which she assembles musicians from all the regions of the globe. Skilful performers with their wondrous sonatas, itinerant minstrels who can only sing short ballads, pilgrims who repeat a thousand and a thousand times the couplets of their long solemn songs, are beheld flocking together from all quarters. The thrush whistles, the swallow twitters, the ringdove coos: the first, perched on the topmost branch of an elm, defies our solitary blackbird, who is in no respect inferior to the stranger; the second, lodged under some hospitable roof, utters his confused cries, as in the days of Evander; the third, concealed amid the foliage of an oak, prolongs her soft moanings like the undulating sound of a horn in the forests. The redbreast, meanwhile, repeats her simple strain on the barn-door, where she has built her compact and mossy nest; but the nightingale disdains to waste her lays amid this symphony. She waits till night has imposed silence, and takes upon herself that portion of the festival which is celebrated in its shades.

When the first silence of night and the last murmurs of day struggle for the mastery on the hills, on the banks of the rivers, in the woods and in the valleys; when the forests have hushed their thousand voices; when not a whisper is heard among the leaves; when the moon is high in the heavens, and the ear of man is all attention,—then Philomela, the first songstress of creation, begins her hymn to the Eternal. She first strikes the echoes with lively bursts of pleasure. Disorder pervades her strains. She passes abruptly from flat to sharp, from soft to loud. She pauses; now she is slow and now quick. It is the expression of a heart intoxicated with joy—a heart palpitating under the pressure of love. But her voice suddenly fails. The bird is silent. She begins again; but how changed are her accents! What tender melody! Sometimes you hear a languid modulation, though varied in its form; sometimes a tune more monotonous, like the chorus of our ancient ballads—those master-pieces of simplicity and melancholy Singing is as often an expression of sadness as of joy. The bird that has lost her young still sings. She still repeats the notes of her happy days, for she knows no other; but, by a stroke of her art, the musician has merely changed her key, and the song of pleasure is converted into the lamentation of grief.

It would be very gratifying to those who seek to disinherit man and to snatch from him the empire of nature, if they could prove that nothing has been made for him. But the song of birds, for example, is ordained so expressly for our ears, that in vain we persecute these tenants of the woods, in vain we rob them of their nests, pursue, wound, and entangle them in snares. We may give them the acutest pain, but we cannot compel them to be silent In spite of our cruelty, they cannot forbear to charm us, as they are obliged to fulfil the decree of Providence. When held captives in our houses, they multiply their notes There must be some secret harmony in adversity, for all the victims of misfortune are inclined to sing Even when the bird-catcher, with a refinement of barbarity, scoops out the eyes of a nightingale, it has the extraordinary effect of rendering his voice still more melodious. This Homer of the feathered tribes earns a subsistence by singing, and composes his most enchanting airs after he has lost his sight "Demodocus," says the poet of Chios, describing himself in the person of the Phæacian bard "was beloved by the Muse; but she bestowed upon him the good and the bad. She deprived him of the blessing of sight, but she gave him the sweetness of song."

Τον περι μους' εφιλησε, διδου δ' αγαθον τε, κακοντε,
Οφθαλμων μεν, αμερσε, διδου δ' ηθειαν αοιδην.

The bird seems to be the true emblem of the Christian here below. Like him, it prefers solitude to the world, heaven to earth, and its voice is ever occupied in celebrating the wonders of the Creator There are certain laws relative to the cries of animals which we believe have not yet been observed, though they are highly deserving of notice. The varied language of the inhabitants of the desert appears to be adapted to the grandeur or the charms of the places in which they live, and to the hours of the day at which they make their appearance. The roaring of the lion, loud, rough, and harsh, is in accordance with the burning regions where it is heard at sunset; while the lowing of our cattle charms the rural echoes of our valleys. The bleating of the goat has in it something tremulous and wild, like the rocks and ruins among which he loves to climb; the warlike horse imitates the shrill sound of the clarion, and, as if sensible that he was not made for rustic occupations, he is silent under the lash of the husbandman, and neighs beneath the bridle of the warrior. Night, according as it is pleasant or gloomy, brings forth the nightingale or the owl; the one seems to sing for the zephyrs, the groves, the moon, and for lovers; the other hoots for the winds, aged forests, darkness, and death. In short, almost all carnivorous animals have a particular cry, which resembles that of their prey: the sparrow-hawk squeaks like the rabbit and mews like a kitten; the cat herself has a kind of whining tone like that of the little birds of our gardens; the wolf bleats, lows, or barks; the fox clucks or cries; the tiger imitates the bellowing of the bull; and the sea-bear has a kind of frightful roar, like the noise of the breakers among which he seeks his prey. The law of which we speak is very astonishing, and perhaps conceals some tremendous secret. We may observe that monsters among men follow the same law as carnivorous animals. There have been many instances of tyrants who exhibited some mark of sensibility in their countenance and voice, and who affected the language of the unhappy creatures whose destruction they were meditating. Providence, however, has ordained that we should not be absolutely deceived by men of this savage character: we have only to examine them closely, to discover, under the garb of mildness, an air of falsehood and rapacity a thousand times more hideous than their fury itself.

13*

CHAPTER VI.

NESTS OF BIRDS.

How admirably is the providence of the great Creator displayed in the nests of birds! Who can contemplate without emotion this divine beneficence, which imparts industry to the weak and foresight to the thoughtless?

No sooner have the trees expanded their first blossoms, than a thousand diminutive artisans begin their labors on every side. Some convey long straws into the hole of an ancient wall; others construct buildings in the windows of a church; others, again, rob the horse of his hair, or carry off the wool torn by the jagged thorn from the back of the sheep. There wood-cutters arrange small twigs in the waving summit of a tree; here spinsters collect silk from a thistle. A thousand palaces are reared, and every palace is a nest; while each nest witnesses the most pleasing changes; first a brilliant egg, then a young one covered with down. This tender nestling becomes fledged; his mother instructs him by degrees to rise up on his bed. He soon acquires strength to perch on the edge of his cradle, from which he takes the first survey of nature. With mingled terror and transport, he drops down among his brothers and sisters, who have not yet beheld this magnificent sight; but, summoned by the voice of his parents, he rises a second time from his couch, and this youthful monarch of the air, whose head is still encircled by the crown of infancy, already ventures to contemplate the waving summits of the pines and the abysses of verdure beneath the paternal oak. But, while the forests welcome with pleasure their new guest, some aged bird, who feels his strength forsake him, alights beside the current; there, solitary and resigned, he patiently awaits death, on the brink of the same stream where he sang his first loves, and beneath the trees which still bear his nest and his harmonious posterity.

We will notice here another law of nature. Among the smaller species of birds, the eggs are commonly tinged with one of the prevailing colors of the male. The bullfinch builds in the hawthorn, the gooseberry, and other bushes of our gardens; her eggs are slate-colored, like the plumage of her back. We recollect having once found one of these nests in a rose-bush: it resembled a shell of mother-of-pearl containing four blue gems; a rose, bathed in the dews of morning, was suspended above it: the male bullfinch sat motionless on a neighboring shrub, like a flower of purple and azure. These objects were reflected in the water of a stream, together with the shade of an aged walnut-tree, which served as a back-ground to the scene, and behind which appeared the ruddy tints of the morning. In this little picture the Almighty presented us an idea of the graces with which he has decked all nature.

Among the larger birds the law respecting the color of the egg varies. We are of opinion that, in general, the egg is white among those birds the male of which has several females, or among those whose plumage has no fixed color for the species. Among those which frequent the waters and forests, and build their nests on the sea or on the summits of lofty trees, the egg is generally of a bluish green, and, as it were, of the same tint as the elements by which it is surrounded. Certain birds, which reside on the tops of ancient and deserted towers, have green eggs like ivy,[1] or reddish like the old buildings they inhabit.[2] It is, therefore, a law, which may be considered as invariable, that the bird exhibits in her egg an emblem of her loves, her habits, and her destinies. The mere inspection of this brittle monument will almost enable us to determine to what tribe it belonged, what were its dress, habits, and tastes; whether it passed its days amid the dangers of the sea, or, more fortunate, among the charms of a pastoral life; whether it was tame or wild, and inhabited the mountain or the valley. The antiquary of the forest is conducted by a science much less equivocal than the antiquary of the city: a scathed oak, with all its mosses, proclaims much more plainly the hand that gave it existence than a ruined column declares by what architect it was reared. Among men, tombs are so many leaves of their history; Nature, on the contrary, records her facts on living tablets. She has no need of granite or marble to per-

[1] The jack-daw and others.

[2] The white owl, &c.

petuate her writings. Time has destroyed the annals of the sovereigns of Memphis, once inscribed on their funereal pyramids, but has it been able to efface a single letter of the history marked on the egg-shell of the Egyptian ibis?

CHAPTER VII.

MIGRATIONS OF BIRDS—AQUATIC BIRDS—THEIR HABITS—GOODNESS OF PROVIDENCE.

THE reader is acquainted with the following charming lines of the younger Racine on the migration of birds:—

> Ceux qui, de nos hivers redoutant le courroux,
> Vont se réfugier dans des climats plus doux,
> Ne laisseront jamais la saison rigoureuse
> Surprendre parmi nous leur troupe paresseuse.
> Dans un sage conseil par les chefs assemblé,
> Du depart général le grand jour est réglé;
> Il arrive; tout part; le plus jeune peut-être
> Demande, en regardant les lieux qui l'ont vu naitre,
> Quand viendra le printemps par qui tant d'exilés
> Dans les champs paternels se verront rappelés![1]

We have known unfortunate persons whose eyes would be suffused with tears in reading the concluding lines. The exile prescribed by nature is not like that which is ordered by man. If the bird is sent away for a moment, it is only for its own advantage. It sets out with its neighbors, its parents, its sisters and brothers; it leaves nothing behind; it carries with it all the objects of its affection. In the desert it finds a subsistence and a habitation; the forests are not armed against it; and it returns, at last, to die on the spot which gave it birth. There it finds again the river, the tree, the nest, and the sun, of its forefathers. But

[1] Those which, dreading the rigors of our winters, repair to a more genial climate, will never suffer their tardy troop to be overtaken by the inclement season. Assembled in prudent council by their chiefs, the great day of their general departure is fixed. It arrives, the whole tribe departs; the youngest perhaps inquires, while he casts his eyes over his native fields, when spring will arrive, to recall so many exiles to their paternal plains.

is the mortal, driven from his native home, sure of revisiting it again? Alas! man, in coming into the world, knows not what corner of the earth will collect his ashes, nor in what direction the breath of misfortune will scatter them. Happy still, indeed, if he only could expire in peace. But no sooner does fortune frown upon him than he becomes an object of persecution; and the particular injustice which he suffers becomes general. He finds not, like the bird, hospitality in his way; he knocks, but no one opens; he has no place to rest his weary limbs, except, perhaps, the post on the highway, or the stone that marks the limit of some plantation. But sometimes he is denied even this place of repose, which would seem to belong to no one; he is forced onward, and the proscription which has banished him from his country seems to have expelled him from the world. He dies, and has none to bury him. His corpse lies forsaken on its hard couch, whence the commissioner is obliged to have it removed, not as the body of a man, but as a nuisance dangerous to the living. Ah! how much happier, did he expire in a ditch near the way-side, that the good Samaritan might throw, as he passes, a little foreign earth upon his remains! Let us place all our hope in heaven, and we shall no longer be afraid of exile: in religion we invariably find a country!

While one part of the creation daily publishes in the same place the praises of the Creator, another travels from one country to another to relate his wonders. Couriers traverse the air, glide through the waters, and speed their course over mountains and valleys. Some, borne on the wings of spring, show themselves among us; then, disappearing with the zephyrs, follow their movable country from climate to climate. Others repair to the habitation of man, as travellers from distant climes, and claim the rights of ancient hospitality. Each follows his inclination in the choice of a spot. The redbreast applies at the cottage; the swallow knocks at the palace of royal descent. She still seems to court an appearance of grandeur, but of grandeur melancholy like her fate. She passes the summer amid the ruins of Versailles and the winter among those of Thebes.

Scarcely has she disappeared when we behold a colony advancing upon the winds of the north, to supply the place of the travellers to the south, that no vacancy may be left in our fields. On some hoary day of autumn, when the northeast wind is sweeping over the plains and the woods are losing the last remains of their foliage, you will see a flock of wild ducks, all ranged in a line, traversing in silence the sombre sky. If they perceive, while aloft in the air, some Gothic castle surrounded by marshes and forests, it is there they prepare to descend. They wait till night, making long evolutions over the woods. Soon as the vapors of eve enshroud the valley, with outstretched neck and whizzing wing they suddenly alight on the waters, which resound with their noise A general cry, succeeded by profound silence, rises from the marshes. Guided by a faint light, which perhaps gleams through the narrow window of a tower, the travellers approach its walls under the protection of the reeds and the darkness. There, clapping their wings and screaming at intervals, amid the murmur of the winds and the rain, they salute the habitation of man.

One of the handsomest among the inhabitants of these solitudes is the water-hen. Her peregrinations, however, are not so distant. She appears on the border of the sedges, buries herself in their labyrinths, appears and vanishes again, uttering a low, wild cry. She is seen walking along the ditches of the castle, and is fond of perching on the coats of arms sculptured on the walls. When she remains motionless upon them, you would take her, with her sable plumage and the white patch on her head, for a heraldic bird, fallen from the escutcheon of an ancient knight. At the approach of spring, she retires to unfrequented streams. The root of some willow that has been undermined by the waters affords an asylum to the wanderer. She there conceals herself from every eye, to accomplish the grand law of nature. The convolvulus, the mosses, the water maidenhair, suspend a verdant drapery before her nest. The cress and the lentil supply her with a delicate food. The soft murmuring of the water soothes her ear; beautiful insects amuse her eye, and the Naiads of the stream, the more completely to conceal this youthful mother, plant around her their distaffs of reeds, covered with empurpled wool.

Among these travellers from the north, there are some that become accustomed to our manners, and refuse to return to their native land Some, like the companions of Ulysses, are captivated by delicious fruits; others, like the deserters from the vessels of the British circumnavigator, are seduced by enchantresses that detain them in their islands. Most of them, however, leave us after a residence of a few months. They are attached to the winds and the storms which disturb the pellucid stream, and afford them that prey which would escape from them in transparent waters. They love wild and unexplored retreats, and make the circuit of the globe by a series of solitudes.

Fitness for the scenes of nature, or adaptation to the wants of man, determines the different migrations of animals. The birds that appear in the months of storms have dismal voices and wild manners, like the season which brings them. They come not to be heard, but to listen. There is something in the dull roaring of the woods that charms their ear. The trees which mournfully wave their leafless summits are covered only with the sable legions which have associated for the winter. They have their sentinels and their advanced guards. Frequently a crow that has seen a hundred winters, the ancient Sybil of the deserts, remains perched on an oak which has grown old with herself. There, while all her sisters maintain a profound silence, motionless, and, as it were, full of thought, she delivers prophetic sounds to the winds.

It is worthy of remark that the teal, the goose, the duck, the woodcock, the plover, the lapwing, which serve us for food, all arrive when the earth is bare; while, on the contrary, the foreign birds, which visit us in the season of fruits, administer only to our pleasures. They are musicians sent to enhance the joy of our banquets. We must, however, except a few, such as the quail and the wood-pigeon, (though the season for taking them does not commence till after the harvest,) which fatten on our corn, that they may afterward supply our table. Thus the birds of winter are the manna of the rude northern blasts, as the nightingales are the gift of the zephyrs. From whatever point of the compass the wind may blow, it fails not to bring us a present from Providence.

CHAPTER VIII.

SEA-FOWL—IN WHAT MANNER SERVICEABLE TO MAN—IN ANCIENT TIMES THE MIGRATIONS OF BIRDS SERVED AS A CALENDAR TO THE HUSBANDMAN.

THE goose and the duck, being domestic animals, are capable of living wherever man can exist. Navigators have found innumerable battalions of these birds under the antarctic pole itself, and on the coasts of New Zealand. We have ourselves met with thousands, from the Gulf of St. Lawrence to the extremity of Florida. We beheld one day, in the Azores, a company of little bluebirds, of the species of teal, that were compelled by fatigue to alight on a wild fig-tree. The tree had no leaves, but its red fruit hung chained together in pairs like crystals. When it was covered by this flock of birds, that dropped their weary wings, it exhibited a very pleasing appearance. The fruit, suspended from the shadowed branches, seemed to have the color of a brilliant purple, while the tree appeared all at once clothed with the richest foliage of azure.

Sea-fowl have places of rendezvous where you would imagine they were deliberating in common on the affairs of their republic. These places are commonly the rocks in the midst of the waves. In the island of St. Pierre,[1] we used often to station ourselves on the coast opposite to an islet called by the natives *Colombier*, (*Pigeon-house*,) on account of its form, and because they repair thither in spring for the purpose of gathering eggs.

The multitude of birds that assemble on that rock was so great that we could frequently distinguish their cries amid the howlings of the tempests. These birds had an extraordinary voice, resembling the sounds that issued from the sea. If the ocean has its Flora, it has likewise its Philomela. When the curlew whistles at sunset on the point of some rock, accompanied by the hollow murmur of the billows, which forms the bass to the concert, it produces one of the most melancholy harmonies that can

[1] At th[illegible] of Newfoundland.

possibly be conceived Never did the wife of Ceix breathe forth such lamentations on the shores that witnessed her misfortunes

The best understanding prevailed in the republic of Colombier. Immediately after the birth of a citizen, his mother precipitated him into the waves, like those barbarous nations who plunged their children into the river to inure them to the fatigues of life. Couriers were incessantly despatched from this Tyre with numerous attendants, who, under the direction of Providence, sought different points in the ocean, for the guidance of the mariner. Some, stationed at the distance of forty or fifty leagues from an unknown land, serve as a certain indication to the pilot, who discovers them like corks floating on the waves. Others settle on a reef, and in the night these vigilant sentinels raise their doleful voices to warn the navigator to stand off; while others, again, by the whiteness of their plumage, form real beacons upon the black surface of the rocks. For the same reason, we presume, has the goodness of the Almighty given to the foam of the waves a phosphoric property, rendering it more luminous among breakers in proportion to the violence of the tempest. How many vessels would perish amid the darkness were it not for these wonderful beacons kindled by Providence on the rocks!

All the accidents of the seas, the flux and reflux of the tide, and the alternations of calm and storm, are predicted by birds. The thrush alights on a desolate shore, draws her neck under her plumage, conceals one foot in her down, and, standing motionless on the other, apprises the fisherman of the moment when the billows are rising. The sea-lark, skimming the surface of the wave, and uttering a soft and melancholy cry, announces, on the contrary, the moment of their reflux Lastly, the little storm-bird stations herself in the midst of the ocean [1] This faithful companion of the mariner follows the course of ships and predicts the storm. The sailor ascribes to her something sacred, and reli-

[1] The procellaria, or stormy-petrel, is about the size and form of the house-swallow. Except in breeding time, these birds are always at sea, and are seen on the wing all over the vast Atlantic Ocean, at the greatest distance from any land. They presage bad weather, whence they take their name, and they caution sailors of the approach of a storm by collecting under the stern of the ship. This bird braves the utmost fury of the tempest, sometimes skimming with incredible velocity along the hollow and sometimes on the summit of the waves.

giously fulfils the duties of hospitality when the violence of the wind tosses her on board his vessel. In like manner, the husbandman pays respect to the red-breast, which predicts fine weather. In like manner, he receives him beneath his thatch during the intense cold of winter. These men, placed in the two most laborious conditions of life, have friends whom Providence has prepared for them. From a feeble animal they receive counsel and hope, which they would often seek in vain among their fellow-creatures. This reciprocity of benefits between little birds and men struggling through the world, is one of those pleasing incidents which abound in the works of God. Between the red-breast and the husbandman, between the storm-bird and the sailor, there is a resemblance of manners and of fortunes exceedingly affecting. Oh, how dry and unmeaning is nature when explained by the sophist! but how significant and interesting to the simple heart that investigates her wonders with no other view than to glorify the Creator!

If time and place permitted, we would have many other migrations to describe, many other secrets of Providence to reveal. We would treat of the cranes of Florida, whose wings produce such harmonious sounds, and which steer their flight so beautifully over lakes, savannas, and groves of orange and palm-trees; we would exhibit the pelican of the woods, visiting the solitary dead, and stopping only at Indian cemeteries and hillocks of graves; we would state the reasons of these migrations, which have always some reference to man; we would mention the winds, the seasons chosen by the birds for changing their climate, the adventures they meet with, the obstacles they encounter, the disasters they undergo; how they sometimes land on unknown coasts, far from the country to which they were bound; how they perish on their passage over forests consumed by the lightnings of heaven or plains fired by the hands of savages.

In the early ages of the world, it was by the flowering of plants, the fall of the leaves, the departure and arrival of birds, that the husbandman and shepherd regulated their labors. Hence arose among certain people the art of divination; for it was supposed that animals which predicted the seasons and tempests could be no other than the interpreters of the Deity. The ancient naturalists and poets, to whom we are indebted for the little simplicity that is left among us, show how wonderful was this mode of reckoning by the incidents of nature, and what a charm it diffused over life. God is a profound secret; man, created in his image, is likewise incomprehensible; it was therefore perfectly consonant to the nature of things to see the periods of his days regulated by timekeepers as mysterious as himself.

Beneath the tents of Jacob or of Booz, the arrival of a bird set every thing in motion: the patriarch made the tour of his encampment, at the head of his servants, provided with sickles; and if it was rumored that the young larks had been seen making their first efforts to fly, the whole people, trusting in God, entered joyfully upon the harvest. These charming signs, while they directed the labors of the present season, had the advantage of predicting the changes of the succeeding ones. If the geese and the ducks appeared in great numbers, it was known with certainty that the winter would be long. If the crow began to build her nest in January, the shepherds expected in April the flowers of May. The marriage of a young female, on the margin of a fountain, had its relation with the blooming flowers; and the aged, who often die in autumn, fell with the acorns and the ripe fruits. While the philosopher, curtailing or lengthening the year, made the winter encroach upon the domain of spring, the husbandman had no reason to apprehend that the bird or the flower, the astronomer sent him by Heaven, would lead him astray. He knew that the nightingale would not confound the month of frosts with that of roses, or warble the strains of summer at the winter solstice. Thus all the labors, all the diversions, all the pleasures of the countryman were regulated, not by the uncertain calendar of a philosopher, but by the infallible laws of Him who has traced the course of the sun. That supreme Director himself decreed that the festivals of his worship should be determined by the simple epochs borrowed from his own works; and hence, in those days of innocence, according to the season and occupations of men, it was the voice of the zephyr or the storm, of the eagle or the dove, that summoned them to the temple of the God of nature.

Our peasants still make use occasionally of these charming tables, on which are engraven the seasons of rustic labor. The natives of India also have recourse to them, and the negroes and

American savages retain the same method of computation. A Seminole of Florida will tell you that his daughter was married at the arrival of the humming-bird;—his child died in the moulting season of the nonpareil;—his mother had as many young warriors as there are eggs in the nest of the pelican.

The savages of Canada mark the sixth hour after noon by the moment when the wood-pigeon repairs to the stream to drink, and the savages of Louisiana by that in which the day-fly issues from the waters. The passage of various birds regulates the season of the chase; and the time for reaping the crops of corn, maple-sugar, and wild oats, is announced by certain animals, which never fail to appear at the hour of the banquet.

CHAPTER IX.

THE SUBJECT OF MIGRATIONS CONCLUDED—QUADRUPEDS.

Migration is more frequent among fishes and birds than among quadrupeds, on account of the multiplicity of the former, and the facility of their journeys through the two elements by which the earth is surrounded. There is nothing astonishing in all this but the certainty with which they reach the shores to which they are bound. It appears natural that an animal, driven by hunger, should leave the country he inhabits in search of food and shelter; but is it possible to conceive that *matter* causes him to arrive at one place rather than another, and conducts him, with wonderful precision, to *the very spot* where this food and shelter are to be found? How should he know the winds and the tides, the equinoxes and the solstices? We have no doubt that if the migratory tribes were abandoned for a single moment to *their own instinct*, they would almost all perish. Some, wishing to pass to a colder climate, would reach the tropics; others, intending to proceed under the line, would wander to the poles. Our redbreasts, instead of passing over Alsace and Germany in search of little insects, would themselves become the prey of some enormous beetle in Africa; the Greenlander, attracted by a plaintive cry issuing from the rocks, would draw near, and find poor philomela in the agony of death.

Such mistakes are not permitted by the Almighty. Every thing in nature has its harmonies and its relations: zephyrs accord with flowers, winter is suited to storms, and grief has its seat in the heart of man. The most skilful pilots will long miss the desired port before the fish mistakes the longitude of the smallest rock in the ocean. Providence is his polar star, and, whatever way he steers, he has constantly in view that luminary which never sets.

The universe is like an immense inn, where all is in motion. You behold a multitude of travellers continually entering and departing. In the migrations of quadrupeds, nothing perhaps can be compared to the journeys of the bisons across the immense prairies of Louisiana and New Mexico.[1] When the time has arrived for them to change their residence, and to dispense abundance to savage nations, some aged buffalo, the patriarch of the herds of the desert, calls around him his sons and daughters. The rendezvous is on the banks of the Meschacebe; the close of day is fixed for the time of their departure. This moment having arrived, the leader, shaking his vast mane, which hangs down over his eyes and his curved horns, salutes the setting sun with an inclination of the head, at the same time raising his huge back like a mountain. With a deep, rumbling sound, he gives the signal for departure. Then, suddenly plunging into the foaming waters, he is followed by the whole multitude of bulls and heifers, bellowing after him in the expression of their love.

While this powerful family of quadrupeds is crossing with tremendous uproar the rivers and forests, a peaceful squadron is seen moving silently over the solitary lake, with the aid of the starlight and a favorable breeze. It is a troop of small, black squirrels, that having stripped all the walnut trees of the vicinity, resolve to seek their fortune, and to embark for another forest. Raising their tails, and expanding them as silken sails to the

[1] The bison is the wild bull or ox, from which several races of common cattle are descended. It is found wild in many parts of the old and new continents, and is distinguished by its large size and the shagginess of its hair about the head, neck, and shoulders. In the western territories of the United States they are seen in herds innumerable, intermixed with deer.

wind, this intrepid race boldly tempt the inconstant waves. O imprudent pirates, transported by the desire of riches! The tempest arises, the waves roar, and the squadron is on the point of perishing. It strives to gain the nearest haven, but sometimes an army of beavers oppose the landing, fearful lest these strangers are come to pillage their stores In vain the nimble battalions, springing upon the shores, think to escape by climbing the trees, and from their lofty tops to defy the enemy. Genius is superior to artifice;—a band of sappers advance, undermine the oak, and bring it to the ground, with all its squirrels, like a tower, filled with soldiers, demolished by the ancient battering-ram.

Our adventurers experience many other mishaps, which, however, are in some degree compensated by the fruit they have discovered and the sports in which they indulge. Athens, reduced to captivity by the Lacedemonians, was not, on that account, of a less amiable or less frivolous character.

In ascending the North River in the packet-boat from New York to Albany, we ourselves beheld one of these unfortunate squirrels, which had attempted to cross the stream. He was unable to reach the shore, and was taken half-drowned out of the water; he was a beautiful creature, black as ebony, and his tail was twice the length of his body. He was restored to life, but lost his liberty by becoming the slave of a young female passenger.

The reindeer of the north of Europe, and the elks of North America, have their seasons of migration, invariably calculated, like those of birds, to supply the necessities of man. Even the white bear of Newfoundland is sent by a wonderful Providence to the Esquimaux Indians, that they may clothe themselves with its skin. These marine monsters are seen approaching the coasts of Labrador on islands of floating ice, or on fragments of vessels, to which they cling like sturdy mariners escaped from shipwreck. The elephants of Asia also travel, and the earth shakes beneath their feet, yet man has nothing to fear; chaste, tender, intelligent. Behemoth is gentle because he is strong; peaceful, because he is powerful. The first servant of man, but not his slave, he ranks next to him in the scale of the creation When the animals, after the original fall, removed from the habitation of man, the elephant, from the generosity of his nature, appears to have retired with the greatest reluctance; for he has always remained near the cradle of the world. He now goes forth occasionally from his desert, and advances toward an inhabited district, to supply the place of some companion that has died without progeny in the service of the children of Adam.[1]

CHAPTER X.

AMPHIBIOUS ANIMALS AND REPTILES.

In the Floridas, at the foot of the Appalachian Mountains, there are springs which are called natural wells. Each well is scooped out of the centre of a hill planted with orange-trees, evergreen oaks, and catalpas. This hill opens in the form of a

[1] The eloquent writers who have described the manners of this animal render it unnecessary for us to enlarge on the subject. We shall merely observe that the conformation of the elephant appears so extraordinary to us, only because we see it separated from the plants, the situations, the waters, the mountains, the colors, the light, the shade, and the skies, which are peculiar to it. The productions of our latitudes, planned on a smaller scale, the frequent roundness of objects, the firmness of the grasses, the slight denticulation of the leaves, the elegant bearing of the trees, our languid days and chilly nights, the fugitive tints of our verdure, in short, even the color, clothing and architecture of Europeans, have no conformity with the elephant. Were travellers more accurate observers, we should know in what manner this quadruped is connected with that nature which produces him. For our own part, we think we have a glimpse of some of these relations. The elephant's trunk, for example, has a striking coincidence with the wax-tree, the aloe, the lianne, the rattan, and in the animal kingdom with the long serpents of India; his ears are shaped like the leaves of the eastern fig-tree; his skin is scaly, soft, and yet rigid, like the substance which covers part of the trunk of the palm, or rather like the ligneous coat of the cocoanut; many of the large plants of the tropics support themselves on the earth in the manner of his feet, and have the same square and heavy form; his voice is at once shrill and strong, like that of the Caffre in his deserts, or like the war-cry of the Sepoy. When, covered with a rich carpet, laden with a tower resembling the minarets of a pagoda, he carries some pious monarch to the ruins of those temples which are found in the peninsula of India, his massive form, the columns which support him, his irregular figure, and his barbarous pomp, coincide with the colossal structure formed of hewn rocks piled one upon another. The vast animal and the ruined monument both seem to be relics of the giant age.

crescent toward the savanna, and at the aperture is a channel through which the water flows from the well The foliage of the trees bending over the fountain causes the water beneath to appear perfectly black; but at the spot where the aqueduct joins the base of the cone, a ray of light, entering by the bed of the channel, falls upon a single point of the liquid mirror, which produces an effect resembling that of the glass in the *camera obscura* of the painter. This delightful retreat is commonly inhabited by an enormous crocodile, which stands motionless in the centre of the basin;[1] and from the appearance of his greenish hide, and his large nostrils spouting the water in two colored ellipses, you would take him for a dolphin of bronze in some grotto among the groves of Versailles.

The crocodiles or caymans of Florida live not always in solitude. At certain seasons of the year they assemble in troops, and lie in ambush to attack the scaly travellers who are expected to arrive from the ocean. When these have ascended the rivers, and, wanting water for their vast shoals, perish stranded on the shores, and threaten to infect the air, Providence suddenly lets loose upon them an army of four or five thousand crocodiles. The monsters, raising a tremendous outcry and gnashing their horrid jaws, rush upon the strangers. Bounding from all sides, the combatants close, seize, and entwine each other. Plunging to the bottom of the abyss, they roll themselves in the mud, and then to the surface of the waves. The waters, stained with blood, are covered with mangled carcasses and reeking with entrails. It is impossible to convey an idea of these extraordinary scenes described by travellers, and which the reader is always tempted to consider as mere exaggerations. Routed, dispersed, and panic-struck, the foreign legions, pursued as far as the Atlantic, are obliged to return to its abyss, that by supplying our wants at some future period, they may serve without injuring us.[2]

This species of monsters has sometimes proved a stumbling-block to atheistic minds; they are, however, extremely necessary in the general plan. They inhabit only the deserts where the absence of man requires their presence: they are placed there

[1] See Bartram. *Voyage dans les Carolines et dans les Florides*

[2] The immense advantages derived by man from the migrations of fishes are so well known that we shall not enlarge on that subject

for the express purpose of destroying, till the arrival of the great destroyer. The moment we appear on the coast, they resign the empire to us; certain that a single individual of our species will make greater havoc than ten thousand of theirs.[1]

"And why," it will be asked, "has God made superfluous creatures, which render destruction a necessary consequence?" For this great reason, that God acts not, like us, in a limited way. He contents himself with saying, "increase and multiply," and in these two words exists infinity. Henceforth, we shall perhaps measure the wisdom of the Deity by the rule of mediocrity; we shall deny him the attribute of infinitude, and reject altogether the idea of immensity. Wherever we behold it in nature, we shall pronounce it an "excess," because it is above our comprehension. What! If God thinks fit to place more than a certain number of suns in the expanse of heaven, shall we consider the excess as superfluous, and, in consequence of this profusion, declare the Creator convicted of folly and imbecility?

Whatever may be the deformity of the beings which we call monsters, if we consider them individually, we may discover in their horrible figures some marks of divine goodness. Has a crocodile or a serpent less affection for her young than a nightingale or a dove? And is it not a contrast equally wonderful and pleasing to behold this crocodile building a nest and laying an egg like a hen, and a little monster issuing from that egg like a chicken? After the birth of the young one, the female crocodile evinces for it the most tender solicitude. She walks her rounds among the nests of her sisters, which are cones of eggs and of clay, and are ranged like the tents of a camp on the bank of a river. The amazon keeps a vigilant guard, and leaves the fires of day to operate; for, if the delicate tenderness of the mother is, as it were, represented in the egg of the crocodile, the strength and the manners of that powerful animal are denoted by the sun which hatches that egg and by the mud which aids it to ferment.

---

[1] It has been observed that, in the Carolinas, where the *caymans* have been destroyed, the rivers are often infected by the multitude of fishes which ascend from the ocean, and which perish for want of water during the dog-days.

The cayman is commonly known by the name of *Antilles Crocodile*, because it abounds in those islands. It is the most hideous, terrible, and destructive of the *Lacerta* genus of animals.

As soon as one of the broods is hatched, the female takes the young monsters under her protection; they are not always her own children, but she thus serves an apprenticeship to maternal care, and acquires an ability equal to her future tenderness. When her family, at length, burst from their confinement, she conducts them to the river, she washes them in pure water, she teaches them to swim, she catches small fishes for them, and protects them from the males, by whom otherwise they would frequently be devoured.

A Spaniard of Florida related to us that, having taken the brood of a crocodile, which he ordered some negroes to carry away in a basket, the female followed him with pitiful cries. Two of the young having been placed upon the ground, the mother immediately began to push them with her paws and her snout; sometimes posting herself behind to defend them, sometimes walking before to show them the way. The young animals, groaning, crawled in the footsteps of their mother; and this enormous reptile, which used to shake the shore with her bellowing, then made a kind of bleating noise, as gentle as that of a goat suckling her kids.

The rattlesnake vies with the crocodile in maternal affection. This superb reptile, which gives a lesson of generosity to man,[1] also presents to him a pattern of tenderness. When her offspring are pursued, she receives them into her mouth:[2] dissatisfied with every other place of concealment, she hides them within herself, concluding that children can have no better refuge than the bosom of their mother. A perfect example of sublime love, she never survives the loss of her young; for it is impossible to deprive her of them without tearing out her entrails.

Shall we mention the poison of this serpent, always the most violent at the time she has a family? Shall we describe the tenderness of the bear, which, like the female savage, carries maternal affection to such a pitch as to suckle her offspring after their death?[3] If we follow these monsters, as they are called, in all their instincts; if we study their forms and their weapons of

---

[1] It is never the first to attack.

[2] See Carver's *Travels in Canada* for a confirmation of this statement.

[3] See Cook's *Voyages*.

defence; if we consider the link which they make in the chain of creation; if we examine the relations they have among themselves, and those which they have to man; we shall be convinced that final causes are, perhaps, more discernible in this class of beings than in the most favored species of nature. In a rude and unpolished work, the traits of genius shine forth the more prominently amid the shadows that surround them.

The objections alleged against the situations which these monsters inhabit appear to us equally unfounded. Morasses, however noxious they may seem, have, nevertheless, very important uses. They are the urns of rivers in champagne countries, and reservoirs for rain in those remote from the sea. Their mud and the ashes of their plants serve the husbandman for manure. Their reeds supply the poor with fuel and with shelter—a frail covering, indeed, though it harmonizes with the life of man, lasting no longer than himself. These places even possess a certain beauty peculiar to themselves. Bordering on land and water, they have plants, scenery, and inhabitants, of a specific character. Every object there partakes of the mixture of the two elements. The corn-flag forms the medium between the herb and the shrub, between the leek of the seas and the terrestrial plant. Some of the aquatic insects resemble small birds. When the dragon-fly, with his blue corslet and transparent wings, hovers round the flower of the white water-lily, you would take him for a humming-bird of the Floridas on a rose of magnolia. In autumn these morasses are covered with dried reeds, which give to sterility itself the appearance of the richest harvests. In the spring they exhibit forests of verdant lances. A solitary birch or willow, on which the gale has suspended tufts of feathers, towers above these moving plains, and when the wind passes over their bending summits, one bows its head while another rises; but suddenly, the whole forest inclining at once, you discover either the gilded bittern or the white heron, standing motionless on one of its long paws, as if fixed upon a spear.

CHAPTER XI.

OF PLANTS AND THEIR MIGRATIONS.

We now enter that kingdom of nature in which the wonders of Providence assume a milder and more charming character. Rising aloft in the air, and on the summits of the mountains, plants would seem to borrow something of that heaven to which they make approaches. We often see, at the first dawn of day, in a time of profound stillness, the flowers of the valley motionless on their stems, and inclining in various directions toward every point of the horizon. At this very moment, when all appears so tranquil, a great mystery is accomplishing. Nature conceives, and all these plants become so many youthful mothers, looking toward the mysterious region from which they derive their fecundity. The sylphs have sympathies less aerial, communications less imperceptible. The narcissus consigns her virgin progeny to the stream. The violet trusts her modest posterity to the zephyrs. A bee, collecting honey from flower to flower, unconsciously fecundates a whole meadow. A butterfly bears a whole species on his wings All the loves of the plants, however, are not equally peaceful. Some are stormy, like the passions of men. Nothing less than a tempest is required to marry, on their inaccessible heights, the cedar of Lebanon to the cedar of Sinai; while, at the foot of the mountain, the gentlest breeze is sufficient to produce a voluptuous commerce among the flowers. Is it not thus that the rude blast of the passions agitates the kings of the earth upon their thrones, while the shepherds enjoy uninterrupted happiness at their feet?

The flower yields honey. It is the daughter of the morning, the charm of spring, the source of perfumes, the graceful ornament of the virgin, the delight of the poet. Like man, it passes rapidly away, but drops its leaves gently to the earth Among the ancients it crowned the convivial cup and the silvery hair of the sage. With flowers the first Christians bedecked the remains of martyrs and the altars of the catacombs; and, in commemoration of those ancient days, we still use them for the decoration of our temples. In the world, we compare our affections to the colors of the flower. Hope has its verdure, innocence its whiteness, modesty its roseate hue. Some nations make it the interpreter of the feelings,—a charming book, containing no dangerous error, but recording merely the fugitive history of man's changing heart.

By a wise distribution of the sexes in several families of plants, Providence has multiplied the mysteries and the beauties of nature. By this means the law of migrations is reproduced in a kingdom destitute, apparently, of every locomotive faculty. Sometimes it is the seed or the fruit, sometimes it is a portion of the plant, or even the whole plant, that travels. The cocoa-tree frequently grows upon rocks in the midst of the ocean. The storm rages, the fruits fall and are carried by the billows to inhabited coasts, where they are transformed into stately trees—an admirable symbol of Virtue, who fixes herself upon the rock, exposed to the tempest. The more she is assailed by the winds, the more she lavishes treasures upon mankind.

On the banks of the Yare, a small river in the county of Suffolk, England, we were shown a very curious species of the cress It changes its place, and advances, as it were, by leaps and bounds. From its summit descend several fibres, and when those which happen to be at one extremity are of sufficient length to reach the bottom of the water, they take root. Drawn away by the action of the plant, which settles upon its new foot, that on the opposite looses its hold, and the tuft of cresses, turning on its pivot, removes the whole length of its bed. In vain you seek the plant on the morrow in the place where you left it the preceding night. You perceive it higher up or lower down the current of the river, producing, with the other aquatic families, new effects and new beauties. We have not seen this singular species of cress, either in its flowering or bearing state; but we have given it the name of *migrator*, or the traveller.[1]

Marine plants are liable to change their climate. They seem to partake of the adventurous spirit of those nations whose geographical position has rendered them commercial. The *fucus giganteus* issues with the tempests from the caverns of the north.

[1] None of the naturalists consulted upon this subject have verified the description of this curious species of cress.

Borne upon the sea, it moves along encircling an immense mass of water. Like a net stretched across the ocean from shore to shore, it carries along with it the shells, seals, thornbacks, and turtles which it meets in its way. Sometimes, as if fatigued with swimming on the waves, it extends one leg to the bottom of the abyss, and remains stationary; then, pursuing its voyage with a favorable breeze, after having floated beneath a thousand different latitudes, it proceeds to cover the Canadian shores with garlands torn from the rocks of Norway.

The migrations of marine plants, which, at the first view, would seem to be the mere sport of chance, have, nevertheless, very interesting relations with man.

Walking one evening along the seashore at Brest, we perceived a poor woman wandering, in a stooping posture, among the rocks She surveyed with attention the fragments of a wreck, and examined particularly the plants which adhered to it, as if she sought to ascertain, from their age, the exact period of her misfortune. She discovered, beneath some stones, one of those chests in which mariners are used to keep their bottles. Perhaps she had once filled it herself, for her husband, with cordials purchased with the fruit of her economy; at least so we judged, for we saw her lift the corner of her apron to wipe the tears from her eyes Sea-mushrooms now replaced the offerings of her affection. Thus, while the report of cannon announces to the great ones of this earth the destruction of human grandeur, Providence brings the tale of sorrow, on the same shore, to the weak and lowly, by secretly disclosing to them a blade of grass or a ruin.

CHAPTER XII.

TWO VIEWS OF NATURE.

WHAT we have said respecting animals and plants leads us to a more general view of the scenes of nature. Those wonders which, separately considered, so loudly proclaimed the providence of God, will now speak to us of the same truth in their collective capacity

We shall place before the reader two views of nature; one an ocean scene, the other a land picture; one sketched in the middle of the Atlantic, the other in the forests of the New World. Thus, no one can say that the imposing grandeur of this scenery has been derived from the works of man.

The vessel in which we embarked for America having passed the bearing of any land, space was soon enclosed only by the two-fold azure of the sea and of the sky. The color of the waters resembled that of liquid glass. A great swell was visible from the west, though the wind blew from the east, while immense undulations extended from the north to the south, opening in their valleys long vistas through the deserts of the deep. The fleeting scenes changed with every minute. Sometimes a multitude of verdant hillocks appeared to us like a series of graves in some vast cemetery. Sometimes the curling summits of the waves resembled white flocks scattered over a heath. Now space seemed circumscribed for want of an object of comparison; but if a billow reared its mountain crest, if a wave curved like a distant shore, or a squadron of sea-dogs moved along the horizon, the vastness of space again suddenly opened before us. We were most powerfully impressed with an idea of magnitude, when a light fog, creeping along the surface of the deep, seemed to increase immensity itself. Oh! how sublime, how awful, at such times, is the aspect of the ocean! Into what reveries does it plunge you, whether imagination transports you to the seas of the north, into the midst of frosts and tempests, or wafts you to southern islands, blessed with happiness and peace!

We often rose at midnight and sat down upon deck, where we found only the officer of the watch and a few sailors silently smoking their pipes. No noise was heard, save the dashing of the prow through the billows, while sparks of fire ran with a white foam along the sides of the vessel. God of Christians! it is on the waters of the abyss and on the vast expanse of the heavens that thou hast particularly engraven the characters of thy omnipotence! Millions of stars sparkling in the azure of the celestial dome—the moon in the midst of the firmament—a sea unbounded by any shore—infinitude in the skies and on the waves—proclaim with most impressive effect the power of thy arm! Never did thy greatness strike me with profounder awe than in those nights, when, suspended between the stars and the ocean, I beheld immensity over my head and immensity beneath my feet!

I am nothing; I am only a simple, solitary wanderer, and often have I heard men of science disputing on the subject of a Supreme Being, without understanding them; but I have invariably remarked, that it is in the prospect of the sublime scenes of nature that this unknown Being manifests himself to the human heart. One evening, after we had reached the beautiful waters that bathe the shores of Virginia, there was a profound calm, and every sail was furled I was engaged below, when I heard the bell that summoned the crew to prayers. I hastened to mingle my supplications with those of my travelling companions. The officers of the ship were on the quarter-deck with the passengers, while the chaplain, with a book in his hand, was stationed at a little distance before them; the seamen were scattered at random over the poop; we were all standing, our faces toward the prow of the vessel, which was turned to the west.

The solar orb, about to sink beneath the waves, was seen through the rigging, in the midst of boundless space; and, from the motion of the stern, it appeared as if it changed its horizon every moment. A few clouds wandered confusedly in the east, where the moon was slowly rising The rest of the sky was serene; and toward the north, a water-spout, forming a glorious triangle with the luminaries of day and night, and glistening with all the colors of the prism, rose from the sea, like a column of crystal supporting the vault of heaven.

He had been well deserving of pity who would not have recognised in this prospect the beauty of God When my companions, doffing their tarpaulin hats, entoned with hoarse voice their simple hymn to Our Lady of Good Help, the patroness of the seas, the tears flowed from my eyes in spite of myself How affecting was the prayer of those men, who, from a frail plank in the midst of the ocean, contemplated the sun setting behind the waves! How the appeal of the poor sailor to the Mother of Sorrows went to the heart! The consciousness of our insignificance in the presence of the Infinite,—our hymns, resounding to a distance over the silent waves,—the night approaching with its dangers,—our vessel, itself a wonder among so many wonders,—a religious crew, penetrated with admiration and with awe,—a venerable priest in prayer,—the Almighty bending over the abyss, with one hand staying the sun in the west, with the other raising the moon in the east, and lending, through all immensity, an attentive ear to the feeble voice of his creatures,—all this constituted a scene which no power of art can represent, and which it is scarcely possible for the heart of man to feel.

Let us now pass to the terrestrial scene.

I had wandered one evening in the woods, at some distance from the cataract of Niagara, when soon the last glimmering of daylight disappeared, and I enjoyed, in all its loneliness, the beauteous prospect of night amid the deserts of the New World.

An hour after sunset, the moon appeared above the trees in the opposite part of the heavens. A balmy breeze, which the queen of night had brought with her from the east, seemed to precede her in the forests, like her perfumed breath. The lonely luminary slowly ascended in the firmament, now peacefully pursuing her azure course, and now reposing on groups of clouds which resembled the summits of lofty, snow-covered mountains. These clouds, by the contraction and expansion of their vapory forms, rolled themselves into transparent zones of white satin, scattering in airy masses of foam, or forming in the heavens brilliant beds of down so lovely to the eye that you would have imagined you felt their softness and elasticity.

The scenery on the earth was not less enchanting: the soft and bluish beams of the moon darted through the intervals between the trees, and threw streams of light into the midst of the most profound darkness. The river that glided at my feet was now lost in the wood, and now reappeared, glistening with the constellations of night, which were reflected on its bosom. In a vast plain beyond this stream, the radiance of the moon reposed quietly on the verdure. Birch-trees, scattered here and there in the savanna, and agitated by the breeze, formed shadowy islands which floated on a motionless sea of light. Near me, all was silence and repose, save the fall of some leaf, the transient rustling of a sudden breath of wind, or the hooting of the owl; but at a distance was heard, at intervals, the solemn roar of the Falls of Niagara, which, in the stillness of the night, was prolonged from desert to desert, and died away among the solitary forests.

The grandeur, the astonishing solemnity of this scene, cannot be expressed in language; nor can the most delightful nights of Europe afford any idea of it. In vain does imagination attempt to soar in our cultivated fields; it everywhere meets with the habitations of men: but in those wild regions the mind loves to penetrate into an ocean of forests, to hover round the abysses of cataracts, to meditate on the banks of lakes and rivers, and, as it were, to find itself alone with God.

CHAPTER XIII.

PHYSICAL MAN.

To complete the view of final causes, or the proofs of the existence of God, deducible from the wonders of nature, we have only to consider man in his physical or material aspect; and here we shall quote the observations of those who were thoroughly acquainted with the subject.

Cicero describes the human body in the following terms:[1]

"With respect to the senses, by which exterior objects are conveyed to the knowledge of the soul, their structure corresponds wonderfully with their destination, and they have their seat in the head as in a fortified town. The eyes, like sentinels, occupy the most elevated place, whence, on discovering objects, they may give the alarm. An eminent position was suited to the ears, because they are destined to receive sounds, which naturally ascend. The nostrils required a similar situation, because odors likewise ascend, and it was necessary that they should be near the mouth, because they greatly assist us in judging of our meat and drink. Taste, by which we are apprised of the quality of the food we take, resides in that part of the mouth through which nature gives a passage to solids and liquids. As for the touch, it is generally diffused over the whole body, that we might neither receive any impression, nor be attacked by cold or heat, without feeling it. And as an architect will not place the sewer of a

[1] *De Naturâ Deorum*, lib. ii.

house before the eyes or under the nose of his employer, so Nature has removed from our senses every thing of a similar kind in the human body.

"But what other artist than Nature, whose dexterity is incomparable, could have formed our senses with such exquisite skill? She has covered the eyes with very delicate tunics, transparent before, that we might see through them, and close in their texture, to keep the eyes in their proper situation. She has made them smooth and moveable, to enable them to avoid every thing by which they might be injured and to look with facility to whatever side they please. The pupil, in which is united all that constitutes the faculty of sight, is so small that it escapes without difficulty from every object capable of doing it mischief. The eyelids have a soft and polished surface, that they may not hurt the eyes Whether the fear of some accident obliges us to shut them, or we choose to open them, the eyelids are formed in such a manner as to adapt themselves to either of these motions, which are performed in an instant; they are, if we may so express it, fortified with palisades of hair, which serve to repel whatever may attack the eyes when they are open, and to envelop them that they may repose in peace when sleep closes and renders them useless to us. Our eyes possess the additional advantage of being concealed and defended by eminences; for, on the one hand, to stop the sweat that trickles down from the head and forehead, they have projecting eyebrows; and on the other, to preserve them from below, they have cheeks which likewise advance a little. The nose is placed between both like a wall of partition.

"With respect to the ear, it remains continually open, because we have occasion for its services, even when asleep. If any sound then strikes it, we are awaked. It has winding channels, lest, if they were straight and level, some object might find its way into them. . . . . .

"And then our hands,—how convenient are they, and how useful in the arts! The fingers are extended or contracted without the least difficulty, so extremely flexible are their joints. With their assistance the hands use the pencil and the chisel, and play on the lyre and the lute: so much for the agreeable. As to what is necessary, they cultivate the earth, build houses, make clothes, and work in copper and iron. The imagination invents, the senses examine, the hand executes; so that, if we are lodged, clothed, and sheltered,—if we have cities, walls, habitations, temples,—it is to our hands that we are indebted for all these."

It must be allowed that matter alone could no more have fashioned the human body for so many admirable purposes, than this beautiful discourse of the Roman orator could have been composed by a writer destitute of eloquence and of skill.[1]

Various authors, and Nieuwentyt in particular, have proved that the bounds within which our senses are confined, are the very limits that are best adapted to them, and that we should be exposed to a great number of inconveniences and dangers were the senses in any degree enlarged.[2] Galen, struck with admiration in the midst of an anatomical analysis of a human body, suddenly drops the scalpel, and exclaims:

"O Thou who hast made us! in composing a discourse so sacred, I think that I am chanting a hymn to thy glory! I honor thee more by unfolding the beauty of thy works, than by sacrificing to thee whole hecatombs of bulls or by burning in thy temples the most precious incense. True piety consists in first learning to know myself, and then in teaching others the greatness of thy bounty, thy power, and thy wisdom. Thy bounty is conspicuous in the equal distribution of thy presents, having allotted to each man the organs which are necessary for him; thy wisdom is seen in the excellence of thy gifts, and thy power is displayed in the execution of thy designs."[3]

---

[1] Cicero borrowed what he says concerning the service of the hand from Aristotle. In combating the philosophy of Anaxagoras, the Stagyrite observes, with his accustomed sagacity, that man is not superior to the animals because he has hands, but that he has hands because he is superior to the animals. Plato likewise adduces the structure of the human body as a proof of a divine intelligence; and there are some sublime sentences in Job on the same subject.

[2] See note M.

[3] Galen, *de Usu Part.*, lib iii. c. 10.

CHAPTER XIV.

LOVE OF OUR NATIVE COUNTRY.

As we have considered the instincts of animals, it is proper that we should allude to those of physical man; but as he combines in himself the feelings of different classes of the creation, such as parental tenderness, and many others, we shall select one quality that is peculiar to him.

The instinct with which man is pre-eminently endued—that which is of all the most beautiful and the most moral—is the love of his native country. If this law were not maintained by a never-ceasing miracle, to which, however, as to many others, we pay not the smallest attention, all mankind would crowd together into the temperate zones, leaving the rest of the earth a desert. We may easily conceive what great evils would result from this collection of the human family on one point of the globe. To prevent these calamities, Providence has, as it were, fixed the feet of each individual to his native soil by an invincible magnet, so that neither the ices of Greenland nor the burning sands of Africa are destitute of inhabitants.

We may remark still further, that the more sterile the soil, the more rude the climate, of a country, or, what amounts to the same thing, the greater the injustice and the more severe the persecution we have suffered there, the more strongly we are attached to it. Strange and sublime truth!—that misery should become a bond of attachment, and that those who have lost but a cottage should most feelingly regret the paternal habitation! The reason of this phenomenon is, that the profusion of a too fertile soil destroys, by enriching us, the simplicity of the natural ties arising from our wants; when we cease to love our parents and our relations because they are no longer necessary to us, we actually cease also to love our country.

Every thing tends to confirm the truth of this remark. A savage is more powerfully attached to his hut than a prince to his palace, and the mountaineer is more delighted with his native rocks than the inhabitant of the plain with his golden corn-fields. Ask a Scotch Highlander if he would exchange his lot with the first potentate of the earth. When far removed from his beloved mountains, he carries with him the recollection of them whithersoever he goes; he sighs for his flocks, his torrents, and his clouds. He longs to eat again his barley-bread, to drink goat's milk, and to sing in the valley the ballads which were sung by his forefathers. He pines if he is prevented from returning to his native clime. It is a mountain plant which must be rooted among rocks; it cannot thrive unless assailed by the winds and the rain; in the soil, the shelter, and the sunshine of the plain, it quickly droops and dies.

With what joy will he again fly to his roof of furze! with what delight will he visit all the sacred relics of his indigence!

> "Sweet treasures!" he exclaims, "O pledges dear!
> That lying and envy have attracted ne'er,
> Come back: from all this royal pomp I flee,
> For all is but an idle dream to me."

Who can be more happy than the Esquimaux, in his frightful country? What to him are all the flowers of our climates compared to the snows of Labrador, and all our palaces to his smoky cabin? He embarks in spring, with his wife, on a fragment of floating ice.[2] Hurried along by the currents, he advances into the open sea on this frozen mass. The mountain waves over the deep its trees of snow, the sea-wolves revel in its valleys, and the whales accompany it on the dark bosom of the ocean. The daring Indian, under the shelter afforded by his frozen mountain, presses to his heart the wife whom God has given him, and finds with her unknown joys in this mixture of perils and of pleasures.

It should be observed, however, that this savage has very good reasons for preferring his country and his condition to ours. Degraded as his nature may appear to us, still, we may discover in him, or in the arts he practises, something that displays the dignity of man. The European is lost every day, in some vessel

---

[1] "Doux trêsors!" se dit-il: "chers gages, qui jamais
N'attirâtes sur vous l'envie et le mensonge,
Je vous reprends: sortons de ces riches palais,
Comme l'on sortiroit d'un songe.

[2] See *Histoire de la Nouvelle France*, by Charlevoix.

which is a master-piece of human industry, on the same shores where the Esquimaux, floating in a seal's skin, smiles at every kind of danger. Sometimes he hears the ocean which covers him roaring far above his head; sometimes mountain-billows bear him aloft to the skies: he sports among the surges, as a child balances himself on tufted branches in the peaceful recesses of the forest. When God placed man in this region of tempests, he stamped upon him a mark of royalty. "Go," said he to him from amidst the whirlwind, "go, wretched mortal; I cast thee naked upon the earth; but, that thy destiny may not be misconceived, thou shalt subdue the monsters of the deep with a reed, and thou shalt trample the tempests under thy feet."

Thus, in attaching us to our native land, Providence justifies its dealings toward us, and we find numberless reasons for loving our country. The Arab never forgets the well of the camel, the antelope, and, above all, the horse, the faithful companion of his journeys through his paternal deserts; the negro never ceases to remember his cottage, his javelin, his banana, and the track of the zebra and the elephant in his native sands.

It is related that an English cabin-boy had conceived such an attachment for the ship in which he was born that he could never be induced to leave it for a single moment. The greatest punishment the captain could inflict was to threaten him with being sent ashore; on these occasions he would run with loud shrieks and conceal himself in the hold. What inspired the little mariner with such an extraordinary affection for a plank beaten by the winds? Assuredly not associations purely local and physical. Was it a certain moral conformity between the destinies of man and those of a ship? or did he perhaps find a pleasure in concentrating his joys and his sorrows in what we may justly call his cradle? The heart is naturally fond of contracting itself; the more it is compressed, the smaller is the surface which is liable to be wounded. This is the reason why persons of delicate sensibility—such the unfortunate generally are—prefer to live in retirement. What sentiment gains in energy it loses in extent. When the Roman republic was bounded by the Aventine Mount, her citizens joyfully sacrificed their lives in her defence: they ceased to love her when the Alps and Mount Taurus were the limits of her territory. It was undoubtedly some reason of this kind that cherished in the heart of the English youth a predilection for his paternal vessel An unknown passenger on the ocean of life, he beheld the sea rising as a barrier between him and our afflictions; happy in viewing only at a distance the melancholy shores of the world!

Among civilized nations the love of country has performed prodigies The designs of God have always a connection; he has grounded upon nature this affection for the place of our nativity, and hence, the animal partakes, in a certain degree, of this instinct with man; but the latter carries it farther, and transforms into a virtue what was only a sentiment of universal concordance Thus the physical and moral laws of the universe are linked together in an admirable chain. We even doubt whether it be possible to possess one genuine virtue, one real talent, without the love of our native country. In war this passion has accomplished wonders; in literature it produced a Homer and a Virgil. The former delineates in preference to all others the manners of Ionia, where he drew his first breath, and the latter feasted on the remembrance of his native place Born in a cottage, and expelled from the inheritance of his ancestors, these two circumstances seem to have had an extraordinary influence on the genius of Virgil, giving to it that melancholy tint which is one of its principal charms. He recalls these events continually, and shows that the countr where he passed his youth was always before his eyes:

Et dulcis moriens reminiscitur Argos.[1]

But it is the Christian religion that has invested patriotism with its true character. This sentiment led to the commission of crime among the ancients, because it was carried to excess; Christianity has made it one of the principal affections in man, but not an exclusive one. It commands us above all things to be just; it requires us to cherish the whole family of Adam, since we ourselves belong to it, though our countrymen have the first claim to our attachment. This morality was unknown before the coming of the Christian lawgiver, who has been unjustly accused of attempting to extirpate the passions: God destroys not

---

[1] *Æneid.* lib. x

his own work. The gospel is not the destroyer of the heart, but its regulator. It is to our feelings what taste is to the fine arts; it retrenches all that is exaggerated, false, common, and trivial; it leaves all that is fair, and good, and true. The Christian religion, rightly understood, is only primitive nature washed from original pollution.

It is when at a distance from our country that we feel the full force of the instinct by which we are attached to it. For want of the reality, we try to feed upon dreams; for the heart is expert in deception, and there is no one who has been suckled at the breast of woman but has drunk of the cup of illusion. Sometimes it is a cottage which is situated like the paternal habitation; sometimes it is a wood, a valley, a hill, on which we bestow some of the sweet appellations of our native land. Andromache gives the name of Simois to a brook. And what an affecting object is this little rill, which recalls the idea of a mighty river in her native country! Remote from the soil which gave us birth, nature appears to us diminished, and but the shadow of that which we have lost.

Another artifice of the love of country is to attach a great value to an object of little intrinsic worth, but which comes from our native land, and which we have brought with us into exile. The soul seems to dwell even upon the inanimate things which have shared our destiny: we remain attached to the down on which our prosperity has slumbered, and still more to the straw on which we counted the days of our adversity. The vulgar have an energetic expression, to describe that languor which oppresses the soul when away from our country. "That man," they say, "is home-sick." A sickness it really is, and the only cure for it is to return. If, however, we have been absent a few years, what do we find in the place of our nativity? How few of those whom we left behind in the vigor of health are still alive! Here are tombs where once stood palaces; there rise palaces where we left tombs. The paternal field is overgrown with briers or cultivated by the plough of a stranger; and the tree beneath which we frolicked in our boyish days has disappeared.

In Louisiana there were two females, one a negro, the other an

Indian, who were the slaves of two neighboring planters Each of the women had a child; the black a little girl two years old, and the Indian a boy of the same age. The latter died. The two unfortunate women having agreed upon a solitary spot, repaired thither three successive nights The one brought her dead child, the other her living infant; the one her *Manitou*, the other her *Fetiche*. They were not surprised thus to find themselves of the same religion, both being wretched. The Indian performed the honors of the solitude: "This is the tree of my native land," said she; "sit down there and weep." Then, in accordance with the funeral custom of savage nations, they suspended their children from the branch of a catalpa or sassafras-tree, and rocked them while singing some patriotic air. Alas! these maternal amusements, which had oft lulled innocence to sleep, were incapable of awaking death! Thus these women consoled themselves; the one had lost her child and her liberty, the other her liberty and her country. We find a solace even in tears.

It is said that a Frenchman, who was obliged to fly during the reign of terror, purchased with the little he had left a boat upon the Rhine. Here he lived with his wife and two children. As he had no money, no one showed him any hospitality When he was driven from one shore, he passed without complaining to the other; and, frequently persecuted on both sides, he was obliged to cast anchor in the middle of the river. He fished for the support of his family; but even this relief sent by divine Providence he was not allowed to enjoy in peace At night he went to collect some dry grass to make a fire, and his wife remained in cruel anxiety till his return.. Obliged to lead the life of outcasts, among four great civilized nations, this family had not a single spot on earth where they durst set their feet; their only consolation was, that while they wandered in the vicinity of France they could sometimes inhale the breeze which had passed over their native land.

Were we asked, what are those powerful ties which bind us to the place of our nativity, we would find some difficulty in answering the question. It is, perhaps, the smile of a mother, of a father, of a sister; it is, perhaps, the recollection of the old preceptor who instructed us and of the young companions of our childhood; it is, perhaps, the care bestowed upon us by a tender nurse, by some aged *domestic*, so essential a part of the household; finally, it is something most simple, and, if you please, most trivial,—a dog that barked at night in the fields, a nightingale that returned every year to the orchard, the nest of the swallow over the window, the village clock that appeared above the trees, the churchyard yew, or the Gothic tomb. Yet these simple things demonstrate the more clearly the reality of a Providence, as they could not possibly be the source of patriotism, or of the great virtues which it begets, unless by the appointment of the Almighty himself.

BOOK VI.

THE IMMORTALITY OF THE SOUL PROVED BY THE MORAL LAW AND THE FEELINGS.

CHAPTER I.

DESIRE OF HAPPINESS IN MAN.

WERE tnere no other proofs of the existence of God than the wonders of nature, these evidences are so strong that they would convince any sincere inquirer after truth. But if they who deny a Providence are, for that very reason, unable to explain the wonders of the creation, they are still more puzzled when they undertake to answer the objections of their own hearts. By renouncing the Supreme Being, they are obliged to renounce a future state. The soul nevertheless disturbs them; she appears, as it were, every moment before them, and compels them, in spite of their sophistry, to acknowledge her existence and her immortality.

Let them inform us, in the first place, if the soul is extinguished at the moment of death, whence proceeds the desire of happiness which continually haunts us? All our passions here below may easily be gratified; love, ambition, anger, have their full measure of enjoyment: the desire of happiness is the only one that cannot be satisfied, and that fails even of an object, as we know not what that felicity is which we long for. It must be admitted, that if every thing is *matter*, nature has here made a strange mistake, in creating a desire without any object.

Certain it is that the soul is eternally craving. No sooner has it attained the object for which it yearned, than a new wish is formed; and the whole universe cannot satisfy it. Infinity is the only field adapted to its nature; it delights to lose itself in numbers, to conceive the greatest as well as the smallest dimensions, and to multiply without end. Filled at length, but not satisfied with all that it has devoured, it seeks the bosom of the Deity, in whom centre all ideas of infinity, whether in perfection, duration, or space. But it seeks the bosom of Deity only because he is a being full of mystery, "a hidden God."[1] If it had a clear apprehension of the divine nature, it would undervalue it, as it does all other objects that its intellect is capable of measuring; for, if it could fully comprehend the eternal principle, it would be either superior or equal to this principle. It is not in divine as it is in human things. A man may understand the power of a king without being a king himself; but he cannot understand the divinity without being God.

The inferior animals are not agitated by this hope which manifests itself in the heart of man; they immediately attain their highest degree of happiness; a handful of grass satisfies the lamb, a little blood is sufficient for the tiger. If we were to assert, with some philosophers, that the different conformation of the organs constitutes all the difference between us and the brute, this mode of reasoning could, at the farthest, be admitted only in relation to purely material acts. But of what service is my hand to my mind, when amid the silence of night I soar through the regions of boundless space, to discover the Architect of so many worlds? Why does not the ox act in this respect as I do? His eyes are sufficient; and if he had my legs or my arms, they would for this purpose be totally useless to him. He may repose upon the turf, he may raise his head toward the sky, and by his bellowing call upon the unknown Being who fills the immense expanse. But no: he prefers the grass on which he treads; and while those millions of suns that adorn the firmament furnish the strongest evidences of a Deity, the animal consults them not; he is insensible to the prospect of nature, and unconscious that he is himself thrown beneath the tree at the foot of which he lies, as a slight proof of a divine Intelligence.

Man, therefore, is the only creature that wanders abroad, and looks for happiness out of himself. The vulgar, we are told, feel not this mysterious restlessness. They are undoubtedly less unhappy than we, for they are diverted by laborious occupations from attending to their desires, and drown the thirst of felicity in the sweat of their brow. But when you see them toil six

[1] Is. xlv. 15.

days in the week that they may enjoy a little pleasure on the seventh,—when, incessantly hoping for repose and never finding it, they sink into the grave without ceasing to desire,—will you say that they share not the secret aspiration of all men after an unknown happiness? You may reply, that in the class of which we are speaking this wish is at least limited to terrestrial things; but your assertion remains to be proved. Give the poorest wretch all the treasures in the world, put an end to his toils, satisfy all his wants, and you will observe that, before a few months have elapsed, his heart will conceive new desires and new hopes.

Besides, is it true that the lower classes, even in their state of indigence, are strangers to that thirst of happiness which extends beyond this life? Whence proceeds that air of seriousness often observed in the rustic? We have often seen him on Sundays and other festive days, while the people of the village were gone to offer up their prayers to that Reaper who will separate the wheat from the tares,—we have often seen him standing alone at the door of his cottage; he listened with attention to the sound of the bell; his air was pensive, and the sparrows that played around him and the insects that buzzed in every direction seemed not to distract him. Behold that noble figure, placed like the statue of a god upon the threshold of a cabin; that brow, sublime though wrinkled with care; and then say if this being, so majestic, though indigent, could be thinking of nothing, or reflecting only on things of this world. Ah, no! such was not the expression of those half-open lips, of that motionless body, of those eyes fixed on the ground: recollections of God surely accompanied the sound of the religious bell.

If it is impossible to deny that man cherishes hopes to the very tomb,—if it is certain that all earthly possessions, so far from crowning our wishes, only serve to increase the void in the soul,—we cannot but conclude that there must be a something beyond the limits of time. "The ties of this world," says St. Augustin, "are attended with real hardship and false pleasure; certain pains and uncertain joys; hard labor and unquiet rest; a situation fraught with wo and a hope void of felicity."[1] Instead

[1] Vincula hujus mundi asperitatem habent veram, jucunditatem falsam; certum dolorem, incertam voluptatem, durum laborem, timidam quietem; rem plenam miseriæ, spem beatitudinis inanem.—*Epist* 30

of complaining that the desire of happiness has been placed in this world, and its object in the other, let us admire in this arrangement the beneficence of God. Since we must sooner or later quit this mortal life, Providence has placed beyond the fatal boundary a charm which attracts us, in order to diminish our horror of the grave: thus, the affectionate mother who wishes her child to cross a certain limit, holds some pleasing object on the other side to encourage him to pass it.

CHAPTER II.

REMORSE AND CONSCIENCE.

CONSCIENCE furnishes a second proof of the immortality of the soul. Each individual has within his own heart a tribunal, where he sits in judgment on himself till the Supreme Arbiter shall confirm the sentence. If vice is but a physical consequence of our organization, whence arises this dread which embitters the days of prosperous guilt? Why is remorse so terrible that many would choose rather to submit to poverty and all the rigors of virtue than enrich themselves with ill-gotten goods? What is it that gives a voice to blood and speech to stones? The tiger devours his prey, and slumbers quietly; man takes the life of his fellow-creature, and keeps a fearful vigil! He seeks some desert place, and yet this solitude affrights him; he skulks about the tombs, and yet the tombs fill him with horrors. His eyes are wild and restless; he dares not fix them on the wall of the banqueting-room, for fear he should discover there some dreadful signs. All his senses seem to become more acute in order to torment him: he perceives at night threatening corruscations; he is always surrounded by the smell of carnage; he suspects the taste of poison in the food which he has himself prepared; his ear, now wonderfully sensitive, hears a noise where for others there is profound silence; and when embracing his friend, he fancies that he feels under his garments a hidden dagger.

Conscience! is it possible that thou canst be but a phantom of the imagination, or the fear of the punishment of men? I ask my own heart, I put to myself this question: "If thou couldst by a mere wish kill a fellow-creature in China, and inherit his fortune in Europe, with the supernatural conviction that the fact would never be known, wouldst thou consent to form such a wish?" In vain do I exaggerate my indigence; in vain do I attempt to extenuate the murder, by supposing that through the effect of my wish the Chinese expires instantaneously and without pain that, had he even died a natural death, his property, from the situation of his affairs, would have been lost to the state; in vain do I figure to myself this stranger overwhelmed with disease and affliction; in vain do I urge that to him death is a blessing, that he himself desires it, that he has but a moment longer to live: in spite of all my useless subterfuges, I hear a voice in the recesses of my soul, protesting so loudly against the mere idea of such a supposition, that I cannot for one moment doubt the reality of conscience.

It is a deplorable necessity, then, that compels a man to deny remorse, that he may deny the immortality of the soul and the existence of an avenging Deity. Full well we know, that atheism, when driven to extremities, has recourse to this disgraceful denial. The sophist, in a paroxysm of the gout, exclaimed, "O pain! never will I acknowledge that thou art an evil!" Were it even true that there exist men so unfortunate as to be capable of stifling the voice of conscience, what then? We must not judge of him who possesses the perfect use of his limbs by the paralytic who is deprived of his physical strength. Guilt, in its highest degree, is a malady which sears the soul. By overthrowing religion we destroy the only remedy capable of restoring sensibility in the morbid regions of the heart. This astonishing religion of Christ is a sort of supplement to the deficiency of the human mind. Do we sin *by excess*, by too great prosperity, by violence of temper? she is at hand to warn us of the fickleness of fortune and the danger of angry excitement. Are we exposed, on the contrary, to sin by defect, by indigence, by indifference of soul? she teaches us to despise riches, at the same time warms our frigid hearts, and, as it were, kindles in us the fire of the passions. Toward the criminal, in particular, her charity is inexhaustible; no man is so depraved but she admits him to repentance, no ıeper so disgusting but she cures him with her pure hands. For the past she requires only remorse, for the future only virtue: "where sin abounded," she says, "grace did much more abound."[1] Ever ready to warn the sinner, Jesus Christ established his religion as a second conscience for the hardened culprit who should be so unfortunate as to have lost the natural one,—an evangelical conscience, full of pity and indulgence, to which the Son of God has given the power to pardon, which is not possessed by the conscience of man.

Having spoken of the remorse which follows guilt, it would be unnecessary to say any thing of the satisfaction attendant on virtue. The inward delight which we feel in doing a good action is no more a combination of matter than the accusation of conscience, when we commit a bad one, is fear of the laws.

If sophists maintain that virtue and pity are but self-love in disguise, ask them not if they ever felt any secret satisfaction after relieving a distressed object, or if it is the fear of returning to the state of childhood that affects them when contemplating the innocence of the new-born infant. Virtue and tears are for men the source of hope and the groundwork of faith; how then should he believe in God who believes neither in the reality of virtue nor in the truth of tears?

It would be an insult to the understanding of our readers, did we attempt to show how the immortality of the soul and the existence of God are proved by that inward voice called conscience. "There is in man," says Cicero, "a power which inclines him to that which is good and deters him from evil; which was not only prior to the origin of nations and cities, but as ancient as that God by whom heaven and earth subsist and are governed: for reason is an essential attribute of the divine intelligence; and that reason which exists in God necessarily determines what is vice and what is virtue."[2]

---

[1] Rom. v. 20.

[2] *Ad. Attic.*, xii. !8.

CHAPTER III.

THERE CAN BE NO MORALITY IF THERE BE NO FUTURE STATE—PRESUMPTION IN FAVOR OF THE IMMORTALITY OF THE SOUL DEDUCED FROM THE RESPECT OF MAN FOR TOMBS.

Morality is the basis of society; but if man is a mere mass of matter, there is in reality neither vice nor virtue, and of course morality is a mere sham. Our laws, which are ever relative and variable, cannot serve as the support of morals, which are always absolute and unalterable; they must, therefore, rest on something more permanent than the present life, and have better guarantees than uncertain rewards or transient punishments. Some philosophers have supposed that religion was *invented* in order to uphold morality: they were not aware that they were taking the effect for the cause. It is not religion that springs from morals, but morals that spring from religion; since it is certain, as we have just observed, that morals cannot have their principle in *physical* man or *mere matter;* and that men no sooner divest themselves of the idea of a God than they rush into every species of crime, in spite of laws and of executioners

It is well known that a religion which recently aspired to erect itself on the ruins of Christianity, and fancied that it could surpass the gospel, enforced in our churches that precept of the Decalogue: *Children, honor your parents.* But why did the Theophilanthropists retrench the latter part of this precept,—*that ye may live long?*[1] Because a secret sense of poverty taught them that the man who has nothing can give nothing away. How could he have promised length of years who is not sure himself of living two minutes? We might with justice have said to him, "Thou makest me a present of life, and perceivest not that thou art thyself sinking into dust? Like Jehovah, thou assurest me

---

[1] The Theophilanthropists, hardly deserving the name of a religious sect, arose out of the infatuation of the French revolution. Their system was partly positive and partly negative; they were advocates of some scraps of morality, and they denied the doctrine of the resurrection K.

a protracted existence, but where is thy eternity like his from which to dispense it? Thoughtless mortal! even the present rapid hour is not thine own; thine only inheritance is death: what then but nothingness canst thou draw forth from the bottom of thy sepulchre to recompense my virtue?"

There is another moral proof of the immortality of the soul on which it is necessary to insist,—that is, the veneration of mankind for tombs. By an invisible charm, life and death are here linked together, and human nature proves itself superior to the rest of the creation, and appears in all its high destinies. Does the brute know any thing about a coffin, or does he concern himself about his remains? What to him are the bones of his parent, or, rather, can he distinguish his parent after the cares of infancy are past? Whence comes, then, the powerful impression that is made upon us by the tomb? Are a few grains of dust deserving of our veneration? Certainly not; we respect the ashes of our ancestors for this reason only—because a secret voice whispers to us that all is not extinguished in them. It is this that confers a sacred character on the funeral ceremony among all the nations of the globe; all are alike persuaded that the sleep even of the tomb is not everlasting, and that death is but a glorious transfiguration.

CHAPTER IV.

OF CERTAIN OBJECTIONS.

Without entering too deeply into metaphysical proofs, which we have studiously avoided, we shall nevertheless endeavor to answer certain objections which are incessantly brought forward. Cicero has asserted, after Plato, that there is no people among whom there exists not some notion of the Deity. But this universal consent of nations, which the ancient philosophers considered as a law of nature, has been denied by modern infidels, who maintain that certain tribes of savages have no idea of God

In vain do atheists strive to conceal the weakness of their cause. The result of all their arguments is that their system is grounded on *exceptions* alone, whereas the belief of a God forms the *general rule.* If you assert that all mankind believe in a Supreme Being, the infidel first objects to you some particular tribe of savages, then some particular individual, or himself, who are of a different opinion. If you assert that chance could not have formed the world, because there could have been but one single favorable chance against innumerable impossibilities, the infidel admits the position, but replies that *this chance actually did exist;* and the same mode of reasoning he pursues on every subject. Thus, according to the atheist, nature is a book in which truth is to be found only in the notes and never in the text; a language the genius and essence of which consist in its barbarisms.

When we come to examine these pretended exceptions, we discover either that they arise from local causes, or that they even fall under the established law. In the case alleged, for example, it is false that there are any savages who have no notion of a Deity. The early travellers who advanced this assertion have been contradicted by others who were better informed. Among the infidels of the forest were numbered the Canadian hordes; but we have seen these sophists of the cabin, who were supposed to have read in the book of nature, as our sophists have in theirs, that there is no God, nor any future state for man; and we must say that these Indians are absurd barbarians, who perceive the soul of an infant in a dove, and that of a little girl in the sensitive plant. Mothers among them are so silly as to sprinkle their milk upon a grave; and they give to man in the sepulchre the same attitude which he had in the maternal womb. May not this be done to intimate that death is but a second mother, by whom we are brought forth into another life? Atheism will never make any thing of those nations which are indebted to Providence for lodging, food, and raiment; and we would advise the infidel to beware of these bribed allies, who secretly receive presents from the enemy.

Another objection is this: "Since the mind acquires and loses its energies with age,—since it follows all the alterations of matter,—it must be of a material nature, consequently *divisible* and liable to perish."

Either the mind and the body are two distinct beings, or they are but one and the same substance. If there are *two,* you must admit that the mind is comprehended in the body; hence it follows that, as long as this union lasts, the mind cannot but be affected in a certain degree by the bonds in which it is held. It will appear to be elevated or depressed in the same proportion as its mortal tabernacle. The objection, therefore, is done away in the hypothesis by which the mind and the body are considered as *two distinct substances.*

If you suppose that they form but one and the same substance, partaking alike of life and death, *you are bound to prove the assertion.* But it has long been demonstrated that the mind is essentially different from motion and the other properties of matter, being susceptible neither of extension nor division.

Thus the objection falls entirely to the ground, since the only point to be ascertained is, whether matter and thought be *one and the same thing:* a position which cannot be maintained without absurdity.

Let it not be imagined that, in having recourse to prescription for the solution of this difficulty, we are, therefore, unable to sap its very foundation. It may be proved that even when the mind seems to follow the contingencies of the body, it retains the distinguishing characters of its essence. For instance, atheists triumphantly adduce, in support of their views, insanity, injuries of the brain, and delirious fevers. To prop their wretched system, these unfortunate men are obliged to enrol all the ills of humanity as allies in their cause. Well, then, what, after all, is proved by these fevers, this insanity, which atheism—that is to say, the genius of evil—so properly summons in its defence? I see a *disordered imagination* connected with a *sound understanding.* The lunatic and the delirious perceive objects which *have no existence;* but do they reason *falsely* respecting those objects? They only draw logical conclusions from unsound premises.

The same thing happens to the patient in a paroxysm of fever. His mind is beclouded in that part in which images are reflected, because the senses, from their imbecility, transmit only fallacious notions; but the region of ideas remains uninjured and unalterable. As a flame kindled with a substance ever so vile is nevertheless pure fire, though fed with impure aliments, so the mind, a celestial flame, rises incorruptible and immortal from the midst of corruption and of death.

With respect to the influence of climate upon the mind, which has been alleged as a proof of the material nature of the soul, we request the particular attention of the reader to our reply; for, instead of answering a mere objection, we shall deduce from the very point that is urged against us a remarkable evidence of the immortality of the soul.

It has been observed that nature displays superior energies in the north and in the south; that between the tropics we meet with the largest quadrupeds, the largest reptiles, the largest birds, the largest rivers, the highest mountains; that in the northern regions we find the mighty cetaceous tribes, the enormous fucus, and the gigantic pine If all things are the effects of matter, combinations of the elements, products of the solar rays, the result of cold and heat, moisture and drought, why is man alone excepted from this general law? Why is not his physical and moral capacity expanded with that of the elephant under the line and of the whale at the poles? While all nature is changed by the latitude under which it is placed, why does man alone remain everywhere the same? Will you reply that man, like the ox, is a native of every region? The ox, we answer, retains his *instinct* in every climate; and we find that, in respect to man, the case is very different.

Instead of conforming to the general law of nature,—instead of acquiring higher energy in those climates where matter is supposed to be most active,—man, on the contrary, dwindles in the same ratio as the animal creation around him is enlarged. In proof of this, we may mention the Indian, the Peruvian, the Negro, in the south; the Esquimaux and the Laplander in the north. Nay, more: America, where the mixture of mud and water imparts to vegetation all the vigor of a primitive soil—America is pernicious to the race of man, though it is daily becoming less so in proportion as the activity of the material principle is reduced Man possesses not all his energies except in those regions where the elements, being more temperate, allow a freer scope to the mind; where that mind, being in a manner released from its terrestrial clothing, is not restrained in any of its motions or in any of its faculties.

Here, then, we cannot but discover something in direct opposition to passive nature Now this *something* is our *immortal soul.* It accords not with the operations of matter. It sickens and languishes when in too close contact with it. This languor of the soul produces, in its turn, debility of body. The body which, had it been alone, would have thriven under the powerful influence of the sun, is kept back by the dejection of the mind. If it be said that, on the contrary, the body, being incapable of enduring the extremities of cold and heat, causes the soul to degenerate together with itself, this would be mistaking a second time the effect for the cause. It is not the mud that acts upon the current, but the current that disturbs the mud; and, in like manner, all these pretended effects of the body upon the soul are the very reverse—the effects of the soul upon the body.

The twofold debility, mental and physical, of people at the north and south, the gravity of temper which seems to oppress them, cannot, then, in our opinion, be ascribed to too great relaxation or tension of the fibre, since the same accidents do not produce the same effects in the temperate zones. This disposition of the natives of the polar and tropical regions is a real intellectual dejection, produced by the state of the soul and by its struggles against the influence of matter. Thus God has not only displayed his wisdom in the advantages which the globe derives from the diversity of latitudes, but, by placing man upon this species of ladder, he has demonstrated, with almost mathematical precision, the immortality of our essence; since the soul possesses the greatest energy where matter operates with the least force, and the intellectual powers of man diminish where the corporeal mass of the brute is augmented.

Let us consider one more objection: "If the idea of God is naturally impressed upon our souls, it ought to precede education and reason, and to manifest itself in earliest infancy. Now children have no idea of God, consequently," &c.

God being a *spirit,* which cannot be comprehended but by a *spirit,* a child, in whom the intellectual faculties are not yet developed, is incapable of forming a conception of the Supreme Being. How unreasonable to require the heart to exercise its noblest function when it is not yet fully formed—when the wonderful work is yet in the hands of the Maker!

It may be asserted, however, that the child has at least the *instinct* of his Creator. Witness his little reveries, his inquietudes, his terrors in the night, and his propensity to raise his eyes to heaven. Behold that infant folding his innocent hands and repeating after his mother a prayer to the God of mercy. Why does this young angel of the earth stammer forth with such love and purity the name of that Supreme Being concerning whom he knows nothing?

Who, at the mere sight of a new-born infant, could doubt the presence of God within it? Look at the little creature which a nurse is carrying in her arms. What has it said that excites such joy in that venerable veteran, in the man who has just reached his prime, and in that youthful female? Two or three half-articulate syllables, which nobody could understand; and this alone is sufficient to fill rational beings with transport, from the grandfather, who knows all the incidents of life, to the inexperienced mother, who has yet to learn them. Who, then, has conferred such power on the accents of man? Why is the sound of the human voice so irresistibly moving? What so deeply affects you in this instance is a mystery attached to higher causes than the interest which you may take in the age of this infant. Something whispers you that these inarticulate words are the first expressions of an immortal soul

CHAPTER V.

DANGER AND INUTILITY OF ATHEISM.

THERE are two classes of atheists totally distinct from each other: the one composed of those who are consistent in their principles, declaring without hesitation that there is no God, consequently no essential difference between good and evil, and that the world belongs to those who possess the greatest strength or the most address; the other embraces those good people of the system—the hypocrites of infidelity; absurd characters, a thousand times more dangerous than the first, and who, with a feigned benevolence would indulge in every excess to support their pretensions; they would call you *brother*, while cutting your throat ·

the words morality and humanity are continually on their lips: they are trebly culpable, for to the vices of the atheist they add the intolerance of the sectary and the self-love of the author.

These men pretend that atheism is not destructive either of happiness or virtue, and that there is no condition in which it is not as profitable to be an infidel as a pious Christian; a position which it may not be amiss to examine.

If a thing ought to be esteemed in proportion to its greater or less utility, atheism must be very contemptible, for it is of use to nobody.

Let us survey human life; let us begin with the poor and the unfortunate, as they constitute the majority of mankind. Say, countless families of indigence, is it to you that atheism is serviceable? I wait for a reply; but not a single voice is raised in its behalf. But what do I hear? a hymn of hope mingled with sighs ascending to the throne of the Lord! These are believers. Let us pass on to the wealthy.

It would seem that the man who is comfortably situated in this world can have no interest in being an atheist. How soothing to him must be the reflection that his days will be prolonged beyond the present life! With what despair would he quit this world if he conceived that he was parting from happiness forever! In vain would fortune heap her favors upon him; they would only serve to inspire him with the greater horror of annihilation. The rich man may likewise rest assured that religion will enhance his pleasures, by mingling with them an ineffable satisfaction; his heart will not be hardened, nor will he be cloyed with enjoyment, which is the natural result of a long series of prosperity. Religion prevents aridity of heart, as is intimated in her ceremonial. The holy oil which she uses in the consecration of authority, of youth and of death, teaches us that they are not destined to a moral or eternal sterility.

Will the soldier who marches forth to battle—that child of glory—be an atheist? Will he who seeks an endless life consent to perish forever? Appear upon your thundering clouds, ye countless Christian warriors, now hosts of heaven! appear! From your exalted abode, from the holy city, proclaim to the heroes of our day that the brave man is not wholly consigned to the tomb, and that something more of him survives than an empty name.

All the great generals of antiquity were remarkable for their piety. Epaminondas, the deliverer of his country, had the character of the most religious of men; Xenophon, that philosophic warrior, was a pattern of piety; Alexander, the everlasting model of conquerors, gave himself out to be the son of Jupiter. Among the Romans, the ancient consuls of the republic, a Cincinnatus, a Fabius, a Papirius Cursor, a Paulus Æmilius, a Scipio, placed all their reliance on the deity of the Capitol; Pompey marched to battle imploring the divine assistance; Cæsar pretended to be of celestial descent; Cato, his rival, was convinced of the immortality of the soul; Brutus, his assassin, believed in the existence of supernatural powers; and Augustus, his successor, reigned only in the name of the gods.

In modern times was that valiant Sicambrian, the conqueror of Rome and of the Gauls, an unbeliever, who, falling at the feet of a priest, laid the foundation of the empire of France? Was St. Louis, the arbiter of kings,—revered by infidels themselves,—an unbeliever? Was the valorous Du Guesclin, whose coffin was sufficient for the capture of cities,—the Chevalier Bayard, without fear and without reproach,—the old Constable de Montmorenci, who recited his beads in the camp,—were these men without religion? But, more wonderful still, was the great Turenne, whom Bossuet brought back to the bosom of the Church, an unbeliever?

No character is more admirable than that of the Christian hero The people whom he defends look up to him as a father; he protects the husbandman and the produce of his fields; he is an angel of war sent by God to mitigate the horrors of that scourge. Cities open their gates at the mere report of his justice; ramparts fall before his virtue; he is beloved by the soldier, he is idolized by nations; with the courage of the warrior he combines the charity of the gospel; his conversation is impressive and instructing; his words are full of simplicity; you are astonished to find such gentleness in a man accustomed to live in the midst of dangers. Thus the honey is hidden under the rugged bark of an oak which has braved the tempests of ages. We may safely conclude that in no respect whatever is atheism profitable for the soldier.

Neither can we perceive that it would be more useful in the different states of nature than in the conditions of society. If the moral system is wholly founded on the doctrine of the existence of God and the immortality of the soul, a father, a son, the husband, the wife, can have no interest in being unbelievers. Ah! how is it possible, for instance, to conceive that a woman can be an atheist? What will support this frail reed if religion do not sustain her? The feeblest being in nature, ever on the eve of death or exposed to the loss of her charms, who will save her if her hopes be not extended beyond an ephemeral existence? For the sake of her beauty alone, woman ought to be pious. Gentleness, submission, suavity, tenderness, constitute part of the charms which the Creator bestowed on our first mother, and to charms of this kind philosophy is a mortal foe.

Shall woman, who is naturally prone to mystery, who takes delight in concealment, who never discloses more than half of her graces and of her thoughts, whose mind can be conjectured but not known, who as a mother and a maiden is full of secrets, who seduces chiefly by her ignorance, whom Heaven formed for virtue and the most mysterious of sentiments, modesty and love,—shall woman, renouncing the engaging instinct of her sex, presume, with rash and feeble hand, to withdraw the thick vei which conceals the Divinity? Whom doth she think to please by this effort, alike absurd and sacrilegious? Does she hope, by mingling her foolish impiety and frivolous metaphysics with the imprecations of a Spinosa and the sophistry of a Bayle, to give us a high opinion of her genius? Assuredly she has no thoughts of marriage; for what sensible man would unite himself for life to an impious partner?

The infidel wife seldom has any idea of her duties: she spends her days either in reasoning on virtue without practising its precepts, or in the enjoyment of the tumultuous pleasures of the world. Her mind vacant and her heart unsatisfied, life becomes a burden to her; neither the thought of God, nor any domestic cares, afford her happiness.

But the day of vengeance approaches. Time arrives, leading Age by the hand. The spectre with silver hair and icy hands plants himself on the threshold of the female atheist; she perceives him and shrieks aloud. Who now will hear her voice? Her husband? She has none; long, very long, has he withdrawn from the theatre of his dishonor. Her children? Ruined by an impious education and by maternal example, they concern themselves not about their mother. If she surveys the past, she beholds a pathless waste; her virtues have left no traces behind them. For the first time her saddened thoughts turn toward heaven, and she begins to think how much more consolatory it would have been to have a religion. Unavailing regret! The crowning punishment of atheism in this world is to desire faith without being able to acquire it. When, at the term of her career, she discovers the delusions of a false philosophy,—when annihilation, like an appalling meteor, begins to appear above the horizon of death,—she would fain return to God; but it is too late: the mind, hardened by incredulity, rejects all conviction. Oh! what a frightful solitude appears before her, when God and man retire at once from her view! She dies, this unfortunate woman,—expiring in the arms of a hireling nurse, or of some man, perhaps, who turns with disgust from her protracted sufferings. A common coffin now encloses all that remains of her. At her funeral we see no daughter overpowered with grief, no sons-in-law or grandchildren in tears, forming, with the blessing of the people and the hymns of religion, so worthy an escort for the mother of a family. Perhaps only a son, who is unknown, and who knows not himself the dishonorable secret of his birth, will happen to meet the mournful convoy, and will inquire the name of the deceased, whose body is about to be cast to the worms, to which it had been promised by the atheist herself!

How different is the lot of the religious woman! Her days are replete with joy; she is respected, beloved by her husband, her children, her household; all place unbounded confidence in her, because they are firmly convinced of the fidelity of one who is faithful to her God. The faith of this Christian is strengthened by her happiness, and her happiness by her faith; she believes in God because she is happy, and she is happy because she believes in God.

It is enough for a mother to look upon her smiling infant to be convinced of the reality of supreme felicity. The bounty of Providence is most signally displayed in the cradle of man. What affecting harmonies! Could they be only the effects of inanimate matter? The child is born, the breast fills; the little guest has no teeth that can wound the maternal bosom: he grows, the milk becomes more nourishing; he is weaned, and the wonderful fountain ceases to flow. This woman, before so weak, has all at once acquired such strength as enables her to bear fatigues which a robust man could not possibly endure. What is it that awakens her at midnight, at the very moment when her infant is ready to demand the accustomed repast? Whence comes that address which she never before possessed? How she handles the tender flower without hurting it! Her attentions seem to be the fruit of the experience of her whole life, and yet this is her first-born! The slightest noise terrified the virgin: where are the embattled armies, the thunders, the perils, capable of appalling the mother? Formerly this woman required delicate food, elegant apparel, and a soft couch; the least breath of air incommoded her: now, a crust of bread, a common dress, a handful of straw, are sufficient; nor wind, nor rain, scarcely makes any impression, while she has in her breast a drop of milk to nourish her son and in her tattered garments a corner to cover him.

Such being the state of things, he must be extremely obstinate who would not espouse the cause in behalf of which not only reason finds the most numerous evidences, but to which morals, happiness, and hope, nay, even instinct itself, and all the desires of the soul, naturally impel us; for if it were as true as it is false, that the understanding keeps the balance even between God and atheism, still it is certain that it would preponderate much in favor of the former; for, besides half of his reason, man puts the whole weight of his heart into the scale of the Deity.

Of this truth you will be thoroughly convinced if you examine the very different manner in which atheism and religion proceed in their reasoning.

Religion adduces none but general proofs; she founds her judgment only on the harmony of the heavens and the immutable laws of the universe; she views only the graces of nature, the charming instincts of animals, and their exquisite conformities with man.

Atheism sets before you nothing but hideous exceptions; it sees naught but calamities, unhealthy marshes, destructive volcanoes, noxious animals; and, as if it were anxious to conceal itself in the mire, it interrogates the reptiles and insects that they may furnish it with proofs against God.

Religion speaks only of the grandeur and beauty of man. Atheism is continually setting the leprosy and plague before our eyes.

Religion derives her reasons from the sensibility of the soul, from the tenderest attachments of life, from filial piety, conjugal love, and maternal affection.

Atheism reduces every thing to the instinct of the brute, and, as the first argument of its system, displays to you a heart that naught is capable of moving.

Religion assures us that our afflictions shall have an end; she comforts us, she dries our tears, she promises us another life.

On the contrary, in the abominable worship of atheism, human woes are the incense, death is the priest, a coffin the altar, and annihilation the Deity.

CHAPTER VI.

CONCLUSION OF THE DOCTRINES OF CHRISTIANITY—STATE OF PUNISHMENTS AND REWARDS IN A FUTURE LIFE—ELYSIUM OF THE ANCIENTS.

THE existence of a Supreme Being once acknowledged, and the immortality of the soul granted, there can be no farther difficulty to admit a state of rewards and punishments after this life; this last tenet is a necessary consequence of the other two. All that remains for us, therefore, is to show how full of morality and poetry this doctrine is, and how far superior the religion of the gospel is in this respect to all other religions.

In the Elysium of the ancients we find none but heroes and persons who had either been fortunate or distinguished on earth. Children, and, apparently, slaves and the lower class of men,—that is to say, misfortune and innocence,—were banished to the infernal regions. And what rewards for virtue were those feasts and dances, the everlasting duration of which would be sufficient to constitute one of the torments of Tartarus!

Mahomet promises other enjoyments. His paradise is a land

of musk and of the purest wheaten flour, watered by the river of life and the Acawtar, another stream which rises under the roots of *Tuba*, or the tree of happiness. Streams springing up in grottos of ambergris, and bordered with aloes, murmur beneath golden palm-trees. On the shores of a quadrangular lake stand a thousand goblets made of stars, out of which the souls predestined to felicity imbibe the crystal wave. All the elect, seated on silken carpets, at the entrance of their tents, eat of the terrestrial globe, reduced by Allah into a wonderful cake. A number of eunuchs and seventy-two black-eyed damsels place before them, in three hundred dishes of gold, the fish Nun and the ribs of the buffalo Balam. The angel Israfil sings, without ceasing, the most enchanting songs; the immortal virgins with their voices accompany his strains; and the souls of virtuous poets, lodged in the throats of certain birds that are hovering round the tree of happiness, join the celestial choir. Meanwhile the crystal bells suspended in the golden palm-trees are melodiously agitated by a breeze which issues from the throne of God.[1]

The joys of the Scandinavian heaven were sanguinary, but there was a degree of grandeur in the pleasures ascribed to the martial shades, and in the power of gathering the storm and guiding the whirlwind which they were said to possess. This paradise was the image of the kind of life led by the barbarian of the north. Wandering along the wild shores of his country, the dreary sounds emitted by ocean plunged his soul into deep reveries; thought succeeded thought, as in the billows murmur followed murmur, till, bewildered in the mazes of his desires, he mingled with the elements, rode upon the fleeting clouds, rocked the leafless forest, and flew across the seas upon the wings of the tempest.

The hell of the unbelieving nations is as capricious as their heaven. Our observations on the Tartarus of the ancients we shall reserve for the literary portion of our work, on which we are about to enter. Be this as it may, the rewards which Christianity promises to virtue, and the punishments with which it threatens guilt, produce at the first glance a conviction of their truth. The heaven and hell of Christians are not devised after the manners of any particular people, but founded on the general

---

[1] The Koran and the Arabic poets.

ideas that are adapted to all nations and to all classes of society. What can be more simple, and yet more sublime, than the truths conveyed in these few words!—the felicity of the righteous in a future life will consist in the full possession of God; the misery of the wicked will arise from a knowledge of the perfections of the Deity, and from being forever deprived of their enjoyment.

It may perhaps be said that here Christianity merely repeats the lessons of the schools of Plato and Pythagoras. In this case, it must at least be admitted that the Christian religion is not the religion of *shallow minds*, since it inculcates what are acknowledged to have been the doctrines of *sages*.

The Gentiles, in fact, reproached the primitive Christians with being nothing more than a sect of philosophers; but were it certain (what is not proved) that the sages of antiquity entertained the same notions that Christianity holds respecting a future state, still, a truth confined within a narrow circle of chosen disciples is one thing, and a truth which has become the universal consolation of mankind is another. What the brightest geniuses of Greece discovered by a last effort of reason is now publicly taught in every church; and the laborer, for a few pence, may purchase, in the catechism of his children, the most sublime secrets of the ancient sects.

We shall say nothing here on the subject of Purgatory, as we shall examine it hereafter under its moral and poetical aspects. As to the principle which has produced this place of expiation, it is founded in reason itself, since between vice and virtue there is a state of tepidity which merits neither the punishment of hell nor the rewards of heaven.

CHAPTER VII.

THE LAST JUDGMENT.

THE Fathers entertained different opinions respecting the state of the soul of the righteous immediately after its separation from the body. St. Augustin thinks that it is placed in an abode of peace till it be reunited to its incorruptible body.[1] St. Bernard believes that it is received into heaven, where it contemplates the humanity of Jesus Christ, but not his divinity, which it will enjoy only after the resurrection;[2] in some other parts of his sermons he assures us that it enters immediately into the plenitude of celestial felicity;[3] and this opinion the Church seems to have adopted.[4]

But, as it is just that the body and soul, which have together committed sin or practised virtue, should suffer or be rewarded together, so religion teaches us that he who formed us out of dust will summon us a second time before his tribunal. The stoic school believed, as Christians do, in hell, paradise, purgatory, and the resurrection of the body;[5] and the Magi had also a

---

[1] *De Trinit.*, lib. xv. c. 25.

[2] *Serm. in Sanct. omn.*, 1, 2, 3; *De Considerat.*, lib. v. c. 4.

[3] *Serm.* 2, *de S. Malac.* n. 5; *Serm. de S. Vict.*, n. 4.

[4] It is an article of Catholic faith, that the souls of the just, who have nothing to atone for after their departure from this life, are admitted immediately to the beatific vision. Though some of the early fathers supposed that this happiness would be deferred until after the resurrection, they were not on that account taxable with heresy, because the tradition of the Church was not yet plainly manifested. This tradition is gathered, not from the opinions of a few fathers or doctors, but from the sentiment generally held. The declarations of the second Council of Lyons in 1274, that of Florence in 1439, and the Tridentine Synod in the sixteenth century, have explicitly determined the question. St. Augustine, after his elevation to the episcopacy, coincided with the prevailing sentiment on this point. Tract. 26 and 49 in Ioan, lib. 9; *Confess.* c. 3. The passages from St. Bernard which seem to conflict with that sentiment are all susceptible of an orthodox interpretation. T.

[5] Senec., *Epist* 90; Id., *ad. Marc.*; Laert., lib. vii.; Plut., *in Resig. Stoic. et in fac. lun.*

confused idea of this last doctrine.[1] The Egyptians hoped to revive after they had passed a thousand years in the tomb;[2] and the Sybilline verses mention the resurrection and the last judgment.[3]

Pliny, in his strictures on Democritus, informs us what was the opinion of that philosopher on the subject of the resurrection: *Similis et de asservandis corporibus hominum; ac reviviscendi promissa à Democrito vanitas, qui non vixit ipse.*[4]

The resurrection is clearly expressed in these verses of Phocylides on the ashes of the dead:—

> Ου καλον ἁρμονίην αναλυεμεν ανθρωποιο.
> Και ταχα δ'ἐκ γαίης ἐλπίζομεν ἐς φαος ἐλθειν
> Λειψαν αποιχομενων οπισω δε θεοὶτελεθονται.

"It is impious to disperse the remains of man; for the ashes and the bones of the dead shall return to life, and shall become like unto gods"

Virgil obscurely hints at the doctrine of the resurrection in the sixth book of the Æneid.

But how is it possible for atoms dispersed among all the elements to be again united and to form the same bodies? It is a long time since this objection was first urged, and it has been answered by most of the Fathers.[5] "Tell me what thou art," said Tertullian, "and I will tell thee what thou shalt be."[6]

Nothing can be more striking and awful than the moment of the final consummation of ages foretold by Christianity. In those days baleful signs will appear in the heavens; the depths of the abyss will open; the seven angels will pour out their vials filled with wrath; nations will destroy each other; mothers will hear the wailings of their children yet in the womb; and Death, on his pale horse, will speed his course through the kingdoms of the earth.[7]

---

[1] Hyde, *Relig. Pers.*; Plut., *de Is. et Osir.*

[2] Diod. et Herodot.

[3] Bocchus, *in Solin.*, c. 8; Lact., lib. viii., c. 29; lib. iv. c. 15, 18, 19.

[4] Lib. vii. c. 55.

[5] St. Cyril. bishop of Jerusalem, *Catech*, xviii. St Greg Nat. *Oret. pro Res. Carn*: St. August, *de Civ. Dei*, lib xx, St. Chrys., *Homil in Resur. Carn.*: St. Gregor. pope, *Dial*, iv.; St. Amb., *Serm. in Fid. res.*, St. Epiph. Ancyrot.

[6] *In Apologet.*

[7] *Apocalypse.*

Meanwhile the globe begins to tremble on its axis; the moon is covered with a bloody veil; the threatening stars hang half detached from the vault of heaven, and the agony of the world commences. Then, all at once, the fatal hour strikes; God suspends the movements of the creation, and the earth hath passed away like an exhausted river.

Now resounds the trump of the angel of judgment; and the cry is heard, "Arise, ye dead!" The sepulchres burst open with a terrific noise, the human race issues all at once from the tomb, and the assembled multitudes fill the valley of Jehoshaphat.

Behold, the Son of Man appears in the clouds: the powers of hell ascend from the depths of the abyss to witness the last judgment pronounced upon ages; the goats are separated from the sheep, the wicked are plunged into the gulf, the just ascend triumphantly to heaven, God returns to his repose, and the reign of eternity commences.

CHAPTER VIII.

HAPPINESS OF THE RIGHTEOUS.

It has been asked, what is that plenitude of celestial happiness promised to virtue by Christianity? we have heard complaints of its too great mysteriousness. In the mythological systems, it is said, "people could at least form an idea of the pleasures of the happy shades; but who can have any conception of the felicity of the elect?"

Fenelon, however, had a glimpse of that felicity in his relation of the descent of Telemachus to the abode of the manes: his Elysium is evidently a Christian paradise. Compare his description with the Elysium of the Æneid, and you will perceive what progress has been made by the mind and heart of man under the influence of Christianity.

"A soft and pure light is diffused around the bodies of those righteous men, and environs them with its rays like a garment. This light is not like the sombre beams which illumine the eyes of wretched mortals; it is rather a celestial radiance than a light; it pervades the thickest bodies more completely than the sun's rays penetrate the purest crystal; it doth not dazzle, but, on the contrary, strengthens the eyes, and conveys inexpressible serenity to the soul; by this alone the blest are nourished; it issues from them and it enters them again; it penetrates and is incorporated with them as aliments are incorporated with the body. They see, they feel, they breathe it; it causes an inexhaustible source of peace and joy to spring up within them; they are plunged into this abyss of delight, as the fishes are merged in the sea; they know no wants; they possess all without having any thing; for this feast of pure light appeases the hunger of their hearts.

"An eternal youth, a felicity without end, a radiance wholly divine, glows upon their faces. But their joy has nothing light or licentious; it is a joy soothing, noble, and replete with majesty; a sublime love of truth and virtue, which transports them; they feel every moment, without interruption, the same raptures as a mother who once more beholds her beloved son whom she believed to be dead; and that joy, which is soon over for the mother, never leaves the hearts of these glorified beings."[1]

The most glowing passages of the Phædon of Plato are less divine than this picture; and yet Fénélon, confined within the limits of his story, could not attribute to the shades all the felicity which he would have ascribed to the elect in heaven

The purest of our sentiments in this world is admiration; but this terrestrial admiration is always mingled with weakness, either in the person admiring or in the object admired. Imagine, then, a perfect being, the source of all beings, in whom is clearly and sacredly manifested all that was, and is, and is to come; suppose, at the same time, a soul exempt from envy and wants, incorruptible, unalterable, indefatigable, capable of attention without end; figure to yourself this soul contemplating the Omnipotent, incessantly discovering in him new attributes and new perfections, proceeding from admiration to admiration, and conscious of its existence only by the ceaseless feeling of this very admiration; consider, moreover, the Deity as supreme beauty,

[1] *Telem.*, book xiv.

as the universal principle of love; represent to yourself all the friendships of the earth meeting together, and lost in this abyss of sentiments like drops of water in the vast ocean, so that the happy spirit is wholly absorbed by the love of God, without, however, ceasing to love the friends whom it esteemed here below; lastly, persuade yourself that the blest are thoroughly convinced of the endless duration of their happiness:[1] you will then have an idea—though very imperfect, it is true—of the felicity of the righteous; you will then comprehend that the choir of the redeemed can do nothing but repeat the song of *Holy! holy! holy!* which is incessantly dying away, and incessantly reviving, in the everlasting ecstasies of heaven.

[1] St. Augustin.

Part the Second.

THE POETIC OF CHRISTIANITY.

BOOK I.

GENERAL SURVEY OF CHRISTIAN EPIC POEMS[1]

CHAPTER I.

THE POETIC OF CHRISTIANITY IS DIVIDED INTO THREE BRANCHES: POETRY, THE FINE ARTS, AND LITERATURE THE SIX BOOKS OF THIS SECOND PART TREAT IN AN ESPECIAL MANNER OF POETRY.

THE felicity of the blessed sung by the Christian Homer naturally leads us to consider the effects of Christianity in poetry In treating of the spirit of that religion, how could we forget its influence on literature and the arts—an influence which has in a manner changed the human mind, and produced in modern Europe nations totally different from those of ancient times?

The reader, perhaps, will not be displeased if we conduct him to Horeb and Sinai, to the summits of Ida and of the Taygetus, among the sons of Jacob and of Priam, into the company of the gods and of the shepherds. A poetic voice issues from the ruins which cover Greece and Idumæa, and cries from afar to the traveller, "There are but two brilliant names and recollections in history—those of the Israelites and of the ancient Greeks."

The twelve books which we have devoted to these literary investigations compose, as we have observed, the second and third parts of our work, and separate the six books on the *doctrines* from the six books on the *ceremonies* of the Christian religion.

---

[1] Now *ten* only, *Atala* and *René*, two episodes of the original work, having been retrenched by the author. T.

We shall, in the first place, take a view of the poems in which that religion supplies the place of mythology, because the epic is the highest class of poetic compositions. Aristotle, it is true, asserts that the epic poem is wholly comprised in tragedy; but might we not think, on the contrary, that the drama is wholly comprised in the epic poem? The parting of Hector and Andromache, Priam in the tent of Achilles, Dido at Carthage, Æneas at the habitation of Evander or sending back the body of the youthful Pallas, Tancred and Erminia, Adam and Eve, are real tragedies, in which nothing is wanting but the division into scenes and the names of the speakers. Was it not, moreover, the Iliad that gave birth to tragedy, as the Margites was the parent of comedy?[1] But if Calliope decks herself with all the ornaments of Melpomene, the former has charms which the latter cannot borrow; for the marvellous, the descriptive, and the digressive, are not within the scope of the drama. Every kind of tone, the comic not excepted, every species of poetic harmony, from the lyre to the trumpet, may be introduced in the epic. The epic poem, therefore, has parts which the drama has not: it consequently requires a more universal genius; it is of course a more complete performance than a tragedy. It seems, in fact, highly probable that there should be less difficulty in composing the five acts of an Œdipus than in creating the twenty-four books of an Iliad. The result of a few months' labor is not the monument that requires the application of a lifetime. Sophocles and Euripides were, doubtless, great geniuses; but have they obtained from succeeding ages that admiration and high renown which have been so justly awarded to Homer and Virgil? Finally, if the drama holds the first rank in composition, and the epic only the second, how has it happened that, from the Greeks to the present day, we can reckon but five epic poems, two ancient and three modern: whereas there is not a nation but can boast of possessing a multitude of excellent tragedies.

[1] The Margites was a comic or satirical poem attributed to Homer. It is mentioned by Aristotle in his Treatise on Poetry, but no part of it is known to have escaped the ravages of time.

CHAPTER II.

GENERAL SURVEY OF THE POEMS IN WHICH THE MARVELLOUS OF CHRISTIANITY SUPPLIES THE PLACE OF MYTHOLOGY—THE INFERNO OF DANTE—THE JERUSALEM DELIVERED OF TASSO.

Let us first lay down certain principles.

In every epic poem, men and their passions are calculated to occupy the first and most important place.

Every poem, therefore, in which any religion is employed as the *subject* and not as an *accessory*, in which the *marvellous* is the *ground* and not the *accident* of the picture, is essentially faulty.

If Homer and Virgil had laid their scenes in Olympus, it is doubtful whether, with all their genius, they would have been able to sustain the dramatic interest to the end. Agreeably to this remark, we must not ascribe to Christianity the languor that pervades certain poems in which the principal characters are supernatural beings; this languor arises from the fault of the composition. We shall find in confirmation of this truth, that the more the poet observes a due medium in the epic between divine and human things, the more *entertaining* he is, if we may be allowed to use an expression of Boileau. To amuse, for the purpose of instructing, is the first quality required in poetry.

Passing over several poems written in a barbarous Latin style, the first work that demands our attention is the *Divina Comedia* of Dante. The beauties of this singular production proceed, with few exceptions, from Christianity: its faults are to be ascribed to the age and the bad taste of the author. In the pathetic and the terrific, Dante has, perhaps, equalled the greatest poets. The details of his poem will be a subject of future consideration.

Modern times have afforded but two grand subjects for an epic poem—the *Crusades*, and the *Discovery of the New World*. Malfilâtre purposed to sing the latter. The Muses still lament the premature decease of this youthful poet before he had time to accomplish his design. This subject, however, has the disadvantage of being foreign for a Frenchman; and according to another principle, the truth of which cannot be contested, a poet ought to adopt an ancient subject, or, if he select a modern one, should by all means take his own nation for his theme.

The mention of the Crusades reminds us of the *Jerusalem Delivered*. This poem is a perfect model of composition. Here you may learn how to blend subjects together without confusion. The art with which Tasso transports you from a battle to a love-scene, from a love-scene to a council, from a procession to an enchanted palace, from an enchanted palace to a camp, from an assault to the grotto of an anchorite, from the tumult of a besieged city to the hut of a shepherd, is truly admirable. His characters are drawn with no less ability. The ferocity of Argantes is opposed to the generosity of Tancred, the greatness of Solyman to the splendor of Rinaldo, the wisdom of Godfrey to the craft of Aladin; and even Peter the hermit, as Voltaire has remarked, forms a striking contrast with Ismeno the magician. As to the females, coquetry is depicted in Armida, sensibility in Erminia, and indifference in Clorinda. Had Tasso portrayed *the mother*, he would have made the complete circle of female characters. The reason of this omission must, perhaps, be sought in the nature of his talents, which possessed more charms than truth, and greater brilliancy than tenderness.

Homer seems to have been particularly endowed with genius, Virgil with sensibility, Tasso with imagination. We should not hesitate what place to assign to the Italian bard, had he some of those pensive graces which impart such sweetness to the sighs of the Mantuan swan; for he is far superior to the latter in his characters, battles, and composition. But Tasso almost always fails when he attempts to express the feelings of the heart; and, as the traits of the soul constitute the genuine beauties of a poem he necessarily falls short of the pathos of Virgil.

If the *Jerusalem Delivered* is adorned with the flowers of exquisite poetry,—if it breathes the youth, the loves, and the afflictions, of that great and unfortunate man who produced this master-piece in his juvenile years,—we likewise perceive in it the faults of an age not sufficiently mature for such a high attempt as an epic poem. Tasso's measure of eight feet is hardly ever full; and his versification, which often exhibits marks of haste, cannot be compared to that of Virgil, a hundred times tempered in the fire of the Muses. It must likewise be remarked that the ideas of Tasso are not of so fair a family as those of the Latin bard. The works of the ancients may be known, we had almost said, by their *blood*. They display not, like us, a few brilliant ideas sparkling in the midst of a multitude of commonplace observations, so much as a series of beautiful thoughts, which perfectly harmonize together, and have a sort of family likeness. It is the naked group of Niobe's simple, modest, blushing children, holding each other by the hand with an engaging smile, while a chaplet of flowers, their only ornament, encircles their brows.

After the *Jerusalem Delivered*, it must be allowed that something excellent may be produced with a Christian subject. What would it then have been had Tasso ventured to employ all the grand machinery which Christianity could have supplied? It is obvious that he was deficient in boldness. His timidity has obliged him to have recourse to the petty expedients of magic, whereas he might have turned to prodigious account the tomb of Jesus Christ, which he scarcely mentions, and a region hallowed by so many miracles. The same timidity has occasioned his failure in the description of heaven, while his picture of hell shows many marks of bad taste. It may be added that he has not availed himself as much as he might have done of the Mohammedan religion, the rites of which are the more curious as being the less known. Finally, he might have taken some notice of ancient Asia, of Egypt so highly renowned, of Babylon so vast, and Tyre so haughty, and of the times of Solomon and Isaias. How could the muse, when visiting the land of Israel, forget the harp of David? Are the voices of the prophets no longer to be heard on the summits of Lebanon? Do not their holy shades still appear beneath the cedars and among the pines? Has the choir of angels ceased to sing upon Golgotha, and the brook Cedron to murmur? Surely the patriarchs, and Syria, the nursery of the world, celebrated in some part of the *Jerusalem Delivered*, could not have failed to produce a grand effect.[1]

[1] The reader's attention may here be invited to *Palestine*, an Oxford prize poem, written by Mr. Reginald Heber. It derives its various and exquisite

CHAPTER III.

PARADISE LOST.

The *Paradise Lost* of Milton may be charged with the same fault as the *Inferno* of Dante. The marvellous forms the subject, and not the machinery, of the poem; but it abounds with superior beauties which essentially belong to the groundwork of our religion.

The poem opens in the infernal world, and yet this beginning offends in no respect against the rule of simplicity laid down by Aristotle. An edifice so astonishing required an extraordinary portico to introduce the reader all at once into this unknown world, which he was no more to quit.

Milton is the first poet who has closed the epic with the misfortune of the principal character, contrary to the rule generally adopted. We are of opinion, however, that there is something more interesting, more solemn, more congenial with the condition of human nature, in a history which ends in sorrows, than in one which has a happy termination. It may even be asserted that the catastrophe of the Iliad is tragical; for if the son of Peleus obtains the object of his wishes, still the conclusion of the poem leaves a deep impression of grief.[1] After witnessing the funeral of Patroclus, Priam redeeming the body of Hector, the anguish

---

beauties chiefly from Scriptural sources. Mr. Heber, endued with a large portion of Tasso's genius, has supplied many of Tasso's deficiences, so ably enumerated by our author. K.

[1] This sentiment, perhaps, arises from the interest which is felt for Hector. Hector is as much the hero of the poem as Achilles, and this is the great fault of the Iliad. The reader's affections are certainly engaged by the Trojans, contrary to the *intention* of the poet, because all the dramatic scenes occur within the walls of Ilium. The aged monarch, Priam, whose only crime was too much love for a guilty son,—the generous Hector, who was acquainted with his brother's fault, and yet defended that brother,—Andromache, Astyanax, Hecuba,—melt every heart; whereas the camp of the Greeks exhibits naught but avarice, perfidy, and ferocity. Perhaps, also, the remembrance of the Æneid secretly influences the modern reader and he unintentionally espouses the side of the heroes sung by Virgil.

of Hecuba and Andromache at the funeral pile of that hero, we still perceive in the distance the death of Achilles and the fall of Troy.

The infancy of Rome, sung by Virgil, is certainly a grand subject; but what shall we say of a poem that depicts a catastrophe of which we are ourselves the victims, and which exhibits to us not the founder of this or that community, but the father of the human race? Milton describes neither battles, nor funeral games, nor camps, nor sieges: he displays the grand idea of God manifested in the creation of the universe, and the first thoughts of man on issuing from the hands of his Maker

Nothing can be more august and more interesting than this study of the first emotions of the human heart. Adam awakes to life; his eyes open; he knows not whence he originates. He gazes on the firmament; he attempts to spring toward this beautiful vault, and stands erect, with his head nobly raised to heaven. He examines himself, he touches his limbs; he runs, he stops; he attempts to speak, and his obedient tongue gives utterance to his thoughts. He naturally names whatever he sees, exclaiming, "O sun, and trees, forests, hills, valleys, and ye different animals!" and all the names which he gives are the proper appellations of the respective beings. And why does he exclaim, "O sun, and ye trees, know ye the name of Him who created me?" The first sentiment experienced by man relates to the existence of a Supreme Being; the first want he feels is the want of a God! How sublime is Milton in this passage! But would he have conceived such grand, such lofty ideas, had he been a stranger to the true religion?

God manifests himself to Adam; the creature and the Creator hold converse together; they discourse on solitude. We omit the reflections. God knew that it was not good for man to be alone. Adam falls asleep; God takes from the side of our common father the substance out of which he fashions a new creature, whom he conducts to him on his waking

> Grace was in all her steps, Heaven in her eye,
> In every gesture dignity and love.
> ——— Woman is her name, of man
> Extracted; for this cause he shall forego
> Father and mother, and to his wife adhere;
> And they shall be one flesh, one heart, one soul.

Wo to him who cannot perceive here a reflection of the Deity!

The poet continues to develop these grand views of human nature, this sublime reason of Christianity. The character of the woman is admirably delineated in the fatal fall. Eve transgresses by self-love; she boasts that she is strong enough alone to encounter temptation. She is unwilling that Adam should accompany her to the solitary spot where she cultivates her flowers. This fair creature, who thinks herself invincible by reason of her very weakness, knows not that a single word can subdue her. Woman is always delineated in the Scripture as the slave of vanity. When Isaias threatens the daughters of Jerusalem, he says, "The Lord will take away your ear-rings, your bracelets, your rings, and your veils." We have witnessed in our own days a striking instance of this disposition. Many a woman, during the reign of *terror*, exhibited numberless proofs of heroism, whose virtue has since fallen a victim to a dance, a dress, an amusement. Here we have the development of one of those great and mysterious truths contained in the Scriptures. God, when he doomed woman to bring forth with pain, conferred upon her an invincible fortitude against pain; but at the same time, as a punishment for her fault, he left her weak against pleasure. Milton accordingly denominates her "this fair defect of nature."

The manner in which the English bard has conducted the fall of our first parents is well worthy of our examination. An ordinary genius would not have failed to convulse the world at the moment when Eve raises the fatal fruit to her lips; but Milton merely represents that—

> Earth felt the wound, and Nature from her seat,
> Sighing, through all her works gave signs of wo
> That all was lost.

The reader is, in fact, the more surprised, because this effect is much less surprising. What calamities does this present tranquillity of nature lead us to anticipate in future! Tertullian, inquiring why the universe is not disturbed by the crimes of men, adduces a sublime reason. This reason is, the PATIENCE of God.

When the mother of mankind presents the fruit of knowledge to her husband, our common father does not roll himself in the dust, or tear his hair, or loudly vent his grief. On the contrary,—

> Adam, soon as he heard
> The fatal trespass done by Eve, amaz'd,
> Astonied stood and blank, while horror chill
> Ran through his veins, and all his joints relax'd.
> Speechless he stood, and pale.

He perceives the whole enormity of the crime. On the one hand, if he disobey, he will incur the penalty of death; on the other, if he continue faithful, he will retain his immortality, but will lose his beloved partner, now devoted to the grave. He may refuse the fruit, but can he live without Eve? The conflict is long. A world at last is sacrificed to love. Adam, instead of loading his wife with reproaches, endeavors to console her, and accepts the fatal apple from her hands. On this consummation of the crime, no change yet takes place in nature. Only the first storms of the passions begin to agitate the hearts of the unhappy pair.

Adam and Eve fall asleep; but they have lost that innocence which renders slumber refreshing. From this troubled sleep they rise as from unrest. 'Tis then that their guilt stares them in the face. "What have we done?" exclaims Adam. "Why art thou naked? Let us seek a covering for ourselves, lest any one see us in this state!" But clothing does not conceal the nudity which has been once seen.

Meanwhile their crime is known in heaven. A holy sadness seizes the angels, but

> Mix'd
> With pity, violated not their bliss.

A truly Christian and sublime idea! God sends his Son to judge the guilty. He comes and calls Adam in the solitude: "Where art thou?" Adam hides himself from his presence: "Lord, I dare not show myself, because I am naked." "How dost thou know thyself to be naked? Hast thou eaten the fruit of knowledge?" What a dialogue passes between them! It is not of human invention. Adam confesses his crime, and God pronounces sentence:[1] "Man! in the sweat of thy brow shalt thou eat bread. In sorrow shalt thou cultivate the earth, till thou re-

[1] Genesis, iii.; Paradise Lost, book x.

turn unto dust from which thou wast taken. Woman, thou shalt bring forth children with pain." Such, in a few words, is the history of the human race. We know not if the reader is struck by it as we are; but we find in this scene of Genesis something so extraordinary and so grand that it defies all the comments of criticism. Admiration wants terms to express itself with adequate force, and art sinks into nothing.

The Son of God returns to heaven. Then commences that celebrated drama between Adam and Eve in which Milton is said to have recorded an event of his own life—the reconciliation between himself and his first consort. We are persuaded that the great writers have introduced their history into their works. It is only by delineating their own hearts, and attributing them to others, that they are enabled to give such exquisite pictures of nature; for the better part of genius consists in recollections.

Behold Adam now retiring at night in some lonely spot. The nature of the air is changed. Cold vapors and thick clouds obscure the face of heaven. The lightning has scathed the trees. The animals flee at the sight of man. The wolf begins to pursue the lamb, the vulture to prey upon the dove. He is overwhelmed with despair. He wishes to return to his native dust. Yet, says he,

> One doubt
> Pursues me still, lest all I cannot die;
> Lest that pure breath of life, the spirit of man,
> Which God inspired, cannot together perish
> With corporeal clod; then in the grave,
> Or in some other dismal place, who knows
> But I shall die a living death?

Can philosophy require a species of beauties more exalted and more solemn? Not only the poets of antiquity furnish no instance of a despair founded on such a basis, but moralists themselves have conceived nothing so sublime.

Eve, hearing her husband's lamentations, approaches with timidity. Adam sternly repels her. Eve falls humbly at his feet and bathes them with her tears. Adam relents, and raises the mother of the human race. Eve proposes to him to live in continence, or to inflict death upon themselves to save their posterity. This despair, so admirably ascribed to a woman, as well for its vehemence as for its generosity, strikes our common father What reply does he make to his wife?

> Eve, thy contempt of life and pleasure seems
> To argue in thee something more sublime
> And excellent than what thy mind contemns.

The unfortunate pair resolve to offer up their prayers to God, and to implore the mercy of the Almighty. Prostrating themselves on the ground, they raise their hearts and voices, in a spirit of profound humility, toward Him who is the source of forgiveness. These accents ascend to heaven, where the Son himself undertakes the office of presenting them to his Father. The suppliant prayers which follow *Injury*, to repair the mischiefs she has occasioned, are justly admired in the Iliad. It would indeed be impossible to invent a more beautiful allegory on the subject of prayer. Yet those first sighs of a contrite heart, which find the way that the sighs of the whole human race are soon destined to follow,—those humble prayers which mingle with the incense fuming before the Holy of Holies,—those penitent tears which fill the celestial spirits with joy, which are presented to the Almighty by the Redeemer of mankind, and which move God himself, (such is the power of this first prayer in repentant and unhappy man,) —all those circumstances combined have in them something so moral, so solemn, and so pathetic, that they cannot be said to be eclipsed by the *prayers* of the bard of Ilium.

The Most High relents, and decrees the final salvation of man. Milton has availed himself with great ability of this first mystery of the Scriptures, and has everywhere interwoven the impressive history of a God, who, from the commencement of ages, devotes himself to death to redeem man from destruction. The fall of Adam acquires a higher and more tragic interest when we behold it involving in its consequences the Son of the Almighty himself.

Independently of these beauties which belong to the subject of the *Paradise Lost*, the work displays minor beauties too numerous for us to notice. Milton had, in particular, an extraordinary felicity of expression. Every reader is acquainted with his *darkness visible*, his *pleased silence*, &c. These bold expressions, when sparingly employed, like discords in music, produce a highly brilliant effect They have a counter air of genius; but great care must be taken not to abuse them. When too studiously sought after, they dwindle into a mere puerile play upon words, as injurious to the language as they are inconsistent with good taste.

We shall, moreover, observe that the bard of Eden, after the example of Virgil, has acquired originality in appropriating to himself the riches of others; which proves that the original style is not the style which never borrows of any one, but that which no other person is capable of reproducing.

This art of imitation, known to all great writers, consists in a certain delicacy of taste which seizes the beauties of other times, and accommodates them to the present age and manners. Virgil is a model in this respect. Observe how he has transferred to the mother of Euryalus the lamentations of Andromache on the death of Hector. In this passage Homer is rather more natural than the Mantuan poet, whom he has moreover furnished with all the striking circumstances, such as the work falling from the hands of Andromache, her fainting, &c., while there are others, which are not in the Æneid, as Andromache's presentiment of her misfortune, and her appearance with dishevelled tresses upon the battlements; but then the episode of Euryalus is more tender, more pathetic. The mother who alone, of all the Trojan women, resolved to follow the fortunes of her son; the garments with which her maternal affection was engaged and now rendered useless; her exile, her age, her forlorn condition at the very moment when the head of her Euryalus was carried under the ramparts of the camp;—such are the conceptions of Virgil alone. The lamentations of Andromache, being more diffuse, lose something of their energy. Those of the mother of Euryalus, more closely concentrated, fall with increased weight upon the heart. This proves that there was already a great difference between the age of Virgil and Homer, and that in the time of the former all the arts, even that of love, had arrived at a higher perfection.

CHAPTER IV.

OF SOME FRENCH AND FOREIGN POEMS.

HAD Christianity produced no other poem than *Paradise Lost*,—had its genius inspired neither the *Jerusalem Delivered*, nor *Polyeuctes*, nor *Esther*, nor *Athalie*, nor *Zara*, nor *Alzira*,—still we might insist that it is highly favorable to the Muses. We shall notice in this chapter, between *Paradise Lost* and the *Henriad*, some French and foreign productions, on which we have but a few words to say.

The more remarkable passages in the *Saint Louis* of Father Lemoine have been so frequently quoted that we shall not refer to them here. This poem, rude as it is, possesses beauties which we would in vain look for in the *Jerusalem*. It displays a gloomy imagination, well adapted to the description of that Egypt, so full of recollections and of tombs, which has witnessed the succession of the Pharaohs, the Ptolemies, the anchorets of Thebais, and the sultans of the barbarians.

The *Pucelle* of Chapelain, the *Moïse Sauvé* of Saint-Amand, and the *David* of Coras, are scarcely known at present, except by the verses of Boileau. Some benefit may, however, be derived from the perusal of these works: the last, in particular, is worthy of notice.

The prophet Samuel relates to David the history of the chiefs of Israel:—

> Ne'er shall proud tyrants, said the sainted seer,
> Escape the vengeance of the King of kings;
> His judgments justly poured on our last chiefs
> Stand of this truth a lasting monument.
>
> . . . .
>
> Look but at Heli, him whom God's behest
> Appointed Israel's judge and pontiff too!
> His [illegible] zeal had nobly serv'd the state
> If not extinguish'd by his worthless sons.
>
> . . . .

> Over these youths, on vicious courses bent,
> Jehovah thundered forth his dread decree;
> And by a sacred messenger denounced
> Destruction 'gainst them both and all their race.
> Thou knowest, O God! the awful sentence past,
> What horrors racked old Heli's harrowed soul!
> These eyes his anguish witnessed, and this brow
> He oft bedewed with grief-extorted tears.

These lines (in the original) are remarkable, because they possess no mean poetic beauties. The apostrophe which terminates them is not unworthy of a first-rate poet.

The episode of Ruth, which is related in the sepulchral grotto, the burial-place of the ancient patriarchs, has a character of simplicity:—

> We know not which, the husband or the wife,
> Had purer soul, or more of happiness.

Coras is sometimes felicitous in description. Witness the following:—

> Meanwhile the sun, with peerless glory crowned,
> Lessening in form, more burning rays dispensed.

Saint Amand, whom Boileau extols as a man of some genius, is nevertheless inferior to Coras. The *Moïse Sauvé* is a languid composition, the versification tame and prosaic, and the style marked by antithesis and bad taste. It contains, however, some fine passages, which no doubt won the favor of the critic who wrote the *Art Poétique.*

It would be useless to waste our time upon the *Araucana,* with its three parts and thirty-five original songs, not forgetting the supplementary ones of Don Diego de Santisteban Ojozio It contains nothing of the *Christian marvellous.* It is an historical narrative of certain events which occurred in the mountains of Chili. The most interesting feature in the poem is the figure made in it by Ercylla himself, who appears both as a warrior and a writer. The *Araucana* is in eight-line stanzas, like the *Orlando* and the *Jerusalem.* Italian literature at this period gave the law of versification to all European nations. Ercylla among the Spaniards, and Spenser among the English, have adopted this kind of stanza, and imitated Ariosto even in the arrangement of their subjects.

Ercylla says:—

> No las damas, amor, no gentilezas,
> De cabelleros canto enamorados,
> Ni las muestras, regalos y ternezas
> De amorosos afectos y cuidados:
> Mas el valor, los hechos, las proezas
> De aquellos Españoles esforzados,
> Que á la cerviz de Arauco no domada
> Pusiéron duro yugo por la espada.

The subject of the Lusiad is a very rich one for an epic poem. It is difficult to conceive how a man possessing the genius of Camoens should not have had the art to turn it to better account than he has done. At the same time, it should be recollected that this is the first modern epic, that he lived in a barbarous age, that there are many pathetic[1] and even sublime touches in the details of his poem, and that after all the bard of the Tagus was the most unfortunate of mortals. It is a false notion, worthy of our hard-hearted age, that the noblest works are produced in adversity;[2] for it is not true that a man can write best under the pressure of misfortune. All those inspired men who devote themselves to the service of the muses are sooner overwhelmed by affliction than vulgar minds. A mighty genius speedily wears out the body which it animates; great souls, like large rivers, are liable to lay waste their banks.

The manner in which Camoens has intermixed fable and Christianity renders it unnecessary for us to say any thing of the *marvellous* of his performance.

Klopstock has also committed the fault of taking the *marvellous* of Christianity for the *subject* of his poem. His principal character is the Divinity, and this alone would be sufficient to destroy the tragic effect. There are, however, some beautiful passages in the Messiah. The two lovers whom Christ raised from the dead furnish a charming episode, which the mythologic

---

[1] We nevertheless differ on this subject from other critics. The episode of Ines is, in our opinion, chaste and pathetic, but has been upon the whole too highly praised, and is far from having the developments of which it was susceptible.

[2] Juvenal has applied a similar observation to the epic poet:

> Nam si Virgilio puer, et tolerabile deesset
> Hospitium, caderent omnes a crinibus hydri,
> Surda nihil gemeret grave buccina.

times could never have produced. We recollect no characters recalled from the grave among the ancients, except Alceste, Hippolytus, and Heres of Pamphylia.[1]

Richness and grandeur are the particular characteristics of the marvellous in the *Messiah*. Those spheres inhabited by beings of a different nature from man—the multitude of angels, spirits of darkness, unborn souls, and souls that have already finished the career of mortality,—plunge the mind into the ocean of immensity. The character of Abbadona, the penitent angel, is a happy conception. Klopstock has also created a species of mystic seraphs, wholly unknown before his time.

Gessner has left us in his *Death of Abel* a work replete with tenderness and majesty. It is unfortunately spoiled by that sickly tincture of the idyl which the Germans generally give to subjects taken from Scripture; they are all guilty of violating one of the principal laws of the epic, *consistency of manners*, and transform the pastoral monarchs of the East into innocent shepherds of Arcadia.

As to the author of *Noah*, he was overwhelmed by the richness of his subject. To a vigorous imagination, however, the antediluvian world opens a grand and extensive field. There would be no necessity for creating all its wonders: by turning to the Critias of Plato,[2] the Chronologies of Eusebius, and some treatises of Lucian and Plutarch, an abundant harvest might be obtained. Scaliger quotes a fragment of Polyhistor, respecting certain tables written before the deluge and preserved at *Sippary*, probably the same as the *Sipphara* of Ptolemy.[3] The muses speak and understand all languages: how many things might they decipher on these tables!

---

[1] In Plato's *Republic*, book x. Since the appearance of the first edition, we have been informed by Mr. Boissonade, a philologist equally learned and polite, that several other personages are mentioned by Apollodorus and Telesarchus as having been resuscitated in pagan antiquity.

[2] The Critias or Atlanticus is an unfinished dialogue of Plato. He describes an *atlantic* island that existed in the infancy of the world. Its climate was genial and its soil fertile. It was inhabited by a happy race of mortals, who cultivated arts similar to those of Greece. This island, according to the beautiful tradition of the Egyptian priests, was swallowed up by an inundation prior to the deluge of Deucaleon.

[3] Unless we derive *Sippary* from the Hebrew word *Sepher*, which signifies a

CHAPTER V.

THE HENRIAD.

If a judicious plan, a spirited and well-sustained narrative, excellent versification, a pure taste, and a correct and flowing style, were the only qualities necessary for the epic, the *Henriad* would be a perfect poem: these, however, are not sufficient, for it requires besides an heroic and supernatural action. But how could Voltaire have made a happy application of the *marvellous* of Christianity—he who directed all his efforts to the destruction of that marvellous? Such is, nevertheless, the power of religious ideas, that to the very faith which he persecuted the author of the *Henriad* is indebted for the most striking passages of his epic poem, as well as for the most exquisite scenes in his tragedies.

A tincture of philosophy and a cold and grave morality become the historic muse; but this spirit of severity transferred to the epic is a sort of contradiction. When, therefore, Voltaire, in the invocation of his poem, exclaims—

> From thy celestial seat, illustrious *Truth*,
> Descend———

he has fallen, in our opinion, into a gross mistake. Epic poetry

> Is built on fable, and by fiction lives.

Tasso, who also treated a Christian subject, followed Plato and Lucretius[1] in his charming lines beginning—

> Sai che la torre in mondo, ove piu versi
> Di sue dolcezze il lusinghier Parnasso, &c.

---

library. Josephus (*de Antiq. Jud.*, lib. i. c. 2) mentions two columns, one of brick, the other of stone, on which Seth's children had engraved the human sciences, that they might not be swept away by the deluge, which Adam had predicted. These two columns are said to have existed long after the time of Noah.

[1] "As the physician who, to save his patient, mixes pleasant draughts with the medicines proper for curing him, and, on the contrary, introduces bitter drugs into such aliments as are pernicious," &c. Plato, *de Leg.*, lib. i. *Ac veluti pueris absinthia tetra medentes*, &c. Lucret., lib. v.

"There can be no good poetry where there is no fiction," observes Plutarch.[1]

Was semi-barbarous France no longer sufficiently covered with forests to present some castle of the days of yore, with its portcullis, dungeons, and towers overgrown with ivy, and teeming with marvellous adventures? Was there no Gothic temple to be found in a solitary valley, embosomed in woods? Had not the mountains of Navarre some druid, a child of the rock, who, beneath the sacred oak, on the bank of the torrent, amid the howling of the tempest, celebrated the deeds of the Gauls and wept over the tombs of heroes? I am sure there must have been still left some knight of the reign of Francis I., who within his antique mansion regretted the tournaments of former days and the good old times when France went to war with recreants and infidels. How many circumstances might have been gleaned from that Batavian revolution, the neighbor, and, as it were, the sister, of the League! The Dutch were just then forming settlements in the Indies, and Philip was receiving the first treasures from Peru. Coligny had even sent a colony to Carolina; the Chevalier de Gourgues would have furnished the author of the *Henriad* with a splendid and pathetic episode. An epic poem should embrace the universe.

Europe, by the happiest of contrasts, exhibited a pastoral nation in Switzerland, a commercial nation in England, and a nation devoted to the arts in Italy. France also presented a most favorable epoch for epic poetry; an epoch which ought always to be chosen, as it was by Voltaire, at the conclusion of one age and at the commencement of another; an epoch bordering upon old manners on the one hand and new manners on the other. Barbarism was expiring, and the brilliant age of the great Louis began to dawn. Malherbe was come, and that hero, both a bard and a knight, could lead the French to battle, at the same time chanting hymns to victory.

It is admitted that the *characters* in the *Henriad* are but *por-*

---

[1] If we were to be told that Tasso had also invoked Truth, we should reply that he has not done it like Voltaire. Tasso's Truth is a *muse*, an angel, a vague something without a name, a *Christian* being, and not *Truth directly personified*, like that of the *Henriad*.

traits, and this species of painting, of which Rome in her decline exhibited the first models, has been perhaps too highly extolled.

The *portrait* belongs not to the epic. Its beauties are destitute of action and motion.

Some have likewise questioned whether *consistency of manners* be sufficiently preserved in the *Henriad*. The heroes of that poem spout very fine verses, which serve as vehicles for the philosophical principles of Voltaire; but are they good representatives of warriors such as they actually were in the sixteenth century? If the speeches of the Leaguers breathe the spirit of the age, are we not authorized to think that the actions of the characters should display this spirit still more than their words? At least the bard who has celebrated Achilles has not thrown the Iliad into dialogue.

As to the *marvellous*, it amounts to little more than nothing in the *Henriad*. If we were not acquainted with the wretched system which froze the poetic genius of Voltaire, we should be at a loss to conceive how he could have preferred allegorical divinities to the marvellous of Christianity. He has imparted no warmth to his inventions except in those passages where he has ceased to be a philosopher that he may become a Christian. No sooner does he touch upon religion, the source of all poetry, than the current freely flows. The oath of the sixteen in the cavern, the appearance of the ghost of Guise, which comes to furnish Clement with a dagger, are circumstances highly epic, and borrowed even from the superstitions of an ignorant and unhappy age.

Was not the poet guilty of another error when he introduced his philosophy into heaven? His Supreme Being is, doubtless, a very equitable God, who judges with strict impartiality both the Bonze and the Dervise, the Jew and the Mohammedan; but was this to be expected of the muse? Should we not rather require of her *poetry*, a *Christian heaven*, sacred songs, Jehovah, in a word, the *mens divinior*—religion?

Voltaire has, therefore, broken with his own hand the most harmonious string of his lyre, in refusing to celebrate that sacred host, that glorious army of martyrs and angels, with which his talents would have produced an admirable effect. He might have found among our saints powers as great as those of the goddesses of old and names as sweet as those of the graces. What a pity that he did not choose to make mention of those shepherdesses transformed, for their virtues, into beneficent divinities; of those Genevieves who, in the mansions of bliss, protect the empire of Clovis and Charlemagne! In our opinion, it must be a sight not wholly destitute of charms for the muses, to behold the most intelligent and the most valiant of nations consecrated by religion to the daughter of simplicity and peace. Whence did the Gauls derive their troubadours, their frankness of mind, and their love of the graces, except from the pastoral strains, the innocence, and the beauty, of their patroness?

Judicious critics have observed that there are two individuals in Voltaire—the one abounding in taste, science, and reason, and the other marked by the contrary defects. It may be questioned whether the author of the *Henriad* possessed a genius equal to Racine, but he had perhaps more varied talents and a more flexible imagination. Unfortunately, what we are able to do is not always the measure of what we actually accomplish. If Voltaire had been animated by religion, like the author of Athalie, and like him had profoundly studied the works of the fathers and antiquity,—if he had not grasped at every species of composition and every kind of subject,—his poetry would have been more nervous, and his prose would have acquired a decorum and gravity in which it is but too often deficient. This great man had the misfortune to pass his life amid a circle of scholars of moderate abilities, who, always ready to applaud, were incapable of apprising him of his errors. We love to represent him to ourselves in the company of his equals—the Pascals, the Arnauds, the Nicoles, the Boileaus, the Racines. By associating with such men he would have been obliged to alter his tone. The jests and the blasphemies of Ferney would have excited indignation at Port Royal. The inmates of that institution detested works composed in a hurry, and would not, for all the world, have deceived the public by submitting to it a poem which had not cost them the labor of twelve long years at least; and a circumstance truly astonishing is, that, amid so many occupations, these excellent men still found means to fulfil every, even the least important, of their religious duties, and to carry with them into society the urbanity of their illustrious age.[1]

Such a school Voltaire wanted. He is greatly to be pitied for having possessed that twofold genius which extorts at the same time our admiration and our hatred. He erects and overthrows; he gives the most contradictory examples and precepts; he extols the age of Louis XIV. to the skies, and afterward attacks in detail the reputation of its great men. He alternately praises and slanders antiquity; he pursues through seventy volumes what he denominates the *wretch*, and yet the finest passages in his works were inspired by religion. While his imagination enchants you, he throws around him the glare of a fallacious reason, which destroys the marvellous, contracts the soul, and shortens the sight. Except in some of his master-pieces, he considers only the ludicrous side of things and times, and exhibits man to man in a light hideously diverting. He charms and fatigues by his versatility; he both delights and disgusts you; you are at a loss to decide what form is peculiarly his own; you would think him insane, were it not for his good sense, and a misanthropist, did not his life abound with acts of beneficence. You can perceive, amid all his impieties, that he hated sophists.[2] To love the fine arts, letters, and magnificence, was so natural to him that it is nothing uncommon to find him in a kind of admiration of the court of Rome. His vanity caused him, throughout his life, to act a part for which he was not formed, and which was very far beneath him. He bore, in fact, no resemblance to Diderot, Raynal, or D'Alembert. The elegance of his manners, the urbanity of his demeanor, his love of society, and, above all, his humanity, would probably have rendered him one of the most inveterate enemies of the revolutionary system. He is most decidedly in favor of social order, while he unconsciously saps its foundations by attacking the institutions of religion. The most equitable judgment that can be passed upon him is that his

---

[1] It is much to be regretted that the *excellence* of these writers and their literary labors were so deeply sullied by their attachment to the cause of Jansenism. Though Voltaire was not the cotemporary of Pascal, he knew how to combat Christianity with the same weapons of ridicule that the latter had employed against the Society of Jesus, the great bulwark of Catholicism in that age. T.

[2] See note N.

infidelity prevented his attaining the height for which nature qualified him, and that his works (with the exception of his fugitive poems) have fallen very short of his actual abilities—an example which ought to be an everlasting warning to all those who pursue the career of letters.[1] Voltaire was betrayed into all these errors, all these contradictions of style and sentiment, only because he wanted the great counterpoise of religion; and he is an instance to prove that grave morals and piety of thought are more necessary even than a brilliant genius for the successful cultivation of the muse.

[1] "Voltaire's pen was fertile and very elegant; his observations are very acute, yet he often betrays great ignorance when he treats on subjects of ancient learning. Madame de Talmond once said to him, 'I think, sir, that a philosopher should never write but to endeavor to render mankind less wicked and unhappy than they are. Now you do quite the contrary; you are always writing against that religion which alone is able to restrain wickedness and to afford us consolation under misfortunes.' Voltaire was much struck, and excused himself by saying that he only wrote for those who were of the same opinion with himself. Tronchin assured his friends that Voltaire died in great agonies of mind. 'I die forsaken by Gods and men!' exclaimed he, in those awful moments when truth will force its way. 'I wish,' added Tronchin, 'that those who had been perverted by his writings had been present at his death. It was a sight too horrid to support." Seward's *Anecdotes*, vol. v. p. 274.

BOOK II.

OF POETRY CONSIDERED IN ITS RELATION TO MAN

Characters.

CHAPTER I.

NATURAL CHARACTERS.

FROM the general survey of epic poems we shall pass to the details of poetic compositions. Let us first consider the natural characters, such as the husband and wife, the father, the mother, &c., before we enter upon the examination of the social characters, such as the priest and the soldier; and let us set out from a principle that cannot be contested.

Christianity is, if we may so express it, a double religion. Its teaching has reference to the nature of intellectual being, and also to our own nature: it makes the mysteries of the Divinity and the mysteries of the human heart go hand-in-hand; and, by removing the veil that conceals the true God, it also exhibits man just as he is.

Such a religion must necessarily be more favorable to the delineation of *characters* than another which dives not into the secrets of the passions. The fairer half of poetry, the dramatic, received no assistance from polytheism, for morals were separated from mythology.[1] A god ascended his chariot, a priest offered a sacrifice; but neither the god nor the priest taught what man is, whence he comes, whither he goes, what are his propensities, his vices, his virtues, his ends in this life and his destinies in another.

In Christianity, on the contrary, religion and morals are one and the same thing. The Scripture informs us of our origin; it

[1] See note O.

makes us acquainted with our twofold nature; the Christian mysteries all relate to us; we are everywhere seen; for us the Son of God is sacrificed. From Moses to Jesus Christ, from the apostles to the last fathers of the Church, every thing presents the picture of the internal man, every thing tends to dispel the obscurity in which he is enveloped; and one of the distinguishing characteristics of Christianity is that it invariably introduces man in conjunction with God, whereas the false religions have separated the Creator from the creature.

Here, then, is an incalculable advantage which poets ought to have observed in the Christian religion, instead of obstinately continuing to decry it. For if it is equal to polytheism in the *marvellous*, or in the relations of *supernatural things*, as we shall in the sequel attempt to prove, it has moreover the drama and moral part which polytheism did not embrace.

In support of this great truth, we shall adduce examples; we shall institute comparisons, which, while they refine our taste, may serve to attach us to the religion of our forefathers by the charms of the most divine among the arts.

We shall commence the study of the *natural characters* by that of *husband and wife*, and contrast the conjugal love of Adam and Eve with the conjugal love of Ulysses and Penelope. It will not be said of us that we have purposely selected inferior subjects in antiquity, in order to heighten the effect of the Christian subjects.

CHAPTER II.

THE HUSBAND AND WIFE.

Ulysses and Penelope.

THE suitors having been slain by Ulysses, Euryclea goes to awaken Penelope, who long refuses to believe the wonderful story related by her nurse. She rises, however, and, "descending the steps, passed the stone threshold, and sat down opposite to Ulysses, who was himself seated at the foot of a lofty column, and, his eyes fixed on the ground, was waiting to hear what his wife would say. But she kept silence, for great astonishment had seized her heart."[1]

Telemachus accuses his mother of coldness. Ulysses smiles, and makes an excuse for Penelope. The princess still doubts; and, to try her husband, commands the bed of Ulysses to be prepared out of the nuptial chamber; upon which the hero immediately exclaims, "Who, then, has removed my couch? Is it no longer spread on the trunk of the olive, around which I built with this hand a bower in my court?"

"He said; and suddenly the heart and knees of Penelope at once failed her; she recognised Ulysses by this indubitable sign. Soon running to him, bathed in tears, she threw her arms about her husband's neck; she kissed his sacred head, and cried, 'Be not angry, thou who wast always the wisest of men! Let me not move thy wrath, if I forbore to throw myself into thine arms. My heart trembled for fear a stranger should betray my faith by deceitful words. . . . . . . But now I have a manifest proof that it is thyself, by that which thou hast said concerning our couch, which no other man has ever seen, which is known to ourselves and to Actoris alone, (the slave whom my father gave to me when I came to Ithaca, and who is the only attendant on our nuptial chamber.) Thou restorest confidence to this heart rendered distrustful by grief.'

"She said: and Ulysses, unable to restrain his tears, wept over this chaste and prudent spouse, whom he pressed to his heart. As mariners gaze at the wished-for land, when Neptune has shattered their rapid vessel, the sport of the winds and the mountain billows,—when a small number of the crew, floating on the bosom of the ocean, swim to the shore, and, covered with briny foam, gain the strand, overjoyed at their narrow escape from destruction,—so Penelope fixed her delighted eyes on Ulysses. She could not take her arms from the hero's neck, and rosy-fingered Aurora would have beheld the sacred tears of the royal pair had not Minerva held back the sun in the wavy main. . . . . Meanwhile, Eurynome, with a torch in her hand, goes before Ulysses and Penelope, and conducts them to the nuptial chamber.

---

[1] *Odyss.*, b. xxiii. v. 88.

. . . . . . The king and his consort, after yielding to the blandishments of love, enchanted each other by the mutual recital of their sorrows. . . . . . . Scarcely had Ulysses finished the last words of his history, when beneficent slumber, stealing upon his weary limbs, produced a sweet forgetfulness of all his cares."

This meeting of Ulysses and Penelope is, perhaps, one of the most exquisite specimens of ancient genius. Penelope sitting in silence, Ulysses motionless at the foot of a column, and the scene illumined by the blaze of the hospitable hearth—what grandeur and what simplicity of design! And by what means do they recognise each other? By the mention of a circumstance relative to the nuptial couch. Another object of admiration is, that the couch itself was formed by the hand of a king upon the trunk of an olive-tree, the tree of peace and of wisdom, worthy of supporting that bed which never received any other man than Ulysses. The transports which succeed the discovery; that deeply affecting comparison of a widow finding her long-lost husband to a mariner who descries land at the very moment of shipwreck; the conjugal pair conducted by torch-light to their apartment; the pleasures of love followed by the joys of grief or the mutual communication of past sorrows; the twofold delight of present happiness and recollected misfortunes; that sleep which gradually steals on, and at length closes the eyes and lips of Ulysses, while relating his adventures to the attentive Penelope: all these traits display the hand of a master, and cannot be too highly admired.

It would be a truly interesting study to consider what course a modern writer would have pursued in the execution of some particular part of the works of an ancient author. In the foregoing picture, for instance, there is every reason to suspect that the scene, instead of passing in action between Ulysses and Penelope, would have been described in the narrative form by the poet. This narration would have been interspersed with philosophical reflections, brilliant verses, and pretty turns of expression. Instead of adopting this showy and laborious manner, Homer exhibits to you a pair who meet again after an absence of twenty years, and who, without uttering any vehement exclamations, seem as if they had parted only the preceding day. Wherein, then, consists the beauty of its delineation? In its *truth*.

The moderns are, in general, more scientific, more delicate, more acute, and frequently even more interesting, in their compositions than the ancients. The latter, on the other hand, are more simple, more august, more tragic, more fertile, and, above all, more attentive to truth, than the moderns. They have a better taste, a nobler imagination: they work at their composition as a whole, without affectation of ornament. A shepherd giving way to his lamentations, an old man relating a story, a hero fighting, are sufficient with them for a whole poem; and we are puzzled to tell how it happens that this poem, which contains nothing, is nevertheless better filled than our novels that are most crowded with incidents and characters. The art of writing seems to have followed the art of painting: the pallet of the modern poet is covered with an infinite variety of hues and tints; the poet of antiquity composes all his pieces with the three colors of Polygnotus. The Latins, placed between the Greeks and us, partake of both manners; they resemble Greece in the simplicity of the ground, and us in the art of detail. It is probably this happy combination of both styles that renders the productions of Virgil so enchanting.

Let us now turn to the picture of the loves of our first parents. The Adam and Eve of the blind bard of Albion will form an excellent match for the Ulysses and Penelope of the blind bard of Smyrna.

CHAPTER III.

THE HUSBAND AND WIFE, (CONTINUED.)

Adam and Eve.

SATAN, having penetrated into the terrestrial paradise, surveys the animals of the new creation. Among these,

> Two of far nobler shape, erect and tall,
> Godlike èrect, with native honor clad,
> In naked majesty seemed lords of all,
> And worthy seemed: for in their looks divine
> The image of their glorious Maker shone.

Truth, wisdom, sanctitude severe and pure,
(Severe, but in true filial freedom placed,)
Whence true authority in men: though both
Not equal as their sex not equal seemed;
For contemplation he and valor formed,
For softness she, and sweet attractive grace;
He for God only, she for God in him.
His fair large front and eye sublime declared
Absolute rule, and hyacinthine locks
Round from his parted forelock manly hung
Clustering, but not beneath his shoulders broad:
She as a veil down to the slender waist
Her unadorned golden tresses wore
Dishevelled, but in wanton ringlets waved
As the vine curls her tendrils, which implied
Subjection, but required with gentle sway,
And by her yielded, by him best received,
Yielded with coy submission, modest pride,
And sweet reluctant amorous delay.
Nor those mysterious parts were then concealed:
Then was not guilty shame; dishonest shame
Of Nature's works, honor dishonorable,
Sin-bred, how have ye troubled all mankind
With shows instead, mere shows of seeming pure,
And banished from man's life his happiest life,
Simplicity and spotless innocence!
So passed they naked on, nor shunned the sight
Of God or angels, for they thought no ill:
So hand-in-hand they passed, the loveliest pair
That ever since in love's embraces met;
Adam the goodliest man of men since born
His sons, the fairest of her daughters Eve.[1]

Our first parents retire beneath a *tuft of shade by a fresh fountain's side.* Here they take their evening repast amid the animals of the creation, which frisk around their human sovereigns. Satan, disguised under the form of one of these creatures, contemplates the happy pair, and his enmity is almost overcome by their beauty, their innocence, and the thoughts of the calamities which through his means will soon succeed such exquisite felicity — a truly admirable trait! Meanwhile Adam and Eve enter into sweet converse beside the fountain, and Eve thus addresses her husband:—

That day I oft remember, when from sleep
I first awaked, and found myself reposed

[1] *Paradise Lost,* b. iv.

Under a shade of flowers, much wondering where
And what I was, whence thither brought and how.
Not distant far from thence a murmuring sound
Of waters issued from a cave, and spread
Into a liquid plain, then stood unmoved
Pure as the expanse of Heaven: I thither went
With unexperienced thought, and laid me down
On the green bank, to look into the clear
Smooth lake, that to me seemed another sky.
As I went down to look, just opposite
A shape within the watery gleam appeared,
Bending to look on me: I started back,
It started back; but, pleased, I soon returned;
Pleased, it returned as soon, with answering looks
Of sympathy and love. There had I fixed
Mine eyes till now, and pined with vain desire,
Had not a voice thus warned me · What thou seest,
What there thou seest, fair creature, is thyself.
With thee it comes and goes, but follow me,
And I will bring thee where no shadow stays
Thy coming, and thy soft embraces, he
Whose image thou art, him thou shalt enjoy,
Inseparably thine; to him shalt bear
Multitudes like thyself, and thence be called
Mother of human race. What could I do
But follow straight, invisibly thus led?
Till I espied thee, fair, indeed, and tall,
Under a platan, yet, methought, less fair,
Less winning soft, less amiably mild,
Than that smooth watery image. Back I turned;
Thou, following, criedst aloud, "Return, fair Eve;
Whom flyest thou? whom thou flyest, of him thou art;
His flesh, his bone. To give thee being, I lent
Out of my side to thee, nearest my heart,
Substantial life, to have thee by my side
Henceforth an individual solace dear.
Part of my soul, I seek thee, and thee claim,
My other half" With that, thy gentle hand
Seized mine; I yielded, and from that time see
How beauty is excelled by manly grace
And wisdom, which alone is truly fair.
So spake our general mother, and with eyes
Of conjugal attraction, unreproved,
And meek surrender, half embracing, leaned
On our first father. Half her swelling breast
Naked met his, under the flowing gold
Of her loose tresses hid. He, in delight
Both of her beauty and submissive charms,
Smiled with superior love, as Jupiter

On Juno smiles when he impregns the clouds
That shed May flowers, and pressed her matron lip
With kisses pure. . . . .
. . . . . . The sun had fallen
Beneath the Azores. Whether the prime orb,
Incredible how swift, had thither rolled
Diurnal, or this less volubil earth,
By shorter flight to the east, had left him there,
Arraying with reflected purple and gold
The clouds that on his western throne attend.
Now came still evening on, and twilight gray
Had in her sober livery all things clad.
Silence accompanied; for beast and bird,
They to their grassy couch, these to their nests,
Were slunk,—all but the wakeful nightingale;
She all night long her amorous descant sung.
Silence was pleased. Now glowed the firmament
With living sapphires. Hesperus, that led
The starry host, rode brightest till the moon,
Rising in clouded majesty, at length,
Apparent queen, unveiled her peerless light,
And o'er the dark her silver mantle threw.

Adam and Eve, having offered up their prayers to the Almighty retire to the nuptial bower. Proceeding to its inmost covert, they lie down upon a bed of flowers. The poet, remaining as it were at the entrance, entones a canticle to Hymen, in the presence of the starry host. Without preliminary, and as by an impulse of inspiration, he bursts forth into this magnificent epithalamium, after the manner of the ancients:—

Hail wedded love, mysterious law, true source
Of human offspring———

Thus, after Hector's death, does the Grecian army all at once sing:—

Ηράμεθα μέγα κῦδος, ἐπέφνομεν Ἕκτορα δῖον.

"We have gained great glory! We have slain the divine Hector

In like manner, the Salii, celebrating the festival of Hercules, in Virgil, abruptly shout:—

Tu nubigenas, invicte, bimembres, &c.
"Thy arms, unconquered hero, could subdue
The cloud-born Centaurs and the monster crew!"

This hymn to conjugal fidelity puts the finishing stroke to

Milton's picture, and completes the delineation of the loves of our first parents.[1]

We are not afraid that the reader will find fault with us for the length of this quotation. "In all other poems," says Voltaire, "love is considered as a weakness. In Milton alone it is a virtue. The poet has had the art to remove, with chaste hand, the veil which elsewhere conceals the pleasures of this passion. He transports the reader into the garden of bliss. He makes him a partaker, as it were, of the pure raptures with which Adam and Eve are filled. He rises not above human nature, but above *corrupt* human nature; and, as there is no example of such love, neither is there any of such poetry."[2]

If we compare the loves of Ulysses and Penelope with those of Adam and Eve, we shall find that the simplicity of Homer is more ingenious,—that of Milton more magnificent. Ulysses, though a monarch and a hero, has, nevertheless, something rustic about him. His artifices, his attitudes, his words, bear the stamp of unpolished nature. Adam, though but just created, and without experience, is already the perfect model of man. It is evident that he must have sprung, not from the womb of a feeble woman, but from the hands of the living God. He is noble, majestic, perfectly innocent, and at the same time full of intelligence. He is such as the sacred volume describes him, worthy to be respected by the angels and to walk in the garden with his Creator.

As to the two females, if Penelope is at first more coy and afterward more tender than the mother of mankind, the reason is, because she has been tried by adversity, and adversity both creates distrust and heightens the sensibilities. Eve, on the contrary, is complying, communicative, and attracting; nay, she has even a slight tincture of coquetry. How, indeed, can she possess the gravity and reserve of Penelope, when all around smiles upon her? If affliction contracts the soul, happiness expands it. In the former case, we find not deserts enough wherein

[1] There is another passage in which the loves of Adam and Eve are described. It is in the eighth book, where Adam relates to Raphael the first sensations of his life, his conversation with God on solitude, the formation of Eve, and his first interview with her. This passage is not inferior to that which we have just quoted, and likewise owes all its beauty to the spirit of a sacred and pure religion.

[2] *Essai sur la Poésie Epique*, chap. ix.

to bury our sorrows; in the latter, not hearts enough to which to communicate our pleasures. Milton, however, meant not to make his Eve a perfect character. He has represented her as irresistible by her charms, but somewhat indiscreet and loquacious, that the reader might foresee the calamity into which this failing in the sequel hurries her.

We may here remark, that in the description of the pleasures of love the great poets of antiquity evince at once a simplicity and a chastity that are astonishing. Nothing can be more modest than their idea, nothing more free than their expression. We, on the contrary, inflame the senses, though we spare the eye and the ear. Whence arises this magic of the ancients, and why does a perfectly naked Venus by Praxiteles charm the mind rather than the eye? Because it exhibits a beautiful *ideal*, which makes a deeper impression upon the soul than upon matter. Then the genius alone, and not the body, becomes enamored. It is this that burns with desire to unite closely with the master-piece. All terrestrial ardor is extinguished and absorbed by a love more divine. The impassioned soul entwines itself round the beloved object, and spiritualizes even the grosser terms which it is obliged to employ in order to express its feeling.

But neither the love of Penelope and Ulysses, nor that of Dido for Æneas, nor of Alceste for Admetus, can be compared with the tenderness displayed by the august pair in Eden. The true religion alone could have furnished the character of a love so sacred, so sublime. What an association of ideas!—the nascent universe—the ocean affrighted, as it were, at its own immensity—the planets pausing, as if terrified in their new career—the angels thronging to behold these wonders—the Almighty surveying his yet recent work—and two beings, half spirit and half clay, astonished at their bodies, still more astonished at their souls, essaying at one and the same time their first thoughts and their first loves!

To make the picture perfect, Milton has had the art to introduce the spirit of darkness as a deep shadow. The rebel angel seeks out the two noble creatures. From their own lips he learns the fatal secret. He rejoices in the idea of their future misery; and this whole description of the felicity of our first parents is in reality but the first step toward tremendous calamities. Ponelope and Ulysses remind us of past troubles; Adam and Eve point to impending woes. Every drama is fundamentally defective that represents joys without any mixture of sorrows past or sorrows in reserve. We are tired by unalloyed happiness and shocked by absolute misery. The former is destitute of recollections and of tears, the latter of hope and of smiles. If you ascend from pain to pleasure, (as in the scene of Homer,) you will be more pathetic, more melancholy, because the soul then looks back on the past and reposes in the present. If, on the contrary, you descend from prosperity to tears, as in Milton's immortal poem, you will be more sad, more sensitive, because the heart scarcely pauses on the present, and already anticipates the calamities with which it is threatened. We ought, therefore, in our pictures, invariably to combine felicity and adversity, and to make the pains rather more than counterbalance the pleasures, as in nature. Two liquids, the one sweet and the other bitter, are mingled together in the cup of life; but, in addition to the bitterness of the latter, there is the sediment which both liquids alike deposit at the bottom of the chalice.

CHAPTER IV.

THE FATHER.

Priam.

FROM the *conjugal* character let us proceed to that of the *father*. Let us consider paternity in the most sublime and affecting situations of life — old age and misfortune. Priam, that monarch whose favor was sought by the mighty of the earth, *dum fortuna fuit*, but now fallen from the height of glory — Priam, his venerable locks sullied with ashes, his cheeks bedewed with tears, has penetrated alone at midnight into the camp of the Greeks. Low bowed at the knees of the merciless Achilles, kissing those terrible, those devouring[1] hands yet reeking with the blood of his sons, he humbly begs the body of his Hector:—

Μνησαι πατρος σειο, &c.[2]

---

[1] Ανδροφονος, *men-devouring.*

[2] *Iliad*, b. xxiv.

"Remember thy father, O godlike Achilles! He is bowed down with years, and, like me, approaches the termination of his career. Perhaps at this very moment he is overwhelmed by powerful neighbors, and has no one at hand to defend him; and yet, when he is informed that thou livest, he rejoices in his heart. Each day he hopes to see his son return from Troy. But I, the most unfortunate of fathers, of all the sons that I numbered in spacious Ilion scarcely one is left me. I had fifty when the Greeks landed on these shores. Nineteen were the offspring of the same mother. Different captives bore me the others. Most of them have fallen beneath the strokes of cruel Mars. Yet one there was who singly defended his brothers and the walls of Troy. Him thou hast slain, fighting for his country—Hector! For his sake I have repaired to the Grecian fleet. I am come to redeem his body, and have brought thee an immense ransom. Respect the gods, O Achilles! Have compassion upon me. Remember thy father. Oh! how wretched am I! No mortal was ever reduced to such excess of misery. I kiss the hands that have killed my sons!"

What beauties in this address! what a scene unfolded to the view of the reader! Night—the tent of Achilles—that hero, seated beside the faithful Automedon, deploring the loss of Patroclus—Priam abruptly appearing amid the obscurity and throwing himself at the feet of Pelides. There in the dark stand the cars and the mules which have brought the presents of the venerable sovereign of Troy, and at some distance the mangled remains of the generous Hector are left unhonored on the shore of the Hellespont.

Examine Priam's address: you will find that the second word pronounced by the unfortunate monarch, is *πατρος*, *father;* the second thought in the same verse is a panegyric on the haughty chieftain, *θεοις επεικελ' Αχιλλευ*, *godlike Achilles.* Priam must do great violence to his feelings to speak in such terms to the murderer of Hector. All these traits discover a profound knowledge of the human heart.

The most affecting image that the unfortunate monarch could present to the violent son of Peleus, after reminding him of his father, was, without doubt, the age of that father. So far, Priam has not ventured to utter a word concerning himself, but suddenly an opportunity occurs, and he seizes it with the most moving simplicity. *Like me,* he says, *he approaches the termination of his career.* Thus Priam still avoids mentioning himself except in conjunction with Peleus, and he forces Achilles to view only his own father in the person of a suppliant and unfortunate king. The image of the forlorn situation of the aged monarch, *perhaps overwhelmed by powerful neighbors* during the absence of his son, —the picture of his affliction suddenly forgotten when he learns that his son is *full of life,*—finally, the transient sorrows of Peleus contrasted with the irreparable misfortunes of Priam,—all this displays an admirable mixture of grief, address, propriety, and dignity.

With what respectable and sacred skill does the venerable sovereign of Ilium afterward lead the haughty Achilles to listen, even with composure, to the praise of Hector himself! At first he takes care not to name the Trojan hero. *Yet one there was,* says he, without mentioning the name of Hector to his conqueror, till he has told him that *by his hand he fell while fighting for his country!*—

Τὸν σὺ πρώην κτεῖνας, ἀμυνόμενον περὶ πάτρης :

And then he adds the single word *Ἕκτορα, Hector.* It is very remarkable that this insulated name is not comprehended in the poetical period; it is introduced at the commencement of a verse, where it breaks the measure, surprises the eye and ear, forms a complete sense, and is wholly unconnected with what follows:—

Τὸν σὺ πρώην κτεῖνας, ἀμυνόμενον περὶ πάτρης,
Ἕκτορα.

Thus the son of Peleus is reminded of his vengeance before he recollects his enemy. Had Priam named Hector first, Achilles would at once have thought of Patroclus; but 'tis no longer Hector who is presented to his view, 'tis a mangled body, a disfigured corpse, consigned to the dogs and vultures; and even this is not shown to him without an excuse—ἀμυνόμενον περὶ πάτρης—*he fought for his country.* The pride of Achilles is gratified with having triumphed over one who had alone defended *his brothers and the walls of Troy.*

Lastly, Priam, after speaking of men to the son of Thetis, reminds him of the just gods, and once more leads him back to the recollection of Peleus. The trait which concludes the address of the Trojan monarch is most sublimely pathetic.

CHAPTER V.

CONTINUATION OF THE FATHER.

Lusignan.

We shall find in the tragedy of *Zara* a father to contrast with Priam. The two scenes, indeed, cannot be compared, either in point of arrangement, strength of design, or beauty of poetry; but the triumph of Christianity will on that account be only the more complete, since that religion is enabled by the charm of its recollections singly to sustain a competition with the mighty genius of Homer. Voltaire himself does not deny that he sought success in the power of this charm; since he thus writes in allusion to *Zara:*—"I shall endeavor to introduce into this piece whatever appears most pathetic and most interesting in the Christian religion."[1] This venerable Crusader, covered with glory, and bowed down with misfortune, steadfastly adhering to his religion in the solitude of a dungeon,—this Lusignan imploring a young enamored female to hearken to the voice of the God of her fathers,—presents a striking scene, the force of which lies entirely in its evangelical morality and Christian sentiments.

For thee, O God, and in thy glorious cause,
These threescore years old Lusignan hath fought,
But fought in vain; hath seen thy temple fall,
Thy goodness spurned, thy sacred right profaned.
For twenty summers in a dungeon hid,
With tears have I implored thee to protect
My children; thou hast given them to my wishes
And in my daughter now I find thy foe.
I am myself, alas! the fatal cause
Of thy lost faith; had I not been a slave . . .
But, O my daughter! thou dear, lovely object
Of all my cares, O think on the pure blood
Within thy veins,—the blood of twenty kings,
All Christians like myself, the blood of heroes,
Defenders of the faith, the blood of martyrs.

[1] *Œuvr. Complèt.* de Volt., tome 78; *Corresp. gen.*, Lett. 57, p. 119; edit. 1785.

Thou art a stranger to thy mother's fate;
Thou dost not know that, in the very moment
She gave thee birth, I saw her massacred
By those barbarians whose detested faith
Thou hast embraced: thy brothers, the dear martyrs,
Stretch forth their hands from heaven, and wish to embrace
A sister: O remember them! That God
Whom thou betrayest, for us and for mankind
Even in this place expired; where I so oft
Have fought for him, where now his blood by me
Calls loudly on thee. See yon temple, see
These walls: behold the sacred mountain where
Thy Saviour bled; the tomb whence he arose
Victorious; in each path, where'er thou tread'st
Shalt thou behold the footsteps of thy God.
Wilt thou renounce thy honor and thy father?
Wilt thou renounce thy Maker?[1]

A religion which furnishes its enemy with such beauties deserves at least to be heard before it be condemned. Antiquity affords nothing so interesting, because it had not such a religion. Polytheism, laying no restraint upon the passions, could not occasion those inward conflicts of the soul which are so common under the gospel dispensation, and produce the most affecting situations. The pathetic character of Christianity also strongly tends to heighten the charms of *Zara*. Were Lusignan to remind his daughter of nothing but the happy deities, the banquets and the joys of Olympus, all this would have but a very slight interest for her, and would only form a harsh contradiction to the tender emotions which the poet aims to excite. But the misfortunes of Lusignan, his blood, his sufferings, are blended with the misfortunes, the blood, and the sufferings, of Jesus Christ. Could Zara deny her Redeemer on the very spot where he gave himself a sacrifice for her? The cause of a father and the cause of God are mingled together; the venerable age of Lusignan and the blood of the martyrs exert the authority of religion; the mountain and the tomb both cry out. The place, the man, the divinity,—every thing is tragic in this picture.

[1] Voltaire's *Dramatic Works*, translated by Franklin, vol v. p. 36-38.

CHAPTER VI.

THE MOTHER.

Andromache.

"A VOICE was heard on high," says Jeremias,[1] "of lamentation, of mourning, and weeping, of Rachel weeping for her children, and refusing to be comforted because they are not." How beautiful is this expression—*because they are not!* It breathes all the tenderness of the mother.[2] Most assuredly, the religion which has consecrated such an expression must be thoroughly acquainted with the maternal heart.

Our veneration for the Virgin Mary, and the love of Jesus Christ for children, likewise prove that the spirit of Christianity has a tender sympathy with the character of mother. We here propose to open a new path for criticism, by seeking in the sentiments of a *pagan* mother, delineated by a modern author, those *Christian* traits which that author may have introduced into his picture without being aware of it himself. In order to demonstrate the influence of a moral or religious institution on the heart of man, it is not necessary that the instance adduced for this purpose should be selected from the more visible effects of that institution. 'Tis sufficient if it breathe its spirit; and thus it is that the *Elysium* of *Telemachus* is evidently a *Christian paradise.*

Now the most affecting sentiments of Racine's *Andromache* emanate for the most part from a *Christian* poet. The Andromache of the Iliad is the wife rather than the mother; that of Euripides is of a disposition at once servile and ambitious, which destroys the maternal character; that of Virgil is tender and melancholy, but has less of the mother than of the wife: the widow of Hector says not, *Astyanax ubi est*, but *Hector ubi est.*

---

[1] Jer. xxxi. 15.

[2] We know not why Sacy, in his French translation, has rendered *Rama*, by *Rama*, a town. The Hebrew *Rama* (whence comes the ῥάχμος of the Greeks) is applied to a branch of a tree, an arm of the sea, a chain of mountains. The latter is the signification of the Hebrew in this place, and the Vulgate, as seen in the context, has *vox in excelso.*

Racine's *Andromache* has greater sensibility, is more interesting in every respect, than the ancient *Andromache*. That verse which is so simple, yet so full of love,—

> Je ne l'ai point encore embrassé d'aujourd'hui,
>
> I've not yet kissed my child to-day,—

is the language of a Christian mother, and is not in accordance with the Grecian taste, still less that of the Romans.

Homer's *Andromache* deplores the future misery of Astyanax, but scarcely bestows a thought on his present condition. The mother, under the Christian dispensation, more tender without being less provident, sometimes forgets her sorrows while embracing her son. The ancients bestowed upon infancy no great portion of their attention; they seem to have considered swaddling-clothes and a cradle as too simple for their notice The God of the gospel alone was not ashamed to speak of the *little children*,[1] and to hold them up as an example to men. "And, taking a child, he set him in the midst of them. Whom when he had embraced, he saith unto them: Whosoever shall receive one such child in my name, receiveth me."[2]

When Hector's widow says to Cephisus, in Racine,—

> Qu'il ait de ses aieux un souvenir modeste;
> Il est du sang d'Hector, mais il en est le reste.
>
> Teach him with modesty to bear in mind
> His great forefathers he's of Hector's blood,
> But all of Hector's self that now survives,—

who does not perceive the Christian? 'Tis the *deposuit potentes de sede*—"He hath put down the mighty from their seat." Antiquity never speaks in this manner, for it imitates no sentiments but those of nature; but the sentiments expressed in these verses of Racine are not derived purely from nature; so far from this, they contradict the voice of the heart. Hector, in the Iliad, exhorts not his son to retain a modest remembrance of his forefathers Holding up Astyanax toward heaven, he exclaims:

> Ζευ ἄλλοι τε θεοὶ, δότε δὴ καὶ τόνδε γενεσθαι,
> Παῖδ ἔμὸν, ὡς καὶ ἐγώ περ, αριπρετεα Τρώεσσιν,
> Ωδε βιην, τ' ἀγαθὸν, καὶ 'Ιλίου ιφι ανάσσειν.
> Και ποτέ τὶς ἔιπησι, Πατρὸς δ' ὅγε πυλλὸν ἀμείνωι
> 'Εκ πολέμυ ἀνιόντα.

[1] Matt. xviii. 3. [2] Mark ix. 36-37.

O thou! whose glory fills th' ethereal throne,
And all ye deathless powers, protect my son!
Grant him, like me, to purchase just renown,
To guard the Trojans, to defend the crown,
Against his country's foes the war to wage,
And rise the Hector of the future age!
So, when triumphant from successful toils
Of heroes slain he bears the reeking spoils,
Whole hosts may hail him with deserved acclaim,
And say, This chief transcends his father's fame.[1]

Æneas says to Ascanius:—

Et te animo repetentem exempla tuorum,
Et pater Æneas, et avunculus excitet Hector.

Thou, when thy riper years shall send thee forth
To toils of war, be mindful of my worth:
Assert thy birthright, and in arms be known
For Hector's nephew, and Æneas' son.[2]

The modern Andromache, indeed, expresses herself nearly in the same manner respecting the ancestors of Astyanax. But after this line,

Tell by what feats they dignified their names,

she adds,

Tell what they did, rather than what they were.

Now, such precepts are in direct opposition to the suggestions of pride. We here behold amended nature—improved evangelical nature. This humility, which the Christian religion has introduced into the sentiments, and which, as we shall presently have occasion to observe, has changed the relation of the passions, runs through the whole character of the modern Andromache. When Hector's widow, in the Iliad, figures to herself the destiny that awaits her son, there is something mean in the picture which she draws of his future wretchedness. Humility in our religion speaks no such language; it is not less dignified than affecting. The Christian submits to the severest vicissitudes of life; but his resignation evidently springs from a principle of virtue, for he abases himself under the hand of God alone, and not under the hand of man. In fetters he retains his dignity; with a fidelity unmixed with fear, he despises the chains which he is to wear but for a moment, and from which Providence will soon release him;

[1] *Iliad*, b. vi., Pope's translation. [2] *Æneid*, b. xii., Dryden's translation.

he looks upon the things of this life as naught but dreams, and endures his condition without repining, because there is little difference in his eyes between liberty and servitude, prosperity and adversity, the diadem of the monarch and the livery of the slave.

CHAPTER VII.

THE SON.

Gusman.

THE dramatic works of Voltaire furnish us with the example of another Christian character—the character of the son. This is neither the docile Telemachus with Ulysses, nor the fiery Achilles with Peleus; it is a young man with strong passions, but who combats and subdues them by religion.

There is something very attractive in the tragedy of *Alzire*, though consistency of manners is not much observed. You here soar into those lovely regions of Christian morality, which, rising far above the morality of the vulgar, is of itself a divine poetry. The peace that reigns in the bosom of Alvarez is not the mere peace of nature. Let us figure to ourselves Nestor striving to moderate the passions of Antilochus. He would adduce examples of young men who have been undone because they would not listen to the counsels of their parents; then, following up these examples with a few trite maxims on the indocility of youth and the experience of age, he would crown his remonstrances with a panegyric on himself, and look back with regret on the days that are past.

The authority employed by Alvarez is of a very different kind. He makes no mention of his age and his paternal authority, that he may speak in the name of religion alone. He seeks not to dissuade Gusman from the commission of a *particular* crime; he preaches to him a *general* virtue, *charity*,—a kind of celestial humanity which the Son of man brought down with him to earth, where it was a stranger before his coming.[1] Finally,

[1] The ancients themselves owed to their religion the little humanity that is to be found among them. Hospitality, respect for the suppliant and the unfor-

Alvarez commanding his son as a *father*, and obeying him as a *subject*, is one of those traits of exalted morality as far superior to the morality of the ancients as the gospel surpasses the dialogues of Plato for the inculcation of the virtues.

Achilles mangles the body of his enemy and insults him when vanquished. Gusman is as proud as that hero; but, sinking beneath Zamor's dagger, expiring in the flower of youth, cut off at once from an adored wife and the command of a mighty empire, hear the sentence which he pronounces upon his rival and his murderer! behold the admirable triumph of religion and of paternal example over a Christian son!—

[*To Alvarez.*] My soul is on the wing,
And here she takes her flight, but waits to see
And imitate Alvarez. O my father!
The mask is off; death has at last unveiled
The hideous scene, and shown me to myself;
New light breaks in on my astonished soul:
Oh! I have been a proud, ungrateful being,
And trampled on my fellow-creatures! Heaven
Avenges earth: my life can ne'er atone
For half the blood I've shed. Prosperity
Had blinded Gusman; death's benignant hand
Restores my sight; I thank the instrument
Employed by heaven to make me what I am,—
A penitent. I yet am master here,
And yet can pardon: Zamor, I forgive thee;
Live and be free, but oh! remember how
A Christian acted, how a Christian died.

[*To Montezuma, who kneels to him.*]
Thou, Montezuma, and ye hapless victims
Of my ambition, say, my clemency
Surpassed my guilt, and let your sovereigns know
That we were born your conquerors.

[*To Zamor.*]
Observe the difference 'twixt thy gods and mine;
Thine teach thee to revenge an injury,
Mine bids me pity and forgive thee, Zamor.[1]

To what religion belongs this morality and this death? Here reigns an *ideal of truth* superior to every *poetic ideal.* When we

tunate, were the offspring of religious ideas. That the wretched might find some pity upon earth, it was necessary that Jupiter should declare himself their protector. Such is the ferocity of man without religion!

[1] Voltaire's *Works*, translated by Franklin, vol. vi. pp. 260, 261.

say an *ideal of truth*, it is no exaggeration; every reader knows that the concluding verses—

Observe the difference 'twixt thy gods and mine, &c.—

are the very expressions of François de Guise.[1] As for the rest of this passage, it comprehends the whole substance of the morality of the gospel:—

Death has at last unveiled
The hideous scene, and shown me to myself. . . .
Oh! I have been a proud, ungrateful being,
And trampled on my fellow-creatures!

One trait alone in this piece has not the stamp of Christianity It is this:—

Let your sovereigns know
That we were born your conquerors.

Here Voltaire meant to make nature and Gusman's haughty character burst forth again. The dramatic intention is happy, but, taken as an abstract beauty, the idea expressed in these lines is very low amid the lofty sentiments with which it is surrounded. Such is invariably the appearance of *mere nature* by the side of *Christian nature.* Voltaire is very ungrateful for calumniating that religion which furnished him with such pathetic scenes and with his fairest claims to immortality. He ought constantly to have borne in mind these lines, composed, no doubt, under an involuntary impulse of admiration:—

Can Christians boast
Of such exalted virtue? 'twas inspired
By heaven. The Christian law must be divine.

Can they, we may add, boast of so much *genius*, of so *many poetic beauties?*

---

[1] It is not so generally known that Voltaire, in making use of the expression of François de Guise, has borrowed the words from another poet. Rowe had previously availed himself of this incident in his *Tamerlane*, and the author of *Alzira* has been content to translate the passage *verbatim* from the English dramatist:

Now learn the difference 'twixt thy faith and mine. . . .
Thine bids thee lift thy dagger to my throat;
Mine can forgive the wrong, and bid thee live.

CHAPTER VIII.

THE DAUGHTER.

Iphigenia and Zara.

For the character of the *Daughter*, *Iphigenia* and *Zara* will supply us with an interesting parallel. Both, under the constraint of paternal authority, devote themselves to the religion of their country. Agamemnon, it is true, requires of Iphigenia the twofold sacrifice of her love and of her life, and Lusignan requires Zara to forget the former alone; but for a female passionately in love to live and renounce the object of her affections is perhaps a harder task than to submit to death itself. The two situations, therefore, may possess nearly an equal degree of *natural* interest. Let us see whether they are the same in regard to *religious* interest.

Agamemnon, in paying obedience to the gods, does no more, after all, than immolate his daughter to his ambition. Why should the Greek virgin bow submissive to Jupiter? Is he not a tyrant whom she must detest? The spectator sides with Iphigenia against Heaven. Pity and terror, therefore, spring solely from *natural* considerations; and if you could retrench religion from the piece, it is evident that the theatrical effect would remain the same.

In *Zara*, on the contrary, if you meddle with the religion you destroy the whole. Jesus Christ is not bloodthirsty. He requires no more than the sacrifice of a passion. Has he a right to demand this sacrifice? Ah! who can doubt it? Was it not to redeem Zara that he was nailed to the cross, that he endured insult, scorn, and the injustice of men, that he drank the cup of bitterness to the very dregs? Yet was Zara about to give her heart and her hand to those who persecuted this God of charity! —to those who daily sacrificed the professors of his religion!—to those who detained in fetters that venerable successor of Bouillon, —that defender of the faith, the *father* of Zara! Certainly religion is not useless here, and he who would suppress that would annihilate the piece.

Zara, as a *tragedy*, is, in our opinion, more interesting than *Iphigenia*, for a reason which we shall endeavor to explain. This obliges us to recur to the principles of the art.

It is certain that the characters of tragedy ought to be taken from the upper ranks alone of society. This rule is the result of certain proprieties which are known to the fine arts as well as to the human heart. The picture of the sorrows which we ourselves experience pains without interesting or instructing us. We need not go to the theatre to learn the secrets of our own family. Can fiction please us when sad reality dwells beneath our roof? No moral is attached to such an imitation. On the contrary, when we behold the picture of our condition, we sink into despair, or we envy a state that is not our own, and in which we imagine that happiness exclusively resides. Take the lower classes to the theatre. They seek not there men of straw or representations of their own indigence, but persons of distinguished rank, invested with the purple. Their ears would fain be filled with illustrious names, and their eyes engaged with the misfortunes of kings.

Morality, curiosity, the dignity of art, refined taste, and perhaps nature, envious of man, impose the necessity, therefore, of selecting the characters for tragedy from the more elevated ranks of society. But, though the person should be *distinguished*, his distresses ought to be *common;* that is to say, of such a nature as to be felt by all. Now it is in this point that *Zara* seems to us more affecting than *Iphigenia*.

When the daughter of Agamemnon is doomed to die to facilitate the departure of a fleet, the spectator can scarcely feel interested by such a motive; but in *Zara* the reason is brought home to the heart, and every one can appreciate the struggle between a passion and a duty. Hence is derived that grand rule of the drama, that the interest of tragedy must be founded, not upon a *thing*, but upon a *sentiment*, and that the character should be remote from the spectator by his rank, but near to him by his misfortune.

We might now examine the subject of Iphigenia, as it has been handled by the Christian pen of Racine; but the reader can pursue this consideration at his discretion. We shall make only one observation.

Father Brumoy remarks that Euripides, in ascribing to Iphigenia a horror of death and a desire to escape it, has adhered more closely to nature than Racine, whose Iphigenia seems too resigned. The observation is good in itself, but Brumoy overlooked the circumstance that the modern Iphigenia is the *Christian daughter.* Her father and Heaven have commanded, and nothing now remains but to obey. Racine has given this courage to his heroine merely from the secret influence of a religious institution, which has changed the groundwork of ideas and of morals. Here Christianity goes farther than nature, and consequently harmonizes better with poetry, which aggrandizes objects and is fond of exaggeration. The daughter of Agamemnon banishing her fears and attachment to life is a much more interesting character than Iphigenia deploring her fate. We are not affected only by what is natural. The fear of death is natural to man; yet he who laments his own approaching death excites no great compassion around him. The human heart desires more than it accomplishes. It is chiefly prone to admiration, and feels a secret impetus toward that unknown beauty for which it was originally formed.

Such is the constitution of the Christian religion that it is itself a kind of poetry, viewing, as it does, every character in its beau-ideal. Witness, for instance, the representation of martyrs by our painters, of knights by our poets, &c. The portraiture of vice is susceptible of as much strength and vividness from the Christian pen as that of virtue; because the heinousness of crime is in proportion to the number of bonds which the guilty man has broken asunder. The Muses, therefore, who are averse to mediocrity, find ample resources in that religion which always exhibits its characters above or below the ordinary standard of humanity.

To complete the circle of the *natural* characters, we should treat of fraternal affection; but all that we have said concerning the *son* and the *daughter* is equally applicable to two *brothers*, or to *brother* and *sister.* For the rest, we find in the Bible the history of Cain and Abel, the great and first tragedy that the world beheld; and we shall speak in another place of Joseph and his brethren.

Finally, the Christian religion, while it deprives the poet of none of the advantages enjoyed by antiquity for the delineation of the *natural* characters, offers him, in addition, all its *influence* in those same characters, necessarily augments his *power* by increasing his *means*, and multiplies the *beauties* of the drama by multiplying the sources from which they spring.

CHAPTER IX.

SOCIAL CHARACTERS.

The Priest.

THOSE characters which we have denominated *social* are reduced by the poet to two—the *priest* and the *soldier*. Had we not set apart the fourth division of our work for the history of the clergy and the benefits which they confer, it would be an easy task to show here how far superior, in point of variety and grandeur, is the character of the Christian priest to that of the priest of polytheism. What exquisite pictures might be drawn, from the pastor of the rustic hamlet to the pontiff whose brows are encircled with the papal tiara; from the parish priest of the city to the anchoret of the rock; from the Carthusian and the inmate of La Trappe to the learned Benedictine; from the missionary, and the multitude of religious devoted to the alleviation of all the ills that afflict humanity, to the inspired prophet of ancient Sion! The order of virgins is not less varied or numerous, nor less varied in its pursuits. Those daughters of charity who consecrate their youth and their charms to the service of the afflicted,—those inhabitants of the cloister who, under the protection of the altar, educate the future wives of men, while they congratulate themselves on their own union with a heavenly spouse,—this whole innocent family is in admirable correspondence with the nine sisters of fable. Antiquity presented nothing more to the poet than a high-priest, a sorcerer, a vestal, a sibyl. These characters, more over, were but accidentally introduced; whereas the Christian priest is calculated to act one of the most important parts in the epic.

M. de la Harpe has shown in his *Melanie* what effects may be produced with the character of a village curate when delineated by an able hand. Shakspeare, Richardson, Goldsmith, have brought the priest upon the stage with more or less felicity. As to external pomp, what religion was ever accompanied with ceremonies so magnificent as ours? Corpus Christi day, Christmas, Holy-week, Easter, All-souls, the funeral ceremony, the Mass, and a thousand other rites, furnish an inexhaustible subject for splendid or pathetic descriptions.[1] The modern muse that complains of Christianity cannot certainly be acquainted with its riches. Tasso has described a procession in the *Jerusalem*, and it is one of the finest passages in his poem. In short, the ancient sacrifice itself is not banished from the Christian subject; for nothing is more easy than, by means of an episode, a comparison, or a retrospective view, to introduce a sacrifice of the ancient covenant.

CHAPTER X.

CONTINUATION OF THE PRIEST.

The Sibyl—Joiada—Parallel between Virgil and Racine.

ÆNEAS goes to consult the Sibyl. Having reached the aperture of the cavern, he awaits the awful words of the prophetess. He soothes her with a prayer. The Sibyl still struggles. At length the god overpowers her. The hundred doors of the cavern open with a tremendous noise, and these words float in the air: "Oh thou who hast at last completed thy mighty dangers upon the ocean!"

What vehemence, when the god begins to agitate the Sibyl! Take notice of the rapidity of these turns: *Deus! ecce Deus!* She touches—she grapples with—the spirit. *The God! behold*

---

[1] We shall treat of all these ceremonies in another part of our work.

the God! is her exclamation. These expressions—*non vultus, non color unus*—admirably delineate the agitation of the prophetess. Virgil is remarkable for his negative turns of expression; and it may be observed in general that they are very numerous in writers of a pensive genius. May it not be that souls endowed with the finer sensibilities are naturally inclined to complain, to desire, to doubt, to express themselves with a kind of timidity; and that complaint, desire, doubt, and timidity, are *privations* of something? The feeling mind does not positively say, *I am familiar with adversity;* but characterizes itself, like Dido, as *non ignara mali, not unacquainted with evil.* In short, the favorite images of the pensive poets are almost always borrowed from negative objects, as the silence of night, the shade of the forests, the solitude of the mountains, the peace of the tombs, which are nothing but the absence of noise, of light, of men, and of the tumults and storms of life.[1]

However exquisite the beauty of Virgil's verse may be, Christian poetry exhibits something superior. The high-priest of the Hebrews, ready to crown Joas, is seized with the divine spirit in the temple of Jerusalem :—

> Behold, Eternal Wisdom! in thy cause
> What champions arm themselves,—children and priests!
> But if the Almighty smile, who can resist them?
> When he commands, the grave resigns its tenants;

---

[1] Thus, Euryalus, speaking of his mother, says—

> *Genetrix* . . . .
> . . . . *Quam miseram tenuit* non *Ilia tellus,*
> *Mecum excedentem* non *mœnia regis Acestæ.*

"My unfortunate mother, who determined to accompany me, and whom *neither* her native soil *nor* the walls of the king of Acesta had the power to detain."

A moment afterward he adds—

> Nequeam *lacrymas perferre parentis.*
> "I could *not* resist the tears of my mother."

Volscens is preparing to despatch Euryalus when Nisus exclaims—

> *Me, me, (adsum qui feci,)*
> . . . . . *Mea fraus omnis.* Nihil *iste* nec *ausus,*
> Nec *potuit.*
> "Mine, mine is all the fault: *nothing* durst he, *nor* could he, do."

The conclusion of this admirable episode is also of a negative character.

'Tis he who wounds and heals, destroys and saves!
They trust not, as thou seest, in their own merits,
But in thy name so oft by them invoked,
In oaths sworn by thee to their holiest king,
And in this temple, with thy presence crowned,
Which, like the sun, from age to age shall last.
  What holy awe is this that thrills my heart?
Is it the Spirit Divine that seizes on me?
'Tis He himself! He fires my breast, he speaks;
My eyes are opened, and dark, distant ages
Spring forth to view! . . . .
Hearken, O Heavens! thou Earth, attention keep!
O Jacob, say no more thy God doth sleep.
Vanish, ye sinners, and with terror fly,
The Lord awakes, arrayed in majesty!
. . . .
How into drossy lead is changed the gold!
Who is that bleeding priest I there behold?
Jerusalem, thou faithless city, weep,
Who in thy prophet's blood thy sword dost steep.
Thy God hath banished all his former love,
And odious now thy fuming odors prove.
Ah! whither are those youths and women driven?
The Queen of cities is destroyed by Heaven;
Her captive priests and kings to strangers bow,
And God her solemn pomp no longer will allow.
Ye towering cedars, burn; thou temple, fall,
And in one common ruin mingle all.
  Jerusalem, dear object of my grief,
What daring hand thy strength disarms
And in one day has ravished all thy charms?
  Oh that, to give me some relief,
Mine eyes could like two fountains flow,
With never-ceasing streams to weep thy wo![1]

This passage requires no comment.

As Virgil and Racine recur so frequently in our criticisms, let us endeavor to form a just idea of their talents and their genius. These two great poets so nearly resemble each other, that they might deceive the eyes of the Muse herself, like those twins mentioned in the Æneid, who occasioned their own mother agreeable mistakes.

Both of them carefully polish their works; they are both full of taste, bold, yet natural in expression; sublime in the portrayal of love, and, as if one had followed the other step by step,

[1] *Athalie*, act iii. scene vii. From Duncombe's translation.

Racine has introduced into his *Esther* a certain sweetness of melody, with which Virgil has, in like manner, filled his second eclogue. The difference, however, in their respective strains is that which exists between the voice of a tender maiden and that of a youth, between the sighs of innocence and those of sinful love.

These are, perhaps, the points in which Virgil and Racine resemble each other; the following are, perhaps, those in which they differ.

The latter is in general superior to the former in the invention of character. Agamemnon, Achilles, Orestes, Mithridates, Acomates, are far superior to all the heroes of the *Æneid.* Æneas and Turnus are not finely drawn, except in two or three passages. Mezentius alone is boldly delineated.

In the soft and tender scenes, however, Virgil bursts forth in all his genius. Evander, the venerable monarch of Arcadia, living beneath a roof of thatch, and defended by two shepherds' dogs on the very spot where, at a future period, will rise the magnificent residence of the Cæsars, surrounded by the Prætorian guard; the youthful Pallas; the comely Lausus, the virtuous son of a guilty father; and, lastly, Nisus and Euryalus, are characters perfectly divine.

In the delineation of females Racine resumes the superiority. Agrippina is more ambitious than Amata, and Phædra more impassioned than Dido.

We shall say nothing of *Athalie,* because in this piece Racine stands unrivalled; it is the most perfect production of genius inspired by religion.

In another particular, however, Virgil has the advantage over Racine; he is more pensive, more melancholy. Not that the author of *Phædra* would have been incapable of producing this melody of sighs. The *role* of *Andromache, Berenice* throughout, some stanzas of hymns in imitation of the Bible, several strophes of the choruses in *Esther* and *Athalie,* exhibit the powers which he possessed in this way. But he lived too much in society, and too little in solitude. The court of Louis XIV., though it refined his taste and gave him the majesty of forms, was, perhaps, detrimental to him in other respects; it placed him at too great a distance from nature and rural simplicity.

We have already remarked[1] that one of the principal causes of Virgil's melancholy was, doubtless, the sense of the hardships which he had undergone in his youth. Though driven from his home, the memory of his Mantua was never to be effaced. But he was no longer the Roman of the republic, loving his country in the harsh and rugged manner of a Brutus; he was the Roman of the monarchy of Augustus, the rival of Homer, and the nursling of the Muses.

Virgil cultivated this germ of melancholy by living in solitude. To this circumstance must, perhaps, be added some others of a personal nature. Our moral or physical defects have a powerful influence upon our temper, and are frequently the secret origin of the predominant feature of our character. Virgil had a difficulty in pronunciation,[2] a weakly constitution, and rustic appearance. He seems in his youth to have had strong passions; and these natural imperfections, perhaps, proved obstacles to their indulgence. Thus, family troubles, the love of a country life, wounded self-love, and passions debarred of gratification, concurred in giving him that tincture of melancholy which charms us in his productions.

We meet with no such thing in Racine as the *Diis aliter visum* —the *Dulces moriens reminiscitur Argos*—the *Disce puer virtutem ex me, fortunam ex aliis*—the *Lyrnessi domus alta: sola Laurente sepulchrum.* It may not, perhaps, be superfluous to observe that almost all these expressions fraught with melancholy occur in the last six books of the *Æneid,* as well as the episodes of Evander and Pallas, Mezentius and Lausus, and Nisus and Euryalus. It would seem that as he approached the tomb the Mantuan bard transfused something more divine than ever into his strains; like those swans of the Eurotas, consecrated to the Muses, which just before they expired were favored, according to Pythagoras, with an inward view of Olympus, and manifested their pleasure by strains of melody.

Virgil is the friend of the solitary, the companion of the private hours of life. Racine is, perhaps, superior to the Latin poet, because he was the author of *Athalie;* but in the latter

[1] Part I., book v., chap. 14.

[2] *Sermone tardissimum, ac pene indocto similem . . . . . . facie rusticanâ,* &c. Donat., *de P. Virg. vit.*

there is something that excites softer emotions in the heart. We feel greater admiration for the one, greater love for the other The sorrows depicted by the first are too royal; the second addresses himself more to all ranks of society. On surveying the pictures of human vicissitudes delineated by Racine, we may imagine ourselves wandering in the deserted parks of Versailles; they are vast and dull, but amid the growing solitude we perceive the regular hand of art and the vestiges of former grandeur:—

> Naught meets the eye but towers reduced to ashes,
> A river tinged with blood, and desert plains.

The pictures of Virgil, without possessing less dignity, are not confined to certain prospects of life. They represent all nature; they embrace the solitudes of the forests, the aspect of the mountains, the shores of ocean, where exiled females fix their weeping eyes on its boundless billows:—

> Cunctæque profundum
> Pontum adspectabant flentes.

CHAPTER XI.

THE WARRIOR—DEFINITION OF THE BEAUTIFUL IDEAL.

THE heroic ages are favorable to poetry, because they have that antiquity and that uncertainty of tradition which are required by the Muses, naturally somewhat addicted to fiction. We daily behold extraordinary events without taking any interest in them; but we listen with delight to the relation of the obscure facts of a distant period. The truth is, that the greatest events in this world are extremely little in themselves: the mind, sensible of this defect in human affairs, and tending incessantly toward immensity, wishes to behold them only through an indistinct medium, that it may magnify their importance.

Now, the spirit of the heroic ages is formed by the union of an imperfect civilization with a religious system at the highest point of its influence. Barbarism and polytheism produced the heroes of Homer; from barbarism and Christianity arose the knights of Tasso.

Which of the two—the *heroes* or the *knights*—deserve the preference either in morals or in poetry? This is a question that it may not be amiss to examine.

Setting aside the particular genius of the two poets, and comparing only man with man, the characters of the *Jerusalem* appear to us superior to those of the *Iliad*.

What a vast difference, in fact, between those knights so ingenuous, so disinterested, so humane, and those perfidious, avaricious, ferocious warriors of antiquity, who insulted the lifeless remains of their enemies,—as poetical by their vices as the former were by their virtues!

If by heroism is meant an effort against the passions in favor of virtue, then, most assuredly, Godfrey is the genuine hero, not Agamemnon. Now, we would ask how it happens that Tasso, in delineating his characters, has exhibited the pattern of the perfect soldier, while Homer, in representing the men of the heroic ages, has produced but a species of monsters? The reason is, that Christianity, ever since its first institution, has furnished the beau-ideal in morals, or the beau-ideal of character, while polytheism was incapable of bestowing this important advantage on the Grecian bard. We request the reader's attention for a moment to this subject; it is of too much consequence to the main design of our work not to be placed in its clearest light.

There are two kinds of the *beautiful ideal*, the moral and the physical, both of which are the offspring of society, and to both such people as are but little removed from the state of nature—the savages, for instance—are utter strangers. They merely aim in their songs at giving a faithful representation of what they see. As they live in the midst of deserts, their pictures are noble and simple; you find in them no marks of bad taste, but then they are monotonous, and the sentiments which they express never rise to heroism.

The age of Homer was already remote from those early times. When a savage pierces a roebuck with his arrows, strips off the skin in the recess of the forest, lays his victim upon the coals of a burning oak, every circumstance in this action is poetic. But in the tent of Achilles there are already bowls, spits, vessels. A few more details, and Homer would have sunk into meanness in his descriptions, or he must have entered the path of the beautiful ideal by beginning to *conceal.*

Thus, in proportion as society multiplied the wants of life, poets learned that they ought not, as in past times, to exhibit every circumstance to the eye, but to throw a veil over certain parts of the picture.

Having advanced this first step, they perceived that it was likewise necessary to select; and then that the object selected was susceptible of a more beautiful form, or produced a more agreeable effect in this or in that position.

Continuing thus to *hide* and to *select,* to *add* and to *retrench,* they gradually attained to forms which ceased to be natural, but which were more perfect than nature; by artists these forms were denominated the *beautiful ideal.*

The *beautiful ideal* may, therefore, be defined the art of *selecting* and *concealing.*

This definition is equally applicable to the beautiful ideal in the moral and to that in the physical order. The latter consists in the dexterous concealment of the weak part of objects; the former in hiding certain foibles of the soul—for the soul has its low wants and blemishes as well as the body.

Here we cannot forbear remarking that naught but man is susceptible of being represented more perfect than nature, and, as it were, approaching to the Divinity. Who ever thought of delineating the *beautiful ideal* of a horse, an eagle, or a lion? We behold here an admirable proof of the grandeur of our destiny and the immortality of the soul.

That society in which morals first reached their complete development must have been the first to attain the *beautiful moral ideal,* or, what amounts to the same thing, the *beautiful ideal of character.* Now, such was eminently the case with that portion of mankind who were formed under the Christian dispensation. It is not more strange than true that, while our forefathers were barbarous in every other respect, morals had, by means of the gospel, been raised to the highest degree of perfection among them; so that there existed men who, if we may be allowed the expression, were at the same time savages in body and civilized in mind.

This circumstance constitutes the beauty of the ages of chivalry, and gives them a superiority over the heroic as well as over modern times.

If you undertake to delineate the early ages of Greece, you will be as much shocked by their rudeness of character as you will be pleased with the simplicity of their manners. Polytheism furnishes no means of correcting barbarous nature and supplying the deficiencies of the primitive virtues.

If, on the other hand, you wish to sketch a modern age, you will be obliged to banish all truth from your work, and to adopt both the beautiful *moral* ideal and the beautiful *physical* ideal. Too remote from nature and from religion in every respect, you could not faithfully depict the interior of our families, and still less the secret of our hearts.

Chivalry alone presents the charming mixture of *truth* and *fiction.*

In the first place, you may exhibit a picture of manners accurately copied from nature. An ancient castle, a spacious hall, a blazing fire, jousts, tournaments, hunting parties, the sound of the horn, and the clangor of arms, have nothing that offends against taste, nothing that ought to be either *selected* or *concealed.*

In the next place, the Christian poet, more fortunate than Homer, is not compelled to tarnish his picture by introducing into it the barbarous or the *natural* man; Christianity offers him the perfect hero.

Thus, while we see Tasso merged in nature for the description of physical objects, he rises above nature for the perfection of those in the moral order.

Now, *nature* and the *ideal* are the two great sources of all poetic interest—the *pathetic* and the *marvellous.*

CHAPTER XII.

THE WARRIOR, (CONTINUED.)

We shall now show that the virtues of the knights which exalt their character to the *beautiful ideal* are truly Christian virtues.

If they were but mere moral virtues, invented by the poet, they would have neither action nor elasticity. We have an instance of this kind in Æneas, whom Virgil has made a philosophic hero.

The purely moral virtues are essentially frigid; they imply not something added to the soul, but something retrenched from it; it is the absence of vice rather than the presence of virtue.[1]

The religious virtues have wings; they are highly impassioned. Not content with abstaining from evil, they are anxious to do good. They possess the activity of love; they reside in a superior region, the objects in which appear somewhat magnified. Such were the virtues of chivalry.

Faith or fidelity was the first virtue of the knights; faith is, in like manner, the first virtue of Christianity.

The knight never told a lie. Here is the Christian.

The knight was poor, and the most disinterested of men. Here you see the disciple of the gospel.

The knight travelled through the world, assisting the widow and the orphan. Here you behold the charity of Jesus Christ.

The knight possessed sensibility and delicacy. What could have given him these amiable qualities but a humane religion which invariably inculcates respect for the weak? With what benignity does Christ himself address the women in the gospel!

Agamemnon brutally declares that he loves Briseïs as dearly as his wife, because she is not less skilful in ornamental works. Such is not the language of a knight.

Finally, Christianity has produced that valor of modern heroes which is so far superior to that of the heroes of antiquity.

---

[1] The distinction between moral and religious virtues is not exact. The author would have written more correctly on this point by using the word *natural* instead of *moral*. T.

The true religion teaches us that the merit of a man should be measured not by bodily strength, but by greatness of soul. Hence the weakest of the knights never quakes in presence of an enemy; and, though certain to meet death, he has not even a thought of flight.

This exalted valor is become so common that the lowest of our private soldiers is more courageous than an Ajax, who fled before Hector, who in his turn ran away from Achilles. As to the clemency of the Christian knight toward the vanquished, who can deny that it springs from Christianity?

Modern poets have borrowed a multitude of new characters from the chivalrous age. In *tragedy*, it will be sufficient to mention Tancred, Nemours, Couci, and that Nerestan who brings the ransom of his brethren in arms at a moment when all hope of his return has fled, and surrenders himself a prisoner because he cannot pay the sum required for his own redemption. How beautiful these Christian morals! Let it not be said that this is a purely poetical invention; there are a hundred instances of Christians who have resigned themselves into the hands of infidels, either to deliver other Christians, or because they were unable to raise the sum which they had promised.

Everybody knows how favorable chivalry is to the epic poem. How admirable are all the knights of the *Jerusalem Delivered!* Rinaldo so brilliant, Tancred so generous, the venerable Raymond de Toulouse, always dejected and always cheered again! You are among them beneath the walls of Solyma; you hear the young Bouillon, speaking of Armida, exclaim, "What will they say at the court of France when it is known that we have refused our aid to beauty?" To be convinced at once of the immense difference between Homer's heroes and those of Tasso, cast your eyes upon Godfrey's camp and the ramparts of Jerusalem. Here are the knights, there the heroes of antiquity. Solyman himself appears to advantage only because the poet has given him some traits of the generosity of the chevalier; so that even the principal hero of the infidels borrows his majesty from Christianity

But in Godfrey we admire the perfection of the heroic character. When Æneas would escape the seduction of a female, he fixed his eyes on the ground, *immota tenebat lumina;* he concealed his agitation, and gave vague replies: "O queen, I deny not thy favors; I shall ever remember Elisa." Not thus does the Christian chieftain listen to the addresses of Armida. He resists, for too well is he acquainted with the frail allurements of this world; he pursues his flight toward heaven, *like the glutted bird, heedless of the specious food which invites him.*

> Qual saturo augel, che nôn si cali,
> Ove il cibo mostrando, altri l'invita.

In combat, in deliberation, in appeasing a sedition, in every situation, Bouillon is great, is august. Ulysses strikes Thersites with his sceptre, and stops the Greeks when running to their ships. This is natural and picturesque. But behold Godfrey singly showing himself to an enraged army, which accuses him of having caused the assassination of a hero! What noble and impressive beauty in the prayer of this captain, so proudly conscious of his virtue! and how this prayer afterward heightens the intrepidity of the warrior, who, unarmed and bareheaded, meets a mutinous soldiery!

In battle, a sacred and majestic valor, unknown to the warriors of Homer and Virgil, animates the Christian hero. Æneas, protected by his divine armor, and standing on the stern of his galley as it approaches the Rutulian shore, is in a fine epic attitude; Agamemnon, like the thundering Jupiter, displays an image replete with grandeur; but in the last canto of the *Jerusalem*, Godfrey is described in a manner not inferior either to the progenitor of the Cæsars or to the leader of the Atrides.

The sun has just risen, and the armies have taken their position. The banners wave in the wind, the plumes float on the helmets; the rich caparisons of the horses, and the steel and gold armor of the knights, glisten in the first rays of the orb of day. Mounted on a swift charger, Godfrey rides through the ranks of his army; he harangues his followers, and his address is a model of military eloquence. A glory surrounds his head; his face beams with unusual splendor; the angel of victory covers him with his wings. Profound silence ensues. The prostrate legions adore that Almighty who caused the great Goliah to fall by the hand of a youthful shepherd. The trumpets suddenly sound the charge; the Christian soldiers rise, and, invigorated by the strength of the God of Hosts, rush, undaunted, and confident of victory, upon the hostile battalions of the Saracens.

BOOK III

OF POETRY CONSIDERED IN ITS RELATIONS TO MAN—THE SUBJECT CONTINUED.

The Passions.

CHAPTER I.

CHRISTIANITY HAS CHANGED THE RELATIONS OF THE PASSIONS, BY CHANGING THE BASIS OF VICE AND VIRTUE.

FROM the examination of *characters*, we come to that of the *passions*. It is obvious that in treating of the former it was impossible to avoid touching a little upon the latter, but here we purpose to enter more largely into the subject. If there existed a religion whose essential quality it was to oppose a barrier to the passions of man, it would of necessity increase the operation of those passions in the drama and the epopee; it would, from its very nature, be more favorable to the delineation of sentiment than any other religious institution, which, unacquainted with the errors of the heart, would act upon us only by means of external objects. Now, here lies the great advantage which Christianity possesses over the religions of antiquity: it is a heavenly wind which fills the sails of virtue and multiplies the storms of conscience in opposition to vice.

Since the proclamation of the gospel, the foundations of morals have changed among men, at least among Christians. Among the ancients, for example, humility was considered as meanness and pride as magnanimity; among Christians, on the contrary, pride is the first of vices and humility the chief of virtues. This single change of principles displays human nature in a new light, and we cannot help discovering in the passions shades that were not perceived in them by the ancients.

With us, then, *vanity* is the root of evil, and *charity* the source of good; so that the vicious passions are invariably a compound of pride, and the virtuous passions a compound of love.

Apply this principle, and you will be convinced of its truth. Why are all the passions allied to courage more pleasing among the moderns than among the ancients? Why have we given another character to valor, and transformed a brutal impulse into a virtue? Because with this impulse has been associated humility. From this combination has arisen *magnanimity* or *poetic generosity*, a species of passion (for to that length it was carried by the knights) to which the ancients were utter strangers.

One of our most delightful sentiments, and perhaps the only one that absolutely belongs to the soul, (for all the others have some admixture of sense in their nature or their object,) is friendship. How wonderfully has Christianity heightened the charms of this celestial passion, by giving it charity for its foundation! St. John was the disciple whom Jesus loved, and, before he expired on the cross, friendship heard him pronounce those words truly worthy of a God:—"*Woman, behold thy son!*" said he to his mother, and to the disciple, "*Behold thy mother!*"

Christianity, which has revealed our twofold nature and laid open the contradictions of our being and the good and bad of our heart, which, like ourselves, is full of contrasts,—exhibiting to us an incarnate God, an infant who is at the same time the ruler of the spheres, the Creator of the universe receiving life from a creature,—Christianity, we say, viewed in this light of contrasts, is super-eminently the religion of friendship. This sentiment is strengthened as much by oppositions as by resemblances. That two men may be perfect friends, they must incessantly, in some way, attract and repel one another; they must have genius of equal power, but of a different kind; contrary opinions, but similar principles; different antipathies and partialities, but at the bottom the same sensibility; opposite tempers, and yet like tastes: in a word, great contrasts of character and great harmonies of heart.

This genial warmth which *charity* communicates to the virtuous passions imparts to them a divine character. Among the ancients, the reign of the affections terminated with the grave: here every thing suffered shipwreck. Friends, brothers, husband

and wife, parted at the gates of death, and felt that their separation was eternal. The height of their felicity consisted in mingling their ashes together; but how mournful must have been an urn containing naught but recollections! Polytheism had fixed man in the regions of the past; Christianity has placed him in the domain of hope. The joys derived from virtuous sentiments on earth are but a foretaste of the bliss that is reserved for us. The principle of our friendships is not in this world: two beings who mutually love each other here below are only on the road to heaven, where they will arrive together if virtue be their guide; so that this strong expression employed by the poets—*to transfuse your soul into that of your friend*—is literally true in respect of two Christians. In quitting their bodies, they merely disencumber themselves of an obstacle which prevented their more intimate union, and their souls fly to be commingled in the bosom of the Almighty.

It must not be supposed, however, that Christianity, in revealing to us the foundations upon which rest the passions of men, has stripped life of its enchantments. Far from sullying the imagination by allowing it to indulge in unbounded curiosity, it has drawn the veil of doubt and obscurity over things which it is useless for us to know; and in this it has shown its superiority over that false philosophy which is too eager to penetrate into the nature of man and to fathom the bottom of every thing. We should not be continually sounding the abysses of the heart; the truths which it contains belong to the number of those that require half light and perspective. It is highly imprudent to be incessantly applying our judgment to the loving part of our being, to transfer the reasoning spirit to the passions. This curiosity gradually leads us to doubt of every thing generous and noble; it extinguishes the sensibilities, and, as it were, murders the soul. The mysteries of the heart are like those of ancient Egypt; every profane person who strives to penetrate into their secrets without being initiated by religion, as a just punishment for his audacity is suddenly struck dead.

CHAPTER II.

IMPASSIONED LOVE.

Dido.

WHAT in our times we properly call love is a sentiment the very name of which was unknown to remote antiquity. That mixture of the senses and of the soul,—that species of love of which friendship is the moral element,—is the growth of modern ages. To Christianity also we are indebted for this sentiment in its refined state; for Christianity, invariably tending to purify the heart, has found means to transfuse spirituality even into the passion that seemed least susceptible of it. Here, then, is a new source of poetic description, with which this much reviled religion has furnished the very authors who insult it. In numberless novels may be seen the beauties that have been elicited from this demi-christian passion. The character of Clementina in *Sir Charles Grandison*, for instance, is one of those master-pieces of composition of which antiquity affords no example. But let us penetrate into this subject: let us first consider *impassioned love*, and afterward take a view of *rural love*.

The first kind of love is neither as pure as conjugal affection nor as graceful as the sentiment of the shepherd, but fiercer than either; it ravages the soul in which it reigns. Resting neither upon the gravity of marriage nor upon the innocence of rural manners, and blending no other spells with its own, it becomes its own illusion, its own insanity, its own substance. Unknown by the too busy mechanic and the too simple husbandman, this passion exists only in those ranks of society where want of employment leaves us oppressed with the whole weight of our heart, together with its immense self-love and its everlasting inquietudes.

So true is it that Christianity sheds a brilliant light into the abyss of our passions, that the orators of the pulpit have been most successful in delineating the excesses of the human heart and painting them in the strongest and most impressive colors. What a picture has Bourdaloue drawn of ambition! How Massillon has penetrated into the inmost recesses of our souls, and drawn forth our passions and our vices into open day! "It is the character of this passion," observes that eloquent preacher, when speaking of love, "to fill the whole heart: we can think of nothing else; it absorbs, it intoxicates us; we find it wherever we are; there is nothing but what revives its fatal images, but what awakens its unjust desires. Society and solitude, presence and absence, the most indifferent objects and the most serious occupations, the holy temple itself, the sacred altars, the awful mysteries of religion, renew its recollections."[1]

"It is culpable," says the same preacher in another place,[2] "to love for its own sake what cannot tend to our felicity, our perfection, or consequently to our peace: for in love we seek happiness in what we love; we desire to find in the beloved object all that the heart stands in need of; we call upon it as a remedy for the dreadful void which we feel within us, and flatter ourselves that it will be capable of filling it; we consider it as a resource for all our wants, the cure for all our sorrows, the author of all our happiness. . . . . . But this love of the creature is attended with the keenest anxiety; we always doubt whether we are beloved with a warmth of affection equal to our own; we are ingenious in tormenting ourselves, assiduous in accumulating fears, suspicions, and jealousies; the more sincere our passion, the more acutely we suffer; we become the victims of our own distrust. All this you know, and it is not for me to come hither to address you in the language of your insensate passions."

This great disease of the soul bursts forth in all its fury on the appearance of the object which is destined to develop the seeds of it. Dido is still engaged with the works of her infant city; a tempest arises, and a hero is cast upon her shores. The queen is agitated; a *secret fire* circulates in her veins, indiscretions begin, pleasures follow, disappointment and remorse succeed. Dido is soon forsaken; she looks round her with horror, and perceives naught but precipices. How has that structure of happiness fallen, of which an exalted imagination had been the amorous

[1] Massillon's Sermon on the *Prodigal Son,* part i.

[2] Sermon on the *Adulteress,* part i.

architect, like those palaces of clouds tinged for a few moments with the roseate hues of the setting sun? Dido flies in quest of her lover; she calls the faithless Æneas:—

"Perfidious man, hopest thou to conceal from me thy designs and escape clandestinely from this country? Can neither our love, nor this hand which I have given to thee, nor Dido ready to ascend the fatal pile—can nothing stay thy treacherous steps?"[1]

What anguish, what passion, what truth, in the eloquence of this betrayed woman! Her feelings so throng in her heart that she produces them in confusion, incoherent, and separate, just as they accumulate on her lips. Take notice of the authorities which she employs in her prayers. Is it in the name of the gods, in the name of a vain sovereignty, that she speaks? No; she does not even insist upon Dido forsaken; but, more humble and more affectionate, she implores the son of Venus only by tears, only by the very hand of the traitor. If to this she adds the idea of love, it is only to extend it to Æneas: "By our nuptials, by our union already begun." *Per connubia nostra, per inceptos hymenæos.* She also appeals to the places that had witnessed her transports; for the unfortunate are accustomed to associate surrounding objects with their sentiments. When forsaken by men, they strive to create a support for themselves by animating the insensible objects around them with their sorrows. That roof, that hospitable hearth, to which she once welcomed the ungrateful chieftain, are therefore the real deities of Dido. Afterward, with the address of a woman, and of a woman in love, she successively calls to mind Pygmalion and Iarbas, in order to awaken the generosity or the jealousy of the Trojan hero. As the finishing stroke of her passion and her distress, the haughty queen of Carthage goes so far as to wish that "a little Æneas," *parvulus Æneas*, may be left behind at her court to soothe her grief, even while attesting her shame. She imagines that so many tears, so many imprecations, so many entreaties, are arguments which it is impossible for Æneas to withstand; for in these moments of insanity, the passions, incapable of pleading their cause, conceive that they are availing themselves of all their resources when they are only putting forth a turbulent clamor.

[1] *Æneid*, b. iv.

CHAPTER III.

CONTINUATION OF THE PRECEDING SUBJECT.

The Phædra of Racine.

We might be content with opposing to Dido the Phædra of Racine. More impassioned than the queen of Carthage, she is a *Christian wife.* The fear of the avenging flames and the awful eternity of hell is manifest throughout the whole part of this guilty woman,[1] and particularly in the celebrated scene of jealousy, which, as everybody knows, is the invention of the modern poet. Incest was not so rare and monstrous a crime among the ancients as to excite such apprehensions in the heart of the culprit. Sophocles, it is true, represents Jocasta as expiring the moment she is made acquainted with her guilt, but Euripides makes her live a considerable time afterward. If we may believe Tertullian,[2] the sorrows of Œdipus excited nothing but the ridicule of the spectators in Macedonia. Virgil has not placed Phædra in the infernal regions, but only in those myrtle groves, "those mournful regions" where wander lovers "*whom death itself has not relieved from their pains.*"[3]

Thus the Phædra of Euripides, as well as the Phædra of Seneca, is more afraid of Theseus than of Tartarus. Neither the one nor the other expresses herself like the Phædra of Racine:—

What! Phædra jealous! and doth she implore
Thy pity, Theseus? and while Theseus lives
Doth her lewd breast burn with unhallowed fire?
And ah! whose love doth she aspire to gain?
At that dread thought what horrors rend my soul!
The measure of my crimes is surely full,
Swelled as it is with incest and imposture;
My murderous hands, athirst with vengeance, burn
To bathe them in the blood of innocence.
Still, miscreant, canst thou live? canst thou support
The light of his pure beams from whom thou'rt sprung?

---

[1] This fear of Tartarus is slightly alluded to in Euripides.
[2] Tertu'., *Apolog.*
[3] *Æneid*, lib. vi. 444.

Where shall I hide? The awful sire and sovereign
Of all the gods is my forefather too,
And heaven and earth teem with my ancestors.
What if I hasten to the realms of night
Infernal, there my father holds the urn,
Which Fate, 'tis said, gave to his rigid hands;
There Minos sits in judgment on mankind.
How will his venerable shade, aghast,
Behold his daughter, when at his tribunal
Constrained to avow her manifold misdeeds
And crimes perhaps unheard-of even in hell?
How, O my parent, how wilt thou endure
This racking spectacle? Methinks I see
The fateful urn drop from thy trembling hand;
Methinks, with brow austere, I see thee sit,
Devising some new penalty for guilt
Without a parallel. But ah! relent!
Have mercy on thine offspring, whom the rage
Of an incensed deity hath plunged
In nameless woes. Alas! my tortured heart
Hath reaped no harvest from the damning crime
That steeps my name in lasting infamy!

This incomparable passage exhibits a gradation of feeling, a knowledge of the sorrows, the anguish, and the transports of the soul, which the ancients never approached. Among them we meet with fragments, as it were, of sentiments, but rarely with a complete sentiment; here, on the contrary, the whole heart is poured forth. The most energetic exclamation, perhaps, that passion ever dictated, is contained in the concluding lines:—

Alas! my tortured heart
Hath reaped no harvest from the damning crime
That steeps my name in lasting infamy.

In this there is a mixture of sensuality and soul, of despair and amorous fury, that surpasses all expression. This woman who would *console herself for an eternity of pain* had she but enjoyed a *single moment of happiness*—this woman is not represented in the *antique character;* she is the *reprobate Christian;* the sinner fallen alive into the hands of God; her words are the words of the self-condemned to everlasting tortures.

CHAPTER IV.

CONTINUATION OF THE PRECEDING SUBJECT.

Julia d' Etange—Clementina.

But now the scene will change: we shall hear that impassioned love, so terrible in the Christian Phædra, eliciting only tender sighs from the bosom of the *pious* Julia; hers is the voice of melancholy, issuing from the sanctuary of peace. Hers are the accents of love, softened and prolonged by the religious echo of the holy place.

"The region of chimeras is the only one in this world that is worth living in; and such is the vanity of all human things, that, except the Supreme Being, there is nothing excellent but what has no existence. . . . . . . A secret languor steals through the recesses of my heart; it feels empty and unsatisfied, as you told me yours formerly did; my attachment to whatever is dear to me is not sufficient to engage it; a useless strength is left which it knows not what to do with. This pain is extraordinary, I allow, but it is not the less real. My friend, I am too happy; I am weary of felicity. . . . . .

"Finding, therefore, nothing here below to satisfy its craving, my eager soul elsewhere seeks wherewith to fill itself. Soaring aloft to the source of feeling and existence, it there recovers from its languor and its apathy. It is there regenerated and revived. It there receives new vigor and new life. It acquires a new existence which is independent of the passions of the body; or rather, it is no longer attached to the latter, but is wholly absorbed in the immense Being whom it contemplates; and, released for a moment from its shackles, it returns to them with the less regret after this experience of a more sublime state which it hopes at some future period to enjoy. . . . . . .

"When reflecting on all the blessings of Providence, I am ashamed of taking to heart such petty troubles and forgetting such important favors. . . . . When, in spite of myself, my melancholy pursues me, a few tears shed before Him who can dispense comfort instantly soothe my heart. My reflections are never bitter or painful. My repentance itself is devoid of apprehensions. My faults excite in me less fear than shame. I am acquainted with regret, but not with remorse.

"The God whom I serve is a God of clemency, a Father of mercies. What most deeply affects me is his goodness, which, in my eyes, eclipses all his other attributes. It is the only one of which I have a conception. His power astonishes; his immensity confounds; his justice . . . . He has made man feeble, and he is merciful because he is just. The God of vengeance is the God of the wicked. I can neither fear him for myself nor invoke him against another. Oh, God of peace! God of goodness! thee I adore! Thy work, full well I know it, I am; and I hope at the day of judgment to find thee such as thou speakest in this life to my troubled heart."

How happily are love and religion blended in this picture! This style, these sentiments, have no parallel in antiquity.[1] What folly to reject a religion which dictates to the heart such tender accents, and which has added, as it were, new powers to the soul!

Would you have another example of this new language of the passions, unknown under the system of polytheism? Listen to Clementina. Her expressions are still more unaffected, more pathetic, and more sublimely natural, than Julia's:—

"This one thing I have to say—but turn your face another way; I find my blushes come already. Why, Chevalier, I did intend to say—but stay; I have wrote it down somewhere—[She pulled out her pocket-book]—Here it is. [She read:] 'Let me beseech you, sir,—I was very earnest, you see,—to hate, to despise, to detest—now don't look this way—the unhappy Clementina with all your heart; but, for the sake of your immortal soul, let me conjure you to be reconciled to our Holy Mother Church!' Will you, sir? [following my averted face with her sweet face; for I *could not* look toward her.] Say you will. Tender-hearted man! I always thought you had sensibility. Say you will,—not for my

---

[1] The mixture, however, of metaphysical and natural language in this extract is not in good taste. The *Almighty*, the *Lord*, would be better than *source of existence*, &c.

sake. I told you that I would content myself to be still despised. It shall not be said that you did this for a wife! No, sir; your conscience shall have all the merit of it!—and, I'll tell you what, I will lay me down in peace, [She stood up with a dignity that was augmented by her piety;] and I will say, 'Now do thou, O beckoning angel!'—for an angel will be on the other side of the river; the river shall be death, sir,—'now do thou reach out thy divine hand, O minister of peace! I will wade through these separating waters, and I will bespeak a place for the man who, many, many years hence, may fill it!' and I will sit next you forever and ever;—and this, sir, shall satisfy the poor Clementina, who will then be richer than the richest."[1]

Christianity proves a real balm for our wounds, particularly at those times when the passions, after furiously raging in our bosoms, begin to subside, either from misfortune or from the length of their duration. It lulls our woes, it strengthens our

---

[1] It would have been much to our author's purpose to have expatiated more at large upon the works of *Richardson*, as he has founded the excellence of his good characters entirely upon a *Christian* basis. He has exemplified the *beautiful ideal* of human nature. The characters of Clementina, Sir Charles Grandison, and Clarissa Harlowe, are the most virtuous, amiable, accomplished, and noble that can well be imagined. They are supported with strict propriety, are elevated by uncommon dignity, and charm the reader while they command his admiration. They show that mankind are truly happy only in proportion as they listen to the dictates of conscience and follow the path of duty. Where could Richardson, a bookseller and a printer, immersed in the occupation of his shop and his press, acquire such a correct acquaintance with high life and refined society,—such exalted sentiments of religion, honor, love, friendship, and philanthropy,—as he has displayed in his works? Where did he acquire such a command over our feelings,—such a power "to ope the sacred source of sympathetic tears"?

The best answer to these questions is that he derived these treasures from the rich resources of his own mind, from the study of the Bible, and a quick insight into human nature and human character. He has been justly styled "the great master of the human heart," "the Shakspeare of Romance." *Clarissa Harlowe* and *Sir Charles Grandison* are *long* works, because they are designed to develop the springs of human action, and to give a distinct view of the progressive, various, and complex movements of the human mind. *Prolixity* is made the pretext of the frivolous novel-readers of the present age to neglect these invaluable works; although, if they be weighed in the balance of literary justice, they will be found to comprise as much, if not more, sterling excellence than half the novels that have been written since their publication.

wavering resolution, it prevents relapses by combating the dangerous power of memory in a soul scarcely yet cured. It sheds around us peace, fragrance, and light. It restores to us that harmony of the spheres which was heard by Pythagoras during the silence of his passions. As it promises a recompense for every sacrifice, we seem to be giving up nothing for it when we are giving up every thing. As it presents, at each successive step, a still more lovely object to our desires, it gratifies the natural inconstancy of our hearts. It fills us with the ecstasies of a love which is always beginning, and this love is ineffable, because its mysteries are those of purity and innocence.

CHAPTER V.

CONTINUATION OF THE PRECEDING SUBJECT.

Eloisa.

JULIA was brought to a sense of religion by ordinary disappointments. She continued in the world, and, being constrained to conceal from it the passion of her heart, she betook herself in secret to God, certain of finding in this indulgent Father a pity which her fellow-creatures would have refused her. She delights to pour forth her confessions before the Supreme Judge, because he alone has the power to absolve her, and perhaps also—involuntary relic of her weakness!—because it affords her an opportunity of calling to mind her love.

If we find such relief from the communication of our sorrows to some superior mind, to some peaceful conscience, which strengthens and enables us to share the tranquillity which itself enjoys, how soothing must it be to address ourselves on the subject of our passions to that impassible Being whom our secrets cannot disturb, and to complain of our frailty to that Omnipotent Deity who can impart to us some of his strength! We may form some conception of the transports of those holy men who, retiring to the summits of mountains, placed their whole life at the feet of God, penetrated by means of love into the region of eternity, and at length soared to the contemplation of primitive light. Julia's end, unknown to herself, approaches; but when she first perceives the shadows of the tomb that begin to involve her, a ray of divine excellence beams from her eyes. The voice of this dying female is soft and plaintive. It is like the last rustling of the winds sweeping over the forests,—the last murmurs of a sea forsaking its shores.

The accents of Eloisa are stronger. The wife of Abelard, she lives and lives for God.[1] Her afflictions have been equally unexpected and severe. Cut off from the world and plunged into solitude, she has been ushered suddenly, and with all her fire, into the privacy of the cloister. Religion and love at once sway her heart. It is rebellious nature seized, while full of energy, by grace, and vainly struggling in the embraces of heaven. Give Racine to Eloisa for an interpreter, and the picture of her woes will be a thousand times more impressive than that of Dido's misfortunes, from the tragical effect, the place of the scene, and a certain awfulness which Christianity throws around objects to which it communicates its grandeur.

> In these deep solitudes and awful cells,
> Where heavenly pensive contemplation dwells,
> And ever-musing melancholy reigns,
> What means this tumult in a vestal's veins?
> Why rove my thoughts beyond this last retreat?
> Why feels my heart its long-forgotten heat?
> Yet, yet I love! . . . .
> Ah, wretch! believed the spouse of God in vain—
> Confessed within the slave of love and man.

[1] Abelard, a distinguished dialectician of France in the twelfth century, has acquired more renown by his amours with Eloisa than by his subtlety and learning. The author calls Eloisa his wife; for, although their intercourse at first was only that of lovers, they were afterward secretly married. This circumstance, however, did not suffice to appease Eloisa's uncle, who, indignant at the seduction of his neice, caused a serious injury to be inflicted upon the body of Abelard. The latter, to conceal his disgrace, retired into the monastery of St. Denys, and subsequently gathered around him an immense number of students. His teaching, however, was infected with various errors, which were condemned in his own country and at Rome. Abelard repented both of his errors and his pleasures before his death, which took place in 1142. After the disgrace of her consort, Eloisa also retired into a convent, where she led a holy life. T.

Assist me, heaven! but whence arose that prayer
Sprung it from piety, or from despair?
Even here, where frozen chastity retires,
Love finds an altar for forbidden fires.
I ought to grieve, but cannot what I ought;
I mourn the lover, not lament the fault;
I view my crime, but kindle at the view,
Repent old pleasures, and solicit new;
Now, turned to heaven, I weep my past offence,
Now think of thee, and curse my innocence.
Oh come! Oh teach me nature to subdue—
Renounce my love, my life, myself, and you;
Fill my fond heart with God alone, for he
Alone can rival—can succeed to thee.[1]

It would be impossible for antiquity to furnish such a scene, because it had not such a religion. You may take for your heroine a Greek or Roman vestal; but never will you be able to produce that conflict between the flesh and the spirit which constitutes all the charm in the situation of Eloisa, and which belongs to the Christian doctrine and morality. Recollect that you here find united the most impetuous of the passions and a commanding religion which never submits to any compromise with carnal appetites. Eloisa loves; Eloisa burns; but within the convent walls every thing calls upon her to quench her earthly fires, and she knows that everlasting torments or endless rewards await her fall or her triumph. No accommodation is to be expected. The creature and the Creator cannot dwell together in the same soul. Dido loses only an ungrateful lover. How different the anguish that rends the heart of Eloisa! She is compelled to choose between God and a faithful lover whom she has involved in misfortunes. Neither must she flatter herself that she shall be able to devote the smallest portion of her heart to Abelard. The God of Sinai is a jealous God—a God who insists on being loved in preference—who punishes the very shadow of a thought, nay, even the dream, that is occupied with any other object than himself.

We shall here take the liberty of remarking an error into which Colardeau has fallen, because it is tinctured with the spirit of his age, and strongly tends to illustrate the subject of which we are treating. His translation of the epistle from

---

[1] Pope's *Eloisa.*

Eloisa has a philosophic cast, which is far different from the truly poetical spirit of Pope. After the passage quoted above, we find these lines:—

Dear sisters, guiltless partners of my chains,
Who know not Eloisa's amorous pains;
Ye captive doves, within these hallowed walls,
To none obedient but Religion's calls:
In whom her *feeble* virtues only shine,—
Those virtues, now, alas! no longer mine:
Who ne'er amid the *convent's languors* prove
The almighty empire of tyrannic love;
Who with a heavenly spouse alone content,
Love but from *habit*, not from sentiment;
How smoothly glide your days, your nights how free
From all the pangs of sensibility!
By storms of passion as unvexed they roll,
Ah! with what envy do they fill the soul![1]

These lines, it is true, are not deficient either in ease or tenderness; but they are not to be found in the English poet. Faint indeed are the traces of them discoverable in the following passage:—

How happy is the blameless vestal's lot,
The world forgetting, by the world forgot!
Eternal sunshine of the spotless mind,
Each prayer accepted and each wish resigned;
Labor and rest, that equal periods keep;
Obedient slumbers, that can wake and weep;
Desires composed, affections ever even,
Tears that delight, and sighs that waft to heaven.
Grace shines around her with serenest beams,
And whispering angels prompt her golden dreams;
For her the unfading rose of Eden blooms,
And wings of seraphs shed divine perfumes;
To sounds of heavenly harps she dies away,
And melts in visions of eternal day.[2]

It is difficult to conceive how a *poet* could have prevailed upon himself to substitute a wretched commonplace on *monastic languors* for this exquisite description. Who is so blind as not to see how beautiful, how dramatic, is the contrast which Pope intended to produce between the pains of Eloisa's love and the serenity and chastity of a religious life? Who is so dull as not

[1] Translation of F. Su. berl.

[2] Pope's *Eloisa*.

to perceive how sweetly this transition soothes the soul agitated by the passions, and what heightened interest it afterward gives to the renewed operations of these same passions? Whatever may be the value of philosophy, it certainly does not become it to act a part in the troubles of the heart, because its object should be to appease them. Eloisa, philosophizing on the *feeble* virtues of religion, neither speaks the language of truth nor of her age, neither of a woman nor of love. We here discover nothing but the *poet*, and, what is still worse, the era of sophistry and declamation.

Thus it is that the spirit of irreligion invariably subverts truth and spoils the movements of nature. Pope, who lived in better times, has not fallen into the same error as Colardeau.[1] He retained the worthy spirit of the age of Louis XIV., of which the age of Queen Anne was a kind of prolongation or reflection. We must go back to religious ideas, if we attach any value to works of genius; religion is the genuine philosophy of the fine arts, because, unlike human wisdom, it separates not poetry from morality or tenderness from virtue.

On the subject of Eloisa many other interesting observations might be made in regard to the solitary convent in which the scene is laid. The cloisters, the vaults, the tombs, the austere manners, contrasted with all the circumstances of love, must augment its force and heighten its melancholy. What a vast difference between the Queen of Carthage seeking a speedy death on the funeral pile, and Eloisa slowly consuming herself on the altar of religion! But we shall speak at length on the subject of convents in another part of our work.

[1] Pope, moreover, being a Catholic, could not have drawn the false picture of conventual life which fell from the pen of the infidel Colardeau. T.

CHAPTER VI.

RURAL LOVE.

The Cyclop and Galatea of Theocritus.

As a subject of comparison among the ancients under the head of rural love, we shall select the idyl of the *Cyclop and Galatea*. This little poem is one of the master-pieces of Theocritus. The *Sorceress* is superior to it in warmth of passion, but it is less pastoral.

The Cyclop, seated upon a rock on the coast of Sicily, thus gives vent to his pain, while overlooking the billows that roll beneath him:—

"Charming Galatea, why dost thou scorn the attentions of a lover, thou whose face is fair as the curd pressed by the soft net-work of rushes? . . . . . thou who art more tender than the lamb, more lovely than the heifer, fresher than the grape not yet softened by the sun's powerful rays? Thou glidest along these shores when sound slumbers enchain me; thou fleest me when I am not visited by refreshing sleep; thou fearest me as the lamb fears the wolf grown gray with years. Never have I ceased to adore thee since thou camest with my mother to pluck the young hyacinths on the mountains: it was I who guided thy steps. From that day even to the present moment I find it impossible to live without thee. And yet, dost thou heed my pains? In the name of Jupiter, hast thou any feeling for my anguish? . . . But, unsightly as I am, I have a thousand ewes whose rich udders my hand presses and whose foaming milk is my beverage. Summer, autumn, and winter, always find cheeses in my cavern; my nets are always full of them. No Cyclop could play so well to thee upon the pastoral reed as I can, O lovely maiden! None could with such skill celebrate all thy charms during the storms of night. For thee I am rearing eleven does which are ready to drop their fawns. I am also bringing up four bears' cubs stolen from their savage mothers. Come, and all these riches shall be thine. Let the sea furiously lash its shores; thy nights shall be more happy if thou wilt pass them in my cave by my side. Laurels and tall cypresses murmur there; the dark ivy and the vine laden with clusters line its dusky sides; close to it runs a limpid stream which white Ætna discharges from his snow-clad summits and down his sides covered with brown forests. What! wouldst thou still prefer the sea and its thousands of billows? If my hairy bosom offends thy sight, I have oak wood and live embers remaining beneath the ashes; burn,—for any thing from thy hand will give me pleasure,—burn, if thou wilt, mine only eye, this eye, which is dearer to me than life itself Ah! why did not my mother give to me, as to the fish, light oars wherewith to cleave the liquid waves! O! how I would then descend to my Galatea! how I would kiss her hand if she refused me her lips! Yes, I would bring the white lilies, or tender poppies with purple leaves; the first grow in summer, and the others adorn the winter, so that I could not present them both to thee at once. . . . .

"In this manner did Polyphemus apply to his wounded heart the immortal balm of the Muses, thus soothing the sorrows of life more sweetly than he could have done by any thing that gold can purchase."

This idyl breathes the fire of passion. The poet could not have made choice of words more delicate or more harmonious. The Doric dialect also gives to his verses a tone of simplicity which cannot be transfused into our language. The frequent repetition of the first letter of the alphabet, and a broad and open pronunciation, seem to represent the tranquillity of the scenes and the unaffected language of the shepherd. The naturalness of the Cyclop's lament is also remarkable. He speaks from the heart; yet no one would suspect for a moment that his sighs are any thing else than the skilful imitation of a poet. With what simplicity and warmth does the unhappy lover depict his own ugliness! Even that eye, which renders him so offensive, suggests to Theocritus an affecting idea: so true is the remark of Aristotle, conveyed by Boileau in these lines:—

D'un pinceau délicat l'artifice agréable
Du plus affreux objet fait un objet aimable.

It is well known that the moderns, and the French in particular, have not been very successful in pastoral composition.[1] We are of opinion, however, that Bernardin de Saint-Pierre has surpassed the bucolic writers of Italy and Greece. His novel, or rather his poem, of *Paul and Virginia*, belongs to the small number of works which in a few years acquire an antiquity that authorizes us to quote them without being afraid of having our taste called in question.

CHAPTER VII.

CONTINUATION OF THE PRECEDING SUBJECT.

Paul and Virginia.

THE old man seated on the mountain relates the history of the two exiled families; he gives an account of their labors, their loves, their sports, and their cares.

"Paul and Virginia had neither clocks nor almanacs, neither books of chronology, history, nor philosophy. The periods of their lives were regulated by those of nature. They knew the hours of the day by the shadow of the trees; the seasons by the times when they produce their flowers or their fruits; and the years by the number of their harvests. These pleasing images imparted the greatest charms to their conversation. ''Tis dinner-time,' said Virginia to the family: 'the shadows of the bananas are at their feet;' or, 'night approaches: the tamarind-trees are shutting up their leaves.' 'When will you come to see us?' asked some young friends who lived not far off. 'In cane-time,' replied Virginia. When any person inquired her

[1] The Revolution deprived us of a man who gave promise of first-rate talents in the eclogue; we allude to André Chenier. We have seen a collection of manuscript idyls by him, in which there are passages worthy of Theocritus. This explains the expression used by that unfortunate young man when upon the scaffold. "Die!" exclaimed he, striking his forehead; "and yet I had something here!" It was the Muse revealing his talents to him at the moment of death.—See note P.

age, or that of Paul, she would answer, 'My brother is as old as the great cocoa-tree beside the fountain, and I am as old as the smaller; the mangoes have borne fruit twelve times, and the orange-trees have flowered twice as often, since I was born.' Their lives seemed to be attached to those of the trees, like the existence of the fauns and dryads. They knew no other historical epochs than those of their mothers' lives, no other chronology than that of the orchards, and no other philosophy than that of doing good to everybody, and of resignation to the will of the Almighty. . . . .

"Sometimes, when alone with Virginia, Paul said to her on his return from work, 'When I am fatigued, the sight of you refreshes me; and when from the top of the hill I look down into this valley, you look just like a rose-bud in the midst of our orchards. . . . Though I lose sight of you among the trees, still I discern something of you which I cannot describe in the air through which you pass or on the turf upon which you have been sitting. . . . .

"'Tell me by what spell you have enchanted me. It cannot be by your understanding, for our mothers have more than we. Neither is it by your caresses, for they kiss me much oftener than you. I suppose it must be by your kindness. Here, my beloved, take this citron branch covered with blossom, which I broke in the forest. Place it at night beside your bed. Eat this honey-comb, which I climbed to the top of a rock to take for you; but first sit down on my knee, and I shall be refreshed.'

"'Oh my brother!' Virginia would reply, 'the beams of the morning sun that gild the summits of these rocks give me less joy than your presence.' . . . . You ask why you love me. Have not all those creatures that are brought up together a mutual affection for each other? Look at our birds, reared in the same nests; they love like us, and, like us, they are always together. Hear how they call and answer one another from tree to tree; just as, when echo wafts to me the notes which you play on your flute, I repeat the words at the bottom of this valley. . . . . . . I daily pray to God for my mother and yours, for you and for our poor servants; but when I pronounce your name my fervor seems to increase. How ardently I implore the Almighty that no misfortune may befall you! Why do you go so far and climb so high in quest of fruits and flowers for me? Have we not plenty in the garden? How you have fatigued yourself! You are bathed in sweat!' With these words she wiped his forehead and his cheeks with her little white handkerchief, and gave him several kisses."

The point to be examined in this picture is not why it is superior to that of *Galatea*, (a superiority too evident not to be acknowledged by every reader,) but why it owes its excellence to religion, and, in a word, in what way it is Christian.

It is certain that the charm of Paul and Virginia consists in a certain pensive morality which pervades the whole work, and which may be compared to that uniform radiance which the moon throws upon a wilderness bedecked with flowers. Now, whoever has meditated upon the truths of the gospel must admit that its divine precepts have precisely this solemn and affecting character. Saint-Pierre, who, in his *Studies of Nature*, endeavors to justify the ways of God and to demonstrate the beauty of religion, must have nourished his genius by the perusal of the sacred volume. If his eclogue is so pathetic, it is because it represents two little exiled Christian families, living under the eye of the Lord, guided by his word in the Bible and his works in the desert. To this add indigence and those afflictions of the soul for which religion affords the only remedy, and you will have the whole of the subject. The characters are as simple as the plot: they are two charming children, whose cradle and whose grave are brought under your notice, two faithful slaves, and two pious mistresses. These good people have a historian every way worthy of their lives: an old man residing alone upon the mountain, and who has survived all that he loved, relates to the traveller the misfortunes of his friends over the ruins of their cottages.

We may observe that these Southern bucolics are full of allusions to the Scriptures. In one, we are reminded of Ruth, of Sephora; in another, of Eden and our first parents. These sacred recollections throw an air of antiquity over the scenes of the whole picture, by introducing into it the manners of the primitive East. The mass, the prayers, the sacraments, the ceremonies of the Church, to which the author is every moment referring, likewise shed their spiritual beauty over the work. Is not the mysterious dream of Madame de la Tour essentially connected with what is grand and pathetic in our religious doctrines? We also discover the Christian in those lessons of resignation to the will of God, of obedience to parents, charity to the poor, strictness in the performance of the duties of religion,—in a word, in the whole of that delightful theology which pervades the poem of Saint-Pierre. We may even go still farther, and assert that it is religion, in fact, which determines the catastrophe. Virginia dies for the preservation of one of the principal virtues enjoined by Christianity. It would have been absurd to make a Grecian woman die for refusing to expose her person; but the lover of Paul is a *Christian* virgin, and what would be ridiculous according to the impure notions of heathenism becomes in this instance sublime.

This pastoral is not like the idyls of Theocritus, or the eclogues of Virgil; neither does it exactly resemble the grand rural scenes of Hesiod, Homer, and the Bible; but, like the parable of the *Good Shepherd*, it produces an ineffable effect, and you are convinced that none but a Christian could have related the evangelical loves of Paul and Virginia.

It will perhaps be objected that it is not the charm borrowed from the sacred Scriptures which confers on Saint-Pierre the superiority over Theocritus, but his talent for delineating nature. To this we reply that he owes this talent also, or at least the development of this talent, to Christianity; since it is this religion which has driven the petty divinities from the forests and the waters, and has thus enabled him to represent the deserts in all their majesty. This we shall attempt to demonstrate when we come to treat of mythology; let us now proceed with the investigation of the passions.

CHAPTER VIII.

THE CHRISTIAN RELIGION ITSELF CONSIDERED AS A PASSION.

NOT satisfied with enlarging the sphere of the passions in the drama and the epic poem, the Christian religion is itself a species of passion, which has its transports, its ardors, its sighs, its joys, its tears, its love of society and of solitude. This, as we know, is by the present age denominated *fanaticism*. We might reply in the words of Rousseau, which are truly remarkable in the mouth of a philosopher: "Fanaticism, though sanguinary and cruel,[1] is nevertheless a great and powerful passion, which exalts the heart of man, which inspires him with a contempt of death, which gives him prodigious energy, and which only requires to be judiciously directed in order to produce the most sublime virtues. On the other hand, irreligion, and a *reasoning and philosophic* spirit in general, strengthens the attachment to life, debases the soul and renders it effeminate, concentrates all the passions in the meanness of private interest, in the abject motive of self, and thus silently saps the real foundations of all society; for so trifling are the points in which private interests are united, that they will never counterbalance those in which they oppose one another."[2]

But this is not the question; we treat at present only of dramatic effect. Now, Christianity considered itself as a passion supplies the poet with immense treasures. This religious passion is the stronger as it is in contradiction to all others, and must swallow them up to exist itself. Like all the great affections, it is profoundly serious; it attracts us to the shade of convents and of mountains. The beauty which the Christian adores is not perishable; it is that eternal beauty for which Plato's disciples were so anxious to quit the earth. Here below she always appears veiled to her lovers; she shrouds herself in the folds of the universe as in a mantle; for if but one of her glances were to meet the eye and pierce the heart of man, unable to endure it he would expire with transport.

---

[1] Is Philosophy less so?

[2] *Emile*, tome iii. p. 193, note.

To attain the enjoyment of this supreme beauty, Christians take a very different course from that which the Athenian philosophers pursued; they remain in this world in order to multiply their sacrifices, and to render themselves more worthy, by a long purification, of the object of their desires.

Whoever, according to the expression of the Fathers, have the least possible commerce with the flesh, and descend in innocence to the grave,—such souls, relieved from doubts and fears, wing their flight to the regions of life, where in never-ending transports they contemplate that which is true, immutable, and above the reach of opinion. How many glorious martyrs has this hope of possessing God produced! What solitude has not heard the sighs of illustrious rivals contending for the enjoyment of Him who is adored by the cherubim and seraphim? Here an Anthony erects an altar in the desert, and for the space of forty years sacrifices himself, unknown to all mankind; there a St. Jerome forsakes Rome, crosses the seas, and, like Elias, seeks a retreat on the banks of the Jordan. Even there hell leaves him not unmolested, and the attractive figure of Rome, decked with all her charms, appears in the forests to torment him. He sustains dreadful assaults; he fights hand-to-hand with his passions. His weapons are tears, fasting, study, penance, and, above all, love. He falls at the feet of the divine beauty, and implores its succor. Sometimes, like a criminal doomed to the most laborious toils, he loads his shoulders with a burden of scorching sand, to subdue the rebellious flesh, and to extinguish the unholy desires which address themselves to the creature.

Massillon, describing this sublime love, exclaims, "To such the Lord alone appears good and faithful and true, constant in his promises, amiable in his indulgence, magnificent in his gifts, real in his tenderness, merciful even in his wrath; he alone appears great enough to fill the whole immensity of our hearts, powerful enough to satisfy all its desires, generous enough to soothe all its woes; he alone appears immortal, and worthy of our endless affection; finally, he alone excites no regret, except that we learned too late to love him."[1]

The author of the *Following of Christ* has selected from St

[1] *La Pecheresse,* part i.

Augustine and the other Fathers whatever is most mystic and most ardent in the language of divine love.[1]

"The love of God is generous; it impels the soul to great actions, and excites in it the desire of that which is most perfect.

"Love always aspires to a higher sphere, and suffers not itself to be detained by base considerations.

"Love is determined to be free and independent of all the terrestrial affections, lest its inward light should be obscured, and it should either be embarrassed with the goods or dejected by the ills of the world.

"There is nothing in heaven or upon earth that is more delicious or more powerful, more exalted or more comprehensive, more agreeable, more perfect, or more excellent, than love, because love is the offspring of God, and, soaring above all created beings, cannot find repose except in God.

"Those alone who love can comprehend the language of love, and those words of fire in which a soul deeply imbued with the Deity addresses him when it ejaculates, 'Thou art my God; thou art my love; thou art completely mine, and I am entirely thine! Extend my heart that I may love thee still more; and teach me by an inward and spiritual taste how delicious it is to love thee, to swim, and to be, as it were, absorbed in the ocean of thy love.'"

"He who loves generously," adds the same author, "stands firm amid temptations, and suffers himself not to be surprised by the subtle persuasions of his enemy."

It is this Christian passion, this immense conflict between a terrestrial and a celestial love, which Corneille has depicted in that celebrated scene of his *Polyeuctes*,—for this great man, less delicate than the philosophers of the present day, had no notion that Christianity was beneath his genius.

Pol. If death be noble in a sovereign's cause,
What must his be who suffers for his God?
Paul. What God is that thou speakest of?
Pol. Ah! Paulina,
He hears thy every word.—'Tis not a God,
Deaf and insensible and impotent,
Of marble, or of wood, or shining gold.

[1] Book iii. ch. 5.

I mean the Christian's God—my God and thine,
Than whom nor earth nor heaven confess another.

Paul. Be then content within thy heart's recess
To adore in silence.

Pol. Why not tell me rather
To be at once idolater and Christian?

Paul. Feign but a moment, till Severus' absence,
And give my father's mercy scope to act.

Pol. My Heavenly Father's mercy—ah! how far
To be preferred! He my unconscious steps
From lurking danger guides. His hand sustains,
And when but entering on my new career,
His grace decrees the crown of victory.
My bark just launched he safely wafts to port,
And me from baptism's rites to heaven conveys.
Oh that thou knewest the vanity of life,
And all the bliss that after death awaits us!
God of all mercy, thou hast given to her
Too many virtues, and too high perfections,
Which claim her for a Christian, that 'twere grievous
To think her destined to remain estranged
From thee and from thy love, to live the slave,
The unhappy slave, of thine arch-enemy,
And die, as born, beneath his odious yoke!

Paul. What wish escaped thy too presumptuous tongue?

Pol. One whose fulfilment gladly would I purchase
With every purple drop that fills these veins.

Paul. Sooner shall————

Pol. Hold, Paulina: 'tis in vain
To struggle 'gainst conviction. Unawares
The God of Christians melts the obdurate heart;
The happy moment, though not yet arrived,
Will come, but when, is not to me revealed.

Paul. Give up such idle fancies, and assure
Me of thy love.

Pol. Ah! doubt me not, Paulina;
I love thee more than life, nay, more than aught
In heaven or earth, save God.

Paul. Then, by that love
Leave me not, I conjure thee!

Pol. By that love
Let me implore thee, do as I have done.

Paul. What, not content to abandon, wouldst thou too
Seduce me from my faith?

Pol. Is't then a hardship
To go to heaven? for thither I'd conduct thee!

Paul. No more of these chimeras!

Pol. Sacred truths!

Paul. Infatuation!

Pol No; celestial light.
Paul. Thou choosest death before Paulina's love.
Pol. Attached to earth, thou spurnest grace divine.[1]

Such are those admirable dialogues in Corneille's manner, in which the sincerity of the speakers, the rapidity of the transitions, the warmth and elevation of the sentiments, never fail to delight the audience. How sublime is Polyeuctes in this scene! what greatness of soul, what dignity, what divine enthusiasm he displays! The gravity and nobleness of the Christian character appear, even in the opposition of the plural and singular pronouns *vous* and *tu*, the mere use of which in this way places a whole world between the martyr Polyeuctes and the pagan Paulina.

Finally, Corneille has exhibited all the energy of the Christian passion in that dialogue which, to use Voltaire's expression, is "admirable, and always received with applause."

Felix proposes to Polyeuctes to sacrifice to his false gods; but Polyeuctes refuses to comply;—

Fel. At length to my just wrath my clemency
Gives place. Adore, or yield thy forfeit life.
Pol. I am a Christian.
Fel. Impious wretch! adore,
Or death shall be thy doom.
Pol. I am a Christian.
Fel. Oh bosom most obdurate! Soldiers, haste
And execute the orders I have issued.
Paul. Ah! whither lead ye him?
Fel. To death.
Pol. To glory.[2]

Those words—*I am a Christian*—twice repeated are equal to the most exalted expression of the *Horaces*. Corneille, who was so excellent a judge of the sublime, well knew to what a height the love of religion is capable of rising; for the Christian loves God as the supreme beauty, and heaven as his native land.

But, on the other hand, could polytheism ever inspire an idolater with anything of the enthusiasm of Polyeuctes? What could be the object of his passionate love? Would he submit to death for some lewd goddess or for a cruel and unfeeling god? The religions which are capable of exciting any ardor are those

[1] Act iv. scene iii.

[2] Act v. scene iii.

which approach more or less to the doctrine of the unity of a God; otherwise, the heart and mind, being divided among a multitude of divinities, cannot be strongly attached to any. No love, moreover, can be durable that has not virtue for its object. Truth will ever be the predominant passion of man; if he loves error, it is because at the time he considers error as truth. We have no affection for falsehood, though we are continually falling into it; but this weakness proceeds from our original depravity; we have lost strength while retaining desire, and our hearts still seek the light which our eyes are now too feeble to endure.

The Christian religion, in again opening to us, by the merits of the Son of Man, those luminous paths which death had covered with its shades, has recalled to us our primitive loves. Heir of the benedictions of Jacob, the Christian burns to enter that celestial Sion to which are directed all his sighs. This is the passion which our poets may celebrate, after the example of Corneille. It is a source of beauty which was wholly unknown to antiquity, and which Sophocles and Euripides would not have overlooked.

CHAPTER IX.

OF THE UNSETTLED STATE OF THE PASSIONS.

We have yet to treat of a state of the soul which, as we think, has not been accurately described; we mean that which precedes the development of the strong passions, when all the faculties, fresh, active, and entire, but confined in the breast, act only upon themselves, without object and without end. The more nations advance in civilization, the more this unsettled state of the passions predominates; for then the many examples we have before us, and the multitude of books we possess, give us knowledge without experience; we are undeceived before we have enjoyed; there still remain desires, but no illusions. Our imagination is rich, abundant, and full of wonders; but our existence is poor, insipid, and destitute of charms. With a full heart, we dwell in an empty world, and scarcely have we advanced a few steps when we have nothing more to learn.

It is inconceivable what a shade this state of the soul throws over life; the heart turns a hundred different ways to employ the energies which it feels to be useless to it. The ancients knew but little of this secret inquietude, this irritation of the stifled passions fermenting all together; political affairs, the sports of the Gymnasium and of the Campus Martius, the business of the forum and of the popular assemblies, engaged all their time, and left no room for this tedium of the heart.

On the other hand, they were not disposed to exaggerations, to hopes and fears without object, to versatility in ideas and sentiments, and to perpetual inconstancy, which is but a continual disgust,—dispositions which we acquire in the familiar society of the fair sex. Women, independently of the direct passion which they excite among all modern nations, also possess an influence over the other sentiments. They have in their nature a certain ease which they communicate to ours; they render the marks of the masculine character less distinct; and our passions, softened by the mixture of theirs, assume, at one and the same time, something uncertain and delicate.

Finally, the Greeks and Romans, looking scarcely any farther than the present life, and having no conception of pleasures more perfect than those which this world affords, were not disposed, like us, by the character of their religion, to meditation and desire. Formed for the relief of our afflictions and our wants, the Christian religion incessantly exhibits to our view the twofold picture of terrestrial griefs and heavenly joys, and thus creates in the heart a source of present evils and distant hopes, whence spring inexhaustible abstractions and meditations. The Christian always looks upon himself as no more than a pilgrim travelling here below through a vale of tears and finding no repose till he reaches the tomb. The world is not the object of his affections, for he knows that the days of man are few, and that this object would speedily escape from his grasp.

The persecutions which the first believers underwent had the effect of strengthening in them this disgust of the things of this life. The invasion of the barbarians raised this feeling to the highest pitch, and the human mind received from it an impression of melancholy, and, perhaps, even a slight tincture of misanthropy, which has never been thoroughly removed. On all sides arose convents; hither retired the unfortunate, smarting under the disappointments of the world, or souls who chose rather to remain strangers to certain sentiments of life than to run the risk of finding themselves cruelly deceived.[1] But, nowadays, when these ardent souls have no monastery to enter, or have not the virtue that would lead them to one, they feel like strangers among men. Disgusted with the age, alarmed by religion, they remain in the world without mingling in its pursuits; and then we behold that culpable sadness which springs up in the midst of the passions, when these passions, without object, burn themselves out in a solitary heart.

---

[1] Though the author does not assert in this passage that misanthropy had any part in the introduction of the monastic institute, or is compatible with its essential spirit, this meaning might be inferred by the reader who would not attend particularly to the language which he employs. He wishes to convey the idea that the conventual life, by removing the occasions of sin and fixing the mind and heart upon God alone, afforded the remedy of that morbid condition of the soul which follows from misanthropy and a natural aversion for the world. These sentiments are transformed by the religious or monastic spirit into sentiments of charity and self-denial. It is well known that the introduction of the religious orders was the inauguration of a new era in the history of Christian charity, as it opened immense additional resources for the alleviation of almost every species of human misery. The monastic spirit, moreover, was founded essentially on the love of God, as the only end of man. But the love of God and the love of the neighbor go hand-in-hand. Misanthropy, therefore, is a sentiment, both historically and intrinsically, opposed to the spirit of the monastic state. That a tinge of melancholy in regard to earthly things should pervade the religious and even the ordinary Christian life, is in accordance with the gospel itself, since it teaches us to look upon ourselves as exiles in this world, and beatifies those who yield to the spiritual sadness which this consideration inspires. "Blessed are they that mourn, for they shall be comforted." T.

BOOK IV.

OF THE MARVELLOUS; OR, OF POETRY IN ITS RELATIONS TO SUPERNATURAL BEINGS.

CHAPTER I.

MYTHOLOGY DIMINISHED THE GRANDEUR OF NATURE—THE ANCIENTS HAD NO DESCRIPTIVE POETRY, PROPERLY SO CALLED.

WE have already shown in the preceding books that Christianity, by mingling with the affections of the soul, has increased the resources of the drama. Polytheism did not concern itself about the vices and virtues; it was completely divorced from morality. In this respect, Christianity has an immense advantage over heathenism. But let us see whether, in regard to what is termed the *marvellous,* it be not superior in beauty to mythology itself.

We are well aware that we have here undertaken to attack one of the most inveterate scholastic prejudices. The weight of authority is against us, and many lines might be quoted from Racine's poem on the *Poetic Art* in our condemnation.

However this may be, it is not impossible to maintain that mythology, though so highly extolled, instead of embellishing nature destroys her real charms; and we believe that several eminent characters in the literary world are at present of this opinion.

The first and greatest imperfection of mythology was that it circumscribed the limits of nature and banished truth from her domain. An incontestable proof of this fact is that the poetry which we term *descriptive* was unknown throughout all antiquity;[1] so that the very poets who celebrated the works of nature did not enter into the *descriptive* in the sense which we attach to the word. They have certainly left us admirable delineations of the

[1] See note Q.

employments, the manners, and the pleasures, of rural life; but as to those pictures of scenery, of the seasons, and of the variations of the sky and weather, which have enriched the modern Muse, scarcely any traits of this kind are to be found in their compositions.

The few that they contain are indeed excellent, like the rest of their works. Homer, when describing the cavern of the Cyclop, does not line it with *lilacs and roses;* like Theocritus, he has planted laurels and tall pines before it. He embellishes the gardens of Alcinöus with flowing fountains and useful trees; in another place he mentions the hill *assaulted by the winds and covered with fig-trees,* and he represents the smoke of Circe's palace ascending above a forest of oaks.

Virgil has introduced the same truth into his delineations. He gives to the pine the epithet of *harmonious,* because the pine actually sends forth a kind of soft murmur when gently agitated; the clouds in the Georgics are compared to fleeces of wool rolled together by the winds; and the swallows in the Æneid twitter on the thatched roof of king Evander or skim the porticoes of palaces. Horace, Tibullus, Propertius, and Ovid, have also left some sketches of this nature; but they consist of nothing more than a favorite grove of Morpheus, a valley into which the Cytherean goddess is about to descend, or a fountain where Bacchus reposes in the lap of the Naiads.

The philosophic age of antiquity produced no alteration in this manner. Olympus, whose existence was no longer believed, now sought refuge among the poets, who in their turn protected the gods that had once protected them. Statius and Silius Italicus advanced no further than Homer and Virgil; Lucan alone made some progress in this species of composition, and in his Pharsalia we find the description of a forest and a desert, which remind us of the colors of modern artists.[1]

Lastly, the naturalists were as sober as the poets, and followed nearly the same road. Thus Pliny and Columella, who came the last, take more pains to describe nature than Aristotle. Among the historians and the philosophers, Xenophon, Plato,

[1] This description is full of bombast and bad taste; though we have nothing to do here with the execution of the piece, but with the class to which it belongs.

Tacitus, Plutarch, and Pliny the younger, are remarkable for some beautiful pictures [1]

It can scarcely be supposed that men endued with such sensibility as the ancients could have wanted eyes to perceive the charms of nature and talents for depicting them, had they not been blinded by some powerful cause. Now, this cause was their established mythology, which, peopling the universe with elegant phantoms, banished from the creation its solemnity, its grandeur, and its solitude. It was necessary that Christianity should expel the whole hosts of fauns, of satyrs, and of nymphs, to restore to the grottos their silence and to the woods their scope for uninterrupted contemplation. Under our religion the deserts have assumed a character more pensive, more vague, and more sublime; the forests have attained a loftier pitch; the rivers have broken their petty urns, that in future they may only pour the waters of the abyss from the summit of the mountains; and the true God, in returning to his works, has imparted his immensity to nature.

The prospect of the universe could not excite in the bosoms of the Greeks and Romans those emotions which it produces in our souls. Instead of that setting sun, whose lengthened rays sometimes light up the forest, at others form a golden tangent on the rolling arch of the seas,—instead of those beautiful accidents of light which every morning remind us of the miracle of the creation,—the ancients beheld around them naught but a uniform system, which reminds us of the machinery of an opera.

If the poet wandered in the vales of the Taygetus, on the banks of the Sperchius, on the Mænalus, beloved of Orpheus, or in the plains of the Elorus, whatever may have been the charm of this Grecian geography, he met with nothing but fauns, he heard no sounds but those of the dryads. Apollo and the Muses were there, and Vertumnus with the Zephyrs led eternal dances. Sylvans and Naiads may strike the imagination in an agreeable

---

[1] See in Xenophon the Retreat of the Ten Thousand, and the Treatise on Hunting: in Plato, the exordium of the Dialogue on the Laws: in Tacitus, the description of the forsaken camp where Varus was massacred with his legions, (*Annal.*, lib. i.;) in Plutarch, the lives of Brutus and of Pompey; in Pliny, the description of his garden.

manner, provided they be not incessantly brought forward. We would not

——Expel the Tritons from the watery waste,
Destroy Pan's pipe, snatch from the Fates their shears.

But then what impression does all this leave on the soul? What results from it for the heart? What moral benefit can the mind thence derive? Oh, how far more highly is the Christian poet favored! Free from that multitude of absurd deities which circumscribed them on all sides, the woods are filled with the immensity of the Divinity; and the gift of prophecy and wisdom, mystery and religion, seem to have fixed their eternal abode in their awful recesses.

Penetrate into those forests of America coeval with the world. What profound silence pervades these retreats when the winds are hushed! What unknown voices when they begin to rise! Stand still, and every thing is mute; take but a step, and all nature sighs. Night approaches: the shades thicken; you hear herds of wild beasts passing in the dark; the ground murmurs under your feet; the pealing thunder roars in the deserts; the forest bows; the trees fall; an unknown river rolls before you. The moon at length bursts forth in the east; as you proceed at the foot of the trees, she seems to move before you at their tops, and solemnly to accompany your steps. The wanderer seats himself on the trunk of an oak to await the return of day; he looks alternately at the nocturnal luminary, the darkness, and the river: he feels restless, agitated, and in expectation of something extraordinary. A pleasure never felt before, an unusual fear, cause his heart to throb, as if he were about to be admitted to some secret of the Divinity; he is alone in the depth of the forests, but the mind of man is equal to the expanse of nature, and all the solitudes of the earth are less vast than one single thought of his heart. Even did he reject the idea of a Deity, the intellectual being, alone and unbeheld, would be more august in the midst of a solitary world than if surrounded by the ridiculous divinities of fabulous times. The barren desert itself would have some congeniality with his discursive thoughts, his melancholy feelings, and even his disgust for a life equally devoid of illusion and of hope.

There is in man an instinctive melancholy, which makes him harmonize with the scenery of nature. Who has not spent whole hours seated on the bank of a river contemplating its passing waves? Who has not found pleasure on the sea-shore in viewing the distant rock whitened by the billows? How much are the ancients to be pitied, who discovered in the ocean naught but the palace of Neptune and the cavern of Proteus! It was hard that they should perceive only the adventures of the Tritons and the Nereids in the immensity of the seas, which seems to give an indistinct measure of the greatness of our souls, and which excites a vague desire to quit this life, that we may embrace all nature and taste the fulness of joy in the presence of its Author.

CHAPTER II.

OF ALLEGORY.

METHINKS I hear some one ask, do you find nothing beautiful in the allegories of the ancients? We must make a distinction.

The *moral* allegory, like that of the *prayers* in Homer, is beautiful in all ages, in all countries, in all religions; nor has it been banished by Christianity. We may, as much as we will, place at the foot of the throne of the Supreme Judge the two vessels filled with good and evil; we shall possess this advantage, that our God will never act unjustly or at random, like Jupiter; he will pour the floods of adversity upon the heads of mortals, not out of caprice, but for a purpose known to himself alone. We are aware that our happiness here below is co-ordinate with a general happiness in a chain of beings and of worlds that are concealed from our sight; that man, in harmony with the spheres, keeps pace with them in their progress to accomplish a revolution which God envelops in his eternity.

But if the *moral* allegory still continues to exist for us, this is not the case with the *physical* allegory. Let Juno be the *air*, and Jupiter the *ether*, and thus, while brother and sister, still remain husband and wife,—where is the charm, where is the grandeur, of this personification? Nay, more, this species of allegory is contrary to the principles of taste and even of sound logic.

We ought never to personify a being itself, but only a *quality* or *affection* of that being; otherwise there is not a real personification, but merely a change in the name of the object. I may give speech to a stone; but what shall I gain by assigning to this stone an allegorical name? Now the soul, whose nature is life, essentially possesses the faculty of producing; so that one of her vices, one of her virtues, may be considered as her *son*, or as her *daughter*, since she has actually given birth to it. This passion, active as its parent, may, in its turn grown up, develop itself, acquire features, and become a distinct being. But the *physical object*—a being purely passive by its very nature, which is not susceptible either of pleasure or of pain, which has no passions, but merely accidents, and accidents as inanimate as itself—affords nothing to which you can impart life. Would you transform the *obduracy* of the flint or the *sap* of the oak into an allegorical being? It should be observed that the understanding is less shocked by the creation of dryads, naiads, zephyrs, and echoes, than by that of nymphs attached to mute and motionless objects; for in trees, water, and the air, there are motions and sounds which convey the idea of life, and which may consequently furnish an allegory, like the movement of the soul. But this *minor* species of physical allegory, though not quite so bad as the *greater*, is always of inferior merit, cold and incomplete; it resembles at best the fairies of the Arabs and the genii of the Orientals.

As to the vague sort of deities placed by the ancients in solitary woods and wild situations, they doubtless produced a pleasing effect, but they had no kind of connection with the mythological system: the human mind here fell back into natural religion. What the trembling traveller adored as he passed through these solitudes was something *unknown*, something with whose name he was not acquainted, and which he called the *divinity of the place;* sometimes he gave it the name of Pan, and Pan was the *universal God.* These powerful emotions, excited by wild nature, have not ceased to exist, and the forests still retain for us their awful divinity.

In short, it is so true that the *physical allegory*, or the deities of fable, destroyed the charms of nature, that the ancients had no genuine landscape painters for the same reason that they had no descriptive poetry.[1] This species of poetry, however, was more or less known among other idolatrous nations, who were strangers to the mythologic system; witness the Sanscrit poems, the tales of the Arabs, the Edda of the Scandinavians, the songs of the negroes and the savages.[2] But, as the infidel nations have always mingled their false religion, and consequently their bad taste, with their compositions, it is under the Christian dispensation alone that nature has been delineated with truth.

CHAPTER III.

HISTORICAL PART OF DESCRIPTIVE POETRY AMONG THE MODERNS.

No sooner had the apostles begun to preach the gospel to the world than descriptive poetry made its appearance. All things returned to the way of truth, *before Him who*, in the words of St. Augustin, *holds the place of truth on earth.* Nature ceased to speak through the fallacious organ of idols; her ends were discovered, and it became known that she was made in the first place for God, and in the second for man. She proclaims, in fact, only two things: God glorified by his works, and human wants supplied.

This great discovery changed the whole face of the creation. From its intellectual part, that is to say, from the divine intelligence which it everywhere displays, the soul received abundance of food; and from its material part the body perceived that every thing had been formed for itself. The vain images attached to inanimate beings vanished, and the rocks became much more really animated, the oaks pronounced more certain oracles, the winds and the waves emitted sounds far more impressive, when man had discovered in his own heart the life, the oracles, and the voice of nature.

Hitherto solitude had been looked upon as frightful, but Chris-

[1] The facts on which this assertion is grounded are developed in note W, at the end of the volume. [2] See note R.

tians found in it a thousand charms. The anchorets extolled the beauties of rocks and the delights of contemplation; and this was the first stage of descriptive poetry. The religious who published the lives of the first fathers of the desert were also obliged to describe the retreats in which these illustrious recluses had buried their glory. In the works of a Jerome and of an Athanasius[1] may still be seen descriptions of nature which prove that they were not only capable of observing, but also of exciting a love for what they delineated.

This new species of composition introduced into literature by Christianity rapidly gained ground. It insinuated itself even into the historic style, as may be remarked in the collection known by the name of the Byzantine, and particularly in the histories of Procopius. It was in like manner propagated, but in a degenerate form, by the Greek novelists of the Lower Empire and by some of the Latin poets in the West.

When Constantinople had passed under the yoke of the Turks, a new species of descriptive poetry, composed of the relics of Moorish, Greek, and Italian genius, sprang up in Italy. Petrarch, Ariosto, and Tasso, raised it to a high degree of perfection. But this kind of description is deficient in truth. It consists of certain epithets incessantly repeated and always applied in the same manner. It was impossible to quit the *shady forest*, the *cool cavern*, or the banks of the *limpid stream*. Nothing was to be seen but groves of orange-trees and bowers of jessamine and roses.

Flora returned with her basket, and the eternal *Zephyrs* failed not to attend her; but they found in the woods neither the *Fauns* nor the *Naiads*, and, had they not met with the *Fairies* and the *Giants* of the Moors, they would have run the risk of losing themselves in this immense solitude of Christian nature. When the human mind advances a step, every thing must advance with it; all nature changes with its lights or its shadows. Hence, it would be painful to us now to admit petty divinities where we see naught but wide-extended space. Place, if you will, the mistress of Tithonus upon a car, and cover her with flowers and with dew; nothing will prevent her appearing dis-

[1] Hieron., *in Vit. Paul.*; Athan., *in Vit. Anton.*

proportionate, while shedding her feeble light through the boundless firmament which Christianity has expanded; let her then leave the office of enlightening the world to Him by whom it was created.

From Italy this species of descriptive poetry passed into France, where it was favorably received by a Ronsard, a Lemoine, a Coras, a St. Amand, and the early novelists. But the great writers of the age of Louis XIV., disgusted with this style of delineation, in which they discovered no marks of truth, banished it both from their prose and their poetry; and it is one of the distinguishing characteristics of their works that they exhibit no traces of what we denominate *descriptive poetry*.[1]

Thus repulsed from France, the rural muse sought refuge in England, where Spenser, Milton, and Waller had paved the way for her reception. Here she gradually lost her affected manner, but she fell into another excess. In describing real nature alone, she attempted to delineate every thing, and overloaded her pictures either with objects too trivial or with ridiculous circumstances. Thomson himself, in his *Winter*, so superior to the other parts of his poem, has some passages that are very tedious. Such was the second epoch of descriptive poetry.

From England she returned to France, with the works of Pope and the bard of the *Seasons*. Here she had some difficulty in gaining admission, being opposed by the ancient Italian style, which Dorat and some others had revived; she nevertheless triumphed, and for the victory was indebted to Delille and St. Lambert. She improved herself under the French muse, submitted to the rules of taste, and reached the third epoch.

It must, however, be observed that she had preserved her purity, though unknown, in the works of some naturalists of the time of Louis XIV., as Tournefort and Dutertre. The latter displays a lively imagination, added to a tender and pensive genius: he even uses the word *melancholy*, like Lafontaine, in the sense in which we at present employ it. Thus the age of Louis XIV. was not wholly destitute of genuine descriptive poetry, as we might at first be led to imagine; it was only confined to the

[1] Fénélon, Lafontaine, and Chaulieu, must be excepted. Racine the younger, the father of this new poetic school, in which Delille has excelled, may also be considered as the founder of descriptive poetry in France.

letters of our missionaries;[1] and here it is that we have studied this kind of style, which we consider so new at the present day.

The admirable passages interspersed in the Bible afford a twofold proof that descriptive poetry is among us the offspring of Christianity. *Job*, the *Prophets*, *Ecclesiasticus*, and the *Psalms*, in particular, are full of magnificent descriptions. What a master-piece of this kind is the one hundred and third psalm!—

"Bless the Lord, O my soul! O Lord, my God, thou art exceedingly great! . . . . . Thou hast appointed darkness, and it is night: in it shall all the beasts of the woods go about. The young lions roaring after their prey, and seeking their meat from God The sun ariseth, and they are gathered together: and they shall lie down in their dens. Man shall go forth to his work, and to his labor until the evening. How great are thy works, O Lord! thou hast made all things in wisdom: the earth is filled with thy riches. So is this great sea, which stretcheth wide its arms; there are creeping things without number: creatures little and great. There the ships shall go. This sea-dragon which thou hast formed to play therein." . . . . . .

Pindar and Horace have fallen far short of this poetry.

We were, therefore, correct in the observation that to Christianity St. Pierre owes his talent for delineating the scenery of nature; to Christianity he owes it, because the doctrines of our religion, by destroying the divinities of mythology, have restored truth and majesty to the deserts; to Christianity he owes it, because he has found in the system of Moses the genuine system of nature.

But here another advantage presents itself to the Christian poet. If his religion gives him a *solitary* nature, he likewise may have an *inhabited* nature. He may, if he choose, place angels to take care of the forests and the abysses of the deep, or commit to their charge the luminaries and spheres of heaven. This leads us to the consideration of the *supernatural beings*, or the *marvellous*, of Christianity.

---

[1] The reader will see some fine examples of this when we come to treat of the Missions.

CHAPTER IV.

HAVE THE DIVINITIES OF PAGANISM, IN A POETICAL POINT OF VIEW, THE SUPERIORITY OVER THE CHRISTIAN DIVINITIES?[1]

"We admit," impartial persons may say, "that, in regard to men, Christianity has furnished a department of the drama which was unknown to mythology, and that it has likewise created the genuine descriptive poetry. Here are two advantages which we acknowledge, and which may, in some measure, justify your principles, and counterbalance the beauties of fable. But now, if you are candid, you must allow that the divinities of paganism, when they act *directly* and *for themselves*, are more poetic and more dramatic than the Christian divinities."

At first sight, we might be inclined to this opinion. The gods of the ancients, sharing our virtues and our vices,—having, like us, bodies liable to pain and irritable passions,—mingling with the human race, and leaving here below a mortal posterity,—these gods are but a species of superior men. Hence we may be led to imagine that they furnish poetry with greater resources than the incorporeal and impassible divinities of Christianity; but on a closer examination we find this dramatic superiority reduced to a mere trifle.

In the first place, there have always been, in every religion, two species of deity,—one for the poet and the other for the philosopher.[2] Thus the abstract Being so admirably delineated by Tertullian and St. Augustin is not the Jehovah of David or of Isaias: both are far superior to the Theos of Plato or the Jupiter of Homer. It is not, therefore, strictly true that the poetic divinities of the Christians are wholly destitute of passions. The God

[1] The word divinities here is employed in a wide sense, embracing the inhabitants of the spirit-world. T.

[2] That is, in the representation or delineation of the Deity by means of human language. T.

of the Scriptures repents, he is jealous, he loves, he hates, his wrath is roused like a whirlwind; the Son of man takes pity on our distresses; the Virgin, the saints, and the angels, are melted by the spectacle of our afflictions, and *Paradise*, in general, is much more deeply interested in behalf of man than *Olympus*.

There are passions, therefore, among our celestial powers,[1] and these passions have this great advantage over those of the gods of paganism, that they never lead to any idea of depravity and vice. It is indeed very remarkable that, in depicting the indignation or the sorrow of the Christian heaven, it is impossible to destroy the sentiment of tranquillity and joy in the imagination of the reader; such is the sanctity and the justice of the God that is pointed out by our religion.

This is not all: for if you positively insist that the God of the Christians is an impassible being, still you may have impassioned divinities, equally dramatic and equally malignant with those of antiquity. In hell are concentrated all the passions of men. To us our theological system appears more beautiful, more regular, more scientific, than the fabulous doctrine which intermingled men, gods, and demons. In our heaven the poet finds perfect beings, but yet endued with sensibility and ranged in a brilliant hierarchy of love and power; the abyss confines its gods impassioned and potent in evil, like the gods of mythology; men hold the middle place,—men, allied to heaven by their virtues and to hell by their vices,—men, beloved of the angels, hated by the devils, the unfortunate objects of a war that shall never terminate but with the world.

These are powerful agents, and the poet has no reason to complain. As to the actions of the Christian intelligences, it will not be a difficult task to prove that they are more vast and more mighty than those of the mythological divinities. Can the God who governs the spheres, who propels the comets, who creates the universe and light, who embraces and comprehends all ages, who penetrates into the most secret recesses of the human heart, —can this God be compared with a deity who rides abroad in a car, who lives in a palace of gold on a petty mountain, and who

[1] Or rather, they are attributed to them by mankind.

has not even a clear foresight of the future? There is not so much as the slight advantage arising from visible forms and the difference of sex but what our divinities share with those of Greece, since the angels in Scripture frequently assume the human figure, and the hierarchy of saints is composed of men and women.

But who can prefer a saint whose history sometimes offends against elegance and taste, to the graceful Naiad attached to the sources of a stream? It is necessary to separate the terrestrial from the celestial life of this saint; on earth she was but a woman; her divinity begins only with her happiness in the regions of eternal light. You must, moreover, continue to bear in mind that the Naiad was incompatible with descriptive poetry, that a stream represented in its natural course is much more pleasing than in its allegorical delineation, and that we gain on one hand what we seem to lose on the other.

In regard to battles, whatever has been advanced against Milton's angels may be retorted upon the gods of Homer. In the one case, as in the other, they are divinities for whom we have nothing to fear, since they are not liable to death. Mars overthrown and covering nine acres with his body,—Diana giving Venus a blow on the ear,—are as ridiculous as an angel cut in two and the severed parts uniting again like a serpent. The supernatural powers may still preside over the engagements of the epic; but, in our opinion, they ought not to interfere except in certain cases, which it is the province of taste alone to determine; this the superior genius of Virgil suggested to him more than eighteen hundred years ago.

That the Christian divinities, however, have a ridiculous position in battle is not a settled point. Satan preparing to engage with Michael in the terrestrial paradise is magnificent; the God of Hosts advancing in a dark cloud at the head of his faithful legions is not a puny image; the exterminating sword, suddenly unsheathed before the rebel angels, strikes with astonishment and terror; the sacred armies of heaven, sapping the foundations of Jerusalem, produce as grand an effect as the hostile gods besieging Priam's palace: finally, there is nothing more sublime in Homer than the conflict between Emanuel and the reprobate spirits in Milton, when, plunging them into the abyss, the Son of man, *"checked his thunder in mid-volley,"* lest he should annihilate them.

> Hell heard the unsufferable noise; hell saw
> Heaven running from heaven, and would have fled
> Affrighted; but strict fate had cast too deep
> Her dark foundations, and too fast had bound.

CHAPTER V.

CHARACTER OF THE TRUE GOD.

We are filled with admiration when we consider that the God of Jacob is also the God of the gospel; that the God who hurls the thunderbolt is likewise the God of peace and innocence.

> He forms the bud, he swells the ripening fruit,
> And gives the flowers their thousand lovely hues,
> Dispenses sun or rain as best may suit,
> And bids cool night distil refreshing dews.

We are of opinion that there is no need of proof to demonstrate how superior, in a poetical point of view, the God of Christians is to the Jupiter of antiquity. At the command of the former, rivers roll back to their sources, the heavens are folded like a book, the seas are divided, the dead rise from their tombs, and plagues are poured forth upon nations. In him the sublime exists of itself; and you are spared the trouble of seeking it. The Jupiter of Homer, shaking the heavens with a nod, is doubtless highly majestic; but Jehovah descends into the chaos; he pronounces the words, *"Let there be light,"* and the fabulous son of Saturn dwindles to nothing.

When Jupiter would give the other deities an idea of his power, he threatens to carry them off by the end of a chain. Jehovah needs no chain, nor any thing of the kind.

> What needs his mighty arm our puny aid?
> In vain the monarchs of the earth combined
> Would strive to shake his throne; a single glance
> Dissolves their impious league; he speaks, and straight
> His foes commingle with their native dust.

At his dread voice affrighted ocean flees,
And heaven itself doth tremble. In his sight
The countless spheres that glow in yon expanse
Are nothing, and the feeble race of mortals
As though it ne'er had been.[1]

When Achilles prepares to avenge Patroclus, Jupiter announces to the immortals that they are at liberty to take part in the conflict. All Olympus is immediately convulsed:—

Above, the sire of gods his thunder rolls,
And peals on peals redoubled rend the poles.
Beneath, stern Neptune shakes the solid ground;
The forests wave, the mountains nod around;
Through all their summits tremble Ida's woods,
And from their sources boil her hundred floods.
Troy's turrets totter on the rocking plain;
And the tossed navies beat the heaving main.
Deep in the dismal regions of the dead
The infernal monarch reared his horrid head, &c.[2]

This passage has been quoted by all critics as the utmost effort of the sublime. The Greek verses are admirable: they present successively the thunder of Jupiter, the trident of Neptune, and the shriek of Pluto. You imagine that you hear the thunder's roar reverberating through all the valleys of Ida.

Δεινον δ' εβροντησε πατηρ ανδρων τε Θεων τε.

The sounds of the words which occur in this line are a good imitation of the peals of thunder, divided, as it were, by intervals of silence, *ων, τε, ων, τε.* Thus does the voice of heaven, in a tempest, alternately rise and fall in the recesses of the forests. A sudden and painful silence, vague and fantastic images, rapidly succeed the tumult of the first movements. After Pluto's shriek you feel as if you had entered the empire of death; the expressions of Homer drop their force and coloring, while a multitude of hissings imitate the murmur of the inarticulate voices of the shades.

Where shall we find a parallel to this? Has Christian poetry the means of equalling such beauties? Let the reader judge. In the following passage the Almighty describes himself:—

"There went up a smoke in his wrath, and a fire flamed from his face; coals were kindled by it. He bowed the heavens and came down, and darkness was under his feet. And he ascended

[1] Racine's *Esther*. [2] Pope's *Homer*, book xx. 75–84.

upon the cherubim, and he flew upon the wings of the winds. And he made darkness his covert, his pavilion round about him dark waters in the clouds of the air. And the Lord thundered from heaven, and the highest gave his voice; hail and coals of fire. At the brightness before him the clouds passed, hail and coals of fire. And he sent forth his arrows, and he scattered them: he multiplied lightnings, and troubled them. Then the fountains of waters appeared, and the foundations of the world were discovered. At thy rebuke, O Lord, at the blast of the spirit of thy wrath."[1]

"It must be admitted," says La Harpe, "that there is as much difference between this species of the sublime and any other as between the spirit of God and the spirit of man. Here we behold the conception of the grand in its principle. The rest is but a shadow of it, as created intelligence is but a feeble emanation of the Intelligence that creates,—as a fiction, however excellent, is but a shadow of truth, and derives all its merit from a fundamental resemblance."

CHAPTER VI.

OF THE SPIRITS OF DARKNESS.

THE deities of polytheism, nearly equal in power, shared the same antipathies and the same affections. If they happened to be opposed to each other, it was only in the quarrels of mortals. They were soon reconciled by drinking nectar together.

Christianity, on the contrary, by acquainting us with the real constitution of supernatural beings, has exhibited to us the empire of virtue eternally separated from that of vice. It has revealed to us spirits of darkness incessantly plotting the ruin of mankind, and spirits of light solely intent on the means of saving them. Hence arises an eternal conflict, which opens to the imagination a source of numberless beauties.

---

[1] Psalm xvii.

This sublime species of the marvellous furnishes an ther kind of an inferior order; that is to say, *magic*. This last was known to the ancients; but among us it has acquired, as a poetic machine, higher importance and increased extent. Care must, however, be always taken to employ it with discretion, because it is not in a style sufficiently chaste. It is above all deficient in grandeur; for, borrowing some portion of its power from human nature, men communicate to it something of their own insignificance.

A distinguishing feature in our supernatural beings, especially in the infernal powers, is the attribution of a character. We shall presently see what use Milton has made of the character of pride, assigned by Christianity to the prince of darkness. Having, moreover, the liberty to assign a wicked spirit to each vice, he thus disposes of a host of infernal divinities. Nay, more; he then obtains the genuine allegory without having the insipidity which accompanies it; as these perverse spirits are, in fact, real beings, and such as our religion authorizes us to consider them.

But, if the demons are as numerous as the crimes of men, they may also be coupled with the tremendous incidents of nature. Whatever is criminal and irregular in the moral or in the physical world is alike within their province. Care must only be taken when they are introduced in earthquakes, volcanic eruptions, and the gloomy recesses of an aged forest, to give these scenes a majestic character. The poet should, with exquisite taste, make a distinction between the thunder of the Most High and the empty noise raised by a perfidious spirit. Let not the lightnings be kindled but in the hands of God. Let them never burst from the storm excited by the powers of hell. Let the latter be always sombre and ominous. Let not its clouds be reddened by *wrath* or propelled by the wind of *justice*. Let them be pale and livid, like those of *despair*, and be driven by the impure blasts of *hatred* alone. In these storms there should be felt a power mighty only in destruction. There should be found that incongruity, that confusion, that kind of energy for evil, which has something disproportionate and gigantic, like the chaos whence it derives its origin.

CHAPTER VII.

OF THE SAINTS.

It is certain that the poets have not availed themselves of all the stores with which the *marvellous* of Christianity is capable of supplying the Muses. Philosophers may laugh at the saints and angels; but had not the ancients themselves their demi-gods? Pythagoras, Plato, Socrates, recommend the worship of those mortals whom they denominate heroes. "Honor the heroes full of benignity and intelligence," says the first in his *Golden Verses;* and, that the term *heroes* may not be mistaken, Hierocles interprets it exactly in the same manner as Christianity explains the appellation of *saint.* "These heroes, full of benignity and intelligence, are always thinking of their Creator, and are resplendent with the light reflected by the felicity which they enjoy in him." "The term *heroes,*" says he in another place, "comes from a Greek word that signifies love, to intimate that, full of love for God, the heroes seek only to assist us to pass from this earthly state to a divine life, and to become citizens of heaven."[1] The fathers of the Church also give to the saints the appellation of *heroes.* In this sense they say that baptism is the priesthood of the laity, and that it makes all Christians *kings and priests unto God;*[2] and heroes assuredly were all those illustrious martyrs who, subduing the passions of their hearts and defying the malignity of men, have, by their glorious efforts, deserved a place among the celestial powers. Under polytheism sophists sometimes appeared more moral than the religion of their country; but among us, never has a philosopher, however extraordinary his wisdom, risen higher than Christian morality. While Socrates honored the memory of the just, paganism held forth to the veneration of the people villains, whose corporeal strength was their only virtue and who were polluted with every species of crime. If the honors of apotheosis were conferred on good kings, had not also

---

[1] Hierocl., *Com. in Pyth.*

[2] Hieron., *Dial. cont. Lucif.*, t. ii. p. 136.

a Tiberius and a Nero their priests and their temples? Holy mortals whom the Church of Christ commands us to revere, ye were neither the strong nor the mighty among men! Born, many of you, in the cottage of indigence, ye have exhibited to the world nothing more than an humble life and obscure misfortunes. Shall we never hear aught but blasphemies against a religion which, deifying indigence, hardship, simplicity, and virtue, has laid prostrate at their feet wealth, prosperity, splendor, and vice?

What is there so incompatible with poetry in those anchorets of Thebais, with their white staves and their garments of palm-leaves? The birds of heaven bring them food;[1] the lions of the desert carry their messages[2] or dig their graves.[3] Familiars of the angels, they fill with miracles the deserts where Memphis once stood,[4] and Horeb and Sinai, Carmel and Lebanon, the brook Cedron and the valley of Jehoshaphat, still proclaim the glory of the monk and of the hermit of the rock. The Muses love to meditate in these antique cloisters, peopled with the shades of an Anthony, a Pachomius, a Benedict, and a Basil. The apostles preaching the gospel to the first believers in catacombs, or beneath the date-tree of the desert, were not, in the eyes of a Michael Angelo or a Raphael, subjects so exceedingly unfavorable to genius.

As we shall recur to the subject in the sequel, we shall at present say nothing concerning all those benefactors of mankind who founded hospitals and devoted themselves to the miseries of poverty, pestilence, and slavery, in order to relieve the afflicted. We shall confine ourselves to the Scriptures alone, lest we become bewildered in a subject so vast and so interesting. May we not suppose, then, that the Josues, the Eliases, the Isaiases, the Jeremiases, the Daniels, in a word, all those prophets who are now enjoying eternal life, could breathe forth their sublime lamentations in exquisite poetry? Cannot the urn of Jerusalem still be filled with their tears? Are there no more willows of Babylon upon which they may hang their unstrung harps? As for us, though we pretend not to a rank among the poets, we think that

---

[1] Hieron., *in Vit. Paul.* [2] Theod., *Hist. Relig.*, chap. vi. [3] Hieron., *Ibid.*

[4] We here make but slight mention of these recluses, because we shall speak of them in another place.

these sons of prophecy would form very striking groups among the clouds. Picture to yourselves their heads encircled with radiance, silvery beards sweeping their immortal breasts, and the Spirit of God himself beaming from their resplendent eyes.

But what a host of venerable shades is roused by the strains of the Christian Muse in the cavern of Mambre! Abraham, Isaac, Jacob, Rebecca, and all ye children of the East,—ye patriarchs, kings, and ancestors of Jesus Christ,—sing the ancient covenant between God and man! Repeat to us that history, dear to heaven, the history of Joseph and his brethren! The choir of holy monarchs, with David at their head,—the army of confessors and martyrs clad in bright robes,—would also furnish us with some exquisite touches of the *marvellous*. The latter supply the pencil with the tragic style in its highest elevation. Having depicted their sufferings, we might relate what God accomplished for those holy victims, and touch upon the gift of miracles with which he honored their tombs. Then we would station near these august choirs the band of heavenly virgins, the Genevieves, the Pulcherias, the Rosalias, the Cecilias, the Lucillas, the Isabellas, the Eulalias. The marvellous of Christianity presents the most pleasing contrasts.

'Tis well known how Neptune,

> Rising from the deep,
> Calms with a single word the infuriate waves.

Our doctrines furnish us with a very different kind of poetry. A ship is on the point of perishing. The chaplain, by mysterious words which absolve the soul, remits to each one the guilt of his sins. He addresses Heaven in that prayer which, amid the uproar of the elements, commends the spirits of the shipwrecked to the God of tempests. Already the abysses of ocean yawn to engulf the ill-fated vessel. Already the billows, raising their dismal voices among the rocks, seem to begin the funeral dirge; but suddenly a ray of light bursts through the storm. Mary, the *star of the sea*, the patroness of mariners, appears in the midst of a cloud. She holds her child in her arms, and calms the waves with a smile. Charming religion, which opposes to what is most terrific in nature what is most lovely on earth and in heaven,—to the tempests of ocean a little infant and a tender mother!

CHAPTER VIII.

OF THE ANGELS.

SUCH is the kind of *marvellous* which may be derived from our saints without entering into the varied history of their lives. But we discover also in the hierarchy of the angels, a doctrine as ancient as the world, an immense treasure for the poet. Not only are the commands of the Most High conveyed from one extremity of the universe to the other by these divine messengers,—not only are they the invisible guardians of men, or assume, when they would manifest themselves, the most lovely forms,—but religion permits us to assign tutelary angels to the beautiful incidents of nature as well as to the virtuous sentiments. What an innumerable multitude of divinities is thus all at once introduced to people the spheres!

Among the Greeks, heaven terminated at the summit of Mount Olympus, and their gods ascended no higher than the vapors of the earth. The *marvellous* of Christianity, harmonizing with reason, astronomy, and the expansion of the soul, penetrates from world to world, from universe to universe, through successions of space from which the astonished imagination recoils. In vain does the telescope explore every corner of the heavens; in vain does it pursue the comet through our system; the comet at length flies beyond their reach; but it cannot delude the *archangel*, who rolls it on to its unknown pole, and who, at the appointed time, will bring it back by mysterious ways into the very focus of our sun.

The Christian poet alone is initiated into the secret of these wonders. From globe to globe, from sun to sun, with the *seraphim*, *thrones*, and *dominations* that govern the spheres, the weary imagination again descends to earth, like a river which, by a magnificent cascade, pours forth its golden current opposite to the sun setting in radiant majesty. From grand and imposing images you pass to those which are soft and attractive. In the shady forest you traverse the domain of the *Angel of Solitude;*

in the soft moonlight you find the *Genius of the musing heart;* you hear his sighs in the murmur of the woods and in the plaintive notes of Philomela. The roseate tints of the dawn are the streaming hair of the *Angel of Morning*. The *Angel of Night* reposes in the midst of the firmament like the moon slumbering upon a cloud; his eyes are covered with a bandage of stars, while his feet and his forehead are tinged with blushes of twilight and Aurora; an *Angel of Silence* goes before him, and he is followed by the *Angel of Mystery*. Let us not wrong the poets by thinking that they look upon the *Angel of the Seas*, the *Angel of Tempests*, the *Angel of Time*, and the *Angel of Death*, as spirits disagreeable to the Muses. The *Angel of Holy Love* gives the virgin a celestial look, and the *Angel of Harmony* adorns her with graces; the good man owes the uprightness of his heart to the *Angel of Virtue* and the power of his words to the *Angel of Persuasion*. There is nothing to prevent our assigning to these beneficent spirits attributes distinctive of their powers and functions. The *Angel of Friendship*, for instance, might wear a girdle infinitely more wonderful than the cestus of Venus; for here might be seen, interwoven by a divine hand, the consolations of the soul, sublime devotion, the secret aspirations of the heart, innocent joys, pure religion, the charm of the tombs, and immortal hope.[1]

[1] If we except Milton, never was a more poetical use made of the agency of the heavenly messengers than by Addison in the *Campaign*. He thus sublimely depicts the Angel of Vengeance:—

> So, when an angel by divine command
> With rising tempests shakes a guilty land,
> Such as of late o'er pale Britannia past,
> Calm and serene he drives the furious blast,
> And, pleased the Almighty's orders to perform,
> Rides in the whirlwind and directs the storm.

CHAPTER IX.

APPLICATION OF THE PRINCIPLES ESTABLISHED IN THE PRECEDING CHAPTERS—CHARACTER OF SATAN

FROM precepts let us pass to examples. On resuming the subject of the preceding chapters, we shall begin with the character ascribed to the fallen angels by Milton.

Dante and Tasso had, prior to the English poet, depicted the monarch of hell. The imagination of Dante, exhausted by nine circles of torment, has made simply an atrocious monster of Satan, locked up in the centre of the earth. Tasso, by giving him horns, has almost rendered him ridiculous. Misled by these authorities, Milton had, for a moment, the bad taste to measure his Satan; but he soon recovers himself in a sublime manner. Hear the exclamation of the Prince of Darkness from the summit of a mountain of fire, whence he surveys, for the first time, his new dominions:[1]—

Farewell, happy fields,
Where joy forever dwells! hail, horrors, hail!
Infernal world, and thou profoundest hell,
Receive thy new possessor; one who brings
A mind not to be changed by place or time!
. . . . Here at least
We shall be free. . . . .
Here we may reign secure, and, in my choice,
To reign is worth ambition, though in hell.

What a mode of taking possession of the infernal abyss!

The council of fallen spirits being assembled, the poet thus represents Satan in the midst of his senate:[2]—

His form had not yet lost
All her original brightness, nor appeared
Less than archangel ruined, and the excess
Of glory, obscured; as when the sun new risen
Looks through the horizontal, misty air,
Shorn of his beams, or from behind the moon
In dim eclipse disastrous twilight sheds
On half the nations, and with fear of change
Perplexes monarchs. Darkened so, yet shone

[1] *Paradise Lost*, b. i. 249.

[2] *Paradise Lost*, b. i. 591.

Above them all the Archangel: but his face
Deep scars of thunder had intrenched, and care
Sat on his faded cheek. . . . .

Let us complete the delineation of the character of Satan. Having escaped from hell and reached the earth, overwhelmed with despair, while contemplating the universe, he thus apostrophizes the sun:[1]—

Oh thou, that, with surpassing glory crowned,
Look'st from thy sole dominion, like the God
Of this new world,—at whose sight all the stars
Hide their diminished heads,—to thee I call,
But with no friendly voice, and add thy name,
O Sun, to tell thee how I hate thy beams,
That bring to my remembrance from what state
I fell, how glorious once above thy sphere;
Till pride and worse ambition threw me down,
Warring in heaven against heaven's matchless King.
Ah, wherefore! he deserved no such return
From me, whom he created what I was
In that bright eminence. . . . .
. . . . Lifted up so high,
I 'sdained subjection, and thought one step higher
Would set me highest, and in a moment quit
The debt immense of endless gratitude. . . . . . .
Oh, had his powerful destiny ordained
Me some inferior angel, I had stood
Then happy; no unbounded hope had raised
Ambition. . . . .
Me miserable! which way shall I fly
Infinite wrath and Infinite despair?
Which way I fly is hell; myself am hell. . . . . .
Oh then at last relent: is there no place
Left for repentance, none for pardon left?
None left but by submission; and that word
Disdain forbids me, and the dread of shame
Among the spirits beneath, whom I seduced
With other promises and other vaunts,
Than to submit, boasting I could subdue
The Omnipotent. Ah me! they little know
How dearly I abide that boast so vain,
Under what torments inwardly I groan,
While they adore me on the throne of hell. . . .
But say I could repent, and could obtain
By act of grace my former state; how soon
Would height recall my thoughts! how soon unsay
What feigned submission swore! . . . . . .

[1] *Paradise Lost*, b. iv., from verse 33 to 113, with a few omissions. See note S.

This knows my punisher; therefore as far
From granting he as I from begging peace:
All hope excluded thus, behold, instead
Of us outcast, exiled, his new delight,
Mankind created, and for him this world.
So farewell hope, and, with hope, farewell fear,
Farewell remorse; all good to me is lost;
Evil, be thou my good: by thee, at least,
Divided empire with heaven's King I hold
By thee, and more than half perhaps will reign,
As man ere long and this new world shall know.

How exalted soever may be our admiration of Homer, we are obliged to admit that he has nothing which can be compared to this passage. When, in conjunction with the grandeur of the subject, the excellence of the poetry, the natural elevation of the characters, so intimate an acquaintance with the passions is displayed, what more can justly be required of genius? Satan repenting when he beholds the light, which he hates because it reminds him how much more glorious was once his own condition; afterward wishing that he had been created of an inferior rank; then hardening himself in guilt by pride, by shame, and by mistrust itself of his ambitious character; finally, as the sole result of his reflections, and as if to atone for a transient remorse, taking upon himself the empire of evil throughout all eternity — this is certainly one of the most sublime conceptions that ever sprang from the imagination of a poet.

An idea here strikes us, which we cannot forbear to communicate. Whoever possesses discernment and a knowledge of history, must perceive that Milton has introduced into the character of Satan the perverseness of those men, who about the middle of the seventeenth century filled England with mourning and wretchedness. You even discover in him the same obstinacy, the same enthusiasm, the same pride, the same spirit of rebellion and intolerance; you meet with the principles of those infamous levellers, who, seceding from the religion of their country, shook off the yoke of all legitimate government, revolting at once against God and man. Milton had himself imbibed this spirit of perdition; and the poet could not have imagined a Satan so detestable, unless he had seen his image in one of those reprobates, who, for such a length of time, transformed their country into a real abode of demons.

CHAPTER X.

POETICAL MACHINERY.

Venus in the woods of Carthage—Raphael in the bowers of Eden.

We shall now quote some examples of poetical machinery. Venus appearing to Æneas in the woods of Carthage is a passage composed in the most graceful style. "His mother, pursuing the same path across the forest, suddenly stands before him. She had the figure and the face of a nymph, and was armed after the manner of the virgins of Tyre."

This poetry is charming; but has the bard of Eden fallen short of it, when describing the arrival of the angel Raphael at the bower of our first parents?

Six wings he wore, to shade
His lineaments divine; the pair that clad
Each shoulder broad came mantling o'er his breast
With regal ornament; the middle pair
Girt like a starry zone his waist;
. . . . the third his feet
Shadowed from either heel with feathered mail
Sky-tinctured grain. . . . . He stood
And shook his plumes, that heavenly fragrance filled
The circuit wide. . . . .
. . . . He now is come
Into the blissful field through groves of myrrh
And flowering odors, cassia, nard, and balm,
A wilderness of sweets; for Nature here
Wantoned as in her prime, and played at will
Her virgin fancies. . . . .
Him through the spicy forest onward come,
Adam discerned, as in the door he sat,
. . . . and thus he called:—
Haste hither, Eve, and worth thy sight behold,
Eastward among those trees what glorious shape
Comes this way moving; seems another morn
Risen on mid-noon.

In this passage, Milton, little inferior in grace to Virgil, surpasses the Roman poet in sanctity and grandeur. Raphael is more beautiful than Venus, Eden more delicious than the woods of Carthage, and Æneas is a cold and insignificant character in comparison with the majestic father of mankind.

Here is a description of one of Klopstock's mystical angels:—

"The first-born of the Thrones quickly descended toward Gabriel, to conduct him in solemn state into the presence of the Most High. By the Eternal he is called *the Elect*, and by Heaven, *Eloa*. He is the highest of all created beings, and next in rank to the Essence increate; a single thought of his is as beautiful as the whole soul of man when, worthy of immortality, it is absorbed in profound meditation. His looks are more lovely than the vernal morn; brighter than the stars when, in youthful splendor, they issued from their Creator's hands to run their appointed courses. He was the first being that God created. From the crimson dawn he formed his ethereal body. When he received existence, a heaven of clouds floated around him; God himself raised him from them in his arms, and, blessing him, said, *Creature, here am I!*"[1]

Raphael is the *external*, Eloa the *internal*, angel. The Mercuries and the Apollos of mythology seem to us less divine than these genii of Christianity.

The gods in Homer fight with each other on several occasions; but we there meet with nothing superior to the preparations of Satan for giving battle to Gabriel in paradise, or to the overthrow of the rebel legions by the thunderbolts of Emanuel. The divinities of the Iliad several times rescue their favorite heroes by covering them with a cloud; but this machine has been most happily transferred to Christian poetry by Tasso, when he introduces Solyman into Jerusalem.[2] The car enveloped in vapor,—the invisible journey of an aged enchanter and a hero through the camp of the Christians,—the secret gate of Herod,—the allusions to ancient times interwoven with a rapid narrative,—the warrior who attends a council without being seen, and who shows himself only to urge Jerusalem to make a longer resistance,—all this marvellous machinery, though of the magic kind, possesses extraordinary excellence.

It may perhaps be objected that paganism has at least the

---

[1] *Messias*, Erst. ges. v. 286, &c.

[2] Book x.

superiority over Christianity in the description of the voluptuous What shall we say, then, of Armida? Is she devoid of charms when, leaning over the forehead of the slumbering Renaud, the dagger drops from her hand and her hatred is transformed into love? Is Ascanius, concealed by Venus in the Cytherean forests, more pleasing than the young hero of Tasso who is bound with flowery chains and transported to the Fortunate Isles? There is certainly no excess of the serious in those gardens whose only fault is to be too enchanting or in those loves that require only to be covered with a veil. We find in this episode even the cestus of Venus, the omission of which in other places has been so much regretted. If discontented critics would have the use of magic altogether banished from poetry, the spirits of darkness might become the principal actors themselves, instead of being the agents of men. The facts recorded in the Lives of the Saints would authorize such imagery, and the demon of sensualism has always been considered as one of the most dangerous and most powerful among the infernal spirits.

CHAPTER XI.

DREAM OF ÆNEAS—DREAM OF ATHALIE.

We have now but two species of poetic machinery to treat of —the *journeys of the gods*, and *dreams*.

To begin with the latter, we shall select the dream of Æneas on the fatal night of the destruction of Troy, which the hero himself thus relates to Dido:—

'Twas in the dead of night, when sleep repairs
Our bodies worn with toils, our minds with cares,
When Hector's ghost before my sight appears:
A bloody shroud he seemed, and bathed in tears,
Such as he was when, by Pelides slain,
Thessalian coursers dragged him o'er the plain.
Swoln were his feet, as when the thongs were thrust
Through the bored holes, his body black with dust;
Unlike that Hector who returned from toils
Of war triumphant in Æacian spoils,

Or him who made the fainting Greeks retire,
And launched against their navy Phrygian fire.
His hair and beard stood stiffened with his gore,
And all the wounds he for his country bore
Now streamed afresh, and with new purple ran.
I wept to see the visionary man,
And while my trance continued thus began:
O light of Trojans and support of Troy,
Thy father's champion and thy country's joy!
O long-expected by thy friends! from whence
Art thou so late returned for our defence?
Do we behold thee, wearied as we are
With length of labors and with toils of war?
After so many funerals of thy own,
Art thou restored to our declining town?
But say, what wounds are these? what new disgrace
Deforms the manly features of thy face?
To this the spectre no reply did frame,
But answered to the cause for which he came,
And, groaning from the bottom of his breast,
This warning in these mournful words expressed:
O goddess-born! escape, by timely flight,
The flames and horrors of this fatal night;
The foes already have possessed the wall;
Troy nods from high and totters to her fall.
Enough is paid to Priam's royal name,
More than enough to duty and to fame.
If by a mortal hand my father's throne
Could be defended, 'twas by mine alone:
Now Troy to thee commends her future state,
And gives her gods companions of thy fate:
From their assistance happier walls expect,
Which, wandering long, at last thou shalt erect.
He said, and brought me from their blest abodes
The venerable statues of the gods,
With ancient Vesta from the sacred choir,
The wreaths and relics of the immortal fire.[1]

This dream deserves particular attention, because it is an epitome, as it were, of Virgil's genius, and displays, in a narrow compass, all the species of beauties peculiar to that poet.

We are struck, in the first place, with the contrast between this terrific dream and the peaceful hour in which it is sent by the gods to Æneas. No one has referred to times and places with more impressive effect than the Mantuan poet. Here it is

[1] Dryden's *Virgil*, book ii.

a tomb, there some affecting adventure, that determines the limits of a country; a new city bears an ancient appellation; a foreign stream assumes the name of a river in one's native land. As to the hours, Virgil has almost always coupled the most tranquil time with the most distressing events, producing a contrast replete with melancholy, and which recalls the philosophic moral that nature fulfils her laws undisturbed by the petty revolutions in human things.

The delineation of Hector's ghost is also worthy of notice. The phantom, surveying Æneas in silence, his *big* tears, his *swollen* feet, are minor circumstances of which the great painter invariably avails himself to give identity to the object. The words of Æneas—*quantum mutatus ab illo!*—are the exclamation of a hero, duly sensible of Hector's merits and taking a retrospective view of the whole history of Troy. In the *squallentem barbam et concretos sanguine crines* you see the perfect spectre. But Virgil, after his manner, suddenly changes the idea:—*Vulnera . . . . . circum plurima muros accepit patrios.* How comprehensive are these words!—a eulogy on Hector, the memory of his misfortunes and those of his country, for which he received so many wounds. *O lux Dardaniæ! Spes ô fidissima Teucrum!* are exclamations fraught with genuine ardor. How deeply pathetic and how keenly painful do they render the succeeding words: *ut te post multa tuorum funera . . . adspicimus!* Alas! this is the history of those who leave their country. On their return we may address them in the words of Æneas to Hector:—

> After so many funerals of thy own,
> Art thou restored to our declining town?[1]

The silence of Hector, his deep sigh, followed by the exhortation,—*fuge, eripe flammis,*—are also striking circumstances, and cannot fail to produce effects of terror and consternation in the mind of the reader. The last trait in the picture combines the twofold imagery of dream and vision; and it seems as if the spectre were removing Troy itself from the earth when he hurries off with the statue of Vesta and the sacred fire in his arms.

There is, moreover, in this dream, a beauty derived from the

---

[1] The author could not refrain from this observation, after having experienced the truth of it in all its terrible reality. E.

very nature of the thing. Æneas at first rejoices to see Hector, under the impression that he is yet alive; he then alludes to the misfortunes that have befallen Troy since the *death* of the hero. The state in which he beholds him is not sufficient to remind him of his fate; he asks, *whence proceed those wounds?* and yet tells you that he thus appeared the day on which he was dragged round the walls of Ilion. Such is the incoherence of the ideas, sentiments, and images, of a dream.

It is a high gratification to us to find among the Christian poets something that rivals, and that perhaps surpasses, this dream. In poetry, tragic effect, and religion, these two delineations are equal, and Virgil is once more repeated in Racine.

Athalie, under the portico of the temple of Jerusalem, thus relates her dream to Abner and Mathan:—

> 'Twas in the dead of night, when horror reigns,
> My mother Jezabel appeared before me,
> Richly attired as on the day she died.
> Her sorrows had not damped her noble pride;
> She even still retained those borrowed charms
> Which, to conceal the irreparable ravage
> Of envious time, she spread upon her cheeks.
> "Tremble," said she, "O daughter worthy of me!
> The Hebrews' cruel God 'gainst thee prevails;
> I grieve that into his tremendous hands
> Thou too must fall, my daughter!" As she spoke
> These awful words, her shadow toward my bed
> Appeared to stoop; I stretched my arms to meet her
> But grasped in my embrace a frightful mass
> Of bones and mangled flesh besmeared with mire,
> Garments all dyed with gore, and shattered limbs,
> Which greedy dogs seemed eagerly to fight for.

It would be difficult to decide, in this place, between Virgil and Racine. Both dreams are alike drawn from the character of their respective religions. Virgil is more melancholy, Racine more terrific. The latter would have missed his object, and betrayed an ignorance of the gloomy spirit of the Hebrew doctrines, if, after the example of the former, he had placed the dream of Athalie in a peaceful hour. As he is about to perform much, so also he promises much in the verse—

> 'Twas in the dead of night, when horror reigns.

In Racine there is a conformity, and in Virgil a contrast, of images.

The scene announced by the apparition of Hector—that is to say, the destruction of a great nation and the foundation of the Roman empire—would be much more magnificent than the fall of a single queen, if Joas, *rekindling the torch of David*, did not show us in the distance the coming of the Messiah and the reformation of all mankind.

The two poets exhibit the same excellence, though we prefer the passage in Racine. As Hector first appeared to Æneas, so he remained to the end; but the borrowed pomp of Jezabel, so suddenly contrasted with her gory and lacerated form, is a change of person which gives to Racine's verse a beauty not possessed by that of Virgil. The mother's ghost, also, bending over her daughter's bed, as if to conceal itself, and then all at once transformed into mangled bones and flesh, is one of those frightful circumstances which are characteristic of the phantom.

CHAPTER XII.

POETICAL MACHINERY, CONTINUED.

Journeys of Homer's gods—Satan's expedition in quest of the New Creation.

We now come to that part of poetic machinery which is derived from the *journeys* of supernatural beings. This is one of the departments of the *marvellous* in which Homer has displayed the greatest sublimity. Sometimes he tells you that the car of the god flies like the thought of a traveller, who calls to mind in a moment all the regions that he has visited; at others he says, "Far as a man seated on a rock on the brink of ocean can see around him, so far the immortal coursers sprang forward at every bound."

But, whatever may be the genius of Homer and the majesty of his gods, his *marvellous* and all his grandeur are nevertheless eclipsed by the *marvellous* of Christianity.

Satan, having reached the gates of hell, which are opened for him by sin and death, prepares to go in quest of the creation.[1]

The gates wide open stood,
. . . . And like a furnace mouth
Cast forth redounding smoke and ruddy flame.
Before their eyes in sudden view appear
The secrets of the hoary deep, a dark
Illimitable ocean, without bound,
Without dimension, where length, breadth, and height,
And time and place, are lost; where eldest Night
And Chaos, ancestors of Nature, hold
Eternal anarchy, amidst the noise
Of endless wars, and by confusion stand. . . .
Into this wild abyss the wary fiend
Stood on the brink of hell, and looked a while,
Pondering his voyage, for no narrow frith
He had to cross. . . . .
. . . . At last his sail-broad vans
He spreads for flight, and, in the surging smoke
Uplifted, spurns the ground; thence many a league,
As in a cloudy chair, ascending rides
Audacious; but that seat soon failing, meets
A vast vacuity; all unawares,
Fluttering his pennons vain, plump down he drops
Ten thousand fathom deep, and to this hour
Down had been falling, had not, by ill chance,
The strong rebuff of some tumultuous cloud,
Instinct with fire and nitre, hurried him
As many miles aloft; that fury stayed
Quenched in a boggy syrtis, neither sea,
Nor good dry land; nigh foundered, on he fares,
Treading the crude consistence, half on foot,
Half flying. . . . . . .
. . . . The fiend
O'er bog or steep, through strait, rough, dense, or rare,
With head, hands, wings, or feet, pursues his way,
And swims, or sinks, or wades, or creeps, or flies.
At length, a universal hubbub wild
Of stunning sounds and voices all confused,
Borne through the hollow dark, assaults his ear
With loudest vehemence; thither he plies,
Undaunted to meet there whatever power
Or spirit of the nethermost abyss
Might in that noise reside, of whom to ask
Which way the nearest coast of darkness lies

[1] *Paradise Lost*, book ii. v. 888 to 1050; book iii. v. 501 to 544, with the omission of passages here and there.

Bordering on light, when straight behold the throne
Of Chaos, and his dark pavilion spread
Wide on the wasteful deep; with him enthroned,
Sat sable-vested Night, eldest of things,
The consort of his reign; and by them stood
. . . . Rumor and Chance,
And Tumult and Confusion all embroiled,
And Discord with a thousand various mouths,
To whom Satan, turning boldly, thus: Ye Powers
And Spirits of this nethermost abyss,
Chaos, and ancient Night, I come no spy
With purpose to explore or to disturb
The secrets of your realm, but by constraint
Wandering this darksome desert, as my way
Lies through your spacious empire up to light—
. . . . Direct my course.
Thus Satan; and him thus the Anarch old,
With faltering speech and visage incomposed,
Answered: I know thee, stranger, who thou art;—
That mighty leading angel, who of late
Made head against heaven's King, though overthrown.
. . . . I upon my frontiers here
Keep residence, ...
That little which is left so to defend,
Encroached on still through your intestine broils,
Weakening the sceptre of old Night; first hell,
Your dungeon stretching far and wide beneath;
Now lately heaven and earth, another world,
Hung o'er my realm, linked in a golden chain
To that side heaven from whence your legions fell.
. . . . Go and speed;
Havoc and spoil and ruin are my gain!
He ceased; and Satan stayed not to reply,
But, glad that now his sea should find a shore,
With fresh alacrity and force renewed,
Springs upward like a pyramid of fire
Into the wild expanse. . . . .
But now at last the sacred influence
Of light appears, and from the walls of heaven
Shoots far into the bosom of dim night
A glimmering dawn; here nature first begins
Her farthest verge, and Chaos to retire—
That Satan with less toil, and now with ease,
Wafts on the calmer wave by dubious light,
And like a weather-beaten vessel holds
Gladly the port, ...
Weighs his spread wings, at leisure to behold
Far off the empyreal heaven extended wide—
With opal towers and battlements adorned

Of living sapphire. . . . . . .
. . . . Far distant he descries,
Ascending, by degrees magnificent,
Up to the wall of heaven, a structure high—
Direct against which opened from beneath
A passage down to the earth.——
Satan from hence now on the lower stair,
That scaled by steps of gold to heaven gate,
Looks down with wonder at the sudden view
Of all this world at once.

In the opinion of any impartial person, a religion which has furnished such a sublime species of the marvellous, and moreover inspired the idea of the loves of Adam and Eve, cannot be an *anti-poetical* religion. What is Juno, repairing to the limits of the earth in Ethiopia, to Satan speeding his course from the depths of Chaos up to the frontiers of nature? The passages which we have omitted still heighten the effect; for they seem to protract the journey of the prince of darkness, and convey to the reader a vague conception of the infinite space through which he has passed.

CHAPTER XIII.

THE CHRISTIAN HELL.

Among the many differences which distinguish the Christian hell from the Tartarus of the ancients, one in particular is well worthy of remark;—that is, the torments which the devils themselves undergo. Pluto, the Judges, the Fates, the Furies, shared not the tortures of the guilty. The pangs of our infernal spirits are therefore an *additional field* for the imagination, and consequently a *poetical advantage* which our hell possesses over that of antiquity.

In the Cimmerian plains of the *Odyssey*, the indistinctness of the place, the darkness, the incongruity of the objects, the ditch where the shades assemble to quaff blood, give to the picture something awful, and that perhaps bears a nearer resemblance to the Christian hell than the Tænarus of Virgil. In the latter may be perceived the progress of the philosophic doctrines of

Greece. The Fates, the Cocytus, the Styx, are to be found with all their details in the works of Plato. Here commences a distribution of punishments and rewards unknown to Homer. We have already observed[1] that misfortune, indigence, and weakness, were, after death, banished by the pagans to a world as painful as the present. The religion of Jesus Christ has not thus repudiated the souls of men; on the contrary, it teaches the unhappy that when they are removed from this world of tribulation they shall be conveyed to a place of repose, and that, if they have thirsted after righteousness in time, they shall enjoy its rewards in eternity.[2]

If philosophy be satisfied, it will not be difficult perhaps to convince the Muses. We must admit that no Christian poet has done justice to the subject of hell. Neither Dante, nor Tasso, nor Milton, is unexceptionable in this respect. There are some excellent passages, however, in their descriptions, which show that if all the parts of the picture had been retouched with equal care they would have produced a place of torment as poetical as those of Homer and Virgil.

CHAPTER XIV.

PARALLEL BETWEEN HELL AND TARTARUS.

Entrance of Avernus—Dante's gate of Hell—Dido—Francisca d'Arimino—Torments of the damned.

THE description of the entrance of Avernus in the sixth book of the Æneid contains some very finished composition:—

> Ibant obscuri solâ sub nocte per umbram,
> Perque domos ditis vacuas et inania regna.
> . . . .
> Pallentes habitant morbi, tristisque senectus,

[1] Part i. book vi.

[2] The pagan view respecting the infernal region was so manifestly unjust that Virgil himself was compelled to notice it:—

. . . . sortemque animo miseratus iniquam. *Æneid,* b. vi.

Et metus, et malesuada fames, et turpis egestas,
Terribiles visu formæ; letumque, laborque,
Tum consanguineus leti sopor, et mala mentis
Gaudia.

Every one who can read Latin must be struck with the mournful harmony of these lines. You first hear the bellowing of the cavern in which the Sibyl and Æneas are walking:—

Ibant obscuri solâ sub nocte per umbram;

then you are all at once ushered into *desert spaces,* into the *regions of vacuity:*—

Perque domos ditis vacuas et inania regna.

Next come the dull and heavy syllables which admirably represent the deep sighs of hell:—

Tristisque senectus, et metus—letumque, laborque,—

consonances which moreover evince that the ancients were no strangers to the species of beauty attached by us to rhyme. The Latins, as well as the Greeks, employed the repetition of sounds in their pastoral pictures and sombre harmonies.

Dante, like Æneas, at first wanders in a wild forest which conceals the entrance to his hell. Nothing can be more awful than this solitude. He soon reaches the gate, over which he discovers the well-known inscription:—

Per me si và nella città dolente;
Per me si và nell' eterno dolore:
Per me si và tra la perduta gente.
. . . .
Lasciat' ogni speranza, voi ch' entrate.

Here we find precisely the same species of beauties as in the Latin poet. Every ear must be struck with the monotonous cadence of these repeated rhymes, in which the everlasting outcry of pain which ascends from the depths of the abyss seems alternately to burst forth and expire. In the thrice reiterated *per me si và* you may fancy the *knell* of the dying Christian. The *lasciat' ogni speranza* is comparable to the grandest trait in the hell of Virgil.

Milton, after the example of the Mantuan poet, has placed Death at the entrance of his hell (*Letum*) as well as Sin, which is nothing else than the *mala mentis gaudia*, the guilty joys of the heart. The former is thus described by him:—

> The other shape,—
> If shape it might be called that shape had none,—
> . . . . Black it stood as Night,
> Fierce as ten furies, terrible as hell,
> And shook a dreadful dart. What seemed his head,
> The likeness of a kingly crown had on.

Never was phantom represented in a manner more vague and more terrific. The origin of Death, related by Sin,—the manner in which the echoes of hell repeat the tremendous name when for the first time pronounced,—form altogether a species of dark sublime unknown to antiquity.[1]

Advancing into the infernal regions, we go with Æneas into the *lugentes campi*, the plain of tears. He there meets with the unfortunate Dido. He discovers her in the shade of a wood, *as you perceive, or fancy that you perceive, the new moon rising through the clouds.*

> Qualem primo qui surgere mense
> Aut videt aut vidisse putat per nubila lunam.

The whole of this passage displays exquisite taste; but Dante is perhaps not less pathetic in the description of the *plain of tears.* Virgil has placed lovers among myrtle groves and solitary alleys. Dante has surrounded his with a lurid atmosphere and tempests, which incessantly drive them to and fro. The one has assigned to love its own reveries as a punishment. The other has sought that punishment in the image of the excesses to which the passion gives birth. Dante accosts an unhappy couple in the midst of a whirlwind. Francisca d'Arimino, being questioned by the poet, relates the history of her misfortunes and of her love.

---

[1] Harris, in his *Hermes*, remarks that this passage derives great beauty from the masculine gender which is here given to Death. If Milton had said, *shook her dart*, instead of *shook his dart*, the sublime would be diminished. *Death* is masculine in Greek, (*θανατος*,) and Racine has also given it the masculine gender in French, *La mort est le seul dieu que j'osois implorer.* Voltaire has not approved himself much as a critic in finding fault with the use of the masculine for *death* and of the feminine for *sin*, as, in English, *death* may be any of the three genders, and *sin* is properly made feminine by the general rule which applies this gender to nouns implying either *weakness* or *capacity.*

One day,
For our delight, we read of Lancelot,—
How him love thralled. Alone we were, and no
Suspicion near us. Oft-times, by that reading,
Our eyes were drawn together, and the hue
Fled from our altered cheek. But at one point
Alone we fell. When of that smile we read,—
The wished smile, so rapturously kissed
By one so deep in love,—then he, who ne'er
From me shall separate, at once my lips
All trembling kissed. The book and writer both
Were love's purveyors. In its leaves that day
We read no more.[1]

What admirable simplicity in this recital of Francisca! What delicacy of expression in the concluding lines! They are not surpassed by the language of Virgil in the fourth book of the *Æneid*, where allusion is made to the love of Dido:

Then first the trembling earth the signal gave,
And flashing fires enlighten all the cave;
Hell from below, and Juno from above,
And howling nymphs, were conscious to their love.[2]

Not far from the field of tears, Æneas descries the field of the warriors. Here he meets with Deiphobus, cruelly mutilated. Interesting as his story may be, the mere name of Ugolino reminds us of a far more exquisite passage. That Voltaire should have discovered nothing but burlesque objects in the flames of a Christian hell is a circumstance that may be conceived; but we would ask whether poetry at least does not find its advantage in the scenes in which Count Ugolino appears, and which form the subject of such exquisite verse, such tragic episode?

When we pass from all these details to a general view of hell and of Tartarus, we find in the latter the Titans blasted with lightning, Ixion threatened with the fall of a rock, the Danaids with their tun, Tantalus disappointed by the waters, &c.

Whether it be that we are familiarized with the idea of these torments, or that they have nothing in them capable of producing the terrible because they are measured by the standard of hardships known in life, so much is certain, that they make but little impression on the mind. But would you be deeply affected,—

[1] Canto v.

[2] Dryden's Translation.

would you know how far the imagination of pain can extend,—would you become acquainted with the poetry of torments and the hymns of flesh and blood,—descend into the hell of Dante. Here spirits are tossed about by the whirlwinds of a tempest; there burning sepulchres enclose the followers of heresy. Tyrants are plunged into a river of warm blood. Suicides, who have disregarded the noble nature of man, are sunk toward that of the plant, and are transformed into stunted trees which grow in a burning sand and whose branches the harpies are incessantly breaking off. These spirits will not be united to their bodies on the day of the general resurrection. They will drag them into the dreary forest, and there suspend them to the boughs of the trees to which they are attached.

Let it not be asserted that any Greek or Roman author could have produced a Tartarus as awful as Dante's Inferno. Such a remark, were it even correct, would prove nothing decisive against the poetic resources of the Christian religion; but those who have the slightest acquaintance with the genius of antiquity will admit that the sombre coloring of Dante is not to be found in the pagan theology, and that it belongs to the stern doctrines of our faith.

CHAPTER XV.

PURGATORY.

THAT the doctrine of purgatory opens to the Christian poet a source of the marvellous which was unknown to antiquity will be readily admitted.[1] Nothing, perhaps, is more favorable to the inspiration of the muse than this middle state of expiation between the region of bliss and that of pain, suggesting the idea of a confused mixture of happiness and of suffering. The grada-

[1] Some trace of this dogma is to be found in Plato and in the doctrine of Zeno. (See Diog. Laer.) The poets also appear to have had some idea of it; (*Æneid*, b. vi.;) but these notions are all vague and inconsequent. (See note T.)

tion of the punishments inflicted on those souls that are more or less happy, more or less brilliant, according to their degree of proximity to an eternity of joy or of wo, affords an impressive subject for poetic description. In this respect it surpasses the subjects of heaven and hell, because it possesses a future, which they do not.

The river Lethe was a graceful appendage of the ancient Elysium; but it cannot be said that the shades which came to life again on its banks exhibited the same poetical progress in the way to happiness that we behold in the souls of purgatory. When they left the abodes of bliss to reappear among men, they passed from a perfect to an imperfect state. They re-entered the ring for the fight. They were born again to undergo a second death. In short, they came forth to see what they had already seen before. Whatever can be measured by the human mind is necessarily circumscribed. We may admit, indeed, that there was something striking and true in the circle by which the ancients symbolized eternity; but it seems to us that it fetters the imagination by confining it always within a dreaded enclosure. The straight line extended *ad infinitum* would perhaps be more expressive, because it would carry our thoughts into a world of undefined realities, and would bring together three things which appear to exclude each other,—hope, mobility, and eternity.

The apportionment of the punishment to the sin is another source of invention which is found in the purgatorial state, and is highly favorable to the sentimental. What ingenuity might be displayed in determining the pains of a mother who has been too indulgent—of a maiden who has been too credulous—of a young man who has become the victim of a too ardent temperament! If violent winds, raging fires, and icy cold, lend their influence to the torments of hell, why may not milder sufferings be derived from the song of the nightingale, from the fragrance of flowers, from the murmur of the brook, or from the moral affections themselves? Homer and Ossian tell us of the joy of grief, *χρυεροῦ τεταρπώμεσθα γόοιο.*

Poetry finds its advantage also in that doctrine of purgatory which teaches us that the prayers and other good works of the faithful may obtain the deliverance of souls from their temporal pains. How admirable is this intercourse between the living son and the deceased father—between the mother and daughter—between husband and wife—between life and death! What affecting considerations are suggested by this tenet of religion! My virtue, insignificant being as I am, becomes the common property of Christians; and, as I participate in the guilt of Adam, so also the good that I possess passes to the account of others. Christian poets! the prayers of your Nisus will be felt, in their happy effects, by some Euryalus beyond the grave. The rich, whose charity you describe, may well share their abundance with the poor; for the pleasure which they take in performing this simple and grateful act, will receive its reward from the Almighty in the release of their parents from the expiatory flame. What a beautiful feature in our religion, to impel the heart of man to virtue by the power of love, and to make him feel that the very coin which gives bread for the moment to an indigent fellow-being, entitles perhaps some rescued soul to an eternal position at the table of the Lord!

CHAPTER XVI.

PARADISE.

THE characteristic which essentially distinguishes *Paradise* from *Elysium* is this, that in the former the righteous souls dwell in heaven with God and the angels, whereas in the latter the happy shades are separated from Olympus. The philosophic system of Plato and Pythagoras, which divides the soul into two essences—*the subtle form*, which flies beneath the moon, and the *spirit*, which ascends to the Divinity,—this system is not within our province, which embraces the poetical theology alone.

We have shown in various parts of this work the difference which exists between the felicity of the elect and that of the manes in Elysium. 'Tis one thing to dance and to feast, and another to know the nature of things, to penetrate into the secrets of futurity, to contemplate the revolutions of the spheres—in a word, to be associated in the omniscience if not in the omnipotence, of the Eternal. It is, however, not a little extraordinary that, with so many advantages, the Christian poets have all been unsuccessful in their description of heaven. Some have failed through timidity, as Tasso and Milton; others from fatigue, as Dante; from a philosophical spirit, as Voltaire; or from overdrawing the picture, as Klopstock.[1] This subject, therefore, must involve some hidden difficulty, in regard to which we shall offer the following conjectures:—

It is natural to man to show his sympathy only in those things which bear some relation to him and which affect him in a particular way, for instance, misfortune. Heaven, the seat of unbounded felicity, is too much above the human condition for the soul to be touched by it; we feel but little interest in beings perfectly happy. On this account, the poets have always succeeded better in the description of hell; humanity, at least, is here, and the torments of the wicked remind us of the afflictions of life; we are affected by the woes of others, like the slaves of Achilles, who, while shedding many tears for the death of Patroclus, secretly deplored their own unhappy lot.

To avoid the coldness resulting from the eternal and ever uniform felicity of the just, the poet might contrive to introduce into heaven some kind of hope or expectation of superior happiness, or of some grand unknown epoch in the revolution of beings;[2] he might remind the reader more frequently of human things, either by drawing comparisons or by giving affections and even passions to the blessed. Scripture itself mentions the *hopes* and the sacred *sorrows of heaven.* Why should there not be in paradise tears such as saints might be capable of shedding?[3]

---

[1] It is singular enough that Chapelain, who has produced choirs of martyrs, virgins, and apostles, has alone represented the Christian paradise in its true light.

[2] The essential happiness of the blessed in heaven, viz., that which consists in the intuitive vision of God, cannot be increased either before or after the resurrection; but their accidental happiness, or that which may be derived from creatures, is susceptible of augmentation; for instance, when they witness the conversion of sinners, or behold new saints, especially their own relatives or friends, added to the number of the elect. Such events cannot fail to heighten their joy, on account of the love which they have for God and for their neighbor. In this sense only can there be any hope in heaven. (See Witasse, *de Deo.*, quæst. xi. sect. xii.) T.

[3] Milton has seized this idea when he represents the angels dismayed at the

By these various means he would produce harmonies between our feeble nature and a more sublime constitution, between our short-lived existence and eternal things; we should be less disposed to consider as an agreeable fiction a happiness which, like our own, would be mingled with vicissitudes and tears.

From all these considerations on the employment of the Christian marvellous in poetry, we may at least doubt whether the marvellous of Paganism possesses so great an advantage over it as has generally been supposed. Milton, with all his faults, is everlastingly opposed to Homer, with all his beauties. But suppose for a moment that the bard of Eden had been born in France, that he had flourished during the age of Louis XIV., and that with the native grandeur of his genius he had combined the taste of Racine and Boileau; we ask, what in this case the *Paradise Lost* would have been, and whether the *marvellous* of that poem would not have equalled the *marvellous* of the *Iliad* and *Odyssey?* If we formed our judgment of mythology from the *Pharsalia*, or even from the *Æneid*, would we have that brilliant idea of it which is conveyed by the father of the graces, the inventor of the cestus of Venus? When we possess a work on a Christian subject as perfect in its kind as the performances of Homer, we will then have a fair opportunity of deciding between the *marvellous* of fable and the *marvellous* of our own religion; and till then we shall take the liberty of doubting the truth of that precept of Boileau:—

> The awful mysteries of the Christian's faith
> Admit not of the lighter ornaments.

We might, indeed, have abstained from bringing Christianity into the lists against mythology, on the single question concerning the *marvellous*. If we have entered into this subject, it is only to exhibit the superabundant resources of our cause. We might cut short the question in a simple and decisive manner; for were it as certain as it is doubtful that Christianity is incapable of furnishing as rich a *marvellous* as that of fable, still it is true that it possesses a certain poetry of the soul, an imagination of the heart, of which no trace is to be found in mythology; and the impressive beauties which emanate from this source would

intelligence of the fall of man; and Fénélon in like manner assigns emotions of pity to the happy shades.

alone compensate the loss of the ingenious fictions of antiquity. In the pictures of paganism, every thing has a physical character, every thing is external and adapted only to the eye; in the delineations of the Christian religion, all is sentiment and mind, all is internal, all is created for the soul. What food for thought! what depth of meditation! There is more sweetness in one of those divine tears which Christianity draws from the eyes of the believer than in all the smiling errors of mythology. A poet has only to contemplate the *Mother of Sorrows*, or some obscure saint, the patron of the blind and the orphan, to compose a more affecting work than with all the gods of the Pantheon Is there not poetry here? Do we not find here also the marvellous? But, if you would have a marvellous still more sublime, contemplate the life, actions, and sufferings of the Redeemer, and recollect that your *God* bore the appellation of the *Son of man!* Yes, we venture to predict that a time will come when men will be lost in astonishment to think how they could have overlooked the admirable beauties which exist in the mere names, in the mere expressions, of Christianity, and will be scarcely able to conceive how it was possible to aim the shafts of ridicule at this religion of reason and of misfortune [1]

Here we conclude the survey of the direct relations between Christianity and the Muses, having considered it in its relations to *men* and in its relations to supernatural beings. We shall close our remarks on this subject with a general view of the Bible, the source whence Milton, Dante, Tasso, and Racine, derived a part of their wonderful imagery, as the great poets of antiquity had borrowed their grandest traits from the works of Homer.

---

1 The religion of reason or truth, established by the Son of God, must, by its very nature, be always a butt of opposition for every variety of religious error, and consequently expose its professors to obloquy and persecution. It is therefore a religion of misfortune or suffering, as well as of reason or truth. Our Saviour himself announced this external characteristic of his church, and it is a source of immense consolation to its faithful but persecuted members of the present day to recall those words, "You shall be hated by all men for my name's sake." On the other hand, it is a melancholy evidence of the strange blindness that seizes upon the mind, that there are men who boast of their Christianity, and yet, despite the positive declarations of Christ, do not recognise in the storm of opposition continually raging against the Church one of the most striking characteristics of its truth. (See St. Matt. x.) T.

BOOK V.

THE BIBLE AND HOMER.

CHAPTER I.

OF THE SCRIPTURES AND THEIR EXCELLENCE.

How extraordinary that work which begins with Genesis and ends with the Apocalypse! which opens in the most perspicuous style, and concludes in the most figurative language! May we not justly assert that in the books of Moses all is grand and simple, like that creation of the world and that innocence of primitive mortals which he describes, and that all is terrible and supernatural in the last of the prophets, like that corrupt society and that consummation of ages which he has represented?

The productions most foreign to our manners, the sacred books of infidel nations, the Zendavesta of the Parsees, the Vidam of the Brahmins, the Coran of the Turks, the Edda of the Scandinavians, the maxims of Confucius, the Sanscrit poems, excite in us no surprise. We find in all these works the ordinary chain of human ideas; they have all some resemblance to each other both in tone and idea. The Bible alone is like none of them; it is a monument detached from all the others. Explain it to a Tartar, to a Caffre, to an American savage; put it into the hands of a bonze or a dervise; they will be all equally astonished by it —a fact which borders on the miraculous. Twenty authors, living at periods very distant from one another, composed the sacred books; and, though they are written in twenty different styles, yet these styles, equally inimitable, are not to be met with in any other performance. The New Testament, so different in its spirit from the Old, nevertheless partakes with the latter of this astonishing originality.

But this is not the only extraordinary thing which men unanimously discover in the Scriptures. Those who do not believe in the authenticity of the Bible nevertheless believe, in spite of themselves, that there is something more than common in this same Bible. Deists and atheists, great and little, all attracted by some hidden magnet, are incessantly referring to that work, which is admired by the one and reviled by the others. There is not a situation in life for which we may not find in the Bible a text apparently dictated with an express reference to it. It would be a difficult task to persuade us that all possible contingencies, both prosperous and adverse, had been foreseen, with all their consequences, in a book penned by the hands of men. Now it is certain that we find in the Scriptures—

The origin of the world and the prediction of its end:

The groundwork of all the human sciences:

Political precepts, from the patriarchal government to despotism; from the pastoral ages to the ages of corruption:

The moral precepts, applicable in prosperity and adversity, and to the most elevated as well as the most humble ranks of life:

Finally, all sorts of styles, which, forming an inimitable work of many different parts, have, nevertheless, no resemblance to the styles of men.

CHAPTER II.

OF THE THREE PRINCIPAL STYLES OF SCRIPTURE.

Among these divine styles, three are particularly remarkable:—

1. The historic style, as that of Genesis, Deuteronomy, Job, &c.

2. Sacred poetry, as it exists in the Psalms, in the Prophets, in the moral treatises, &c.

3. The evangelical or gospel style

The first of these three styles has an indescribable charm, sometimes imitating the narrative of the epic, as in the history of Joseph, at others bursting into lyric numbers, as after the passage of the Red Sea; here sighing forth the elegies of the holy Arab, there with Ruth singing affecting pastorals. That chosen people, whose every step is marked with miracles,—that people, for whom the sun stands still, the rock pours forth waters, and the heavens shower down manna,—could not have any ordinary annals. All known forms are changed in regard to them: their revolutions are alternately related with the trumpet, the lyre, and the pastoral pipe; and the style of their history is itself a continual miracle, that attests the truth of the miracles the memory of which it perpetuates.

Our astonishment is marvellously excited from one end of the Bible to the other. What can be compared to the opening of Genesis? That simplicity of language, which is in an inverse ratio to the magnificence of the objects, appears to us the utmost effort of genius.

"In the beginning God created heaven and earth.

"And the earth was void and empty, and darkness was upon the face of the deep; and the spirit of God moved over the waters.

"And God said, Be light made, and there was light.

"And God saw the light that it was good, and he divided the light from the darkness."

The beauty of this style cannot be described; and, if it were criticized, we should scarcely know how to answer. We shall merely observe that God, seeing the light, and, like a man satisfied with his work, congratulating himself and finding it good, is one of those traits which are not in the order of human things; it does not come naturally to the mind. Homer and Plato, who speak with so much sublimity of the gods, have nothing comparable to this majestic simplicity. God stoops to the language of men, to reduce his wonders to the level of their comprehension; but he still is God.

When we reflect that Moses is the most ancient historian in the world, and that he has mingled no fabulous story with his narrative; when we consider him as the deliverer of a great people, as the author of one of the most excellent legislative codes that we know of, and as the most sublime writer that ever existed; when we behold him floating in his cradle upon the Nile, afterward concealing himself for many years in the deserts, then returning to open a passage through the sea, to produce streams of water from the rock, to converse with God in a cloud, and finally to disappear on the summit of a mountain, we cannot forbear feeling the highest astonishment. But when, with a reference to Christianity, we come to reflect that the history of the Israelites is not only the real history of ancient days, but likewise the type of modern times; that each fact is of a twofold nature, containing within itself an *historic truth* and a *mystery;* that the Jewish people is a symbolical epitome of the human race, representing in its adventures all that has happened and all that ever will happen in the world; that Jerusalem must always be taken for another city, Sion for another mountain, the Land of Promise for another region, and the call of Abraham for another vocation; when it is considered that the *moral* man is likewise disguised under the *physical* man in this history; that the fall of Adam, the blood of Abel, the violated nakedness of Noah, and the malediction pronounced by that father against a son, are still manifested in the pains of parturition, in the misery and pride of man, in the oceans of blood which since the first fratricide have inundated the globe, and in the oppressed races descended from Cham, who inhabit one of the fairest portions of the earth;[1] lastly, when we behold the Son promised to David appearing at the appointed time to restore genuine morality and the true religion, to unite all the nations of the earth, and to substitute the sacrifice of the internal man for blood-stained holocausts, we are at a loss for words, and are ready to exclaim, with the prophet, "God is our king before ages!"

In Job the historic style of the Bible changes, as we have observed, into elegy. No writer—not even Jeremias, *he alone whose lamentations*, according to Bossuet, *come up to his feelings*—has carried the sadness of the soul to such a pitch as the holy Arab. It is true that the imagery, borrowed from a southern clime, from the sands of the desert, the solitary palm-tree, the sterile mountain, is in singular unison with the language and sentiment of an afflicted soul; but in the melancholy of Job there is something supernatural. The individual man, however wretched, cannot draw forth such sighs from his soul. Job is the emblem of *suffering humanity;* and the inspired writer has found lamentations sufficient to express all the afflictions incident to the whole human race. As, moreover, in Scripture every thing has a final reference to the new covenant, we are authorized in believing that the

[1] The negroes.

elegies of Job were composed also for the days of mourning of the Church of Jesus Christ. Thus God inspired his prophets with funeral hymns worthy of departed Christians, two thousand years before these sacred martyrs had conquered life eternal.

"Let the day perish wherein I was born, and the night in which it was said, A man-child is conceived."[1]

Extraordinary kind of lamentation! Such expressions are to be met with only in the Scripture.

"For now I should have been asleep and still, and should have rest in my sleep."

This expression, *should have rest in* MY *sleep*, is particularly striking. Omit the word *my*, and the whole beauty of it is destroyed. *Sleep* YOUR *sleep, ye opulent of the earth,* says Bossuet, *and remain in* YOUR *dust.*[2]

"Why is light given to him that is in misery, and life to them that are in bitterness of soul?"[3]

Never did an exclamation of deeper anguish burst from the recesses of a human bosom.

"Man born of a woman, living for a short time, is filled with many miseries."[4]

The circumstance—*born of a woman*—is an impressive redundance; we behold all the infirmities of man in the infirmity of his mother. The most elaborate style would not express the vanity of life with such force as those few words—"living for *a short time,* is filled with *many* miseries."

Every reader is acquainted with that exquisite passage in which God deigns to justify his power to Job by confounding the reason of man; we shall therefore say nothing concerning it in this place.

The third species of *historical* style that we find in the Bible is the bucolic; but of this we shall have occasion to speak at some length in the two following chapters.

As to the second general style of the Holy Scriptures, namely, *sacred poetry*, a great number of excellent critics having exerted their abilities on this subject, it would be superfluous for us to go over the grou id again. Who is unacquainted with the choruses of

---

[1] Job iii. 3.
[2] *Funer. Orat.* for the Chancellor Le Tellier.
[3] Job iii. 20.
[4] Job xiv. 8.

Esther and Athalie? Who has not read the odes of Rousseau and of Malherbe? Dr. Lowth's Essay is in the hands of every scholar,[1] and La Harpe has left us an excellent prose translation of the Psalmist.

The third and last style of the sacred volume is that of the *New Testament.* Here the sublimity of the prophets is softened into a tenderness not less sublime; here love itself speaks, here the *Word* is really *made flesh.* What beauty! What simplicity!

Each evangelist has a distinct character, except St. Mark, whose gospel seems to be only an abridgment of St. Matthew's St. Mark, however, was a disciple of St Peter, and several critics are of opinion that he wrote under the dictation of the prince of the apostles It is worthy of remark that he has recorded the fall of his master. That Jesus Christ should have chosen for the head of his church the very one among his disciples who had denied him appears to us a sublime and affecting mystery. The whole spirit of Christianity is unfolded in this circumstance. St Peter is the Adam of the new law; the guilty and penitent father of the new Israelites. His fall teaches us, moreover, that the Christian religion is a religion of mercy, and that Jesus Christ has established his law among men subject to error less for the flowers of innocence than for the fruits of repentance.

The Gospel of St. Matthew is particularly precious for its moral precepts. It contains a greater number of those pathetic lessons which flowed so abundantly from the heart of Jesus than any other gospel.

The narrative of St John has something sweeter and more tender. In him we really behold the disciple whom Jesus loved; the disciple whom he wished to have with him in the garden of Olives during his agony Sublime distinction! for it is only the

---

[1] The deep and various learning of Bishop Lowth, and his elegant and refined taste, give him the strongest claims to the praise here attributed to his work on the sacred poetry of the Hebrews

"What," said he, "is there in the whole compass of poetry, or what can the human mind conceive more grand, more noble, or more animated,—what is there more beautiful or interesting,—than the sacred writings of the Hebrew prophets? They equal the almost inexpressible greatness of the subjects by the splendor of their diction and the majesty of their poetry; and, as some of them are of higher antiquity than even the Fables of the Greeks, so they excel the Greek compositions as much in sublimity as in age."—*Louth's Prælections.* S.

friend of our soul that we deem worthy of entering into the secret of our grief. John was also the only apostle who accompanied the Son of Man to Calvary. It was there that the Saviour confided to him his mother. "Woman, behold thy son!" after that, he saith to the disciple, "Behold thy mother!" Heavenly words, full of love and confidence! The beloved disciple had received an indelible impression of his Master from having reposed on his bosom; hence, he was the first to recognise him after his resurrection. The heart of John could not mistake the features of his divine friend; his faith was the offspring of his charity. The whole Gospel of St. John is characterized by the spirit of that maxim which he repeated so continually in his old age. Full of days and good works, and no longer able to discourse at length to the people whom he had brought forth in Christ, he contented himself with saying, "My little children, love one another."

St. Jerome informs us that St. Luke belonged to the medical profession, (which was so noble and excellent in ancient times,) and that his gospel is a medicine for the soul. The language of this evangelist is pure and elevated, and indicates him to have been a man of letters and acquainted with the affairs and the men of his time. He commences his narrative after the manner of the ancient historians, and you imagine yourself reading an introduction of Herodotus:—

"Forasmuch as many have taken in hand to set forth in order a narrative of the things that have been accomplished among us; according as they have delivered them unto us, who from the beginning were eye-witnesses and ministers of the word; it seemed good to me also, having diligently attained to all things from the beginning, to write to thee in order, most excellent Theophilus."

Such is the ignorance of our times that many who pretend to a liberal education will be surprised to learn that St. Luke is a writer of high rank, and that his gospel breathes the genius of Græco-Hebræic antiquity. What narrative is more beautiful than the whole passage which precedes the birth of Christ?

"There was in the days of Herod the king of Judea, a certain priest named Zachary, of the course of Abia, and his wife was of the daughters of Aaron, and her name was Elizabeth. And they were both just before God; . . . . and they had nc son, for that Elizabeth was barren, and they both were well advanced in years."

Zachary is offering up sacrifice in the temple, when an angel appears to him "standing on the right side of the altar of incense." He announces that he shall have a son, and that this son shall be called John, who will be the precursor of the Messiah and will turn "the hearts of the fathers unto the children." The same angel then repairs to the humble dwelling of an Israelitic virgin, and says to her, "Hail, full of grace, the Lord is with thee!" Mary hastens to the mountains of Judea, where she meets Elizabeth, and the infant in the womb of the latter leaps with joy at the salutation of her who was to bring forth the Saviour of the world. Filled all at once with the Holy Ghost, Elizabeth exclaims, "Blessed art thou among women, and blessed is the fruit of thy womb! And whence is this to me, that the mother of my Lord should come to me? For behold, as soon as the voice of thy salutation sounded in my ears, the infant in my womb leaped for joy" Then Mary entones that magnificent canticle, "My soul doth magnify the Lord," &c. Here follows the history of the Redeemer's birth and of the shepherds who come to adore him. A numerous multitude of the celestial army are heard singing, "Glory to God in the highest, and on earth peace to men of good will:" a hymn worthy of the angels, and an abridgment, as it were, of the Christian religion.

We know something of antiquity, and we venture to assert that a long search would be necessary among the brightest geniuses of Rome and Greece, before any thing could be found to rival the simplicity and grandeur of the passage which we have just quoted

Whoever reads the gospel with attention will discover something admirable at every moment, which at first might escape his notice on account of its extreme simplicity. St. Luke, for instance, in recording the genealogy of Christ, ascends to the very origin of the world. Having reached the primitive generations, and continuing the names of the different races, he says: "Cainan, who was of Henos, who was of Seth, who was of Adam, who was of GOD." The simple expression, *who was of God,* without comment or reflection, to relate the creation, the origin, the nature, the end, and the mystery, of man, appears to us an illustration of the grandest sublimity.

The religion of the Son of Mary is the essence, as it were, of all religions, or that which is most celestial in them all. The character of the evangelical style may be delineated in a few words: it is a tone of parental authority mingled with a certain fraternal indulgence, with I know not what commiseration of a God who, to redeem us, deigned to become the son and the brother of men.

To conclude: the more we read the epistles of the apostles, and especially those of St. Paul, the more we are astonished; we look in wonder upon the man who, in a kind of common exhortation, familiarly introduces the most sublime thoughts, penetrates into the deepest recesses of the human heart, explains the nature of the Supreme Being, and predicts future events.[1]

CHAPTER III.

PARALLEL BETWEEN THE BIBLE AND HOMER.

Terms of Comparison.

So much has been written on the Bible,—it has been so repeatedly commented upon,—that the only method perhaps now left to produce a conviction of its beauties is to compare it with the works of Homer. Consecrated by ages, these poems have become invested with a venerable character which justifies the parallel and removes all idea of profanation. If Jacob and Nestor are not of the same family, both at least belong to the early ages of the world, and you feel that it is but a step from the palace of Pylos to the tents of Israel.

In what respect the Bible is more beautiful than Homer—what resemblances and what differences exist between it and the productions of that poet,—such are the subjects which we purpose to examine in these chapters. Let us contemplate those two magnificent monuments, which stand like solitary columns at the entrance to the temple of genius, and form its simple, its majestic peristyle.

[1] See note U.

In the first place, it is a curious spectacle to behold the competition of the two most ancient languages in the world, the languages in which Moses and Lycurgus published their laws and David and Pindar chanted their hymns. The Hebrew, concise, energetic, with scarcely any inflection in its verbs, expressing twenty shades of a thought by the mere apposition of a letter, proclaims the idiom of a people who, by a remarkable combination, unite primitive simplicity with a profound knowledge of mankind.

The Greek displays, in its intricate conjugations, in its endless inflections, in its diffuse eloquence, a nation of an imitative and social genius,—a nation elegant and vain, fond of melody and prodigal of words.

Would the Hebrew compose a verb, he needs but know the three radical letters which form the third person singular of the preterite tense. He then has at once all the tenses and moods, by introducing certain *servile* letters before, after, or between, those three radical letters.

The Greek meets with much more embarrassment. He is obliged to consider the *characteristic*, the *termination*, the *augment*, and the *penultima*, of certain *persons* in the *tenses* of the verbs; modifications the more difficult to be discovered, as the characteristic is lost, transposed, or takes up an unknown letter, according to the very letter before which it happens to be placed.

These two conjugations, Hebrew and Greek, the one so simple and so short, the other so compounded and so prolix, seem to bear the stamp of the genius and manners of the people by whom they were respectively formed The first retraces the concise language of the Patriarch who goes alone to visit his neighbor at the well of the palm-tree; the latter reminds you of the prolix eloquence of the Pelasgian on presenting himself at the door of his host.

If you take at random any Greek or Hebrew substantive, you will be still better able to discover the genius of the two languages. *Nesher,* in Hebrew, signifies an *eagle;* it is derived from the verb *shur,* to *contemplate,* because the eagle gazes steadfastly at the sun. The Greek for *eagle* is *'αιετος, rapid flight.*

The children of Israel were struck with what is most sublime in the eagle; they beheld him motionless on the mountain rock watching the orb of day on his return.

The Athenians perceived only the impetuous flight of the bird and that motion which harmonized with the peculiar movement of their own thoughts. Such are precisely those images of *sun*, *fire*, and *mountains*, so frequently employed in the Bible, and those allusions to *sounds*, *courses*, and *passages*, which so repeatedly occur in Homer.[1]

Our terms of comparison will be, Simplicity; Antiquity of Manners; Narration; Description; Comparisons or Images; the Sublime. Let us examine the first of these terms.

1. SIMPLICITY.

The simplicity of the Bible is more concise and more solemn; the simplicity of Homer more diffuse and more lively: the former is sententious, and employs the same terms for the expression of new ideas; the latter is fond of expatiating, and often repeats in the same phrases what has been said before. The simplicity of Scripture is that of an ancient priest, who, imbued with all the sciences, human and divine, pronounces from the recess of the sanctuary the precise oracles of wisdom. The simplicity of the poet of Chios is that of an aged traveller, who, beside the hearth of his host, relates all that he has learned in the course of a long and chequered life.

2. ANTIQUITY OF MANNERS.

The sons of the shepherds of the East tend their flocks like the sons of the king of Ilium. But if Paris returns to Troy, it is to reside in a palace among slaves and in the midst of luxury. A tent, a frugal table, rustic attendants,—this is all that Jacob's children have to expect at the paternal home.

No sooner does a visitor arrive at the habitation of a prince in Homer than the women, and sometimes even the king's daughter herself, lead the stranger to the bath. He is anointed with

---

[1] *Αἰετός* seems to come from the Hebrew HAIT, *to go forth impetuously*, unless it be derived from ATE, *soothsayer*, or ATH, *prodigy*. The art of divination might thus be traced to an etymology. The Latin *aquila* comes evidently from the Hebrew *aiouke*, *animal with claws*, by giving it the Latin termination *a*, pronouncing the *u* like *ou*, and transposing the *k* and changing it into *q*.

perfumes, water is brought him in ewers of gold and silver, he is invested with a purple mantle, conducted to the festive hall, and seated in a beautiful chair of ivory raised upon a step of curious workmanship. Slaves mingle wine and water in goblets, and present the gifts of Ceres in a basket; the master of the house helps him to the juicy portion of the victim, of which he gives him five times more than to any of the others. The greatest cheerfulness prevails during the repast, and hunger is soon appeased in the midst of plenty. When they have finished eating, the *stranger* is requested to relate his history. At length, when he is about to depart, rich presents are made him, let his appearance at first have been ever so mean; for it is supposed that he is either a god who comes thus disguised to surprise the heart of kings, or at least an unfortunate man, and consequently a favorite of Jupiter.

Beneath the tent of Abraham the reception is different. The patriarch himself goes forth to meet his guest; he salutes him, and then pays his adorations to God. The sons lead away the camels, and the daughters fetch them water to drink. The feet of the *traveller* are washed; he seats himself on the ground, and partakes in silence of the repast of hospitality. No inquiries are made concerning his history; no questions are asked him; he stays or pursues his journey as he pleases. At his departure a covenant is made with him, and a stone is erected as a memorial of the treaty This simple altar is designed to inform future ages that two men of ancient times chanced to meet in the road of life, and that, after having behaved to one another like two brothers, they parted never to come together again, and to interpose vast regions between their graves.

Take notice that the unknown guest is a *stranger* with Homer and a *traveller* in the Bible. What different views of humanity! The Greek implies merely a political and local idea, where the Hebrew conveys a moral and universal sentiment.

In Homer, all civil transactions take place with pomp and parade. A judge seated in the midst of the public place pronounces his sentences with a loud voice Nestor on the seashore presides at sacrifices or harangues the people. Nuptial rites are accompanied with torches, epithalamiums, and garlands suspended from the doors; an army, a whole nation, attends the funeral of a king; an oath is taken in the name of the Furies, with dreadful imprecations.

Jacob, under a palm-tree at the entrance of his tent, administers justice to his shepherds. "Put thy hand under my thigh," said the aged Abraham to his servant, "and swear to go into Mesopotamia"[1] Two words are sufficient to conclude a marriage by the side of a fountain. The servant conducts the bride to the son of his master, or the master's son engages to tend the flocks of his father-in-law for seven years in order to obtain his daughter. A patriarch is carried by his sons after his death to the sepulchre of his ancestors in the field of Ephron. These customs are of higher antiquity than those delineated by Homer, because they are more simple; they have also a calmness and a solemnity not to be found in the former.

3. NARRATION.

The narrative of Homer is interrupted by digressions, harangues, descriptions of vessels, garments, arms, and sceptres, by genealogies of men and things. Proper names are always surcharged with epithets. A hero seldom fails to be *divine*, *like the immortals*, or *honored by the nations as a God*. A princess is sure to have *handsome arms;* her shape always resembles *the trunk of the palm-tree of Delos*, and she owes her locks to *the youngest of the graces*.

The narrative of the Bible is rapid, without digression, without circumlocution; it is broken into short sentences, and the persons are named without flattery. These names are incessantly recurring, and the pronoun is scarcely ever used instead of them,—a circumstance which, added to the frequent repetition of the conjunction *and*, indicates by this extraordinary simplicity a society much nearer to the state of nature than that sung by Homer. All the selfish passions are awakened in the characters of the Odyssey, whereas they are dormant in those of Genesis.

---

[1] The custom of swearing by the generation of men is a natural image of the manners of that primeval age when a great portion of the earth was still a desert waste, and man was the chief and most precious object in the eyes of his fellow-man. This custom was also known among the Greeks, as we learn from the life of Crates; Diog. Laer., l. vi.

4. DESCRIPTION.

The descriptions of Homer are prolix, whether they be of the pathetic or terrible character, melancholy or cheerful, energetic or sublime

The Bible, in all its different species of description, gives in general but one single trait; but this trait is striking, and distinctly exhibits the object to our view.

5. COMPARISONS.

The comparisons of Homer are lengthened out by incidental circumstances; they are little pictures hung round an edifice to refresh the eye of the spectator, fatigued with the elevation of the domes, by calling his attention to natural scenery and rural manners.

The comparisons of the Bible are generally expressed in few words; it is a lion, a torrent, a storm, a conflagration, that roars, falls, ravages, consumes. Circumstantial similes, however, are also met with; but, then, an oriental turn is adopted, and the object is personified, as pride in the cedar, &c.

6. THE SUBLIME.

Finally, the sublime in Homer commonly arises from the general combination of the parts, and arrives by degrees at its acme.

In the Bible it is always unexpected; it bursts upon you like lightning, and you are left wounded by the thunderbolt before you know how you were struck by it.

In Homer, again, the sublime consists in the magnificence of the words harmonizing with the majesty of thought.

In the Bible, on the contrary, the highest sublimity often arises from a vast discordance between the majesty of the ideas and the littleness, nay, the triviality, of the word that expresses them. The soul is thus subjected to a terrible shock; for when, exalted by thought, it has soared to the loftiest regions, all on a sudden the expression, instead of supporting it, lets it fall from heaven to earth, precipitating it from the bosom of the divinity into the mire of this world. This species of sublime—the most impetuous of all—is admirably adapted to an immense and awful being, allied at once to the greatest and the most trivial objects.

CHAPTER IV.

CONTINUATION OF THE PARALLEL BETWEEN THE BIBLE AND HOMER—EXAMPLES.

A FEW examples will now complete the development of our parallel. We shall reverse the order which we before pursued,—that is, we shall begin with addresses, from which short and detached passages may be quoted, in the nature of the *sublime* and the *simile,* and conclude with the *simplicity and antiquity of manners.*

There is a passage remarkably sublime in the *Iliad;* it is that which represents Achilles, after the death of Patroclus, appearing unarmed at the entrenchments of the Greeks, and striking terror into the Trojan battalions by his shouts.[1] The golden cloud which encircles the brows of Pelides, the flame which plays upon his head, the comparison of this flame with a fire kindled at night on the top of a besieged tower, the three shouts of Achilles which thrice throw the Trojan army into confusion, form altogether that Homeric sublime which, as we have observed, is composed of the combination of several beautiful incidents with magnificence of words.

Here is a very different species of the sublime; it is the movement of the ode in its highest enthusiasm.

"The burden of the valley of vision. What aileth thee also, that thou, too, art wholly gone up to the house-tops? Full of clamor, a populous city, a joyous city: thy slain are not slain by the sword, nor dead in battle. . . . . . Behold, the Lord . . . . will crown thee with a crown of tribulation; he will toss thee like a ball into a large and spacious country; there shalt thou die, and there shall the chariot of thy glory be, the shame of the house of thy Lord."[2]

Into what unknown world does the prophet all at once transport you? Who is it that speaks, and to whom are these words addressed? Movement follows upon movement, and each verse

---

[1] *Iliad,* lib. xviii. 204.

[2] Isaias xxii. 1, 2, 18.

produces greater astonishment than that which precedes it The city is no longer an assemblage of edifices; it is a female, or rather a mysterious character, for the sex is not specified. This person is represented *going to the house-tops to mourn;* the prophet, sharing her agitation, asks in the singular, "Wherefore dost thou ascend"? and he adds *wholly,* in the collective: "He shall throw you like a ball into a spacious field, and to this shall the chariot of your glory be reduced." Here are combinations of words and a poetry truly extraordinary.

Homer has a thousand sublime ways of characterizing a violent death; but the Scripture has surpassed them all in this single expression:—"*The first-born of death* shall devour his strength."

The *first-born of death,* to imply the most cruel death, is one of those metaphors which are to be found nowhere but in the Bible. We cannot conceive whither the human mind has been in quest of this; all the paths that lead to this species of the sublime are unexplored and unknown.[1]

It is thus also that the Scriptures term death *the king of terrors;*[2] and thus, too, they say of the wicked man, *he hath conceived sorrow, and brought forth iniquity.*[3]

When the same Job would excite a high idea of the greatness of God, he exclaims:—*Hell is naked before him,*[4]—*he withholdeth the waters in the clouds,*[5]—*he taketh the scarf from kings, and girdeth their loins with a cord.*[6]

The soothsayer Theoclimenus is struck, while partaking of the banquet of Penelope, with the sinister omens by which the suitors are threatened. He addresses them in this apostrophe:—

O race to death devote! with Stygian shade
Each destined peer impending fates invade:
With tears your wan, distorted cheeks are drowned;
With sanguine drops the walls are rubied round:
Thick swarms the spacious hall with howling ghosts,
To people Orcus and the burning coasts!
Nor gives the sun his golden orb to roll,
But universal night usurps the pole.[7]

[1] Job xviii. 13 We have followed here the Hebrew text, with the polyglott of Ximenes, the versions of Sanctes Pagnin, Arius Montanus, &c. The Vulgate has, "first-born death," *primogenita mors.*

[2] Ibid. v. 14. [3] Ibid. xv. 35. [4] Ibid. xxvi. 6.

[5] Ibid. xii. 15. [6] Ibid. xii. 18.

[7] Pope's *Homer's Odyss.*, book xx. 423–430.

Awful as this sublime may be, still it is inferior in this respect to the vision of Eliphaz, in the book of Job:—

"In the horror of a vision by night, when deep sleep is wont to hold men, fear seized upon me, and trembling, and all my bones were affrighted; and when *a spirit passed before me, the hair of my flesh stood up.* There stood one whose countenance I knew not, an image before my eyes, and I heard the voice as it were of a gentle wind."[1]

Here we have much less blood, less darkness, and fewer tears, than in Homer; but that unknown countenance and gentle wind are, in fact, much more awful.

As to that species of the sublime which results from the collision of a great idea and a feeble image, we shall presently see a fine example of it when we come to treat of comparisons.

If the bard of Ilium represents a youth slain by the javelin of Menelaus, he compares him to a young olive-tree covered with flowers, planted in an orchard, screened from the intense heat of the sun, amid dew and zephyrs; but, suddenly overthrown by an impetuous wind upon its native soil, it falls on the brink of the nutritive waters that conveyed the sap to its roots. Such is the long simile of Homer, with its elegant and charming details:—

Καλον, τηλεθαον, τοδε τε πνοιαι δονεουσι
Παντοιων ανεμων, και τεβρυει ανθει λευκω.

As the young olive in some sylvan scene,
Crowned by fresh fountains with eternal green,
Lifts the gay head in snowy flow'rets fair,
And plays and dances to the gentle air;
When lo! a whirlwind from high heaven invades
The tender plant, and withers all its shades;
It lies uprooted from its genial bed,
A lovely ruin, now defaced and dead.[2]

In reading these lines, we seem to hear the sighings of the wind through the summit of the olive.

The Bible, instead of all this, has but a single trait. "The wicked," it says, "shall be blasted as a vine when its grapes are in the first flower, and as an olive-tree that casteth its flowers."[3]

"With shaking shall the earth be shaken as a drunken man,"

---

[1] Job iv. 13–16. [2] *Iliad*, lib. xvii. 55, 56. [3] Job xv. 33.

exclaims Isaias, "and shall be removed as the tent of one night."[1]

Here is the sublime in contrast. At the words, *it shall be removed,* the mind remains suspended, and expects some great comparison, when the prophet adds, *like the tent of one night* You behold the earth, which to us appears so vast, spread out in the air, and then carried away with ease by the mighty God by whom it was extended, and with whom the duration of ages is scarcely as a rapid night.

Of the second species of comparison which we have ascribed to the Bible, that is, the *long* simile, we meet with the following instance in Job:—

"He (the wicked man) seemeth to have moisture before the sun cometh, and at his rising his blossom shall shoot forth. His roots shall be thick upon a heap of stones, and among the stones he shall abide. If one swallow him up out of his place, he shall deny him, and shall say, I know thee not."[2]

How admirable is this simile, or, rather, this prolonged metaphor! Thus, the wicked are denied by those sterile hearts, by those *heaps of stones,* in which, during their guilty prosperity, they foolishly struck root. Those flints which all at once acquire the faculty of speech exhibit a species of personification almost unknown to the Ionian bard.[3]

Ezekiel, prophesying the destruction of Tyre, exclaims:— "Now shall the ships be astonished in the day of thy terror; and the islands in the sea shall be troubled, because no one cometh out of thee."[4]

Can any thing be more awful and more impressive than this image? You behold in imagination that city, once so flourishing and so populous, still standing with all her towers and all her edifices, but not a living creature traversing her desert streets or passing through her solitary gates.

Let us proceed to examples of the narrative kind, which exhibit a combination of *sentiment, description, imagery, simplicity,* and *antiquity of manners.*

---

[1] Isaias xxiv 20. [2] Job viii. 16–18.

[3] Homer has represented the shore of the Hellespont as weeping

[4] Ezek. xxvi. 18

The most celebrated passages, the most striking and most admired traits in Homer, occur almost word for word in the Bible, but here they invariably possess an incontestable superiority.

Ulysses is seated at the festive board of king Alcinoüs, while Demodocus sings the Trojan war and the misfortunes of the Greeks:—

> Touched at the song, Ulysses straight resigned
> To soft affliction all his manly mind:
> Before his eyes the purple vest he drew,
> Industrious to conceal the falling dew;
> But when the music paused, he ceased to shed
> The flowing tear, and raised his drooping head;
> And, lifting to the gods a goblet crowned,
> He poured a pure libation to the ground.
> Transported with the song, the listening train
> Again with loud applause demand the strain:
> Again Ulysses veiled his pensive head,
> Again unmanned, a shower of sorrow shed.[1]

Beauties of this nature have, from age to age, secured to Homer the first place among the greatest geniuses. It reflects no discredit upon his memory that he has been surpassed in such pictures by men who wrote under the immediate inspiration of heaven. But vanquished he certainly is, and in such a manner as to leave criticism no possible subterfuge.

They who sold Joseph into Egypt, the own brothers of that powerful man, return to him without knowing who he is, and bring young Benjamin with them, according to his desire.

"Joseph, courteously saluting them again, asked them, saying, Is the old man, your father, in health, of whom you told me?—is he yet living?

"And they answered, Thy servant, our father, is in health,—he is yet living. And, bowing themselves, they made obeisance to him.

"And Joseph, lifting up his eyes, saw Benjamin, his brother by the same mother, and said, Is this your young brother of whom you told me? And he said, God be gracious to thee, my son.

"And he made haste, because his heart was moved upon his brother, and tears gushed out; and, going into his chamber, he wept.

[1] Pope's *Homer's Odyss.*, b. viii. 79–90.

"And when he had washed his face, coming out again, he refrained himself, and said, Set bread on the table."[1]

Here are Joseph's tears in opposition to those of Ulysses Here are beauties of the very same kind, and yet what a difference in pathos! Joseph weeping at the sight of his ungrateful brethren and of the young and innocent Benjamin—this manner of inquiring concerning his father—this adorable simplicity—this mixture of grief and kindness—are things wholly ineffable. The tears naturally start into your eyes, and you are ready to weep like Joseph

Ulysses, disguised in the house of Eumæus, reveals himself to Telemachus He leaves the habitation of the herdsman, strips off his rags, and, restored to his beauty by a touch of Minerva's wand, he returns magnificently attired.

> The prince, o'erawed,
> Scarce lifts his eyes, and bows as to a god.
> Then with surprise, (surprise chastised by fears,)
> How art thou changed! he cries; a god appears!
> Far other vests thy limbs majestic grace;
> Far other glories lighten from thy face!
> If heaven be thy abode, with pious care,
> Lo! I the ready sacrifice prepare,
> Lo! gifts of labored gold adorn thy shrine,
> To win thy grace. Oh save us, power divine
>   Few are my days, Ulysses made reply,
> Nor I, alas! descendant of the sky.
> I am thy father. Oh my son! my son!
> That father for whose sake thy days have run
> One scene of wo—to endless cares consigned
> And outraged by the wrongs of base mankind.
> Then, rushing to his arms, he kissed his boy
> With the strong raptures of a parent's joy.
> Tears bathe his cheek, and tears the ground bedew
> He strained him close, as to his breast he grew.[2]

We shall recur to this interview; but let us first turn to that between Joseph and his brethren

Joseph, after a cup has been secretly introduced by his direction into Benjamin's sack, orders the sons of Jacob to be stopped. The latter are thunder-struck Joseph affects an intention to

---

[1] Genesis xliii. 26–31. [2] Pope's *Homer's Odyssey*, book xvi. 194–213

detain the culprit. Juda offers himself as a hostage for Benjamin. He relates to Joseph that, before their departure for Egypt, Jacob had said to them:—

"You know that my wife bore me two.

"One went out, and you said a beast devoured him; and hitherto he appeareth not.

"If you take this, also, and any thing befall him in the way, you will bring down my gray hairs with sorrow unto hell. . . . .

"Joseph could no longer refrain himself before many that stood by; whereupon he commanded that all should go out, and no stranger be present at their knowing one another.

"And he lifted up his voice with weeping, which the Egyptians and all the house of Pharao heard.

"And he said to his brethren, I am Joseph; is my father yet living? His brethren could not answer him, being struck with exceeding great fear.

"And he said mildly to them, Come nearer to me. And when they were come near him he said, I am Joseph, your brother, whom ye sold into Egypt.

"Be not afraid; . . . . not by your counsel was I sent hither, but by the will of God.

"Make haste and go ye up to my father.

"And, falling upon the neck of his brother Benjamin, he embraced him and wept; and Benjamin in like manner wept also on his neck.

"And Joseph kissed all his brethren, and wept upon every one of them."[1]

Such is the history of Joseph, which we find not in the work of a sophist, (for that which springs from the heart and from tears is not understood by him;) but we find this history in the volume which forms the groundwork of that religion so despised by sophists and freethinkers, and which would have a just right to return contempt for contempt, were not charity its essence. Let us examine in what respects the interview between Joseph and his brethren surpasses the discovery of Ulysses to Telemachus.

Homer, in our opinion, has, in the first place, fallen into a great

---

[1] Genesis xliv. and xlv.

error in employing the *marvellous* in his picture. In dramatic scenes, when the passions are agitated and all the wonders ought to emanate from the soul, the intervention of a divinity imparts coldness to the action, gives to the sentiment the air of fable, and discloses the falsehood of the poet where we expected to meet with nothing but truth. Ulysses, making himself known in his rags by some natural mark, would have been much more pathetic. Of this Homer was himself aware, since the king of Ithica was revealed to Euryclea, his nurse, by an ancient scar, and to Laertes by the little circumstance of the pear-trees which the good old man had given him when a child. We love to find that the heart of the *destroyer of cities* is formed like those of other men, and that the simple affections constitute its principal element.

The discovery is much more ably conducted in Genesis By an artifice of the most harmless revenge, a cup is put into the sack of the young and innocent Benjamin The guilty brethren are overwhelmed with grief when they figure to themselves the affliction of their aged father; and the image of Jacob's sorrow, taking the heart of Joseph by surprise, obliges him to discover himself sooner than he had intended. As to the pathetic words, *I am Joseph*, everybody knows that they drew tears of admiration from Voltaire himself. Ulysses found in Telemachus a dutiful and affectionate son. Joseph is speaking to his brethren who *had sold him*. He does not say to them, *I am your brother*, but merely, I am *Joseph;* and this name awakens all their feelings. Like Telemachus, they are deeply agitated; but it is not the majesty of Pharao's minister; 'tis something within their own consciences that occasions their consternation He desires them *to come near to him;* for he raised his voice to such a pitch as to be heard by the whole house of Pharao when he said, *I am Joseph.* His brethren alone are to hear the explanation, which he adds in a *low tone;* I am Joseph, YOUR BROTHER, WHOM YE SOLD INTO EGYPT. Here are delicacy, simplicity, and generosity, carried to the highest degree

Let us not fail to remark with what kindness Joseph cheers his brethren, and the excuses which he makes for them when he says that, so far from having injured him, they are, on the contrary, the cause of his elevation The Scripture never fails to introduce Providence in the perspective of its pictures. The great counsel of God, which governs all human affairs at the moment when they seem to be most subservient to the passions of men and the laws of chance, wonderfully surprises the mind. We love the idea of that hand concealed in the cloud which is incessantly engaged with men. We love to imagine ourselves something in the plans of Infinite Wisdom, and to feel that this transitory life is a pattern of eternity.

With God every thing is great; without God every thing is little: and this remark applies even to the sentiments. Suppose all the circumstances in Joseph's story to happen as they are recorded in Genesis,—suppose the son of Jacob to be as kind, as tender, as he is represented, but, at the same time, to be a *philosopher*, and, instead of telling his brethren, *I am here by the will of the Lord*, let him say, *fortune has favored me.* The objects are instantly diminished; the circle becomes contracted, and the pathos vanishes together with the tears.

Finally, Joseph kisses his brethren as Ulysses embraces Telemachus; but he begins with Benjamin. A modern author would not have failed to represent him falling in preference upon the neck of the most guilty of the brothers, that his hero might be a genuine tragedy character. The Bible, more intimately acquainted with the human heart, knew better how to appreciate that exaggeration of sentiment by which a man always appears to be striving to perform or to say what he considers something extraordinary. Homer's comparison of the sobs of Telemachus and Ulysses with the cries of an eagle and her young, had, in our opinion, been better omitted in this place. "And he fell upon Benjamin's neck, and kissed him, and wept; and Benjamin wept also, as he held him in his embrace." Such is the only magnificence of style adapted to such occasions.

We might select from Scripture other narratives equally excellent with the history of Joseph; but the reader himself may easily compare them with passages in Homer. Let him take, for instance, the story of Ruth, and the reception of Ulysses by Eumæus. The book of Tobias displays a striking resemblance to several scenes of the Iliad and Odyssey. Priam is conducted by Mercury in the form of a handsome youth, as Tobias is accompanied by an angel in the like disguise.

The Bible is particularly remarkable for certain modes of ex pression—far more pathetic, we think, than all the poetry of Homer. When the latter would delineate old age he says:—

> Slow from his seat arose the Pylean sage,—
> Experienced Nestor, in persuasion skilled;
> Words sweet as honey from his lips distilled.
> Two generations now had passed away,
> Wise by his rules, and happy by his sway;
> Two ages o'er his native realm he reigned,
> And now the example of the third remained.[1]

This passage possesses the highest charms of antiquity, as well as the softest melody. The second verse, with the repetitions of the letter L, imitates the sweetness of honey and the pathetic eloquence of an old man:—

> Τυ καὶ ἀπὸ γλώσσης μέλιτος γλυκίων ῥῦεν αὐδή.

Pharao having asked Jacob his age, the patriarch replies:—

"The days of my pilgrimage are one hundred and thirty years, few and evil; and they are not come up to the days of the pilgrimage of my fathers."[2]

Here are two very different kinds of antiquity. The one lies in the image, the other in the sentiments; the one excites pleasing ideas, the other melancholy; the one, representing the chief of the nation, exhibits the old man only in relation to a certain condition of life, the other considers him individually and exclusively Homer leads us to reflect rather upon men in general, and the Bible upon the particular person.

Homer has frequently touched upon connubial joys, but has he produced any thing like the following?

"Isaac brought Rebecca into the tent of Sarah, his mother, and took her to wife, and he loved her so much that it moderated the sorrow which was occasioned by his mother's death."[3]

We shall conclude this parallel, and the whole subject of Christian poetics, with an illustration which will show at once the difference that exists between the style of the Bible and that of Homer; we shall take a passage from the former and present it in colors borrowed from the latter. Ruth thus addresses Noemi:—

---

[1] *Iliad*, b. i. [2] Gen. xlvii. 9. [3] Gen. xxiv. 67.

"Be not against me to desire that I should leave thee and depart; for whithersoever thou shalt go I will go, and where thou shalt dwell I also will dwell. Thy people shall be my people, and thy God my God. The law that shall receive thee dying, in the same will I die."[1]

Let us endeavor to render this passage in the language of Homer.

The fair Ruth thus replies to the wise Noemi, honored by the people as a goddess: "Cease to oppose the determination with which a divinity inspires me. I will tell thee the truth, just as it is, and without disguise. I will remain with thee, whether thou shalt continue to reside among the Moabites, so dexterous in throwing the javelin, or shalt return to Judea, so fertile in olives. With thee I will demand hospitality of the nations who respect the suppliant. Our ashes shall be mingled in the same urn, and I will offer agreeable sacrifices to the God who incessantly accompanies thee.

"She said; and as, when a vehement wind brings a cool refreshing rain from the western sky, the husbandmen prepare the wheat and the barley, and make baskets of rushes nicely interwoven, for they foresee that the falling shower will soften the soil and render it fit for receiving the precious gifts of Ceres, so the words of Ruth, like the fertilizing drops, melted the whole heart of Noemi."

Something like this, perhaps,—so far as our feeble talents allow us to imitate Homer,—would be the style of that immortal genius. But has not the verse of Ruth, thus amplified, lost the original charm which it possesses in the Scripture? What poetry can ever be equivalent to that single stroke of eloquence, *Populus tuus populus meus, Deus tuus Deus meus.* It will now be easy to take a passage of Homer, to efface the colors, and to leave nothing but the groundwork, after the manner of the Bible.

We have thus endeavored, to the best of our limited abilities, to make our readers acquainted with some of the innumerable beauties of the sacred Scriptures. Truly happy shall we be, if

---

[1] Ruth i. 16.

we have succeeded in exciting within them an admiration of that grand and sublime corner-stone which supports the church of Jesus Christ!

"If the Scripture," says St. Gregory the Great, "comprehends mysteries capable of perplexing the most enlightened understandings, it also contains simple truths fit for the nourishment of the humble and the illiterate; it carries externally wherewith to suckle infants, and in its most secret recesses wherewith to fill the most sublime geniuses with admiration; like a river whose current is so shallow in certain parts that a lamb may cross it, and deep enough in others for an elephant to swim there."

Part the Third.

THE FINE ARTS AND LITERATURE.

BOOK I.

THE FINE ARTS.

CHAPTER I.

MUSIC.

Of the Influence of Christianity upon Music.

To the Fine Arts, the sisters of poetry, we have now to direct our attention. Following the steps of the Christian religion, they acknowledged her for their mother the moment she appeared in the world; they lent her their terrestrial charms, and she conferred on them her divinity. Music noted down her hymns; Painting represented her in her mournful triumphs; Sculpture delighted in meditating with her among the tombs; and Architecture built her temples sublime and melancholy as her thoughts.

Plato has admirably defined the real nature of music. "We must not judge of music," said he, "by the pleasure which it affords, nor prefer that kind which has no other object than pleasure, but that which contains in itself a resemblance to the beautiful."

Music, in fact, considered as an art, is an imitation of nature; its perfection, therefore, consists in representing *the most beautiful nature possible.* But pleasure is a matter of opinion which varies according to times, manners, and nations, and which cannot be the *beautiful,* since the *beautiful* has an absolute existence. Hence every institution that tends to purify the soul, to banish from it trouble and discord, and to promote the growth of virtue, is by this very quality favorable to the *best* music, or to the most perfect imitation of the *beautiful*. But if this institution is moreover of a religious nature, it then possesses the two essential conditions of harmony:—the *beautiful* and the *mysterious* Song has come to us from the angels, and symphony has its source in heaven

It is religion that causes the vestal to sigh amid the night in her peaceful habitation; it is religion that sings so sweetly beside the bed of affliction. To her Jeremias owed his lamentations and David the sublime effusions of his repentance. If, prouder under the ancient covenant, she depicted only the sorrows of monarchs and of prophets,—more modest, and not less royal, under the new law, her sighs are equally suited to the mighty and the weak, because in Jesus Christ she has found humility combined with greatness

The Christian religion, we may add, is essentially melodious, for this single reason, that she delights in solitude. Not that she has any antipathy to society; there, on the contrary, she appears highly amiable: but this celestial Philomela prefers the desert; she is coy and retiring beneath the roofs of men; she loves the forests better, for these are the palaces of her father and her ancient abode. Here she raises her voice to the skies amid the concerts of nature; nature is incessantly celebrating the praises of the Creator, and nothing can be more religious than the hymns chanted in concert with the winds by the oaks of the forest and the reeds of the desert.

Thus the musician who would follow religion in all her relations is obliged to learn the art of imitating the harmonies of solitude. He ought to be acquainted with the melancholy notes of the waters and the trees; he ought to study the sound of the winds in the cloister and those murmurs that pervade the Gothic temple, the grass of the cemetery and the vaults of death.

Christianity has invented the organ and given sighs to brass itself. To her music owed its preservation in the barbarous ages; wherever she has erected her throne, there have arisen a people who sing as naturally as the birds of the air. Song is the daughter of prayer, and prayer is the companion of religion. She has civilized the savage, only by the means of hymns; and the Iroquois who would not submit to her doctrines was overcome by her concerts. O religion of peace! thou hast not, like other systems, inculcated the precepts of hatred and discord; thou hast taught mankind nothing but love and harmony.

CHAPTER II.

THE GREGORIAN CHANT.

If it were not proved by history that the Gregorian chant is a relic of that ancient music of which so many wonderful things are related, the examination of its scale would itself suffice to convince us of its great antiquity.[1] Before the time of Guido Aretino, it rose no higher than the fifth, beginning with *ut:—ut, re, mi, fa, sol,* or *c, d, e, f, g.* These five notes are the natural gamut of the voice, and produce a full and musical scale.[2]

Burette has left us some Greek tunes. On comparing them with the plain chant, we find in both the same system. Most of the Psalms are sublimely solemn, particularly the *Dixit Dominus Domino meo,* the *Confitebor tibi,* and the *Laudate pueri.* The *In Exitu,* arranged by Rameau, is of a less antique character, belonging, perhaps, to the same age as the *Ut queant laxis,*—that is to say, the age of Charlemagne.

[1] The Gregorian chant is so called from St. Gregory the Great, who introduced it, and who flourished in the sixth century. The chief points in which it differs from modern music are the following:—It has not as great a variety of notes; its melodies are more grave; and, chiefly, it excludes harmonization. It is also called *plain-chant,* and is often sung in unison by the choir and congregation. T.

[2] Guido, a Benedictine monk of Italy, lived in the eleventh century. He introduced the gamut, and is supposed to have been acquainted with counterpoint. He was the first to employ the syllables *ut, re, mi,* &c. for the designation of musical notes, deriving them from the first stanza of the hymn in honor of St. John Baptist:—

Ut queant laxis *re*sonare fibris,
*Mi*ra gestorum *fa*muli tuorum,
*Sol*ve polluti *la*bii reatum,
Sancte Joannes. —T.

Christianity is serious as man, and her very smile is grave. Nothing is more exquisite than the sighs which our afflictions extort from religion. The whole of the service for the dead is a master-piece; you imagine that you hear the hollow murmurs of the grave. An ancient tradition records that the *chant which delivers the dead*, as it is termed by one of our best poets, is the same that was performed at the funeral obsequies of the Athenians about the time of Pericles

The chant of the *Passion*, or history of our Saviour's sufferings, during the holy week, is worthy of remark. The recitative of the historian, the cries of the Jewish populace, the dignity of the answers of Jesus, form a musical drama of the most pathetic character.

Pergolesi has displayed in his *Stabat Mater* all the riches of his art; but has he surpassed the simple music of the Church? He has varied the melody with each strophe; and yet the essential character of melancholy consists in the repetition of the same sentiment, and, if we may so express ourselves, in the monotony of grief. Various reasons may draw tears from our eyes, but our tears have always the same bitterness; besides, rarely do we weep over a number of sorrows at once; when the wounds are numerous, there is always one more severe than the rest, which at length absorbs all inferior pains Such is the cause of the charm which pervades our old French ballads. The repetition of the notes at each couplet to different words is an exact imitation of nature.

Pergolesi, then, manifested a want of acquaintance with this truth, which is intimately connected with the theory of the passions, when he determined that not a sigh of the soul should resemble the sigh that had gone before it. Wherever variety is, there is distraction; and wherever distraction is, sorrow is at an end: so necessary is unity to sentiment: so weak is man in this very part in which lies all his strength, we mean, in grief.[1]

---

[1] These remarks of the author are unquestionably true when the musical subject possesses a unity of incident as well as of sentiment. Here the repetition of the same notes is very expressive But when the subject, like the *Stabat*, recalls to the mind a variety of scenes, does not the perfection of the musical art require that these scenes should be represented with all the expressiveness of which it is capable? The *Requiem* of Mozart is a master-piece,

The lesson of the Lamentations of Jeremiah is stamped with a peculiar character. It may have been retouched by the moderns, but to us the ground appears to be of Hebrew origin, for it bears no resemblance to the Greek tunes in the church music. The Pentateuch was sung at Jerusalem, like pastorals, in a full and soft strain; the prophecies were repeated in a harsh and emphatic tone; and the psalms had an ecstatic mode belonging exclusively to them.[1] Here we fall into those grand recollections which the Catholic worship assembles from all quarters:—Moses and Homer, Lebanon and Cytheron, Solyma and Rome, Babylon and Athens, have deposited their remains at the foot of our altars.

Finally, it was enthusiasm itself that inspired the *Te Deum*. When, halting in the plains of Lens or Fontenoy, amid clouds of smoke and yet reeking blood, a French army, scathed with the thunderbolts of war, bowed the knee to the flourishes of clarions and trumpets, and joined in a hymn of praise to the God of battles,—or when, in the midst of lamps, altars of gold, torches, perfumes, the swelling tones of the organ, and the full accompaniment of various instruments, this grand hymn shook the windows, the vaults, and the domes of some ancient cathedral,—there was not a soul but felt transported, not one but experienced some portion of that rapture which inspired Pindar in the groves of Olympia or David on the banks of the Cedron.

The reader will observe that, in treating of the Greek chants only of the Church, we have not employed all our means, since we might have exhibited an Ambrose, a Damasus, a Leo, a Gregory, laboring themselves for the restoration of the science of music; we might have enumerated all those master-pieces of modern music composed for Christian solemnities, as well as all those great masters, Vinci, Leo, Hasse, Galuppi, and Durante, educated or patronized in the oratories of Rome and at the court of the sovereign pontiff.[2]

---

because it has an imitative power, an objective excellence, while at the same time its general tone is in accordance with the solemn feelings which the subject inspires. T.

[1] Bonnet's *History of Music and its Effects*.

[2] In the whole range of musical literature, nothing can be found to excel the compositions to which the worship and piety of the Catholic Church have given birth. T

CHAPTER III.

HISTORICAL PAINTING AMONG THE MODERNS.

The pleasing writers of Greece relate that a young female, perceiving the shadow of her lover upon a wall, chalked the outline of the figure. Thus, according to antiquity, a transient passion produced the art of the most perfect illusions.

The Christian school has sought another master. It has discovered him in that Great Artist who, moulding a morsel of earth in his mighty hands, pronounced those words, *Let us make man in our own image!* For us, then, the first stroke of design existed in the eternal idea of God; and the first statue which the world beheld was that noble figure of clay animated by the breath of the Creator.

There is a force of error which compels silence, like the force of truth; both, carried to the highest pitch, produce conviction, the former negatively, the latter affirmatively. When, therefore, we hear it asserted that Christianity is inimical to the arts, we are struck dumb with astonishment, for we cannot forbear calling to mind Michael Angelo, Raphael, the Caracci, Domenichino, Lesueur, Poussin, Coustou, and crowds of other artists, whose names alone would fill whole volumes.

About the middle of the fourth century, the Roman empire, invaded by barbarians and torn in pieces by heresy, crumbled into ruin on every side. The arts found no asylum except with the Christians and the orthodox emperors Theodosius, by a special law,—*de excusatione artificum,*—exempted painters and their families from all taxes and from the quartering of troops. The fathers of the Church bestow never-ceasing praises on painting. St. Gregory thus expresses himself:—"I frequently gazed at the figure, and could not pass it without shedding tears, as it placed the whole story before my eyes in the most lively manner."[1] This was a picture representing the sacrifice of Abraham. St

[1] Second Nicene Coun. Act., xi.

Basil goes still further; for he asserts that painters *accomplish as much by their pictures as orators by their eloquence.*[1] A monk, named Methodius, executed, in the ninth century, that *Last Judgment* which converted Bogoris, king of the Bulgarians.[2] The clergy had collected at the college of Orthodoxy, at Constantinople, the finest library in the world, and all the master-pieces of antiquity: here, in particular, was to be seen the Venus of Praxiteles,[3] which proves, at least, that the founders of the Catholic worship were neither *barbarians* without taste, *bigoted monks*, nor the votaries of *absurd superstition.*

This college was demolished by the iconoclast emperors.[4] The professors were burnt alive, and it was at the risk of meeting with a similar fate that some Christians saved the dragon's skin, one hundred and twenty feet long, on which the works of Homer were written in letters of gold. The pictures belonging to the churches were consigned to the flames. Stupid and furious bigots, nearly resembling the Puritans of Cromwell's time, hacked to pieces with their sabres the admirable mosaic-works in the church of the Virgin Mary at Constantinople, and in the palace of Blaquernæ. To such a height was this persecution carried that it involved the painters themselves; they were forbidden, under pain of death, to prosecute their profession. Lazarus, a *monk*, had the courage to become a martyr to his art. In vain did Theophilus cause his hands to be burned, to prevent him from holding the pencil. This illustrious friar, concealed in the vault of St. John the Baptist, painted with his mutilated fingers the great saint whose protection he sought;[5] worthy, undoubtedly, of becoming the patron of painters, and of being acknowledged by that sublime family which the breath of the Spirit exalts above the rest of mankind.

Under the empire of the Goths and Lombards, Christianity continued to lend her assisting hand to talent. These efforts are particularly remarkable in the churches erected by Theodoric,

[1] St. Basil, *hom.* 20.

[2] Curopal. Cedren. Zonar. Maimb., *Hist. of the Iconocl.*

[3] Cedren. Zonar. Constant., and Maimb., *Hist. of the Iconocl.*

[4] The *Iconoclasts* or Image-breakers, a fanatical sect that originated in the seventh century. At a later period, the name was applied to all who were opposed to the veneration of images. T.

[5] Maimb., *Hist. of the Iconocl.*, Cedren. Curopal.

Luitprand, and Desiderius. The same spirit of religion actuated Charlemagne; and the Church of the APOSTLES, erected by that great prince at Florence, is, even at the present day, accounted a fine structure.

At length, about the thirteenth century, the Christian religion, after encountering a thousand obstacles, brought back the choir of Muses in triumph to the earth Every thing was done for the churches, both by the patronage of the pontiffs and of religious princes. Bouchet, a Greek by birth, was the first architect, Nicolas the first sculptor, and Cimabue the first painter, that recovered the antique style from the ruins of Rome and Greece. From that time the arts were raised by different hands and different geniuses to the pitch of excellence which they attained in the great age of Leo X., when Raphael and Michael Angelo burst forth like resplendent luminaries.

The reader is aware that our subject does not require us to give a technical history of the art. All that we undertake to show is in what respect Christianity is more favorable to painting than any other religion Now, it is an easy task to prove three things—Firstly, that the Christian religion, being of a spiritual and mystic nature, furnishes the painter with the *beautiful ideal* more perfect and more divine than that which arises from a material worship; secondly, that, correcting the deformity of the passions, or powerfully counteracting them, it gives a more sublime expression to the human countenance, and more clearly displays the soul in the muscles and conformation of the body; thirdly, and lastly, that it has furnished the arts with subjects more beautiful, more rich, more dramatic, more pathetic, than those of mythology.

The first two propositions have been amply discussed in our examination of poetry; we shall, therefore, confine our attention to the third only.

CHAPTER IV.

OF THE SUBJECTS OF PICTURES.

FUNDAMENTAL truths.

Firstly. The subjects of antiquity continue at the disposal of modern painters; thus, in addition to the mythological scenes, they have the subjects which Christianity presents.

Secondly. A circumstance which shows that Christianity has a more powerful influence over genius than fable, is that our great masters, in general, have been more successful in sacred than in profane subjects.

Thirdly. The modern styles of dress are ill adapted to the arts of imitation; but the Catholic worship has furnished painting with costumes as dignified as those of antiquity.[1]

Pausanias,[2] Pliny,[3] and Plutarch,[4] have left us a description of the pictures of the Greek school.[5] Zeuxis took for the subjects of his three principal productions, Penelope, Helen, and Cupid; Polygnotus had depicted, on the walls of the temple of Delphi, the sacking of Troy and the descent of Ulysses into hell; Euphranor painted the twelve gods, Theseus giving laws, and the battles of Cadmea, Leuctra, and Mantinea; Apelles drew Venus Anadyomene with the features of Campaspe; Ætion represented the nuptials of Alexander and Roxana, and Timantes delineated the sacrifice of Iphigenia.

Compare these subjects with the Christian subjects, and you

---

[1] These costumes of the fathers and the first Christians (which have been transmitted to our clergy) are no other than the robe of the ancient Greek philosophers, denominated *περιβολαιον*, or *pallium*. It was even a cause of persecution for the believers; for when the Romans or the Jews perceived them thus attired, they would exclaim, Ο *Γραικος επιθετης*, *Oh the Greek impostor!* (Jerom., *ep.* 10, *ad Furiam.*) Consult Kortholt. *de Morib. Christ.*, cap. iii. p. 23, and Bar., an. lvi. n. 11. Tertullian has written a work expressly on this subject, (*de Pallio.*)

[2] Paus., lib. v.

[3] Plin., lib. xxxv. c. 8 9.

[4] Plut., in *Hipp.*, *Pomp.*, *Lucul.*, &c.

[5] See note V.

will perceive their inferiority. The sacrifice of Isaac, for example, is in a more simple style than that of Iphigenia, and is equally affecting Here are no soldiers, no group of people, none of that bustle which serves to draw off the attention from the principal action. Here is the solitary summit of a mountain, a patriarch who numbers a century of years, the knife raised over an only son, and the hand of God arresting the paternal arm The histories of the Old Testament are full of such pictures; and it is well known how highly favorable to the pencil are the patriarchal manners, the costumes of the East, the largeness of the animals and the vastness of the deserts of Asia.

The New Testament changes the genius of painting. Without taking away any of its sublimity, it imparts to it a higher degree of tenderness. Who has not a hundred times admired the *Nativity*, the *Virgin and Child*, the *Flight in the Desert*, the *Crowning with Thorns*, the *Sacraments*, the *Mission of the Apostles*, the *Taking down from the Cross*, the *Women at the holy Sepulchre.* Can bacchanals, festivals of Venus, rapes, metamorphoses, affect the heart like the pictures taken from the Scripture? Christianity everywhere holds forth virtue and misfortune to our view, and polytheism is a system of crimes and prosperity. Our religion is our own history; it was for us that so many tragic spectacles were given to the world: we are parties in the scenes which the pencil exhibits to our view. A Greek, most assuredly, felt no kind of interest in the picture of a demi-god who cared not whether he was happy or miserable; but the most moral and the most impressive harmonies pervade the Christian subjects. Be forever glorified, O religion of Jesus Christ, that hast represented in the Louvre[1] the *Crucifixion of the King of Kings*, the *Last Judgment* on the ceiling of our court of justice, a *Resurrection* at the public hospital, and the *Birth of our Saviour* in the habitation of those orphans who are forsaken both by father and mother!

We may repeat here, respecting the subjects of pictures, what we have said elsewhere concerning the subjects of poems. Christianity has created a dramatic department in painting far superior to that of mythology. It is religion also that has given us a Claude

[1] The Museum of the Fine Arts at Paris.

Loraine, as it has furnished us with a Delille and a St. Lambert.[1] But what need is there of so many arguments? Step into the gallery of the Louvre, and then assert, if you can, that the spirit of Christianity is not favorable to the fine arts.

CHAPTER V.

SCULPTURE.

WITH a few variations required by the technical part of the art, our remarks on painting are equally applicable to sculpture.

The statue of Moses by Michael Angelo, at Rome; Adam and Eve by Baccio, at Florence; the Vow of Louis XIII. by Coustou, at Paris; St. Denys by the same; the tomb of Cardinal Richelieu, the production of the joint genius of Lebrun and Girardon; the monument of Colbert, executed after the design of Lebrun, by Coyzevox and Tuby; Christ, the Mother of Pity, and the Eight Apostles, by Bouchardon, and several other statues of the religious kind, prove that Christianity understands the art of animating the marble full as well as the canvas.

It were, however, to be wished that sculptors would in future banish from their funeral compositions those skeletons which they have frequently introduced in monuments. Such phantoms are not suggested by the genius of Christianity, which depicts death so fair for the righteous.

It is equally necessary to avoid representations of corpses,[2] (however meritorious the execution,) or humanity sinking under protracted infirmities.[3] A warrior expiring on the field of honor in the full vigor of manhood may be very fine; but a body emaciated by disease is an image which the arts reject, unless accom-

[1] See note W.

[2] As in the mausoleum of Francis I. and Anne of Bretagne.

[3] As in the tomb of the Duke d'Harcourt.

panied by some miracle, as in the picture of St. Charles Borromeo.[1] Exhibit, then, upon the monument of the Christian, on the one hand his weeping family and his dejected friends, on the other, smiling hope and celestial joys. Such a sepulchre, displaying on either side the scenes of time and of eternity, would be truly admirable. Death might make his appearance there, but under the features of an angel at once gentle and severe; for the tomb of the righteous ought always to prompt the spectator to exclaim, with St. Paul, *O grave, where is thy victory? O death, where is thy sting?*

CHAPTER VI.

ARCHITECTURE.

Hotel des Invalides.

In treating of the influence of Christianity on the arts, there is no occasion for either subtlety or eloquence. The monuments are there to confute the depreciators of religion. It is sufficient, for example, to mention St. Peter's at Rome, St. Sophia's at Constantinople, and St. Paul's in London, to prove that we are indebted to religion for the three master-pieces of modern architecture.

In architecture, as in the other arts, Christianity has re-established the genuine proportions. Our churches, neither so small as the temples of Athens nor so gigantic as those of Memphis, maintain that due medium in which beauty and taste eminently reside. By means of the *dome*, unknown to the ancients, religion has produced a happy combination of the boldness of the Gothic and the simplicity and grace of the Grecian orders.

---

[1] Painting may be more easily reconciled to the representation of a dead body than sculpture, because the marble, exhibiting more palpable forms, approaches too near to the truth.

This dome, which in most of our churches is transformed into a steeple, imparts to our hamlets and towns a moral character which the cities of antiquity could not possess. The eyes of the traveller are first struck by that religious spire the sight of which awakens in his bosom a multitude of feelings and recollections. It is the funeral pyramid around which the rude forefathers of the hamlet sleep; but it is also the monument of joy beneath which the sacred brass records the life of the believer. Here husband and wife are united Here Christians fall prostrate at the foot of the altar,—the weak to pray to the God of might, the guilty to implore the God of mercy, the innocent to sing the praises of the God of love. Does a country-place appear naked, dreary, and desolate?—introduce a rural steeple, and the whole instantly becomes animated. The soothing ideas of *pastor* and *flock*, of an asylum for the traveller, of alms for the pilgrim, of hospitality and Christian fraternity, spring up on every side.

The more those ages which reared our monuments were distinguished for piety and faith, the more striking are those monuments for grandeur and elevation of character. Of this an exquisite specimen may be seen in the *Hotel of the Invalids* and the *Military School.* You would say that, at the voice of religion, the domes of the former aspire to heaven, while, at the command of an atheistical age, the latter has been made to grovel upon the earth.

Three sides, forming with the church an oblong square, compose the whole structure of the *Invalids.* But what perfect taste in this simplicity! What beauty in that court, which, nevertheless, is but a military cloister, where art has blended martial with religious ideas, and combined the image of a camp of aged soldiers with the affecting recollections of an hospital! It is at once the monument of the *God of hosts* and the *God of the gospel.* The rust of years with which it begins to be covered gives it a noble affinity to those living ruins—the veterans who walk beneath its ancient porticos. In the forecourts every thing reminds you of war—ditches, glacis, ramparts, cannon, tents, sentinels. Proceed, and the noise gradually diminishes till it wholly subsides at the church, where profound silence reigns. It was a grand idea to place the religious structure in the rear of all the military edifices, like the image of rest and hope at the end of a life exposed to a thousand hardships and dangers.

The age of Louis XIV. is perhaps the only one that has duly appreciated these admirable moral harmonies, and always performed in the arts just what was becoming, without doing either too little or too much. The wealth of commerce has erected the magnificent colonnades of *Greenwich Hospital;* but there is something prouder and more imposing in the general mass of the *Invalids.* You are convinced that a nation which rears such palaces for the old age of its armies has received the sword of might as well as the sceptre of the arts.[1]

CHAPTER VII

VERSAILLES.

PAINTING, architecture, poetry, and the higher species of eloquence, have invariably degenerated in philosophic ages; because a reasoning spirit, by destroying the imagination, undermines the foundation of the fine arts. We fancy ourselves more enlightened because we correct a few errors in natural philosophy, substituting, however, all the errors of reason in their stead; and we are, in fact, going backward, since we are losing one of the finest faculties of the mind.

It was at Versailles that all the splendors of the religious age of France were combined. Scarcely a century has elapsed since those groves rang with the sounds of festivity, and now they are animated only by the music of the grasshopper and the nightingale. This palace, which of itself is like a large town,—those marble staircases, which seem to ascend to the skies,—those statues, those basins of water, those wōods,—are now either crumbling into ruin, or covered with moss, or dried up, or overthrown; and yet this abode of kings never appeared more magnificent or less solitary. All these places were formerly empty The little

[1] Our author's subject would not have suffered by a more particular notice of St. Peter's at Rome and St. Paul's Cathedral in London.

court of the last of the Bourbons (before adversity had completely overwhelmed that court) seemed lost in the vast habitation of Louis XIV.

When time has given a mortal blow to empires, some great name associates itself with them and covers their relics. If the noble poverty of the soldier has now succeeded the magnificence of courts at Versailles,—if the views of miracles and martyrs have there taken the place of profane pictures,—why should the shade of Louis XIV. be offended? He conferred lustre on religion, on the arts, and on the army. It is consistent, therefore, that the ruins of his palace should afford an asylum to the ruins of the army, of the arts, and of religion.

CHAPTER VIII.

GOTHIC CHURCHES.

Every thing ought to be in its proper place. This is a truth become trite by repetition; but without its due observance there can be nothing perfect. The Greeks would not have been better pleased with an Egyptian temple at Athens than the Egyptians with a Greek temple at Memphis. These two monuments, by changing places, would have lost their principal beauty; that is to say, their relations with the institutions and habits of the people. This reflection is equally applicable to the ancient monuments of Christianity. It is even curious to remark how readily the poets and novelists of this infidel age, by a natural return toward the manners of our ancestors, introduce dungeons, spectres, castles, and Gothic churches, into their fictions,—so great is the charm of recollections associated with religion and the history of our country. Nations do not throw aside their ancient customs as people do their old clothes. Some part of them may be discarded; but there will remain a portion, which with the new manners will form a very strange mixture.

In vain would you build Grecian temples, ever so elegant and well-lighted, for the purpose of assembling the *good people* of St. Louis and Queen Blanche, and making them adore a *metaphysical God;* they would still regret those *Notre Dames* of Rheims and Paris,—those venerable cathedrals, overgrown with moss, full of generations of the dead and the ashes of their forefathers; they would still regret the tombs of those heroes, the Montmorencys, on which they loved to kneel during mass; to say nothing of the sacred fonts to which they were carried at their birth. The reason is that all these things are essentially interwoven with their manners; that a monument is not venerable, unless a long history of the past be, as it were, inscribed beneath its vaulted canopy, black with age. For this reason, also, there is nothing marvellous in a temple whose erection we have witnessed, whose echoes and whose domes were formed before our eyes. God is the eternal law; his origin, and whatever relates to his worship, ought to be enveloped in the night of time.

You could not enter a Gothic church without feeling a kind of awe and a vague sentiment of the Divinity. You were all at once carried back to those times when a fraternity of cenobites, after having meditated in the woods of their monasteries, met to prostrate themselves before the altar and to chant the praises of the Lord, amid the tranquillity and the silence of night. Ancient France seemed to revive altogether; you beheld all those singular costumes, all that nation so different from what it is at present; you were reminded of its revolutions, its productions, and its arts. The more remote were these times the more magical they appeared, the more they inspired ideas which always end with a reflection on the nothingness of man and the rapidity of life.

The Gothic style, notwithstanding its barbarous proportions, possesses a beauty peculiar to itself.[1]

[1] Gothic architecture, as well as the sculpture in the same style, is supposed to have been derived from the Arabs. Its affinity to the monuments of Egypt would rather lead us to imagine that it was transmitted to us by the first Christians of the East; but we are more inclined to refer its origin to nature.

The forests were the first temples of the Divinity, and in them men acquired the first idea of architecture. This art must, therefore, have varied according to climates. The Greeks turned the elegant Corinthian column, with its capital of foliage, after the model of the palm-tree.[1] The enormous pillars of the ancient Egyptian style represent the massive sycamore, the oriental fig, the banana, and most of the gigantic trees of Africa and Asia.

The forests of Gaul were, in their turn, introduced into the temples of our ancestors, and those celebrated woods of oaks thus maintained their sacred character. Those ceilings sculptured into foliage of different kinds, those buttresses which prop the walls and terminate abruptly like the broken trunks of trees, the coolness of the vaults, the darkness of the sanctuary, the dim twilight of the aisles, the secret passages, the low doorways,—in a word, every thing in a Gothic church reminds you of the labyrinths of a wood; every thing excites a feeling of religious awe, of mystery, and of the Divinity.

The two lofty towers erected at the entrance of the edifice overtop the elms and yew-trees of the churchyard, and produce the most picturesque effect on the azure of heaven. Sometimes their twin heads are illumined by the first rays of dawn; at others they appear crowned with a capital of clouds or magnified in a foggy atmosphere. The birds themselves seem to make a mistake in regard to them, and to take them for the trees of the forest; they hover over their summits, and perch upon their pinnacles. But, lo! confused noises suddenly issue from the top of these towers and scare away the affrighted birds. The Christian architect, not content with building forests, has been

[1] Vitruvius gives a different account of the invention of the Corinthian capital; but this does not confute the general principle that architecture originated in the woods. We are only astonished that there should not be more variety in the column, after the varieties of trees. We have a conception, for example, of a column that might be termed *Palmist*, and be a natural representation of the palm-tree. An orb of foliage slightly bowed and sculptured on the top of a light shaft of marble would, in our opinion, produce a very pleasing effect in a portico.

desirous to retain their murmurs; and, by means of the organ and of bells, he has attached to the Gothic temple the very winds and thunders that roar in the recesses of the woods. Past ages, conjured up by these religious sounds, raise their venerable voices from the bosom of the stones, and are heard in every corner of the vast cathedral. The sanctuary re-echoes like the cavern of the ancient Sibyl; loud-tongued bells swing over your head, while the vaults of death under your feet are profoundly silent

BOOK II.

PHILOSOPHY.

CHAPTER I.

ASTRONOMY AND MATHEMATICS.

Let us now consider the effects of Christianity upon literature in general. It may be classed under these three principal heads:—philosophy, history, and eloquence.

By *philosophy* we here mean the study of every species of science.

It will be seen that, in defending religion, we by no means attack *wisdom*. Far be it from us to confound sophistical pride with the solid qualifications of the mind and heart. *Genuine philosophy* is the innocence of the old age of nations, when they have ceased to possess virtues by instinct, and owe such as they have to reason. This second innocence is less certain than the first, but, when it can be attained, it is more sublime.

On whatever side you view the religion of the gospel, you find that it enlarges the understanding and tends to expand the feelings. In the sciences, its tenets are not hostile to any natural truth; its doctrine forbids not any study. Among the ancients, a philosopher was continually meeting with some divinity in his way; he was doomed by the priests of Jupiter or Apollo, under pain of death or exile, to be absurd all his life. But, as the God of the Christians has not confined himself within the narrow limits of a sun, he has left all the luminaries of heaven open to the researches of scholars: "He hath delivered the world to their consideration."[1] The natural philosopher may weigh the air in his tube without any apprehension of offending Juno; it is not of the elements of his body, but of the virtues of his soul, that the Supreme Judge will one day require an account.

[1] Ecclesiastes iii. 11.

We are aware that we shall not fail to be reminded of certain bulls of the Holy See, or certain decrees of the Sorbonne, which condemn this or that philosophical discovery; but, on the other hand, how many ordinances of the court of Rome in favor of these same discoveries might we not enumerate! What can be said in this case, except that the clergy, who are men like ourselves, have shown themselves more or less enlightened, according to the natural course of ages? If Christianity *itself* has never appeared in opposition to the sciences, we have a sufficient authorization for our first assertion.

Let it be observed that the Church has at all periods protected the arts, though she has sometimes discouraged abstract studies; and in this she has displayed her accustomed wisdom. In vain do men perplex their understandings; they never will fully comprehend any thing in nature, because it is not they who have said to the ocean, "Hitherto thou shalt come, and shalt go no farther, and here thou shalt break thy swelling waves."[1] Systems will eternally succeed systems, and truth will ever remain unknown. "If nature," says Montaigne, "should one day be pleased to reveal her secrets to us, oh heavens! what errors, what mistakes, shall we find in our paltry sciences!"[2]

The legislators of antiquity, agreeing on this point, as in many others, with the principles of the Christian religion, discouraged philosophers[3] and lavished honors upon artists.[4] All these alleged persecutions of the sciences by Christianity may, therefore, with equal justice, be laid to the charge of the ancients, in whom, however, we discover such profound wisdom. In the year of Rome 591, the senate issued a decree banishing all philosophers from the city, and six years afterward Cato lost no time in procuring the dismissal of Carneades, the Athenian ambassador, "lest," as he said, "the Roman youth, acquiring a taste for the subtleties of the Greeks, should lose the simplicity of the ancient manners." If the system of Copernicus was

---

1 Job xxxviii 11. 2 *Essays*, book ii. ch. 12

3 Xenoph., *Hist. Græc.*; Plut., *Mor.*: Plat, *in Phæd.*, *in Repub.*

4 The Greeks carried this hatred of philosophers to a criminal height, since they put Socrates to death.

condemned by the court of Rome, did it not meet with a similar fate among the Greeks?[1] "Aristarchus," says Plutarch, "was of opinion that the Greeks ought to bring Cleanthes, the Samian, to trial, and to find him guilty of blasphemy against the gods, as a disturber of the public faith; because this man, endeavoring to save appearances, supposed that the firmament was motionless, and that the earth moved along the oblique circle of the zodiac, revolving upon its axis."[2]

It is true, moreover, that modern Rome showed superior intelligence; for the same ecclesiastical tribunal which at first condemned the system of Copernicus, six years afterward allowed it to be taught as an hypothesis.[3] Besides, could a greater proficiency in astronomical science be reasonably expected of a Roman priest than of Tycho Brahe, who continued to deny the motion of the earth? Lastly, were not a Pope Gregory, who reformed the calendar, a Friar Bacon, probably the inventor of the telescope, Cuza, a cardinal, Gassendi, a priest, either the patrons or the luminaries of astronomy?[4]

---

[1] The assertion that the system of Copernicus, proclaimed by Galileo, was condemned by the Court of Rome, is proved to be utterly unfounded in truth. Galileo was arraigned before the tribunals at Rome, not as an astronomer, but as a bad theologian. He was censured, not for teaching that the earth revolved round the sun, but for obstinately declaring that his opinion was contained in the Bible, and pretending that the ecclesiastical authorities should publish a decision to this effect. That such were the facts of the case we learn from the letters of Guicciardini and the Marquis Nicolini, both disciples and friends of Galileo, and from the letters of the distinguished astronomer himself. Mr. Mallet du Pau, an impartial Protestant writer, has presented all this evidence in a lengthy dissertation on the subject, which appeared in the *Mercure de France*, July 17, 1784. T.

[2] Plut., *On the Face which appears in the Moon's Disc*, chap. 4. It is scarcely necessary to observe that there is an error in Plutarch's text, and that it was, on the contrary, Aristarchus of Samos against whom Cleanthes endeavored to raise a persecution on account of his opinion respecting the motion of the earth; but this makes no alteration in what we are attempting to demonstrate.

[3] The theory of Galileo, once divested of its theological aspect, met with no opposition whatever from the ecclesiastical authorities. T. See note X.

[4] Cardinal Cuza, equally distinguished for virtue and learning, died in 1454. He taught without censure the same astronomical system which afterward formed the pretended charge against Galileo—a fact which corroborates the remark in a preceding note, that the question in the case of Galileo was not of an astronomical, but a theological, nature. T.

Plato, that genius so deeply enamored of the loftier sciences, expressly says, in one of his finest works, *that the higher studies are not useful to all, but only to a small number;* and to this reflection, confirmed by experience, he adds the remark, "that absolute ignorance is neither the greatest of evils nor the most to be feared, but that an accumulation of ill-digested knowledge is infinitely worse."[1]

If religion, therefore, stood in need of any justification on this head, we should not want authorities among the ancients, or even among the moderns. Hobbes has written several treatises[2] against the uncertainty of the most certain of all sciences,—the mathematics. In that which he has entitled *Contra Geometras, sive contra fastum Professorum*, he censures the definitions of Euclid, one after another, and shows how much in them is false, vague, or arbitrary The manner in which he expresses himself is remarkable:—*Itaque per hanc epistolam hoc ago ut ostendam tibi non minorem esse dubitandi causam in scriptis mathematicorum quàm in scriptis physicorum, ethicorum, &c.*[3] "I shall therefore endeavor to prove to you, in this epistle, that there is not less cause for doubt in the works of mathematicians, than in those of natural philosophers, moralists, &c"

Bacon has expressed himself in still stronger language against the sciences, even when he appears to be defending them. According to that great writer, it is proved that a slight tincture of philosophy may lead to a disbelief of a first cause; but that more profound knowledge conducts man unto God[4]

How dreadful this idea, if true! For one single genius capable of attaining that plenitude of knowledge required by Bacon, and where, according to Pascal, *you merely find yourself in another sort of ignorance*, how many inferior minds must there be, that can never soar so high, but remain involved in those clouds of science which enshroud the Divinity!

The rock upon which the multitude will invariably strike is pride; you will never be able to persuade them that they know nothing at the moment when they imagine themselves in posses-

---

[1] *De Leg.*, lib. vii.

[2] *Examinatio et emendatio mathematicæ hodiernæ, Dial. IV., contra geometras.*

[3] Hob., *Opera omn. Amstelod.*, edit. 1667.

[4] *De Aug Scient.*, lib. v.

sion of all the stores of science. Great minds alone can form a conception of that last point of human knowledge, at which the treasures which you have amassed vanish from your sight and you find yourself reduced to your original poverty. For this reason, almost all wise men have considered philosophical studies as fraught with extreme danger for the multitude. Locke employs the first three chapters of the fourth book of his *Essay on the Human Understanding* in fixing the limits of our knowledge, which are at so small a distance from us as to be really alarming.

"Our knowledge," says he, "being so narrow as I have showed, it will perhaps give us some light into the present state of our minds if we look a little into the dark side and take a view of our ignorance; which, being infinitely larger than our knowledge, may serve much to the quieting of disputes; if, discovering how far we have clear and distinct ideas, we confine our thoughts within the contemplation of those things that are within the reach of our understandings, and launch not out into that abyss of darkness, (where we have not eyes to see nor faculties to perceive any thing,) *out of a presumption that nothing is beyond our comprehension*."[1]

Lastly, it is well known that Newton, disgusted with the study of the mathematics, could not for several years bear to hear it mentioned; and even in our days, Gibbon, who was so long the apostle of the new ideas, wrote as follows:—"The precision of the sciences has accustomed us to despise moral evidence, so fruitful in exquisite sensations, and which is capable of deciding the opinions and the actions of our lives."

In fact, many people have thought that science, in the hands of man, contracts the heart, robs nature of her charms, leads weak minds to atheism, and from atheism to crimes of every kind; that the fine arts, on the contrary, impart a magic coloring to life, melt the soul, fill us with faith in the Divinity, and conduct us by religion to the practice of every virtue.

We shall not quote Rousseau, whose authority on this subject might be called in question; but Descartes, for example, has expressed himself in a most extraordinary manner, respecting the science on which a considerable share of his reputation is founded.

[1] Locke on the *Human Understanding*, vol. ii. book iv. ch. 3, p. 22.

"Accordingly," says the learned author of his life, "nothing appeared to him less useful than to devote the whole attention to simple numbers and imaginary figures, as if we ought to stop at such *trifles*, without extending our views beyond them. He ever saw in them something worse than useless; he looked upon it as dangerous to apply too assiduously to those superficial demonstrations which are less frequently the result of industry and experience than of accident.[1] His maxim was that this application weans us by degrees from the use of our reason, and renders us liable to lose the track which its light directs us to pursue."[2] This opinion of the author of the application of algebra to geometry is worthy of serious attention.

Father Castel, also, who has written on the subject of the mathematics, has not hesitated to express his conviction of the over-importance attached to it. "In general," says he, "the science of mathematics is too highly esteemed. . . . . . . Geometry has sublime truths; it embraces objects but little developed, and points of view that have, as it were, passed unobserved: but why should we be afraid to speak out? It contains paradoxes, apparent contradictions, conclusions of system and concessions, opinions of sects, conjectures, and even false arguments."[3]

According to Buffon, "what are called mathematical truths are nothing more than identities of ideas, and have no reality."[4] Lastly, the Abbé Condillac, affecting the same contempt for mathematicians as Hobbes, says, "that when they quit their calculations to pursue researches of a different nature, we find in them neither the same perspicuity, nor the same precision, nor the same depth of understanding. We have four celebrated metaphysicians, Descartes, Mallebranche, Leibnitz, and Locke; the last is the only one who was not a mathematician, and how superior is he to the three others!"[5]

This opinion is not correct. In pure metaphysics, Mallebranche and Leibnitz far surpassed the English philosopher. Mathematical geniuses, it is true, are often wrong in the ordinary affairs

---

[1] Letters of 1638, p. 412; Cartes. *lib. de direct. ingen. regula*, n. 5.

[2] *Œuvres de Desc*, tome i. p. 112. [3] *Math. univ.*, pp. 3, 4.

[4] *Hist. nat.*, tome i. prem. disc. p. 77.

[5] *Essai sur l'Origine des Connoissances humaines*, tome ii. sect. 2, ch 4, p. 239, edit. Amst. 1788.

of life; but this proceeds from their extreme accuracy. They would everywhere discover absolute truths; whereas, in morals and in politics, all truths are relative. It is strictly true that two and two make four; it is an identical proposition, one and all, independent of time and place. But it is not equally clear that a good law at Athens is a good law at Paris. It is a fact that liberty is an excellent thing; but ought we, for this reason, to shed torrents of blood to establish it among a people, how unfit soever that people may be to enjoy the blessing?

In mathematics, we ought to consider nothing but the principle; in morals, nothing but the consequence. The one is a simple, the other a compound, truth. Besides, nothing deranges the compasses of the mathematician, whereas every thing deranges the heart of the philosopher. When the instrument of the latter will be as true as that of the former, we may hope to penetrate to the bottom of things. Till that time we must expect errors. He who would introduce mathematical strictness into the social relations must be either the most stupid or the most wicked of men.

The mathematics, moreover, far from proving vastness of understanding in most of those who employ them, should, on the contrary, be considered as the prop of their weakness, as a supplement to their insufficient capacity, as a method of abbreviation adapted to the classing of results in heads incapable of accomplishing this of themselves. They are, in fact, but general signs of ideas, which spare us the trouble of thinking; the numbered tickets of a treasure which we have not counted; the instruments with which we work, and not the things on which we operate. Let us suppose one idea to be represented by A, and another by B. What a prodigious difference will there be between the man who develops these two ideas in all their bearings, moral, political, and religious, and him who, with pen in hand, patiently multiplies A by B, finding curious combinations, but without having any thing else before his mind than the properties of tw barren letters!

But if, excluding every other science, you instruct a boy in this, which certainly furnishes very few ideas, you run the risk of drying up the very source of his ideas, of spoiling the finest genius, of extinguishing the most fertile imagination, of circumscribing the most extensive understanding. You fill his young head with a multitude of numbers and unmeaning figures, which represent nothing at all; you accustom him to be satisfied with a given sum, not to take a single step without the aid of a theory, never to put forth his strength; you teach him to relieve his memory and his mind by artificial operations, to know and eventually to love none but those strict principles and those absolute truths which overturn society.

It has been asserted that the mathematics serve to rectify the errors of the reasoning faculty in youth. To this a very ingenious, and at the same time a very sound, answer has been given:—that you must first have the ideas before you can class them, that to pretend to arrange the understanding of a boy would amount to the same thing as to pretend to set in order an empty room. First give him clear notions of his moral and religious duties; store his mind with knowledge, human and divine; and when you have bestowed the necessary attention on the education of his heart, when his mind is sufficiently furnished with objects of comparison and sound principles, then place them in order, if you please, by means of geometry.[1]

But is it true that the study of the mathematics is so necessary in life? If you must have magistrates, ministers, civil and religious classes, what have the properties of a circle or of a triangle to do with their respective professions? Every thing must be of a positive nature, you will say. But what is less positive than the sciences, the theories of which change several times in a century? Of what consequence is it to the husbandman that the element of the earth be not *homogeneous*, or to the wood-cutter that the wood be of a *pyroligneous* substance? One eloquent page of Bossuet on morals is more useful and more difficult to be written than a volume of philosophical abstractions. But,

---

[1] These remarks are fully confirmed by Dr. Johnson. "Whether we provide for action or conversation, whether we wish to be useful or pleasing, the first requisite is the religious and moral knowledge of right and wrong; the next is an acquaintance with the history of mankind, and with those examples which may be said to embody truth and prove by events the reasonableness of opinions. Prudence and justice are virtues and excellences of all times and of all places, we are *perpetually moralists*, but we are *geometricians* only by *chance*."—Johnson's *Life of Milton*.

you will say, we apply the discoveries of the sciences to the mechanical arts. All these notable discoveries scarcely ever produce the effects that are expected from them. The high perfection of agriculture in England is not so much the result of scientific experiments, as of the patient toil and industry of the farmer, obliged to bestow incessant pains upon an ungrateful soil.

We erroneously ascribe to our science what belongs to the natural progress of society. The number of hands and of rustic animals has increased; the manufactures and products of the earth must have been proportionably augmented and improved. To have lighter ploughs and more perfect machines for the various classes of artisans is certainly an advantage; but to imagine that the whole of genius, the whole of human wisdom, is comprised in the circle of mechanical inventions, is an egregious mistake.

As to the mathematics, properly so called, it has been proved that a person may in a short time learn as much of them, as is requisite to make him a good engineer. All beyond this practical geometry is but *speculative geometry*, which has its fancies, its inutilities, and, if we may be allowed the expression, its romances, like the other sciences. "A proper distinction should be made," says Voltaire, "between useful geometry and curious geometry. Square curves as long as you please, and you may display a good deal of sagacity; but you will resemble an arithmetician who investigates the properties of numbers instead of calculating his fortune. . . . . When Archimedes discovered the specific gravity of bodies, he rendered a service to mankind; but of what service would it be to find three numbers, such that the difference between the squares of two of them, added to the number three, will always form a square, and the sum of their three differences, added to the same cube, will still produce a square? *Nugæ difficiles!*"[1]

Unpleasant as this truth may be to mathematicians, it must, however, be told: nature has not destined them to hold the first rank. With the exception of a few distinguished for their discoveries, she has doomed them all to a melancholy obscurity; and

[1] *Quest. sur l'Encyc. Geom.*

those geniuses themselves would be threatened with oblivion, did not the historian undertake the task of introducing them to the world. Archimedes owes his glory to Polybius, and Voltaire laid the foundation of Newton's fame. Plato and Pythagoras survive as moralists and legislators, and Leibnitz and Descartes as metaphysicians, rather, perhaps, than as mathematicians. D'Alembert would, at the present day, share the fate of Varignon and Duhamel,—whose names, though still respected in the schools, are scarcely known to the world except by academic eulogies,—had he not combined the reputation of a scholar with that of a man of science. A poet, by means of a few verses, lives to the remotest posterity, immortalizes his age, and transmits to future times those whom he deigns to celebrate in his compositions; the man of science, scarcely known during his lifetime, is forgotten the day after his death. Involuntarily ungrateful, he can do nothing for the great man or the hero by whom he is patronized. To no purpose will he give his name to a chemical furnace or a philosophical machine; such expedients, however praiseworthy, will not confer distinguished fame. Glory is born without wings; she is obliged to borrow those of the Muses when she would soar to the skies. Corneille, Racine, Boileau, the orators and artists, contributed to immortalize Louis XIV. much more than the celebrated men of science who flourished during his time. All ages, all countries, present the same example. Let mathematicians then cease to complain, if nations, by one general instinct, give to letters the precedence over the sciences; because the man who has bequeathed to the world one single moral precept, one single affecting sentiment, renders a greater service to society than the mathematician who discovered the beautiful properties of the triangle.

After all, it is, perhaps, no very difficult task to reconcile those who declaim against mathematics and those who prefer them to all the other sciences. This difference of opinion proceeds from a very common error, which is to confound a *great* with a *skilful* mathematician. There is a *material* geometry composed of lines, of points, of A+B, with which a very inferior understanding can, with time and perseverance, perform prodigies. It is then a species of geometrical machine which executes of itself highly complicated operations, like the arithmetical machine invented by Pascal. In the sciences, he who comes last is sure to know the most, so that many a scholar of the present day seems to be a greater proficient than Newton; and, for the same reason, many a one who now passes for a man of science will be deemed ignorant by the next generation. Proud of their calculations, mechanical geometricians hold the arts of the imagination in sovereign contempt; they smile with pity when you talk to them of literature, of morals, of religion; they *are intimately acquainted*, they will tell you, with all nature. Are you not as much pleased with the *ignorance* of Plato, who terms this same nature a *mysterious poetry?*

Fortunately, there exists another geometry,—an intellectual geometry. It is necessary to have studied this in order to obtain admission among the disciples of Socrates; it is this that beholds the Deity behind the circle and the triangle, and has formed such men as Pascal, Leibnitz, Descartes, and Newton. In general, all the inventive mathematical geniuses have been religious.[1]

But it cannot be denied that this geometry of great minds is very rare. For one single genius who pursues his course through the higher regions of science, how many others are bewildered in its inextricable mazes! Here we may notice one of those reactions so frequent in the laws of Providence:—the irreligious ages necessarily lead to the sciences, and the sciences necessarily produce irreligious ages. When, in an impious age, man proceeds so far as to disbelieve the existence of God, this truth being the only one which he cannot shake off, and feeling an imperious necessity for positive truths, he seeks to create new ones, and imagines that he discovers them in the abstractions of the sciences. On the other hand, it is natural that ordinary minds, or young and unthinking persons, on meeting with mathe-

---

[1] This remark, so just and so honorable to science, recalls to our minds the beautiful lines of Ovid.

> Felices animæ! quibus hæc cognoscere primis,
> Inque domos superas scandere cura fuit.
> Credibile est illas pariter vitiisque locisque
> Altius humanis exseruisse caput.
> Non Venus et Vinum sublimia pectora fregit,
> Officiumve fori, militiæve labor.—Ovid, *Fasti*, lib. i.

matical truths throughout the whole universe,—on discovering them in the heavens with Newton, in chemistry with Lavoisier, in minerals with the Abbé Hauy,—it is natural, we say, that they should take them for the principles of things, and not see any object beyond them. That beautiful simplicity of nature which should lead them to recognise, with Aristotle, *a primary moving principle,* and with Plato, an eternal *geometrician,* serves but to bewilder them. God soon becomes for them nothing more than the properties of bodies, and the very chain of numbers conceals from their view the grand unity of being.

CHAPTER II.

CHEMISTRY AND NATURAL HISTORY.

SUCH are the abuses that have given so many advantages to the enemies of the sciences, and produced the eloquent declamations of Rousseau and his followers. Nothing is more admirable, say they, than the beautiful discoveries of a Spallanzani, a Lavoisier, and a Lagrange; but all is spoiled by the consequences which perverted minds pretend to draw from them. What! because men have demonstrated the simplicity of the digestive juices and varied those of generation; because chemistry has increased, or, if you please, diminished, the number of the elements; because every student comprehends the laws of gravitation, and every schoolboy can scrawl geometrical figures; because this or that writer is a subtle metaphysician,—are we thence to conclude that there is neither God nor true religion? What an abuse of reasoning!

Disgust for philosophic studies has been strengthened in timid minds by another consideration. "If," say they, "all these discoveries were certain and invariable, we could understand the pride which they engender, not in the estimable men by whom they were made, but in the multitude who enjoy the benefit of them. But, in those sciences termed positive, does not the experience of to-day destroy the experience of yesterday? All the errors of ancient physics have had their partisans and their defenders A literary work of high merit will enjoy repute in every age; nay, time only adds to its lustre. But the sciences which are engaged solely with the properties of *bodies* cannot maintain their systems; the most renowned theories soon become antiquated. Chemists, for instance, imagined that they had obtained a regular nomenclature,[1] and now they find themselves mistaken. A few more facts, and it will be necessary to break up the drawers of modern chemistry. Of what use has it been to introduce such confusion in names, calling the atmospheric air oxygen, &c.? The sciences are a labyrinth in which you find yourself more than ever bewildered at the very moment when you imagine that you are just at the end of it.

These objections are plausible, but they are not more applicable to chemistry than to the other sciences. To reproach chemists with undeceiving themselves by their experiments, would be finding fault with their honesty and accusing them of being unacquainted with the essence of things. To whom, then, is this secret known, except to that Supreme Intelligence which has existed from all eternity? The shortness of life, the weakness of our senses, the imperfections of our instruments and of our means, are so many insurmountable obstacles to the discovery of that general formula which the Almighty hath forever concealed from us. Our sciences, as it is well known, *decompose* and *recompose*, but they cannot *compose*. It is this inability to create that always discovers the weak side and the insignificance of man. In spite of all his efforts he can do nothing; he everywhere meets with an invincible resistance. He cannot make matter subservient to his purposes, without

[1] By means of the famous terminations of acids in *ous* and *ic*. It has been recently demonstrated that nitric acid and sulphuric acid were not the result of the addition of oxygen to *nitrous acid* and *sulphureous acid*. There has been, from the beginning, a chasm left in the system by the muriatic acid, which had no positive in *ous*. M. Bertholet, we are told, is on the point of proving that *azote*, hitherto considered as a simple essence combined with *caloric*, is a compound substance. There is but one certain fact in chemistry, fixed by Boërhave and developed by Lavoisier,—namely, that *caloric*, or the substance which, combined with light, composes fire, has a continual tendency to expand bodies, or to separate their constituent particles from one another.

hearing its groans and complaints, and he seems to unite his own sighs and his turbulent heart with all his works.

In the productions of the Creator, on the contrary, all is silent, because it is not the result of effort; all is still, because all is submissive. He spoke; chaos was mute, and the spheres rolled without noise into the expanse of the firmament The united powers of matter are to one single word of God as nothing is to every thing, as created things are to necessity. Behold man in the midst of his labors: what a terrible collection of machines! He whets the steel, he distils the poison, he summons the elements to his aid, he causes the water to roar, the air to hiss, his furnaces are kindled. Armed with fire, what is this new Prometheus about to attempt? Is he going to create a world? No. The end of his work is destruction; all that he can bring forth is death!

Whether it be from the prejudices of education, or from the habit of wandering in the deserts and bringing our heart alone to the study of nature, we must confess that it gives us some pain to see the spirit of analysis and classification predominating in the amiable sciences, in which we should look for nothing but the graces of the Divinity We think it very pitiful, if we may be allowed to express the opinion, that *mammiferous* man should be classed nowadays, according to the system of Linnæus, with monkeys, bats, and sloths Would it not have been full as well to have left him at the head of the creation, where he was placed by Moses, Aristotle, Buffon, and nature? Connected by his soul with heaven, and by his body with the earth, we loved to see him form that link in the chain of beings which unites the visible with the invisible world and time with eternity.

"Even in this age," says Buffon, "in which the sciences seem to be cultivated with extraordinary care, it is, in my opinion, very easy to perceive that philosophy is neglected, and, perhaps, to a greater degree than in any preceding age; the arts which people are pleased to term scientific have usurped its place; the methods of calculation and of geometry, those of botany and of natural history,—in a word, formulas and dictionaries,—engage almost everybody's attention; we imagine that we know more because we have increased the number of symbolical expressions and scientific phrases, without observing that all these arts are but scaffolds to enable us to climb to science, and are not science itself; that we ought never to employ them when they can be dispensed with, and ought always to be afraid lest they should fail us when we would apply them to the edifice."[1]

These remarks are judicious; but, in our opinion, *classifications* are pregnant with still more danger. Is there not reason to fear lest this rage for reducing all things to physical signs, for discovering in the different races of the creation nothing but claws, teeth, and beaks, may gradually lead youth into materialism? If, however, there is a science in which the inconveniences of incredulity are felt in their fullest extent, that science is natural history. You there blight whatever you touch; the perfumes, the brilliant tints, the elegant forms of plants, disappear before the botanist who attaches to them neither morality nor feeling. Without religion the heart is insensible and dead to beauty; for beauty is not a thing that exists out of us; it is in the heart of man that all the charms of nature reside.

As for him who studies the nature and properties of animals, what else is it, if he is an infidel, than studying inanimate bodies? Whither do his researches conduct him? what can be their end? It is for him that those cabinets have been formed —schools in which death, with scythe in hand, is the lecturer; cemeteries in which clocks have been placed to count the minutes for skeletons and to mark the hour in eternity!

It is in these tombs where nothingness has collected its wonders, where the relics of the ape insult the relics of man; 'tis there we must seek the cause of that phenomenon—an *atheistical naturalist.* By frequenting the atmosphere of sepulchres, his soul has inhaled death.

When science was poor and solitary, when she roved through the valley and the forest, when she watched the bird carrying food to her young or the quadruped returning to his lair, when her laboratory was all nature, her amphitheatre the heavens and the earth, when she was simple and marvellous as the wilds in which she passed her life, then she was religious. Seated

---

[1] Buffon, *Hist. Nat.*, tome i., *prem. disc.*, p. 79.

beneath a spreading oak, her brow encircled with a wreath of flowers, which her innocent hands had plucked from the mountain, she was content to paint on her tablets the surrounding scenery. Her books were but catalogues of remedies against corporeal infirmities, or collections of sacred hymns, whose words in like manner relieved the sorrows of the soul. But when societies of learned men were formed,—when philosophers, seeking reputation and not nature, attempted to treat of the works of God without ever having felt a love for them,—infidelity sprang up together with vanity, and science was reduced to the petty instrument of a petty renown.

The Church has never spoken with such severity against philosophic studies as the various philosophers whom we have quoted in these pages. If you accuse her of having looked rather coldly upon that knowledge *which*, to use the words of Seneca, *cures us of nothing*, you must also condemn that multitude of legislators, statesmen, and moralists, who, in every age, have protested much more strongly than she has done against the danger, the uncertainty, and the obscurity of the sciences.[1]

Where will she discover truth? Is she to seek it in Locke, so highly extolled by Condillac? in Leibnitz, who deemed Locke so weak in metaphysics? or in Kant, who now attacks both Locke and Condillac? Must she take up the maxims of Minos, Lycurgus, Cato, Rousseau, who banish the sciences from their republics? or adopt the opinion of the legislators by whom they are tolerated? What dreadful lessons, if she but looks around her! What an ample subject for reflection, in that well-known history of the *tree of knowledge which produces death!* The ages of philosophy have invariably bordered upon the ages of destruction

In a question, therefore, which divided the world, the Church could adopt no other course than that which she has pursued.

These remarks were never more applicable than at the present day, when men have dared in the name of philosophy to degrade religion to the level of their blind reason. While metaphysicians, with their pretended science have discarded revelation, geologists have proclaimed man to be but an improved species of the monkey! "Professing themselves to be wise, they became fools:" Rom i. T.

What could she do more than accommodate herself to times and circumstances: oppose morality to the abuse which man makes of his knowledge, and endeavor to maintain in him, for the sake of his own happiness, a simple heart and an humble mind?

To conclude: the vice of the day consists in separating abstract studies rather too much from literary studies. The one belongs to the understanding, the others to the heart; we should, therefore, beware of cultivating the former to the exclusion of the latter, and of sacrificing the part which *loves* to the part which *reasons*. It is by a happy combination of natural and moral science, and above all by the inculcation of religious ideas, that we shall succeed in again giving to our youth that education which of old produced so many great men. It must not be supposed that our soil is exhausted. The beautiful plains of France might again be made to yield abundant harvests, were they but cultivated somewhat in the manner of our forefathers: 'tis one of those happy regions where reign those tutelar *genii* of mankind and that *divine breath* which, according to Plato, distinguish climates favorable to virtue.[1]

CHAPTER III.

CHRISTIAN PHILOSOPHERS—METAPHYSICIANS.

EXAMPLES come to the support of principles; and a religion which can claim a Bacon, a Newton, a Boyle, a Clarke, a Leibnitz, a Grotius, a Pascal, an Arnaud, a Nicole, a Mallebranche, a La Bruyère, (to say nothing of the fathers of the Church, or of Bossuet, Fénélon, Massillon, and Bourdaloue, whom we shall here consider only as orators,) such a religion may boast of being favorable to philosophy.[2]

[1] Plat., *de Leg.*, lib. v.

[2] As to such men as Pascal, Nicole, and Arnaud, it is much to be lamented that, while on the one hand they lent their talents to the defence of religion, on the other they were misled by a sectarian spirit to foment scandals in the Church. T.

Bacon owes his immortality to his essay *On the Advancement of Learning*, and to his *Novum Organum Scientiarum*. In the former he examines the circle of the sciences, classing each object under its respective faculty; he admits four faculties—the *soul* or *sensation*, the *memory*, the *imagination*, and the *understanding*. The sciences are here reduced to three:—*poetry*, *history*, and *philosophy*.

In the second work he rejects the mode of reasoning by syllogism, and proposes experimental physics as the only guide in nature. We still read with pleasure the profession of faith of the illustrious Lord-Chancellor, and the prayer which he was accustomed to repeat before he repaired to business. This Christian simplicity in a great man is deeply affecting. When Newton and Bossuet respectfully uncovered their august heads while pronouncing the name of God, they were perhaps more worthy of admiration at that moment than when the former weighed those worlds the dust of which the other taught mankind to despise.

Clarke in his *Treatise on the Existence of God*, Leibnitz in his *Theodicea*, Mallebranche in his *Inquiry concerning Truth*, have accomplished so much in metaphysics that they have left nothing to be done by their successors.

It is very extraordinary that our age should imagine itself superior to the last in logic and metaphysics. The facts are against us. Certainly the Abbé de Condillac, who has said nothing new, cannot singly counterbalance Locke, Descartes, Mallebranche, and Leibnitz. He merely dissects the first-mentioned philosopher, and bewilders himself whenever he attempts to advance without his guide. Let us observe, also, that the metaphysical science of the present age differs from that of antiquity in this particular—that it separates the imagination as much as possible from abstract perceptions. We have insulated all the faculties of our understanding, reserving thought for one thing, reason for another, and so of the rest. The consequence is, that our works have no unity, and our minds, thus divided into chapters, are subjected to the inconveniences of those histories in which every subject is separately treated of. While we are beginning a new article, the preceding one escapes our memory. We lose the connection which the facts have with each other.

We fall into confusion from being too methodical, and the multitude of particular conclusions prevents us from arriving at the general deduction.

When it is the design of a work, like that of Clarke, to attack men who pride themselves on their powers of reasoning, and to whom you must prove that you can reason as well as they, you cannot do better than to adopt the firm and close manner of the English divine; but in any other case, why should this dry style be preferred to one that is perspicuous and yet animated? Why should you not transfuse your feelings into a serious performance as well as into a merely entertaining book? The metaphysical works of Plato are still read with delight, because they are colored with a brilliant imagination. Our late metaphysicians have fallen into an egregious error in separating the history of the human mind from the history of divine things; in maintaining that the latter leads to nothing positive, and that the former alone is of any immediate utility. Where is the necessity for investigating the operations of the mind of man unless it be to refer them to God? Of what advantage is it to me to know whether or not I receive my ideas by means of the senses? "All metaphysicians," exclaims Condillac, "have bewildered themselves in enchanted worlds. I alone have discovered truth. My science is of the highest utility. I am going to explain to you the nature of conscience, of attention, of recollection!" And whither will all this lead me? Nothing is good, nothing is positive, except inasmuch as it aims at a moral end. Now, all metaphysical science which is not, like that of the ancients and of Christians, based upon theology, — all metaphysics which interpose an abyss between man and God—which assert that, as the latter is but darkness, it would be absurd to bestow a thought on the subject,—such metaphysics are at once futile and dangerous, because they have no object.

The other kind of knowledge, on the contrary,—by associating me with the divinity, by giving me an immense idea of my greatness, and of the perfection of my being,—disposes me to think justly and to act virtuously. All moral ends are connected by this link with the higher metaphysics, which present but a more sublime road to arrive at virtue. This is what Plato termed, by way of eminence, *the science of the gods*, and Pythagoras the *divine geometry.* Beyond this, metaphysics are but a microscope that curiously displays some minute objects which would have escaped the naked eye, but the ignorance or knowledge of which will neither create nor fill up a chasm in our existence.

CHAPTER IV.

CHRISTIAN PHILOSOPHERS, CONTINUED

Political Writers.

WE have, of late years, made an extraordinary parade of our political knowledge. It might almost be imagined that before our time the modern world had never heard of liberty or of the different social constitutions. It is probably for this reason that we have tried them all with such skill and success Nevertheless, Machiavel, Sir Thomas More, Mariana, Bodin, Grotius, Puffendorf, and Locke, all Christian philosophers, had devoted their attention to the nature of governments long before Mably and Rousseau.

We shall not enter into any analysis of the works of those publicists whose names we need only mention to prove that every species of literary glory belongs to Christianity. We shall elsewhere show what the liberties of mankind owe to this same religion, which is accused of inculcating the maxims of slavery.

It were sincerely to be wished that, if any writers are yet engaged in the discussion of political subjects, (which God forbid!) they would introduce into works of this kind those graces which the ancients gave to theirs. Xenophon's *Cyropædia*, Plato's *Republic and Laws*, are at the same time serious treatises and books replete with charms. Plato excels in giving an admirable turn to the most barren discussions. He possesses the art of infusing enchantment into the very exposition of a law. Here we see three old men conversing on the way from Gnossus to the cavern of Jupiter, and reposing in flowery meads under lofty cypresses. There, the involuntary murderer, standing with one foot in the sea, offers lib' tions to Neptune. Farther on, a foreign poet is received with songs and perfumes. He is greeted with the appellation of a man wholly divine. He is crowned with laurels and covered with honors. He is escorted beyond the limits of the Republic. Thus Plato has a hundred pleasing ways of setting forth his ideas. He softens down the severest sentences by considering crime in a religious point of view.

It is worthy of remark that modern political writers have ex tolled the republican form of government, whereas those of Greece generally gave the preference to monarchy. What is the reason of this? Both were dissatisfied with what they had, and conceived a predilection for what they had not. Such is the history of all mankind.

We may observe, also, that the sages of Greece viewed society in its moral relations; but our latest philosophers have considered it in its political bearings. The former insisted that the government should flow from the manners of the people; the latter, that the manners should be derived from the government. The philosophy of the one was founded on religion; the philosophy of the others on atheism. "Be virtuous and ye shall be free," cried Plato to the people; but they are told nowadays, "Be free and ye shall be virtuous." Greece, with such sentiments, was happy. What advantages shall we reap from the contrary principles?

CHAPTER V.

MORALISTS.

La Bruyère.

THE writers of the same age, whatever be their difference in point of genius, have all, nevertheless, something in common with each other. You may know those of the brilliant era of France by the energy of their thoughts, the unaffected plainness of their expressions, and yet a certain Greek and Latin construction of phrase, which, without injuring the genius of the French language, denotes the excellent models which those authors had studied.

Writers are, moreover, divided into groups, if we may be allowed the expression, who follow this or that master—this or the other school. Thus the writers of *Port Royal* may be distinguished from the writers of *the Society* Thus Fénélon, Massillon, and Flechier, correspond in certain points; and Pascal, Bossuet, and La Bruyère, in others. The latter are particularly remarkable for a kind of abruptness of thought and style which is peculiar to them; but it must be admitted that La Bruyère, who is fond of imitating Pascal,[1] sometimes weakens the proofs and the original manner of that great genius. When the author of the *Caractères*, with a view to demonstrate the insignificance of man, says, *You are placed, O Lucia, somewhere on this atom*, &c , he remains far behind that famous passage of the author of the *Pensées:—What is a man in the midst of infinity? Who can form a conception of this?*

La Bruyère further observes:—*There are but three events for man—to be born, to live, and to die. He has no perception of his birth, he suffers at his death, and he forgets to live.* Pascal impresses us much more deeply with our nothingness. *The last act*, says he, *is always painful, however pleasing all the rest of the comedy may have been. A little earth is thrown upon our heads, and 'tis over with us forever* How terrible are the concluding words! You first see the *comedy*, and then the *grave*, and then the *earth*, and then *eternity*. The carelessness with which the expression is thrown out admirably denotes the insignificance of life. What freezing indifference in this brief and cold history of man![2]

[1] See in particular his chapter on *Freethinkers*.

[2] This reflection is omitted in the small edition of Pascal, with notes. The editors probably thought that it was not in a *fine style*. We have heard the prose of the age of Louis XIV. censured as deficient in harmony, elegance, and precision. We have heard people observe, *If Bossuet and Pascal were to come to life again, they would not write in that manner* "'Tis we," they assert, "who excel in writing prose, and who far surpass all our predecessors in the art of arranging words." Is it not true that we express ordinary ideas in a lofty and elaborate style? whereas, the writers of the age of Louis XIV. conveyed the grandest conceptions in the most simple language.

La Bruyère is, nevertheless, one of the best writers of the age of Louis XIV. No man ever understood the art of giving more variety to his style, a greater diversity of forms to his language, and more rapid transitions to his ideas. He descends from the heights of eloquence to familiarity, and passes from pleasantry to argument, without once offending against taste or shocking the reader. Irony is his favorite weapon. Equally philosophical with Theophrastus, his view embraces a greater number of objects, and his remarks are more original and more profound. Theophrastus conjectures, La Rochefoucault divines, and La Bruyère shows what is passing in the recesses of the heart.

It is a great triumph for Religion that she can number among her philosophers a Pascal and a La Bruyère; and, after such examples, it should not be quite so readily asserted that none but persons of *shallow understanding* can be Christians.

"If my religion be false," says the author of the *Caractères*, "it is, I must own, the most artful snare that could possibly be devised. It is impossible to avoid falling into it and being caught. What majesty, what magnificence, in its mysteries! What coherency, what connection, in all its doctrines! What sound reason! What candor! What innocence of morals! What an invincible and overwhelming body of evidence is given successively, and for three whole centuries, by millions of the most learned and most considerate persons then in the world, and whom the conviction of one and the same truth supported in exile, in fetters, at the approach of death, and under the most cruel torments!"

Could La Bruyère revisit the earth, what would be his astonishment to find that religion whose beauty and excellence were acknowledged by the greatest men of his age, now termed *infamous, ridiculous*, and *absurd!* He would doubtless imagine that the new *freethinkers* are far superior to the writers who preceded them, and that, in comparison with them, Pascal, Bossuet, Fénélon, and Racine, are authors destitute of genius. He would open their works with profound attention and a respect mingled with fear. In every line he would expect to find some important discovery of the human mind, some lofty idea, perhaps even some historical fact, before unknown, to prove irrefragably the falsehood of Christianity. What then would he say, what would he think, in his second astonishment, which would very soon succeed the first?

We want a La Bruyère. The Revolution has produced a total change in characters. Avarice, ignorance, selfishness, appear in a thousand new lights. These vices, in the age of Louis XIV., were compounded with religion and politeness; now they are mixed up with impiety and coarseness of manners. In the seventeenth century, therefore, they must have had finer tints and more delicate shades. At that period they might have been ridiculous; but it is certain that now they are detestable.

CHAPTER VI.

MORALISTS, CONTINUED.

THERE was a genius who, at the age of twelve years, had with *bars* and *rings* created the mathematics; who, at sixteen, had composed the ablest treatise on conic sections that had appeared since the time of the ancients; who, at nineteen, reduced to a machine a science existing entirely in the understanding; who, at twenty-three, demonstrated the phenomena of the gravity of the air, and overthrew one of the great errors of ancient physics; who, at an age when the intellectual faculties scarcely begin to expand in others, having gone through the whole circle of human sciences, discovered their inanity, and turned all his thoughts toward religion; who, from that moment till his death, (which happened in his thirty-ninth year,) amid incessant bodily infirmities, fixed the language spoken by Bossuet and Racine, and furnished a model of the most perfect facetiousness as well as of the strongest reasoning; finally, who, in the short intervals of ease, resolved, unassisted, one of the profoundest problems of geometry, and scattered at random upon paper thoughts not less indicative of a superhuman than of a human mind. The name of this stupendous genius was BLAISE PASCAL.[1]

[1] In portraying the genius of Pascal, our author followed the opinion of some authors who appear to have awarded him honors which belonged to

It is difficult not to be overwhelmed with astonishment when, on opening the *Thoughts* of the Christian philosopher, we light upon the six chapters in which he treats of the nature of man The sentiments of Pascal are particularly remarkable for their profound melancholy and a certain immensity which I cannot describe: you are suspended among these sentiments as in the midst of infinity. Metaphysicians speak of that *abstract thought* which has none of the properties of matter, which explores all things without moving from the spot, which lives of itself, which is imperishable because indivisible, and which positively proves the immortality of the soul. This definition of thought seems to have been suggested to metaphysicians by the works of Pascal.

There exists a curious monument of Christian philosophy and the philosophy of the present day: it is the *Thoughts* of Pascal with the annotations of editors.[1] It is like the ruins of Palmyra, the superb relics of genius and of past ages, at the foot of which the Arab of the desert has built his miserable hut.

"Pascal," says Voltaire, "a sublime madman, born a century too early." The signification of this *century too early* must be obvious to every reader. One single observation will suffice to show how inferior Pascal *the sophist* would have been to Pascal *the Christian*.

In what part of his works has the recluse of Port Royal soared above the greatest geniuses? In his six chapters on man. Now these six chapters, which turn entirely on the original fall of man, *would not exist had Pascal been an unbeliever*.

We shall here make an observation of the highest importance. Among those who have embraced the philosophic opinions, some are incessantly decrying the age of Louis XIV., while others, priding themselves on their impartiality, allow that age the *faculties of imagination*, but deny it those of reason. The eighteenth century, say they, is pre-eminently the thinking age.

Any impartial person who reads with attention the writers of

---

others. Torricelli and Descartes had preceded him in the demonstration of the gravity of the atmosphere; and as to his treatise on conic sections, he himself admitted that he had derived his information from a work of Des-Argues. But, independently of these discoveries, Pascal has undoubted claims to be ranked among the profoundest minds that ever existed. T.

[1] See note Y.

the age of Louis XIV., will soon discover *that nothing escaped their sight;* but that, contemplating objects from a higher standpoint than we do, they disdained the routes which we pursue, and at the end of which their piercing eyes discovered a fatal abyss.

This assertion we might support with a thousand proofs. Was it from ignorance of the objections against religion that so many great men were religious? Was it not at this very period that Bayle published his doubts and his sophisms? Is it no longer known that Clarke and Leibnitz were then wholly engaged in combating infidelity? that Pascal had planned a defence of religion? that La Bruyère composed his chapter on *Freethinkers,* and Massillon his sermon on the *Reality of a Future State?* that, finally, Bossuet hurled at the heads of atheists those overwhelming words:—"What have they seen—these *extraordinary geniuses,* —what have they seen *more than others?* What ignorance is theirs! and how easy it would be to confound them, if, weak and presumptuous, they were not afraid of being instructed! For do they think that they have more clearly perceived the difficulties because they sink under them and because others who *have seen them* have despised them? They have seen nothing; they know nothing; they have not even the means to establish that annihilation for which they hope after this life, and which, miserable lot as it is, they are not sure of enjoying."

And what relations, moral, political, or religious, escaped the observation of Pascal? What aspect of things has he not examined? If he considers human nature in general, he draws that well-known and astonishing picture:—"The first thing that presents itself to man, when he surveys himself, is his body," &c In another place he says, "Man is but a thinking reed," &c. Has Pascal, we would ask, shown himself in all this a shallow *thinker?*

Modern writers have expatiated much on the power of opinion, and Pascal was the first who made the observation. One of the strongest political reflections thrown out by Rousseau is found in his discourse on the *Inequality of Conditions:*—"The first," says he, "who, having enclosed a piece of ground, took it into his head to say, *This is mine,* was the real founder of civil society." Now this is almost word for word the awful idea which the recluse of Port Royal has expressed with a very different kind of energy:—"This dog is mine, said those poor children; that is my place in the sunshine; such was the commencement and the image of the usurpation of the whole earth."

This, too, is one of those thoughts which make us tremble for Pascal. What would have become of that great man had he not been a Christian? How adorable is that curb of religion, which, without restraining our comprehensive views, holds us back from the brink of the precipice!

'Tis the same Pascal who has also observed:—"Three degrees of latitude overthrow all jurisprudence. A meridian determines truth, or a few years of possession. Fundamental law changes; right has its epochs; a pretty sort of justice that is bounded by a river or a mountain! Truth on this side of the Pyrenees may be error on the other."

Surely, the boldest spectator of the present age, the writer most intent on generalizing ideas in order to convulse the world, never pronounced a keener satire on the justice of governments and the prejudices of nations.

All the insults which by means of philosophy we have heaped upon human nature have been in a greater or lesser degree derived from the works of Pascal. But in robbing this extraordinary genius of his ideas on the miseries of man, we have not known, like him, how to discover the greatness of man. Bossuet and Fénélon, the former in his *Histoire Universelle*, his *Avertissemens*, and his *Politique tiré de l'Écriture sainte*, the latter in his *Télémaque*, have said every thing essential on the subject of governments. Montesquieu himself, as it has very justly been remarked, has often done no more than develop the principles of the Bishop of Meaux. We might fill volumes were we to select all the passages favorable to liberty and the love of country which occur in the authors of the seventeenth century.

What improvement was unattempted in that age?[1] The equalization of weights and measures, the abolition of provincial customs, the reformation of the civil and criminal code, the equal division of taxes,—all those plans of which we so loudly boast, were proposed, discussed, and even executed when the

[1] See note Z.

advantages of the reform appeared to counterbalance its inconveniencies. Did not Bossuet even project a union between the Protestant Church and that of Rome? When we consider that Bagnoli, Le Maitre, Arnaud, Nicole, and Pascal, devoted themselves to the education of youth, we shall scarcely imagine that education at the present day is better understood or more scientifically conducted. The best classical books that we even now possess are those of Port Royal, and in all our elementary works we do no more than repeat them, often taking especial care to conceal our thefts.

Our superiority, then, is reduced to some little progress in the natural sciences,—a progress resulting from that of time, and by no means compensating for the loss of the imagination which is the consequence of it. The *mind* is the same in all ages; but it is more particularly accompanied either by the arts or by the sciences: it is only with the former that it possesses all its poetic grandeur and moral beauty.

But it may be asked, if the age of Louis XIV. conceived all kinds of liberal ideas, how happens it that it neglected to make the same use of them as we have done? Ah! let us not boast of our experiments Pascal, Bossuet, Fénélon, saw much farther than we do; for, at the same time that they were as well acquainted with the nature of things as we are, and even better, they were aware of the danger of innovations. Did their works furnish no evidence of philosophical thought, yet could we suppose that these great men were not struck with the abuses which creep in on every side, and that they were unacquainted with the weak and the strong side of human affairs? But their principle was that *a small evil ought not to be done even for the sake of a great good,*[1] and still less in behalf of vain systems, which are almost invariably productive of deplorable results. It was certainly not from any want of genius that this same Pascal, who, as we have already shown, understood so well the defect of laws in the *absolute sense*, observed in the *relative sense*, "How wise it is to distinguish men by external qualities! Which of us two shall give way to the other? the least clever? But I am as clever as he is; we must fight it out. He has four lacqueys, and

[1] *History of Port Royal.*

I have but one; that is clear, if I will but count: I must give way, and I am a fool if I dispute the point."

Here is a reply to volumes of sophisms. The author of the *Thoughts* submitting to four *lacqueys* is a very different sort of philosopher from all those *thinkers* whom the four lacqueys have shocked.

In a word, the age of Louis XIV. continued tranquil, not because this or that thing was unperceived by it, but because, on making a discovery, it examined it thoroughly, considering it on every side and exploring all its dangers. If it did not plunge into the ideas of the times, the reason is that it was superior to them. We take its strength for its weakness; its secret and ours are comprised in this reflection of Pascal:—

"The sciences have two extremities, which touch one another: the first is pure natural ignorance, the state of all mankind at their birth; the other extremity is that at which all great minds arrive, who, after traversing the whole circle of human knowledge, discover that they know nothing, and find themselves in the same ignorance from which they set out, but it is a scientific ignorance, which is acquainted with itself. Those who have left the state of natural ignorance, and have not been able to reach the other, have some tincture of that self-sufficient science, and are puffed up with conceit. These are disturbers of society, and their judgments are more false than those of any of the others. The vulgar and the real scholars compose the mass of the world; the others despise them, and are despised by them."

Here we cannot forbear to make a sorrowful reflection on ourselves. Pascal had undertaken to give to the world the work of which we now publish so small a portion. What a master-piece would such a philosopher have produced! If God permitted him not to execute his design, it was, probably, because it is not fit that all doubts on the subject of faith should be removed; that there may be matter left for those temptations and trials which produce saints and martyrs.

BOOK III.

HISTORY.

CHAPTER I.

OF CHRISTIANITY AS IT RELATES TO THE MANNER OF WRITING HISTORY.

If Christianity has so greatly conduced to the advancement of philosophical ideas, it must of course be favorable to the genius of history, which is but a branch of moral and political philosophy. Whoever rejects the sublime notions of nature and her Author which religion inspires wilfully deprives himself of an abundant source of images and ideas.

He, in fact, will be most intimately acquainted with man who has long meditated on the designs of Providence; he will be best able to fathom human wisdom who has penetrated into the depths of the divine intelligence. The designs of kings, the vices of cities, the unjust and crooked measures of civil policy, the restlessness of the heart from the secret working of the passions, those long agitations with which nations are at times seized, those changes of power from the king to the subject, from the noble to the plebeian, from the rich to the poor,—all these subjects will be inexplicable to you, if you have not, as it were, attended the council of the Most High, and considered the spirit of strength, of prudence, of weakness, or of error, which he dispenses to the nations whose salvation or whose ruin he decrees.

Eternity, therefore, should be the groundwork of the history of time, every thing being referred to God as the universal cause. You may extol, as much as you please, the writer who, penetrating into the secrets of the human heart, deduces the most important events from the most trivial sources: a God watching over the kingdoms of the earth; impiety, that is to say, the absence of moral virtues, becoming the immediate cause of the calamities of nations; this, in our opinion, is an historical foundation far more noble and far more solid than the other.

The French revolution will afford an illustration of this remark. Were they any ordinary causes, we would ask, which in the course of a few years perverted all our affections and banished from among us that simplicity and greatness peculiar to the heart of man? The spirit of God having withdrawn from the people, no force was left except that of original sin, which resumed its empire as in the days of Cain and his race. Whoever would have followed the dictates of reason felt a certain incapability of good; whoever extended a pacific hand beheld that hand suddenly withered; the bloody flag waved over the ramparts of every city; war was declared against all nations; then were fulfilled the words of the prophet: "They shall cast out the bones of the kings of Judah, and the bones of the princes thereof, and the bones of the priests, and the bones of the inhabitants of Jerusalem, out of their graves."[1] Streams of blood flowed in all quarters: culpable in regard to the past, fanaticism swept away the old institutions; culpable in regard to the future, it founded nothing new for posterity; the tombs of our ancestors and the rising generation were alike profaned. In that line of life which was transmitted to us by our ancestors, and which it is our duty to prolong beyond our own existence, each confined his views to the present, and, consecrating himself to his own corruption as to an abominable worship, lived as if nothing had preceded and as if nothing was to follow him.

But, while this spirit of destruction was internally devouring France, a spirit of salvation was protecting her against external injury. She had neither prudence nor greatness except on her frontiers; within all was devastation, without all was triumph. The country no longer resided in the homes of her children; it exists in a camp on the Rhine, as in the time of the Merovingian dynasty. You would have imagined that you beheld the Jewish nation expelled from the land of Gessen, and subduing the barbarous nations in the desert.

Such a combination of things has no natural principle in human events. The religious writer alone can here discover the profound

[1] Jerem. viii. 1.

counsels of the Most High. Had the combined powers attempted only to put an end to the excesses of Robespierre, and then left France entire to repair her calamities and her errors, they had, perhaps, gained their point. But God beheld the iniquity of courts, and said to the foreign soldier, "I will break the sword in thy hand, and thou shall not destroy the people of St Louis."

Thus religion seems to lead to the explanation of the most in comprehensible facts in history. There is, moreover, in the name of God something sublime, which imparts to the style a certain wonderful power, so that the most religious writer is almost invariably the most eloquent. Without religion, it is possible to have wit, but very difficult to possess genius. Add to this, you perceive in the Christian historian the tone, we had almost said the taste, of an honest man, which renders you disposed to give implicit credit to all that he relates. On the contrary, you mistrust the sophistical historian; for, as he almost always represents society in an unfavorable light, you are inclined to look upon him as a deceiver.

CHAPTER II.

OF THE GENERAL CAUSES WHICH HAVE PREVENTED MODERN WRITERS FROM SUCCEEDING IN HISTORY.

First Cause—The Beauties of the Ancient Subjects.

A POWERFUL objection here occurs: If Christianity is favorable to the genius of history, how happens it that modern writers are in general inferior to those of antiquity in this profound and important department of literature?

In the first place, the fact assumed in this objection is not strictly true, since one of the most beautiful historical monuments that exists among men—the *Discourse on Universal History*—was dictated by the spirit of Christianity. But, deferring for a moment our considerations on that work, let us inquire into the causes of our inferiority in history, if that inferiority actually exists. These causes are, in our opinion, of two kinds; some belonging to *history*, and others to the *historian*.

Ancient history presents a picture which has no parallel in modern times. The Greeks were particularly remarkable for the greatness of men—the Romans for the greatness of things. Rome and Athens, setting out from a state of nature and attaining the highest degree of civilization, traversed the entire scale of the virtues and the vices, of ignorance and the arts. You observe the growth of man and of his intellect. At first a child, then the sport of all the passions in youth, strong and wise in maturer years, infirm and corrupt in his old age. The state follows the man, passing from the royal or paternal government to the republican constitution, and then sinking with decrepitude into despotism.

Though modern nations exhibit, as we shall presently have occasion to observe, some interesting epochs, some celebrated reigns, some brilliant portraits, some illustrious actions, yet it must be confessed that they do not furnish the historian with that combination of things, that sublimity of lessons, which make ancient history a complete whole and a finished picture. They did not begin with the first step. They did not form themselves by degrees. They were suddenly transported from the recesses of forests and the savage state into the midst of cities and civilization. They are but young branches engrafted upon an aged trunk. Thus their origin is involved in darkness. You perceive there at the same time the greatest virtues and the greatest vices; gross ignorance and gleams of light; vague notions of justice and of government; a confused medley in manners and in language. These nations have not passed either through that state in which good manners make the laws, or that in which good laws make the manners.

These nations having established themselves upon the ruins of the ancient world, another phenomenon strikes the historian. Every thing suddenly assumes a regular appearance, a uniform aspect. He discovers monarchies on every side, while the few petty republics intermixed with them are either converted into principalities or absorbed by the neighboring kingdoms. At the same time, the arts and sciences are developed; but in silence and obscurity. They separate themselves, as it were, from the destinies of man. They cease to influence the fate of empires. Confined to a small class of citizens, they become rather an object of luxury and curiosity than an additional element of national life.

Thus every thing is consolidated at once. A religious and political balance keeps all the different parts of Europe upon a evel. None of them is now liable to destruction. The most insignificant modern state may boast of a duration equal to that of the empire of a Cyrus or a Cæsar. Christianity is the sheet-anchor which has fixed so many floating nations and kept them in port; but their ruin is almost certain if they come to break the common chain by which religion holds them together.

Now, by diffusing over nations that uniformity, and, if we may so express it, that monotony of manners which the laws produced in ancient Egypt, and which they still occasion in India and China, Christianity has of course rendered the colors of history less vivid. Those general virtues of all ages and of all countries, such as humanity, modesty, charity, which it has substituted instead of the doubtful political virtues, have also less scope on the theatre of the world As they are genuine virtues, they shun the glare of light and the clamor of fame. Among the modern nations there is a certain silence in affairs which disconcerts the historian. Far be it from us to complain of this! The moral man among us is far superior to the moral man of the ancients. Our reason is not perverted by an abominable religion. We adore no monsters. Obscenity walks not forth with unblushing face among Christians. We have neither gladiators nor slaves. It is not very long since the sight of blood thrilled us with horror. Ah! let us not envy the Romans their Tacitus if it be necessary to purchase him with a Tiberius!

CHAPTER III.

THE SAME SUBJECT, CONTINUED.

Second Cause—The Ancients Exhausted all the Historical Styles except the Christian Style.

To this first cause of the inferiority of our historians, arising from the very nature of the subjects, must be added a second, originating in the manner in which the ancients wrote history. They exhausted all its colors, and if Christianity had not furnished a new order of reflections and ideas, the doors of history would have been forever closed against the moderns.

Young and brilliant in the time of Herodotus, she held forth to the view of Greece natural pictures of the birth of society and the primitive manners of men. The historian of those days enjoyed the incalculable advantage of writing the annals of fable while writing those of truth. He needed but to paint, and not to reflect. The vices and virtues of nations were as yet only in their poetical age.

Other times brought with them other manners. Thucydides was deprived of those admirable delineations of the cradle of the world; but he entered a hitherto uncultivated field of history. He traced with energy and gravity the evils occasioned by political dissensions, leaving to posterity examples by which it never profits.

Xenophon, in his turn, discovered a new path. Without becoming dull, or sacrificing any portion of Attic elegance, he took a pious view of the human heart, and became the father of moral history.

Placed on a more extensive stage, and in the only country where two species of eloquence—that of the bar and that of politics—flourished, Livy transfused them both into his works. He was the orator, as Herodotus was the poet, of history.

Finally, the corruption of mankind—the execrable reigns of a Tiberius and a Nero—gave birth to the last species of history, the philosophical The causes of events—which Herodotus had sought in the gods, Thucydides in political constitutions, Xenophon in morals, and Livy in the concurrence of all these different circumstances combined—Tacitus discovered in the depravity of the human heart.

We would not, however, be understood to assert that these great historians shine exclusively in the characters which we have taken the liberty to assign to them; but it appears to us that these are the distinctive features of their works. Between these primitive characters of history there are tints which were seized by historians of an inferior rank. Thus, Polybius takes his place between Thucydides the politician and Xenophon the philosophic soldier. Sallust partakes at once of the respective manners of Tacitus and Livy; but the former surpasses him in energy of thought, and the latter in beauty of narration. Suetonius wrote biography without reflection and without reserve. Plutarch added morality to it. Velleius Paterculus learned to generalize without distorting history. Florus produced a philosophical epitome of it. Lastly, Diodorus Siculus, Dionysius of Halicarnassus, Cornelius Nepos, Quintus Curtius, Aurelius Victor, Ammianus Marcellinus, Justin, Eutropius, and others whom we forbear to mention or whose names have slipped our memory, conducted history down to the period when it fell into the hands of Christian authors,—a period when a total change took place in the minds and in the manners of men.

Between truths and illusions the case is widely different. The latter are inexhaustible, and the circle of the former is confined. Poetry is ever new, and this it is that constitutes its charm in the eyes of men. But in morals and in history you are limited to the narrow sphere of truth Do what you will, you cannot avoid the repetition of known observations. What historical field, then, was left for the moderns which had not been previously explored? They could do no more than imitate; and in these imitations several causes prevented their attaining to the elevation of their originals. As poetry, the origin of the Catti, the Tencteri, the Mattiaci, in the depths of the Hercynian Forest. displayed nothing of that brilliant Olympus, of those cities reared by the sounds of the lyre, and of the whole enchanted infancy of the Hellenes and of the Pelasgi, planted on the banks of the

Achelous and the Eurotas. In politics, the feudal system forbade important lessons. As to eloquence, there was only that of the pulpit. As to philosophy, the nations were not yet sufficiently miserable or sufficiently corrupt for it to begin to make its appearance.

Imitations were, however, produced with more or less success. Bentivoglio in Italy copied Livy, and would be eloquent were he not affected. Davila, Guicciardini, and Fra Paolo, had more simplicity, and Mariana, in Spain, displayed considerable talents; but this fiery Jesuit disgraced a department of literature whose highest merit is impartiality.[1] Hume, Robertson, and Gibbon, have more or less followed Sallust or Tacitus; but the latter historian has produced two writers not inferior to himself,—Machiavel and Montesquieu.

Tacitus, however, should not be chosen for a model without great caution. The adoption of Livy is liable to fewer inconveniences. The eloquence of the former is too peculiarly his own to be attempted by any one who is not possessed of his genius. Tacitus, Machiavel, and Montesquieu, have formed a dangerous school, by introducing those ambitious expressions, those dry phrases,

[1] Mariana, a native of Spain, flourished in the fifteenth and sixteenth centuries. Our author very probably borrowed his opinion of Mariana's historical merit from the Abbé Mably's work on the *manner* of writing history. Mably, however, admits that his knowledge of Mariana was not derived from his own personal reading. What rendered Mariana obnoxious to the French was not the defect of his style as the historian of Spain, but his fierce denunciation of tyranny and fearless advocacy of democratic principles in his work, *De Rege et Regis institutione*. To men who, like Chateaubriand, had just emerged from the horrors of the French revolution, an author like Mariana might well have appeared *fiery*, though teaching the simple truth. The character of doctrines depends much upon the times in which they appear. The fact is, the Jesuits have had a difficult position amid the inconsistencies of the human mind. When they have vindicated the rights of authority in defending the fundamental principles of order and law, they have been condemned as the friends of tyranny; and when, pursuing the same line of truth, they have denounced despotism and advocated the rights of the people, they have been held up as the enemies of social order! Thus, when John the Baptist came, neither eating bread nor drinking wine, the Jews declared that he had a devil; and when Christ appeared, eating and drinking, the same Jews pronounced him a glutton. The Jesuits, therefore, will always answer the world as he answered the Jews:—"And wisdom is justified by all her children." Luke vii. T.

those abrupt turns, which, under the appearance of brevity, border on obscurity and bad taste.

Let us, then, leave this manner to those immortal geniuses who, from different causes, have created a peculiar style; a style which they alone can support, and which it is dangerous to imitate. Be it remembered that the writers of the most brilliant eras of literature were strangers to that studied conciseness of ideas and language. The ideas of Livy and Bossuet are copious, and strictly concatenated; with them, every word arises out of that which goes before it, and gives birth to the word which is to follow. Great rivers, if we may be allowed to use this simile, flow not at intervals in a right line; their currents, slowly rolling from their distant sources, are continually increasing; they take a large and circuitous sweep in the plains, embracing cities and forests with their mighty arms, and discharging into the ocean streams of water capable of filling its deepest caverns.

CHAPTER IV.

OF THE REASONS WHY THE FRENCH HAVE NO HISTORICAL WORKS, BUT ONLY MEMOIRS.

HERE is another question, which relates exclusively to the French:—Why have we nothing but memoirs instead of history, and why are almost all of these memoirs excellent?

The Frenchman, in all ages, even while yet a barbarian, was vain, thoughtless, and sociable. He reflects little upon objects in general, but he is an inquisitive observer of details, and his eye is quick, penetrating, and accurate. He must always be upon the stage himself, and even in the quality of an historian he cannot make up his mind to keep entirely out of sight. Memoirs leave him at full liberty to follow the bent of his genius. There, without quitting the theatre, he introduces his observations, which are always intelligent and sometimes profound. He is fond of saying, *I was there, and the King said to me—The prince informed me—I gave my advice, I foresaw the benefit or the mischief.* In this manner his vanity gratifies itself; he makes a display of his wit to the reader; and his solicitude to gain credit for ingenious ideas often leads him to think well. In this kind of history, moreover, he is not obliged to renounce his passions, from which he finds it difficult to part. He is an enthusiast in this or that cause, in behalf of this or that person; and, sometimes insulting the adverse party, at others jeering his own, he at once indulges his revenge and gives vent to his spleen.

From the Sire de Joinville to the Cardinal de Retz, from the memoirs of the time of the League to those of the time of the Fronde, this character is everywhere conspicuous; it betrays itself even in the grave Sully. But when you would tranfer to history this art of details, the whole scene is changed; for weak tints are lost in large pictures, like slight undulations on the surface of the ocean. Compelled in this case to generalize our observations, we fall into the spirit of system. Add to this that, being prevented from speaking openly of ourselves, we appear behind all the characters of our history. In the narrative we become jejune, prolix, and circumstantial, because we chat much better than we relate; in general reflections we are trivial or vulgar, because we are intimately acquainted with him only with whom we associate.[1]

Finally, the private life of the French is, perhaps, another circumstance unfavorable to the genius of history. Tranquillity of mind is necessary for him who would write well upon men. Now our *literati*, living in general without families, or at least out of their families, their passions restless and their days miserably devoted to the gratification of vanity, acquire habits which are directly at variance with the gravity of history. This practice of confining our whole existence within a certain circle must, of course, shorten our sight and contract our ideas. Too attentive to a nature that is but the creature of compact, genuine nature

---

[1] We know that there are exceptions, and that some French writers have distinguished themselves as historians; we shall presently do justice to their merit. But it seems to us that it would be unfair to found an objection upon this fact, which could not affect the truth of our general assertion. Otherwise, there would be no truth in criticism. General theories partake not of the nature of man, in which the purest truth contains always some mixture of error. Truth in man is like a triangle, which can have but one right angle, as if nature had wished to impress an image of our defective virtue upon the very science which alone we consider certain.

eludes our observation; we scarcely ever reason upon it, except by an extraordinary effort, and, as it were, by accident; and when we happen to be right, it is the result of conjecture more than of judgment.

We may therefore safely conclude that to the revolution in human affairs, to a different order of things and of times, to the difficulty of striking out new tracks in morals, in politics, and in philosophy, we must ascribe the inferiority of the moderns in history; and as to the French, if they have in general good memoirs only, it is in their peculiar character that we must seek the reason of this singularity.

By some, it has been referred to political causes; if, say they, history has not risen among us to the standard of antiquity, it is because her independent genius has always been fettered. This assertion seems to be flatly contradicted by facts. In no age, in no country, under no form of government, was greater freedom of thought enjoyed than in France during the time of the monarchy. Some acts of oppression, some severe or unjust proceedings of the censors of the press, may, no doubt, be adduced; but would they counterbalance the numberless contrary examples?[1] Turn to our memoirs, and in every page of them you will find the severest and often the most offensive truths levelled against kings, priests, and nobles. The Frenchman has never bowed with abject servility to the yoke; he has always indemnified himself by the independence of his opinion for the constraint imposed upon him by monarchical forms. The *Tales* of Rabelais, the treatise on *Voluntary Slavery* by La Beotie, the *Essays* of Montaigne, the *Morals* of Charron, the *Republics* of Boddin, all the works in favor of the League, the treatise in which Mariana even goes so far as to defend regicide, are sufficient proofs that the privilege of unlimited discussion belonged to other times as well as to the present. If the citizen rather than the subject constituted the historian, how happens it that Tacitus, Livy himself, and among us the Bishop of Meaux and Montesquieu, gave their severe lessons under the most absolute masters that ever reigned? Never did they imagine, while censuring dishonorable actions and praising the virtuous, that the liberty of writing consisted in abusing

[1] See note AA.

governments and shaking the foundations of duty. Had they made so pernicious a use of their talents, Augustus, Trajan, and Louis would most assuredly have compelled them to be silent; but is not this kind of dependence a benefit rather than an evil? When Voltaire submitted to a lawful censure, he gave us *Charles XII.* and the *Age of Louis XIV.;* when he broke through all restraint, he produced only the *Essay on Manners.* There are truths which prove the source of the greatest disorders, because they inflame all the passions; and yet, unless a just authority closes our lips, it is precisely these that we take the highest pleasure in revealing, because they gratify, at one and the same time, the malignity of our hearts corrupted by the fall, and our primitive propensity to the truth.

CHAPTER V.

EXCELLENCE OF MODERN HISTORY.

It is now but just to consider the reverse of the picture, and to show that modern history is still capable of being highly interesting, if treated by some skilful hand. The establishment of the Franks in Gaul, Charlemagne, the crusades, chivalry, a battle of Bouvines, the last branch of an imperial family perishing at Naples on a scaffold, a battle of Lepanto, a Henry IV. in France, a Charles I. in England, present at least memorable epochs, singular manners, celebrated events, tragic catastrophes. But the grand point to be seized in modern history is the change produced by Christianity in social order. By erecting morals on a new basis, it has modified the character of nations, and created in Europe a race of men totally different from the ancients in opinions, government, customs, manners, arts, and sciences.

And what characteristic traits do the new nations exhibit! Here are the Germans, a people among whom the radical corruption of the higher classes has never extended its influence to the lower; where the indifference of the former toward their country has never prevented the latter from being sincerely attached to it; a people among whom the spirit of revolt and of fidelity, of slavery and of independence, has never changed since the days of Tacitus.

There you behold the laborious Batavians, whose information comes from their good sense, their ingenuity from industry, their virtues from coldness, and their passions from reason.

Italy, with her hundred princes and magnificent recollections, forms a strong contrast to obscure and republican Switzerland.

Spain, cut off from other nations, still presents a more original character to the historian. The kind of stagnation of manners in which she lies will, perhaps, one day prove of advantage to her, and, when all the other European nations will have been exhausted by corruption, she alone will be able to appear with lustre upon the stage of the world, because there the groundwork of morals will still subsist.

A mixture of German and French blood, the English nation displays in every thing its double origin. Its government, a compound of royalty and aristocracy; its religion, less pompous than the Catholic, but more brilliant than the Lutheran; its soldiers, at once robust and active; its literature and its arts; finally, the language, the very features and persons, of the English, partake of the two sources from which they are descended. With German simplicity, sedateness, good sense, and deliberation, they combine the fire, impetuosity, levity, vivacity, and elegance of mind, which distinguish the French.

The English have public spirit, and we have national honor; our good qualities are rather the gifts of divine favor than the effects of a political education. Like the demi-gods, we are more nearly allied to heaven than to earth.

The French, the eldest sons of antiquity, are Romans in genius and Greeks in character. Restless and fickle in prosperity, constant and invincible in adversity; formed for all the arts; polished even to excess during the tranquillity of the state; rude and savage in political commotions; tossed, like ships without ballast, by the vehemence of all the passions,—one moment in the skies, the next in the abyss; enthusiasts alike in good and in evil, doing the former without expecting thanks and the latter without feeling remorse; remembering neither their crimes nor their virtues; pusillanimously attached to life in time of peace, prodigal of their blood in battle; vain, satirical, ambitious, fond at once of old fashions and of innovations; despising all mankind except themselves; individually the most amiable, collectively the most disagreeable of men; charming in their own country, insupportable abroad; alternately more gentle, more innocent than the lamb submitting to the knife, and more merciless, more ferocious than the tiger springing upon his prey:—such were the Athenians of old, and such are the French of the present day.

Having thus balanced the advantages and the disadvantages of modern history and of ancient history, it is time to remind the reader that, if the historians of antiquity are, in general, superior to ours, this truth is nevertheless liable to great exceptions. We shall now proceed to show that, thanks to the spirit of Christianity, French genius has almost attained the same perfection in this noble department of literature as in its other branches.

CHAPTER VI.

VOLTAIRE CONSIDERED AS AN HISTORIAN.

"VOLTAIRE," says Montesquieu, "will never compose a good history; he is like the monks, who write not for the sake of the subject of which they treat, but for the glory of their order. Voltaire writes for his convent."

This opinion, applied to the *Age of Louis XIV.* and the *History of Charles XII.*, is far too severe, but perfectly accurate in regard to the *Essay on the Manners of Nations.*[1] Two authors, in particular, were formidable to those who combated Christianity, Pascal, and Bossuet. These, then, it was necessary to attack, and to endeavor, indirectly, to destroy their authority.

[1] An unguarded word in Voltaire's *Correspondence* shows what was his design, and what the historical truth he aimed at, in writing the *Essay.* "I have made a burlesque of the whole world: it is a good hit.' —*Corresp. Gen.*, tome v. p. 94.

Hence the edition of Pascal with notes, and the *Essay*, which was held up in opposition to the *Discourse on Universal History*. But never did the anti-religious party, in other respects too successful, commit a grosser error or afford Christianity a greater triumph. It is scarcely conceivable how Voltaire, with so much taste and discrimination, should not have understood the danger of a conflict, hand to hand, with Bossuet and Pascal. The observation which applies to all his poetical works holds good in regard to his historical productions: while he declaims against religion, his finest pages are inspired by Christianity. Witness the following portrait of St. Louis:—

"Louis IX.," says he, "appeared to be a prince destined to reform Europe, if Europe could have been reformed, to polish France and render her triumphant, and to be in all things a pattern to mankind. His piety, which was that of an anchoret, took from him none of the virtues of a king. A wise economy lessened not his liberality. He knew how to combine profound policy with strict justice, and perhaps he is the only monarch who deserves that encomium. Prudent and firm in council, intrepid in battle without being rash, compassionate as though he had all his life been unfortunate, it is not given to man to carry virtue to a higher pitch. . . . Seized with the plague before Tunis, he was, by his own command, laid upon ashes, and expired, at the age of fifty-five years, with all the piety of a monk and all the fortitude of a truly great man."

Was it the design of Voltaire, in this portrait, which is so elegantly drawn, to depreciate his hero by introducing an anchoret? It can scarcely be denied that such was his intention; but how egregious was the mistake! It is precisely the contrast between the religious and the military virtues, between Christian humility and royal grandeur, that constitutes the pathos and the beauty of this picture.

Christianity necessarily heightens the effect of historical delineations, by making the characters start, as it were, from the canvas, and laying the warm colors of the passions on a cold and tranquil ground. To renounce its grave morality would be to reject the only new method of eloquence which the ancients have left us. We have no doubt that Voltaire, had he been religious, would have excelled in history. He wants nothing but seriousness; and, notwithstanding his imperfections, he is perhaps, with the exception of Bossuet, the best historian that France has produced.

CHAPTER VII.

PHILIP DE COMMINES AND ROLLIN.

A Christian eminently possesses the qualities which one of the ancients[1] requires in an historian—"a quick perception of the things of the world, and a pleasing way of expressing himself."

As a biographer, Philip de Commines bears an extraordinary resemblance to Plutarch; his simplicity is even more unaffected than that of the ancient writer, who frequently has no other merit than that of being simple. Plutarch loves to run after ideas, and in many of his artless turns he is but a very agreeable impostor.

It must indeed be admitted that he is better informed than Commines; and yet this old French gentleman, with the gospel and his confidence in the hermits, has, notwithstanding his ignorance, left memoirs replete with instruction. Among the ancients, erudition was indispensably necessary for a writer; among us, an illiterate Christian, whose only study has been the love of God, has often produced an admirable volume. For this reason it is that St. Paul observes, "Though I understand all mysteries and all knowledge, and have not charity, I am nothing."

Rollin is the Fénélon of history, and, like the latter, has embellished Egypt and Greece. The first volumes of the *Ancient History* are fraught with the spirit of antiquity: the narrative of this virtuous author is full, simple, and tranquil; and Christianity, inspiring his writings, has imparted to him something that deeply affects the mind. His works denote

[1] Lucian, in his *Inquiry how History ought to be written.*

that *good man, whose heart*, according to the admirable expression of Scripture, *is a continual feast.*[1] Rollin has diffused over the crimes of men the serenity of a conscience void of reproach, and the grace and charity of an apostle of Christ. Shall we never witness the return of those times, when the education of youth and the hopes of posterity were intrusted to such hands?

CHAPTER VIII.

BOSSUET CONSIDERED AS AN HISTORIAN.

But it is in the *Discourse on Universal History* that the influence of the genius of Christianity over the genius of history appears eminently conspicuous. Political like Thucydides, moral like Xenophon, eloquent like Livy, as profound and graphic as Tacitus, the Bishop of Meaux has, moreover, that solemnity and elevation of style of which no example is to be found except in the admirable exordium of the book of Maccabees.

Bossuet is more than an historian; he is a father of the Church, an inspired priest, on whose brow oft plays a lambent flame as on that of the legislator of the Hebrews. What a survey has he taken of the earth! he is in a thousand places at once! A patriarch under the palm-tree of Tophel, a minister at the court of Babylon, a priest at Memphis, a legislator at Sparta, a citizen at Athens and at Rome, he changes time and place at pleasure; he passes along with the rapidity and the majesty of ages. With the rod of the law in hand, and with irresistible authority, he drives before him *pêle-mêle* both Jews and Gentiles to the grave; he brings up the rear of the funeral procession of all generations, and, supported by Isaias and Jeremias, he raises his prophetic lamentations amid the ruins and the wrecks of the human race.

The first part of the *Discourse on Universal History* is admi

[1] Ecclesiastic. xxx. 27.

rable for the narration; the second, for sublimity of style and lofty metaphysical ideas; the third, for the profundity of its moral and political views. Have Livy and Sallust any observations on the ancient Romans superior to these words of the Bishop of Meaux?

"The groundwork of a Roman, if we may be allowed the expression, was the love of his liberty and of his country: one of these principles caused him to love the other; because he loved his liberty, he also loved his country, as a mother that brought him up in sentiments equally generous and free.

"Under this name of liberty, the Romans as well as the Greeks figured to themselves a state in which no individual was subject to any power but the law, and in which the law was stronger than any individual."

In hearing people declaim against religion, you would suppose that a priest is necessarily a slave, and that before our times no one ever spoke worthily on the subject of liberty; but read the observations of Bossuet on the Greeks and Romans. Who has excelled him in treating of the virtues and vices? Who has formed a juster estimate of human things? Some of those strokes from time to time escape him which have no parallel in ancient eloquence and which originate in the very spirit of Christianity. For example, after speaking of the pyramids of Egypt, he adds, "But, in spite of all the efforts of men, their insignificance is invariably apparent; these pyramids were tombs. Nay, more, the kings by whom they were erected had not the satisfaction of being interred in them, and consequently did not enjoy their sepulchres."[1]

In this passage we know not which to admire most, the grandeur of the idea or the boldness of the expression. The term *enjoy* applied to a *sepulchre* at once proclaims the magnificence of that sepulchre, the vanity of the Pharaohs by whom it was erected, the rapidity of our existence,—in a word, the inconceivable nothingness of man, who, incapable of possessing any real good here below except a tomb, is sometimes deprived even of that barren inheritance.

Tacitus, be it observed, has treated of the Pyramids,[2] but all

[1] *Disc. on Univ. Hist.*, part iii. [2] *Annal.*, lib. ii.

his philosophy suggested to him nothing to be compared to the beautiful reflection with which religion inspired Bossuet A striking example of the influence of Christianity on the mind of a great man!

The most finished historical portrait in Tacitus is that of Tiberius; but it is eclipsed by the portrait of Cromwell, for in his *Funeral Orations* also Bossuet is an historian. What shall we say of the exclamation of joy that escapes from Tacitus when speaking of the Bructarii who slaughtered one another within view of a Roman camp? "By the favor of the gods," says he, "we had the pleasure to behold this conflict without taking any part in it. Merely spectators, we witnessed (and an extraordinary sight it was) sixty thousand men cutting each other's throats for our amusement. May the nations not in amity with us continue to cherish in their hearts these mutual animosities!"[1]

Now let us hear Bossuet.—"After the deluge first appeared those ravagers of provinces denominated conquerors, who, impelled by the thirst of dominion, have exterminated so many innocent people . . . Since that period, ambition has known no bounds in sporting with human life; and to this point are men arrived that they slaughter without hating one another. This business of mutual destruction is even deemed the height of glory and the most excellent of all the arts"[2]

It is difficult to forbear adoring a religion which causes so wide a difference between the morality of a Bossuet and that of a Tacitus.

The Roman historian, after relating that Thrasyllus had predicted the elevation of Tiberius to the empire, adds:—"From these circumstances, and some others, I cannot tell whether the affairs of life be subject to an immutable necessity, or whether they depend on chance alone" Then come the opinions of the philosophers, which Tacitus gravely repeats, at the same time giving the reader clearly to understand that he believes in the predictions of astrologers

Reason, sound morality, and eloquence, are also, in our opinion, on the side of the Christian prelate. "This long chain of particular causes which create and dissolve empires is de-

[1] Tacitus *On the Manners of the Germans.* [2] *Disc. on Univ. History.*

pendent on the secret decrees of Divine Providence. From the heaven of heavens God guides the reins of every kingdom; all hearts are in his hand. Sometimes he curbs the passions; at others he relaxes the bridle, and thereby agitates the whole human race. . . . . He knows the extent of human wisdom, which always falls short in some respect or other; he enlightens it, he extends its views, and then abandons it to its ignorance. He blinds, he urges it on, he confounds it; it is involved, it becomes embarrassed in its own subtleties, and its very precautions prove a snare in which it is entrapped . . . . . He it is who prepares these effects in the most remote causes, and who strikes these mighty blows, the rebound of which is felt so far. . . . . . But let not men deceive themselves; God, when he pleases, can restore the bewildered mind; he who exults over the infatuation of others may himself be plunged into the thickest darkness, and it often requires no other instrument to derange his understanding than long prosperity."

How does the eloquence of antiquity shrink from a comparison with this Christian eloquence![1]

[1] It seems almost superfluous to add to this detailed recital of the beauties of Bossuet. But there is *one* passage in his *Universal History* so remarkable for simple and sublime energy that we wish to treat the reader with the perusal of it. Speaking of the extent of the Roman empire under Augustus, Bossuet says, "Their mountains cannot defend the Rhæti from his arms; Pannonia acknowledges and Germany dreads him; victorious by sea and by land, he shuts the temple of Janus. The whole earth lives in peace under his power, *and Jesus Christ comes into the world.*"

BOOK IV.

ELOQUENCE.

CHAPTER I.

OF CHRISTIANITY AS IT RELATES TO ELOQUENCE

CHRISTIANITY furnishes so many proofs of its excellence, that, when you think you have no further subject to treat of, another suddenly starts up under your pen We have been speaking of philosophers, and, behold, the orators appear and inquire whether we have forgotten them; we have reasoned upon Christianity in the arts and sciences, and Christianity calls upon us to exhibit to the world the most powerful effects of eloquence ever known. To the Catholic religion the moderns owe that oratorical art which, had our literature been destitute of it, would have given the genius of antiquity a decided superiority over ours. Here is one of the proudest triumphs of our religion; and, notwithstanding all that may be said in praise of Demosthenes and Cicero, Massillon and Bossuet may, without fear, stand a comparison with them.

The only species of eloquence known to the ancients were judicial and political eloquence. Moral eloquence—that is to say, the eloquence of every age, of every government, of every country—appeared not upon earth until the gospel dispensation. Cicero defends a client; Demosthenes combats an adversary, or endeavors to rekindle the love of country in a degenerate people; both only know how to rouse the passions, and they found all their hopes of success on the agitation which they excite in the heart. The eloquence of the pulpit has sought its hopes in a higher region. By opposing the movements of the soul, she hopes to persuade it; by appeasing all the passions, she makes them listen to her voice. God and charity, such is her text, ever the same, ever inexhaustible She needs neither the cabals of party, nor popular commotions, nor important events, in order to shine; in the most profound peace, over the bier of the obscurest citizen, she exerts her most sublime influences; she knows how to excite interest in behalf of a virtue that is unknown; she draws tears from your eyes for a person whose name you never heard. Incapable of fear and of injustice, she gives lessons to kings, but without insulting them; she comforts the indigent, but without flattering their vices. She is no stranger to politics or to any other terrestrial things; but these, though the primary springs of ancient eloquence, are with her but secondary reasons; she beholds them from the elevated region where she reigns, as an eagle from the summit of the mountain perceives the lowly objects in the plain.

What particularly distinguishes Christian eloquence from the eloquence of the Greeks and Romans is, in the words of La Bruyère, *that evangelical sadness which is the soul of it*, that majestic melancholy on which it feeds. You read once, perhaps twice, the orations of Cicero against Verres and Catiline; the oration for the crown and the philippics of Demosthenes; but you meditate all your life on the *Funeral Orations* of Bossuet, and turn over night and day the sermons of Bourdaloue and Massillon. The discourses of the Christian orators are so many books, while those of antiquity are but orations. What wonderful taste is displayed by the sacred teachers in their reflections on the vanities of the world! "Your whole life," say they, "is but the intoxication of a day, and you spend that day in the pursuit of the most empty illusions. Granting that you attain the summit of all your wishes, that you become a king, an emperor, the master of the world,—it is but for a moment, and then death will sweep away all these vanities together with your nothingness."

This kind of meditation, so grave, so solemn, and tending so naturally to the sublime, was wholly unknown to the orators of antiquity. The heathens exhausted themselves *in the pursuit of the shadows of life;*[1] they knew not that real existence begins not until death. The Christian religion has alone founded that great school of the grave where the apostle of the gospel imbibes instruction; she no longer allows him, like the demi-sages of

[1] Job.

Greece, to squander the immortal intellect of man on things of a moment.

In short, religion in all ages and in all countries has been the source of eloquence. If Demosthenes and Cicero were great orators, the reason is because they were above all religious.[1] The members of the Convention, on the contrary, displayed only mutilated talents, and scraps, as it were, of eloquence, because they attacked the faith of their forefathers, and thus cut themselves off from all the inspirations of the heart.[2]

CHAPTER II.

CHRISTIAN ORATORS—FATHERS OF THE CHURCH.

THE eloquence of the Fathers of the Church has in it something that overawes, something energetic, something royal, as it were, and whose authority at once confounds and subdues. You are convinced that their mission comes from on high, and that they teach by the express command of the Almighty. In the midst of these inspirations, however, their genius retains its majesty and serenity.

---

[1] The names of the gods are incessantly in their mouths. See the apostrophe of the former to the gods plundered by Verres, and the invocation of the latter to the manes of the heroes of Marathon.

[2] Let it not be said that the French had not time to acquire practice in the new career upon which they had entered. Eloquence is a fruit of revolutions, in which it grows spontaneously and without culture, the savage and the negro have sometimes spoken like Demosthenes There was, besides, no want of models, since they possessed the master-pieces of the ancient forum and those also of that sacred forum in which the Christian orator explains the eternal law When Montlosier, descending from the mountains of Auvergne, where he had, doubtless, paid but little attention to the study of rhetoric, exclaimed, when speaking of the clergy in the Constituent Assembly, "Drive them from their palaces, and they will seek refuge in the hut of the indigent whom they have fed; rob them of their golden crosses, and they will take up wooden ones in their stead; it was a cross of wood that saved the world!" this beautiful apostrophe was not inspired by anarchy, but by religion. If, finally, Vergniaud attained the heights of eloquence, in his speech for Louis XVI., it was because his subject raised him into the region of religious ideas—the pyramids death, silence, and the tomb.

St. Ambrose is the Fénélon of the Latin Fathers. He is flowery, smooth, and rich; and, with the exception of a few defects, which belong to the age in which he lived, his works are equally entertaining and instructive. To be convinced of this the reader need only turn to the *Treatise on Virginity* and the *Praise of the Patriarchs.*

At the present day, when you make mention of a saint, people figure to themselves some rude fanatical monk, addicted, from weakness of intellect or of character, to a ridiculous superstition. Augustin, however, exhibits a very different picture. A young man of an ardent temperament and superior genius, he gives himself up to the gratification of his passions; he has soon completed the circle of pleasure, and he is astonished that the joys of the earth should be incapable of filling the void of his heart. His restless soul turns toward heaven; something whispers that there dwells that sovereign beauty to which he aspires. God himself speaks to him; and this man of the world, whom the world was unable to satisfy, at length finds repose and the fulfilment of his desires in the bosom of religion.

Montaigne and Rousseau have left us their confessions. The former has imposed upon the credulity of the reader; the latter has revealed his shameful depravity, at the same time holding himself forth, even to the divine judgment, as a model of virtue. In the confessions of St. Augustin we are made acquainted with man as he is. He confesses his sins not to earth, but to heaven: he conceals nothing from Him who is omniscient. A Christian on his knees in the tribunal of penance, he deplores his infirmities, and discloses them that the physician of souls may apply a remedy to the wound. He was not afraid of tiring, by prolixity, Him of whom he wrote those sublime words:—*He is patient because he is eternal.* And what a magnificent portrait has he drawn of the God to whom he confesses his errors!

"Thou art infinitely great," says he, "infinitely good, merciful, just; thy beauty is incomparable, thy might irresistible, thy power unbounded. Ever in action, ever at rest, thou upholdest, thou fillest, thou preservest, the universe; thou lovest without passion, thou art jealous without pain; thou changest thine operations, but never thy designs. But what am I saying, O my God! and what can any one say unto thee!"

The same individual who drew this brilliant image of the true God will now speak to us with the most amiable simplicity of his youthful errors:—

"I finally set out for Carthage. I was no sooner arrived there than I found myself besieged by a crowd of culpable attractions, that pressed upon me from every side. . . . A quiet life appeared to me intolerable, and I followed a path which was covered with snares and precipices. My happiness was then to be loved as well as to love, because man desires to find life in that which he loves. . . . At length I fell into the net in which I had wished to be caught: I was loved, and I possessed what I loved. But, O my God! thou didst then make me sensible of thy goodness and mercy, in filling my soul with bitterness: for, instead of the delights I had anticipated, I experienced only jealousy, suspicion, fear, anger, quarrelling, and excitement."

The simple, melancholy, and impassioned tone of this narrative, that return to God and the peace of heaven at a moment when the saint seems most agitated by the illusions of the world and the recollection of his past follies,—all this mixture of regret and repentance is replete with charms. We are acquainted with no expression of feeling more delicate than the following.—"My happiness was to be loved as well as to love, for man wishes to find life in the object of his love." It was St. Augustin also that said:—"A contemplative soul finds a solitude in herself." *The City of God*, the *Epistles*, and some of the *Treatises* of the same Father, abound with thoughts of this kind.

St. Jerome is particularly distinguished for a vigorous imagination, which his immense learning was incapable of extinguishing. The collection of his letters is one of the most curious monuments of patristic literature. As in the case of St. Augustin, the pleasures of the world proved the rock upon which he struck.

He loves to dwell on the nature and delights of solitude. From the recess of his cell at Bethlehem he beheld the fall of the Roman empire. What a vast subject of reflection for a holy anchoret! Accordingly, death and the vanity of human life are ever present to his view.

"We are dying, we are changing every hour," says he, in a letter to one of his friends, "and yet we live as if we were immortal. The very time which it takes to pen these lines must be retrenched from my days. We often write to one another, my dear Heliodorus; our letters traverse the seas, and as the ship scuds along so life flies: a moment of it passes with every wave."[1]

As Ambrose is the Fénélon of the Fathers, so Tertullian is the Bossuet. Part of his vindication of religion might, even at the present day, be of service to the same cause. How wonderful that Christianity should now be obliged to defend herself before her own children as she formerly defended herself before her executioners, and that the *Apology to the* GENTILES should have become the *Apology to the* CHRISTIANS!

The most remarkable feature of this work is the intellectual development which it displays. You are ushered into a new order of ideas; you feel that what you hear is not the language of early antiquity or the scarcely-articulate accents of man. Tertullian speaks like a modern; the subjects of his eloquence are derived from the circle of eternal truths, and not from the reasons of passion and circumstance employed in the Roman tribune or in the public place at Athens. This progress of the genius of philosophy is evidently the effect of our holy religion Had not the false deities been overthrown and the true worship of God been established, man would have continued in endless infancy; for, persevering in error in regard to the first principle, all his other notions would have been more or less tinctured with the fundamental vice.

The other tracts of Tertullian, particularly those on *Patience*, the *Shows*, the *Martyrs*, the *Ornaments of Women*, and the *Resurrection of the Body*, contain numberless beautiful passages. "*I doubt*," says the orator, reproaching the Christian females with their luxury, "I doubt whether hands accustomed to bracelets will be able to endure the weight of chains; whether feet adorned with fillets will become habituated to galling fetters. I much question whether a head covered with a network of pearls and diamonds would not yield to the sword." These words, addressed to the women who were daily conducted to the scaffold, glow with courage and with faith.

We regret that we cannot here quote the whole of the beautiful epistle to the martyrs, which has acquired additional interest

[1] *Hieron. Epist.*

with us since the persecution of Robespierre. "Illustrious confessors of Jesus Christ," exclaims Tertullian, "a Christian finds in prison the same joys as the prophets tasted in the desert. Call it not a dungeon, but a solitude. When the soul is in heaven, the body feels not the weight of fetters; it carries the whole man along with it." This concluding sentiment is sublime.

From the priest of Carthage Bossuet borrowed that thrilling passage which has been so much admired in his funeral discourse on the Duchess of Orleans. "Our flesh soon changes its nature; our body takes another name: even that of corpse, says Tertullian, 'as it still leaves some trace of human form, will not long be applicable to it. It becomes I know not what, something for which no language has a name:' so true is it that every thing in him dies, even those doleful words which convey an idea of his earthly remains."

Tertullian possessed extensive erudition, though he accuses himself of ignorance; and in his works we find particulars respecting the private life of the Romans which we would elsewhere seek in vain. A barbarous and African Latinity disfigures the works of this great orator. He often falls into declamation, and his taste is not always correct. "Tertullian's is an iron style," says Balzac, "but it must be allowed that with this metal he has forged excellent weapons."

According to Lactantius, surnamed the Christian Cicero, Cyprian was the *first eloquent Father of the Latin Church.* But Cyprian almost everywhere imitates Tertullian, diminishing alike the beauties and the defects of his model. Such is the judgment of La Harpe, whose authority should be always quoted in matters of criticism.

Among the Fathers of the Greek Church, two only are highly eloquent, SS. Chrysostom and Basil. The homilies of the former on *Death*, and the *Disgrace of Eutropius*, are real master-pieces.[1] The diction of St. Chrysostom is pure but labored, and his style is rather forced, after the manner of Isocrates. Before the young orator embraced Christianity,[2] Libanius had selected him for his successor in the chair of rhetoric.

---

[1] See note BB.

[2] That is, before he had received the sacrament of baptism. Born of Christian parents, he studied rhetoric and philosophy, after which he embraced the

With greater simplicity, St. Basil possesses less elevation than St. Chrysostom. He closely adheres to the mystical tone and the paraphrase of the Scripture.[1] St. Gregory Nazianzen,[2] surnamed the Theologian, has left, besides his prose works, several poetical pieces on the mysteries of Christianity.

"He always resided at his solitary retreat of Arianzum in his native country," says the Abbé Fleury. A garden, a fountain, and trees which afforded him shade, constituted his whole delight. He fasted, he prayed with abundance of tears. . . . . These sacred poems were the occupations of St. Gregory in his last retirement. He there relates the history of his life and sufferings. . . . . He prays, he teaches, he explains the mysteries, and gives rules of moral conduct. . . . . He designed to furnish those who are fond of poetry and music with useful subjects of amusement, and not to yield to the pagans the advantage of deeming themselves alone capable of succeeding in the *belles-lettres*.[3]

Finally, St. Lernard, who before the appearance of Bossuet was called the last of the fathers, combined with extensive talents extensive learning. He was particularly successful in the delineation of manners, and was endowed with something of the genius of Theophrastus and La Bruyère.

"The proud man," says he, "is loud when he talks and sullen in silence; he is dissolute in prosperity, furious in adversity; dishonest within, honest without; he is rude in his behaviour, morose in his replies, always strong in attack, always feeble in defence; he yields with an ill grace, he importunes to gain his point; he does not what he can and what he ought to do, but he is ready to do what he ought not and what he cannot perform."[4]

---

legal profession; but, having resolved to devote himself entirely to the service of God, he was instructed, baptized, and ordained lector by St. Meletius. T.

[1] He has written a celebrated Letter on Solitude; it is the first of his epistles, and furnished the groundwork of his Rule.

[2] In the different French editions of the *Génie du Christianisme*, a singular historical error occurs in a note appended to this passage, which states that St. Gregory the Theologian had a son of the same name and sanctity with himself. But it should be observed that St. Gregory the Theologian, of whom our author speaks in the text, was the son, and not the father, of St. Gregory, Bishop of Nazianzum. T.

[3] Fleury's *Eccl. Hist.*, vol. iv. book xix. c. 9. [4] *De Mor.*, lib. xxxiv. c. 16.

We must not forget that phenomenon of the thirteenth century,—the book on the *Following of Christ.* How did a monk, shut up in his convent, acquire that propriety of expression, that exquisite knowledge of man, in an age when the passions were rude and taste still more unpolished? Who revealed to him in his solitude those mysteries of the heart and of eloquence? One master, and one alone—JESUS CHRIST.

CHAPTER III.

MASSILLON.

IF we now leap over several centuries, we shall come to orators whose names alone throw a certain class of people into great embarrassment; for full well they know that all their sophistry avails nothing when opposed to Bossuet, Fénélon, Massillon, Bourdaloue, Fléchier, Mascaron. and Poulle.

It is painful to be obliged to pass with such rapidity over such stores of wealth, and to be unable to pause at each of these great orators But how shall we select from among all these treasures, or how point out to the reader excellences which he has not observed? Would we not swell these pages too much by filling them with these illustrious proofs of the beauty of Christianity? We shall not, therefore, make use of all our weapons; we will not abuse our advantages, lest, by pressing the evidence too closely, we should urge the enemies of Christianity to an obstinate rejection of its truths,—the last refuge of the spirit of sophistry when driven to extremities.

We shall not adduce, in support of our arguments, Fénélon, so sweet and so full of grace in Christian meditations; nor the great Bourdaloue, a tower of strength and victory to the doctrines of the gospel; we shall not avail ourselves of the learned compositions of Fléchier, nor of the brilliant imaginations of Poulle, the last of the Christian orators. O religion, how great have been thy triumphs! Who could doubt thy beauty when Fénélon and Bossuet occupied thy episcopal chairs? when Bour daloue, in solemn accents, instructed a monarch then blest with prosperity, but who, in his misfortunes, was favored by a merciful Heaven with the soothing counsels of Massillon?

It must not, however, be supposed that the Bishop of Clermont possesses only the sensibility of genius: he has also a masculine and nervous language at his command. In our opinion, his *Petit Carême* has been too exclusively extolled. The author, indeed, there displays an intimate knowledge of the human heart, just views respecting the vices of courts. He there inculcates moral truths, written with elegance and yet with simplicity; but there is certainly a higher eloquence, a bolder style, more pathetic movements, and more profound ideas, in some of his other sermons, such as those on *Death*, on *Final Impenitence*, on the *Small Number of the Elect*, on the *Death of the Sinner*, on the *Necessity of a Future State*, and on the *Passion of Christ.* Read, for example, this description of the dying sinner:—

"At length, amid all these painful struggles, his eyes become fixed, his features altered, his face distorted, and his livid lips involuntarily open; a shivering seizes his whole frame, and by this last effort his soul is reluctantly disengaged from this body of clay, and finds itself alone at the foot of the awful tribunal."[1]

To this picture of the death of the wicked let us subjoin that of the vanity of human things:—

"Look at the world such as you saw it in early life and such as you now behold it. A new court has succeeded that which your first years witnessed; new characters have occupied the stage, and the principal parts are filled by new actors. There are new events, new intrigues, new passions, new heroes in virtue as in vice which are the subjects of applause, of derision, of public censure. Nothing is lasting; all things change, wear out, and become extinct; God alone remains forever the same. The torrent of time, which carries away each succeeding age, flows before his eyes, and with indignation he sees feeble mortals, hurried along by its rapid current, insult him as they pass."

---

[1] Advent Sermon *on the Death of the Sinner*, part i.

This example of the vanity of earthly things, taken from the age of Louis XIV, which was drawing to a close, and presented, perhaps, to the consideration of aged Christians who had beheld all its glory, is highly pathetic. The expression which terminates the period seems as if it had dropped from the lips of Bossuet, such is its frankness and at the same time its sublimity.

We shall give another example of that nervous eloquence which Massillon might be supposed not to have possessed, as his richness and sweetness are in general the only topics of praise. We shall select a passage in which the orator quits his favorite style—that is to say, sentiment and imagery—for mere argument. In his sermon on the *Truth of a Future State* he thus addresses the unbeliever:—

"What shall I say more? If all dies with us, our anxiety for reputation and posterity must be frivolous; the honor paid to the memory of illustrious men a puerile error, since it is ridiculous to honor that which no longer has existence; our veneration for the tomb a vulgar illusion; the ashes of our ancestors and of our friends no more than vile dust, which ought to be given to the winds and which belongs to none; the injunctions of the dying, held so sacred among the most barbarous nations, merely the last sounds of a machine that is falling to pieces. And, if we must speak out, the laws are, in this case, a senseless servitude; kings and sovereigns only phantoms set up by the weakness of nations; justice is an encroachment upon the liberty of man; the law of marriage a vain scruple; chastity a prejudice; honor and integrity chimeras; incest, parricide, the blackest perfidy, sports of nature, and names which the policy of legislators has invented.

"Such is the point to which the philosophy of the wicked is reduced; such is that energy, that reason, that wisdom, of which they are eternally boasting. Admit their maxims, and the universe returns to a frightful chaos; all things are thrown into disorder upon the earth; all the notions of virtue and vice are overthrown; and the most inviolable laws of society are abolished; and the discipline of morality is swept away; and the government of states and empires ceases to be subject to any rule; and the whole harmony of political institutions is dissolved; and the human race becomes an assemblage of madmen, barbarians, cheats, unnatural wretches who have no other laws than force, no other curb than their passions and the dread of authority, no other tie than irreligion and independence, no other gods than themselves. Such is the world of the impious; and, if you are pleased with this scheme of a republic, form, if you can, a society of these monsters; all we shall say is that you are worthy to fill a place in it."

Compare Massillon with Cicero, and Bossuet with Demosthenes, and you will always find the differences that we have specified between their styles of eloquence. In the Christian orators there is a more general order of ideas, a more profound knowledge of the human heart, a stronger chain of reasoning, a religious and solemn tone of eloquence, unknown to antiquity. Massillon has written some funeral orations, but they are inferior to his other discourses. His eulogy on Louis XIV. is not remarkable, except for the sentence with which it opens:—*God alone is great, my brethren!* How beautiful is this expression pronounced before the coffin of Louis the Great![1]

CHAPTER IV.

BOSSUET AS AN ORATOR.

But what shall we say of Bossuet as an orator? To whom shall we compare him? and which of the harangues of Cicero and Demosthenes are not eclipsed by his *Funeral Orations?* The Christian orator seems to be indicated in those words of a King:—"There is gold, and a multitude of jewels; but the lips of knowledge are a precious vessel"[2] Looking always upon the grave, and bending as it were over the gulf of futurity, Bossuet is incessantly dropping the awful words of *time* and *death*, which are re-echoed in the silent abysses of eternity. He gathers around him an indescribable sadness; he becomes merged in sorrows inconceivable. The heart, after an interval of more than a century, is yet struck with that celebrated exclamation:—

[1] See note CC.

[2] Prov. xx. 15.

"The princess is dying; the princess is dead!" Did monarchs ever receive such lessons? Did philosophy ever express itself with greater independence? The diadem is as nothing in the eyes of the preacher; by him the poor are raised to an equality with the monarch, and the most absolute potentate in the world must submit to be told, before thousands of witnesses, that all his grandeur is but vanity, that his power is but a dream, and himself is but dust.

There are three things continually succeeding one another in Bossuet's discourses:—the stroke of genius or of eloquence; the quotation so admirably blended with the text as to form but one piece with it; lastly, the reflection, or the survey taken with eagle eye of the causes of the event of which he treats. Often, too, does this star of the Church throw a light upon discussions in the most abstruse metaphysics or the most sublime theology. To him nothing is obscure. He has created a language employed by himself alone, in which frequently the simplest term and the loftiest idea, the most common expression and the most tremendous image, serve, as in Scripture, to produce the most striking effect.

Thus, when pointing to the coffin of the Duchess of Orleans, he exclaims, *There you see, notwithstanding her great heart, that princess so admired and so beloved! There you behold her, such as Death has made her!* Why do we shudder at the simple expression—*such as Death has made her?* 'Tis on account of the opposition between that *great heart*, that *princess so admired*, and the inevitable stroke of death, which has laid her low as the meanest of mankind. 'Tis because the verb *make*, applied to death, which *unmakes* all, produces a contradiction in the words and a clashing of the ideas which agitate the whole soul; as if, to describe an event so sudden and so afflicting, the terms had changed their signification, and the language itself were thrown into confusion as well as the heart.

We have already remarked that, with the exception of Pascal, Bossuet, Massillon, and La Fontaine, the writers of the age of Louis XIV., from having lived too little in retirement, were strangers to that species of melancholy sentiment which, at the present day, is so strangely abused.

How happens it, then, that the Bishop of Meaux, incessantly

surrounded with the splendors of Versailles, is remarkable for such profound contemplations? It is because he enjoyed a solitude in religion—because his body was in the world and his mind in the desert—because he had found a refuge for his heart in the secret tabernacles of the Lord—because, as he himself said of Maria Theresa of Austria, "he repaired to the altars, there to enjoy with David an humble tranquillity, and retired to his oratory, where, in spite of the bustle of the court, he found the Carmel of Elias, the desert of John, and the mountain which so often witnessed the sorrows of Jesus."

All of Bossuet's funeral orations are not equal in merit; but they are all in some respect sublime. That on the *Queen of England* is a master-piece of style and a model of philosophical and political composition.

The oration on the *Duchess of Orleans* is the most remarkable of all, because it is wholly created by genius. Here are none of those pictures of the troubles of nations,—none of those developments of public affairs which commonly keep up the tone of the orator. It seems natural to suppose that the interest excited by a princess expiring in the prime of life would be speedily exhausted. The whole subject is limited to a few commonplace topics of beauty, youth, grandeur, and death; and yet upon this slender foundation Bossuet has reared one of the most solid and splendid monuments of his eloquence. From this point he sets out to display the misery of man by his perishable part, and his greatness by the immortal portion of his being. He first debases him below the worms which prey upon him in the grave, and then describes him resplendent with virtue in the regions of incorruptibility.

Every reader knows with what genius he has, in the funeral oration on the *Princess Palatine*, descended, without derogating from the majesty of the rhetorical art, even to the simple interpretation of a dream; though he has evinced in the same discouse his high capacity for philosophical abstractions.

If, in his sermons on *Maria Theresa* and the *Chancellor of France*, the panegyrist dwells not on the usual subjects of eulogy, his thoughts move in a more enlarged sphere—in more profound contemplations. Alluding to Le Tellier and Lamoignon, he says:—"Now do those two pious souls who on earth were desirous of effecting the ascendency of the laws behold clearly those eternal laws from which ours are derived; and, if any trace whatever of our short-sighted distinctions is apparent in this simple and luminous vision, they adore God in the attribute of supreme justice and rule."

In this theology of Bossuet how many other beautiful features present themselves, as the sublime, the graceful, the sad, or the pleasing! Turn to the picture of the Fronde.[1] "The monarchy shaken to its very foundations, war at home, war abroad, fire and sword within and without. . . . . Was this one of those storms in which Heaven sometimes finds it necessary to pour forth its wrath? . . . . or may it be considered as the throes of France ready to bring forth the miraculous reign of Louis?"[2] This is followed by some reflections on the illusions of earthly friendships, which "expire with years and interests," and on the profound obscurity of the human heart, "which never knows what it will in future desire; which frequently cannot tell what it at present wishes, and which uses not less concealment and deceit with itself than with others."[3]

"But the trumpet sounds, and Gustavus appears. He appears to surprised and betrayed Poland like a lion holding his prey in his talons, and ready to tear it in pieces. What has become of that formidable cavalry which once was seen to rush upon the enemy with the swiftness of the eagle? Where are those martial spirits, those vaunted battle-axes, and those bows which used never to be bent in vain? The horses are now swift, the men are now active, only to flee before the conqueror."[4]

As we advance, our ears tingle with the words of a prophet. Is it Isaias or Jeremias who apostrophizes the island of conference and the nuptial ceremonies of the Fourteenth Louis? "Sacred festival! auspicious marriage! nuptial veil, benediction, sacrifice! Let me this day mingle your ceremonies and your splendor with this funeral pomp, and the height of grandeur with its ruins."[5]

The poet—it will not be taken amiss if we apply to Bossuet an appellation which constitutes the glory of David—the poet con

---

[1] The party opposed to the Court was called the *Fronde*.

[2] *Fun. Orat. for An. de Gonz.*

[3] *Fun. Orat. for An. de Gonz.*

[4] *Ibid.*

[5] *Fun. Orat. on Mar. Ther. of Aus.*

tinues his strains. He no longer touches the inspired chords; but, lowering the tone of his lyre to the mode which Solomon adopted to celebrate the flocks of Mount Gilead, he chants those peaceful words:—"In the solitude of St. Fare, as far removed from the ways of secular life as it is separated by its happy situation from all commerce with the world,—on that sacred mountain chosen by God above a thousand years ago—where the spouses of Jesus Christ renewed the charms of ancient days—where the joys of the earth were unknown—where the footsteps of the man of the world, the inquisitive, and the lawless wanderer, never appear,—under the superintendence of the holy abbess, who knew how to dispense milk to babes as well as bread to the strong,—the life of the Princess Anne dawned auspiciously."[1]

This passage, which you would almost suppose to have been extracted from the book of Ruth, does not exhaust the pencil of Bossuet. He has still enough of those antique and soft colors left to delineate a happy death. "Michael Le Tellier," says he, "began the hymn in celebration of the divine mercies. *I will sing forever the mercies of the Lord.* With these words upon his lips he expires, and continues the sacred song with the angels of the Most High."

We were for some time of opinion that the funeral oration on the *Prince of Condé*, with the exception of the incomparable passage with which it concludes, had generally been too highly extolled. We considered it more easy, as it really is, to reach the form of eloquence which appears in the exordium of that eulogy than that in the oration on the *Princess Henrietta*. But when we re-perused that discourse with attention,—when we beheld the orator blowing the epic trumpet during one half of his narrative, and, as it were, sounding an Homeric strain,—when, retiring to Chantilly, he resumes the Christian tone, and recovers all the grand and solemn ideas with which the above-mentioned funeral orations are replete,—when, after having followed Condé to the coffin, he summons nations, princes, prelates, and warriors, around the cenotaph of the hero,—when, finally, advancing with his hoary locks, like a majestic spirit of another world, he exhibits Bossuet

[1] *Fun. Orat. for An. de Gonz.*

declining to the tomb, and the age of Louis XIV. (whose obsequies you would almost conceive him to be celebrating) on the brink of eternity,—at this utmost effort of human eloquence tears of admiration flowed from our eyes and the book dropped from our hands.

CHAPTER V.

INFIDELITY THE PRINCIPAL CAUSE OF THE DECLINE OF TASTE AND THE DEGENERACY OF GENIUS.

THE preceding observations may have led the reader to this reflection, that *infidelity is the principal cause of the decline of taste and the degeneracy of genius.* When the national religion had lost its influence at Athens and at Rome, talents disappeared with the gods, and the Muses consigned to barbarism those who no longer had any faith in them

In an enlightened age one would scarcely believe to what a degree good morals depend on good taste, and good taste on good morals. The works of Racine, gradually becoming more pure in proportion as the author became more religious, at last concluded with his Athalia. Take notice, on the contrary, how the impiety and the genius of Voltaire discover themselves at one and the same time in his productions by a mixture of delightful and disagreeable subjects. Bad taste, when incorrigible, is a perversion of judgment, a natural bias in the ideas. Now, as the mind acts upon the heart, the ways of the latter can scarcely be upright when those of the former are not so. He who is fond of deformity at a time when a thousand master-pieces might apprise him of his error and rectify his taste is not far from loving vice; and 'tis no wonder if he who is insensible to beauty should also be blind to virtue.

Every writer who refuses to believe in a God, the author of the universe and the judge of men, whose soul he has made immortal, in the first place excludes infinity from his works. He confines his intellect within a circle of clay, from which it has then no means of escaping. He sees nothing noble in nature. All her operations are, in his infatuated opinion, effected by impure means of corruption and regeneration. The vast abyss is but a little *bituminous* water; the mountains are small *protuberances* of *calcareous* or *vitrifiable* rock; and the heavens, where the day produces an immense solitude, as if to serve as a camp for the host of stars which the night leads forth in silence,—the heavens are but a petty vault thrown over us for a moment by the capricious hand of Chance.

If the unbeliever is thus limited in regard to physical objects, how can he describe with eloquence the dignity of man? For him language has no richness, and from the treasures of expression he is irrevocably excluded. Contemplate the corpse interred in yonder grave, that statue of nothing, wrapt in a winding-sheet. There is man according to the atheist! Sprung from the impure body of a woman; inferior to the animals in point of instinct; dust like them, and returning, as they do, to dust; having no passions, but impelled by appetites; obeying not moral laws, but only physical influences; looking forward to no other end than a sepulchre and worms,—there is that being who had fancied himself animated by an immortal spirit! Talk no more of the mysteries of the soul, of the secret delights of virtue! Ye graces of infancy, ye loves of truth, generous friendship, elevation of sentiment, charms of the tombs and of our native country, all your enchantments are destroyed!

By a necessary consequence, infidelity also introduced a spirit of cavilling and disputation, abstract definitions, the scientific style, and with it the practice of coining new words, all deadly foes to taste and eloquence.

It is possible that the amount of talent among the authors of the eighteenth century equalled that of the writers in the seventeenth.[1] Why, then, does the latter rank so much above the former? for we can no longer dissemble the fact that the writers of our age have been, in general, placed too high. If, as it is

[1] We make this admission to give the greater weight to the argument; but we are far from being of that opinion. Pascal and Bossuet, Molière and La Fontaine, were four writers absolutely incomparable, and such as we shall never again possess. If we omit Racine, it is because he has a rival in Virgil.

agreed, there are so many faults in the works of Rousseau and Voltaire, what shall we say of those of Raynal and Diderot?[1] The luminous method of our late metaphysicians has, no doubt with reason, been extolled. It should, nevertheless, have been remarked that there are two sorts of perspicuity: the one belongs to a vulgar order of ideas, (a commonplace notion, for example, may be clearly comprehended;) the other proceeds from an admirable faculty of conceiving and expressing with precision a strong and complex idea. The pebbles at the bottom of a brook may easily be seen, because the stream is shallow; but amber, coral, pearls, attract the eye of the diver at immense depths beneath the pellucid waters of the abyss

If our age, in a literary point of view, is inferior to that of Louis XIV., let us seek no other cause for it than our irreligion. We have already shown how much Voltaire would have gained by being a Christian; he would, at this day, dispute the palm of the Muses with Racine. His works would have acquired that moral tint without which nothing is perfect; we should also find in them those charming allusions to other times the want of which occasions so great a void. He who denies the God of his country is almost always destitute of respect for the memory of his forefathers; for him the tombs are without interest, and he considers the institutions of his ancestors as barbarous customs; he takes no pleasure in calling to mind the sentiments, the wisdom, and the manners, of his antique mother.

Religion is the most powerful motive of the love of country; pious writers have invariably disseminated that noble sentiment in their works. With what respect, in what magnificent terms, do the writers of the age of Louis XIV. always mention France! Wo be to him who insults his country! Let our country become weary of being ungrateful before we are weary of loving her; let our heart be greater than her injustice!

If the religious man loves his country, it is because his mind is simple, and the natural sentiments which attach us to the land of our nativity are the ground, as it were, and the habit of his heart. He gives the hand to his forefathers and to his children; he is planted in his native soil, like the oak which sees its aged

[1] See note DD.

roots below striking deep into the earth, while at its top young shoots are aspiring to heaven.

Rousseau is one of the writers of the eighteenth century whose style is the most fascinating, because, designedly eccentric, he created for himself a shadow, at least, of religion. He believed in something, which was not *Christ*, but yet was the *gospel.* This phantom of Christianity, such as it is, has sometimes imparted ineffable graces to his genius. Would not he, who has inveighed with such energy against sophists, have done better to give full scope to the tenderness of his soul, than to bewilder himself, like them, in empty systems, whose obsolete errors he has merely dressed up in the garb of youth?[1]

Buffon would be deficient in nothing, were his sensibility equal to his eloquence. We frequently have occasion to make the remark, which cannot be sufficiently impressed upon the present age, that *without religion there can be no feeling.* Buffon delights us by his style, but seldom excites our sensibility. Read, for instance, his admirable description of the dog: every kind of dog is depicted there—the hunter's dog, the shepherd's dog, the wild dog, the master dog, the foppish dog, &c. But what is wanting to complete the list? The blind man's dog. This is the first that would have struck the mind of a Christian.

Buffon has paid little attention to the tender relations of life. We must, however, do justice to this great painter of nature, who possesses a rare excellence of style. He who can observe such an exact propriety, who is never either too high or too low, must have a great command over his mind and conduct. It is well known that Buffon respected whatever it becomes a man to respect. He did not think that philosophy consisted in the public profession of infidelity and in wantonly insulting the altars of twenty-four millions of men. He was regular in the performance of his duties as a Christian, and set an excellent example to his domestics. Rousseau, embracing the groundwork and rejecting the forms of Christianity, displays in his performances the tenderness of religion, together with the bad tone of the sophist; Buffon, for the contrary reason, has the dryness of philosophy, with the decorum of piety. Christianity has infused into the style of

---

[1] See note EE.

the former its charm, its ease, its warmth, and invested the style of the latter with order, perspicuity, and magnificence. Thus the works of both these celebrated men bear, in their good as well as in their bad qualities, the stamp of what they themselves chose and rejected in religion.

In naming Montesquieu, we call to mind the truly great man of the eighteenth century. The *Spirit of Laws*, and the essay *on the Causes of the Greatness and Decline of the Roman Empire*, will live as long as the language in which they are written. If Montesquieu, in a production of his youth, unfortunately assailed religion with some of those shafts which he aimed at our manners, this was but a transient error, a species of tribute paid to the corruption of the regency.[1] But in the work which has placed Montesquieu in the rank of illustrious men, he has made a magnificent reparation for the injury by the panegyric he pronounces on that religion which he had the imprudence to attack. The maturity of his years, and even an interest for his fame, taught him that in order to erect a durable monument he must lay its foundations in a more stable soil than the dust of this world, his genius, which embraced all ages, rested upon religion alone, to which all ages are promised.

From all our observations we conclude that the writers of the eighteenth century owe most of their defects to a delusive system of philosophy, and that, if they had been more religious, they would have approached nearer to perfection.

There has been in our age, with some few exceptions, a sort of general abortion of talents. You would even say that impiety, which renders every thing barren, is also manifested in the impoverishment of physical nature. Cast your eyes on the generations which immediately succeeded the age of Louis XIV. Where are those men with countenances serene and majestic, with dignified port and noble attire, with polished language and air at once military and classical—the air of conquerors and lovers of the arts? You look for them, but you find them not The diminutive, obscure mortals of the present times walk like pigmies beneath the lofty porticos of the structures raised by a former age. On their harsh brows sit selfishness and the contempt of

[1] See note FF.

God; they have lost both the dignity of dress and the purity of language. You would take them not for the descendants, but for the buffoons, of the heroic race which preceded them.

The disciples of the new school blast the imagination with I know not what truth, which is not the real truth. The style of these men is dry, their mode of expression devoid of sincerity, their imagination destitute of love and of warmth; they have no unction, no richness, no simplicity. You find in their works nothing that fills, nothing that satisfies; immensity is not there, because the Divinity is wanting. Instead of that tender religion, that harmonious instrument which the authors of the age of Louis XIV. made use of to pitch the tone of their eloquênce, modern writers have recourse to a contracted philosophy, which goes on dividing and subdividing all things, measuring sentiments with compasses, subjecting the soul to calculation, and reducing the universe, God himself included, to a transient subtraction from nothing.

Thus, the eighteenth century is daily fading away in the perspective, while the seventeenth is gradually magnified, in proportion as we recede from it: the one grovels on the earth, the other soars to the skies. In vain would you strive to depreciate the genius of a Bossuet or a Racine; it will share the immortality of that venerable form of Homer which is seen behind the long lapse of centuries. Sometimes it is obscured by the dust which a crumbling age raises in its fall; but no sooner is the cloud dispersed than you again perceive the majestic figure, but of augmented size, to overlook the new ruins.[1]

---

[1] See note GG.

BOOK V.

HE HARMONIES OF THE CHRISTIAN RELIGION WITH THE SCENES OF NATURE AND THE PASSIONS OF THE HUMAN HEART.

CHAPTER I.

DIVISION OF THE HARMONIES.

Before we proceed to the ceremonies of religion, we have yet to examine some subjects which we could not sufficiently develop in the preceding books. These subjects relate either to the physical or the moral side of the arts. Thus, for example, the sites of monasteries and the ruins of religious monuments belong to the material part of architecture; while the effects of the Christian doctrine, with the passions of the human heart and the scenery of nature, are referable to the dramatic and descriptive departments of poetry.

Such are the subjects which we comprehend in this book under the general head of *Harmonies*.

CHAPTER II.

PHYSICAL HARMONIES.

The Sites of Religious Monuments—The Convents of Maronites, Copts, &c.

There are in human things two kinds of nature, placed the one at the beginning, the other at the end, of society. Were not this the case, man, advancing farther and farther from his origin, would have become a sort of monster: but, by a particular law of Providence, the more civilized he grows the nearer he approaches to his first state; and to this cause is it owing that science, carried to its highest pitch, is ignorance, and that the perfection of the arts is nature.

This last nature—this *nature of society*—is the most beautiful: genius is its instinct, and virtue its innocence: for the genius and virtue of the civilized man are but the improved instinct and innocence of the savage. Now, no one can compare an Indian of Canada with Socrates, though the former may be, strictly speaking, as moral as the latter: you might as well maintain that the peace of the unfolded passions of the infant has equal excellence with the peace of the subdued passions of the man; that the being who has but mere sensations is equal to the being endued with reason, which would be tantamount to the assertion that weakness is as desirable as strength. A petty lake never lays waste its banks, and at this you are not astonished; its impotence occasions its calmness; but the serenity of the ocean fills you with pleasure, because it possesses the power to be tempestuous, and you admire the silence of the abyss, because it arises from the very profundity of its waters.

Between the ages of nature and those of civilization intervene others, which we have denominated *barbarous* ages. These were unknown to the ancients. They resulted from the sudden reunion of a polished people and a savage people. These ages must of course be remarkable for depravity of taste. On the one hand, the savage, applying himself to the arts, could not carry them to a degree of elegance, while the social man had not simplicity enough to follow nature alone.

In such a case nothing pure can be expected, except where a moral cause acts of itself independently of temporary causes. Owing to this, the first recluses, following that delicate and sure religious taste which never deceives when nothing foreign is blended with it, have selected, in every region of the globe, the most striking situations for the erection of their monasteries.[1] There is not a hermit who does not know, as well as Claude Lorrain or Le Nôtre, on what rock he ought to form his cell.

In the chain of Lebanon are seen here and there Maronite convents erected on the brink of precipices. Into some of these you

[1] See note HH.

penetrate through long caverns, the entrance to which is closed by masses of rock: to others you cannot gain access but by means of a basket let down from the edifice. The sacred river gushes from the foot of the mountain; the forest of black cedars overlooks the picture, and is itself surmounted by rounded peaks clothed with a mantle of snow. The wonder is not complete till the moment you reach the monastery. Within are vineyards, streams, groves; without, a dreary nature, and the earth, with its rivers and plains and seas, sunk and lost in the azure abyss. Nourished by religion on these precipitous rocks, between earth and sky, the pious recluses soar aloft to heaven, like the eagles of the mountain.

The circular and detached cells of the Egyptian convents are surrounded by one common wall, which protects them from the Arabs. From the top of the tower erected in the midst of these convents, you behold deserts of sand above which the pyramids rear their gray heads, or stones that direct the traveller on his way. Sometimes an Abyssinian caravan, a troup of roving Bedouins, pass in the distance along one of the horizons of the moving expanse; at others, a southern blast envelops the whole perspective in an atmosphere of dust. The moon illumines a naked soil, where the breezes find not even a blade of grass wherewith to form a sound. No shadows diversify the treeless desert, and amid the buildings of the monastery alone you meet with a semblance of the shades of night.

At the isthmus of Panama, in America, the cenobite may contemplate from the roof of his convent the two seas which bathe either shore of the New World; the one often agitated when the other is at rest, and offering to meditation the twofold picture of calm and tempest.

The convents seated on the Andes behold the waves of the Pacific Ocean subsiding in the distance. A transparent sky rests upon the earth and upon the seas, and seems to enclose the edifice of religion in a concave of crystal The nasturtium, taking the place of the religious ivy, lines the sacred walls with its red flowers; the lama crosses the torrent on a floating bridge of lianas, and the unfortunate Peruvian comes to offer up his prayers to the God of Las Casas.

In Europe, we find ancient abbeys embosomed in woods, and

revealing themselves to the traveller only by their towers which soar above the lofty oaks. Ordinary edifices receive their grandeur from the scenery which surrounds them; the Christian religion, on the contrary, embellishes the site where she erects her altars and suspends her sacred decorations. We have alluded elsewhere to the convents of Europe and their effect amid the scenery of nature. To complete our observations, we shall present the reader with the following beautiful poem, the production of a friend, which will prove to our poets that their muse would gain much more in wandering through the cloister than in becoming the echo of impiety:—

LA CHARTREUSE DE PARIS.

Vieux cloître où de Bruno les disciples cachés
Renferment tous leurs vœux sur le ciel attachés;
Cloître saint, ouvre-moi tes modestes portiques!
Laisse-moi m'égarer dans ces jardins rustiques
Où venait Catinat méditer quelquefois,
Heureux de fuir la cour et d'oublier les rois.
J'ai trop connu Paris: mes légères pensées,
Dans son enceinte immense au hasard dispersées,
Veulent enfin rejoindre et lier tous les jours
Leur fil demi formé, qui se brise toujours.
Seul, je viens recueillir mes vagues rêveries,
Fuyez, bruyants remparts, pompeuses Tuileries,
Louvre, dont le portique à mes yeux éblouis
Vante après cent hivers la grandeur de Louis!
Je préfère ces lieux où l'âme, moins distraite,
Même au sein de Paris peut goûter la retraite:
La retraite me plaît, elle eut mes premiers vers.
Déjà, de feux moins vifs éclairant l'univers,
Septembre loin de nous s'enfuit et décolore
Cet éclat dont l'année un moment brille encore.
Il redouble la paix qui m'attache en ces lieux;
Son jour mélancolique, et si doux à nos yeux,
Son vert plus rembruni, son grave caractère,
Semblent se conformer au deuil du monastère.
Sous ces bois jaunissants j'aime à m'ensevelir.
Couché sur un gazon qui commence à pâlir,
Je jouis d'un air pur, de l'ombre, et du silence.

Ces chars tumultueux où s'assied l'opulence,
Tous ces travaux, ce peuple à grands flots agité,
Ces sons confus qu'élève une vaste cité,
Des enfants de Bruno ne troublent point l'asile;

Le bruit les environne et leur âme est tranquille.
Tous les jours, reproduit sous des traits inconstants,
Le fantôme du siècle emporté par le temps
Passe et roule autour d'eux ses pompes mensongères.
Mais c'est en vain: du siècle ils ont fui les chimères;
Hormis l'éternité tout est songe pour eux.
Vous déplorez pourtant leur destin malheureux!
Quel préjugé funeste à des lois si rigides
Attacha, dites-vous, ces pieux suicides?
Ils meurent longuement, rongés d'un noir chagrin:
L'autel garde leurs vœux sur des tables d'airain;
Et le seul désespoir habite leurs cellules.

Eh bien! vous qui plaignez ces victimes crédules,
Pénétrez avec moi ces murs religieux:
N'y respirez-vous pas l'air paisible des cieux?
Vos chagrins ne sont plus, vos passions se taisent,
Et du cloître muet les ténèbres vous plaisent.
Mais quel lugubre son, du haut de cette tour,
Descend et fait frémir les dortoirs d'alentour?
C'est l'airain qui, du temps formidable interprète,
Dans chaque heure qui fuit, à l'humble anachorète
Redit en longs échos: "Songe au dernier moment!"
Le son sous cette voûte expire lentement;
Et, quand il a cessé, l'âme en frémit encore.
La Méditation, qui, seule dès l'aurore,
Dans ces sombres parvis marche en baissant son œil,
A ce signal s'arrête, et lit sur un cercueil
L'épitaphe à demi par les ans effacée,
Qu'un gothique écrivain dans la pierre a tracée
O tableaux éloquents! oh! combien à mon cœur
Plaît ce dôme noirci d'une divine horreur,
Et le lierre embrassant ces débris de murailles
Où croasse l'oiseau, chantre des funérailles;
Les approches du soir et ces ifs attristés
Où glissent du soleil les dernières clartés;
Et ce buste pieux que la mousse environne,
Et la cloche d'airain à l'accent monotone;
Ce temple où chaque aurore entend de saints concerts
Sortir d'un long silence et monter dans les airs;
Un martyr dont l'autel a conservé les restes,
Et le gazon qui croît sur ces tombeaux modestes
Où l'heureux cénobite a passé sans remord
Du silence du cloître à celui de la mort!

Cependant sur ces murs l'obscurité s'abaisse,
Leur deuil est redoublé, leur ombre est plus épaisse
Les hauteurs de Meudon me cachent le soleil,
Le jour meurt, la nuit vient: le couchant, moins vermeil,
Voit pâlir de ses feux la dernière étincelle.

Tout à coup se rallume une aurore nouvelle
Qui monte avec lenteur sur les dômes noircis
De ce palais voisin qu'éleva Médicis;
Elle en blanchit le faîte, et ma vue enchantée
Reçoit par ces vitraux la lueur argentée.
L'astre touchant des nuits verse du haut des cieux
Sur les tombes du cloître un jour mystérieux,
Et semble y réfléchir cette douce lumière
Qui des morts bienheureux doit charmer la paupière.
Ici, je ne vois plus les horreurs du trépas:
Son aspect attendrit et n'épouvante pas.
Me trompé-je? Écoutons: sous ces voûtes antiques
Parviennent jusqu'à moi d'invisibles cantiques,
Et la Religion, le front voilé, descend:
Elle approche: déjà son calme attendrissant
Jusqu'au fond de votre âme en secret s'insinue;
Entendez-vous un Dieu dont la voix inconnue
Vous dit tout bas: "Mon fils, viens ici, viens à moi;
Marche au fond du desert, j'y serai près de toi."

Maintenant, du milieu de cette paix profonde,
Tournez les yeux: voyez, dans les routes du monde,
S'agiter les humains que travaille sans fruit,
Cet espoir obstiné du bonheur qui les fuit.
Rappelez-vous les mœurs de ces siècles sauvages
Où, sur l'Europe entière apportant les ravages,
Des Vandales obscurs, de farouches Lombards,
Des Goths se disputaient le sceptre des Césars.
La force était sans frein, le faible sans asile:
Parlez, blâmerez-vous les Benoit, les Basile,
Qui, loin du siècle impie, en ces temps abhorrés,
Ouvrirent au malheur des refuges sacrés?
Déserts de l'Orient, sables, sommets arides,
Catacombes, forêts, sauvages Thébaïdes,
Oh! que d'infortunés votre noire épaisseur
A dérobés jadis au fer de l'oppresseur!
C'est là qu'ils se cachaient; et les chrétiens fidèles,
Que la religion protégeait de ses ailes,
Vivant avec Dieu seul dans leurs pieux tombeaux,
Pouvaient au moins prier sans craindre les bourreaux.
Le tyran n'osait plus y chercher ses victimes.
Et que dis-je? accablé de l'horreur de ses crimes,
Souvent dans ces lieux saints l'oppresseur désarmé
Venait demander grâce aux pieds de l'opprimé.
D'héroïques vertus habitaient l'ermitage.
Je vois dans les débris de Thèbes, de Carthage,
Au creux des souterrains, au fond des vieilles tours,
D'illustres pénitents fuir le monde et les cours.
La voix des passions se tait sous leurs cilices;
Mais leurs austérités ne sont point sans délices:

Celui qu'ils ont cherché ne les oubliera pas;
Dieu commande au désert de fleurir sous leurs pas.
Palmier, qui rafraîchis la plaine de Syrie,
Ils venaient reposer sous ton ombre chérie!
Prophétique Jourdain, ils erraient sur tes bordes!
Et vous, qu'un roi charmait de ses divins accords,
Cèdres du haut Liban, sur votre cime altière
Vous portiez jusqu'au ciel leur ardente prière!
Cet antre protégeait leur paisible sommeil;
Souvent le cri de l'aigle avança leur réveil;
Ils chantaient l'Eternel sur le roc solitaire,
Au bruit sourd du torrent dont l'eau les désaltère,
Quand tout à coup un ange, en dévoilant ses traits,
Leur porte, au nom du ciel, un message de paix.
Et cependant leurs jours n'étaient point sans orages.
Cet éloquent Jérôme, honneur des premiers âges,
Voyait sous le cilice, et de cendres couvert,
Les voluptés de Rome assiéger son désert.
Leurs combats exerçaient son austère sagesse.
Peut-être comme lui, déplorant sa faiblesse,
Un mortel trop sensible habita ce séjour.
Hélas! plus d'une fois les soupirs de l'amour
S'élevaient dans la nuit du fond des monastères;
En vain le repoussant de ses regards austères,
La pénitence veille à côté d'un cercueil:
Il entre déguisé sous les voiles du deuil;
Au Dieu consolateur en pleurant il se donne;
A Comminge, à Rancé, Dieu sans doute pardonne:
A Comminge, à Rancé, qui ne doit quelques pleurs?
Qui n'en sait les amours? qui n'en plaint les malheurs
Et toi, dont le nom seul trouble l'âme amoureuse,
Des bois du Paraclet vestale malheureuse,
Toi qui, sans prononcer de vulgaires serments,
Fis connaître à l'amour de nouveaux sentiments;
Toi que l'homme sensible, abusé par lui-même,
Se plaît à retrouver dans la femme qu'il aime;
Héloïse! à ton nom quel cœur ne s'attendrit?
Tel qu'un autre Abailard ton amant te chérit.
Que de fois j'ai cherché, loin d'un monde volage,
L'asile où dans Paris s'écoula ton jeune âge!
Ces vénérables tours qu'allonge vers les cieux
La cathédrale antique où priaient nos aïeux,
Ces tours ont conservé ton amoureuse histoire.
Là tout m'en parle encor: là revit ta mémoire;
Là du toit de Fulbert j'ai revu les débris.
On dit même, en ces lieux, par ton ombre chéris,
Qu'un long gemissement s'élève chaque année
A l'heure où se forma ton funeste hyménée.
La jeune fille alors lit, au déclin du jour,
Cette lettre éloquente où brûle ton amour:

Son trouble est aperçu de l'amant qu'elle adore,
Et des feux que tu peins son feu s'accroît encore.
Mais que fais-je, imprudent? quoi! dans ce lieu sacré
J'ose parler d'amour, et je marche entouré
Des leçons du tombeau, des menaces suprêmes!
Ces murs, ces longs dortoirs, se couvrent d'anathèmes
De sentences de mort qu'aux yeux épouvantés
L'ange exterminateur écrit de tous côtés;
Je lis à chaque pas: *Dieu*, l'*enfer*, la *vengeance*.
Partout est la rigueur, nulle part la clémence.
Cloître sombre, où l'amour est proscrit par le ciel,
Où l'instinct le plus cher est le plus criminel,
Déjà, déjà ton deuil plaît moins à ma pensée.
L'imagination, vers tes murs élancée,
Chercha le saint repos, leur long recueillement;
Mais mon âme a besoin d'un plus doux sentiment.
Ces devoirs rigoureux font trembler ma faiblesse.
Toutefois quand le temps, qui détrompe sans cesse,
Pour moi des passions détruira les erreurs,
Et leurs plaisirs trop courts souvent mêlés de pleurs;
Quand mon cœur nourrira quelque peine secrète,
Dans ces moments plus doux et si chers au poëte,
Où, fatigué du monde, il veut, libre du moins,
Et jouir de lui-même et rêver sans témoins,
Alors je reviendrai, solitude tranquille,
Oublier dans ton sein les ennuis de la ville,
Et retrouver encor, sous ces lambris déserts,
Les mêmes sentiments retracés dans ces vers.

CHAPTER III.

OF RUINS IN GENERAL.

Ruins are of two kinds.

FROM the consideration of the *sites* of Christian monuments we proceed to the effects of the *ruins* of those monuments. They furnish the heart with magnificent recollections and the arts with pathetic compositions.

All men take a secret delight in beholding ruins. This sentiment arises from the frailty of our nature, and a secret conformity between these destroyed monuments and the caducity of our own existence. We find moreover something consoling to our littleness in observing that whole nations, and men once so renowned, could not live beyond the span allotted to our own obscurity. Ruins, therefore, produce a highly moral effect amid the scenery of nature; and, when they are introduced into a picture, in vain does the eye attempt to stray to some other object; they soon attract it again, and rivet it upon themselves. And why should not the works of men pass away, when the sun which shines upon them must one day fall from its exalted station in the heavens? He who placed it in the firmament is the only sovereign whose empire knows no decay.

There are two species of ruins,—the one the work of years, the other that of men. In the former there is nothing disagreeable, because the operations of nature keep pace with those of time. Does time bring forth a heap of ruins? Nature bestrews them with flowers. Does time cause a rent in a tomb? Nature places within it the nest of a dove. Incessantly engaged in the work of reproduction, she surrounds death itself with the sweetest illusions of life.

The ruins of the second class are rather devastations than ruins; they exhibit nothing but the image of annihilation, without any reparative power. The effect of calamity, and not of years, they resemble hoary hair on the head of youth. The destructions of men are, besides, much more violent and much more complete than those of time: the latter undermine, the former demolish. When God, for reasons unknown to us, decrees the acceleration of ruin in the world, he commands time to lend his scythe to man; and time with astonishment beholds us lay waste in the twinkling of an eye what it would have taken him whole ages to destroy.

We were one day walking behind the palace of the Luxembourg, and were accidentally led to the very same Carthusian convent which Fontanes has celebrated. We beheld a church the roof of which had fallen in; the lead had been stripped from the windows, and the doorways blocked with upright planks. Most of the other buildings of the monastery no longer existed. Long did we stroll among the sepulchral stones of black marble scattered here and there upon the ground; some were completely dashed in pieces, others still exhibited some vestiges of inscriptions We advanced into the inner cloister; there grew two wild plum-trees amid high grass and rubbish. On the walls were to be seen paintings half effaced, representing events in the life of St. Bruno; a dial-plate was left on one of the sides of the church; and in the sanctuary, instead of that hymn of peace formerly chanted in honor of the dead, was heard the grating of instruments employed in sawing the tombstones.

The reflections which occurred to us in this place may be made by any of our readers. We left it with a wounded heart, and entered the contiguous suburb without knowing whither we went. Night came on. As we were passing between two lofty walls in a lonely street, all at once the sound of an organ struck our ear, and the words of that triumphal hymn, *Laudate Dominum omnes gentes*, issued from a neighboring church; it happened to be the octave of Corpus Christi. It is impossible to express the emotion excited in us by these religious strains; it seemed as if we heard a voice from heaven saying, "O thou of little faith, why mournest thou as those without hope? Thinkest thou that I change my mind like men? that I forsake because I punish? Instead of arraigning my decrees, follow the example of these faithful servants, who bless my chastening hand even under the ruins beneath which I crush them."

We entered the church just at the moment when the priest was pronouncing the benediction. Old men, poor women, and children, were on their knees. We knelt down among them; our tears flowed, and from the bottom of our heart we said, "Forgive us, O Lord, if we murmured on beholding the desolation of thy temple; forgive our overwhelmed reason! Man himself is but a decayed edifice, a wreck of sin and death; his lukewarm love, his wavering faith, his limited charity, his imperfect sentiments, his insufficient thoughts, his broken heart,—in short, all things about him,—are but ruins!"

CHAPTER IV.

PICTURESQUE EFFECT OF RUINS.

Ruins of Palmyra, Egypt, &c.

RUINS, considered under the aspect of scenery, produce a more magical effect in a picture than the uninjured and entire monument. In temples which the hand of time has not shaken, the walls intercept the view of the surrounding scenery and prevent you from distinguishing the colonnades and arches of the edifice; but when these temples crumble into ruins, nothing is left but detached masses between which the eye discerns, above and in the distance, the stars, the clouds, mountains, rivers, and forests. Then, by a natural effect of optics, the horizon recedes, and the galleries suspended in the air appear painted on the ground of the sky and of the earth. These beautiful effects were not unknown to the ancients; if they erected a circus, it was not an uninterrupted mass of masonry, but constructed with such openings as to admit the illusions of perspective.

Ruins have, in the next place, particular conformities with their desert localities, according to the style of their architecture and the character of the places in which they are situated.

In hot climates, unfavorable to herbage and mosses, they are destitute of those grasses which decorate our Gothic mansions and ancient castles; but then larger vegetables are intermixed with the more massive proportions of their architecture. At Palmyra the date-tree cleaves the heads of the men and the lions which support the capitals of the *Temple of the Sun;* the palm, with its column, supplies the place of the broken pillar, and the peach-tree, consecrated by the ancients to Harpocrates, flourishes in the abode of silence. Here, too, you see a different kind of trees, which, by their dishevelled foliage and fruit hanging in crystals, harmonize admirably with the pendent ruins. A caravan, halting in these deserts, heightens their picturesque effects. The dignity of the oriental dress accords with the dignity of these ruins, and the camels seem to swell their dimensions, when, reposing between fragments of masonry, they exhibit only their russet heads and their protuberant backs.

In Egypt ruins assume a different character; there, in a small space, are frequently comprised various styles of architecture and various kinds of recollections. The pillars in the ancient Egyptian style rise by the side of the elegant Corinthian column; a fabric of the Tuscan order stands contiguous to an Arabic tower, a monument of the pastoral age near a structure of the Roman period. Fragments of the Sphinx, the Anubis, with broken statues and obelisks, are rolled into the Nile and buried in the earth amid rice-grounds, bean-fields, and plains of clover. Sometimes, in the overflowing of the river, these ruins have the appearance of a large fleet on the water; sometimes clouds, pouring like waves over the sides of the ruins, seem to cut them in halves; the jackal, mounted on a vacant pedestal, stretches forth his wolf-like head behind the bust of a Pan with a ram's head; the antelope, the ostrich, the ibis, the jerboa,[1] leap among the rubbish, while the sultana-hen stands motionless upon them, like a hieroglyphic bird of granite and porphyry.

The vale of Tempe, the woods of Olympus, the hills of Attica and of the Peloponnesus, are everywhere bestrewed with the ruins of Greece. There the mosses, the creeping plants, and the rock-flowers, flourish in abundance. A flaunting garland of jessamine entwines an antique Venus, as if to replace her cestus; a beard of white moss hangs from the chin of Hebe; the poppy shoots up on the leaves of the book of Mnemosyne, a lovely emblem of the past renown and the present oblivion of these regions. The waves of the Ægean Sea, which only advance to subside beneath crumbling porticos; Philomela chanting her plaintive notes; Alcyon heaving his sighs; Cadmus rolling his rings around an altar; the swan building her nest in the lap of a Leda,—all these accidents, produced, as it were, by the Graces, pour a magic spell over these poetic ruins. You would say that

[1] An animal about the size of a rat, with two very short fore-legs, and two long hind-legs resembling a kangaroo, and a long tail tufted at the extremity. There are various species of the jerboa, that are natives of Egypt, Siberia, the Cape, India, &c. &c.

a divine breath yet animates the dust of the temples of Apollo and the Muses, and the whole landscape bathed in the sea resembles a beautiful picture of Apelles, consecrated to Neptune and suspended over his shores.

CHAPTER V.

RUINS OF CHRISTIAN MONUMENTS.

THE ruins of Christian monuments have not an equal degree of elegance, but in other respects will sustain a comparison with the ruins of Rome and Greece. The finest of this kind that we know of are to be found in England, principally toward the north, near the lakes of Cumberland, on the mountains of Scotland, and even in the Orkney Islands. The walls of the choir, the pointed arches of the window, the sculptured vaultings, the pilasters of the cloisters, and some fragments of the towers, are the portions that have most effectually withstood the ravages of time.

In the Grecian orders, the vaults and the arches follow in a parallel direction the curves of the sky; so that on the gray hangings of the clouds or in a darkened landscape they are lost in the grounds In the Gothic style, the points universally form a contrast with the circular arches of the sky and the curvatures of the horizon The Gothic being, moreover, entirely composed of *voids*, the more readily admits of the decoration of herbage and flowers than the *fulness* of the Grecian orders. The clustered columns, the domes carved into foliage or scooped out in the form of a fruit-basket, afford so many receptacles into which the winds carry with the dust the seeds of vegetation. The house-leek fixes itself in the mortar; the mosses cover some rugged parts with their elastic coating; the thistle projects its brown burrs from the embrasure of a window; and the ivy, creeping along the northern cloisters, falls in festoons over the arches

No kind of ruin produces a more picturesque effect than these relics. Under a cloudy sky, amid wind and storm, on the coast of that sea whose tempests were sung by Ossian, their Gothic architecture has something grand and sombre, like the God of Sinai of whom they remind you. Seated on a shattered altar in the Orkneys, the traveller is astonished at the dreariness of those places: a raging sea, sudden fogs, vales where rises the sepulchral stone, streams flowing through wild heaths, a few reddish pine-trees scattered over a naked desert studded with patches of snow,—such are the only objects which present themselves to his view. The wind circulates among the ruins, and their innumerable crevices are so many tubes which heave a thousand sighs. The organ of old did not lament so much in these religious edifices. Long grasses wave in the apertures of the domes, and beyond these apertures you behold the flitting clouds and the soaring sea-eagle. Sometimes, mistaking her course, a ship, hidden by her swelling sails, like a spirit of the waters curtained by his wings, ploughs the black bosom of ocean. Bending under the northern blast, she seems to bow as she advances, and to kiss the seas that wash the relics of the temple of God.

On these unknown shores have passed away the men who adored that *Wisdom* which walked beneath the waves. Sometimes in their sacred solemnities they marched in procession along the beach, singing, with the Psalmist, *How vast is this sea which stretcheth wide its arms!*[1] At others, seated in the cave of Fingal on the brink of ocean, they imagined they heard that voice from on high which said to Job, *Who shut up the sea with doors when it brake forth as issuing out of the womb?*[2] At night, when the tempests of winter swept the earth, when the monastery was enveloped in clouds of spray, the peaceful cenobites, retiring within their cells, slept amid the howling of the storm, congratulating themselves on having embarked in that vessel of the Lord which will never perish.

Sacred relics of Christian monuments, ye remind us not, like so many other ruins of blood, of injustice and of violence ye relate only a peaceful history, or at most the mysterious sufferings of the Son of man! And ye holy hermits, who, to secure a place in happier regions, exiled yourselves to the ices of the pole,

[1] Ps. ciii. [2] Job xxxviii. 8.

ye now enjoy the fruit of your sacrifices; and if, among angels, as among men, there are inhabited plains and desert tracts, in like manner as ye buried your virtues in the solitudes of the earth, so ye have doubtless chosen the celestial solitudes, therein to conceal your ineffable felicity!

CHAPTER VI.

MORAL HARMONIES.

Popular Devotions.

WE now take leave of the physical harmonies of religious monuments and the scenes of nature, and enter upon the moral harmonies of Christianity. The first to be considered are *those popular devotions* which consist in certain opinions and practices of the multitude which are neither enjoined nor absolutely prohibited by the Church. They are, in fact, but harmonies of religion and of nature. When the common people fancy that they hear the voices of the dead in the winds, when they talk of nocturnal apparitions, when they undertake pilgrimages to obtain relief from their afflictions, it is evident that these opinions are only affecting relations between certain scenes of nature, certain sacred doctrines, and the sorrows of our hearts. Hence it follows that the more of these popular devotions a religion embraces, the more poetical it must be; since poetry is founded on the emotions of the soul and the accidents of nature rendered mysterious by the intervention of religious ideas.

We should indeed be deserving of pity, if, subjecting every thing to the rules of reason, we rigorously condemned these notions which assist the common people to endure the woes of life and teach them a morality which the best laws will never give.[1] It is good, and it is something beautiful at the same time, that

[1] The object of the author in this chapter is not to examine the philosophical or theological accuracy of certain popular actions and practices, but merely to

all our actions should be full of God, and that we should be incessantly surrounded by his miracles.

The vulgar are wiser than philosophers. Every fountain, every cross beside a road, every sigh of the wind at night, brings with it a prodigy. For him who possesses faith, nature is a continual wonder. Is he afflicted? he looks at his little picture or medal, and finds relief. Is he anxious once more to behold a relative, a friend? he makes a vow, seizes the pilgrim's staff, climbs the Alps or the Pyrenees, visits Our Lady of Loretto, or St. James in Galicia; on his knees he implores the saint to restore to him a son, (a poor sailor, wandering, perhaps, on the high seas,) to prolong the life of a parent or of a virtuous wife. His heart is lightened. He sets out on his return to his cottage: laden with shells, he makes the hamlets resound with his joy, and celebrates, in simple strains, the beneficence of the blessed Virgin, the mother of God. Everybody wishes to have something belonging to the pilgrim. How many ailments have been cured merely by a blessed ribbon! The pilgrim at length reaches home, and the first person that greets him on his arrival is his wife after a happy delivery, a son returned home, or a father restored to health.

Happy, thrice happy they who possess faith! They cannot smile, without thinking that they will rejoice in the eternal smiles of Heaven; they cannot weep, without thinking that the time of their sorrowing will soon be over. Their tears are not lost: religion collects them in her urn, and presents them to the Most High.

The steps of the true believer are never solitary; a good angel

---

show the superiority of convictions that have a religious basis over sentiments of infidelity. The general principle which he wishes to establish is well expressed in the following passage of Paley's Moral Philosophy, p. 391:—

"Whilst the infidel mocks at the superstition of the vulgar, insults over their credulous fear, their childish errors and fantastic rites, it does not occur to him to observe that the most preposterous device by which the weakest devotee ever believed he was securing the happiness of a future life is more rational than unconcern about it. Upon this subject nothing is so absurd as indifference, no folly so contemptible as thoughtlessness and levity."

It must be admitted, however, that the phraseology of our author has not the precision and perspicuity which are desirable in treating such a subject. The invocation of the Blessed Virgin, pilgrimages, the devotional use of holy pictures and other objects blessed by the Church, &c., are not to be ranked among things which she "neither enjoins nor absolutely prohibits;" for such practices are at least approved and encouraged by her. T.

watches by his side, counsels him in his dreams, and protects him from the evil spirit. This heavenly friend is so devoted to his interests that he consents for his sake to be an exile upon earth

Did there exist among the ancients any thing more admirable than the many customs that prevailed among our religious forefathers? If they discovered the body of a murdered man in a forest, they erected a cross on the spot in token of pity. This cross demanded of the Samaritan a tear for the unfortunate traveller, and of the inhabitant of the faithful city a prayer for his brother. And then, this traveller was, perhaps, a poor stranger, who had fallen at a great distance from his native land, like that illustrious Unknown sacrificed by the hands of men far away from his celestial country! What an intercourse between us and God! What prodigious elevation was thus given to human nature! How astonishing that we should thus discover a resemblance between our fleeting days and the eternal duration of the Sovereign of the universe!

We shall say nothing of those jubilees which, substituted for secular games, plunge all Christendom into the bath of repentance, purify the conscience, and offer a religious amnesty to repenting sinners. Neither shall we relate how, in public calamities, both high and low walked barefoot from church to church, to endeavor to avert the wrath of God The pastor headed the solemn procession with a cord about his neck, the humble victim devoted for the welfare of his flock. The fear of these evils was not encouraged among the people by an ebony crucifix, a bit of blessed laurel, or an image of the patron saint. How often has the Christian knelt before these religious symbols to ask of God that assistance which could not be obtained from man!

Who has not heard of our Lady of the Woods, who inhabits the aged thorn or the mossy cavity of a spring, and is so celebrated in the hamlet for her miracles? Many a matron will tell you, that after having invoked the good Mary of the Woods she suffered less from the pains of childbirth. The maiden who had lost her lover would often fancy in the moonlight that she saw the spirit of her young betrothed in this solitary spot, or heard his voice in the low murmur of the stream The doves that drink from these waters have always the power of generation and the flowers that grow on their borders never cease to bloom

It was fitting that the tutelar saint of the forest should accomplish effects as tender in their nature as the moss amid which she dwells, and as charming as the fountain that veils her from human sight.

It is particularly in the great events of life that religious customs impart their consolations to the unfortunate. We once were spectators of a shipwreck. The mariners, on reaching the shore, stripped off all their clothes, with the exception of their wet trousers and shirts. They had made a vow to the Virgin during the storm. They repaired in procession to a little chapel dedicated to St. Thomas, preceded by the captain, and followed by the people, who joined them in singing the *Ave Maris Stella*. The priest said the mass appointed for the shipwrecked, and the sailors hung their garments, dripping with sea-water, as votive offerings, against the walls of the chapel.[1] Philosophy may fill her pages with high-sounding words, but we question whether the unfortunate ever go to hang up their garments in her temple.

Death, so poetical because of its bordering upon things immortal, so mysterious on account of its silence, could not but have a thousand ways of announcing itself to the vulgar. Sometimes its token was heard in the ringing of a distant bell; at others, the person whose dissolution drew nigh heard three knocks upon the floor of his chamber. A nun of St. Benedict, on the point of quitting the world, found a crown of white thorn at the entrance of her cell. Did a mother lose her son abroad, her dreams immediately apprised her of this misfortune. Those who withhold their belief in presentiments will never know the secret channels by which two hearts, bound by the ties of love, hold mutual intercourse from one end of the world to the other. Frequently would some cherished departed one appear to a friend on earth, soliciting prayers for the rescue of his soul from the purgatorial flame, and its admission to the company of the elect. Thus did religion accord to friendship some share in the sublime prerogative which belongs only to God, of imparting eternal happiness.

Opinions of a different kind, but still of a religious character, inspired feelings of humanity; and such is their simplicity that

---

[1] See note II.

they embarrass the writer. To destroy the nest of a swallow, to kill a robin redbreast, a wren, a cricket—the attendant on the rural hearth, a dog grown old in the service of a family, was a deed which never failed, it was said, to be followed by some visitation. From an admirable respect for age, it was thought that persons advanced in years were of propitious influence in a house, and that an old servant brought good luck to his master. Here we meet with some traces of the affecting worship of the *Lares*, and are reminded of the daughter of Laban carrying her household gods along with her.

The vulgar were persuaded that no person could commit a wicked action without being haunted all the rest of his life by frightful apparitions. Antiquity, wiser than we, would have forborne to destroy these useful accordances of religion, of conscience, and of morality. Neither would it have rejected another opinion, according to which it was deemed certain that every man possessing ill-gotten wealth had entered into a covenant with the spirit of darkness and made over his soul to hell.

Finally, wind, rain, sunshine, the seasons, agriculture, birth, infancy, marriage, old age, death, had all their respective saints and images, and never were people so surrounded with friendly divinities as were the Christian people.

It is not the question now to enter into a rigid examination of these opinions. So far from laying any injunctions on the subject, religion served, on the contrary, to prevent the abuse of them, and to check their extravagancies. The only question is whether their aim be moral, whether they have a stronger tendency than the laws themselves to keep the multitude in the paths of virtue What sensible man has any doubt of this? By your incessant declamations against superstition, you will at length open a door for every species of crime. A circumstance that cannot fail to surprise the sophists is, that, amid all the evils which they will have occasioned, they will not even enjoy the satisfaction of seeing the common man more incredulous If he shakes off the influence of religion, he will supply its place with monstrous opinions. He will be seized with a terror the more strange as he will be ignorant of its object: he will shudder in a churchyard, where he has set up the inscription, *Death is an eternal sleep;* and, while affecting to despise the Divine power, he will go to consult the gipsy, and, trembling, seek his destinies in the motley figures of a card.

The marvellous, a future state, and hope, are required by man, because he feels himself formed to survive this terrestrial existence. *Conjuration, sorcery,* are with the vulgar but the instinct of religion, and one of the most striking proofs of the necessity of a public worship. He who believes nothing is not far from believing every thing; you have conjurors when you cease to have prophets, enchantments when you renounce religious ceremonies, and you open the dens of sorcerers when you shut up the temples of the Lord.[1]

[1] These remarks are confirmed by indisputable facts. Julian the apostate, who thought himself very wise, after rejecting Christianity, was a complete dupe of magicians. Another instance may be mentioned, which it is a greater wonder our author omitted, as it occurred in his own country at a period with which he was well acquainted. The Duke of Orleans, the Regent of France, a hardened infidel, had great faith in astrology. Pope's assertion was not less true than poetical, when he said,—

"The godless regent trembled at a star."

Part the Fourth.

WORSHIP.

BOOK I.

CHURCHES, ORNAMENTS, SINGING, PRAYERS, ETC.

CHAPTER I.

OF BELLS.

THE subject which will now occupy us — the worship of the Christian Church — is as interesting as any that we have considered, and forms the concluding part of this work. As we are about to enter the temple, let us first speak of the bell which summons us thither.

To us it seems not a little surprising that a method should have been found, by a single stroke of a hammer, to excite the same sentiment, at one and the same instant, in thousands of hearts, and to make the winds and clouds the bearers of the thoughts of men. Considered merely as harmony, the bell possesses a beauty of the highest kind,—that which by artists is styled *the grand.* Thunder is sublime; but only by its grandeur. Thus it is, also, with the wind, the sea, the volcano, the cataract, or the voice of a whole assembled nation.

With what transport would Pythagoras, who listened to the hammer of the smith, have hearkened to the sound of our bells on the vigil of some religious solemnity! The soul may be moved by the tones of the lyre; but it will not be rapt into enthusiasm as when roused by the thunders of the combat, or when a powerful peal proclaims in the region of the clouds the triumphs of the God of battles

This, however, is not the most remarkable character of the sound of bells. This sound has a thousand secret relations with man. How oft, amid the profound tranquillity of night, has the heavy tolling of the death-bell, like the slow pulsations of an expiring heart, startled the adultress in her guilty pleasures! How often has it caught the ear of the atheist who, in his impious vigils, had perhaps the presumption to write that there is no God! The pen drops from his fingers. He hears with consternation the funeral knell which seems to say to him, *And is there indeed no God?* Oh, how such sounds disturbed the slumbers of our tyrants![1] Extraordinary religion, which, by the mere percussion of the magic metal, can change pleasures into torments, appal the atheist, and cause the dagger to drop from the hand of the assassin!

But more pleasing sentiments have also attached us to the sound of bells. When, about the time for cutting the grain, the tinkling of the little bells of our hamlets was heard intermingled with the sprightly strains of the lark, you would have thought that the angel of harvest was proclaiming the story of Sephora or of Noemi. It seems to us that were we a poet we should not reject the idea of a bell tolled by spectres in the ancient chapel of the forest, that which religious fear set in motion in our fields to keep off the lightning, or that which was rung at night in certain sea-ports to direct the pilot in his passage among the rocks. On our festivals the lively peals of our bells seemed to heighten the public joy. In great calamities, on the contrary, their voice became truly awful. The hair yet stands erect at the remembrance of those days of murder and conflagration, all vibrating with the dismal noise of the tocsin. Who has forgotten those yells—those piercing shrieks succeeded by intervals of sudden silence, during which was now and then heard the discharge of a musket, some doleful and solitary voice, and, above all, the heavy tolling of the alarm-bell, or the clock that calmly struck the hour which had just elapsed?

But, in a well-regulated society, the sound of the tocsin, suggesting the idea of succor, filled the soul with pity and terror, and thus touched the two great springs of tragical sensation.

---

[1] The author alludes, in this chapter, to the incidents of the revolutionary period and of that which preceded it. T.

Such were something like the sentiments awakened by the bells of our temples,—sentiments the more exquisite as a vague recollection of heaven was always blended with them. Had bells been attached to any other edifice than to our churches they would have lost their moral sympathy with our hearts. It was God himself who commanded the angel of victory to strike up the peals that proclaimed our triumphs, or the angel of death to sound forth the departure of a soul that had just returned to him Thus, by numberless secret ways, a Christian society corresponded with the Divinity, and its institutions were mysteriously lost in the Source of all mystery.

Let bells, then, call the faithful together; for the voice of man is not sufficiently pure to summon penitence, innocence, and misfortune to the foot of the altar. Among the savages of America, when suppliants appear at the door of a cabin, it is the child belonging to it that ushers these distressed strangers into the habitation of his father; so, if the use of bells were forbidden us, a child should be chosen to call us to the house of the Lord.

CHAPTER II.

VESTMENTS OF THE CLERGY AND ORNAMENTS OF THE CHURCH.

PEOPLE are incessantly extolling the institutions of antiquity, and they will not perceive that the Christian worship is the only relic of that antiquity which has been transmitted to us. Every thing in the Church retraces those remote ages which men have left so far behind them, and on which they still love to expatiate in idea. Fix your eyes on the Christian priest, and you are instantly transported to the country of Numa, Lycurgus, or Zoroaster The *tiara* shows us the Mede roving among the ruins of Suza and Ecbatan. The *alb*—the Latin name of which reminds us of the dawn of day and of virginal whiteness—presents charming conformities with religious ideas. A sublime recollection or an agreeable harmony is invariably attached to the decorations of our altars. Is there any thing offensive to the eye or repugnant to good taste in those altars formed after the model of an ancient tomb, or in those images of the Living Sun which are enclosed in our tabernacles? Our chalices sought their names among the plants, and the lily lent them her shape. Charming concordance between the Lamb and flowers!

The cross, as the most direct mark of faith, is also, in the eyes of certain persons, the most ridiculous of objects. The Romans scoffed at it, like the new enemies of Christianity; but Tertullian showed them that they themselves employed this sign in their fasces. The attitude in which the cross exhibits the Son of man is sublime. The sinking body and the inclined head form a divine contrast with the arms outstretched toward heaven. Nature, however, has not been so fastidious as unbelievers. She has not scrupled to introduce the form of a cross into a multitude of her works. There is a whole family of flowers which partakes of this form, and this family is distinguished by an inclination to solitude.[1] The hand of the Most High has also placed the standard of our salvation among the stars of heaven.[2]

The urn which contained the perfumes resembled a bo t in shape. Flames and odoriferous vapors floated in a censer at the extremity of a long chain. Here were seen candelabra of gilded bronze,—the work of a Cafieri or a Vassé,—and images of the mystic chandeliers of the royal poet. There the Cardinal Virtues, in a sitting posture, supported the triangular music-desk. Its sides were adorned with lyres; it was crowned with a terrestrial globe; and an eagle of brass, hovering over these beautiful allegories, seemed to be wafting our prayers on his expanded wings toward heaven. On every side were seen pulpits of an airy construction, vases surmounted with flames, balconies, lofty stands, marble balustrades, stalls sculptured by the Charpentiers and Dugoulons, brackets manufactured by the Ballins, and remonstrances designed by the Bertrands and the Cottes. Sometimes the relics of heathen temples served to decorate the temples of

[1] These flowers are called cruciform, and they belong to the *tetradynamia* class of Linnæus.

[2] Our author probably alludes to the constellation *el cruzero*, or *croisiers*, south of the zodiac. It consists of six stars, and was discovered by the navigators to the New World.

the living God The holy-water vases of the church of St. Sulpice were two sepulchral urns brought from Alexandria. The basins, the patens, the lustral water, called to your mind every moment the ancient sacrifices, and incessantly mingled, without confounding, the remembrance of whatever Greece possessed most beautiful with the sublime recollections of Israel.

Finally, the lamps and the flowers which decorated our churches served to perpetuate the memory of those times of persecution when the faithful assembled in tombs for the purpose of prayer. You might almost imagine that you beheld those primitive Christians secretly lighting their torch beneath the sepulchral arches, and young virgins bringing flowers to deck the altar of the catacombs, where a pastor, distinguished only by poverty and good works, consecrated offerings to the Lord. This was truly the reign of Jesus Christ, the God of the humble and the afflicted. His altar was as poor as his servants; but if the chalices in those days were made of wood, says St. Boniface, the priests were of gold, and never were such exalted virtues seen among Christians as in those ages when, in order to worship the Lord of light and life, they were obliged to secrete themselves in the bosom of darkness and of death.

CHAPTER III.

OF SINGING AND PRAYER.

It is objected against the Catholic Church that she employs in her liturgy an unknown tongue; as if the clergy preached in Latin, or the service were not translated in our prayer-books. If Religion had changed her language according to the caprice or customs of men, how could we have known the works of antiquity? Such is the inconsistency of our nature that we censure the very practices to which we are indebted for a portion of our knowledge and our pleasure. But, even considering the custom of the Church in itself, we see not why the language of Virgil (and, under certain circumstances of time and place, the language of Homer) should appear so offensive in our liturgy. It seems to us that an ancient and mysterious language—a language which changes not with the world—is well adapted to the worship of the Eternal, Incomprehensible, and Immutable Being; and, as the sense of our miseries compels us to raise a suppliant cry to the King of kings, is it not natural to address Him in the most beautiful idiom known to man? that in which prostrate nations once presented their petitions to the Cæsars? Moreover, it is worthy of remark that the prayers in Latin seem to increase the religious sentiment of the people. May not this be the effect of our natural disposition to secrecy? Amid the confusion of his thoughts and various trials, man fancies that he asks what he has need of, and what he is ignorant of, when he pronounces words with which he is not familiar or which he does not even understand. The vagueness of his prayer is its charm; and his disquieted soul, little acquainted with its own desires, delights in offering up prayers as mysterious as its own wants.

We have now to examine what some have been pleased to call the *barbarism* of the ecclesiastical chant.

It is generally admitted that, in lyric poetry, the Hebrews are far superior to the other nations of antiquity. The Church, then, which sings every day the psalms and prophetic lessons, has an excellent groundwork to begin with. It would be difficult to see any thing ridiculous or barbarous in the hymns which are drawn from such a source. The ecclesiastical chant is also based upon the Gospels and the Epistles of the apostles. Racine, in imitating various passages of them, thought, like Malherbe and Rousseau, that they were worthy of the highest efforts of his Muse.[1] Chrysostom, Ambrose, Coffin, and Santeuil, alternately swept the Greek and Latin lyre on the tombs of Alcæus and of Horace. Vigilant in praising the great Creator, Religion mingles her matin concerts with those of Aurora:—

Image of the Eternal Sire,
Arise, resplendent source of light!
Thou dayspring from on high, thy glories bright
Eclipse the sun's meridian fire,
Whose purest rays
Are but the reflex of thy beauty's blaze.

---

[1] See the canticle taken from *St. Paul*.

With the setting sun the Church again sings:[1]—

> Great God, whose glistening throne is fixed
> High in the star-bespangled skies;
> Who paint'st the glowing firmament
> With all its variegated dies!

This music of Israel on the lyre of Racine cannot be pronounced destitute of charms We imagine that it is not so much a real sound that we hear, as that *interior and melodious voice*, which, according to Plato, awakes in the morning those who are captivated with virtue *by singing with all its power in their hearts.*

But, without having recourse to these hymns, the common prayers of the Church are admirable; it is only the habit of repeating them from our infancy that renders us insensible to their beauty. The world would resound with the praises of Plato or Seneca if their works contained a profession of faith so simple, so pure, so luminous, as that article of the creed—

"I believe in one God, the Father Almighty, Maker of heaven and earth, and of all things visible and invisible."

The Lord's prayer is the production of a God who understood all our wants. Let us duly consider its words:—

Our Father who art in heaven:—Here is an acknowledgment of one only God

Hallowed be thy name:—These words indicate the duty of worshipping God; the vanity of earthly things: God alone is worthy of being hallowed.

Thy kingdom come:—The immortality of the soul is pointed out.

Thy will be done on earth as it is heaven:—This expression of pious resignation, while it implies the attributes of the Deity, embraces the whole moral and physical order of the universe.

Give us this day our daily bread:—How impressive and philosophical! What is the only real want of man? a little bread; and that he only requires for this day; for, will he be alive to-morrow?

And forgive us our trespasses as we forgive them that trespass against us:—A code of morality and charity comprised in the smallest compass.

---

[1] See note KK.

And lead us not into temptation, but deliver us from evil:—Behold the human heart exposed without reserve! behold man and all his weakness! Let him not ask for strength to overcome; let him pray only that he may not be attacked and may not suffer. None but the author of human nature could be so thoroughly acquainted with his work.

We shall not speak here of the *angelical salutation,*—that prayer so truly full of grace,—nor of the confession which the Christian utters every day in the presence of the Almighty. Never will the laws provide a substitute of equal moral efficacy with the performance of these devotions. Consider only what a curb man must find in that humiliating acknowledgment which he makes at morning and at night:—*I have sinned in thought, word, and deed.* Pythagoras recommended a similar confession to his disciples; but it was reserved for Christianity to realize all those pleasing visions of virtue in which the sages of Rome and Athens indulged.

Christianity, in fact, is at one and the same time a kind of philosophic sect and an antique system of legislation. Hence the abstinences, the fasts, the vigils, of which we find traces in the ancient republics and which were practised by the learned schools of India, Egypt, and Greece. The more closely we scrutinize this question, the more we are convinced that the greater part of the insults aimed at the Christian worship must recoil upon antiquity. But to return to the subject of prayer.

The acts of faith, hope, charity, and repentance, also dispose the heart to virtue; while the prayers used at the different Christian ceremonies relative to civil or religious matters, or only to the mere accidents of life, have a perfect appropriateness, are distinguished for elevated sentiment, awaken grand recollections, and are marked by a style at once simple and magnificent.

At the nuptial mass the priest reads from the Epistle of St. Paul to the Ephesians:—"Let women be subject to their husbands as to the Lord;" and at the gospel he says, "There came to Jesus the Pharisees tempting him, and saying, Is it lawful for a man to put away his wife for every cause? Who, answering, said to them, ... for this cause shall a man leave father and mother, and shall cleave to his wife, and they two shall be in one flesh!"

At the nuptial benediction, the priest, after repeating the words which God himself pronounced over Adam and Eve,—*Increase and multiply,*—adds, "Look, O Lord, we beseech thee, upon these thy servants; . . . . look mercifully upon this thy handmaid; may this wedlock be to her a yoke of love and peace! may she marry in Christ faithful and chaste, and remain a follower of holy women! May she be amiable to her husband like Rachel, wise like Rebecca, long-lived and faithful like Sara! . . . . May she be fruitful in offspring, approved and innocent, and attain unto the rest of the blessed and unto the heavenly kingdom!—that they both may see their children's children unto the third and fourth generation, and arrive at a desired old age."

At the ceremony of *churching* is repeated the psalm, "Unless the Lord build the house, they labor in vain who build it."

At the commencement of Lent, in the ceremony of threatening sinners with the anger of heaven, the following maledictions from Deuteronomy were formerly used:—

"Cursed be he who despiseth his father and mother. Cursed be he who puts the blind out of his way," &c.

In visiting the sick, the priest, on entering the house, says, "Peace be to this house and to all who dwell therein!" Afterward, beside the pillow of the sick person, he pronounces this prayer:—"O most merciful God, open thine eye of mercy upon this thy servant; preserve and continue him in the unity of the Church; consider his contrition, accept his tears, assuage his pain as shall seem to thee most expedient for him." He then reads the psalm, "In thee, O Lord, I have put my trust; deliver me in thy righteousness."

When we recollect that it is almost always the POOR whom the priest thus goes to visit on their couches of straw, these Christian supplications appear still more divine.

Every Christian knows the beautiful prayers recited for those who are in their agony:—"Depart, Christian soul, out of this world," &c. Then a passage from the gospel is read, which describes the agony of our Lord in the garden Afterward follow the psalm *Miserere,* a part of the Apocalypse which represents the glorification of the elect, and finally Ezechiel's vision—an emblematical allusion to the resurrection of the dead:—"The hand of the Lord was upon me, and brought me forth in the spirit of the Lord; and set me down in the midst of a plain that was fall of bones. . . . And he said to me, Prophesy to the spirit, prophesy, O Son of man, and say to the spirit, Thus saith the Lord God; come, spirit, from the four winds, and blow upon these slain, and let them live again."

For conflagrations, for pestilence, for war, and all kinds of calamities, there are particular prayers. Never, while we live, shall we forget the impression produced by the reading of the psalm, "Give glory to the Lord, for he is good," during a shipwreck in which we were ourselves involved. "He said the word, and there arose a storm of wind, and the waves thereof were lifted up. And they cried to the Lord in their affliction, and he brought them out of their distresses. And he turned the storm into a breeze, and its waves were still."

Toward the paschal solemnity Jeremias, with his lamentations, issues from the dust of Sion to deplore the fate of the Son of man. The Church selects whatever is most beautiful and most solemn in the Old and New Testament to compose the service of that week, consecrated by the greatest of mysteries, which heralds the greatest of griefs. Even the litanies which are used by the people in their devotions express the most admirable sentiments and aspirations. Witness the following from the Litany of Providence:—

> "Providence of God, consolation of the pilgrim soul;
> Providence of God, hope of the abandoned sinner;
> Providence of God, calmer of the storm;
> Providence of God, repose of the heart,
> Have mercy on us!"

Lastly, our ancient songs, even the Christmas carols of our forefathers, have also their merits; they breathe the unaffected simplicity, and, as it were, the freshness, of faith. Why have we been so much affected during our country missions in hearing the laboring people sing at the Benediction of the Blessed Sacrament? Those artless strains produced a profound emotion, because they arose from truth and conviction. The carols which describe rural scenes have a peculiarly graceful expression in the mouth of the female peasant. When the sound of the spinning-wheel accompanies her song, when her children, leaning upon her knees, listen with silent attention to the story of the infant Jesus and his manger, in vain would you seek sweeter melodies and a religion better adapted to a mother.

CHAPTER IV.

SOLEMNITIES OF THE CHURCH.

Sunday.

We have already remarked[1] the beauty of this seventh day which corresponds with that when the Creator rested from his work This division of time is of the highest antiquity. It is a question of little importance to us here whether it was an obscure tradition of the creation transmitted by the children of Noah to their posterity, or whether some pastoral people invented this division from the observation of the planets; but so much, at least, is certain, that it is the most *perfect* that was ever employed by any legislator. Exclusively of its exact correspondence with the strength of man and animals, it has those great geometrical harmonies which the ancients always sought to establish between the particular and the general laws of the universe It gives the number six for labor; and six, by two simple multiplications, produces the 360 days of the ancient year, and the 360 degrees of the circumference of the globe. We may, then, perceive both magnificence and philosophy in this religious law which divided the circle of our labors as well as the circle described by the planets in their revolutions; as if man had no other period to his fatigues than the consummation of ages, nor any smaller space to fill with his sorrows than the vast abyss of time.

The decimal calculation may suit a mercantile people; but it is neither beautiful nor convenient in the other concerns of life or in the great celestial equations. It is rarely employed by nature; it does not harmonize with the year and the course of

---

[1] Part i. book ii chap. i.

the sun; and the law of gravity (perhaps the only law of the universe) is accomplished by the *square* and not by the *quintuple* of the distances. Neither does it agree with the birth, the growth, and the development of the different species; almost all females go by three, nine, or twelve, which belong to the calculation by six.[1]

We know by experience that the fifth day comes too soon and the tenth too late for a period of rest. Terror, which was all-powerful in France, never could compel the peasant to observe the *decade*, because the strength of man, and, as it has been remarked, even that of animals, is inadequate to the exertion. The ox cannot labor nine successive days; at the end of the sixth, his lowing seems to demand the hours marked by the Creator for the general rest of nature.[2]

Sunday combines every advantage, for it is at the same time a day of pleasure and of religion. It is doubtless necessary that man should have some recreation after his labors; but, as his leisure is beyond the reach of the civil law, to release him at that moment from the influence of the religious law is to remove every curb, to plunge him again into a state of nature, and to let loose all at once a kind of savage upon society. It was to prevent this danger that the ancients themselves made the day of rest a religious day; and Christianity consecrated this example.

Nevertheless, this great day of the benediction of the earth, this mysterious day of the rest of Jehovah, shocked the enlightened understandings of the members of that convention "who had made a covenant with death, because they were worthy to be of the part thereof."[3] After a universal consent of six thousand years, after sixty ages of Hosannas, the wisdom of Danton presumed to condemn the work which the Almighty had deemed good. He fancied that, by plunging us back into chaos, he could substitute the tradition of its ruins and its darkness for that of the origin of light and the creation of the spheres: he wanted to separate the French people from all other nations, and to make it, like the Jews, a caste hostile to the rest of mankind.

---

[1] See Buffon.

[2] The peasants said, "Our oxen know when Sunday comes, and will not work on that day."

[3] Wisd. i. 16.

A tenth day, which had no other honor than that of heralding the memory of Robespierre, usurped the place of that ancient sabbath, so intimately connected with the birth of ages; that day, sanctified by the religion of our forefathers, hallowed by a hundred millions of Christians on the surface of the globe, celebrated by the saints and the hosts of heaven, and, if we may so express it, observed by the great Creator himself in the ages of eternity.

CHAPTER V.

EXPLANATION OF THE MASS.

THE ceremonial of the mass may be defended by an argument at once so simple and so natural, that it is difficult to conceive how it could have been overlooked in the controversy between Catholics and Protestants. What is it that constitutes the essence of religious worship? It is sacrifice A religion that has no sacrifice has no worship, properly so called. This truth cannot be questioned, since among all the nations of the earth the ceremonies of religion have sprung from the sacrifice, and not the sacrifice from the ceremonies of religion. It follows, therefore, that worship exists only among that Christian people who have an external oblation.

Some may admit this principle without admitting the justness of its application to the mass; but, if the objection turned upon this point, it would not be difficult to prove that the eucharistic offering is the most admirable, the most mysterious, and the most divine, of all sacrifices.

A universal tradition informs us that the creature formerly became guilty in the eyes of the Creator. All nations endeavored to appease the anger of heaven, and believed that a victim was necessary for this purpose. So convinced were they of this that they began by offering man himself as a holocaust. Such was the terrible sacrifice to which the savage had recourse, because by its very nature it was more conformable to the original sentence which condemned man to death

In the course of time the blood of animals was substituted in the place of human victims; but on the occasion of some great calamity the former practice was revived. The oracles demanded even the children of kings; the daughter of Jephte, Isaac, Iphigenia, were claimed by heaven, while Curtius and Codrus devoted themselves to death in behalf of Athens and Rome.

Human sacrifices, however, were the first to be abolished, because they belonged to the state of nature, when man was almost entirely merged in the *physical* order. The offering of animals continued for a long time; but, when society began to grow old, when people reflected upon the relations between God and man, they recognised the inefficacy of the material sacrifice, and understood that the blood of goats and heifers could not redeem a being endowed with intelligence and a capability of virtue. A victim, therefore, more worthy the nature of man, was sought after; and, while philosophers taught that the gods could not be moved by the blood of hecatombs, and would accept only the offering of an humble heart, Jesus Christ confirmed these vague notions of reason. The mystic Lamb succeeded to the firstling of the flock, and the immolation of *physical* man was forever superseded by the immolation of the passions, or the sacrifice of *moral* man.

The more deeply we study Christianity, the more clearly shall we perceive that it is but the development of our natural light, and the necessary result of the advancement of society.[1] Who nowadays could endure at an altar the infected blood of an animal, or believe that the skin of an ox will render Heaven attentive to our prayers? But it is easily conceived that a spiritual victim daily offered for the sins of men may be acceptable to God.

For the preservation, however, of exterior worship, some sign was necessary as a symbol of the moral victim; and Jesus Christ,

[1] It is manifest, from other portions of this work, that the author does not mean in this passage to favor the doctrines of transcendentalism or the perfectibility of man. His expressions, if taken separately from the context, would imply those errors: but, in their application to the point under consideration, it will be seen that they are intended only to signify a necessary accordance between Christianity and right reason, between religion and the advanced condition of society. In this, as in some other passages, the language of the writer is not sufficiently precise. T.

before he left the earth, provided for this want of the senses, which cannot dispense with a material object. He instituted the eucharist, where under the visible elements of bread and wine he concealed the invisible offering of his blood and of our hearts. Such is our explanation of the Christian sacrifice,—an explanation which has nothing contrary to good sense or to philosophy; and whoever reflects a moment on the subject will perhaps discover some new views in relation to the sacred depths of this mystery.

CHAPTER VI.

CEREMONIES AND PRAYERS OF THE MASS.

We have now to consider the ceremonies of the sacrifice.[1] If the mass were a rite the description of which could be found in Horace or in some Greek tragedy, how admirable would the introductory psalm appear to us!

V. I will go into the altar of God.

R. To God who giveth joy to my youth.

V. Judge me, O God, and distinguish my cause from the nation that is not holy, deliver me from the unjust and deceitful man.

R. For thou art God my strength: why hast thou cast me off? And why do I go sorrowful whilst the enemy afflicteth me?

V. Send forth thy light and thy truth: they have conducted me, and brought me into thy holy hill and into thy tabernacles.

R. And I will go into the altar of God: to God who giveth joy to my youth.

V. To thee, O God, my God, I will give praise upon the harp: why art thou sad, O my soul? and why dost thou disquiet me?

R. Hope in God, for I will still give praise to him. the salvation of my countenance and my God.

This dialogue is a real lyric poem between the priest and the clerk who answers for the faithful. The first, full of days and experience, bemoans the misery of man for whom he is going to offer up the adorable sacrifice; the second, full of hope and youth, celebrates the victim by which he is to be redeemed.

Then follows the *Confiteor Deo,* an admirable prayer of devo-

[1] See note LL.

tion and humility. The priest implores the mercy of the Almighty for the congregation and himself.

The holy dialogue recommences. . . .

V. O Lord, hear my prayer!
R. And let my supplication come to thee.

Then the priest ascends the altar, and respectfully kisses the stone in which are some holy relics of the martyrs,—a circumstance which reminds us of the catacombs.

After the introit or preliminary prayer of the mass, the celebrant, seized with a divine fire like the prophets of Israel, begins the canticle sung by angels over the Saviour's crib, and of which Ezechiel in ecstasy heard a part in the cloud.

"Glory be to God on high, and peace on earth to men of good will. We praise thee, we bless thee, we adore thee, we glorify thee, we give thee thanks for thy great glory," &c.

Then follows the Epistle, in which we hear the mild and tender language of St. John, the friend of the Redeemer, or an exposition of the divine mysteries in the sublime words of St. Paul, challenging the power of death. Before reading the gospel, the priest calls upon God to purify his lips with the coal of fire with which he touched the lips of the prophet Isaias. The voice of Jesus Christ is now heard in the assembly, pronouncing judgment upon the adulterous woman, or relating the charitable deeds of the good Samaritan, or blessing the little children whom he called around him.

What may the celebrant and the congregation do, after hearing the Saviour's words, but declare their firm belief in the existence of a God who gave such examples to men? The creed, therefore, is now solemnly chanted. Philosophy, which boasts of being the patron of every thing great, should have observed that Christianity was the first to exhibit the spectacle of a whole people publicly professing their faith in the unity of God:—*Credo in unum Deum.*

Here follows the *offertory*, or the oblation of the bread and wine. In presenting the former, the priest begs the Almighty to accept it for himself, for the living and for the dead. In offering the latter, he says, "We offer to thee, O Lord, the chalice of our salvation." He then blesses the bread and wine,—

"Come, O eternal God, and bless this sacrifice." In washing his fingers, he says, "I will wash my hands among the innocent. . . . . Take not away my soul, O God, with the wicked, nor my life with bloody men," &c. We are here reminded of the persecutions of the Church in the early ages. Turning toward the people, the celebrant says, *Orate, fratres*, "Pray, brethren," to which the clerk answers, in the name of all, "May the Lord receive from thy hands this sacrifice," &c. The priest then recites in a low voice the prayer called *Secreta*, in the concluding words of which he announces eternity—*per omnia secula seculorum*—and continues, *sursum corda*, "lift up your hearts;" to which all answer, *habemus ad Dominum*, "we lift them to the Lord."

The Preface is now sung to an ancient and solemn air, concluding with an invocation to the Dominations, the Powers, the Virtues, the Angels, Archangels, Cherubim and Seraphim, to descend with the august victim of the altar, and to repeat with the faithful the trisagium and the eternal hosanna,—"Holy, holy, holy, Lord God of hosts! the heavens and the earth are full of thy glory; hosanna in the highest!"

Here follows the most important part of the sacrifice The canon, wherein is engraved the eternal law of God, has commenced, and the consecration of the bread and wine is accomplished by the very words of Jesus Christ In a posture of profound reverence, the priest says, "O Lord, may this blessed host be acceptable to thee, as were the offerings of Abel the Just, the sacrifice of our patriarch Abraham, and that of thy high-priest Melchisedech! We beseech thee to grant that these gifts may be presented on thy holy altar by the hands of thy angel in the presence of thy divine majesty."

Oh moment solennel! ce peuple prosterné,
Ce temple dont la mousse a couvert les portiques,
Ses vieux murs, son jour sombre, et ses vitraux gothiques,
Cette lampe d'airain, qui, dans l'antiquité
Symbole du soleil et de l'éternité,
Luit devant le Très-Haut jour et nuit suspendue:
La majesté d'un Dieu parmi nous descendue,
Les pleurs, les vœux, l'encens qui montent vers l'autel,
Et de jeunes beautés, qui sous l'œil maternel
Adoucissent encor par leur voix innocente
De la religion la pompe attendrissante;

Cet orgue qui se tait, ce silence pieux,
L'invisible union de la terre et des cieux,
Tout enflamme, agrandit, émeut l'homme sensible:
Il croit avoir franchi ce monde inaccessible,
Où sur des harpes d'or l'immortel séraphin,
Aux pieds de Jéhovah, chante l'hymne sans fin.
Alors de toutes parts un Dieu se fait entendre;
Il se cache au savant, se révèle au cœur tendre:
Il doit moins se prouver qu'il ne doit se sentir.[1]

CHAPTER VII.

SOLEMNITY OF CORPUS CHRISTI.

CHRISTIAN festivals are not like the ceremonies of paganism. We do not drag an ox-god or a sacred goat in triumph; neither are we obliged, under pain of being torn to pieces, to adore a cat or crocodile, or to roll drunk in the streets, committing all sorts of abominations in honor of Venus, Flora, or Bacchus. In our solemnities all is essentially moral. If the Church has excluded the dance from them, it is because she is aware of the many passions that are disguised under this apparently innocent amusement.[2] The God of the Christians is satisfied with the emotions of the heart and with the uniformity of sentiment which springs from the peaceful reign of virtue in the soul. What pagan festivity can be compared to the solemnity on which we commemorate the eucharistic institution?

As soon as the morning star announces the festival of the King of the Universe, all the houses display their gold and silk embroidery, the streets are all covered with flowers, and the bells

[1] De Fontanes, *Le Jour des Morts.* La Harpe pronounced these twenty lines to be as beautiful a specimen of versification as could be found in the French language. We may add that they give a most faithful description of the Christian sacrifice. See note MM.

[2] In some countries, however, it is still customary to introduce the dance in religious ceremonies, as in South America, where the aborigines converted to the faith are remarkable for their innocence. This practice was no doubt borrowed from Spain, where even at the present day the dance is introduced with a beautiful and impressive effect during the benediction of the blessed sacrament. T.

call thousands of the faithful to the temple. The signal is given; all is ready for the procession. The guilds first appear, with the images of their respective patron saints, and sometimes the relics of those holy men who, though born in an obscure condition, are worthy of being revered by kings for their virtue: sublime lesson, which the Christian religion alone has given to the world. After these confraternities appears conspicuously the standard of Jesus Christ, which is no longer a sign of grief, but of general exultation. Then advances at slow pace, in two ranks, a long train of solitaries,—those children of the rivulet and the rock whose antique costume revives the memory of other times and other manners. The monastic orders are followed by the secular clergy; and sometimes prelates, clad in the Roman purple, lengthen the solemn procession. Finally, the pontiff of the festival appears in the distance, bearing in his hands the holy eucharist, which is seen radiant under a magnificent canopy at the end of the train, like the sun which is sometimes seen glittering under a golden cloud at the extremity of an avenue illumined by its splendors.

A number of graceful youths also take their position in the ranks, some holding baskets of flowers, others vases of perfumes. At a given signal, they turn toward the image of the eternal sun, and scatter rose-leaves in handfuls along the way, while Levites in white tunics skilfully swing the censer in presence of the Most High Now thousands of voices are heard along the lines, pouring forth the hymn of praise, and bells and cannon announce that the Lord of the Universe has entered his holy temple. At intervals the sacred melody ceases, and there reigns only a majestic silence, like that of the vast ocean in a moment of calm. The multitude are bowed in adoration before God; nothing is heard but here and there the cautious footsteps of those who are hastening to swell the pious throng.

But whither will they conduct the God of heaven, whose supreme majesty is thus proclaimed by the powers of earth? To a simple repository, fitted up with linen and green boughs; an innocent temple and rural retreat, like that to which he was welcomed in the days of the ancient covenant. The humble of heart, the poor, the children, march foremost; then come judges, warriors, and other powerful ones of the world. The Son of God is borne along between simplicity and grandeur, as at this time of the year, when his festival is celebrated, he displays h mself tc man between the season of flowers and that of thunders.

The windows and walls of the city are thronged with the inhabitants, whose hearts glow with joy and adoration on this solemnity of the God of their country. The child in his mother's arms lifts his hands to the Jesus of the mountain, and the old man bent toward the grave feels himself suddenly delivered from all his anxieties; he receives a new insurance of life which fills his soul with joy in the presence of the living God.

The festivals of Christianity are arranged with an admirable conformity to the scenes of nature. The feast of Corpus Christi occurs at a time when the heavens and earth proclaim the divine power, when the woods and fields are swarming with new generations of beings. A charming bond unites all things in creation; not a single plant is doomed to widowhood. On the other hand, when the leaves begin to fall, the Church recalls the memory of the faithful departed; because man decays like the foliage of the trees.

In the spring, we have a celebration for the rural population The feast of Corpus Christi admits of all the splendor which worldly greatness can confer, while the Rogation days are more particularly suited to our village people. The soul of the husbandman expands with joy under the influence of religion, as the soil which he cultivates is gladdened by the dews of heaven. Happy the man whose toils result in a useful harvest! whose heart is humbly bowed down by virtue, as the stock is bent by the weight of the grain that surmounts it!

CHAPTER VIII.

THE ROGATION DAYS.

The bells of the village church strike up, and he rustics immediately quit their various employments. The vine-dresser descends the hill, the husbandman hastens from the plain, the wood-cutter leaves the forest: the mothers, sallying from their huts, arrive with their children; and the young maidens relinquish their spinning wheels, their sheep, and the fountains, to attend the rural festival.

They assemble in the parish churchyard on the verdant graves of their forefathers. The only ecclesiastic who is to take part in the ceremony soon appears; this is some aged pastor known only by the appellation of the *curé*, and this venerable name, in which his own is lost, designates less the minister of the temple than the laborious father of his flock He comes forth from his solitary house, which stands contiguous to the abode of the dead, over whose ashes he keeps watch. This pastor in his habitation is like an advanced guard on the frontier of life, to receive those who enter and those who depart from this kingdom of wo and grief. A well, some poplars, a vine climbing about his window, and a few pigeons, constitute all the wealth of this king of sacrifices.

The apostle of the gospel, vested simply in a surplice, assembles his flock before the principal entrance of the church, and delivers a discourse, which must certainly be very impressive, to judge from the tears of his audience. He frequently repeats the words, *My children! my dearly-beloved children!* and herein consists the whole secret of the eloquence of this rustic Chrysostom.

The exhortation ended, the assembly begins to move off, singing, "Ye shall go forth with pleasure, and ye shall be received with joy; the hills shall leap, and shall hear you with delight." The standard of the saints, the antique banner of the days of chivalry, opens the procession of the villagers who follow their pastor pêle-mêle They pursue their course through lanes overshadowed with trees and deeply cut by the wheels of the rustic vehicles; they climb over high barriers formed by a single trunk of a tree; they proceed along a hedge of hawthorn, where the bee hums, where the bullfinch and the blackbird whistle. The budding trees display the promise of their fruit; all nature is a nosegay of flowers. The woods, the valleys, the rivers, the rocks, hear, in their turns, the hymns of the husbandmen. Astonished at these resounding canticles, the hosts of the green cornfields start forth, and at a convenient distance stop to witness the passage of this rural pageant.

At length the rustics return to their labor: religion designed not to make the day on which they implore the Almighty to bless the produce of the earth a day of idleness. With what confidence does the ploughman plunge his share into the soil, after addressing his supplications to Him who governs the spheres and who keeps in his treasuries the breezes of the south and the fertilizing showers! To finish well a day so piously begun, the old men of the village repair at night to converse with their pastor, who takes his evening meal under the poplars in his yard. The moon then sheds her last beams on this festival, which the Church has made to correspond with the return of the most pleasant of the months and the course of the most mysterious of the constellations. The people seem to hear the grain taking root in the earth and the plants growing and maturing. Amid the silence of the woods arise unknown voices, as from the choir of rural angels whose succor has been implored; and the plaintive and sweet notes of the nightingale salute the ears of the veterans, who are seated not far from the solitary tombs.

CHAPTER IX.

OF CERTAIN CHRISTIAN FESTIVALS.

Epiphany, Christmas, &c.

THEY whose hearts have never fondly looked back to those days of faith when an act of religion was a family festival, and who despise pleasures which have no recommendation but their innocence,—such persons, it may with truth be said, are much to be pitied. If they would deprive us of these simple amusements, will they at least give us something in their stead? Alas! they have tried to do it. The Convention had its sacred days; famine was then styled *holy*, and *Hosanna* was changed into the cry of *Death forever!* How extraordinary, that men, speaking in the name of equality and of all the passions, should never have been able to establish one festival; while the most obscure saint, who had preached naught but poverty, obedience, and the renunciation of worldly goods, had his feast even at the moment when its observance endangered life Hence we may learn that those festivals alone are durable which are allied to religion and to the memory of benefits. It is not enough to say to men, *Be joyful*, in order to make them rejoice. Days of pleasure are not to be created like days of mourning, nor is it as easy to elicit smiles as to cause tears to flow.

While the statue of Marat usurped the place of St. Vincent de Paul, while people celebrated all those festivals the anniversaries of which are marked in our calendars as days of eternal grief, many a pious family secretly kept a Christian holiday, and religion still mingled a little joy with that deep affliction. Simple hearts cannot recollect without emotion the happy hours when whole families assembled round their cakes, which recalled to mind the presents of the Magi. The infirm grandfather, confined all the rest of the year to his room, made his appearance on this festive occasion as the ruling spirit of the paternal mansion. His grandchildren, who had long anticipated the expected feast, surrounded his knees, and made him young again with their affectionate vivacity. Joy beamed from each face, and every heart swelled with transport; the festive apartment was unusually decorated, and each individual appeared in his best clothes. Amid the shock of glasses and bursts of merriment, the happy company drew lots for those royalties which cost neither sighs nor tears; and sceptres were given and accepted which did not burden the hands of those who bore them. Ofttimes an artifice, which heightened the mirth of the subject and drew complaints from the queen alone, transferred the highest dignities to the daughter of the house, and the son of some neighbor lately arrived from the army The young people blushed, embarrassed as they were with their crowns; the mothers smiled; the fathers made signs to one another, and the grandfather drank his glass to the prosperity of the new queen.

The pastor, who was present at the festival, received the first portion, styled the portion of the poor, to be distributed among them with other gifts. Diversions handed down from days of yore, a ball at which some aged domestic performed the part of first musician, prolonged the pleasures of the festival till late at night, and the whole company, nurses and children, farmers, servants, and masters, joined all together in the sprightly dance.

These scenes were formerly repeated throughout all Christendom, from the palace to the cottage; there was scarcely a labourer but found means to fulfil on that day the wish of the great Henry. And what a succession of happy days! Christmas, New Year's day, and Twelfth-day! At that time the farmers renewed their leases, the tradesman was paid his bills; it was the time of marriages, of presents, of charity, and of visiting; the judge and his client conferred together; the trades-unions, fraternities, courts of justice, universities, corporations, assembled according to the ancient Gallic custom; the infirm and the indigent were relieved. The obligation you were under to receive your neighbor at this season made you live on good terms with him all the rest of the year; and thus peace and union reigned among men.

It cannot be doubted that these religious institutions powerfully contributed to the maintenance of morals, by cherishing cordiality and affection among relations. We are already far from those times when a wife, on the death of her husband, went to her eldest son, and delivered up the keys and all the household accounts to him as the head of the family. We have no longer that high idea of the dignity of man with which Christianity inspired us. Mothers and children choose rather to depend on the articles of a contract than to rely upon the sentiments of nature, and the law is universally made a substitute for morals.

What heightened the charms of these Christian festivals was that they had existed from the remotest antiquity; and we found with pleasure, on going back to the past, that our ancestors had rejoiced at the same season as ourselves. These festivals were very numerous; so that, in spite of the calamities incident to life, religion found means to give, from generation to generation, a few happy moments to millions of the unfortunate.

In the night of the birth of the Messiah, the companies of children paying adoration at the manger, the churches illuminated and decked with flowers, the people thronging around the cradle of their Saviour, the penitents who in some side-chapel were making their peace with Heaven, the joyful alleluias, the tones of the organ and the bells, altogether formed a scene replete with innocence and majesty. Immediately after the last day of our rejoicing, which was too often characterized by folly and excess, came the awful ceremony of ashes, like death the day after pleasure. "O man!" said the priest, "remember that dust thou art, and to dust thou shalt return." The officer who was stationed near the kings of Persia to remind them that they were mortals, or the Roman soldier who checked the pride of the triumphant general, gave not of old more impressive lessons.

But a volume would not suffice to detail the ceremonies of the Holy Week alone. It is well known how magnificent they were in Rome, the capital of the Christian world, and we shall, therefore, not attempt to describe them. We leave to painters and poets the task of fitly representing the ecclesiastics in mourning; the altars and the temples hung with black; the sublime music; the celestial voices chanting the sorrows of Jeremiah; the Passion, so fraught with incomprehensible mystery; the sacred sepulchre surrounded by a dejected people; the sovereign Pontiff washing the feet of the poor; the profound darkness; the silence interrupted by a startling noise; finally, the shout of victory abruptly issuing from the tomb; the triumphant Saviour opening a way to heaven for redeemed souls, and leaving to the faithful Christian a divine religion, together with never-failing hopes!

CHAPTER X.

FUNERALS—FUNERAL OF THE GREAT.

If the reader recollects what we have said in the first part of this work respecting the last sacrament that is administered to the Christian, he will allow that it possesses more genuine beauties than all the ceremonies employed by the ancients on the like occasion. The Christian religion, considering man only in reference to his eternal destiny, bestows a particular attention upon the funeral couch. Her ceremonial is varied according to the rank and character of the deceased.

Thus does she sweeten for every one that bitter but salutary thought of death which she has implanted in our souls, like the dove that prepares the morsel for her young ones.

Is she summoned to the funeral of some of the mighty of the earth? Fear not that it will be deficient in grandeur. The more unfortunate the deceased has been, the greater will be the pomp which she will lavish around his bier and the more eloquent will be her lessons; she alone is able to measure the heights and the depths, to tell the summits from which monarchs fall and the abysses in which they disappear.

When, therefore, the urn of affliction has been opened, and filled with the tears of royalty, when the double vanities of regal dignity and vast misfortunes are contained in a narrow coffin, Religion assembles the faithful. The vaulted roof of the church, the altars, the columns, the images of the saints, are shrouded in sable hangings. In the middle of the nave is raised a coffin surrounded with torches which burn in mystic number. The funeral mass has been performed in the presence of Him who was not born and who will never die. Now all is silent. In the pulpit, absorbed in divine contemplation, stands a priest, who alone is habited in pure white, amid the general mourning,—his forehead bald, his countenance pale, his eyes closed, and his hands crossed upon his breast. All at once he opens his eyes, he extends his arms, and these words issue from his lips:—

"He who reigns in the heavens, to whom all the nations of the earth are subject, and to whom alone belong glory, majesty, and eternal power, is also the only being who can prescribe laws to kings, and give them, whenever he pleases, the most solemn and instructive lessons. Whether he raises thrones or overturns them, whether he imparts his power to princes or withdraws it and leaves them nothing but their own weakness, he teaches them their duties in a manner truly sovereign, in a manner worthy of himself.

"Ye Christians, whom the memory of a great queen—daughter, wife, and mother, to mighty monarchs—summons together to this mournful ceremony, this address will exhibit to you one of those awful examples which show to the world the full measure of its vanity. You will see in a single life the extreme vicissitudes of human affairs; the heights of felicity, as well as the depth of wretchedness; a long and painful enjoyment of one or the most brilliant crowns of the universe. All the splendors of birth and dignity heaped upon a head afterward exposed to all the storms of fortune; a rebellion, long repressed, and finally triumphant—no curb to licentiousness—laws abolished—regal majesty violated by proceedings heretofore unknown—a throne basely overturned,—such are the instructions which the Almighty gives to kings"[1]

Recollections of an extraordinary age, of an unfortunate princess, and of a memorable revolution, how affecting and sublime do you become, when thus transmitted by religion from generation to generation!

CHAPTER XI.

FUNERAL OF THE SOLDIER, THE RICH, ETC.

What a noble simplicity once presided at the obsequies of the Christian warrior! Before religion was yet entirely banished from among us, we loved to see a chaplain in an open tent performing the burial service upon an altar composed of drums. It was an interesting sight to behold the God of armies in all his power descending at the invocation of his servant upon the tents of a French camp, while veterans, who had so often braved death, fell on their knees before a coffin, a little altar, and a minister of peace. Amid the rolling of muffled drums, amid the interrupted salutes of cannon, grenadiers bore the body of their valiant leader to the grave which they had dug with their bayonets. After these obsequies they had no races for tripods, for goblets, or lions' skins, but they burned with impatience to seek, in the battle, a more glorious field and funeral

[1] This is the beginning of the most sublime and impressive of all funeral sermons, preached by the great Bossuet on the death of Henrietta Maria, widow of Charles I. See chapter iv. part ii. book iv. The reader may observe how closely applicable the whole quotation is to one of the most engaging and most injured of her sex, Marie Antoinette, Queen of France.

games more worthy of their captain; and if they did not sacrifice a black heifer, as was the pagan custom, to the manes of the hero, they at least spilled in his honor less sterile blood—that of the enemies of their country.

Let us now turn to the consideration of those funerals which take place in our cities by the light of torches; of those illuminated chapels; of that long line of carriages hung with black; of those horses decked with nodding plumes and sable drapery; of the profound silence interrupted by the words of that solemn hymn, the *Dies iræ*. Religion conducted to the funeral procession of the great, poor orphans who were clad in their own livery of misfortune; and, by so doing, she taught children who had no parents to feel something of filial piety; she instructed the rich that no mediation is more powerful with God than that of innocence and adversity; finally, she showed to those in extreme indigence the vanity of all that grandeur which is swallowed up in the tomb.

A particular custom was practised at the decease of priests; they were interred with their faces uncovered. The people imagined that they could read in the face of their pastor the decree of the Supreme Judge, and discover through the veil of death the joys that awaited him,—as through the shades of a serene night we perceive the glories of a glistening firmament.

The same custom was observed also in convents. We once saw a young nun thus lying on her bier. Her pallid brow could scarcely be distinguished from the white fillet with which it was half covered; a wreath of white roses was upon her head, and in her hand burned a mysterious taper. After lying some hours in this state, the coffin was again covered and consigned to the grave. Thus youthful graces and peace of heart cannot save from death; and the lily fades, notwithstanding its virgin whiteness and the tranquillity of the valleys which it inhabits.

For him who supported, as for him who defended his country, was reserved the simplicity of funeral obsequies. Four peasants, preceded by the parish-priest, carried the husbandman on their robust shoulders to the tomb of his fathers. If any laborers met the convoy on the road, they interrupted their work, uncovered their heads, and by a sign of the cross showed their respect for their deceased companion. From a distance the departed husbandman was seen carried along among the yellow sheaves which he himself perhaps had cultivated. The coffin, enveloped in black, seemed to swing like a sombre poppy above the golden harvest and the blue and purple flowers. A disconsolate widow and weeping children led the train of pious and real mourners. In passing the cross by the side of the road, or the saint of the rock, the bearers rested for a moment; setting the coffin on some boundary-stone, they invoked Our Lady of the Fields, at whose feet the deceased had so often prayed for a happy death or an abundant harvest. Here he had often sought for his oxen a protecting shade from the noontide heat; and here, surrounded by his family, he had taken his repast of milk and rye-bread amid the chirping of grasshoppers and the warbling of larks. Ah! how different is his repose there now from what it was in former days! The soil will no longer be watered by the sweat of his brow, nor will his paternal heart be again agitated by anxiety; and by the same path along which he repaired to the church he now goes to the grave, surrounded by the most pleasing monuments of his life—virtuous children and flourishing harvests.

CHAPTER XII.

OF THE FUNERAL SERVICE.

Among the ancients the remains of the indigent and the slave were forsaken almost without ceremony; among us the minister of the altar is bound to bestow the same attendance on the corpse of the peasant as on that of the monarch. No sooner has the meanest of Christians expired than he suddenly becomes (sublime truth!) an august and sacred being; scarcely has the beggar, covered with rags, who languished at our gate, an object of scorn and disgust, quitted this troublesome life, than Religion obliges us to bow before his remains. She forcibly impresses upon our minds the conviction of an awful equality, or rather she commands us to respect a sinner redeemed by the blood of Christ who has passed from a state of obscurity and indigence to a celestial crown. Thus, the great name of Christian places all mankind upon a level in death, and the pride of the mightiest of potentates cannot extort from religion any other prayer than what she voluntarily offers for the lowest of peasants.

And how admirable is that prayer!

Sometimes it is a cry of grief; at others it is an exclamation of hope; we hear alternately the wailing and the rejoicing of death, its tremors, its revivals, its moans, and supplications:—

"His spirit shall go forth, and he shall return into his earth: in that day all their thoughts shall perish."[1]

"The sins of my youth, and my ignorances, do not remember."[2]

The lamentations of the Royal Prophet are interrupted by the sighs of the holy Arabian:—

"Spare me, for my days are nothing. What is man, that thou shouldst magnify him? or why dost thou set thy heart upon him? . . . . if thou seek me in the morning, I shall not be.

"My soul is weary of my life. . . . . I will speak in the bitterness of my soul. . . . . Are thy days as the days of man, and are thy years as the times of men?[3]

"Why hidest thou thy face, and thinkest me thy enemy? Against a leaf that is carried away with the wind thou showest thy power; and thou pursuest a dry straw.

"Man born of a woman, living for a short time, is filled with many miseries; who . . . . fleeth as a shadow, and never continueth in the same state.[4]

"My days have passed away, my thoughts are dissipated, tormenting my heart. . . . . I have said to rottenness, Thou art my father; to worms, my mother and my sister."[5]

At intervals the prayer assumes the form of dialogue between the priest and the choir:—

Priest. "My days are vanished like smoke; and my bones are grown dry like fuel for the fire.

Choir. "My days are vanished like smoke.

Priest. "What is your life? It is a vapor which appeareth for a little while

---

[1] Office of the Dead, Vesp., Ps. cxlv. [2] Ibid., 2 Ant. 2 Noct

[3] Ibid., Less. 1, Noct., from Job vii. 10. [4] Ibid., Less. 2, Noct., Job xiii. xiv

[5] Ibid., Less. 3, Noct., Job xvii.

Choir. "My days are vanished like smoke.[1]

Priest. "Those that sleep in the dust of the earth.

Choir. "Shall awake, some unto life everlasting, and others unto reproach, to see it always.

Priest. "We shall all indeed rise again, but we shall not all be changed

Choir. "They shall awake," &c.[2]

At the communion of the mass, the celebrant says, "Blessed are the dead who die in the Lord. From henceforth now, saith the Spirit, that they may rest from their labors: for their works follow them."[3]

In removing the coffin from the house, the priest entones that psalm of grief and of hope, "From the depths I have cried to thee, O Lord; Lord, hear my voice" While the body is carried forth, the dialogue already mentioned above is repeated; and if the deceased is a priest, the following words are added:—"A sacrifice of jubilation has been offered in the tabernacle of the Lord."

In lowering the coffin into the grave, the priest says, "Earth to earth, ashes to ashes, dust to dust;" and in throwing some earth over it, he exclaims, "I heard a voice from heaven, saying to me, Blessed are the dead who die in the Lord."

But these beautiful prayers are not the only ones offered up by the Church for her deceased children. If she decorates the bier on which the infant reposes with white hangings and coronets of flowers, she also adapts her prayers to the age and sex of the victim that death has seized upon. When four virgins, dressed in white and adorned with green foliage, bring the remains of one of their companions into the church, which is similarly decorated, the priest entones over this youthful corpse a hymn in honor of virginity. Sometimes it is the *Ave, maris stella,*—a chant that is characterized by great beauty of sentiment and that pictures the moment of death as the fulfilment of hope. On other occasions, some tender and poetical ideas are borrowed from the Holy Scripture:—"She hath passed away like the grass of the field: this morning we beheld her in all her graceful

---

[1] First Responsor. in Matins of the Dead, according to the Parisian rite, from Ps. ci. and James iv. The extracts which follow are also from the Parisian rite. T.

[2] Seventh Responsor from Daniel xii and 1 Cor. xv

[3] Apoc xiv.

bloom; this evening her charms are withered. Has not the flower drooped after having been touched by the ploughshare? has not the poppy bent its head under the peltings of the rain?"

When the mother in tears presents herself at the church with the corpse of her infant child, what funeral oration does the pastor pronounce over it? He simply entones the hymn which was sung by the three Hebrew children in the fiery furnace:—

Benedicite, omnia opera Domini! . . . . "All ye works of the Lord, bless the Lord: praise and exalt him above all forever!" . . . . Religion blesses God for having crowned the infant by death, and delivered this little innocent creature from all the miseries of life. It invites nature to rejoice around the tomb of angelic innocence: it expresses not cries of grief, but of joy. In the same spirit of exultation does it recite *Laudate, pueri, Dominum!* . . . . "Praise the Lord, ye children!" . . . . and finishes with this verse, *Qui facit habitare sterilem in domo: matrem filiorum lætantem:*—"Who maketh a barren woman to dwell in a house, the joyful mother of children." What a sublime canticle of consolation for afflicted parents! The Church represents their departed child living eternally in heaven, and promises them more children on earth!

Finally, not satisfied with having fulfilled these duties in behalf of each individual, Religion crowns her pious work in honor of the dead by a general ceremonial, which recalls the memory of the innumerable inhabitants of the grave,—that vast community of departed mortals where rich and poor lie together,—that republic of perfect equality where no one can enter without first doffing his helmet or crown to pass under the low door of the tomb. On this solemn occasion, when the obsequies of the entire family of Adam are celebrated, the Christian soul mingles her grief caused by the loss of former friends with the sorrows excited by more recent bereavements; and this union imparts something supremely beautiful to affliction, as a modern grief would acquire an antique character by being expressed in the vein of the old Homeric tragedy. Religion alone can give to the heart of man that expansion, which will render its sighs and its loves commensurate with the multitude of the dead whom it designs to honor.[1]

[1] See note NN.

BOOK II.

TOMBS.

CHAPTER I.

ANCIENT TOMBS—THE EGYPTIANS.

The last duties that we pay to our fellow-creatures would be melancholy indeed, if they were not impressed with the stamp of religion. Religion received birth at the tomb, and the tomb cannot dispense with religion. It is beautiful to hear the voice of hope issuing from the grave, and to see the priest of the living God following the remains of man to their last abode. We behold here, as it were, immortality leading the way before death.

From funerals we proceed to the consideration of tombs, which occupy so large a space in our history. That we may the better appreciate the ceremonies with which they are honored by Christians, let us see what was their state among the idolatrous nations.

Egypt owes part of its celebrity to its tombs, and has been twice visited by the French, who were drawn thither by the beauty of its ruins and monuments. The French nation have a certain innate greatness which compels them to interest themselves in every corner of the globe with objects great like themselves. Is it, however, absolutely certain, that mummies are objects truly worthy of our curiosity? It might be supposed that the ancient Egyptians were apprehensive lest posterity should some day be ignorant what death was, and were therefore desirous of transmitting to distant ages some specimens of corpses. In Egypt you can scarcely move a step without meeting with emblems of mortality. Do you behold an obelisk, a broken column, a subterraneous cavern? they are so many monuments of death: and when the moon, rising behind the great pyramid, appears above the summit of that immense sepulchre, you fancy that you behold the very pharos of death, and are actually wandering on the shore to which of old the ferryman of hell transported the shades.

CHAPTER II.

THE GREEKS AND ROMANS.

Among the Greeks and Romans, the lower classes of the people were interred at the entrance of cities, along the public road, apparently because tombs are the real monuments of the traveller. The distinguished dead were often buried on the sea-coast. These funeral signals, which from afar indicated the shore and the rocks to the mariner, must have suggested to him very serious reflections. How much more secure did he feel on the ocean than on that land which had ruined such vast fortunes and swallowed up so many illustrious lives! Near the city of Alexandria was seen the hillock of sand, erected by the piety of a freedman and an old soldier to the manes of Pompey. Not far from the ruins of Carthage was descried Cato's statue on a rock. On the Italian coast the mausoleum of Scipio indicated the spot where this great man expired in exile, and the tomb of Cicero marked the place where the father of his country had been basely assassinated.

While Rome erected on the sea-coast these memorials of her injustice, Greece offered some consolation to humanity by perpetuating, on a neighboring shore, more pleasing recollections. The disciples of Plato and Pythagoras, in their voyage to Egypt, whither they repaired to acquire knowledge respecting the gods, passed within sight of Homer's tomb, on the island of Io.[1] It was a happy idea that placed the monument of the bard who

---

[1] Homer was buried at *Chios*.

celebrated the exploits of Achilles under the protection of Thetis. Ingenious antiquity could imagine that the shade of the poet still recited the misfortunes of Ilium to the assembled Nereids, as in the soft and genial nights of Ionia he had disputed with the syrens the prize of song.

CHAPTER III.

MODERN TOMBS—CHINA AND TURKEY.

THE Chinese have an affecting custom: they inter their relatives in their gardens It is soothing to hear in every grove the voices of the shades of our forefathers, and to have always some memorials of the friends who are gone, in the midst of the desert.

At the opposite extremity of Asia, the Turks have nearly the same custom. The strait of the Dardanelles affords a highly philosophical spectacle. On the one hand rise the promontories of Europe with all its ruins; on the other wind the coasts of Asia bordered with Mohammedan cemeteries. What different manners have animated these shores! How many nations have there been buried, from the days when the lyre of Orpheus first assembled the savages who inhabited them till the period which again consigned these celebrated regions to barbarism! Pelasgi, Helenes, Greeks, Mæonians; people of Ilus, of Sarpedon, of Æneas; inhabitants of Ida, of Tmolus, of the Meander and Pactolus; subjects of Mithridates, slaves of the Cæsars, Vandals, hordes of Goths, of Huns, of Franks, of Arabs,—ye have all performed on these shores the ceremonies of the tomb, and in this alone have your manners had any resemblance. Death, sporting with human things and human destinies, has lent the mausoleum of a Roman emperor to the ignoble remains of a Tartar, and has deposited the ashes of a Mollah in the sepulchre of a Plato

CHAPTER IV.

CALEDONIA, OR ANCIENT SCOTLAND.

Four moss-covered stones on the moors of Caledonia mark the burial-place of the warriors of Fingal. Oscar and Malvina are gone; but nothing is changed in their solitary country. The Highlander still delights to repeat the song of his ancestors; he is still brave, tender, and generous; his modern habits are like the pleasing recollection of his ancient manners. 'Tis no longer, (if we may be allowed the image,)—'tis no longer the hand of the bard himself that sweeps the harp; the tones we hear are the slight trembling of the strings produced by the touch of a spirit, when announcing at night, in a lonely chamber, the death of a hero.

"Carril accompanied his voice. The music was like the memory of joys that are past, pleasant and mournful to the soul. The ghosts of departed bards heard it from Slimora's side; soft sounds spread along the woods, and the valleys of night rejoice. So, when he sits in the silence of noon in the valley of his breezes, is the murmur of the mountain to Ossian's ear. The gale drowns it often in its course; but the pleasant sound returns again."

CHAPTER V.

OTAHEITE.

Man here below is like the blind Ossian seated on the tombs of the kings of Morven; wherever he stretches out his hand into the shades that surround him he touches the ashes of his fathers. When intrepid mariners first ploughed the vast Pacific, they beheld waves eternally caressed by balmy breezes rolling at a distance. Unknown islands were soon seen rising from the bosom of the deep. Groves of palms, intermixed with large trees resembling magnified fern, covered the coasts and descended in the form of an amphitheatre to the beach, the blue tops of the mountains majestically crowned those forests These islands, belted with coral, seemed to move like fair ships riding at anchor on the tranquil waters of a sheltered port. A poet of ancient Greece would have said that Venus had thrown her cestus around these new Cytheras to protect them from storms.

Amid these unknown shades, Nature had placed a people beautiful as the country which gave them birth. The Otaheitans wore no other garment than a cloth made of the bark of the fig-tree They dwelt in huts embosomed in the foliage of the mulberry, supported by pillars of odoriferous woods, and skimmed the waves in double canoes having sails woven with rushes and streamers of flowers and feathers: they had dances and assemblies devoted to pleasure; and the songs and dramas of love were not unknown on these shores. Here all things breathed voluptuousness, days of tranquillity, and nights of silence. To recline beside the murmuring stream, to gaze with eyes of indolence upon its current, to wander about mantled in foliage, and, as it were, clad in breezes and perfumes,—such was the whole life of the savages of Otaheite. The toils in which other men pass their tedious days were unknown to these islanders; while roaming through their woods, they found, as did the birds close to their nests, milk and bread suspended from the branches of the trees

Such was the appearance of Otaheite to Wallis, Cook, and Bougainville. On a nearer approach to its coast, they distinguished some monuments of art, intermixed with those of nature. These were the props of the *morais*.[1] Oh the vanity of human pleasures! The first banner descried on these enchanted shores is that of death, which waves over all human enjoyments.

---

[1] *Morai* is a family tomb among the Otaheitans, who place their cemeteries in romantic situations, amid the shade of trees, the frowning faces of rocks and the murmurs of streams. T.

Let it not, then, be imagined that a country where at the first glance we discover nothing but a life of unbounded licentiousness, is a stranger to those graver sentiments so necessary for all mankind. The Otaheitans, like other nations, have religious rites and funeral ceremonies; they have, in particular, attached a high idea of mystery to death. When a corpse is conveyed to the *moraï*, every one gets out of the way as it passes; the conductor of the ceremony then whispers a few words in the ear of the deceased. On reaching the burial-place, the corpse is not interred in the earth, but slung in a cradle covered with a canoe turned upside-down—an emblem of the shipwreck of life. Sometimes a female repairs to the *moraï* to vent her griefs; she sits down, with her feet in the sea, her head low bowed, and her dishevelled hair falling over her face. The waves accompany her lamentations, and they are borne aloft to the Omnipotent, mingled with the murmurs of the boundless Pacific.

CHAPTER VI.

CHRISTIAN TOMBS.

In speaking of the Christian sepulchre our tone is raised, our voice acquires greater firmness. We feel that this tomb alone is truly worthy of man. The monument of the idolater tells you of nothing but the past; that of the Christian speaks only of the future. Christianity has, in every thing, done the best that it was possible to do, and has never suggested those demi-conceptions so frequent in other religions. Thus, with respect to burial-places, setting aside all ideas which spring from local and other circumstances, it has distinguished itself from other religions by a sublime custom. It has committed the ashes of the faithful to the protection of the temples of the Lord, and deposited the dead in the bosom of the living God.

Lycurgus was not afraid to place the tombs in the midst of Lacedæmon. He thought, in accordance with our holy religion, that the ashes of the fathers, instead of shortening the days of the children, actually tend to prolong their lives by teaching them moderation and virtue, which are the surest conductors to a happy old age. The human reasons which have been advanced in opposition to these divine reasons are by no means convincing Can the French boast of greater longevity than the natives of other European countries, who still continue to bury in their towns?

When formerly among us the tombs were separated from the churches, the common people, who are not so prudent as scholars and wits, and have not the same reasons to fear the end of life, universally opposed the dereliction of the antique burial-places. And what had the modern cemeteries that could be compared with those of antiquity? Where was their ivy?—where their aged yew-trees—their turf enriched for so many ages with the spoils of the tomb? Could they show the sacred bones of ancestors, the chapel, the house of the spiritual physician, and all the appurtenances of religion which promised, nay, insured, a speedy resurrection? Instead of those frequented cemeteries we had a solitary enclosure, forsaken by the living, and barren of recollections, in some suburb where death, stripped of every sign of hope, could not but seem eternal.

When the foundations of the edifice are thus invaded, kingdoms must fall into ruins. It were well, too, if nothing more had been done than to change the place of interment; but, by a further blow dealt at the existing state of things, the very ashes of our fathers were disturbed, and their remains were carried off like the filth and dirt of our cities, which are removed by the cartman.

It was reserved for our age to witness what was considered as the greatest of calamities among the ancients and was the severest punishment inflicted on criminals,—we mean the dispersion of their ashes,—to hear this dispersion applauded as the masterpiece of philosophy.[1] And what then was the crime of our

[1] The ancients would have considered that state as overthrown in which the asylum of the dead was violated Every reader is acquainted with the excellent laws of Egypt relative to burial-places The laws of Solon interdicted the violator of the tomb from the worship of the temple, and consigned him to the Furies. Justinian's *Institutes* regulate even the bequest, inheritance, sale, and purchase of a sepulchre

ancestors, that their remains should be treated with such indignity, except their having given life to such degenerate children as we? But observe the end of all this. Mark the atrocity of human wisdom. In some of the towns of France dungeons were erected on the site of the churchyards. Prisons for human beings were raised on the spot where God had decreed an end to all slavery. Places of torment succeeded those abodes where all afflictions were wont to cease. In short, but one point of resemblance—and that indeed an awful one—remained between these prisons and those cemeteries; namely, that the iniquitous judgments of men were executed where God had pronounced the decrees of his inviolable justice.[1]

CHAPTER VII.

COUNTRY CHURCHYARDS.

THE ancients had no more agreeable burial-places than were our country churchyards. Meadows, fields, streams, woods, with a smiling prospect, lent their charms to heighten the impressive aspect of a rural cemetery. We loved there to behold the ancient yew, the fruit-trees, the high grass, the poplars, the elm of the

---

[1] We pass over in silence the abominations perpetrated during the days of the Revolution. There is not a domestic animal in any nation, ever so little civilized, but is buried with more decency than the body of a French citizen was at that time. It is well known how funerals were then conducted, and how, for a few pence, a father, a mother, or a wife, was consigned to the highways. Even there the dead were not secure; for persons made a trade of stealing the shroud, the coffin, or the hair, of the deceased. All these things can be ascribed only to a decree of God himself. They were a consequence of the first offences during the monarchy. It were much to be wished that the signs of religion, of which funerals have been deprived, could be restored to them; and, above all, that dogs be no longer posted to guard the cemeteries. Such is the extreme of misery into which man sinks when he loses sight of God that, no longer venturing to confide in his fellow-creatures, in whose fidelity he has no confidence, he is reduced to the necessity of committing his remains to the protection of brutes!

dead, the box, and the little cross of consolation and of grace. Amid the peaceful tombstones and monuments rose the tower of the village temple surmounted by the rustic emblem of vigilance. No sound was heard on this spot save the simple notes of the redbreast and the noise of the sheep cropping the grass upon the grave of their former shepherd.

The different paths which crossed the consecrated enclosure led to the church or the habitation of the pastor. They were all worn by the poor and the pilgrim, who repaired thither to pray to the God of mercy or to solicit the bread of charity from the minister of the gospel. The rich and the thoughtless never passed near these tombs.

The only epitaph to be seen upon them was the name of the deceased, with the year of his birth and that in which he died. Upon some there was not so much as the name The Christian laborer lies forgotten in death, like the useful productions of the earth among which he passed his life. Nature has not engraven the names of the oaks on their trunks that lie prostrate in the forests.

One day, however, in strolling through a country churchyard, we perceived a Latin epitaph on a small stone which marked the grave of a child. Surprised at this unusual display, we went up to it, curious to learn the erudition of the village pastor, and read these words of the gospel, *Suffer the little children to come unto me.*

The cemeteries of Switzerland are sometimes placed on rocks overlooking lakes, precipices, and valleys [1] The chamois and the eagle here fix their abode, and death grows upon these craggy steeps like those Alpine plants the roots of which are fixed in everlasting ice. After death, the peasant of Glaris or St. Gall is conveyed to one of these lofty burial-places by his pastor. No funeral pomp attends him on these ridges of the Alps but the pomp of nature, and no music but those patriotic and pastoral tones which remind the exiled Swiss of his father, his mother, his sisters, and the bleating of the flocks of his native mountain.

Italy presents her catacombs, or the humble monument of a

---

[1] See note OO.

martyr in the gardens of Mæcenas and Lucullus. England has her dead dressed in woollen, and her graves adorned with sweet-brier and flowers. In her churchyards the tears started in our eyes on meeting sometimes with a French name among English epitaphs. But it is time to return to the tombs of our native land.

CHAPTER VIII.

TOMBS IN CHURCHES.

FIGURE to yourself for a moment the ancient monasteries or the Gothic cathedrals, such as they formerly existed in France. Traverse the aisles, the chapels, the dimly-lighted naves, the cloisters and sanctuaries filled with sepulchres. In this labyrinth of tombs which are they that strike you most? Are they monuments of modern construction, loaded with allegorical figures which crush beneath their icy marbles relics less cold than themselves? Vain phantoms, which seem to partake of the double lethargy of the coffin which they enclose, and of the worldly hearts that erected them! On these you scarcely deign to bestow a look; but you pause before that tomb, covered with venerable dust, on which reclines the Gothic figure of some mitred bishop, dressed in his pontifical robes, his hands folded and his eyes shut. You pause before that monument where an abbot, supported on one elbow, and his head resting on his hand, seems absorbed in meditation. The slumber of the prelate and the attitude of the priest have something mysterious. The former appears deeply engaged with what he sees in his dreams of the tomb. The latter, like a traveller, has not even chosen to lie down entirely; so near at hand is the moment when he shall rise again.

And what lady of distinction is it that reposes by the side of her husband? Both are vested in the garb of Gothic magnificence. A cushion supports their heads, which seem to be rendered so heavy by the sleep of death as to press down this pillow of stone. Happy that husband and wife if they had no painful secret to communicate to each other in meeting on the sepulchral couch! Observe at the extremity of that retired chapel the figures of four esquires in marble, cased in mail, armed at all points, with their hands joined, and kneeling at the four corners of the altar-monument. Is it thine, Bayard, who restoredst to the captive maidens the ransom which would enable them to marry the beloved of their hearts? Is it thou, Beaumanoir, who drankest thine own blood in the combat of the Thirty? or is it some other knight that here enjoys the slumbers of the tomb? These esquires seem to pray with fervor; for those gallant chieftains, the honor of the French name, feared God in the secret of their hearts; it was with the shout of Mountjoy and St. Dennis that they rescued France from the English, and performed prodigies of valor for the Church, their lady-love, and their king. Is there nothing, then, worthy of admiration in the times of a Roland, a Godfrey, a Coucy, and a Joinville?—in the times of the Moors and the Saracens?—of the kingdoms of Jerusalem and Cyprus?—in the times when the East and Asia exchanged arms and manners with Europe and the West?—in the times when a Thibaud sang, when the strains of the Troubadours were mingled with the clash of arms, dances with religious ceremonies, and banquets and tournaments with sieges and battles?[1]

[1] The French, we acknowledge, are under great obligations to the artist who collected the fragments of our ancient sepulchres, but, as to the effects produced by the sight of these monuments, it is impossible not to feel that they have been destroyed. Crowded into a narrow space, divided according to centuries, torn from their connection with the antiquity of the temples and of the Christian worship, subservient only to the history of the arts, and not to that of morals and religion, not retaining so much as their dust, they have ceased to speak either to the imagination or the heart When impious miscreants conceived the idea of thus violating the asylum of the dead and dispersing their ashes in order to destroy the memory of the past, the project, horrible as it was, might have seemed, in the eyes of human folly, to possess a certain specious grandeur, but it was tantamount to a conspiracy to overturn the world, not to leave in France one stone upon another, and to advance over the ruins of religion to the attack of all other institutions. To plunge into such excesses merely to strike out of the beaten track and to make a display of folly and absurdity is to be actuated by all the madness of guilt without having its power. What became of these despoilers of the tombs? They fell into the pits which themselves had dug, and their bodies were left with Death as pledges for those of which they had plundered him.

Those times were worthy of admiration; but they are past. How forcibly did religion teach the noble sons of chivalry the vanity of human things, when, after a long enumeration of pompous titles, as, *High and mighty Lord, Messire Anne de Montmorency*, or *Constable of France*, she added, "Pray for him, poor sinners." Here is nothingness itself.[1]

As to subterraneous burial-places, they were generally reserved for monarchs, and for those who belonged to religious orders. When you wished to indulge in serious and religious contemplations, you had only to descend into the vaults of a convent, and survey those recluses locked in the sleep of death, who were not more tranquil in their sepulchral abodes than they had been in their lifetime. Sweet be your slumbers beneath these vaults, ye peaceful mortals, who divided your earthly patrimony among your brethren, and, like the Grecian hero setting out for the conquest of another universe, reserved for yourselves nothing more than hope![2]

CHAPTER IX.

ST. DENNIS.

Sepulchres were formerly to be seen near Paris, famous among all the sepulchres of men. Strangers thronged to behold the wonders of St. Dennis. There they imbibed a profound veneration for France, and returned home, saying to themselves, with St. Gregory, "This is really the greatest kingdom on earth." But the tempest of wrath surrounded the edifice of death; the billows of popular fury burst over it, and men yet ask one an-

[1] Johnson, in his Treatise on Epitaphs, pronounces this simple appeal of religion sublime.

[2] The anecdote here most beautifully alluded to is recorded of Alexander the Great.

other, with astonishment, *How hath the temple of* AMMON *disappeared among the sands of the desert?*

The Gothic abbey in which these great vassals of death were assembled was not deficient in glory. The treasures of France were at its gates; the Seine bounded the plain in which it was situated; a hundred celebrated places filled all the country around with illustrious names and every field with brilliant recollections; not far off was seated the city of Henry IV. and Louis the Great; and the royal sepulchre of St. Dennis stood in the centre of our power and our luxury, like a vast shrine, in which were deposited the relics of time and the superabundant greatness of the French empire.

Here the sovereigns of France were successively entombed. One of them (it was always the last that had descended into the abyss) remained upon the steps, as if to invite his posterity to follow. In vain, however, did Louis XVI. wait for his two last descendants One was precipitated into the vault, leaving his ancestor upon the threshold; the other, like Œdipus, disappeared in a storm Oh, subject worthy of everlasting meditation! the first monarch on whom the emissaries of divine justice laid their hands was that Louis so renowned for the obedience paid to him by the nations! He was yet perfectly entire in his coffin. In vain he seemed to rise in defence of his throne with all the majesty of his age and a rear-guard of eight centuries of kings; in vain did his menacing attitude appal the enemies of the dead when, thrown into one common grave, he fell upon the bosom of Mary de Medicis · All was destroyed God in his wrath had sworn by himself to chastise France. Let us not seek upon earth the causes of such events; they are of higher origin.

As early as the time of Bossuet there was scarcely room in this receptacle of *annihilated princes* for the remains of Henrietta Maria,—"so thronged is every part," exclaims the most eloquent of preachers,—"so expeditious is death in filling these places!" In the presence of so many ages, the rolling of which seems yet to be heard in those solemn depths, the mind is overwhelmed with a torrent of thoughts. The whole soul shudders in contemplating so much nothingness blended with so much grandeur. When, on the one hand, you look for an expression magnificent enough to describe whatever is most elevated, on the other you must find the lowest of terms to express whatever is most vile. Here the shadow of the ancient arches mingles with the gloom of the ancient tombs; there you see iron gratings that vainly surround these precincts of death to protect them from the fury of men. Listen to the dull sound of the sepulchral worm that seems to be weaving in these coffins the indestructible network of death! Every thing proclaims that you have descended into the empire of ruins; and, from a certain smell of ancientness diffused under these funeral arches, you would imagine that you were breathing the dust of bygone ages.

Christian reader, excuse the tears that flow from our eyes while surveying this family of Clovis and St. Louis. If, suddenly throwing aside the winding-sheets which cover them, these monarchs were to rise erect in their coffins, and to fix upon us their ghastly eyes, by the dim light of this sepulchral lamp! . . . . . Yes, we behold them half-raised,—these spectres of kings; we distinguish their dynasties, we recognise each individual, we venture to interrogate these majesties of the tomb. Say, then, royal race of phantoms, say, would you now wish to return to life for the sake of a crown? Are you still tempted by the prospect of a throne? . . . . . But wherefore this profound silence? Wherefore are you all mute beneath these vaults? Ye shake your royal heads, whence falls a cloud of dust; your eyes once more close, and ye again lie slowly down in your coffins!

Ah! had we put the same question to the rustic dead whose ashes we lately visited, gently bursting the turf which covers their graves, and issuing from the bosom of the earth like brilliant meteors, they would have replied, "If God so willed it, why should we refuse to live again? Why should we not once more enjoy happy days in our humble cots? Our toils were not so oppressive as you suppose; our tears were not without their pleasures when dried by an affectionate wife or blessed by a holy religion."

But whither are we hurried by descriptions of those tombs

long since swept from the face of the earth! Those renowned sepulchres are no more. Little children have played with the bones of mighty monarchs. St Dennis is laid waste; the bird has made it her resting-place, the grass grows on its shattered altars; and, instead of the eternal hymn of death which resounded beneath its domes, naught is now to be heard save the pattering of the rain that enters at the roofless top, the fall of some stone dislodged from the ruined walls, or the sound of the clock which still runs its wonted course among empty tombs and plundered sepulchres.[1]

---

[1] See note PP.

BOOK III.

GENERAL VIEW OF THE CLERGY.

CHAPTER I.

OF JESUS CHRIST AND HIS LIFE.

ABOUT the time of the appearance of the Redeemer of mankind upon earth, the nations were in expectation of some extraordinary personage. "An ancient and constant opinion," says Suetonius, "was current all over the East, that persons coming from Judea should obtain universal empire."[1] Tacitus relates the same fact nearly in the same words. According to this great historian, "most of the Jews were convinced, agreeably to a prediction preserved in the ancient books of their priests, that about this time (the time of Vespasian) the East would prevail, and that some native of Judea should obtain the empire of the world."[2] Lastly, Josephus, speaking of the destruction of Jerusalem, informs us that the Jews were chiefly instigated to revolt against the Romans by an obscure[3] prophecy, which foretold that about this period "a man would arise among them and subdue the universe."[4] The New Testament also exhibits traces of this hope shed abroad in Israel. The multitudes who thronged to the desert asked John the Baptist whether he was the great Messiah, the Christ of God, so long expected; and the disciples

---

[1] *Percrebuerat Oriente toto vetus et constans opinio esse in fatis ut eo tempore Judæâ profecti rerum potirentur.* Suet., in *Vespas.*

[2] *Pluribus persuasio inerat antiquis sacerdotum litteris contineri, eo ipso tempore fore ut valesceret Oriens, profectique Judæâ rerum potirentur.* Tacit., *Hist.*, lib. v.

[3] Αμφιβολος, *applicable to several persons,* and therefore referred by the Latin historians to Vespasian.

[4] Joseph., *de Bell. Jud.*

of Emmaus were disappointed to find that their Master was not he "that should have redeemed Israel."[1] The seventy weeks of Daniel, or the four hundred and ninety years from the rebuilding of the temple, were then accomplished. Finally, Origen, after repeating all these traditions of the Jews, adds that "a great number of them acknowledged Jesus Christ as the deliverer promised by the prophets."[2]

Heaven meanwhile prepares the way for the Son of man. States long disunited in manners, government, and language, entertained hereditary enmities; but the clamor of arms suddenly ceases, and the nations, either allied or vanquished, become identified with the people of Rome.

On the one hand, religion and morals have reached that degree of corruption which of necessity produces changes; on the other, the tenets of the unity of God and the immortality of the soul begin to be diffused. Thus the ways are prepared on all sides for the new doctrine which a universal language will serve to propagate. The vast Roman empire is composed of nations, some barbarous, others civilized, but all excessively miserable. For the former, the simplicity of Christ,—for the latter, his moral virtues,—for all, mercy and charity,—are means of salvation contrived by heaven itself. So efficacious are these means, that, only two centuries after the advent of the Messiah, Tertullian thus addressed the judges of Rome:—"We are but of yesterday, and yet we fill every place—your cities, your islands, your fortresses, your camps, your colonies, your tribes, your decuries, your councils, the palace, the senate, the forum; we leave you nothing but your temples"[3]

With the grandeur of natural preparations is combined the splendor of miracles; the oracles of truth which had been long silent in Jerusalem recover their voice, and the false sibyls become mute. A new star appears in the East; Gabriel descends to the Virgin Mary, and a chorus of blessed spirits sings at night from on high, *Glory to God! peace to men of good will!* A rumor

[1] In the second member of this sentence we have substituted "their Master" for "John," which is found in the French copies, and which was most probably a typographical error; the word *Jean* having been printed by mistake for *Jesus*. T.

[2] *Contra Celsum.*

[3] Tertul., *Apologet.*, cap. xxxvii.

rapidly spreads that the Saviour has come into the world; he is not born in purple, but in the humble abode of indigence; he has not been announced to the great and the mighty, but angels have proclaimed the tidings to men of low estate; he has not assembled the opulent, but the needy, round his cradle, and by this first act of his life declared himself in preference the God of the suffering and the poor.

Let us here pause to make one reflection. We have seen, from the earliest ages, kings, heroes, and illustrious men, become the gods of nations. But here the reputed son of a carpenter in an obscure corner of Judea is a pattern of sorrows and of indigence; he undergoes the ignominy of a public execution; he selects his disciples from among the lowest of the people; he preaches naught but sacrifices, naught but the renunciation of earthly pomp, pleasure, and power; he prefers the slave to the master, the poor to the rich, the leper to the healthy man; all that mourn, all that are afflicted, all that are forsaken by the world, are his delight; but power, wealth, and prosperity, are incessantly threatened by him. He overthrows the prevalent notions of morality, institutes new relations among men, a new law of nations, a new public faith. Thus does he establish his divinity, triumph over the religion of the Cæsars, seat himself on the throne, and at length subdue the earth. No! if the whole world were to raise its voice against Jesus Christ, if all the powers of philosophy were to combine against its doctrines, never shall we be persuaded that a religion erected on such a foundation is a religion of human origin. He who could bring the world to revere a cross,—he who held up suffering humanity and persecuted virtue as an object of veneration to mankind,—he, we insist, can be no other than a God.

Jesus Christ appears among men full of grace and truth; the authority and the mildness of his precepts are irresistible. He comes to be the most unhappy of mortals, and all his wonders are wrought for the wretched. "His miracles," says Bossuet, "have a much stronger character of beneficence than of power." In order to inculcate his doctrines, he chooses the apologue or parable, which is easily impressed on the minds of the people. While walking in the fields, he gives his divine lessons. When surveying the flowers that adorn the mead, he exhorts his disciples to put their trust in Providence, who supports the feeble plants and feeds the birds of the air; when he beholds the fruits of the earth, he teaches them to judge of men by their works; an infant is brought to him, and he recommends innocence; being among shepherds, he gives himself the appellation of the *good shepherd*, and represents himself as bringing back the lost sheep to the fold In spring, he takes his seat upon a mountain, and draws from the surrounding objects instruction for the multitude sitting at his feet. From the very sight of this multitude, composed of the poor and the unfortunate, he deduces his beatitudes:—*Blessed are they that mourn—blessed are they that hunger and thirst*, &c. Such as observe his precepts, and those who slight them, are compared to two men who build houses, the one upon a rock, the other upon sand. According to some commentators, he designed in this comparison to describe a flourishing village upon a hill, and huts at the foot of it destroyed by an inundation.[1] When he asks some water of the Samaritan woman, he expounds to her his heavenly doctrine under the beautiful image of a well of living water.

The bitterest enemies of Jesus Christ never dared to attack his character. Celsus, Julian, Volusian,[2] admit his miracles, and Porphyry relates that the very oracles of the Pagans styled him a man illustrious for his piety.[3] Tiberius would have placed him in the rank of the gods;[4] and, according to Lampridius, Adrian erected temples to him, and Alexander Severus venerated him among holy men and placed his image between those of Orpheus and Abraham.[5] Pliny has borne an illustrious testimony to the innocence of the primitive Christians, who closely followed the example of the Redeemer. There are no philosophers of antiquity but have been reproached with some vices: the very patriarchs had their foibles. Christ alone is without blemish: he is the most brilliant copy of that supreme beauty which is seated upon the throne of heaven Pure and sanctified as the tabernacle of the Lord, breathing naught but the love of God and men, infinitely superior by the elevation of his soul to

[1] Jortin, *On the Truth of the Christ Relig*

[2] Orig., *cont. Cels* i. 11, Jul., *ap. Cyril.*, lib. vi Aug., *Ep.* 3, 4, tome ii.

[3] Euseb., dem. iii ev. 3. Tert., *Apologet.*

[5] Lamp, *in Alex. Sev.*, cap iv. and xxxi.

the vain glory of the world, he prosecuted, amid sufferings of every kind, the great business of our salvation, constraining men by the ascendency of his virtues to embrace his doctrine and to imitate a life which they were compelled to admire.

His character was amiable, open, and tender, and his charity unbounded. The evangelist gives us a complete and admirable idea of it in these few words:—*He went about doing good.* His resignation to the will of God is conspicuous in every moment of his life; he loved and felt the sentiment of friendship; the man whom he raised from the tomb, Lazarus, was his friend; it was for the noblest sentiment of life that he performed the greatest of his miracles. In him the love of country may find a model:—"Jerusalem, Jerusalem," he exclaimed, at the idea of the judgments which threatened that guilty city, "how often would I have gathered thy children together, even as a hen gathereth her chickens under her wings, and ye would not!" Casting his sorrowful eyes from the top of a hill over this city doomed for her crimes to a signal destruction, he was unable to restrain his tears:—*He beheld the city,* says the evangelist, *and wept over it.* His tolerance was not less remarkable. When his disciples begged him to command fire to come down from heaven on a village of Samaria which had denied him hospitality, he replied, with indignation, *You know not of what spirit you are.*

Had the Son of man descended from his celestial abode in all his power, it would certainly have been very easy to practise so many virtues, to endure so many afflictions;[1] but herein lies the glory of the mystery: Christ was the man of sorrows, and acquainted with griefs; his heart melted like that of a merely human creature, and he never manifested any sign of anger except against insensibility and obduracy of soul. *Love one another,* was his incessant exhortation. *Father,* he exclaimed, writhing under the torments inflicted by his executioners, *forgive them; for they know not what they do.* When on the point

[1] That is, if he had come into the world *impassible,* he would not have felt, as he did in his mortal state, the trials and contradictions which he encountered. The author's language here is strange, and at variance with that commonly met with among Catholic writers, though it is certain that his ideas on the subject of which he speaks were sound, as may be seen by reference to the chapters on the *Incarnation* and *Redemption,* part i. book i. T.

of quitting his beloved disciples, he was all at once dissolved in tears; he experienced all the terrors of death, all the anguish of the cross; the blood-sweat trickled down his divine cheeks; he complained that his Father had forsaken him. *Father*, said he, *if it be possible, let this chalice pass from me; nevertheless, not as I will, but as thou wilt.* Then it was that that expression, fraught with all the sublimity of grief, fell from his lips:—*My soul is sorrowful, even unto death.* Ah! if the purest morality and the most feeling heart,—if a life passed in combating error and soothing the sorrows of mankind,—be attributes of divinity, who can deny that of Jesus Christ? A pattern of every virtue, Friendship beholds him reclining on the bosom of St. John or bequeathing his mother to his care; Charity admires him in the judgment of the adulteress; Pity everywhere finds him blessing the tears of the unfortunate; his innocence and his tenderness are displayed in his love of children; the energy of his soul shines conspicuous amid the torments of the cross, and his last sigh is a sigh of mercy.

CHAPTER II.

SECULAR CLERGY.

Hierarchy.

Christ, having left his last instructions to his disciples, ascended from Mount Thabor into heaven. From that moment the Church subsisted in the apostles; it was established at the same time among the Jews and among the Gentiles. St. Peter by one single sermon converted five thousand persons at Jerusalem, and St. Paul received his mission to the pagan nations. The prince of the apostles soon laid in the capital of the Roman empire the foundations of the ecclesiastical power.[1] The first Cæsars yet reigned, and already the obscure priest, who was

---

[1] See note QQ.

destined to displace them from the capitol, went to and fro among the crowd at the foot of their throne. The hierarchy began: Peter was succeeded by Linus, and Linus by Clement and that illustrious chain of pontiffs, heirs of the apostolic authority, which has been unbroken for more than eighteen hundred years, and carries us back to Christ himself.

With the episcopal dignity we see the two other grand divisions of the hierarchy—the priesthood and the diaconate—established from the very beginning. St. Ignatius exhorts the Magnesians "to act in unity with their bishop, who fills the place of Jesus Christ; their priests, who represent the apostles; and their deacons, who are charged with the service of the altars."[1] Pius, Clement of Alexandria, Origen, and Tertullian, confirm these degrees.[2]

Though no mention is made of metropolitans or archbishops before the Council of Nice, yet that council speaks of this ecclesiastical dignity as having been long established.[3] Athanasius[4] and Augustin[5] mention instances of it prior to the date of that assembly. As early as the second century Lyons is termed in civil writings a metropolitan city; and Irenæus, who was its bishop, governed the whole Gallican *Church*, (παροχίων.)[6]

Some authors have been of opinion that archbishops were even of apostolical institution;[7] and Eusebius and St. Chrysostom actually assert that Titus, a bishop, had the superintendence of all the bishops of Crete.[8]

Respecting the origin of the patriarchate, opinions differ. Baronius, De Marca, and Richerius, date it as far back as the time of the apostles; but it nevertheless appears that it was not established in the Church till about 385—four years after the general council of Constantinople.

---

[1] Ignat., *Ep. ad Magnes.* n. 6.

[2] Pius, ep. 2; Clem. Alex., *Strom.*. lib. vi. p. 667; Orig., *Hom.* ii. *in num.*; Hom. *in cantic*; Tertul., *de Monogam.*, c. ii.; *De Fuga*, 41; *De Baptismo*, c. 17

[3] *Conc. Nicen.*, can. vi.

[4] Athan., *De Sentent. Dionys.*, tome I. p. 552.

[5] Aug., *Brevis Collat.*, *Tert. Die.*. c. xvi.

[6] Euseb., *Hist. Eccl.*, lib. v. 23. From παροχίων, we have made *parish.*

[7] Usher, *De Orig. Episc. et Metrop. Bevereg. cod. can. vind.*, lib. 2. cap. vi. n. 12; Hamm., *Pref. to Titus in Dissert.* 4, *Cont. Blondel*, cap. v.

[8] Euseb., *Hist. Eccl.*, lib. iii. c. 4.; Chrys., *Hom.* i. *in Tit.*

The title of cardinal was at first given indiscriminately to the highest dignitaries of the Church.[1] As these heads of the clergy were in general men distinguished for their learning and virtues, the Popes consulted them in important matters. They became by degrees the permanent council of the Holy See, and the right of electing the sovereign pontiff was vested in them when the communion of believers grew too numerous to be assembled together.

The same causes that had placed cardinals near the Popes, also gave canons to the bishops. These were a certain number of priests who composed the episcopal court. The business of the diocese increasing, the members of the council were obliged to divide the duties among them. Some were called vicars and others vicars-general, according to the extent of their charge The whole council assumed the name of *chapter*, and the members who composed it that of *canons*, that is, canonical administrators.

Common priests, and even laymen appointed by the bishops to superintend a religious community, were the source of the order of abbots. We shall presently see how serviceable the abbeys proved to letters, to agriculture, and, in general, to the civilization of Europe.

Parishes were formed at the period when the principal orders of the clergy became subdivided The bishoprics being too extensive to allow the priests of the mother Church to extend their spiritual and temporal aid to the extremities of the diocese, churches were erected in the country. The ministers attached to these rural temples took, in the course of time, the name of curates, from the Latin *cura*, which signifies *care, fatigue.* The appellation at least is not a proud one, and no one could find fault with them for it, since they so scrupulously fulfilled the conditions which it implied.[2]

Besides these parochial churches, chapels were also built on the tombs of martyrs and recluses. This kind of temple was called *martyrium* or *memoria;* and, from an idea still more sooth-

---

[1] Hericourt, *Lois Eccl de France*, p. 205.

[2] St. Athanasius, in his second apology, says that, as early as his time, there were ten parish churches in the Mareotis which belonged to the diocese of Alexandria.

ing and philosophical, it was also termed *cemetery*, after a Greek word which signifies *sleep*.[1]

Lastly, the secular benefices owed their origin to the *agapæ*, or love-feasts, of the primitive Christians. Each of the faithful brought something toward the support of the bishop, priest, and deacon, and for the relief of the sick and of strangers.[2] The rich, the princes, and whole cities, in the sequel, gave possessions to the Church in the place of these precarious alms. Such possessions, being divided into several portions by the council of the superior clergy, assumed different names—as prebend, canonicate, benefice with or without care of souls, &c.—according to the ecclesiastical rank of the person to whose superintendence they were committed.[3]

As to the faithful in general, the whole community of Christians was divided into *Πιςοι*, (*believers*,) and *Κατεχυμενοι*, (*catechumens*.)[4] The believers enjoyed the privilege of being admitted to the holy table, of being present at the services of the Church, and of repeating the Lord's prayer,[5] which St. Augustin for this reason calls *Oratio fidelium*, and St. Chrysostom *Ευχη πιςων*. The catechumens were not allowed to be present at all the ceremonies, and the mysteries were not spoken of before them except in obscure parables.[6]

The term *laity* was invented to distinguish such as had not entered among the general body of the clergy. The latter denomination was formed at the same time. The terms *laici* and *clerici* are met with in every page of the ancient writers. The appellation of *ecclesiastic* was used sometimes in speaking of the Christians in opposition to the Gentiles;[7] sometimes in designating the clergy in contradistinction to the rest of the believers. Finally, the glorious title of *catholic*, or universal, was attributed to the Church from its origin, as is attested by Eusebius, Clement of Alexandria, and St. Ignatius.[8] Poleimon the judge having asked

[1] Fleury, *Hist. Eccl.* [2] St. Just., *Apol.*

[3] Heric., *Lois Eccl.*, pp. 204–213.

[4] Euseb., *Demonst. Evang.*, lib. vii. c. 2.

[5] *Constit. Apost.*, lib. viii. c. 8 and 12.

[6] Theodor., *Epit. Div. Dogm.*, c. 24; Aug., *Serm. ad Neophytos*, in append., tome x. p. 845.

[7] Euseb., lib. iv. c. 7., lib. v. c. 27; Cyril, *Catech.*, 15, n. 4.

[8] Euseb., lib. iv. c. 15; Clem. Alex., *Strom.*, lib. vii.; Ignat., c. *ad Smyrn.*, n. 8.

Pionos the martyr of what church he was, the confessor replied, "Of the Catholic Church; for Jesus Christ knows no other."[1]

Let us not forget, in the description of this hierarchy, which St. Jerome compares to that of the angels, the modes in which Christianity displayed its wisdom and its fortitude; we mean the councils and persecutions. "Call to mind," says La Bruyère, "that first and grand council where the fathers who composed it were each remarkable for some mutilated member or for the scars left upon them by the violence of persecution. They seemed to derive from their wounds a right to sit in that general assembly of the whole Church"

How deplorable are the effects of party spirit! Voltaire, who often evinces a horror of blood and a spirit of humanity, endeavored to show that there were but few martyrs in the primitive days of the Church,[2] and, as if he had never read the Roman historians, he almost denies that first persecution of which Tacitus has drawn such a frightful picture. The author of *Zaïre*, who understood the powerful influence of misfortune, was afraid lest the popular mind should be too much affected by a description of the sufferings of the early Christians. He would rather deprive them of the crown of martyrdom, which exhibits them in so interesting a light to a feeling heart, and rob them even of the charm which attaches to their afflictions.

We have thus sketched an outline of the apostolical hierarchy. Add to this the regular clergy, of which we shall presently speak, and you will have the whole Church of Jesus Christ. We will venture to assert that no other religion upon earth ever exhibited such a system of benevolence, prudence, and foresight, of energy and mildness, of moral and religious laws. Nothing is more wisely instituted than those circles which, commencing with the lowest village clerk, rise to the pontifical throne itself, which they support and by which they are crowned. The Church thus answers, by its different degrees, all our wants. Arts, letters, science, legislation, politics, institutions, (literary, civil, and religious,) foundations for humanity,—all these important benefits we derive from the higher ranks of the hierarchy, while the blessings of

---

[1] *Act. Pion. ap. Bar. an.*, 254, n 9.

[2] See note R R.

charity and morality are diffused by the subordinate degrees among the inferior classes of the people. If the Church of old was indigent from the lowest to the highest order, the reason was because all Christendom was poor. But it would have been unreasonable to require that the clergy should remain poor when opulence was increasing all around them. They would then have lost all consideration. Certain classes with whom they could no longer have associated would have withdrawn themselves from their moral authority. The head of the Church was a prince, that he might be able to speak to princes. The bishops, placed upon an equal footing with the nobles, durst instruct them in their duties. The priests, secular and regular, being raised above the necessities of life, mingled with the rich, whose manners they refined; and the simple curate dwelt among the poor, whom he was destined to relieve by his bounty and to console by his example.

Not but that the lowest of ecclesiastics was also capable of instructing the great and recalling them to virtue; but he could neither follow them in their habits of life, like the superior clergy, nor address them in a language which they would perfectly have understood. Even the consideration which he enjoyed he derived in part from the higher orders of the Church. It is moreover befitting a great nation to have a respectable clergy and altars where the distressed may obtain relief.

In short, there is nothing so beautiful in the history of civil and religious institutions as what relates to the authority, the duties, and the investiture, of the Christian prelate. In him you behold the perfect image of the pastor of the people and the minister of the altar. No class of men has reflected greater honor on humanity than that of bishops, and none are more distinguished for their virtue, their true greatness, and their genius.

The apostolic chief was required to be free from corporeal defect, and like the unblemished priest whom Plato describes in his *Laws*. Chosen in the assembly of the people, he was perhaps the only legal magistrate existing in the barbarous ages. As this august station carried with it an immense responsibility, both in this life and in the next, it was by no means coveted. The Basils and the Ambroses fled to the desert for fear of being elevated to a dignity from the duties of which even their virtues shrunk with dismay.

Not only was the bishop obliged to perform his religious functions,—that is, to teach morality, to administer the sacraments, to ordain the clergy,—but upon him devolved likewise the whole weight of the civil laws and of political affairs. There was either a prince to be appeased, a war to be averted, or a city to be defended. When the Bishop of Paris, in the ninth century, saved that capital by his courage, he probably prevented all France from passing under the yoke of the Normans.

"So thoroughly was it understood," says D'Hericourt, "to be a duty incumbent on the episcopacy to entertain strangers, that Gregory the Great, before he would consecrate Florentine, Bishop of Ancona, required an explanation whether it was from inability or avarice that he had not previously practised hospitality toward strangers."[1]

The bishop was expected to hate sin, but not the sinner; to support the weak; to have the feelings of a father for the poor.[2] He was nevertheless to keep within certain bounds in his gifts, and not to entertain persons of dangerous or useless professions, such as stage-players and hunters,[3]—a truly politic injunction, levelled on the one hand against the predominant vice of the Romans, and on the other against that of the barbarians.

If the bishop had needy relations, it was allowable in him to prefer them to strangers, but not to enrich them; "for," says the canon, "it is their indigence, and not the ties of blood, which, in such a case, he ought to consider."[4]

Is it surprising that, with such virtues, the bishops should have gained the veneration of all classes? The people bowed their heads to receive their benediction. They sang *Hosanna* before them They styled them *most holy*, *most beloved of God*—titles the more illustrious as they were deservedly conferred.

When the nations became civilized, the bishops, whose religious duties were now more circumscribed, enjoyed the good which they had done for mankind, and sought to bestow on them

[1] *Lois Eccles. de France*, p 751.
[2] *Id. ib. Can. Odio.*
[3] *Id. ib. Can. Don. qui Venatoribus.*
[4] *Id. ib.* p. 742; *Can. est Probanda.*

further benefits by paying particular attention to the promotion of morality, charity, and learning. Their palaces became the focus of politeness and the arts Summoned by their sovereigns to the administration of public affairs, and invested with the highest dignities of the Church, they displayed talents which commanded the admiration of Europe. Up to the latest times the bishops of France have been patterns of moderation and intelligence. Some exceptions might doubtless be adduced; but, so long as mankind shall have a relish for exalted traits of virtue, it will be remembered that more than sixty Catholic bishops wandered as fugitives into Protestant countries; and that, in spite of all religious prejudices, they gained the respect and veneration of the people of those countries; that the disciple of Luther and of Calvin came to hear the exiled Roman prelate preach, in some obscure retreat, the love of humanity and the forgiveness of injuries.[1] Finally, it will be remembered that these modern Cyprians, persecuted for the sake of their religion,—these courageous Chrysostoms,—divested themselves of the title which was at once the cause of their affliction and their glory, at the mere word of the Head of the Church,—happy to sacrifice, with their former prosperity, the splendor of twelve years of adversity to the peace of their flock.

As to the inferior clergy, it was to them that we were indebted for the remnant of morality which was still to be found among

[1] The sympathy and generosity of different nations in Europe toward the French clergy, who, exiled from their native land during the Revolution, sought refuge among them, is worthy of everlasting admiration. In England especially all national and religious prejudices seemed to be forgotten to make way for the exercise of a noble and munificent hospitality. All classes of persons, clergy and laity, high and low, united, and the government itself took an active part in this work of charity. During the Reign of Terror not less than 8000 Catholic priests landed on the English shore, where every one received a most friendly welcome. From September, 1792, to August, 1793, the disbursement for the relief of those who were in need amounted to £47,000 sterling. The subscriptions, public and private, exceeded £80,000. Besides this, the University of Oxford had printed at its own expense, and distributed gratuitously among the clergy, an edition of the New Testament according to the Catholic version. Our author (*Memoires d' Outre-tombe*) makes honorable mention of the charity of the English clergy toward his countrymen; but, in the *Histoire du Clergé de France*, by the Abbé Barruel, p. 566, *et seq.*, the noble benevolence of the English people on this occasion is the subject of an eloquent and feeling eulogy,—the evident effusion of a grateful heart. T.

the lower classes, both in the cities and in the country. The peasant without religion is a ferocious animal. He knows not the restraint of education or of human respect. A toilsome life has soured his disposition, and the possession of property has taken from him the innocence of the savage. He is timid, coarse, distrustful, avaricious, and, above all, ungrateful. But, by a truly surprising miracle, this man, by nature so perverse, is transformed into a new creature by the hand of religion. As cowardly as he was before, so brave does he now become His propensity to betray is converted into inviolable fidelity, his ingratitude into unbounded attachment, his distrust into implicit confidence. Compare those impious peasants profaning the churches, laying waste estates, burning women, children, and priests with a slow fire,—compare them, I say, with the inhabitants of La Vendée defending the religion of their forefathers, and alone asserting their freedom, when all the rest of France was bowed down by the yoke of terror. Compare them, and behold the difference that religion can make between men.

If the parish priests could be reproached with prejudices arising from their profession or from ignorance, still, after all, simplicity of heart, sanctity of life, evangelical poverty, the charity of Jesus Christ, made them one of the most respectable classes of the nation. Many of them seemed to be not so much human beings as beneficent spirits, who had descended to the earth to relieve the unfortunate. Often did they deny themselves bread to feed the necessitous, and often did they strip themselves of their garments to cover the naked. Who would presume to upbraid such men with some stiffness of opinion? Which of us, with all our boasted philanthropy, would like, in the depth of winter, to be wakened in the middle of the night, to go to a considerable distance in the country for the purpose of attending a poor wretch expiring upon straw? Which of us would like to have his heart incessantly wounded by the sight of misery which it is not in his power to relieve?—to be surrounded by a family whose haggard cheeks and hollow eyes announce the extremity of famine and every want? Would we be willing to accompany the parish priests of Paris—those angels of humanity—into the abodes of guilt and anguish, in order to administer consolation to distress in its most hideous forms, to pour the balm of hope into a heart oppressed with despair? Finally, which of us would cut himself off from the company of the happy, to associate continually with wretchedness, and to receive, when dying, no other recompense for all these sacrifices and for all this kindness than the ingratitude of the poor and the calumny of the rich?

CHAPTER III.

REGULAR CLERGY.

Origin of the Monastic Life.

If it be true, as we might suppose, that a thing is poetically beautiful in proportion to the antiquity of its origin, it must be admitted that the monastic life has some claim to our admiration. It dates from the earliest ages of the world. The prophet Elias, fleeing from the wickedness of Israel, retired to the banks of Jordan, where he lived on herbs and roots with a few disciples. To us this source of religious orders, which renders further researches into history unnecessary, appears truly striking. What would not the poets of Greece have said, had they discovered that the founder of the sacred colleges was a man who had been rapt into heaven in a fiery chariot, and who was again to appear on earth on the great day of the consummation of ages?

From Elias the monastic life is transmitted, by an admirable inheritance, through the prophets and St. John Baptist, to Christ himself, who often retired from the world to pray amid the solitude of the mountains. Soon afterward the *Therapeutæ*,[1] embracing the advantages of retirement, exhibited on the banks of the Lake Mœris, in Egypt, the first models of Christian monasteries. Finally, in the time of Paul, Anthony, and Pachomius, appeared those celebrated recluses of Thebais who filled Carmel

[1] Voltaire laughs at Eusebius for supposing the *Therapeutæ* to be Christian monks. Eusebius lived nearer their time than Voltaire, and was certainly much better informed on the subject of Christian antiquity. Montfaucon, Fleury, Héricourt, Hélyot, and a host of other savans, agree with the Bishop of Cæsarea.

and Lebanon with the highest works of penance. A glorious and a marvellous voice arose from the most frightful deserts. Divine harmony mingled with the murmur of the streams and of the cascades. The seraphim visited the anchoret of the rock, or transported his resplendent spirit upon the clouds. The lions performed the office of messengers. The ravens, as if endued with intelligence, brought to the holy hermit the celestial manna. The jealous cities found their ancient fame shaken to its foundation. It was the era of the renown of the desert.

Proceeding thus from enchantment to enchantment in the establishment of the religious life, we see it springing from other sources, which may be termed *local;* giving rise to certain particular foundations of orders and convents, which are not less curious than the preceding. Behold at the gates of Jerusalem a monastery erected on the site of Pilate's palace, on Mount Sinai the Convent of the *Transfiguration*, marking the awful spot where Jehovah dictated his laws to the Hebrews. Yonder rises another convent on the mountain where Jesus Christ was last seen upon earth. The roof of its church is open at the very place where the Son of man left the traces of his glorious ascension.

And what admirable things may not the West, in its turn, exhibit in the foundation of communities!—those monuments of our Gallic antiquities, places consecrated by interesting adventures or by deeds of humanity! History, the passions of the heart, and beneficence, prefer an equal claim to the origin of our monasteries. In yonder defile of the Pyrenees behold the hospital of Roncevaux, erected by Charlemagne on the very spot where the flower of chivalry, Roland of France, terminated his glorious achievements. An asylum of peace and charity fitly marks the tomb of the warrior who defended the orphan and died for his country. In the plain of Bovines, before that little temple of the Lord, I learn to despise the triumphal arches of a Marius or a Cæsar. I survey with pride that convent within whose walls a king of France offered the crown to the most worthy. But, if you delight in recollections of a different kind, here is a female of Albion who, overtaken by a mysterious slumber, dreams that the moon descends toward her. She soon gives birth to a daughter chaste and melancholy as the orb of night.

and who, founding a monastery, thus becomes the charming luminary of the desert.

We might be accused of an intention to surprise the ear by means of harmonious sounds were we to enumerate all those convents of *Acqua Bella*, of *Belle Monte*, of *Valombrosa*, or of *Columba*, thus named from its founder—a celestial dove, who resided in the depths of the forest. Tell us if *La Trappe* did not preserve the name of Comminges, and the Paraclete the recollection of Heloisa. Ask the peasant of ancient Neustria, "What monastery is that which you see on the top of the hill?" He will reply, "It is the priory of *The Two Lovers*. A youth of lowly birth fell in love with the fair daughter of the lord of Malmain, who agreed to give her to her lover if he could carry her to the top of the hill. He accepted the condition and accomplished the task; but no sooner had he reached the summit than he expired from the exertion. The lady, not long afterward, died of grief. The parents buried them together on that spot, and erected the priory which you see before you."

Lastly, the tender heart, as well as the antiquary and the poet, will find its gratification in the origin of our convents. Behold those institutions consecrated to charity, to the aid of pilgrims, to preparation for a good death, to the burial of the dead, to the relief of the insane, to the care of orphans: discover, if you can, in the long catalogue of human woes, one single infirmity of soul or body for which religion has not founded a place of maintenance or relief.

The persecutions of the Romans contributed at first to people the solitudes. At a later period, the barbarians having invaded the empire and broken all the bonds of society, men had left no other hope than God, no other asylum than the deserts. Pious congregations of the unfortunate were formed in all quarters, in the midst of forests and the most inaccessible situations. The fertile plains became the prey of savages, while on the naked brows of rugged mountains dwelt another race, which had saved upon these crags, as from a second deluge, the relics of the arts and of civilization. But, as the springs gush forth from the elevated places to fertilize the valleys, so the first anchorets by degrees descended from their eminences, to make known to the barbarians the word of God and the comforts of life.

We may be told, perhaps, that, the causes which gave rise to the monastic life having ceased, the religious communities had become useless institutions in our midst. But when did these causes cease to exist? Are there no longer any orphans, any sick, any distressed travellers, any victims of poverty and misfortune? Ah! when the evils of a barbarous age disappeared, society, which is so ingenious and so effective in its means of tormenting man, knew well how to invent a thousand other sources of misery, which drive us into solitude! How often does disappointment, treachery, and profound disgust, make us wish to escape from the world! What a happiness to find in those religious houses a retreat where one would be secured against the shocks of adversity and the storms of his own heart! A female orphan, abandoned by society at an age when beauty and innocence are assailed by the most seductive influences, knew at least where to find an asylum in which she would be free from the apprehension of being deceived. What consolation was it for this poor young stranger, without parents, to be welcomed by the sweet name of sister! What a numerous and peaceful family did she enter, under the guardianship of religion! A heavenly Father opens his house to her and receives her into his arms!

It is a very barbarous philosophy, and a most cruel policy, to compel any person to live against his will in the midst of the world Men have been so devoid of delicacy as to associate for the purpose of sensual pleasure; but there is a noble egotism in adversity, which prefers to enjoy in secret those pleasures which consist in tears If there are establishments for the health of the body, why should not religion have its institutions for the health of the soul, which is much more liable to disease, and whose sufferings are much more poignant, much longer, and much more difficult to be removed?

Certain philanthropists have imagined that there should be establishments at the public expense for those who are in affliction. What profound knowledge of nature and of the human heart philosophers evince! They wish to intrust unfortunate creatures to the pity of men; to place misery and destitution under the protection of those who have caused them! A more magnificent charity than our own is necessary to comfort the afflicted soul. God alone is rich enough to provide the needful alms.

It has been pretended that a great service was rendered to the monks and nuns in compelling them to quit their peaceful abodes: but what was the consequence? Those pious women who could find an asylum in foreign convents did not hesitate to embrace the opportunity. Others lived together in the world, while many died of grief and affliction. The Trappists, who, it was said, were so much to be pitied, instead of being tempted by the charms of liberty and society, continued their life of austerity amid the heaths of England and the wilds of Russia.

It must not be supposed that we are all equally born to handle the spade or the musket, or that there are no men of a particular taste, having an aptitude for intellectual labor as others have for manual toil. It cannot be doubted that the heart suggests a thousand reasons for seeking a life of retirement. Some are drawn thither by a contemplative disposition; others are led to it by a certain natural timidity, which makes them prefer to live within themselves; then there are persons of such excellent qualities that they cannot find in the world congenial spirits with themselves, and are thus doomed to a kind of moral virginity or eternal widowhood. It was particularly for these solitary and generous souls that religion opened her peaceful retreats.

CHAPTER IV.

THE MONASTIC CONSTITUTIONS.

The reader must be aware that it is not the particular history of the religious orders that we are writing, but only their moral history.

We shall therefore say nothing of St. Anthony, the father of the cenobites; of St. Paul, the first of the anchorets; of St. Syncletica, the foundress of convents for females; we shall not treat of the order of St. Augustin, which comprehends all the chapters known by the appellation of *regular;* nor of that of St

Basil, which includes all the monks and nuns of the East; nor of the rule of St Benedict, comprising the greater part of the western monasteries; nor of that of St. Francis, practised by the mendicant orders; but we shall blend all the religious in one general picture, in which we shall attempt to delineate their customs, their manners, their way of life, whether active or contemplative, and the numberless services which they have rendered to society.

We cannot, however, forbear to make one remark. There are persons who, either from ignorance or prejudice, despise these constitutions under which such a number of cenobites have lived for so many centuries. This contempt is any thing but philosophical, especially at a time when people pique themselves on the study and the knowledge of mankind A religious who, by means of a hair-shirt and a wallet, has assembled under his rule several thousands of disciples, is not an ordinary man; the springs which he has employed for this purpose, and the spirit which prevails in his institutions, are well worthy of examination.

It is well worthy of remark that, of all the monastic rules, the most rigid have been most scrupulously observed. The Carthusians have exhibited to the world the matchless example of a congregation which has subsisted seven hundred years without needing reform. This proves that the more the legislator combats the propensities of nature the more he insures the duration of his work. Those, on the contrary, who pretend to erect societies by employing the passions as materials for the edifice, resemble architects who build palaces with that kind of stone which crumbles away upon exposure to the air.

The religious orders have been in many points of view, nothing but philosophic sects, very nearly resembling those of the Greeks. The monks in the early ages were called philosophers, wore their dress and imitated their manners. Some of them even chose the manual of Epictetus for their only rule. St. Basil first introduced the vows of *poverty, chastity,* and *obedience.* This law is profound; and upon reflection we shall find that the spirit of Lycurgus is comprised in these three precepts.

In the order of St. Benedict every thing is prescribed, even to the minutest details of life: bed, food, walks, conversation, prayers To the weak were assigned the more delicate employments; to the strong, such as were more laborious: in short, most of these religious laws display an astonishing knowledge of the art of governing men. Plato did no more than dream of republics, without being able to carry his plans into execution. The Augustins, the Basils, the Benedicts, were real legislators and the patriarchs of several great nations.

Much has been said, in modern times, in condemnation of perpetual vows; but it is not impossible, perhaps, to support them with reasons drawn from the very nature of things and from the real wants of our soul.

The unhappiness of man proceeds chiefly from his inconstancy, and from the abuse of that free-will which is at once his glory and his misfortune, and will be the occasion of his condemnation. His thoughts and his feelings are ever changing. His loves are not more stable than his opinions, and his opinions are as inconstant as his loves. From this disquietude there springs a wretchedness which cannot be removed until some superior power fix his mind upon one only object. He then bears the yoke with cheerfulness; for, though a man may be an infidel, his infidelity nevertheless is hateful to him. Thus, for instance, we see the mechanic more happy than the rich man who is idle, because he is engrossed with a work which effectually shuts out all foreign desires and temptations to inconstancy. The same subjection to power forms the contentment of children; and the law which prohibits divorce is attended with much less inconvenience for the peace of families than the law which permits it.

The legislators of antiquity understood the necessity of imposing a yoke upon man. In fact, the republics of Lycurgus and Minos were nothing more than communities in which men were bound from their very birth by perpetual vows. The citizen was condemned to a uniform or monotonous existence, and subjected to the most troublesome regulations, which extended even to his meals and recreations. He could neither dispose of his time during the day, nor of the different periods of his life. A rigid sacrifice of his inclinations was demanded of him; he had to love, to think, and to act, according to the law. In a word, to render him happy he was deprived of his own will.

The perpetual vow, therefore,—that is, submission to an inviolable rule,—far from producing discontentment or misery, on the contrary is conducive to the happiness of man, especially when the only object of the vow is to protect him against the illusions of the world, as is the case in monastic institutions. The uprising of the passions seldom takes place before the age of twenty, and at that of forty they are commonly extinguished or disabused; and thus an indissoluble obligation deprives us at most of a few years of freedom, while it secures to us a peaceful life and banishes regret and remorse the remainder of our days. If we contrast the evils which spring from our passions with the little enjoyment which they procure, we shall perceive that the perpetual vow is something desirable even during the gay season of youth.

We ask, moreover, whether a nun would be happy if there were no moral restraint to prevent her from leaving the cloister at discretion? After a few years of retirement she would behold society altogether changed; for, on the theatre of life, when we cease for a moment to gaze upon the scene, the decorations change and pleasure vanishes; and, on looking back again, we see only places that have been deserted and actors that are unknown to us. A convent would be a very useless institution if it were a house where the folly of the world could enter and go out at the whim of the moment. The agitated heart would not commune long enough with the heart that is at peace, to acquire something of its blessed repose, and the soul that is calm and cheerful would soon lose its joyful tranquillity amid the troubled spirits of the world. Instead of burying in silence the past evils of life, for which the cloister presents so efficient a remedy, the religious would be entertaining each other with their spiritual maladies, and perhaps mutually creating a disposition to brave again the dangers which they had fled. A woman of the world and a woman of solitude, the unfaithful spouse of Christ would be fit neither for solitude nor for the world. The ebb and flow of the passions—those vows alternately broken and renewed—would banish from convents the peace, subordination, and propriety, which should reign in them; and those sacred retreats, far from putting an end to our disquietudes, would be nothing more than places where we would deplore for a moment the inconstancy of others and plan some new inconstancy for ourselves

But what renders the perpetual vow of religion far superior to that kind of political vow which existed among the people of Sparta and Crete, is its coming from ourselves, its not being imposed by others. Moreover, this vow offers to the heart a compensation for the terrestrial love which it sacrifices. In this alliance of an immortal soul with the eternal principle we see nothing but true greatness. Here are two natures adapted to each other and coming together. What a sublime spectacle! Man, born free, seeks happiness in vain by pursuing his own will; then, wearied out, and convinced that there is nothing here below worthy of his regard, he swears to make God the eternal object of his love, and, as is the case with the Divine Being, he creates for himself by his own act a *necessity* to do so.

CHAPTER V.

MANNERS AND LIFE OF THE RELIGIOUS.

Coptic Monks, Maronites, &c.

Let us now proceed to a delineation of the religious life, and, in the first place, lay down this principle:—wherever we find a great deal of mystery, solitude, silence, and contemplation, many allusions to the Deity, many venerable things in manners, customs, and apparel, there must necessarily be abundance of beauties of every kind. If this observation be correct, we shall presently see how admirably it applies to the subject before us.

Let us return once more to the hermits of Thebais. They dwelt in narrow cells, and wore, like Paul their founder, robes made of the leaves of palm-trees; others were habited in cloth woven of the hair of the antelope; some, like Zeno, merely threw the skins of wild beasts over their shoulders; while Seraphion the anchoret appeared wrapped in the shroud which was to cover him in the grave. The Maronite monks in the solitudes of Lebanon, the Nestorian hermits scattered along the Tigris, those of Abyssinia, near the cataracts of the Nile and on the coasts of the Red Sea, all lead a life as extraordinary as the deserts in which they have buried themselves The Coptic monk, on entering his monastery, renounces every pleasure, and spends all his time in labor, fasting, prayer, and the practice of hospitality. He lies on the ground; and scarcely has he slumbered a few moments when he rises, and, beneath the serene firmament of Egypt, raises his voice amid the silence of night, on the ruins of Thebes and Memphis Sometimes the echo of the pyramids repeats to the shades of the Pharaos the hymns of this member of the mystic family of Joseph; at others the pious recluse celebrates in his matin devotion the true Sun of glory on the very spot where harmonious statues greeted the visible sun of day.[1] There, too, he seeks the European bewildered among those renowned ruins; there, rescuing him from the hands of a horde of Arabs, he conducts him to his lofty tower, and amply supplies this stranger with refreshments which he denies himself. Scholars go, it is true, to visit the ruins of Egypt; but how happens it that, unlike those Christian monks, the objects of their scorn, they repair not thither to fix their abode in those oceans of sand, to endure all sorts of privations, that they may give a glass of water to the fainting traveller and snatch him from the scimetar of the Bedouin?

God of Christians! what marvellous things hast thou done! Which way soever we turn our eyes, we perceive nothing but monuments of thy bounty. Throughout the four quarters of the globe Religion has distributed her soldiers and stationed her sentinels of humanity. The Maronite monk, by the clattering of two boards hung to the top of a tree, calls the stranger who is benighted among the precipices of Lebanon; this poor ignorant artist possesses no more costly means of informing you where he is. The Abyssinian hermit awaits you in yon wood among prowling tigers; and the American missionary watches for your preservation in his boundless forests Cast by tempests upon an unknown coast, you all at once perceive a cross erected on a rock. Unfortunate are you if this emblem of salvation does not make

---

[1] The statue of Memnon was said to utter a melodious sound. This sound was supposed to be caused by the reverberation of the rays of the sun. The geographer Strabo attests the fact. The ruins of this statue are still considerable. S.

your eyes overflow with tears! You are in a friendly country, for here are Christians. You are Frenchmen, it is true, and they are perhaps Spaniards, Germans, or English. But what of that? Are you not of the great family of Jesus Christ? These foreigners will receive you as a brother; it is you whom they invite by this cross; they never saw you before, and yet they weep for joy because you have escaped the perils of the deep.

Observe yon traveller upon the Alps; he has performed but half his journey. Night approaches; the snow begins to fall; alone, trembling, bewildered, he proceeds a few steps, and is to all appearance irrecoverably lost. It grows dark; he finds himself on the brink of a precipice, and dares not venture either to advance or to turn back. The cold soon overpowers him; his limbs are benumbed; a fatal drowsiness oppresses his eyes; his last thoughts dwell on his wife and children. But hark! is it not the sound of a bell that strikes his ear amid the howling of the tempest? or is it the knell of death which his affrighted fancy hears amid the war of winds? No; they are real sounds. Another noise arises; a dog yelps among the snow; he approaches, he arrives, he barks for joy; a benevolent recluse follows, and comes up just in time to rescue him from his perilous situation.

It was not enough, then, for this recluse to have risked his life a thousand times in order to save his fellow-creatures, or to have fixed his permanent abode among the most dreary deserts; but the very animals must be taught to become the instruments of his sublime beneficence, to glow, as it were, with the same sympathy as their holy masters, and, by their barking on the summit of the Alps, to send forth upon the echoes the miracles of our religion.[1]

---

[1] The convents or hospitals here alluded to are situated upon the summit of the great St. Bernard, one of the high mountains in the Alps. They were founded in the tenth century by Bernard of Menthon, an ecclesiastic, to afford assistance and entertainment to the pilgrims in their journey to Rome. Some of the monks who belong to these convents take care of sick travellers, and others search for those who have lost their way in the pathless regions of snow and ice. They make no distinction of age, sex, or religion, but, like the good Samaritan, consider distress as an undeniable claim to their humanity and protection.

Their dogs, of a large size, are trained to go out alone, and they exercise an

Let it not be said that such acts may be prompted by humanity alone; for how happens it that we find nothing of the sort in antiquity, though possessing such sensibility? People talk of philanthropy; the Christian religion is philanthropy itself. Astonishing and sublime idea, which makes the Christian of China a friend of the Christian of France, the converted Indian a brother of the Egyptian monk! We are no longer strangers on the earth; neither can we any longer lose our way in it. Jesus Christ has restored to us the inheritance of which we were deprived by the sin of Adam. O Christian! for thee there is now no unknown ocean or deserts; thou wilt everywhere find the hut of thy father and the language of thy ancestors.

CHAPTER VI.

THE SUBJECT CONTINUED.

Trappists—Carthusians—Sisters of St. Clare—Fathers of Redemption—Missionaries—Ladies of Charity, &c.

SUCH are the manners and customs of some of the religious orders of the contemplative life; but, if these things are so extremely beautiful, it is solely because they are associated with meditation and prayer: take from them the name and presence of God, and the charm is almost entirely destroyed.

Transport yourself now to La Trappe, and contemplate those monks, dressed in sackcloth, digging their own graves! Behold them wandering like spectres in the extensive forest of Mortagne and on the margin of the solitary lake! Silence walks by their

---

astonishing sagacity in tracking travellers that have lost their way and in discovering those who have fallen down amid drifts of snow. Even the warmest colors of our author's description could scarcely do justice to the indefatigable and perilous exertions of these most benevolent monks. S.

These monks still exercise their heroic charity, as far as their means will permit, notwithstanding the spoliations recently suffered from the Swiss government, whose hatred of the true religion is only equalled by its inhumanity. T side, or, if they speak when they meet, all they say to each other is, *Brother, we must die.* These rigorous orders of Christianity were schools of active morality, instituted in the midst of the pleasures of the age, and exhibiting continually to the eyes of vice and prosperity models of penance and striking examples of human misery.

And what a sight was that of an expiring monk of La Trappe! what sublime philosophy! what a warning to mankind! Extended upon a little straw and ashes in the sanctuary of the church, his brethren ranged in silence around him, he exhorts them to persevere in virtue while the funeral bell announces his last agonies. It is usually the task of the living to encourage their departing friends; but here is a spectacle much more sublime; it is the dying man who expatiates on death. Already stepping upon the threshold of eternity, he understands better than those around him what death is, and, with a voice which seems to issue from the sepulchre, he emphatically summons his companions and even his superiors to works of penance. Who does not shudder in perceiving that this religious, after a life of so much holiness, is yet penetrated with fear at the approach of his mortal dissolution? Christianity has drawn from the tomb all the morality that underlies it. By death has morality entered into the life of man. Had he remained immortal after the fall, he would never perhaps have been acquainted with virtue.[1]

Thus religion everywhere presents scenes the most pleasing or the most instructive. Here holy men, like people enchanted by a magic spell, perform in silence the joyful operations of the harvest and the vintage; there the nuns of St. Clare tread with bare feet the ice-cold tombs of their cloister. Imagine not, however, that they are unhappy amid their austerities; their hearts are pure, and their eyes are directed toward heaven, indicative of desire and hope. A gray woollen robe is preferable to magnificent apparel purchased at the price of virtue, and the bread of charity is more wholesome than that of prostitution. From how many afflictions are not these females secured by the simple veil which separates them from the world? To give the reader

[1] See note SS.

an adequate idea of the objects which now suggest themselves to our contemplation would require a talent quite different from ours. The highest eulogy that we could present of the monastic life would be to exhibit a catalogue of the meritorious works to which it has been devoted. Religion, leaving the care of our joys to our own hearts, is like a tender mother, intent only on alleviating our sorrows; but in accomplishing this arduous task she has summoned all her sons and daughters to her aid. To some she has committed the care of those afflicted with disease, as to the multitude of monks and nuns dedicated to the service of hospitals; to others she has consigned the poor, as to the pious Sisters of Charity. The Redemptionist Father embarks at Marseilles; but whither is he bound alone, with his breviary and his staff? This conqueror is speeding to the deliverance of humanity, attended by invisible armies. With the purse of charity in his hand, he goes to brave pestilence, slavery, and martyrdom. He accosts the Dey of Algiers; he addresses him in the name of that heavenly king whose ambassador he is. The barbarian is astonished at the sight of this European stranger who ventures to come alone, across seas and through storms, to demand the release of his captive fellow-creatures. Impelled by an unknown power, he accepts the gold that is offered him, and the heroic deliverer, satisfied with having restored some unfortunate beings to their country, obscure and unknown, humbly sets out on foot to return to his monastery.

Wherever we look, a similar prospect presents itself. The missionary embarking for China meets, in the port, the missionary returning glorious and crippled from Canada; the Gray nun hastens to administer relief to the pauper in his cottage; the Capuchin flies to check the ravages of a conflagration; the friar Hospitaller washes the feet of the traveller; the brother of the *Bona Mors* Society consoles the dying Christian or conveys the body of the poor to the grave; the Sister of Charity mounts to the garret of indigence to distribute money and clothing and to light up the soul with hope; those women so justly denominated *Filles-Dieu* (daughters of God) are always carrying here and there food, lint, and medicaments; the Sister of the *Good Shepherd* extends her arms to the unhappy victim of crime, exclaiming, *I am not come to call the just but sinners to repent-*

ance The orphan finds a father, the lunatic a physician, the ignorant an instructor. All these doers of heavenly works encourage one another. Religion, meanwhile, attentive to their actions, and holding a crown of immortality, thus addresses them:—"Be of good heart, my children, go on! Quicken your pace; be more speedy than the evils which befall human life. Earn this crown which I have prepared for you, and which will secure you from every affliction, from every want."

Among so many pictures, each of which would require whole volumes to enter fully into its details and praises, on what particular scene shall we fix our view? We have already treated of those hospitable houses which religion has erected in the solitudes of the four quarters of the globe; let us now turn our eyes to objects of a different kind.

There are people in whom the mere name of Capuchin excites feelings of contempt. The monks of the order of St Francis were, nevertheless, very often distinguished for simplicity and dignity. Which of us has not seen a couple of those venerable men journeying in the country, commonly toward All-Souls' day, at the approach of winter, about the time of the vintage? They went along soliciting hospitality at the ancient mansions which they passed in their way. At nightfall the two pilgrims reached a solitary edifice; they ascended the antique steps, laid down their long staves and their wallets at the top, knocked at the loud-resounding door, and applied for hospitality. If the master refused admittance to these guests of the Lord, they made a profound obeisance, silently retired, took up their wallets and their staves, and, shaking the dust from their sandals, proceeded, amid the shades of night, to seek the cabin of the husbandman. If, on the contrary, they were received, they were first supplied with water to wash, after the fashion of the days of Jacob and Homer, and then they went and seated themselves at the hospitable fire. As in times of old, they began to caress the children of their hosts, not merely to gain their favor, but because, like their divine Master, they were fond of children; they made them presents of relics and pictures. The young folks, who had at first run away affrighted, being now attracted by these curiosities, soon grew so familiar as to play between the knees of the good friars. The parents with a smile of tenderness beheld their innocent sports, and the interesting contrast between the infantine graces of their offspring and the hoary age of their guests.

Meanwhile the rain poured in torrents; tempestuous winds swept through the leafless woods and howled among the chimneys and battlements of the Gothic mansion; the owl screeched from the top of the turret. Near a large fire, the family sat down to supper; the repast was cordial and the behavior friendly. The youthful daughter of the host timidly questioned her guests, who, with becoming gravity, commended her beauty and modesty. The good fathers entertained the whole family with their agreeable converse; they related some affecting story, for they had always met with many remarkable things in their distant missions among the savages of America or the tribes of Tartary. Their long beard, their dress in the fashion of the ancient East, and the manner in which they came to ask for hospitality, revived the recollection of those times when a Thales and an Anacharsis thus travelled in Asia and Greece.

After supper the mistress called her servants, and one of the fathers was invited to perform the accustomed family devotions; the two monks then retired to rest, wishing their hosts every sort of prosperity. Next morning, upon inquiry for the aged travellers, it was found that they were gone, like those sacred visions which sometimes visit the habitations of the good.

Was there any thing calculated to harrow the soul, any errand which persons, averse to tears, durst not undertake for fear of compromising their pleasures; it was to the inmates of the convent that it was immediately consigned, and more particularly to the fathers of the order of St. Francis. It was supposed that men who had devoted themselves to suffering ought naturally to be the heralds of misfortune. One was obliged to carry to a family the disastrous intelligence of the loss of its fortune, another to inform the parent of the death of an only son. The great Bourdaloue himself performed this painful duty: he presented himself in silence at the door of the father, crossed his hands upon his breast, made a profound inclination, and retired mute as death, of which he was the interpreter.

Can we suppose that it afforded much pleasure, (we mean what the world would deem such,) can we suppose that it was a very agreeable office, for a Carmelite or a Franciscan to go from prison to prison, to announce to the criminal his sentence, to hear his sad tale, to administer consolation to him, and to remain for entire days amid the most agonizing scenes? In the performance of these pious duties, the sweat has often been seen to flow from the brow of these sympathizing monks and to trickle upon their robes, making them forever sacred, in spite of the sarcasms of infidels. And yet what honor, what profit, accrued to these sons of charity from so many sacrifices, except the derision of the world, and, perhaps, the abuse of the very prisoners whom they went to console? Men, ungrateful as they are, at least acknowledged their own insufficiency in these important incidents of life, since they confided them to religion, the only effectual resource in the lowest depths of misfortune. O apostle of Christ! what scenes didst thou witness when, standing beside the executioner, thou wast not afraid of being sprinkled with the blood of the wretched culprit, and wast his last friend upon earth! Here is one of the most impressive sights that the world can exhibit! At the two corners of the scaffold human justice and divine justice are met face to face. The one, implacable, and supported by an avenging sword, is accompanied by despair; the sweet attendants of the other are pity and hope. The one has for her minister a man of blood, the other a man of peace. The one condemns, the other absolves. The former says to the victim, whether innocent or guilty, "Thou must die!" the latter cries, "Child of innocence or of repentance, speed thy flight to heaven!"[1]

---

[1] When our author drew this interesting picture of a pious priest discharging the most painful of all duties, he probably had in his mind a *particular* occurrence. As the innocent Louis XVI. ascended the scaffold, to be murdered by his rebellious subjects, the Abbé Edgeworth, his intrepid and faithful confessor, addressed him with these sublime expressions:—"*Fils de St. Louis, montez au ciel!*" S.

BOOK IV.

MISSIONS.

CHAPTER I.

GENERAL SURVEY OF THE MISSIONS.

HERE s another of those grand and original ideas which belong exclusively to the Christian religion. Idolatrous nations knew nothing of that divine enthusiasm which animates the apostle of the gospel. The ancient philosophers themselves never quitted the enchanting walks of Academus and the pleasures of Athens to go, under the guidance of a sublime impulse, to civilize the savage, to instruct the ignorant, to cure the sick, to clothe the poor, to sow the seeds of peace and harmony among hostile nations; but this is what Christians have done and are still doing every day. Neither oceans nor tempests, neither the ices of the pole nor the heat of the tropics, can damp their zeal. They live with the Esquimaux in his seal-skin cabin; they subsist on train-oil with the Greenlander; they traverse the solitude with the Tartar or the Iroquois; they mount the dromedary of the Arab or accompany the wandering Caffir in his burning deserts; the Chinese, the Japanese, the Indian, have become their converts. Not an island, not a rock in the ocean has escaped their zeal; and, as of old the kingdoms of the earth were inadequate to the ambition of Alexander, so the globe itself is too contracted for their charity

When regenerated Europe presented to the preachers of the true faith but one great family of brethren, they turned their eyes toward those distant regions where so many souls still languished in the darkness of idolatry. They were filled with compassion on beholding this degradation of man, and they felt within them an irresistible desire to sacrifice their lives for the salvation of these benighted strangers. They had to penetrate immense forests, to traverse almost impassable morasses, to cross dangerous rivers, to climb inaccessible rocks; they had to encounter nations who were cruel, superstitious, and jealous; in some they had to struggle with the ignorance of barbarism, in others with the prejudices of civilization. All these obstacles were incapable of daunting them. They who no longer believe in the religion of their fathers must at least admit that, if the missionary is fully persuaded that there is no salvation but in the Christian faith, the act by which he dooms himself to sufferings of every kind to save an idolater far surpasses the greatest personal sacrifices recorded in history.

When a man, in sight of a whole nation, and under the eyes of his relatives and friends, exposes himself to death for his native country, he exchanges a few days of life for ages of glory; he sheds lustre on his family, he raises it to wealth and honor But the missionary whose life is spent in the recesses of the forest, who dies a painful death, without spectators, without applause, without advantage to those who are dear to him,—obscure, despised, characterized as a madman, an idiot, a fanatic, and all to procure eternal happiness to an unknown savage,—by what name shall we call such a death, such a sacrifice?

Various religious congregations devoted themselves to the service of the missions:—the Dominicans, the order of St Francis, the Jesuits, and the priests of the foreign missions. Of these missions there were four different classes:—

1. The missions of the Levant, comprehending the Archipelago, Constantinople, Syria, Armenia, the Crimea, Ethiopia, Persia, and Egypt.

2. The missions of America, beginning at Hudson's Bay and extending through Canada, Louisiana, California, the Antilles, and Guiana, to the celebrated settlements of Paraguay.

3. The missions of India, embracing Hindostan, the peninsula on this and on the other side of the Ganges, Manilla, and the Philippine Islands.

4. The missions of China, to which were annexed those of Tonquin, Cochin-China, and Japan.

Besides these, there were some congregations in Iceland and among the negroes of Africa, but they were not regularly supplied. A Presbyterian mission was recently attempted at Otaheite.

When the Jesuits first published that invaluable correspondence entitled *Lettres Édifiantes*, it was quoted and commended by every writer. Implicit faith was given to its authority, and the facts which it contained were considered as indubitable; but it soon became the fashion to decry what had been so highly admired. These letters were written by Christian priests. How was it possible, then, that they could possess any merit? People were not ashamed to prefer, or rather to feign to prefer, the travels of a Baron de la Hontan, distinguished only for his ignorance and disregard of truth, to those of a Dutertre and a Charlevoix. Scholars who had been at the head of the first tribunals in China, who had passed thirty or forty years at the court of the emperors themselves, who spoke and wrote the language of the country, who associated with the little and lived on familiar terms with the great, who had visited the different parts of the country and closely studied the manners, religion, and laws of that vast empire,—these scholars, whose numerous performances enriched the memoirs of the Academy of Sciences, found themselves treated as impostors by a man who had never been out of the European quarter at Canton, who knew not a single word of Chinese, and whose whole merit consisted in flatly contradicting the accounts of the missionaries. All this is now well known, and justice, though tardy, has been done to the Jesuits. Pompous embassies have been sent at a prodigious expense by mighty nations; but have they furnished us with any information which we had not before received from a Duhalde and a Le Comte? or have they detected any falsehoods in the narratives of those fathers?

A missionary, in fact, cannot but be an excellent traveller. Being obliged to speak the language of the people to whom he preaches the gospel, to conform to their customs, to live for a long time among all classes of society, to endeavor to penetrate into the palace as well as the cottage, if he is but scantily endowed with genius he cannot fail to collect a multitude of valuable facts The man, on the contrary, who travels post-haste with an interpreter, who has neither time nor inclination to expose himself to a thousand dangers in order to acquire a knowledge of manners and customs,—that man, though possessed of all the qualities requisite for an accurate observer, will, nevertheless, be able to gain but very superficial notions respecting people of whom he can catch only a transient glimpse as he hastens through their country.

The Jesuit had likewise the advantage of a learned education over the ordinary traveller. The superiors required various qualities in the students destined for the missions. For the Levant, it was necessary to understand the Greek, Coptic, Arabic, and Turkish languages, and to possess some knowledge of medicine; for India and China were wanted astronomers, mathematicians, geographers, and mechanicians; and America was reserved for the naturalists.[1] And how many pious disguises and artifices, how many changes of life and manners, were they obliged to adopt in order to proclaim the truth to mankind! At Madura the missionary assumed the habit of the Indian penitent, submitted to all his customs, practised all his austerities, however repugnant and puerile; in China he became a mandarin and a literary character; among the Iroquois he turned hunter and savage.

Almost all the French missions were established by Colbert and Louvois, who were aware of the service they would render to the arts, sciences, and commerce. Fathers Fontenay, Tachard, Gerbillon, Le Comte, Bouvet, and Visdelou, were sent to India by Louis XIV.; they were all mathematicians, and by the king's command they were admitted members of the Academy of Sciences previously to their departure.

Father Brêdevent, known for his physico-mathematical dissertation, unfortunately died while traversing Ethiopia; but the public reaped the benefit of part of his labors. Father Sicard visited Egypt with draughtsmen furnished him by M. de Maurepas. His great work, under the title of *Description of Ancient and Modern Egypt*, having been deposited while yet in manuscript in the profession-house of the Jesuits, was thence stolen, and no tidings have ever been heard of it since. Certainly no person was better qualified to acquaint us with the state of Persia

[1] See the *Lettres Édifiantes* and Fleury's work on the qualities necessary for a missionary.

and the history of the renowned Thamas Kouli Khan than Bazin the monk, who was first physician to that conqueror and attended him in all his expeditions. Father Cœur-doux informed us respecting the manufactures and dyes of India. China was as well known to us as France; we had original manuscripts and translations of its history; we had Chinese herbals, geographies, and books of mathematics; and, to crown the singularity of this extraordinary mission, Father Ricci wrote moral works in the language of Confucius, and is still accounted an elegant author at Pekin.

If China is now closed against us, and we are no longer able to dispute with the English the empire of India, it is not the fault of the Jesuits, who were on the point of opening to us those vast regions. "They had succeeded in America," says Voltaire, "in teaching savages the necessary arts; they succeeded also in China in teaching a polished nation the most sublime sciences."[1]

The services which they rendered to their country throughout the Levant are equally well established. Were any authentic proof of this required, it would be found in the following distinguished testimonial:—

THE KING'S WARRANT.

"This day, the seventh of June, one thousand six hundred and seventy-nine, the king being at St. Germain-en-Laye, wishing to gratify and favor the French fathers of the Society of Jesus, who are missionaries in the Levant, in consideration of their zeal for religion, and of *the advantages which his subjects, residing and trafficking in those parts, derive from their instructions,* his majesty has retained and retains them for his chaplains in the church and consular chapel of the city of Aleppo in Syria, &c.[2]

(*Signed,*) LOUIS."

To these same missionaries we are indebted for the attachment to the French name still cherished by the savages in the forests of America. A white handkerchief is sufficient to insure you a safe passage through hostile tribes, and to procure you everywhere lodging and hospitality. The Jesuits of Canada and

[1] *Essai sur les missions chrétiennes,* p. 195. [2] *Lettres édif.* tome i. p. 129.

Louisiana discovered new articles of trade, new dyeing materials and medicines, and directed the attention of the colonists to their cultivation. By naturalizing in our country the insects, birds, and plants of foreign climes,[1] they added to the riches of our manufactories, to the delicacies of our table, and to the shade of our woods.

They, too, were the writers of those simple or elegant annals which we possess in relation to our colonies. What an admirable history is that of the Antilles by Dutertre, or that of New France by Charlevoix! The works of those pious authors are fraught with every species of science; learned dissertations, portraitures of manners, plans of improvement for our settlements, the mention of useful objects, moral reflections, interesting adventures, are all to be found in them. You there find the history of an acacia or Chinese willow, as well as that of an emperor reduced to the necessity of stabbing himself; and the account of the conversion of a Paria in the middle of a treatise on the mathematics of the Bramins. The style of these narratives, sometimes rising to the sublime, is often admirable for its simplicity. Lastly, astronomy, and chiefly geography, were annually enriched by our missionaries with new information. A Jesuit in Tartary meets with a Huron woman whom he had known in Canada; from this extraordinary circumstance he infers that the American continent approached at the northwest to the Asiatic coast, and thus he conjectured the existence of that strait which long afterward conferred glory on a Behring and a Cook. Great part of Canada and all Louisiana were explored by our missionaries. In calling the savages of Nova Scotia to Christianity, they transferred to us those coasts which proved a mine of wealth for our commerce and a nursery for our seamen. Such is a small part of the services which these men, now so despised, found means to render to their country.[2]

---

[1] Two monks, during the reign of Justinian, brought the first silkworms from Serinda to Constantinople. For the turkey-fowl, and several foreign trees and shrubs, naturalized in Europe, we are indebted also to the missionaries.

[2] There can scarcely be a doubt that, if a band of missionaries were employed to Christianize the savages of Florida, New Mexico, and California, the United States government would be spared a vast amount of treasure and the sacrifice of many valuable lives. T.

CHAPTER II.

MISSIONS OF THE LEVANT.

EACH of the missions had a character and a species of sufferings peculiar to itself. Those of the Levant presented a spectacle of a very philosophical nature. How powerful was that Christian voice which resounded amid the tombs of Argos and the ruins of Sparta and Athens! In those same islands of Naxos and Salamis which gave birth to the brilliant theories that turned the heads of the Greeks, a poor Catholic priest, disguised as a Turk, throws himself into a boat, lands at some wretched cabin formed among the broken shafts of columns, administers consolation to a descendant of the conquerors of Xerxes extended on a couch of straw, distributes alms in the name of Jesus Christ, and—doing good, as others do evil, under the veil of darkness—returns in secret to his desert.

The man of science who goes to measure the relics of antiquity in the solitudes of Europe and Asia has undoubtedly some claim to our admiration; but there is a man who commands still higher respect,—some unknown Bossuet expounding the words of the prophets on the ruins of Tyre and Babylon.

It pleased the Almighty that there should be an abundant harvest on so rich a soil: ground like that could not be unfruitful. "We left Serpho," says Father Xavier, "more cheered than I am capable of expressing here; the people loading us with benedictions, and thanking God a thousand times for having inspired us with the design and the resolution of visiting them among their rocks!"[1]

The mountains of Lebanon, as well as the sands of Thebais, witnessed the self-devotion of these missionaries. They are inexpressibly happy in giving a lively interest to the most trifling circumstances. If, for example, they are describing the cedars of Lebanon, they tell you of four stone altars which are seen at

---

[1] *Lettr. édif.*, tome i. p. 15.

the foot of those trees, and where the Maronite monks performed a solemn mass on the anniversary of the Transfiguration. Their religious voices seem to mingle with the murmur of those woods celebrated by Solomon and Jeremias, and with the noise of the torrents falling from the mountains.

Are they speaking of the valley where flows the *holy* river, they say, "In these rocky hills are deep caverns which formerly served as so many cells for a great number of recluses, who had chosen these retreats as the only witnesses upon earth of the severity of their penance. It was the tears of these pious penitents that gave to the river just referred to the name of the holy river. Its source is in the mountains of Lebanon. The sight of those caverns and that river in this frightful desert excites compunction, a love of penance, and compassion for those sensual and worldly souls who prefer a few days of enjoyment and pleasure to an eternity of bliss."[1] In our opinion, this passage is a perfect model both in regard to style and sentiment.

These missionaries possessed a wonderful instinct for tracking out misfortune and pursuing it even to its last hiding-place. The slave-prisons and the galleys infected with the plague could not escape their ingenious charity. Hear what Father Tarillon says in his lettter to Pontchartrain:—

"The services which we render to these poor creatures (the Christian slaves at Constantinople) consist in keeping them in the fear of God and in the faith; in procuring them relief from the charity of the faithful; in attending them during illness; and, lastly, in assisting them to die the death of the righteous. If in the performance of these duties we encounter many hardships and difficulties, I can affirm that God rewards it with great consolations. . . . . .

"In times of pestilence, as it is necessary to be close at hand to attend such persons as are infected, and as we have here only four or five missionaries, our custom is to let only one of our number go into the prison and remain there as long as the disease continues. He who obtains permission for this of the superior prepares himself for the task during a few days of retreat, and takes leaves of his brethren as if he were soon to die. Some-

[1] *Lettr. édif.*, tome i. p. 288.

times he accomplishes his sacrifice there, and sometimes he escapes the danger."[1]

Father Jacques Cachod thus writes to Father Tarillon:—"I am now superior to all the fears excited by contagious distempers; and, if it please God, I shall not die of this disease, after the risks which I have run. I am just leaving the prison, where I have administered the sacrament to eighty-two persons. . . . . In the daytime I felt not the least symptom of fear. It was only at night, during the short slumbers which were allowed me, that my mind was harassed with alarming ideas. The greatest danger that I incurred, or perhaps ever shall go through in my life, was in the hold of a man-of-war of eighty-two guns. The slaves, in concert with their overseers, had made me go down to them in the evening, to confess them all night and to say mass very early in the morning. We were shut up, according to custom, under a double lock. Of fifty-two slaves whom I confessed, twelve were sick, and three died before my departure; judge, then, what an atmosphere I must have breathed in that close place without the smallest aperture! God, who, in his goodness, saved me on this occasion, will preserve me on many others."[2]

A man who voluntarily shuts himself up in a prison in time of pestilence,—who candidly acknowledges his terrors, and nevertheless overcomes them from a motive of charity,—who afterward obtains access by a bribe, as if to enjoy illicit pleasures, to the hold of a man-of-war, in order to attend the infected slaves,—such a man, it must be allowed, obeys not any natural impulse; here is something more than *humanity*. This the missionaries admit, and they assume not the credit of these sublime actions. "It is God," they frequently repeat, "who gives us this strength; none of the merit belongs to us."

A young missionary not yet inured to dangers like those veterans, bending under their hardships and evangelical laurels, is astonished at having escaped the first peril; he fears that it has happened through his fault, and seems mortified at the circumstance. After having given his superior an account of the pestilence, during which he was often obliged *to lay his ear close to the lips of the infected, that he might catch their expiring words,*

[1] *Lettr. édif.*, tome i. p. 288.

[2] Ibid., tome i. p. 24.

he adds:—"I was not worthy that God should be pleased to accept the sacrifice of my life which I offered him. I therefore request your prayers that the Almighty may forget my sins and graciously permit me to die for his sake."

Father Bouchet writes from India in the following terms:—"Our mission is more flourishing than ever; we have this year had *four great persecutions.*" It was this same Father Bouchet who sent to Europe the tables of the Bramins which Bailly made use of in his History of Astronomy. The English Company of Calcutta has not yet made public any monuments of Indian science which had not been explored or mentioned by our missionaries; and yet the enlightened English, now the sovereigns of several extensive kingdoms, having at their disposal all the resources of art and power, must certainly possess superior means of success to those enjoyed by a poor, solitary, wandering, and persecuted Jesuit. "If we were to appear ever so little openly in public," says Royer, "we should easily be discovered by our looks and complexion. In order, therefore, not to raise a still more violent persecution against religion, we are under the necessity of keeping ourselves concealed as much as possible. I pass whole days either confined in a boat, which I never quit but at night, to visit the villages contiguous to the rivers, or concealed in some sequestered habitation."[1] The boat of this good religious was his only observatory; but he who possesses charity is truly rich and ingenious.

CHAPTER III.

MISSIONS OF CHINA.

Two monks of the order of St. Francis, the one a Pole, the other a Frenchman by birth, were the first Europeans who penetrated into China, about the middle of the twelfth century. It was afterward visited at two different times by Marco Paolo, a

[1] *Lettr. édif.*, tome i. p. 8.

Venetian, and his kinsmen Nicholas and Matthew Paolo. The Portuguese, having discovered the passage by sea to India, formed a settlement at Macao; and Father Ricci, a Jesuit, resolved to penetrate into the vast empire of Cathay, concerning which so many extraordinary things were related He first applied himself to the study of the Chinese language, one of the most difficult in the world. His ardor vanquished every obstacle, and, after many dangers and repeated refusals, he, in 1682,[1] obtained permission of the Chinese magistrates to reside at Chouachen.

Ricci, who was a pupil of Clavius, and was himself well versed in the mathematics, by means of this science gained patrons among the mandarins He relinquished the dress of the bonzes, and assumed the habit of the learned class. He gave lessons in geometry, in which he contrived to inculcate the more valuable precepts of Christian morality. He resided successively at Chouachen, Nemcham, Pekin, and Nankin, sometimes meeting with ill-treatment, at others being received with joy; encountering adversity with invincible fortitude, and still cherishing the hope of succeeding in introducing the knowledge of Christianity. At length the emperor himself, charmed with the virtues and the talents of the missionary, permitted him to reside in the capital, and granted several privileges to him, and also to the partners of his toils. The Jesuits conducted themselves with the utmost discretion, and displayed a profound knowledge of the human heart. They respected the customs of the Chinese, and conformed to them in every point that was not at variance with the laws of the gospel. Embarrassments attended them on every side. "Jealousy," says Voltaire, "soon destroyed the fruit of their prudence; and that spirit of restlessness and contention, attached in Europe to knowledge and talents, frustrated the grandest designs."[2]

Ricci was equal to every exigency. He answered the accusations of his enemies in Europe; he superintended the infant congregations in China; he gave lessons in mathematics; he wrote controversial books in the Chinese language against the literati who attacked him; he cultivated the friendship of the emperor,

---

[1] This date, which we find in three different editions of the work, is incorrect. It should be 1582. T.

[2] *Essai sur les Mœurs*, ch. cxcv.

and ingratiated himself with the court, where his polished demeanor gained him the favor of the great. All these harassing occupations shortened his days. He terminated at Pekin a life of fifty-seven years, half of which had been spent in the labors of the apostleship.

After Ricci's death his mission was interrupted by the revolutions which happened in China; but when Cun-chi, the Tartar emperor, ascended the throne, he appointed Father Adam Schall president of the board of mathematics. Cun-chi died, and, during the minority of his son Cang-hi, the Christian religion experienced new persecutions.

When the emperor came of age, the calendar being in great confusion, it was found necessary to recall the missionaries. The young prince conceived a partiality for Verbiest, the successor of Schall. He directed that the doctrines of Christianity should be examined by the tribunal of the states of the empire, and made remarks with his own hand on the memoir of the Jesuits. The judges, after mature investigation, declared that the Christian religion was good, and that it contained nothing inimical to purity of morals and the prosperity of nations.

It was worthy of the disciples of Confucius to pronounce such a sentence in favor of the precepts of Christ. Shortly after this decree, Father Verbiest summoned from Paris those learned Jesuits who carried the glory of the French name to the very centre of Asia.

The Jesuit who was bound for China provided himself with telescope and compasses. He appeared at the court of Pekin with all the urbanity of the court of Louis XIV. and surrounded by the retinue of the arts and sciences. Unrolling maps, turning globes, and tracing spheres, he taught the astonished mandarins both the real course of the stars and the true name of Him who guides them in their orbits. He combated errors in physics only with a view to correct those of morality; he replaced in the heart, as its proper seat, that simplicity which he banished from the understanding, exciting at once by his manners and his attainments a profound veneration for his God and a high esteem for his native land.

It was a proud sight for France to behold her humble religious regulating in China the annals of a great empire. Questions were transmitted from Pekin to Paris: chronology, astronomy, natural history, were so many subjects for curious and learned discussion. Chinese books were translated into French, and French into Chinese. Father Parennin, in his letter addressed to Fontenelle, thus wrote to the Academy of Sciences:—"You will perhaps be surprised that I should send you from this distant part of the globe a treatise on anatomy, a course of medicine, and questions on natural philosophy, written in a language with which you are doubtless unacquainted; but your surprise will cease when you find that it is your own works which I have transmitted to you in a Tartar dress."[1]

The reader should peruse this letter from beginning to end: it breathes that tone of politeness and that style of urbanity almost entirely forgotten at the present day. Voltaire characterizes the writer as a man celebrated for his attainments and discretion, and who spoke the Chinese and Tartar languages very fluently; and continues, "He is more particularly known among us by his luminous and instructive answers to the difficulties started by one of our most eminent philosophers respecting the sciences of China."[2]

In 1711, the emperor of China gave the Jesuits three inscriptions, composed by himself, for a church which they were erecting at Pekin. That for the front was:—*To the true principle of all things.* For one of the two columns of the portico was designed the following:—*He is infinitely good and infinitely just; he enlightens, he supports, he directs all things, with supreme authority and with sovereign justice.* The other column displayed these words:—*He had no beginning; he will have no end: he produced all things from the commencement of time; he it is who governs them and is their real Lord.* Whoever takes any interest in the glory of his country cannot, without deep emotion, behold poor French missionaries imparting such ideas of the Supreme Being to the ruler of many millions. What a truly noble application of religion!

The common people, the mandarins, the men of letters, in crowds embraced the new doctrine; the ceremonies of the church, in particular, found the most favorable reception

[1] *Lettr. édif.*, tome xix. p. 257. [2] *Age of Louis XIV.*, vol. ii. ch 39.

"Before the communion," says Father Prémare, cited by Father Fouquet, "I repeated aloud the acts that ought to be performed on approaching the holy sacrament. Though the Chinese tongue is not fertile in expressions for the affections of the heart, this exercise was very successful. . . . . I remarked in the faces of these good Christians a devotion which I had never yet perceived."[1]

"Loukang," adds the same missionary, "had given me a liking for country missions. I walked out of the town and found numbers of poor people everywhere at work. I accosted one of them, whose looks were prepossessing, and spoke to him concerning God. He seemed pleased with what I said, and invited me, by way of doing me an honor, to pay a visit to the *Hall of Ancestors*. This is the best building in the town, and belongs in common to all the inhabitants, because, having for a long time made it a practice not to intermarry with strangers, they are now all related, and have the same forefathers. Here then it was that several of them, quitting their work, assembled to hear the sacred doctrine."[2] Is not this a scene of the Odyssey, or rather of the Bible?

An empire whose immutable manners had for two thousand years been proof against time, revolutions, and conquest,—this empire is suddenly changed at the voice of a Christian monk, who has repaired thither alone from the extremities of Europe. The most deeply-rooted prejudices, the most ancient customs, a religion consecrated by a long succession of ages, all give way, all disappear, before the mere name of the God of the gospel. At the very moment we are writing, at the moment when Christianity is persecuted in Europe, it is propagated in China. That fire which was thought to be extinguished is rekindled, as is invariably the case after persecutions. When the clergy were massacred in France, when they were stripped of their possessions and honors, many were ordained priests in secret; the proscribed bishops were often obliged to refuse orders to young men desirous of flying to martyrdom. This adds one more to the thousand proofs already existing, how grossly they had mistaken

[1] *Lettr. édif.*

[2] *Lettr. édif.*, tome xvii. p. 152, *et seq.*

the spirit of Christianity who hoped to annihilate it by fire and fagot. Unlike all human things, whose nature is to perish under torments, the true religion flourishes in adversity: for God has impressed it with the same seal that he has set upon virtue.

CHAPTER IV.

MISSIONS OF PARAGUAY.

Conversion of the Savages.[1]

While Christianity flourished among the worshippers of Fohi, and other missionaries were announcing it to the noble Japanese or at the courts of sultans, it was seen gliding, as it were, into the inmost forests of Paraguay, to tame those Indian nations who lived like birds on the branches of trees. What an extraordinary religion must that be which, at its will, unites the political and moral forces, and from its superabundant resources produces governments as excellent as those of Minos and Lycurgus! While Europe had as yet but barbarous constitutions, formed by time and chance, the Christian religion revived in the New World all the wonders of the ancient systems of legislation. The wandering tribes of the savages of Paraguay became fixed, and at the word of God an evangelical republic sprang up in the wildest of deserts. And who were the men of great genius that performed these prodigies? Simply Jesuits, who were often thwarted in their designs by the avarice of their countrymen.

It was a practice generally adopted in Spanish America, tc make slaves of the Indians and to sacrifice them to the labors of the mines. In vain did the clergy, both secular and regular, a thousand times remonstrate against this practice, not less impolitic than barbarous. The tribunals of Mexico and Peru, and even the court of Madrid, re-echoed with the continual com-

---

[1] For this and the following chapter, see *Lettres édifiantes*, vols. viii. and ix.; the *History of Paraguay*, by Charlevoix; Lozano's *Historia de la Compagnia de Jesus en la provincia del Paraguay*; Muratori's *Il Christianesimo felice*; and Montesquieu's *Spirit of the Laws*.

plaints of the missionaries.[1] "We pretend not," said they to the colonists, "to prevent your making a profit of the Indians in legitimate ways; but you know that it never was the king's intention that you should consider them as slaves, and that the law of God expressly forbids this. . . . . We deem it wrong to deprive them of their liberty, to which they have a natural right; and nothing can authorize us to call that right in question."[2]

At the foot of the Cordilleras, on the side next to the Atlantic, between the Oronoko and Rio de la Plata, there was still an immense region, peopled by savages, to which the Spaniards had not extended their devastations. In the recesses of its forests the missionaries undertook to found a Christian republic and to confer at least upon a small number of Indians those blessings which they had not been able to procure for all.

The first step they took was to obtain of the court of Spain the liberty of all the savages whom they might convert to the faith. At this intelligence the colonists took the alarm, and it was only by the aid of wit and address that the Jesuits stole, in some measure, the permission to shed their blood in the forests of the New World. At length, having triumphed over human rapacity and malice, and meditating one of the noblest designs that ever entered into the heart of man, they embarked for Rio de la Plata.

That great river has for its tributary the stream which gave name to the country and the missions whose history we are sketching. Paraguay, in the language of the savages, signifies the *Crowned River*, because it rises in the lake Xarayes, by which it thus seems to be crowned. Before it swells the Rio de la Plata, it receives the waters of the Parana and Uraguay. Forests, in which are embosomed other forests, levelled by the hand of time,—morasses and plains completely inundated in the rainy season,—mountains which rear deserts over deserts,—form part of the vast regions watered by the Paraguay. All kinds of game abound in them, as well as tigers and bears. The woods are full of bees, which produce remarkably white wax and

[1] Robertson's *History of America.*

[2] Charlevoix, *Hist. de Paraguay,* tome ii. pp. 26 and 27.

honey of uncommon fragrance. Here are seen birds with the most splendid plumage, resembling large flowers of red and blue, among the verdant foliage of the trees. A French missionary, who lost himself in these wilds, gives the following description of them:—

"I continued my route without knowing whither it would lead me, and without meeting any person from whom I could obtain information. In the midst of these woods I sometimes met with enchanting spots. All that the study and ingenuity of man could devise to render a place agreeable would fall short of the beauties which simple nature has here collected.

"These charming situations reminded me of the ideas which I had formerly conceived when reading the lives of the ancient recluses of Thebais. I formed a wish to pass the rest of my days in these forests, whither Providence had conducted me, that I might devote all my attention to the affair of my salvation, far from all intercourse with men; but, as I was not the master of my destiny, and the commands of the Lord were expressly signified in those of my superiors, I rejected this idea as an illusion."[1]

The Indians who were found in these retreats resembled their place of habitation only in its worst points. This indolent, stupid, and ferocious race exhibited in all its deformity the degradation of man after his fall. Nothing affords a stronger proof of the degeneracy of human nature than the littleness of the savage amid the grandeur of the desert.

On their arrival at Buenos Ayres, the missionaries sailed up the Rio de la Plata, entered the waters of the Paraguay, and dispersed over its wilds. The ancient accounts portray them with a breviary under the left arm, a large cross in the right hand, and with no other provision than their trust in the Almighty. They represent them forcing their way through forests, wading through morasses where they were up to the waist in water, climbing rugged rocks, searching among caverns and precipices, at the risk of meeting with serpents and ferocious beasts instead of men whom they were seeking.

Several perished with hunger and from the hardships they

[1] *Lettr. édif.*, tome viii. p. 381.

endured. Others were massacred and devoured by the savages. Father Lizardi was found transfixed with arrows upon a rock; half of his body was mangled by birds of prey, and his breviary lay open beside him at the office for the dead. When a missionary thus discovered the remains of one of his companions, he hastened to perform the funeral rites; and, filled with great joy, he sung a solitary *Te Deum* over the grave of the martyr.

Such scenes, perpetually recurring, astonished the barbarous hordes. Sometimes they gathered round the unknown priest who spoke to them concerning God, and looked at the firmament to which he pointed; at others they ran from him as a magician, and were overcome by unusual terrors. The religious followed, stretching out his hands to them in the name of Jesus Christ. If he could not prevail on them to stop, he planted his cross in a conspicuous place and concealed himself in the woods. The savages by degrees approached to examine the standard of peace erected in the wilderness; some secret magnet seemed to attract them to this emblem of their salvation. The missionary then, sallying forth all at once from his ambuscade, and taking advantage of the surprise of the barbarians, invited them to relinquish their miserable way of life, and to enjoy the comforts of society.

When the Jesuits had succeeded in their efforts with a few Indians, they had recourse to another method of winning souls. They had remarked that the savages of that region were extremely sensible to the charms of music: it is even asserted that the waters of the Paraguay impart a finer tone to the voice. The missionaries, therefore, embarked in canoes with the new converts, and sailed up the rivers singing religious hymns. The neophytes repeated the tunes, as tame birds sing to allure the wild ones into the net of the fowler. The savages were always taken by this pious snare. Descending from their mountains, they hastened to the banks of the rivers to listen to the captivating sounds; and many, plunging into the water, swam after the enchanted bark. The bow and arrow dropped from the hand of the savage, and a foretaste of the social virtues and of the first sweets of humanity seemed to take possession of his wondering and confused soul. He beheld his wife and his infant weep for unknown joy; soon, yielding to an irresistible impulse, he fell at the foot of the cross, and mingled torrents of tears with the regenerating waters that were poured upon his head.

Thus the Christian religion realized in the forests of America what fabulous history relates of an Orpheus and an Amphion,—a reflection so natural that it occurred to the missionaries themselves.[1] Certain it is that their relation, though strictly true, wore all the semblance of a fiction.

CHAPTER V.

MISSIONS OF PARAGUAY, CONTINUED.

Christian Republic—Happiness of the Indians.

THE first savages who complied with the exhortations of the Jesuits were the Guaranis,—a tribe scattered along the rivers Paranapane, Pirape, and Uraguay. They formed a large village under the direction of Fathers Maceta and Cataldino, whose names it is but just to preserve among those of the benefactors of mankind. This village was called Loretto; and, in the sequel, as other Indian churches were successively established, they were all comprehended under the general name of *Reductions.* In a few years their number amounted to thirty, and they collectively composed that celebrated *Christian commonwealth* which seemed to be a relic of antiquity discovered in the New World. They confirmed under our own eyes the great truth known to Greece and Rome,—that men are to be civilized and empires founded, not by the abstract principles of philosophy, but by the aid of religion.

Each village was governed by two missionaries who superintended the affairs, both spiritual and temporal, of the little republics. No stranger was permitted to reside there longer than three days; and, to prevent all such intercourse as was liable to corrupt

---

[1] Charlevoix.

the manners of the new Christians, they were not permitted to learn the Spanish language so as to speak it, though all the converts could read and write it correctly.

In each *Reduction* there were two schools, the one for the first rudiments of learning, the other for dancing and music. The latter, which likewise served as a foundation for the laws of the ancient republics, was particularly cultivated by the Guaranis, who could themselves build organs and make harps, flutes, guitars, and our martial instruments.

As soon as a boy had attained the age of seven years, the two superiors began to study his character. If he appeared adapted for mechanical occupations, he was placed in one of the workshops of the Reduction, the choice of which was left to himself. Here he became a goldsmith, gilder, watchmaker, locksmith, carpenter, cabinet-maker, weaver, or founder. All these trades were originally established by the Jesuits themselves, who had learned all the useful arts for the express purpose of instructing the Indians in them without being obliged to have recourse to strangers.

Such of the young people as preferred agricultural pursuits were enrolled in the class of husbandmen; and those who still retained any strolling propensity, from their former way of life, wandered about with the flocks.

The women worked apart from the men, at their own homes. At the beginning of every week a certain quantity of wool and cotton was distributed among them. This they were to return on the Saturday evening following, ready for further operations. They were likewise engaged in rural employments, which occupied their leisure without exceeding their strength.

There were no public markets in the villages; but on stated days each family was supplied with the necessaries of life. One of the missionaries superintended the distribution, and took care that the shares should be proportionate to the number of persons belonging to each cottage.

The ringing of a bell was the signal for beginning and leaving off work. It was heard at the first dawn of day, when the children immediately assembled in the church, and their matin concert, like that of the birds, lasted till sunrise. The men and women afterward attended mass, and then repaired to their respective labors. At the decline of day the bell again summoned the new citizens to the altar, and evening prayers were chanted in two parts, accompanied by a full band . .

The ground was divided into lots, and each family cultivated one of them for the supply of its wants. There was besides a public field called the *Possession of God.*[1] The produce of this common field was destined to make up for the deficiency of bad crops, and to support the widows, orphans, and infirm. It likewise served as a fund for war. If, at the end of the year, any surplus remained in the public exchequer, it went to defray the expenses of the Church and to discharge the tribute of a gold crown paid by every family to the king of Spain.[2]

A *cacique* or war-chief, a *corregidor* for the administration of justice, *regidors* and *alcaldes* for the police and the superintendence of the public works, composed the civil, military, and political establishment of the Reductions. These magistrates were elected by the general assembly of the citizens, but it appears that they were only permitted to choose out of a certain number of persons proposed by the missionaries. This was a law borrowed from the senate and people of Rome. There was, moreover, an officer called *fiscal*, a kind of public controller, elected by the elders. He kept a register of all the males capable of bearing arms. A *teniente* was the prefect of the children. He conducted them to the church, and attended them to the schools, carrying a long stick in his hand. He reported to the missionaries such observations as he had made on the manners, dispositions, and good or bad qualities of his pupils.

Finally, the village was divided into several quarters, each of which had a superintendent. As the Indians are naturally sluggish and improvident, a person was appointed to examine the agricultural implements, and to compel the heads of families to cultivate their lands.

In case of any infringement of the laws, the first fault was punished by a secret reprimand from the missionaries, the second by a public penance at the door of the church, as among the early Christians; the third by the discipline of the whip But, during

[1] Montesquieu was mistaken in supposing that there was a community of property in Paraguay. Here we see what led him into this error.

[2] Charlevoix's *Hist. of Paraguay.* Montesquieu has estimated this tribute at one fifth of the capital.

the century and a half that this republic subsisted, we scarcely find a single instance of an Indian who incurred the last-mentioned chastisement. "All their faults," says Charlevoix, "are the faults of children. They continue such all their lives in many things, and have likewise all the good qualities of childhood."

The indolent were sentenced to cultivate a larger portion of the common field; so that a judicious economy had made the very defects of these innocent creatures subservient to the general prosperity.

In order to prevent licentiousness, care was taken to marry the young people at an early age. Women that had no children retired, during the absence of their husbands, to a particular building called the *House of Refuge*. The sexes were kept separate, very much as in the Grecian republics. They had distinct benches at church, and different doors at which they went in and out without intermingling.

There were fixed regulations for every thing, not excepting dress, which was decent and becoming, yet not ungraceful. The women wore a plain white tunic, fastened round the waist. Their arms and legs were uncovered, and their loosely-flowing hair served them instead of a veil.

The men were habited like the ancient Castilians. When they went to their work they put a white frock over this dignified dress. Those who had signalized themselves by acts of courage or virtue were distinguished by frocks of a purple color.

The Spaniards, and the Portuguese of Brazil in particular, made incursions into the territory of the *Christian Republic*, and often carried off some of its citizens into slavery. Determined to put an end to these depredations, the Jesuits, by delicate management, contrived to obtain permission from the Court of Madrid to arm their converts. They procured the raw materials, established foundries for cannon and manufactories of gunpowder, and trained to war those who were not suffered to live in peace. A regular military force assembled every Monday to perform evolutions and to be reviewed by the cacique. There were prizes for the archers, the pikemen, the slingers, the artillerymen, and the musketeers. The Portuguese, when they returned, instead of finding a few straggling and panic-struck husbandmen, were met by battalions which cut them in pieces and pursued them to their very forts. It was remarked that these new troops never receded, and that they rallied without confusion amid the fire of the enemy. Such was their ardor that they were often hurried away by it in their military exercises, and it was found necessary to interrupt them for fear of accidents.

Paraguay then afforded an example of a state exempt both from the dangers of a wholly military constitution, like that of Lacedæmon, and the inconveniences of a wholly pacific community, such as that of the Quakers. The great political problem was solved. Agriculture, which sustains, and arms, which preserve, were here united. The Guaranis were planters though they had no slaves, and soldiers without being ferocious,—immense and sublime advantages, which they owed to the Christian religion, and which neither the Greeks nor the Romans had ever enjoyed under their system of polytheism.

In every thing a wise medium was observed. The Christian Republic was neither absolutely agricultural, nor exclusively addicted to war, nor entirely cut off from letters and commerce. It had a little of all, and a great number of festivals. It was neither morose like Sparta, nor frivolous like Athens. The citizen was neither oppressed with toil nor intoxicated with pleasure. Finally, the missionaries, while they confined the multitude to the necessaries of life, were capable of distinguishing among the flock those children whom nature had marked for higher destinies. According to Plato's plan, they separated such as gave indications of genius, in order to initiate them in the sciences and letters. This select number was called the *Congregation* The children belonging to it were educated in a kind of seminary, and subjected to the same rigid silence, seclusion, and study, as the disciples of Pythagoras. Such was the emulation which prevailed among them, that the mere threat of being sent back to the inferior schools plunged a pupil into the deepest distress. It was this excellent institution that was destined one day to furnish the country with priests, magistrates, and heroes.

The villages of the Reductions occupied a considerable space, generally on the bank of a river and in an agreeable situation. All the houses were uniform, built of stone, and of a single story; the streets were spacious and straight. In the centre of the village was the public square, formed by the church, the habitation of the missionaries, the arsenal, the public granary, the House of Refuge, and the inn for strangers. The churches were handsome and highly ornamented; the walls were covered with pictures separated by festoons of natural foliage. On festivals, perfumed waters were sprinkled in the nave and the sanctuary was strewed with the flowers of lianas.

The cemetery, situated behind the church, formed an oblong square enclosed with walls about breast high. It was bordered all round by an alley of palm-trees and cypresses, and intersected longitudinally by other alleys of lemon and orange-trees. That in the middle led to a chapel where was celebrated every Monday a mass for the dead.

From the end of the streets of the village, avenues of the finest and largest trees led to other chapels in the country, and which could be seen in the distance. These religious monuments served as boundaries to the processions on occasions of extraordinary solemnity.

On Sunday, after the mass, the ceremonies of betrothing and marriage were performed, and in the evening the catechumens and infants were baptized in the same manner as in the primitive church, with three immersions, with singing, and the use of the white costume.

The principal festivals were announced by extraordinary parade. On the preceding evening bonfires were kindled, the streets were illuminated, and the children danced in the public square. Next morning, at daybreak, the soldiers appeared under arms. The war-cacique who headed them was mounted on a stately charger, and proceeded under a canopy borne by two horsemen at his side. At noon, after divine service, an entertainment was given to such strangers as happened to be at the place, and a small quantity of wine was allowed to be used. In the evening there was the race of the ring, at which the two fathers were present to deliver the prizes to the victors; and as soon as it was dark they gave the signal for retiring, at which all these happy and peaceful families repaired to their homes to enjoy the sweets of repose.

In the midst of these wild forests, and among this ancient people, the celebration of the feast of the Blessed Sacrament presented an extraordinary spectacle. The Jesuits allowed them to dance, after the Greek fashion, as they had nothing to fear for the morals of Christians who were so remarkable for their innocence. We shall here give the description which Father Charlevoix has left us of this ceremony:—

"I have remarked that there was nothing very valuable to be seen at this celebration. All the beauties of simple nature are brought into requisition, with a variety that presents it in the most favorable light. Nature here, if I may so speak, is all life: for, on the flowers and branches of the trees which form the triumphal arches under which the Blessed Sacrament is carried, birds of every variety of plumage are seen hovering, confined by long cords, which give them the appearance of being perfectly free and of coming of their own accord to mingle their notes with the sacred song of the musicians and the people, and to praise in their own way that God whose providence never fails them. . . .

"At certain distances are seen tigers and lions, securely chained, so as not to disturb the celebration, and beautiful fishes sporting in large basins of water. In a word, every species of living creature is made to assist at the ceremony, as if deputed to render homage to the Man-God in his august sacrament.

"The solemnity of this festival is further enhanced by the introduction of whatever is used by the people in times of great rejoicing The first-fruits of the harvest are offered to the Lord, and the grain which is to be sown is presented to receive his blessing. The warbling of the birds, the roaring of the lions, the howling of the tigers, all is heard without confusion, and forms a concert unique in its kind . . .

"As soon as the procession returns to the church, all the eatables that were exposed during the ceremony are presented to the missionaries, who send the choicest portion of them to the sick, and distribute the rest among the people of the village. In the evening there is a display of fireworks, which takes place on all the great solemnities and on days of public rejoicing."

Under a government so paternal and so analogous to the simple and pompous nature of the savage, it is not surprising that the new Christians were the purest and the happiest of men. The change which took place in their habits and morals was a miracle in the eyes of the New World. That spirit of cruelty and vengeance, that subjection to the grossest vices which characterize the

Indian tribes, were transformed into a spirit of meekness, patience, and chastity. We may form some idea of their virtues from an expression of the Bishop of Buenos Ayres in a letter to the king of Spain:—"Sire," said he, "among those numerous tribes of Indians, who are naturally prone to all sorts of vice, there prevails so much innocence that I do not think they ever commit a mortal sin."

In these communities of Christian savages there were neither lawsuits nor quarrels. Even the distinctions of *mine* and *thine* were unknown; for, as Charlevoix observes, he possesses nothing of his own who is always ready to share the little he has with those who are in want. Abundantly supplied with all the necessaries of life, governed by the same persons who had rescued them from barbarism and whom they justly regarded as a kind of divinities, indulging the best feelings of nature in the bosom of their families and among their countrymen at large, enjoying the advantages of civilized life without having ever quitted the desert, and the pleasures of society without having lost those of solitude, these Indians might boast of a happiness unprecedented in the world. Hospitality, friendship, justice, and the tender virtues, flowed naturally from their hearts under the influence of religion, as the ripe fruit of the olive falls by the action of the winds. Muratori has in one single word portrayed this Christian commonwealth, by entitling the description he has given of it *Il Cristianesimo felice.*

In perusing this history, we seem to have but one desire—namely, to cross the ocean, and, far distant from troubles and revolutions, to seek an obscure life in the huts of these savages and a peaceful grave under the palm-trees of the cemeteries. But no deserts are so solitary nor seas so vast as to secure man from the afflictions which pursue him. Whenever we delineate the felicity of a nation, we must at last come to the catastrophe; amid the most pleasing pictures, the heart of the writer is harrowed by this melancholy reflection, which is incessantly recurring:—*All this is no more.* The missions of Paraguay are destroyed; the savages, assembled together with so much trouble, are again wandering in the woods or buried alive in the bowels of the earth; and this destruction of one of the fairest works ever produced by the hand of man has been applauded. It was a creation of Christianity, a field fertilized by the blood of apostles; this was enough to make it an object of hatred and contempt. Nevertheless, at the very moment when infidelity triumphed at the sight of Indians consigned in the New World to an execrable servitude, all Europe re-echoed its pretended philanthropy and love of liberty! These disgraceful variations of human nature, according as it is actuated by contrary passions, stupify the soul, and would be sufficient to excite a hatred of our species were we to keep our eyes too long fixed upon them. Let us then rather say that we are weak creatures, that the ways of the Almighty are inscrutable, and that he is pleased to try his servants. While we here indulge our grief, the simple Christians of Paraguay, now buried in the mines of Potosi, are doubtless adoring the hand which has smitten them, and, by their patient endurance of affliction, are acquiring a place in that republic of the saints which is beyond the reach of the persecutions of men.

CHAPTER VI.

MISSIONS OF GUIANA.

If these missions astonish by their grandeur, there are others which, though less known, are not less worthy of admiration. It is often in the obscure cottage and on the grave of the indigent that the King of kings loves to display the riches of his grace and of his miracles. In proceeding northward from Paraguay to the extremity of Canada, you formerly met with a great number of small missions, where the convert had not become civilized to attach himself to the apostle, but where the apostle had turned savage to accompany the convert. The French religious were at the head of these wandering churches, whose perils and perpetual change of place seemed exactly calculated for our courage and genius.

Father Creuilli, a Jesuit, founded the missions of Cayenne. What he accomplished for the comfort of the negroes and savages seems to surpass the powers of human nature. Lombard and

Ramette, treading in the steps of this holy man, penetrated into the morasses of Guiana. Here they gained the affections of the Galibis, by devoting themselves to the relief of their sufferings, and prevailed on those Indians to intrust them with some of their children, whom they instructed in the Christian religion. On returning to their native forests these civilized youths preached the gospel to their aged and savage parents, who were easily convinced by the eloquence of the new missionaries. The converts assembled at a place called Kourou, where Father Lombard, with two negroes, had erected a hut. Their settlement daily increasing, they resolved to have a church. But how were they to pay the builder, a carpenter of Cayenne, who demanded fifteen hundred francs for the work? The missionary and his disciples, though rich in virtues, were in other respects the poorest of men. Faith and charity are ingenious; the Galibis engaged to hollow out seven canoes, for which the carpenter agreed to allow two hundred francs a piece. To make up the rest of the sum, the women spun as much cotton as would suffice for eight hammocks. Twenty others of the savages labored as voluntary slaves for a planter the whole time that his two negroes, whom he consented to lend for the purpose, were employed in sawing boards for the roof of the edifice. Thus the whole business was accomplished, and a temple of God arose in the desert.

He who from all eternity has marked out the course of things, has recently unfolded in those regions one of those designs whose first principles escape the sagacity of men, and whose depths we cannot penetrate till the very instant of their fulfilment. When Father Lombard, upward of a century ago, laid the foundations of his mission among the Galibis, little did he imagine that he was only disposing the savages to receive at some future period the martyrs of the faith, and that he was preparing the deserts of a new Thebais for persecuted religion. What a fertile subject for reflection! Billaud de Varennes and Pichegru, the one the tyrant, the other the victim, met in the same cabin at Synnamary!—hearts which the extremity of misery itself had proved incapable of uniting[1]. Irreconcilable animosities raged among

[1] Pichegru was a French general of distinguished abilities during the Revolution, but opposed to the excesses of the times. He was banished under the *Directory* to Cayenne, whence he afterward escaped. He had been preceded

the partners of the same chains, and the cries of unfortunate wretches ready to tear one another in pieces were mingled with the yell of tigers in the forests of the New World.

Amid this tumult of the passions, behold evangelical composure and serenity! confessors of Jesus Christ cast among the converts of Guiana, and finding among Christian barbarians that compassion which was denied them by their own countrymen; indigent nuns, who seemed to have exiled themselves to a destructive climate merely to nurse a Collot d'Herbois on his deathbed, and to bestow on him all the attentions of Christian charity,—these pious females making no distinction between the innocent and the guilty in their love of humanity, shedding tears over all, praying to God to bless both the persecutors of his name and the martyrs of his faith. What a lesson! what a scene! How wretched are men, and how beautiful is religion!

CHAPTER VII.

MISSIONS OF THE ANTILLES.

The establishment of the French colonies in the Antilles, or *Ant-Isles*, (thus named because they are the first you come to at the entrance of the Gulf of Mexico,) dates no further back than the year 1627, when M. d'Enambuc built a fort and left a few families in the island of St. Christopher.

It was customary at that time to send missionaries as ministers to distant settlements, that religion might partake in some measure of that spirit of intrepidity and adventure which distinguished those who first went to seek their fortune in the New World. The *Friars Preachers* of the congregation of St. Louis, the Carmelites, the Capuchins, and the Jesuits, devoted themselves to the instruction of the Caribbees and Negroes, and to all the duties required by the infant colonies of St. Christopher's, Guadaloupe, Martinique, and St. Domingo.

---

thither by Billaud de Varennes and Collot d'Herbois, among the most ferocious characters of the *Reign of Terror*, the latter of whom died in that country. T.

Even at the present day, we know of no account of the Antilles more satisfactory and complete than the history of Father Dutertre, a missionary of the congregation of St. Louis.

"The Caribbees," says he, "are greatly prone to musing. Their faces bear the stamp of a pensive and melancholy character. They pass half the day together seated on the summit of a rock or on the shore, their eyes fixed on the earth or on the sea, without uttering a single word. . . . . They are of a kind, gentle, affable, and compassionate disposition, being very often affected even to tears by the distresses of the French, and cruel to none but their sworn enemies.

"Mothers are tenderly attached to their children, and are always on the alert to prevent any accident that may befall them. They keep them almost always at the breast, even in the night; and it is a wonder that, lying as they do in suspended hammocks, which are very inconvenient, they never smother any of their infants. . . . . In all their excursions, either by sea or land, they carry them along under their arms in little beds of cotton, suspended from the shoulder in a scarf, that they may have the objects of their anxious care continually before their eyes."[1]

You almost imagine here that you are reading a passage of Plutarch.

With a disposition to dwell on the simple and tender, Dutertre cannot fail to be deeply affecting when he speaks of the Negroes. He has not represented them, however,—after the manner of the philanthropists,—as the most virtuous of mankind; but he has given us a picture of their sentiments which is characterized by feeling, good-nature, and sound judgment.

"There was an instance at Guadeloupe," says he, "of a young negress so profoundly impressed with the wretchedness of her condition, that her master never could prevail upon her to marry the negro whom he had selected for her. . . . . She waited till the priest (at the altar) asked if she would have such a person for her husband, and then she replied, with a firmness that astonished us, 'No, father; I will neither have him nor any other. I am content to be miserable myself, without bringing into the world children who would, perhaps, be still more miserable than

I am, and whose sufferings would be much more painful to me than my own.' She accordingly remained unmarried, and was commonly called the *Maid of the Isles*."

Thus does the good father delineate the manners of the Negroes, describe the economy of their humble dwellings, and interest the reader in their affection for their children. He intermingles with his narrative sentences from Seneca, who speaks of the simplicity of the cottages inhabited by the people of the Golden Age. Then he quotes Plato, or rather Homer, who says that the gods take from the slave one-half of his energies. He compares the free Caribbean savage with the enslaved Negro savage, and shows how much Christianity assists the latter to endure his afflictions.

It has been the fashion of our times to accuse priests of fostering servitude and countenancing the oppression of the people, while it is certain that no class of men have ever raised their voice with so much courage and energy in behalf of the slave and for the relief of the poor and helpless as the Catholic clergy. They have always maintained that liberty is an imprescriptible right of the Christian. Convinced of this, the Protestant colonist, with a view to conciliate cupidity and conscience, deferred the baptism of the Negro until the hour of death; and, in many cases, he allowed the slave to die without the benefit of this regenerating rite, fearing lest, recovering from his illness, he should claim his liberty on the ground of being a *Christian*.[1]

---

[1] *Histoire des Antil.*, tome ii. p. 503. By her wise legislation the Church contributed vastly to the mitigation of the evils of slavery under the old Roman civilization and during subsequent periods, and finally succeeded in abolishing it from Europe. In the twelfth century Alexander III. forbade Christians to be held in slavery; for it was an axiom which had grown out of the salutary operation of Christianity upon society that a Christian should not be kept as a slave. The Catholic missionaries, however, in the New World, advocated the cause of the Indians who were reduced to slavery by the cruel rapacity of the European colonists, not only on the ground of their being Christians, but of their belonging to the great family of Adam. This was a sufficient title to their liberty; for the latter was a natural right, the invasion of which could not be justified by any motives of human passion. But, as the author well observes in the sequel of this chapter, where the missionaries found domestic slavery existing as a social evil, they strove to mitigate the sufferings of those in bondage, without aiming at the overthrow of the established order or violating the rights of property. T.

Religion here shows itself as noble and beautiful as avarice is mean and hateful.

The compassionate and religious spirit which the missionaries evinced, in speaking of the Negroes in our colonies, was alone in accordance with the dictates of reason and humanity. It rendered the master more merciful and the slave more virtuous. It served the cause of mankind without injury to the country, to the existing order, or to the rights of property. But a vain, boasting philanthropy has ruined every thing. Even the sentiment of pity has been extinguished; for who would now dare to espouse the cause of the blacks after the crimes which they have committed? Such is the result of our pretensions! The most laudable objects have been frustrated by our short-sighted policy.[1]

In natural history Father Dutertre has a happy talent of description. He sometimes gives you an idea of an animal by a single expression. The humming-bird he calls a *celestial flower*, imitating the language of Commire in regard to the butterfly:—

Florem putares nare per liquidum æthera.

"The plumage of the flamingo," says he, "has a flesh-color; and, when flying against the rays of the sun, it shines like a firebrand." Buffon has not described the flight of a bird more successfully than the historian of the Antilles. Speaking of the sea-swallow, he says:—"This bird has much difficulty in rising above the branches of a tree; but when it has once taken its flight it skims peacefully through the air, its wings extended and scarcely moving, yet without its experiencing the slightest fatigue. If a heavy rain or violent wind impedes its way, it makes for the clouds, soaring aloft to the middle region of the atmosphere and disappearing from the sight of man."[2]

He thus describes the female humming-bird in the process of building its nest:—

. . . . . "She cards, as it were, all the cotton that is brought to her by her mate, and turns it over thread after thread with her bill and diminutive feet. Then she forms her nest, which is not

[1] The author had before his eyes the massacres of St. Domingo, which had but recently occurred. His remarks on the ultra philanthropy of his time will be easily applied in our own day and country. T.

[2] *Histoire des Antil.*, tome ii. p. 268, &c.

larger than the half of a pigeon-egg. While raising this little structure, she goes round it innumerable times, smoothing the border of it with her neck and the interior with her tail. . . . . I have never been able to ascertain what food the mother brings her young ones, except that she gives them her tongue to suck, which is all covered, I believe, with the sweets of various flowers."

If perfection in the art of delineation consists in giving a precise idea of objects and always exhibiting them in an agreeable point of view, that perfection must be awarded to the missionary of the Antilles.

CHAPTER VIII.

MISSIONS OF NEW FRANCE.

We shall not treat of the missions of California, because they exhibit no peculiar characteristic; nor of those of Louisiana, which resemble the fearful missions of Canada, where the intrepidity of the apostles of Jesus Christ shone forth in all its glory.

When the French, under the command of Champlain, sailed up the river St. Lawrence, they found the forests of Canada inhabited by savages very different from those who had heretofore been discovered in the New World. They were robust, courageous men, proud of their independence, capable of reasoning and calculation, neither astonished at the manners of the Europeans nor dismayed by their arms;[1] and, instead of admiring us like the innocent Caribbeans, manifesting for our customs naught but scorn and disgust.

Three nations shared the empire of the desert:—the Algonquin, (the principal and most ancient of all, but which, having by its power incurred the hatred, was also about to succumb under the

---

[1] In the first engagement which took place between Champlain and the Iroquois, those Indians sustained the fire of the French without showing the least sign of surprise or terror.

united attacks, of the other two,) the Huron, our ally, and the Iroquois, our enemy.

These were not roving nations. They had fixed habitations and regular governments. We have had opportunities of observing, among the Indians of the New World, all the constitutions of civilized nations. Thus, the Natchez, in Louisiana, afforded an example of despotism in the state of nature; the Creeks, of Florida, had a monarchy; and the Iroquois, in Canada, a republican government.

These last and the Hurons were the Spartans and Athenians of those savage regions. The Hurons—witty, gay, and sprightly, yet deceitful, brave, and eloquent, elated with success, dispirited by adverse fortune, and governed by their women—had more honor than patriotism. The Iroquois—divided into cantons which were under the direction of ambitious old men, politic, taciturn, and demure, burning with the desire of dominion, capable of the greatest vices and of the most sublime virtues, sacrificing every thing to the welfare of their country—were at once the most ferocious and the most intrepid of men. No sooner did the French and English appear in those regions than, by a natural instinct, the Hurons joined the former and the Iroquois sided with the latter, but without feeling any attachment for them, and only making use of them for the purpose of procuring arms. They forsook their new allies whenever they became too powerful, and united with them again when the French proved victorious. Thus did a petty band of savages artfully temporize between two great civilized nations, seeking to destroy the one by the other, frequently on the point of accomplishing this deep design, and of becoming at once the masters and deliverers of this vast portion of the New World.

Such were the nations whom our missionaries undertook to conciliate by means of religion. If France beheld her empire in the New World extended beyond the banks of the Meschacebe,—if she retained Canada for so long a period against the united force of the English and Iroquois,—she owed almost all her success to the Jesuits. They saved the infant colony by placing before it as a bulwark a village of Christian Hurons and Iroquois—by preventing general coalitions of the Indians—by negotiating treaties of peace—by exposing themselves singly to the fury of the Iroquois in order to frustrate the designs of the English. The despatches of the governors of the provinces composing New England are continually characterizing the French missionaries as the most dangerous enemies, and represent them as disconcerting the plans of the British power, discovering its secrets, and bereaving it of the affections and the aid of the savages.

The wretched administration of Canada, the wrong measures taken by the governors, a narrow or oppressive policy, often proved greater obstacles to the good intentions of the Jesuits than the opposition of the enemy. If they presented the most judicious and best-concerted plans for the prosperity of the colony, they were commended for their zeal, while other counsels were adopted; but no sooner did the state of affairs become critical than application was made to them for advice. The governors scrupled not to employ them in the most dangerous negotiations, regardless of the perils to which they exposed them. Of this the history of New France affords a remarkable instance:—

A war had broken out between the French and Iroquois. Fortune favored the latter. They had advanced to the very walls of Quebec, and had massacred and devoured the inhabitants of the adjacent country. Every thing was given up for lost. Father Lamberville was at this very moment living as a missionary among the Iroquois. Though continually in danger of being burned alive by the conquerors, he had been induced to remain with the savages in the hope of bringing them into pacific measures, and thus saving the relics of the colony. The elders loved him, and had protected him against the warriors.

At this juncture he received a letter from the governor of Canada beseeching him to persuade the savages to send ambassadors to Fort Catarocouy to treat of peace. The missionary repaired to the elders, and, by his entreaties, prevailed upon them to accept the truce and depute their principal chiefs. These chiefs, on reaching the place appointed for the meeting, were made prisoners, thrown into irons, and sent to France to the galleys.

Lamberville was ignorant of the secret design of the governor. Such was the sincerity with which he had acted that he still continued to reside as before among the savages. When he received intelligence of what had happened, he gave himself up for lost.

When summoned to appear before the elders, he found them assembled in council with stern looks and a threatening aspect One of them, in terms of just indignation, related the treachery of the governor, and then added:—"It cannot be denied that we have every reason to treat thee as an enemy; but this we cannot prevail upon ourselves to do. We know thee too well not to be convinced that thy heart had no share in the treachery of which thou hast been the instrument; and we are not so unjust as to punish thee for a crime of which we believe thee to be innocent, and for which thou undoubtedly feelest as strong an abhorrence as we. . . . . It is not, however, fit that thou shouldst remain here. All our people would not, perhaps, do thee the same justice; and, when once our young men have sung the war-song, they will consider thee as a traitor who has consigned our chiefs to hard and cruel slavery, and will listen only to their fury, from which it will not then be in our power to deliver thee."[1]

After this they constrained the missionary to depart, and gave him guides to conduct him by unfrequented roads beyond the frontiers of their country. Louis XIV., being informed of the manner in which the Indians had been arrested, gave orders for their release. The chief who had addressed Lamberville was soon afterward converted, and retired to Quebec. His conduct on this occasion was the first-fruits of the virtues of Christianity, which had already begun to spring up in his heart.

But what men, too, were a Brebœuf, a Lallemant, a Jogues, who fertilized with their blood the frozen wastes of New France! I myself met one of these apostles of religion amid the solitudes of America. One morning, as we were slowly pursuing our course through the forests, we perceived a tall, venerable old man, with a white beard, approaching us. He was dressed in a long robe, and walked with the aid of a staff, at the same time reading attentively in a book. He appeared radiantly illumined by the rising sun, which threw a beam upon him athwart the foliage of the trees. Fancy would fain have believed him to be Thermosiris issuing from the sacred wood of the Muses in the deserts of Upper Egypt. He proved to be a missionary of Louisiana on

---

[1] Charlevoix, *Histoire de la Nouv. France*, tome i. livre xi.

his way from New Orleans, returning to the country of the Illinois, where he had the superintendence of a little flock of French people and Christian savages He accompanied us for several days; and, however early we were up in the morning, we always found the aged traveller risen before us, and reading his breviary while walking in the forest. This holy man had suffered much. He related to us many of the afflictions of his life, concerning which he spoke without a murmur, still less with pleasure, but yet with serenity. Never did we behold a more placid smile than his. He frequently and aptly recited verses of Virgil and Homer, which he applied to the enchanting scenes that successively presented themselves to our view or to the thoughts with which we were engaged. He seemed to possess great attainments of every kind, which he scarcely suffered to appear under his evangelical simplicity. Like his predecessors, the apostles, though knowing every thing, he seemed to know nothing. We had one day a conversation on the subject of the French Revolution, and we felt a secret pleasure in talking of the troubles of men amid the most tranquil scenes. We were seated in a valley on the banks of a river whose name we knew not, and which, for a long series of ages, had poured its refreshing waters through this unknown region. On making this observation, we perceived that our aged companion was affected. His eyes filled with tears at this image of a life passed in the deserts in conferring benefits unknown to the world.[1]

Charlevoix describes one of the missionaries of Canada in these terms:—"Father Daniel was too near Quebec not to pay it a visit before he returned to his mission. . . . . He arrived at the port in a canoe with the oar in his hand, and accompanied by three or four savages. He was barefoot, exhausted, his underclothes worn out and his cassock hanging in rags on his emaciated body; yet his countenance was expressive of content and satisfaction with the life which he led, and excited both by his looks and conversation a desire to go and share with him the crosses to

[1] The life led by the missionaries among the bloodthirsty savages of New France, the hardships which they underwent, and the crown of martyrdom which many of them received, form so pathetic a page in the annals of Christianity that no heart can remain unmoved at the perusal S.

which the Lord attached such unction."[1] What a genuine picture of those joys and tears which Jesus Christ has promised to his elect!

Hear what the historian of New France says in another place concerning the missionaries among the Hurons:—"Nothing was more apostolical than the life which they led. All their moments were marked by some heroic action, by conversions, or by sufferings which they considered as a real indemnity when their labors had not produced all the fruit which they had hoped for. From the hour of four in the morning, when they rose, till eight, they generally kept within; this was the time for prayer, and the only part of the day which they had for their private exercises of devotion. At eight, each went whithersoever his duty called him: some visited the sick, others walked into the fields to see those who were engaged in cultivating the earth, others repaired to the neighboring villages which were destitute of pastors. These excursions answered many good purposes; for in the first place no children, or at least very few, died unbaptized; even adults who had refused to receive instruction while in health applied for it when they were sick: they were not proof against the ingenious and indefatigable charity of their physicians."

Were such descriptions to be found in Telemachus, how would the simple and pathetic style of these passages be extolled! The fiction of the poet would be praised with enthusiasm; and yet people are insensible to the truth when presented with the same attractions.

But these were only the least of the labors of these evangelical ministers. Sometimes they accompanied the savages in long hunting excursions, which lasted several years; at others they were exposed to the inconceivable caprices of those Indians, who, like children, are never capable of resisting any impulse of their imagination or their desires. But they deemed themselves rewarded for their trouble if, during their protracted sufferings, they had gained one soul to God, opened the gate of heaven to an infant, relieved one sick person, or dried up the tears of one unfortunate being. We have already seen that their country had not more faithful citizens; the honor of being Frenchmen often

[1] Charlevoix, *Histoire de la Nouv. France,* tome i. livre v.

drew upon them persecution and death. The savages discovered them to be *of the white flesh of Quebec*, by the fortitude which they evinced in enduring the most excruciating torments.

Heaven, satisfied with their virtues, bestowed on several of them that palm which they so anxiously desired, and which has raised them to the rank of the primitive apostles The Huron village where Father Daniel[1] officiated as missionary was surprised by the Iroquois on the morning of July 4, 1648. The young warriors were absent. The Jesuit was just at that moment saying mass, surrounded by his converts; he had only time to finish the consecration and to run to the place whence the shrieks proceeded. A horrid scene met his view: women, children, and old men, lay promiscuously in the agonies of death. All who yet survived fell at his feet soliciting baptism The father dipped a napkin in water, and with it sprinkled the kneeling crowd, thus procuring everlasting life for those whom he was unable to rescue from temporal death. He then recollected having left in the huts some sick persons who had not yet received the seal of Christianity. He flew thither, enrolled them among the number of the faithful, returned to the chapel, hid the sacred vessels, gave a general absolution to the Hurons who had betaken themselves to the altar, exhorted them to attempt their escape, and, to give them time to accomplish it, went forth to meet the enemy At the appearance of this priest advancing alone against an army, the astonished barbarians paused and fell back a few steps; not daring to approach the saint, they pierced him at a distance with their arrows. "Though transfixed with them in every part," says Charlevoix, "he still continued to speak with extraordinary emphasis, sometimes addressing the Almighty, to whom he offered up his blood for his flock, and sometimes his murderers, whom he threatened with the wrath of heaven, assuring them, nevertheless, that they would always find the Lord willing to forgive them if they had recourse to his clemency."[2] He expired, and, by thus attracting the attention of the Iroquois to himself, saved part of his congregation.

Father Garnier displayed equal heroism in another settlement.

---

[1] The same person described by Charlevoix.

[2] *Hist. de la Nouv. Fr.*, tome ii. lib. vii. p 5.

He was but a very young man, and had recently torn himself from his weeping friends for the purpose of saving souls in the forests of Canada. Having received two balls on the field of carnage, he fell senseless, and was stripped by an Iroquois who supposed him to be dead. Some time afterward the father came to himself; he raised his head and beheld at some distance a Huron just expiring. The apostle mustered all his strength to go and absolve the converted Indian; he crawled toward him, but fell down again by the way. A barbarian, perceiving him, ran and dispatched him with his hatchet. "He breathed his last," observes Charlevoix, "in the exercise, and, as it were, in the very bosom, of charity."[1]

Lastly, Father Breboeuf, uncle to the poet of that name, was burned with those excruciating torments which the Iroquois inflicted on their prisoners. "This missionary—who had endured for twenty years hardships the most likely to extinguish the sentiments of nature,—who possessed a courage which nothing could appal,—a virtue familiarized with the prospect of a speedy and cruel death, and so elevated as even to make it the object of his most ardent wishes,—who had moreover been apprised by more than one celestial token that his prayers were heard—was equally proof against menaces and tortures; but the sight of his dear disciples cruelly treated before his face, mingled no small degree of pain with the joy which he felt on finding his hopes accomplished. . . . .

"The Iroquois were fully aware that they had to do with a man from whom they should not have the pleasure of extorting the least sign of weakness; and, as if they were apprehensive that he would communicate his intrepidity to others, they separated him, after a while, from the rest of the prisoners, made him ascend the scaffold alone, and were so exasperated against him that they seemed beside themselves with rage and desperation.

"All this did not prevent the servant of God from speaking in a loud voice, sometimes to the Hurons, who, though they could not see him, were within hearing; sometimes to his executioners, whom he warned that they would incur the wrath

[1] *Hist. de la Nouv. Fr.*, tome ii. lib. vii. p. 24.

of heaven, if they continued to persecute the worshippers of the true God. This boldness astonished the barbarians. Having endeavored, but in vain, to reduce him to silence, they cut off his lower lip and the end of his nose, held lighted torches to every part of his body, and burned his gums," &c.

Another missionary, named Lallemant, was tortured at the same time with Father Breboeuf. He had but just entered upon the ministerial career. The pain sometimes forced from him involuntary cries. He applied to the aged apostle to strengthen his fortitude; but the latter, unable to speak, could merely nod his head and smile with his mangled lips to encourage the young martyr. The smoke of the two funeral piles ascended together toward heaven, and excited in angelic bosoms mingled emotions of joy and grief. The savages made a collar of red-hot hatchets for Father Breboeuf; they cut from him pieces of flesh, which they devoured before his face, telling him that the flesh of Frenchmen was excellent eating.[1] Then, continuing their railleries, "Thou assuredst us just now," cried the barbarians, "that the more a person suffers on earth the more happy he is in heaven; it is, therefore, out of kindness to thee that we study to increase thy tortures."[2]

When, during the reign of terror, the hearts of priests were paraded on the tops of pikes through the streets of Paris, the rabble exclaimed, *Ah! il n'est point de fête quand le cœur n'en est pas!* "Ah! there is no festivity where the heart does not partake of it!"

At length, after enduring many other torments, which we dare not transcribe, Father Breboeuf breathed forth his soul, which winged its flight to the mansions of Him who healeth all the wounds of his servants.

It was in 1649 that these events occurred in Canada; that is to say, at the moment of the highest prosperity of France and during the *fêtes* of Louis XIV. All then triumphed, the missionary as well as the soldier.

Those to whom a priest is an object of hatred and of ridicule will rejoice in these torments of the confessors of the faith. Certain wise men, with a greater spirit of prudence and modera-

[1] *Hist de la Nouv. Fr.*, tome i. livre 7. [2] *Ibid.*

tion, will observe that, after all, the missionaries were the victims of their fanaticism. With a disdainful pity they will ask, *What business had those monks in the wilds of America?* We must admit, indeed, that they did not visit those regions, after the manner of men of science, to attempt some great philosophical discoveries; they went merely in obedience to the injunction of that Master who said to them, "Go ye and teach all nations." Complying in perfect simplicity with this command, they relinquished all the attractions of their native country, and undertook, even at the risk of their lives, to reveal to a barbarian whom they had never seen . . . . . what? In the opinion of the world, nothing—a mere nothing:—*the existence of God and the immortality of the soul!*

CHAPTER IX.

CONCLUSION OF THE MISSIONS.

We have thus indicated the course taken by the different missions, which shows that they were characterized by a spirit of simplicity and heroism, and, at the same time, evinced a great devotion to science and the highest wisdom of legislation. In our opinion it was a just subject of pride for Europe, and, in particular, for France, which furnished the greatest number of missionaries, to behold these men annually quitting her shores to display wonders of the arts, of laws, of humanity, and of courage, in the four quarters of the globe. Hence proceeded the high idea which strangers formed of our nation and of the God whom we adore. The inhabitants of the remotest regions sought our alliance; the ambassador of the savage of the West met at our court the envoy of the nations of the East. We pretend not to the gift of prophecy; but you may rest assured (and experience will prove it) that never will men of science, despatched to distant countries with all the instruments and all the plans of an academy, be able to effect what a poor monk, setting out on foot from his convent, accomplished singly with his rosary and his breviary.[1]

[1] Since the first publication of this work, the Catholic missions have expanded over a much vaster field, and have admitted a fifth geographical division, embracing the islands of Oceanica. They also continue to exhibit all the admirable features here sketched by our author. In China, Tongking, Siam, Oceanica, and even in the western wilds of our own United States, we still behold the apostle, the martyr, and the man of science, among the missionaries of the Catholic Church. The support and extension of missionary enterprise are chiefly due to the aid furnished by the *Association for the Propagation of the Faith*, whose receipts annually exceed $700,000. For full details, in confirmation of these statements, see *Annals of the Association*, &c. T.

BOOK V.

MILITARY ORDERS, OR CHIVALRY

CHAPTER I.

KNIGHTS OF MALTA.

THERE is not one pleasing recollection, not one useful institution, in modern times, that Christianity may not claim as its own. The only poetical period of our history—the age of chivalry—likewise belongs to it. The true religion possesses the singular merit of having created among us the age of fiction and enchantment.

Sainte-Palaye seems inclined to separate military from religious chivalry, whereas every thing would, on the contrary, induce us to blend them together. In his opinion the institution of the former cannot be dated earlier than the eleventh century;[1] but this is precisely the era of the Crusades, which gave rise to the Hospitallers, the Templars, and the Teutonic order.[2] The formal law by which the military knights bound themselves to defend the faith, the resemblance between their ceremonies and those of the sacraments of the Church, their fasts, ablutions, prayers, confessions, monastic engagements,[3] are sufficient evidence that all the knights had the same religious origin. Lastly, the vow of celibacy, which seems to make a wide distinction between chaste heroes and warriors who talk of nothing but love, can form no valid objection to our opinion; for this vow was not general among the Christian military orders. The knights of St. Jago-of-the-Sword, in Spain, were

---

[1] *Mem. sur l'anc. Chev.*, tome i. part ii. p. 66.

[2] Hén., *Hist. de Fr.*, tome i. p. 167; Fleury, *Hist. Eccles.*, tome xiv. p. 387 tome xv. p. 604; Helyot, *Hist. des Ordres Rélig.*, tome iii. pp. 74, 143.

[3] Sainte-Palaye, *loc. cit.*

at liberty to marry;[1] and, in the order of Malta, only such members were obliged to celibacy as attained to the dignities of the order or were presented to its benefices

According to Giustiniani, or the more authentic but less pleasing testimony of Helyot, there were thirty religious military orders:—nine subject to the rule of St Basil, fourteen to that of St. Augustin, and seven belonging to the institution of St. Benedict. We shall confine our observations to the principal of these:—the Hospitallers or knights of Malta in the east, the Teutonic order in the west, and the knights of Calatrava, including those of Alcantara and St. Jago-of-the-Sword, in the south, of Europe.

If authors are correct, we may reckon upward of twenty-eight other military orders, which, not being subject to any particular rules, are considered only as illustrious religious fraternities Such are all those knights of the Lion, the Crescent, the Dragon, the White Eagle, the Lily, the Golden Sword, and those female chevaliers of the Battle-axe, whose names remind you of the Rolands, the Rogers, the Renauds, the Clorindas, the Bradamantes, and the prodigies of the Round Table.

A few traders of Amalfi in the kingdom of Naples obtain permission of Almansor, caliph of Egypt, to build a Latin church at Jerusalem; they annex to it lodgings for the reception of strangers and pilgrims, under the superintendence of Gerard de Provence The Crusades begin. Godfrey de Bouillon arrives, and grants certain lands to the new *Hospitallers.* Gerard is succeeded by Boyant Roger, and Roger by Raymond Dupuy The latter assumes the title of grand-master, and divides the Hospitallers into three classes:—*knights,* whose duty it was to protect the pilgrims on the road and to fight the infidels; *chaplains,* devoted to the ministry of the altar; and *servitors,* who were also required to bear arms.

Italy, Spain, France, England, Germany, and Greece, which successively or all together discharge their hosts on the shores of Syria, are supported by the brave Hospitallers. But fortune changes without abating their valor. Saladin retakes Jerusalem. Acre or Ptolemais is soon the only port left to the Crusaders in

---

[1] Fleury, *Hist. Eccles*, tome xv. p. 406

Palestine. Here you behold assembled the King of Jerusalem and Cyprus, the King of Naples and Sicily, the King of Armenia, the Prince of Antioch, the Count of Jaffa, the Patriarch of Jerusalem, the knights of the Holy Sepulchre, the papal legate, the Count of Tripoli, the Prince of Galilee, the Templars, the Hospitallers, the Teutonic knights, those of St. Lazarus, the Venetians, the Genoese, the Pisans, the Florentines, the Prince of Tarento, and the Duke of Athens. All these princes, all these nations, all these orders, had separate quarters, where they lived wholly independent of one another; "so that there were fifty-eight tribunals," as Fleury remarks, "which exercised the power of life and of death."[1]

It was not long before discord appeared among all these people of such various manners and interests. They came to war in the town. Charles of Anjou and Hugh III., King of Cyprus, who both aspired at the same time to the throne of Jerusalem, increased the confusion. The sultan, Melec-Messor, taking advantage of these intestine broils, advanced with a powerful army with a view to wrest from the Crusaders this their last retreat. He was poisoned on leaving Egypt by one of his emirs; but before he expired he exacted an oath from his son that he would not give the rites of burial to his remains till he had taken Ptolemais. Melec-Seraph punctually fulfilled the last injunction of his father. Acre was besieged and carried by assault on the 18th of May, 1291. On this occasion a community of nuns afforded a memorable example of Christian chastity They mangled their faces, and were found in that state by the infidels, who, filled with disgust and resentment, put them all to the sword.

After the reduction of Ptolemais, the Hospitallers retired to the island of Cyprus, where they remained eighteen years. Rhodes, having revolted against Andronicus, Emperor of the East, invited the Saracens within its walls. Villaret, Grand-Master of the Hospitallers, obtained of Andronicus a grant of the island, in case he could rescue it from the yoke of the Mahommedans. His knights covered themselves with sheep-skins, and, crawling on their hands and knees in the midst of a

[1] *Hist. Eccles.*

flock, they stole into the town in a thick fog, gained possession of one of the gates, dispatched the guards, and introduced the rest of the Christian army into the place.

Four times did the Turks attempt to recover the island of Rhodes from the knights, and four times were they repulsed At the third effort the siege of the city lasted five years, and at the fourth, Mohammed battered the walls with sixteen pieces of cannon of larger calibre than had ever before been seen in Europe.

These same knights had no sooner escaped the overwhelming weight of the Ottoman power than they all at once became its protectors Zizim, a son of that Mohammed II. who had sc lately cannonaded the ramparts of Rhodes, implored the assistance of the knights against his brother Bajazet, who had robbed him of his inheritance. Bajazet, apprehensive of a civil war, hastened to make peace with the order, and agreed to pay it a certain annual sum for the support of Zizim. Thus, by one of those vicissitudes of fortune that are so common, a powerful emperor of the Turks became tributary to a few Christian Hospitallers.

At length, under the Grand-Master Villiers-de-l'Ile-Adam, Solyman made himself master of Rhodes, after losing one hundred thousand men before its walls The knights retired to Malta, which was given to them by the Emperor Charles V Here they were again attacked by the Turks, but, delivered by their courage, they remained in peaceful possession of the island, by whose name they still continue to be known.[1]

---

[1] Vertot, *Hist. des Chev. de Malte;* Fleury, *Hist. Eccles.*; Giustiniani, *Hist degli Ordin. Milit.*; Helyot, *Hist. des Ordres Rélig.*, tome iii.

CHAPTER II.

THE TEUTONIC ORDER.

At the other extremity of Europe, religious chivalry laid the foundation of states which have grown into mighty kingdoms.

The Teutonic order was instituted during the first siege of Acre by the Christians, about the year 1190. In the sequel it was summoned by the Duke of Massovia and Poland to defend his dominions against the incursions of the Prussians. These were then a barbarous people, who, from time to time, sallied from their forests to ravage the neighboring countries. They had reduced the province of Culm to a frightful desert, and had left nothing standing on the banks of the Vistula but the single castle of Plotzko. The Teutonic knights, penetrating by degrees into the woods of Prussia, erected fortresses there. The Warmians, the Barthes, and the Natangues, were successively subdued, and the navigation of the northern seas was rendered secure.

The Knights of the Sword, whose efforts had likewise been directed to the conquest of the northern countries, by uniting with the Teutonic order gave it a truly royal power. The progress of this order was, however, retarded by the long-continued quarrels of the knights with the bishops of Livonia; but at length, the whole North of Europe being subdued, Albert, Margrave of Brandenburg, embraced the doctrine of Luther, drove the knights from their governments, and made himself sole master of Prussia, which then assumed the name of Ducal Prussia. This new duchy was in 1701 erected into a kingdom under the grandfather of Frederick the Great.

The remains of the Teutonic order still subsist in Germany, and the Archduke Charles of Austria is the present grand-master.[1]

---

[1] Schoonbeck, *Ord. Milit.*; Giustiniani, *Hist. degli. Ord. Milit.*; Helyot, *Hist. des Ord. es Relig.*, tome iii.; Fleury, *Hist. Eccles.*

CHAPTER III.

THE KNIGHTS OF CALATRAVA AND OF ST. JAGO-OF-THE-SWORD IN SPAIN.

CHIVALRY made the like progress in the centre as at the extremities of Europe.

About the year 1147, Alphonso the Fighter, King of Castile, took from the Moors the fortress of Calatrava, in Andalusia. Eight years afterward, the Moors prepared to recover it from Don Sanchez, the successor of Alphonso. Don Sanchez, intimidated by their design, caused public proclamation to be made that he would give the town to any person who would defend it. None durst undertake the task but a Benedictine of the Cistercian order, named Don Didacus Velasquez, and Raymond, his abbot. They threw themselves into Calatrava with the peasants and dependants on their monastery of Fiterno; they armed the lay brothers, and fortified the menaced town. The Moors, being informed of these preparations, relinquished their enterprise; Raymond, the abbot, retained the place, and the lay brothers were transformed into knights, who assumed the appellation of Calatrava.

These new knights in the sequel made several conquests from the Moors of Valencia and Jaen. Favera, Maella, Macalon, Valdetormo, La Fresueda, Valderobbes, Calenda, Aquaviva, and Ozpipa, fell successively into their hands. But the order sustained an irreparable check at the battle of Alarcos, where, in 1195, the Moors of Africa defeated the King of Castile. The knights of Calatrava were almost all cut off, together with those of Alcantara and St Jago-of-the-Sword.

We shall not enter into any particulars respecting the latter orders, the object of whose institution also was to fight the Moors and to protect travellers from the incursions of the infidels.[1]

We need but take a general survey of history at the period of

[1] See Schoonbeck, Giustiniani, Helyot, Fleury, and Mariana.

the institution of religious chivalry, to be convinced of the important services which it rendered to society. The order of Malta in the East protected reviving commerce and navigation, and for more than a century was the only bulwark that prevented the Turks from inundating Italy. In the North, the Teutonic order, by subjugating the roving nations on the shores of the Baltic, extinguished the focus of those terrible eruptions which had so often desolated Europe: it afforded time for the progress of civilization, and for the perfecting of those weapons which secure us forever from future Alarics and Attilas.

This will not appear to be mere conjecture, if we observe that the expeditions of the Normans did not cease till about the tenth century, and that the Teutonic knights, on their arrival in the North, found a renewed population, and innumerable barbarians, who had already overflowed the adjacent countries. The Turks, coming down from the East, and the Livonians, Prussians, and Pomeranians, advancing from the West and North, would have harassed Europe with a repetition of the scenes produced by the Huns and Goths, from whose ravages it had scarcely recovered.

The Teutonic knights, indeed, rendered a twofold service to humanity; for, while they brought the savages into subjection, they obliged them to embrace a social life and to attend to agricultural pursuits. Christburg, Bartenstein, Weissemburg, Wesel, Brumberg, Thorn, most of the towns of Prussia, Courland, and Semigalla, were founded by this military religious order; and, while it may boast of having insured the existence of the French and English nations, it may also assume the merit of having civilized the whole of the north of Germany.

But there was another enemy still more dangerous, perhaps, than the Turks and the Prussians, because fixed in the very centre of Europe:—the Moors were several times on the point of enslaving Christendom. Though these people seem to have had in their religion, which allowed polygamy and slavery, and in their despotic and jealous disposition, there was an invincible obstacle to civilization and the welfare of mankind.

The military orders of Spain, therefore, by their opposition to the infidels, like the Teutonic order and that of St. John of Jerusalem, prevented very great calamities. The Christian knights supplied in Europe the place of hired soldiers, and were a kind of regular troops who always repaired to that quarter where the danger was most urgent. The kings and the barons, being obliged to dismiss their vassals after a service of a few months, had frequently been surprised by the barbarians. What experience and the genius of the age could not effect was accomplished by Religion; she formed associations of men who swore in the name of God to spill the last drop of blood for their country. The roads were rendered safe, the provinces were cleared of the banditti by whom they were infested, and external foes found a barrier opposed to their ravages.

Some have censured the knights for pursuing infidels even into their own countries; but such are not aware that, after all, this was but making just reprisals upon nations who had been the first aggressors. The Moors exterminated by Charles Martel justify the Crusades. Did the disciples of the Koran remain quiet in the deserts of Arabia? Did they not, on the contrary, extend their doctrines and their ravages to the walls of Delhi and the ramparts of Vienna? But perhaps a Christian people should have waited until the haunts of these ferocious beasts had been again replenished! Because our forefathers marched against them under the banner of religion, the enterprise, forsooth, was neither just nor necessary! Had the cause been that of Theutates, Odin, Allah, or any other than that of Jesus Christ, it would all be considered right enough.[1]

---

[1] See note TT, at the end. After perusing this extract from Michaud's History of the Crusades, the reader will be better prepared to understand the following chapter of our author on chivalry, in which he seems to include the period when the institution had more or less degenerated. Chivalry, in its first development, was an instrument of peace, an agent of morality. The knight, on his accession to the order, swore "to fear, reverence, and serve God religiously, to battle for the faith, to die rather than renounce Christianity, to be faithful to his lord, to support the rights of the weak, of the widow and the orphan, never to offend the neighbor deliberately, never to undertake an action through a motive of sordid gain, and to keep his faith inviolably in regard to all." Such was the kind of chivalry that the Catholic Church sanctioned, that was extended by the Crusades, and that rose to its loftiest expression in the military orders. Hence it became in the hands of the Church a most powerful auxiliary for the advancement of civilization.

But, as Digby well observes, we must carefully distinguish between this kind of chivalry, which was a form or expression of Catholic life, and that which,

CHAPTER IV.

LIFE AND MANNERS OF THE KNIGHTS.

SUBJECTS that address themselves chiefly to the imagination are not always the easiest to be delineated,—either because, taken altogether, they present a certain vagueness more pleasing than any description that can possibly be produced, or because the reader always goes beyond your representations. The mere word *chivalry*, the mere expression *an illustrious knight*, imply something wonderful in themselves, which no details of explanation can surpass. They embrace every thing, from the fables of Ariosto to the exploits of real knight-errants; from the palaces of Alcina and Armida to the turrets of Cœuvre and Anet.

It is scarcely possible to treat even historically of chivalry without having recourse to the troubadours who sang its exploits, as we adduce the authority of Homer in all that relates to the heroes of antiquity. This the most rigid critics have admitted. But then the writer has the appearance of dealing in nothing but fictions. We are accustomed to such barren and unadorned truth, that whatever is not equally dry has the semblance of falsehood. Like the natives of the icy regions of the pole, we prefer our dreary deserts to those climes where

> La terra molle, e lieta, e dilettossa,
> Simili a segli abitator produce.[1]

The education of the knight began at the age of seven years.[2]

at a later period, was but the embodiment of a worldly principle. The former claims our admiration, because it was an agent of immense good in the diffusion of sound morals. The latter, on the contrary, which aimed solely at the exaltation of material beauty, which pushed virtue to extravagance by assuming the existence of higher motives than those of the Christian faith, which introduced an imaginary and independent principle of honor outside of the duty imposed by the divine law, and which, consequently, undertook to legitimatize the duel, or the resentment of injury by deadly combat,—such chivalry, far from being approved by the Church, was always held in abhorrence. See Mœhler's *Hist. du Moyen Age*, p. 320; Digby, *Ages of Faith*, b. i. and ix. T.

[1] Tasso, canto i. stanza 62.

[2] Sainte-Palaye, tome i. part 1

Duguesclin, while yet a child, amused himself in the venerable avenues to his father's castle by representing sieges and battles with little peasant boys of his own age. He was seen forcing his way through the woods, struggling against the winds, leaping wide ditches, climbing elms and oaks, and among the heaths of Brittany already giving an earnest of the hero destined to be the saviour of France.[1]

The aspirant to knighthood soon passed to the office of page in the castle of some baron. Here were inculcated the first lessons of fidelity to God and the fair sex.[2] Here, too, the youthful page often conceived for the daughter of his lord one of those durable attachments which prodigies of valor were wont to immortalize. Vast Gothic mansions, venerable forests, large solitary lakes, cherished, by their romantic aspect, those passions which nothing was capable of destroying, and which became a kind of enchantment or fatality.

Excited by love to valor, the page practised the manly exercises which opened for him the way to honor. Mounted on a mettlesome steed, he pursued with the lance the wild beasts in the recesses of the woods; or, training the falcon soaring in the skies, he compelled the tyrant of the air to alight, timid and submissive, on his skilful hand. Sometimes, like the young Achilles, he sprang from one horse to another while flying over the plain, at one leap bounding over them or vaulting upon their backs; at others, he climbed, in complete armor, to the top of a bending ladder, and, fancying himself already on the breach, shouted, *Mountjoy and St. Dennis!*[3] In the court of his lord he received all the instructions and examples adapted to his future life. Hither were constantly repairing knights, both known and unknown, who had devoted themselves to perilous adventures, and were returning alone from the kingdoms of Cathay, from the extremities of Asia, and all those extraordinary regions, where they had been redressing wrongs and fighting the infidels

"There you saw," says Froissart, speaking of the house of the Duke de Foy, "there you saw in the hall, the chamber, and the court, knights and esquires going and coming, and heard them

---

[1] *Vie de Duguesclin.*

[2] Sainte-Palaye, tome i. part 7

[3] Sainte-Palaye, tome ii. part 2.

converse on arms and love. All honor was there to be found; all the news, from whatever country or whatever kingdom it might be, was sure to be learned there; for it found its way from all parts to this house, on account of the valor of the master."

The page, having finished his service, became an esquire; and religion always presided over these changes. Illustrious godfathers or beauteous godmothers promised at the altar, for the future hero, religion, fidelity, and love. The duties of the esquire in time of peace consisted in carving at table, in serving up the dishes himself, like the warriors of Homer, and in supplying the guests with water for washing. Men of the highest rank were not ashamed to perform these offices. "At a table before the king," says the Sire de Joinville, "ate the King of Navarre, who was superbly dressed in a coat and mantle of cloth of gold, and adorned with a cincture, clasp, and chain of the same metal, ... and for whom I carved."

The esquire attended the knight in war, carried his lance and his helmet raised on the pommel of the saddle, and with the right hand led his horses. "When he entered the forest, he met four esquires leading four white horses with their right hand." It was his duty in duels and battles to supply his knight with arms, to raise him when overthrown, to give him a fresh horse, to parry the strokes that were aimed at him; but he durst not himself take any part in the combat.

At length, when he had acquired all the necessary qualities, he was admitted to the honors of knighthood. The lists of a tournament, a battle-field, the ditch of a castle, the breach of a tower, were frequently the glorious theatres where the order of the valiant and brave was conferred. Amid the tumult of a battle, gallant esquires fell on their knees before their king or their general, who made them knights by striking them three times over the shoulders with the flat side of his sword. When Bayard had conferred this distinction on Francis I., "How fortunate art thou," said he, addressing his sword, "in having this day given the order of knighthood to such a brave and powerful king! In truth, my good sword, thou shalt be preserved as a relic, and valued beyond any other." "On which," adds the historian, "he gave two leaps, and then returned his sword into the scabbard."

No sooner was the new knight possessed of all his arms than

he burned to distinguish himself by some extraordinary achievements. He explored mountains and valleys in quest of adventures; he traversed venerable forests, vast heaths, and dreary deserts. Toward evening he directed his course to a castle whose solitary towers he perceived at a distance, hoping that he would there find an opportunity of performing some signal exploit. Already he lowered his visor, and commended himself to the lady of his thoughts, when the sound of a horn saluted his ear. On the top of the castle was hoisted a helmet, the conspicuous signal of the habitation of a hospitable knight. The drawbridge was let down, and the adventurous traveller entered the sequestered mansion. If he was desirous of remaining unknown, he covered his shield with a *saddle-cloth*, or with a *green veil*, or a *handkerchief whiter than a lily*. The ladies, with officious haste, took off his armor, furnished him with rich garments, and filled the crystal goblets with generous wine. Sometimes he found his host making merry. "The lord, Amanieu des Escas, on leaving the table, being by the side of a good fire, (for it was winter,) in a hall thickly strewed with rushes or covered with mats, having his esquires about him, conversed with them on arms and love; for everybody in the house, even to the lowest page, was engaged in love."[1]

These festivities of the castle had always something enigmatical about them. At one time it was the feast of the unicorn at another, it was the *vow of the peacock* or of the *pheasant*. The company itself was not less mysterious. Among the guests were Knights of the Swan, of the White Shield, of the Golden Lance, and of Silence,—warriors who were known only by the device of their bucklers and by the penances to which they had submitted.[2]

Toward the end of the feast, troubadours, decked off in peacocks' feathers, entered the hall and commenced an amorous strain:—

> Armes, amours, déduit, joie et plaisance,
> Espoir, désir, souvenir, hardement,
> Jeunesse, aussi manière et contenance,
> Humble regard, trait amoureusement,
> Gents corps, jolis, parez très-richement;

---

[1] Sainte-Palaye.

[2] *Hist. du Maréch. de Boucicault.*

Avisez bien cette saison nouvelle
Le jour de May, cette grande feste et belle,
Qui par le roi se fait à Saint-Denys;
A bien jouter, gardez votre querelle,
Et vous serez honorez et chéris.

The motto of the chivalric profession was—

"Grand bruit au champ, et grand' joie au logis;"
"*Bruit es chans, et joie à l'ostel.*"

But the knight, on his arrival at the castle, did not always witness a scene of rejoicing. Sometimes it was the dwelling of a lady in grief, who was compelled to defend herself against a jealous lover. The handsome, noble, courteous, and gallant chevalier, if refused admittance to the mansion, would pass the night at the foot of a tower, where he could hear the sighs of some Gabriella calling in vain upon the valorous Conci, and with equal sympathy and courage would swear, by his *durandal* and *aquilain*—his faithful sword and swift charger,—to challenge, in single combat, the traitor who thus tormented beauty against every law of honor and of chivalry.

If the knight gained admittance into the gloomy fortress, all his greatness of soul was brought into requisition. Fierce-looking pages conducted him in silence, through long and dismal galleries, to a lonely chamber,—a prison-room which recalled the memory of some remarkable occurrence, and was known as the Chamber of King Richard, or of the Lady of the Seven Towers. The ceiling was covered with the representation of ancient heraldry, and the walls were hung with tapestry, concealing secret doors, and bearing the portraits of distinguished personages, who seemed to follow the knight with their eyes. About midnight, a slight noise was heard; the hangings began to shake, the lamp of the stranger went out, and a coffin arose near his couch. As all his armor would have been useless for protecting him against the dead, he had recourse to the pilgrim's vow, and, rescued by the divine favor from his unpleasant situation, he failed not to consult the Hermit of the Rock, from whom he heard these words :—"If you had the possessions of Alexander, the wisdom of Solomon, and the chivalry of the gallant Hector, pride alone, did you allow it to control thee, would be thy destruction."[1] The good knight understood from this that the visions he had seen were but the punishment of his faults, and he endeavored to acquire a character *sans peur et sans reproche.*

In this manner he continued his course till he had terminated all those adventures sung by our poets and recorded in our ancient chronicles. He delivered princesses detained in caverns, punished miscreants, succored orphans and widows, and defended himself alike against the treachery of dwarfs and the strength of giants. The guardian of morals as well as the protector of the weak, when he passed the mansion of a lady of bad reputation, without deigning to enter, he left a mark of infamy on the gate.[2] If, on the contrary, he came to the habitation of a pious and virtuous female, he addressed her in these words:—"My good friend, (or my good lady,) I pray God to keep you thus in virtue and honor among the number of the good; for you are well worthy of commendation and respect."

The honor of these knights was sometimes carried to that extreme which was witnessed among the primitive Romans, and which excites within us mingled sentiments of admiration and aversion. When Queen Margaret, wife of St. Lewis, was apprised at Damietta, where she was on the point of delivery, of the defeat of the Christian army and of the king being taken prisoner, "she ordered all out of her apartment," says Joinville, "except the knight, (who was eighty years old;) she went on her knees before him, and begged one particular favor, which he pledged himself by oath to confer, and she said, 'I ask you, in virtue of the oath you have taken, that if the Saracens become masters of this city you will cut off my head before I fall into their hands.' And the knight answered, 'Be convinced I shall willingly do so, for I had it already in contemplation to kill you before they should have taken us.'"[3]

Private achievements served the knight as so many steps for attaining to the highest pinnacle of glory. Apprised by the minstrels of the tournaments that were in preparation in beautiful France, he immediately repaired to the rendezvous of the brave. The lists are already arranged. Already the ladies, stationed on

---

[1] Sainte-Palaye. [2] Ducange, *Gloss.* [3] Edit. of Caperronier, p. 84.

scaffolds erected in the form of towers, are looking for the champions adorned with their colors. The lays of the troubadour are heard:—

> Servants d'amour, regardez doulcement,
> Aux échafouds anges de paradis,
> Lors jousterez fort et joyeusement,
> Et vous serez honorez et chéris.

All at once is heard the shout of *Honor to the sons of the brave!* The trumpets sound, the barriers fall; a hundred knights advance from both ends of the lists and meet in the middle; lances fly shattered in the air; front against front, the horses encounter one another and fall. Happy the hero who, like a loyal knight, dexterously applies his thrusts only from the waist to the shoulder, and overthrows without wounding his adversary! All hearts are his; all the ladies are anxious to send him new favors to decorate his arms. Meanwhile heralds stationed in all parts proclaim:—*Remember whose son thou art, and be not degenerate!* Jousts, tilts, and conflicts of every kind, alternately display the valor, strength, and address of the combatants. A thousand shouts, mingled with the clash of arms, rend the skies. Each lady encourages her knight, and throws him a bracelet, a lock of hair, or a scarf. A Sargine, new to the field of glory, but transformed by love into a hero,—a valiant stranger who has fought without arms and without garments, and is distinguished by his *blood-stained shirt*,[1]—are proclaimed the victors. They receive an embrace from their lady-loves, and are greeted with shouts of "The love of the ladies and the death of heroes are the glory and prize of valiant knights."

At these splendid festivities shone the valor and courtesy of a Tremouille, a Boucicault, and a Bayard, whose achievements give probability to the exploits of a Perceforest, a Lancelot, and a Gandifer. The foreign knights who ventured to attack those of France paid dearly for their boldness. During the unfortunate wars in the reign of Charles VI., Sampi and Boucicault alone answered the challenges sent them from all quarters by the conquerors; and, combining generosity with valor, they restored the horses and arms of the rash combatants by whom they had been

[1] Sainte-Palaye. *Hist. des trois Chevaliers et de la Chanise.*

called out. The king wished to prevent his knights from accepting a challenge or resenting such personal insults. But they answered, "Sire, the honor of France is so naturally dear to her children, that, if the devil himself came to challenge us, he would find those among us prepared to fight him"

"At that time," says an old historian, "there were some knights from Spain and Portugal, three of whom, from the latter kingdom of high renown for chivalry, conceived the foolish design of fighting against three knights of France; but, as God is true, in less time than you might go on horseback from the gate of St. Martin to that of St. Antoine, the Portuguese were discomfited by their opponents."[1]

The knights of England were the only champions who could withstand those of France. They, moreover, had fortune on their side, for we were tearing ourselves to pieces with our own hands. The battle of Poictiers, so ruinous to France, was nevertheless honorable to chivalry. The Black Prince, who, out of respect, would never sit down at the table of King John, his prisoner, thus addressed him:—"I am informed that you have great reason to be proud, though the issue has not been according to your wish; for you have this day gained a high reputation for valor, and have surpassed the bravest of your followers. I am not saying this out of compliment to you, sire, for all those of our people who saw both the one and the other are fully convinced of it, and accord you the praise which is your due."

A knight named Ribaumont, in an engagement which took place near the gates of Calais, twice brought Edward III. of England upon his knees; but the monarch, recovering himself, at length compelled Ribaumont to surrender. The English, having gained the victory, returned to the town with their prisoners. Edward, accompanied by the Prince of Wales, gave a grand entertainment to the French knights, and, going up to Ribaumont, said to him, "Never did I see a knight assault his enemies with greater valor than you." The king then took the crown which he wore, and which was both handsome and rich, and, putting it on my lord Eustace, said to him, "My lord, I give you this crown as the most valiant soldier of the day. I

[1] *Journal de Paris sous Charles VI. et VII.*

know that you are of a gay and amorous disposition, and that you are fond of the society of the ladies; therefore, tell them wherever you go that I gave it you. You are no longer a prisoner, and may depart to-morrow if you please."[1]

Joan of Arc revived the spirit of chivalry in France; her arm is said to have wielded the famous sword of Charlemagne, which she had discovered in the church of St. Catherine de Fierbois, in Touraine.

If we were sometimes forsaken by fortune, our courage never failed. Henry IV., at the battle of Ivry, called out to his men, who began to fly, "Turn your heads, if not to fight, at least to see me die." Our soldiers in defeat might always repeat the expression suggested by the genius of the nation to the last French knight at the battle of Pavia, "We have lost every thing but our honor."

Such virtue and valor were certainly entitled to respect. If the hero died in his native land, chivalry in mourning gave him a magnificent funeral. If, on the contrary, he fell in distant expeditions,—if he had no brother in arms, no esquire to afford him the rites of sepulture,—heaven sent one of those recluses to bury him who then inhabited every desert, and who

> . . . . Su'l Libano spesso e su'l Carmelo
> In aera magion fan dimoranza.

It was this that furnished Tasso with his admirable episode of Sweno. Every day an anchoret of Thebais or a hermit of Lebanon rescued the remains of some knight murdered by the infidels. The bard of Solyma has only lent to truth the language of the Muses:—

> "Then from the peaceful region of the night
> I saw descend a ray of slanting light:
> Where on the field the breathless corse was laid,
> There full the lunar beam resplendent played,
> And showed each limb deformed with many a wound,
> 'Midst all the mangled scene of carnage round.
> He lay not prone, but, as his zealous mind
> Still soared beyond the views of human kind,
> In death he sought above the world to rise,
> And claimed, with upward looks, his kindred skies.

[1] Froissart.

One hand was closed, and seemed the sword to rear;
One pressed his bosom with a suppliant air,
As if to Heaven he breathed his humble prayer.

. . . .

While thus intent, the sage's word I heard;
Where Sweno lay a sepulchre appeared
That, rising slow, by miracle disposed,
Within its marble womb a corse enclosed.
'Graved on the monumental stone were read
The name and merits of the warrior dead.
Struck with the sight, I stood with looks amazed,
And on the words and tomb alternate gazed.
Then thus the sage:—"Beside his followers slain
Thy leader's corse shall here enshrined remain;
While in the mansions of the blest above
Their happy souls enjoy celestial love."[1]

But the knight who had formed in his youth these heroic attachments, which were not dissolved but with life itself, had no occasion to be afraid of dying alone in the desert. If the miracles of heaven were not exerted in his behalf, he was at least attended by the miracles of friendship. Constantly accompanied by his *brother-in-arms*, he found in him officious hands to dig his grave and an arm to avenge his death These sacred friendships were confirmed by the most awful oaths. Sometimes the two friends mingled their blood in the same cup; and, as a pledge of their mutual fidelity, they wore either a golden heart, a chain, or a ring. Love, though it so powerfully swayed the bosoms of the knights, had, on these occasions, but a secondary claim upon their hearts; and each succored his friend in preference to his lady.

One circumstance, however, was capable of dissolving these ties, and that was the enmity of their native countries. Two brothers-in-arms of different nations ceased to be united whenever those nations were at variance. Hugh de Carvalay, an English knight, was the friend of Bertrand Duguesclin. When the Black Prince had declared war against Henry of Castile, Hugh, obliged to part from Bertrand, came to take his leave of the latter, and said, "Gentle sir, we must part. We have been good company to one another, and, as we have always had a common purse, and I think I have received more than you, I beg that we

[1] *Jerusalem Delivered*, canto viii.

may settle our accounts together." "No," said Bertrand; "that is but a trifling matter, which I should never have thought of. . . . We have but to do good, and reason commands that you should follow your master. This is the line of conduct which every brave man must pursue. Our attachment was honorable, and so shall our separation also be; but it grieves me much that it must take place." Bertrand then embraced him, and all his companions likewise, and great lamentation attended their parting.[1]

This disinterestedness of the knights—this elevation of soul which acquired for some of them the glorious title of *irreproachable*—shall crown the delineations of their Christian virtues. This same Duguesclin, the flower and glory of chivalry, being a prisoner of the Black Prince, equalled the magnanimity of Porus when in the power of Alexander. The Prince having left the terms of his ransom to himself, he fixed it at an exorbitant sum. "Where will you get all that money?" asked the English hero in astonishment. "Of my friends," replied the haughty constable; "there is not a spinner in France who would not contribute her bobbin to release me out of your hands."

The English Queen, deeply impressed with the virtues of Duguesclin, was the first to give a large sum to procure the liberty of the most formidable enemy of her country. "Ah! madam," cried the Briton knight, throwing himself at her feet, "I thought myself till now the ugliest man in France; but I begin to have not quite so bad an opinion of myself, since ladies make me such presents."

---

[1] *Vie de Bertrand.*

BOOK VI.

SERVICES RENDERED TO MANKIND BY THE CLERGY AND BY THE CHRISTIAN RELIGION IN GENERAL.

CHAPTER I.

IMMENSITY OF THE BENEFITS CONFERRED BY CHRISTIANITY.[1]

To have only a superficial acquaintance with the benefits conferred by Christianity would be, in fact, to know nothing of the subject. If we would understand the extent of her beneficence, we must enter into its details. We must consider the ingenuity with which she has varied her gifts, dispensed her succors, distributed her treasures, her remedies, and her intelligence. In soothing all the sorrows of humanity she has paid a due regard to its imperfection, consulting with a wise condescension even our delicacy of feeling, our self-love, and our frailties. During the few years that we have devoted to these researches, so many acts of charity, so many admirable institutions, so many inconceivable sacrifices, have passed in review before us, that we firmly believe that this merit alone of the Christian religion would be sufficient to atone for all the sins of mankind. Heavenly religion, that compels us to love those wretched beings by whom it is calumniated!

The facts which we are about to state form but a very small portion of the mass which we might have adduced, and many volumes could be filled with what has been omitted. Neither are we sure of having selected the most striking illustrations of Chris-

[1] On the subject of this whole part consult Helyot, *Hist des Ordres Relig et Milit*, 8 vols 4to; Herrmant, *Etab. des Ordres Relig*; Bonnani, *Catal. omn. Ordin. Relig.*, Giustiniani, Mennehius, and Schoonbeck's *Histories of the Military Orders;* Saint Foix, *Essais sur Paris; Vie de Saint Vincent de Paul, Vies des Pères du Desert;* Saint Basil, *Oper.*; and Lobineau, *Hist. de Bretagne.*

tian charity. Impossible as it is to describe every thing, and to judge which of so great a number of charitable works are superior in virtue to the others, we select, almost at random, the subjects of the following pages.

In order to form a just idea of the immensity of these benefits, we should look upon Christendom as a vast republic, where all that we relate concerning one portion is passing at the same time in another. Thus, when we treat of the hospitals, the missions, the colleges, of France, the reader should also picture to himself the hospitals, the missions, and the colleges, of Italy, Spain, Germany, Russia, England, America, Africa, and Asia. He should take into his view two hundred millions of men at least, among whom the like virtues are practised, the like sacrifices are made. He should recollect that for eighteen hundred years these virtues have existed and these same acts of charity have been repeated. Now calculate, if your mind is not lost in the effort, the number of individuals cheered and enlightened by Christianity among so many nations and during such a long series of ages.

CHAPTER II.

HOSPITALS.

CHARITY—an exclusively Christian virtue, unknown to the ancients—originated in Jesus Christ. It was this virtue that principally distinguished him from the rest of mankind, and was in him the seal of the regeneration of human nature. By charity it was that the apostles, after the example of their divine Master, so rapidly won the hearts of their fellow-men and so irresistibly carried conviction home to their bosoms.

The primitive believers, instructed in this great virtue, formed a general fund for the relief of the poor, the sick, and the traveller. This was the commencement of hospitals. The Church, having become more opulent, founded institutions for the afflicted worthy of herself. From that moment works of beneficence had no bounds. A flood of charity may be said to have burst upon the wretched, heretofore unheeded by the prosperous of the world. It will perhaps be asked, How, then, did the ancients manage if they had no hospitals? They had two methods which Christians have not, to rid themselves of the poor and the unfortunate—infanticide and slavery.

The *Lazarettos*, or *Hospitals dedicated to St. Lazarus*, seem to have been the first houses of refuge in the East. Into these establishments were received such leprous persons as, renounced by their relatives, were languishing in the streets of the cities—the horror of the passers-by. These hospitals were attended by the monks of the order of St. Basil.

We have already alluded to the *Trinitarians*, or Fathers for the *Redemption of Captive Slaves.* St. Peter Nolasco in Spain followed the example of St. John of Matha in France. It is impossible to peruse without emotion the austere rules of these orders. By their original constitution the Trinitarians were restricted to a diet of vegetables and milk. But why did they live so austerely? Because the more these fathers denied themselves the necessaries of life the larger was the sum reserved for the barbarians;—because, if the wrath of Heaven required victims, it was hoped that the Almighty would receive the expiations of these religious in exchange for the sufferings from which they might deliver the prisoners.[1]

The order of *Mercy* gave several saints to the world. St. Peter Pascal, Bishop of Jaen, after expending all his revenues in the redemption of captives and the relief of the poor, went among the Turks, by whom he was thrown into prison. The clergy and people of his diocese sent him a sum of money for his ransom. "The saint," says Helyot, "received it very thankfully, but, instead of employing it in obtaining his own liberty, he redeemed a number of women and children, whose weakness made him apprehensive lest they should forsake the Christian religion; and he thus remained in the hands of the barbarians, who procured him the crown of martyrdom in the year 1300."

In this order there was also formed a congregation of females, who devoted themselves to the relief of indigent strangers of

[1] A third reason may be assigned,—viz.: the greater the self-denial of the Redemptionists the more courage would they have to endure the hardships consequent upon the duties of their vocation. T.

their own sex. One of the foundresses was a lady of distinction at Barcelona, who divided her whole fortune among the indigent Her family name is lost; and she is now known only by the appellation of *Mary of Succor*, which the poor have given her.

The order of *Religious Penitents* in Germany and France rescued from vice unfortunate females who were in danger of perishing from want after leading a life of debauchery. It was a sight truly divine to behold religion, by an excess of charity, rising superior to circumstances, however disgusting, and requiring even an evidence of vice, lest its institutions should be diverted from their purposes, and innocence, under the garb of repentance, should usurp a retreat that was intended only for guilt. "You know," says Jehan Simon, Bishop of Paris, in the constitutions of this order, "that some who were virgins have come to us, at the suggestion of their mothers and relatives, who were anxious only to get rid of them; we therefore direct that, if any one apply for admission into your congregation, she be examined," &c.

The tenderest names were employed to cover the past errors of these unfortunate females. They were called daughters of the Good Shepherd, or daughters of Magdalen, to denote their repentance and the forgiveness which awaited them. The vows which they pronounced were but simple. Matches were even sought for such as wished to marry, and a small dowry was granted on those occasions. That every thing about them might suggest ideas of purity, they were dressed in white, whence they were likewise called *White Daughters*. In some cities crowns were placed on their heads, and they were greeted with the words, *Veni, sponsa Christi*, "Come, spouse of Christ." These contrasts were affecting; and this delicacy was truly worthy of a religion which can relieve without wounding the feelings, and spare the weaknesses of the human heart at the same time that it eradicates its vices.[1] At the *Hospital of the Holy Ghost* at Rome it is forbidden to follow such persons as come to deposit orphans at the door of the universal Father.

[1] In the seventeenth century other orders were established having the same object in view, as those of Our Lady of Refuge, and Our Lady of Charity of the Good Shepherd. There are several houses of the latter institute in the United States, which do an immense good. T.

There are many unfortunate persons in society whose situation does not obtrude itself upon your notice, because, descended from respectable but indigent parents, they are obliged to keep up appearances amid the privations of poverty. Scarcely can any situation be more cruel; the heart is wounded on every side; and, to those who possess ever so little elevation of soul, life is a perpetual suffering. What is to become of the unhappy daughters of such persons? Will they go into the families of rich and haughty relatives, and there submit to every kind of contempt? or will they embrace occupations which the prejudices of society and their native delicacy forbid them in spite of all the arguments of sophistry? For this case also religion has provided a remedy. *Our Lady of Pity* opens her pious and respectable retreats for this class of females. Some years since we durst not have mentioned St. Cyr, for it was then understood that women sprung from noble but decayed families deserved neither asylum nor compassion.

God has various ways of calling his servants. Captain Caraffa was soliciting at Naples a recompense for the military services which he had performed for the crown of Spain. One morning, on his way to the palace, he happened to go into the church belonging to a convent. A young nun was singing; he was affected, even to tears, by the sweetness of her voice and the fervent piety of her accents; he concluded that the service of God must be fraught with delight, since it confers such charms on those who have devoted their days to it. He immediately returned home, threw all his certificates of service into the fire, cut off his hair, embraced the monastic life, and founded the order of *Good Works*, whose efforts are directed to the relief of all the afflictions incident to mankind. This order at first made but little progress, because in a pestilence which broke out at Naples all the monks, with the exception of two priests and three lay-brothers, died while attending the infected.

Peter de Betancourt, a friar of the order of St. Francis, being at Guatemala, a town of Spanish America, was deeply affected at the state of the slaves who had no place of refuge during illness. Having obtained by way of alms a small building which he had before used as a school for the poor, he there built himself a kind of infirmary, which he thatched with straw, for the accommodation of such slaves as had no retreat. He soon met with a negro woman, a cripple, who had been turned out by her master. The pious monk immediately took the slave on his shoulders, and, proud of his burden, carried her to the wretched hut which he called his hospital. He then went about through the whole city, endeavoring to procure some relief for his patient. She did not long survive these charitable attentions; but, while shedding her last tears, she promised her attendant a celestial reward.

Several wealthy people, impressed with the virtues of the friar, furnished him with money; and Betancourt saw the hut which had sheltered the negro woman transformed into a magnificent hospital. This religious died young; the love of humanity had exhausted his constitution. As soon as his death became publicly known, the poor and the slaves thronged to the hospital, that they might for the last time behold their benefactor. They kissed his feet; they cut off pieces of his clothes; they would even have torn his body to obtain some relic of him, had not guards been stationed at his coffin. A stranger would have supposed that it was the corpse of a tyrant, which they were defending from the fury of the populace, and not a poor monk, whom they were preserving from its love.

The order of Friar Betancourt prospered after his death;[1] America was filled with hospitals, attended by religious who assumed the name of *Bethlehemites*. The form of their vow was as follows:—"I, Brother . . . . ., make a vow of poverty, chastity, and hospitality, and bind myself to attend poor convalescents, *even though they be unbelievers and infected with contagious diseases.*"[2]

If religion has fixed her stations on the tops of mountains, she has also descended into the bowels of the earth, beyond the reach of the light of heaven, in quest of the unfortunate. The Bethlehemite friars have hospitals at the very bottom of the mines of Peru and Mexico. Christianity has endeavored to repair in the New World the calamities which men have there occasioned, and which have been so unjustly laid to her charge. From this reproach the English historian, Dr. Robertson,—a Protestant, and

---

[1] In 1667. T.

[2] Helyot, tome iii. p. 366.

even a Presbyterian minister,—has completely exonerated the Church of Rome.

"With still greater injustice," says he, "have many authors represented the intolerating spirit of the Roman Catholic religion as the cause of exterminating the Americans, and have accused the Spanish ecclesiastics of animating their countrymen to the slaughter of that innocent people as idolaters and enemies of God. But the first missionaries who visited America, though weak and illiterate, were pious men. They early espoused the defence of the natives, and vindicated their character from the aspersions of their conquerors, who, describing them as incapable of being formed to the offices of civil life or of comprehending the doctrines of religion, contended that they were a subordinate race of men, on whom the hand of nature had set the mark of servitude. From the accounts which I have given of the humane and persevering zeal of the Spanish missionaries in protecting the helpless flock committed to their charge, they appear in a light which reflects lustre upon their function. They were ministers of peace, who endeavored to wrest the rod from the hands of oppressors. To their powerful interposition the Americans were indebted for every regulation tending to mitigate the rigor of their fate. The clergy in the Spanish settlements, regular as well as secular, are still considered by the Indians as their natural guardians, to whom they have recourse under the hardships and exactions to which they are too often exposed."[1]

This passage is formal, and the more remarkable, as the Protestant divine, before he draws this conclusion, furnishes all the evidence that decided his opinion. He quotes the remonstrances of the Dominicans in behalf of the Caribbees: for it was not Las Casas alone who undertook their defence; it was his whole order and the rest of the Spanish ecclesiastics. To this the historian has subjoined the bulls of the popes, and the royal ordinances, issued at the solicitation of the clergy, to ameliorate the condition of the native Americans and to restrain the cruelty of the colonists.

The profound silence which *philosophy* has observed respecting

---

[1] Robertson's *America*, 8vo, vol. iv. pp. 8, 9.

this decisive passage of Robertson is very strange, and deserves to be exposed. Every thing of that author's is quoted excepting the important fact which exhibits the conquest of America in a new light, and which refutes one of the most atrocious calumnies of which history was ever guilty. Sophists have assiduously endeavored to stigmatize religion with a crime which she not only never committed, but of which she felt the utmost abhorrence: in this way have tyrants often accused the victims of their cruelty.[1]

CHAPTER III.

HÔTEL-DIEU—GRAY SISTERS.

We now come to that period when Religion designed to show, as it were, in one single point of view, that there are no human woes which she dares not encounter, that there is no wretchedness beyond the sphere of her love.

The Hôtel-Dieu was founded by St. Landry, the eighth bishop of Paris.[2] The buildings were successively increased by the chapter of Nôtre-Dame, to whom the hospital belonged, by St. Louis, by the Chancellor Duprat, and by Henry IV.; so that it may with truth be said that this receptacle of all human ills expanded in proportion as those sufferings were multiplied, and that charity increased in an equal ratio with affliction.

The hospital was originally attended by monks and nuns

---

[1] See note UU, where the passage from Robertson will be found in full, with an explanation of the massacre of Ireland and that of St. Bartholomew. The extract from the English historian leaves nothing to be desired, and causes those to raise their eyes in astonishment who have been accustomed to all the declamations on the massacres in the New World. The point in question is not whether monsters burned men in honor of the twelve apostles, but whether religion instigated those atrocious proceedings or denounced them to the execration of posterity. One solitary priest undertook to justify the Spaniards; but Robertson will tell how he was treated by the clergy, and what bursts of indignation he excited.

[2] About the middle of the seventh century. T.

under the rule of St. Augustin; but it has for a long time been left exclusively to the latter. "Cardinal Vitry," says Helyot, "doubtless alluded to the nuns of the Hôtel-Dieu when he said that some of them did violence to their feelings, endured with joy and without repugnance the loathsome sight of all human afflictions, and that in his opinion no sort of penance could be compared to this kind of martyrdom."

"There is no one," continues the same author, "who sees the nuns of the Hôtel-Dieu not only dress the wounds of the patients, keep them clean, and make their beds, but also, in the most intense cold of winter, break the ice in the stream which runs through the hospital, and go into it up to their waists to wash their linen, impregnated with filth of the most nauseous description, but must consider them as holy victims, who, from excess of love and charity, in order to serve their fellow-creatures, voluntarily run into the jaws of death, which they defy, in a manner, amid so much infection occasioned by the great number of patients."

We call not in question the virtues which philosophy inspires; but they will appear much more striking to the vulgar when they shall have exhibited acts of self-devotion similar to those just mentioned. The simple recital of Helyot, however, is far from giving a complete idea of the daily sacrifices of these Christian females. He mentions not the abnegation of the pleasures of life, nor the loss of youth and beauty, nor the renunciation of the conjugal character and the endearments of a family. He says nothing concerning all the sacrifices of the heart, the extinction of all the tenderest sentiments except pity, which, among such varieties of wo, becomes only an additional torment.

Yet—would you believe it?—we have seen patients in the agony of death raise themselves on their couches, and muster all their strength to overwhelm with abuse the angels who attended them. And for what reason? Because they were Christians. Ah! wretches, who would attend you but Christians? Other charitable women like these, who were deserving of a religious worship, were publicly *scourged*. We will not disguise the word. After such a return for so much kindness, who would have again returned to the miserable? Who? Why, these same women; they flew at the first signal, or rather they never quitted their post. Behold here religious human nature and impious human nature brought into one view, and judge between them.

The gray sister[1] did not always confine her virtues, like the nuns of the Hôtel-Dieu, within the house of infection; she diffused them abroad like a fragrant odor in the field; she went to visit the infirm husbandman in his cottage. How affecting to see a young woman, beautiful and compassionate, performing, in the name of God, the office of physician for the rustic! We were recently shown, in a meadow, a small house overhung with willows, formerly occupied by three gray sisters. From this rural abode they sallied forth at all hours of the night, as well as day, to administer relief to the country-people. They, as well as all their sisters, were remarkable for the neatness of their external appearance and a look of content, indicating that body and soul were alike free from stain. They were full of tenderness, but yet were not deficient in firmness to endure the sight of human sufferings and to enforce the obedience of their patients They excelled in setting a limb broken by a fall or dislocated by those accidents so common in the country. But a circumstance of still greater importance was that the gray sister never failed to drop a word concerning God in the ear of the husbandman; and never did morality assume forms more divine for the purpose of insinuating itself into the human heart.

While these hospitallers astonished by their charity even those who were accustomed to their sublime acts, other wonders were occurring at Paris. Ladies of distinction exiled themselves from the city and the court and set out for Canada They, doubtless, you would suppose, went to acquire some property, to repair a shattered fortune, or to lay the foundation of a vast estate. Such was not their object They went in the midst of a sanguinary war to found hospitals in the forests for hostile savages

In Europe we fire cannon to announce the destruction of

[1] The Daughters of Charity were so called in several cities of France, from the color of their dress. An excellent institute, bearing the same name, was founded at Montreal, Lower Canada, about the year 1738, by Madame d'Youville, who, with her companions, took charge of the *Hôpital Général* in that city. The sisters devote themselves to various works of mercy. T.

several thousands of men; but in new and distant settlements, where we are nearer to misfortune and to nature, we rejoice only in what is really deserving of thanks and blessings,—that is to say, acts of beneficence and humanity. Three poor nuns, under the conduct of Madame de la Peltrie, land on the Canadian shores, and the whole colony is in a tumult of joy.[1] "The day of the arrival of persons so ardently desired," says Charlevoix, "was a holiday for the whole town. All work was suspended and the shops were closed. The governor received the heroines on the shore at the head of his troops, who were under arms, and with the discharge of cannon. After the first compliments, he led them, amid the acclamations of the people, to the church, where *Te Deum* was sung.

"These pious nuns and their generous conductress, on their part, eagerly kissed the soil after which they had so long sighed, which they hoped to bless with their labors, and which they did not despair even of bedewing with their blood. The French intermingling with the savages, and even unbelievers with the Christians, were unwearied in the expression of their joy. They continued for several days to make the air resound with their shouts of gladness, and gave a thousand thanks to Him who alone could impart such strength and courage to the weakest persons. At the sight of the huts of the savages to which the nuns were conducted the day after their arrival, they were seized with fresh transports of joy. They were not disgusted by the poverty and want of cleanliness which pervaded them; but objects so calculated to abate their zeal tended only to increase its ardor, and they expressed the utmost impatience to enter upon the exercise of their functions.

"Madame de la Peltrie, who had never desired to be rich, and had so cheerfully made herself poor for the sake of Jesus Christ, spared no efforts for the salvation of souls. Her zeal even impelled her to cultivate the earth with her own hands, that she might have wherewith to relieve the poor converts. In a few days she had deprived herself of what she had reserved for her own use, so as to be reduced to the want even of what

[1] Madame Peltrie, with three Ursuline nuns, arrived in Quebec in 1639, and founded there the convent of that order, which is still flourishing. T.

was necessary to clothe the children who were brought to her almost naked; and her whole life, which was a long one, was a series of the most heroic acts of charity."[1]

Is there any thing in ancient history as affecting as this?—any thing capable of extorting tears so pure and so delicious?

CHAPTER IV.

FOUNDLING-HOSPITALS — LADIES OF CHARITY — ACTS OF BENEFICENCE.

LET us listen for a moment to St. Justin the philosopher. In his first Apology, addressed to the emperor, he thus expresses himself:—"It is a common practice, in your empire, to expose infants; and there are persons who afterward bring up these infants for the business of prostitution. Among all the nations subject to you, we meet only with children destined for the most execrable purposes, who are kept like herds of beasts, and upon whom you levy a tribute. . . . . And yet those who abuse these little innocents, besides the crime which they commit against God, may chance to abuse their own offspring. . . . . As for us, Christians, detesting these enormities, we marry only to bring up a family, or we renounce matrimony to live in chastity."[2]

Such, then, were the hospitals which polytheism erected for orphans. O venerable Vincent de Paul, where wast thou? Where wast thou, to address the ladies of Rome as thou didst thy pious countrywomen who seconded thy benevolent designs?—"Now, ladies, see if you can, in your turn, forsake these little innocents, to whom you have become mothers according to grace after they had been abandoned by their mothers according to nature." But in vain shall we look for the *man of mercy* among the votaries of an idolatrous worship.

---

[1] *Hist. de la Nouv. France*, livre v.

[2] See pp. 60, 61.

The age has forgiven Vincent de Paul for being a Christian. Philosophy has been seen to weep over his story. Every reader knows that, though at first but a shepherd's boy and afterward a slave at Tunis, he at length became a priest illustrious for his learning and his good works. It is known that he was the founder of the Foundling-Hospital, of that for the aged poor, of the hospital for the galley-slaves at Marseilles, of the Congregation of Priests of the Mission, (or Lazarists,) of the parochial fraternities of Charity, of the Companies of Ladies for the service of the Hôtel-Dieu, of the Daughters of Charity, who attend on the sick, and, lastly, of the retreats for such as are yet undetermined in the choice of a state of life. Whence does charity derive all her institutions, all her foresight?[1]

St. Vincent de Paul was powerfully seconded by Mademoiselle Legras, who, in conjunction with him, instituted the Daughters of Charity.[2] She had likewise the superintendence of a hospital of the name of Jesus, which, founded for forty poor persons, was the origin of the general hospital of Paris. As the emblem and the reward of a life of incessant toil, Mademoiselle Legras desired that on her tomb should be placed a little cross with these words—*Spes mea*. Her injunctions were fulfilled.

Thus pious families, in the name of Christ, disputed the pleasure of doing good to their fellow-creatures. The wife of the Chancellor of France and Madame Fouquet belonged to the congregation of the Ladies of Charity. They had each their day to visit, instruct, and exhort the sick, and to speak to them in a familiar and pathetic manner concerning the things necessary for salvation. Other ladies received the alms of the charitable. Others again had the care of the linen, furniture, and different articles for the poor. Some author informs us that more than seven hundred Calvinists returned to the bosom of the Catholic Church, having recognised the truth of her doctrines in the excellent *fruits of a charity so ardent and so widely extended*

---

[1] When we reflect that St. Vincent was the thaumaturgus of charity in modern times, and that his life and character have made him venerable, not only among Catholics, but in the eyes of the world at large, it cannot but appear singular that as yet we have no life of this apostolical man in English, worthy of the name. T.

[2] This admirable society, still vigorously engaged in works of mercy all over the world, was commenced in 1633. T

Ye sainted women,—De Miramion, De Chantal, De La Peltrie, De Lamoignon,—your works were the works of peace! The poor accompanied your coffins. They took them from the bearers that they might themselves carry your remains. Your funerals re-echoed their sighs, and a stranger would have supposed that all the benevolent hearts in the world were buried with you in the grave!

We shall conclude this article on the Christian institutions in favor of suffering humanity with an important remark.[1] We are assured that on Mount St. Bernard the sharpness of the air injures the organs of respiration, and that a person seldom lives there longer than ten years. Thus, the monk who retires to its convent may nearly calculate the number of days that he has to spend in the world. All that he gains in the ungrateful service of men is a foreknowledge of the moment of death, which is hidden from the rest of mortals. We are told that the nuns of the Hôtel-Dieu have habitually a slow fever which consumes them, and which proceeds from the vitiated atmosphere they breathe. The monks who reside in the mines of the New World, at the bottom of which, amid eternal night, they have founded hospitals for the unfortunate Indians,—these men also shorten their lives. They are poisoned by the metallic effluvia. Lastly, the fathers who shut themselves up in the infected slave-prisons of Constantinople devote themselves to the most speedy martyrdom.

The reader will forgive us if we here suppress all reflections. We confess our incapacity to find language worthy of acts so sublime. Tears and admiration are all that is left us. How much are those persons to be pitied who would fain destroy religion, and who relish not the sweetness of the fruits which the gospel brings forth! "Stoicism," says Voltaire, "has produced but one Epictetus; and Christianity forms thousands of such philosophers, who know not that they are so, and who carry their virtue to such a length as to be ignorant of possessing any."[2]

---

[1] See note VV.

[2] *Corresp. Gén.*, tome iii. p. 222.

CHAPTER V.

EDUCATION.

Schools, Colleges, Universities, Benedictines, and Jesuits.

To devote one's life to the alleviation of the sufferings of mankind is the first of benefits. The second is to enlighten them. Here again we meet with those *superstitious* priests who have cured us of our ignorance, and who for ten centuries buried themselves in the dust of the schools to rescue us from barbarism. They were not afraid of the light, since they opened to us the sources of it. They were anxious only to impart to us those precious stores which they had collected at the hazard of their lives among the ruins of Greece and Rome.

The Benedictine, who had studied every thing,—the Jesuit, who was acquainted with the sciences and the world,—the Oratorian and the professor of the university,—are perhaps less entitled to our gratitude than those humble friars who devoted themselves throughout all Christendom to the gratuitous instruction of the poor. "The regular clerics of the *pious schools*[1] undertook, out of charity, to teach the lower classes reading, writing, arithmetic, and book-keeping. They likewise taught not only rhetoric and the Greek and Latin languages, but in the towns they also kept schools of philosophy and theology, scholastic and moral, mathematics, geometry, and fortification. When the pupils have finished their lessons, they go in troops to their homes under the superintendence of a religious, lest they should waste their time in playing in the streets."[2]

---

[1] Founded by St. Joseph Calasanctius about the beginning of the seventeenth century. T.

[2] Helyot, tome iv. p. 307. Of all the institutions for gratuitous instruction to which Catholic charity has given birth, that founded in France by the venerable Father La Salle is the most conspicuous. It originated in the middle of the seventeenth century, and its members are known under the name of *Brothers of the Christian Schools.* From a statistical account published in 1842 we

Simplicity of style is always pleasing; but when it is united with simplicity in conferring benefits, it is equally admirable and affecting.

After these primary schools founded by Christian charity, we find learned congregations bound, by the express articles of their institution, to the service of letters and the education of youth. Such are the religious of St. Basil in Spain, who have not less than four colleges in each province. They had one at Soissons in France, and another at Paris—the College of Beauvais, founded by Cardinal Dorman. As early as the ninth century, Tours, Corbeil, Fontenelles, Fulda, St. Gall, St. Denys, St. Germain d'Auxerre, Ferrière, Aniane, and Monte Cassino in Italy, were celebrated seminaries.[1] In the Netherlands the *clergy of the common life* were employed in the collation of original works in the libraries and in restoring the text of manuscripts.[2]

All the European universities were founded either by religious princes, or by bishops or priests, and they were all under the direction of different Christian orders. The famous university of Paris, whence the light of science was diffused over modern Europe, was composed of four faculties. It dates its origin from the time of Charlemagne,—from that barbarous age when Alcuin the monk, struggling alone against ignorance, formed the design of making France *a Christian Athens.*[3] Here a Budæus, a Casaubon, a Grenau, a Rollin, a Coffin, a Lebeau, taught; and here were formed an Abelard, an Amyot, a De Thou, and a Boileau. In England, Cambridge produced a Newton, and Oxford boasts of her Friar Bacon and her Thomas More, her Persian library, her manuscripts of Homer, her Arundelian marbles, and her excellent editions of the classics.[4] Glasgow and Edinburgh in Scotland; Leipsic, Jena, Tübingen, in Germany; Leyden,

---

learn that at that time the congregation had 642 schools, chiefly in Europe, with 171,500 scholars. Since that period these numbers have increased. They have several establishments in the United States. There is a similar institute in Ireland, which has a large number of schools. T.

[1] Fleury, *Hist. Eccles.*, tome x. p. 34.

[2] Instituted in the fourteenth century. T.

[3] Fleury, *Hist. Eccles.*, livre xlv.

[4] Our author would have been more correct if, when speaking of Oxford, he had said nothing upon the subject of *classics*, but had praised that university for *her copious and invaluable treasures of Oriental and other manuscripts.* S.

Utrecht, and Louvain, in the Netherlands; Gandia, Alcala, and Salamanca, in Spain;—all these nurseries of science attest the immense achievements of Christianity. But two orders, the Benedictines and the Jesuits, have been more particularly engaged in the cultivation of letters.

In the year 540 of the Christian era, St. Benedict laid the foundation, at Monte Cassino, in Italy, of that celebrated order destined to enjoy the threefold glory to which no other society ever attained,—of converting Europe to Christianity, of bringing her deserts under cultivation, and of rekindling the torch of science among her barbarous sons.[1]

The Benedictines (and particularly those of the congregation of St. Maur, established in France about the year 543) produced all those men whose learning has become proverbial, and whose laborious and indefatigable researches brought to light the ancient manuscripts buried under the dust of the convents.[2] Of their literary enterprises the most formidable (for we may justly employ that term) was the complete edition of the Fathers of the Church. Those who are acquainted with the difficulty of getting a little volume correctly printed in their native language, will be able to judge how arduous must have been the task of a complete revisal and edition of the Greek and Latin Fathers, forming upward of one hundred and fifty folio volumes! The imagination can scarcely embrace these gigantic labors. To mention the names of a Ruinart, a Lobineau, a Calmet, a Tassin, a Lami, a Mabillon, a Montfaucon, is to recount prodigies of learning and science.

It is impossible to forbear regretting the loss of those great institutions solely dedicated to literary researches and the education of youth. After a revolution which has relaxed the ties of morality and interrupted the course of studies, a society at once religious and literary would apply an infallible remedy to the source of our calamities. In establishments differently constituted

---

[1] England, Frieseland, and Germany, acknowledge as their apostles St. Augustin, St. Willibord, and St. Boniface, all of whom were members of the institute of St. Benedict.

[2] English history is particularly indebted to ecclesiastical writers. What should we know of the early parts of it without their chronicles? Some one has well said:—*Absque monachis nos sane in historiâ patriæ essemus pueri.* S.

there cannot be that regular mode of proceeding, that laborious application to the same subject, which prevail among recluses, and which, when continued for many centuries, at length give birth to truly wonderful productions.

The Benedictines were profound scholars, and the Jesuits men of letters; and both were of as much importance to religion as two illustrious academies are to society.[1]

The order of the Jesuits was divided into three classes,—*approved scholars*, *finished assistants*, and *the professed*. The candidate was first tried by a noviciate of ten years, during which his memory was exercised, but he was not permitted to apply to any particular study. This was done to ascertain the bent of his genius. At the expiration of that time he attended the sick in the hospital for a month, and performed a pilgrimage on foot, at the same time soliciting alms. This was designed to accustom him to the sight of human afflictions, and to prepare him for the fatigues of the missions.

He then proceeded to studies of an extensive or brilliant character. If he had only those qualities which are calculated to shine in society and that polish which pleases the world, he was placed in some conspicuous situation in the capital. He was introduced at court and among the great. Was his genius adapted to solitude? he was employed in the library, or filled some other post in the interior of the society. If he manifested talents for oratory, the pulpit afforded a field for his eloquence. If he possessed a luminous understanding, a correct judgment, and a patient disposition, he was appointed professor in the colleges. If he was ardent, intrepid, full of zeal and faith, he went to sacrifice his life by the scimetar of the Mohammedan or the tomahawk of the savage. Lastly, if he displayed talents for governing men, Paraguay summoned him to its forests, or the order to the superintendence of its concerns.

The general of the company resided at Rome. The provincial fathers in Europe were obliged to correspond with him once a month. The heads of the foreign missions wrote to him whenever ships or caravans visited the remote places in which they

[1] Gibbon said that a single monastery had produced more works than the two English universities. T.

were stationed. There were besides, for urgent cases, missionaries who journeyed from Pekin to Rome, from Rome to Persia, Turkey, Ethiopia, Paraguay, or any other region of the globe.

In Europe, learning sustained an irreparable loss in the Jesuits. Education has never perfectly recovered since their fall. They were particularly agreeable to youth; their polished manners rendered their instructions free from that pedantic tone which is repulsive to youth. As most of their professors were men of letters esteemed in the world, their disciples considered themselves as being only in an illustrious academy. They had contrived to establish among their scholars of different fortunes a kind of patronage which proved beneficial to science. These connections, formed at an age when the heart is readily susceptible of generous sentiments, were never afterward dissolved, and produced between the prince and the man of letters a friendship noble as that which subsisted of old between a Scipio and a Lælius.

They likewise cultivated those venerable relations of master and disciple so dear to the schools of Plato and Pythagoras. They prided themselves in the great man whose genius they had formed, and claimed a portion of his renown. A Voltaire dedicating his *Merope* to Father Porée, and calling him his *dear master*, is one of those amiable traits that are not to be found in more modern education. Naturalists, chemists, botanists, mathematicians, mechanicians, astronomers, poets, historians, translators, antiquaries, journalists,—there is not a branch of science but what the Jesuits have cultivated with distinguished success. Bourdaloue revived the Roman eloquence, Brumoy familiarized France with the Grecian stage, Gresset trod in the steps of Molière; Lecompte, Parennin, Charlevoix, Ducerceau, Sanadon, Duhalde, Noel, Bouhours, Daniel, Tournemine, Maimbourg, Larue, Jouvency, Rapin, Vanière, Commire, Sirmond, Bougeant, Petau, have left names that are not without honor. And what can the Jesuits be accused of? A little ambition,—so natural to genius. "It will always be glorious," says Montesquieu, speaking of these fathers, "to govern mankind by rendering them happy." Consider what the Jesuits have done; recollect all the celebrated writers whom they have given to France or who were educated in their schools, the entire kingdoms gained for our commerce by their skill, their toils, and their blood, the miracles of their missions in China, Canada, and Paraguay, and you will find that the charges brought against them are far from balancing the services which they have rendered to society.[1]

CHAPTER VI.

POPES AND COURT OF ROME.

Modern Discoveries.

Before we undertake to describe the services which the Church has rendered to agriculture, let us take a survey of what the popes have done for the sciences and the fine arts. While the religious orders were engaged throughout all Europe in the education of youth, in the discovery of manuscripts, and in the explanation of antiquities, the Roman pontiffs, by conferring liberal rewards and even ecclesiastical honors on scholars and men of science, took the lead in the general solicitude for the promotion of knowledge. It is, indeed, highly glorious to the Church that a pope should have given his name to the age which commences the era of civilized Europe, and which, rising from among the ruins of Athens and Rome, borrowed its light from the age of an Alexander to reflect it upon that of a Louis.

Those who represent Christianity as checking the advancement of learning manifestly contradict all historical evidences. In

---

[1] The author speaks of the Jesuits in this chapter in the past tense, because, at the time he wrote, they did not exist as a regular body of clergy, if we except the few in Russia. Clement XIV., overpowered by the clamors of infidel and licentious princes, suppressed the order in 1773; but, to the joy of the Catholic world and the friends of education, it was re-established in 1814 by Pius VII. Since that period it has produced some of the most distinguished names of which modern science can boast. When our author alludes to the "little ambition" of which the Jesuits have been accused, he no doubt refers to the errors of a few individuals, without wishing to inculpate the order in general. To make the society at large responsible for the faults of some who belonged to it, as certain superficial or dishonest writers have done, would have been equally opposed to M. Chateaubriand's historical learning and sense of justice. As [illegible]y, the Jesuits have always presented, and still present, a magnificent [illegible] of the spirit and power of Catholicism. T.

every country, civilization has invariably followed the introduction of the gospel. The reverse is the case with the religions of Mohammed, Brama, and Confucius, which have limited the progress of society and forced man to grow old while yet in his infancy.

Christian Rome might be considered as a capacious harbor in which all the wrecks of the arts were collected and preserved. Constantinople falls under the Turkish yoke, and the Church immediately opens a thousand honorable retreats to the illustrious fugitives of Athens and Byzantium. Printing, proscribed in France, finds an asylum in Italy. Cardinals expend their fortunes in researches among the ruins of Greece and in the purchase of manuscripts. So glorious did the age of Leo X. appear to the learned Barthelemi, that at first he preferred it to that of Pericles for the subject of his great work. It was into Christian Italy that he intended to conduct a modern Anacharsis.

"At Rome," says he, "my traveller beholds Michael Angelo raising the cupola of St. Peter's; Raphael painting the galleries of the Vatican; Sadolet and Bembo, who were afterward cardinals, then holding the situation of secretaries to Leo X.; Trissino giving the first representation of Sophonisba,—the first tragedy composed by a modern; Beroaldus, librarian of the Vatican, engaged in the publication of the Annals of Tacitus, then recently discovered in Westphalia and purchased by Leo X. for five hundred gold ducats,—the same pontiff offering places to the learned of all nations who would settle in his dominions, and distinguished rewards to such as would bring manuscripts before unknown. . . . . In all quarters were founded universities, colleges, printing-houses for all kinds of languages and sciences, libraries which were continually receiving accessions of works from those sources, or manuscripts lately brought from regions where ignorance yet maintained her empire. The number of the academies increased to such a degree that there were ten or twelve at Ferrara, about fourteen at Bologna, and sixteen at Sienna. They had for their object the cultivation of the sciences, the belles-lettres, languages, history, and the arts. In two of these academies—one of which was exclusively devoted to Plato, and the other to Aristotle, his disciple—the opinions of the ancient philosophy were discussed and those of modern philosophy partly foreseen. At Bologna, and likewise at Venice, one of these societies superintended the printing establishment, the casting of types, the correction of proofs, the quality of paper, and, in general, whatever could contribute to the perfection of new editions. . . . In every state, the capital, and even the towns of inferior importance, were extremely covetous of knowledge and fame. Almost all of them offered to astronomers observatories; to anatomists amphitheatres; to naturalists botanic gardens; to the studious in general collections of books, medals, and antique monuments; and to talents of every kind distinguished marks of consideration, gratitude, and respect. . . . The progress of the arts encouraged a fondness for public spectacles and magnificence. The study of history and of the monuments of Greece and Rome inspired ideas of propriety, unity, and perfection, which had not before prevailed. Julio de Medicis, brother of Leo X., having been proclaimed a Roman citizen, this proclamation was accompanied with public exhibitions; and in a vast theatre erected for the purpose in the square of the Capitol was performed for two days a comedy of Plautus, the music and extraordinary splendor of which excited universal admiration."

The successors of Leo X. did not permit this noble ardor for the productions of genius to die away. The peaceful bishops of Rome collected in their *villa* the precious relics of ages. In the Borghese and Farnese palaces the traveller admired the masterpieces of Praxiteles and Phidias. It was the popes that purchased at an enormous price the statues of Hercules and Apollo, that preserved the too-much-slighted ruins of antiquity, and covered them with the sacred mantle of religion. Who can help admiring the pious labor of that pontiff who placed Christian images on the beautiful remains of the palace of Adrian? The Pantheon would not now exist, had it not been hallowed by the veneration of the twelve apostles; neither would Trajan's pillar be still standing, had it not been crowned with the statue of St. Peter.

This conservative spirit was manifested in all the orders of the Church. While the ruins collected to adorn the Vatican surpassed the wealth of the ancient temples, a few poor monks protected within the precincts of their convents the ruins of the houses of Tibur and Tusculum,[1] and conducted the stranger through the gardens of Cicero and Horace. A Carthusian

[1] Now Tivoli and Frascati.

pointed out the laurel which grew on Virgil's grave, and a pope was seen crowning Tasso in the Capitol.

Thus for fifteen hundred years the Church has protected the arts and sciences; and at no period has she abated her zeal. If in the eighth century Alcuin the monk taught Charlemagne grammar, in the eighteenth *another ingenious and patient friar*[1] discovered a method of unrolling the manuscripts of Herculaneum; if in 740 Gregory of Tours described the antiquities of Gaul, in 1754 the canon Mazzochi explained the legislative tables of Heraclea. Most of the discoveries which have changed the system of the civilized world were made by members of the Church. For the invention of gunpowder, and perhaps also of the telescope, we are indebted to Friar Bacon; others attribute it to the German monk Berthold Schwartz; bomb-shells were invented by Galen, Bishop of Munster; the mariner's compass was invented by a deacon, Flavio de Gioia, a Neapolitan; spectacles by Despina, a monk; and clockwork either by Pacifico, Archdeacon of Verona, or Pope Sylvester II. How many scholars, a great number of whom we have already named in the course of this work, have shed lustre on the cloister or added dignity to eminent stations in the Church! how many celebrated writers! how many distinguished literary characters! how many illustrious travellers! how many mathematicians, naturalists, chemists, astronomers, antiquaries! how many famous preachers! how many renowned statesmen! In mentioning the names of Suger, Ximenes, Alberoni, Richelieu, Mazarin, Fleury, do we not commemorate at once the greatest ministers and the most important events of modern Europe?

At the very moment (1800) that we are drawing this hasty sketch of the benefits conferred by the Church, Italy, in mourning, is exhibiting an affecting testimonial of love and gratitude to Pius VI. The capital of the Christian world is expecting the remains of the unfortunate pontiff who, by works worthy of an Augustus or a Marcus Aurelius, drained pestilential morasses, discovered the road of the consuls, and repaired the aqueducts of the first monarchs of Rome.[2] As a last instance of that love of

---

[1] Barthelemi, *Voyage en Italie.*

[2] This aged and venerable pontiff was unfortunate indeed; insulted by the

the arts so natural to the heads of the Church, be it observed that Pius VII., at the same time that he is restoring peace to the faithful, still finds means, amid his noble indigence, to replace with new statues those master-pieces which Rome, the patroness of the fine arts, has yielded to the heir of Athens.

After all, the progress of letters was inseparable from the progress of religion, since it was in the language of Homer and Virgil that the fathers explained the principles of the faith. The blood of martyrs, which was the seed of Christians, likewise caused the laurel of the orator and the poet to flourish.

Christian Rome has been to the modern what pagan Rome was to the ancient world,—the common centre of union. This capital of nations fulfils all the conditions of its destiny, and seems in reality to be the *eternal city* There may, perhaps, come a time when it will be universally admitted that the pontifical power is a magnificent institution. The spiritual father, placed amid the nations, binds together all the different parts of Christendom. What a venerable character is a pope truly animated with the apostolic spirit! The general shepherd of the flock, he either keeps it within the bounds of duty or defends it against oppression His dominions, sufficiently extensive to make him independent, too small to give room for any apprehension from his political rank, leave him the power of opinion alone; —an admirable power, when it embraces in its empire no other works than those of peace, charity and beneficence.

The transient mischief which some bad popes occasioned disappeared with them; but we still daily feel the influence of the immense and inestimable benefits for which the whole world is indebted to the court of Rome. That court has almost always proved itself superior to the age. It had ideas of legislation and civil administration, was acquainted with the fine arts and the sciences, and possessed refinement, when all around was involved in the darkness of the Gothic institutions. Nor did it keep the light exclusively to itself, but shed it abroad upon all. It broke down the barriers which prejudice erects between nations;

---

infidel French General Duphot, who placed a national cockade upon his head while per[illegible] of devotion in his own chapel. Driven from Ro[illegible] the I[illegible]ian princes who ought to have protected him, he [illegible] persecution. S.

it studied to soften our manners, to withdraw us from our ignorance, to wean us from our rude or ferocious customs. In the time of our ancestors the popes were missionaries of the arts sent among barbarians, legislators among savages. "Only the reign of Charlemagne," says Voltaire, "had a tincture of politeness, which was probably the consequence of his visit to Rome."

It is, therefore, generally admitted that to the Holy See Europe owes her civilization, part of her best laws, and almost all her arts and sciences. The sovereign pontiffs are now about to seek other means of being useful to mankind; a new career awaits them, and we have a presentiment that they will pursue it with glory. Rome has returned to that evangelical poverty which constituted all her wealth in days of yore. By a remarkable similarity, there are now Gentiles to be converted, nations to be restored to harmony, animosities to be extinguished, tears to be wiped away, and wounds which require all the balm of religion to be healed. If Rome is thoroughly sensible of her situation, never had she before her greater hopes and more brilliant destinies. We say *hopes*, for we reckon tribulations among the objects desired by the Church of Christ. The degenerate world requires a second preaching of the gospel; Christianity, in renewed vigor, is rising victorious over the most tremendous assault that the infernal powers ever made upon her. Who knows if what we have taken for the fall of the Church be not her re-establishment? She was declining in the enjoyment of luxury and repose; she forgot the cross: the cross has again appeared, and she will be saved.[1]

---

[1] Long-continued prosperity has often led to a relaxation of morals and of ecclesiastical discipline; but the faith of the Church ever remains in its purity and integrity, guarded against all the contingencies of the world by the promises of Christ. This faith is revived in times of suffering and persecution, which direct the Christian's attention more forcibly to his eternal welfare and to that divine truth on which it depends. But the enemies of the Church, disregarding these facts, imagine that the efforts of human power against her must necessarily effect her ruin, while these efforts, on the contrary, are the very means employed by the providence of God to exalt her before the world, and to exhibit her supernatural character and divine commission by signal and perpetual triumphs over the passions of men. This has always been the case; but a remarkable instance of this truth was recently witnessed when Pius IX. was driven from Rome and an impious rabble held dominion in the holy city. The enemies of Catholicity predicted with the utmost confidence that popery

CHAPTER VII.

AGRICULTURE.

To the clergy, secular and regular, we are indebted for agriculture, as well as for our colleges and hospitals. The tillage of uncultivated lands, the construction of roads, the enlargement of towns and villages, the institution of post-houses and inns, arts, trades, and manufactures, commerce internal and external, laws, civil and political,—in a word, every thing, we originally received from the Church. Our ancestors were barbarians, whom Christianity was obliged to teach even the art of raising the necessaries of life.

Almost all the grants made to the monasteries in the early ages of the Church, consisted of wastes which the monks brought into cultivation with their own hands. Trackless forests, impassable morasses, extensive heaths, were the sources of that wealth with which we have so vehemently reproached the clergy.

While the monks of Prémontré were tilling the deserts of Poland and part of the forest of Coucy in France, the Benedictines were giving fertility to our moors. Molesme, Colan, and Citeaux, now covered with vineyards and corn-fields, were then wastes overrun with briers and thorns; where the first monks dwelt in cabins made of boughs, like the American settlers, in the midst of their improvements.

St. Bernard and his disciples cultivated the sterile valleys granted them by Thibaud, Count of Champagne. Fontevrault was a real colony, established by Robert d'Arbissel in a wilderness on the confines of Anjou and Brittany. Whole families sought an asylum under the direction of these Benedictines, in

---

was at an end. The milk-white hind, however, is more vigorous than ever. When the adversaries of the Catholic Church venture to form an opinion as to the effect of persecution upon her vitality, they should remember the words of our author:—"Who knows if what we have taken for the fall of the Church be not her re-establishment?" T.

whose vicinity were formed communities of widows, unmarried women, laymen, infirm persons, and aged soldiers. All became husbandmen, after the example of the fathers, who themselves felled trees, guided the plough, sowed the grain, and crowned that portion of France with flourishing crops which it had never borne before.

The colony was soon obliged to send away a portion of its members, and to give up to other deserts the surplus of its laborious hands. Raoul de la Futaye, a companion of Robert, settled in the forest of Nid du Merle, and Vital, another Benedictine, in the woods of Savigny. The forest of L'Orges, in the diocese of Angers; Chaufournois, now Chantenois, in Touraine; Bellay, in the same province; La Puie, in Poitou; L'Encloitre, in the forest of Gironde; Gaisne, a few miles from Loudon; Luçon, in the wood of the same name; La Lande, on the heaths of Garnache; La Magdeleine, on the Loire; Boubon, in Limousin; Cadouin, in Perigord; lastly, Haute Bruyère, near Paris, were so many colonies from Fontevrault, and from uncultivated tracts were transformed into productive fields.

We should tire the reader were we to attempt to enumerate all the furrows made by the ploughs of the Benedictines in the wilds of Gaul. Maurecourt, Longpré, Fontaine, Le Charme, Colinance, Foici, Bellomer, Cousanie, Sauvement, Les Epines, Eube, Vanassel, Pons, Charles, Vairville, and a hundred other places in Brittany, Anjou, Berry, Auvergne, Gascony, Languedoc, and Guyenne, attest their immense labors. St. Columban converted the desert of Vauge into a garden; and even Benedictine nuns, after the example of the fathers of their order, devoted themselves to the cultivation of the soil. Those of Montreuil-les-Dames "employed themselves," says Hermant, "in sewing, spinning, and clearing the forest, in imitation of Laon and all the monks of Clairvaux."[1]

In Spain, the Benedictines displayed the same activity. They purchased waste lands on the bank of the Tagus, near Toledo and there founded the convent of Venghalia, after they had planted the whole surrounding country with vines and orange-trees.

---

[1] *De Mirac.*, lib. iii. chap. 17.

Monte Cassino, in Italy, was an absolute wilderness When St. Benedict retired thither, the face of the country was soon changed, and in a short time the new abbey became so opulent, by its attention to agriculture, that it was enabled to defend itself, in 1037, against the Normans, who made war upon it.

St. Boniface and the monks of his order were the first farmers in the four bishoprics of Bavaria. The Benedictines of Fulda brought into cultivation a tract of land between Hesse, Franconia, and Thuringia, eight thousand geometrical paces in diameter,—that is, twenty-four thousand paces, or near fifty miles, in circumference; and they soon reckoned eighteen thousand farms in Bavaria and Suabia. The monks of St. Benedict of Polironna, near Mantua, employed more than three thousand pair of oxen in husbandry.

It should be remarked that the almost general rule which forbade the use of meat to the monastic orders doubtless proceeded, in the first place, from a principle of rural economy.[1] The religious societies being then very numerous, the voluntary abstinence of so many persons from animal food could not but be extremely favorable to the propagation of cattle. Thus our fields, now so flourishing, are partly indebted for their harvest and their flocks to the industry and frugality of the monks.

Moreover, example, which is frequently of so little avail in morality, because the passions destroy the good effects of it, has a powerful influence over the material part of life. The sight of several thousands of monks cultivating the earth gradually undermined those barbarous prejudices which looked with contempt upon the art of agriculture. The peasant learned in the convent to turn up the glebe and to fertilize the soil. The baron began to seek in his fields treasures less precarious than what he procured by arms. The monks, therefore, were in reality the

---

[1] The author has not displayed in this sentence his usual accuracy. The object of the monastic institute was the observance of the evangelical counsels, among which is bodily mortification. It is therefore but natural to suppose, even if the rules of the monastic orders did not establish the fact, that the members of those bodies abstained from flesh-meat with a view chiefly, if not altogether, to deny the sensual appetite. The mortification of the passions was the principal end at which they aimed, and hence we must infer that their self-denial did not proceed from a principle of rural economy, but that rural economy was a consequence of their self-denial. T.

founders of agriculture, both as husbandmen themselves, and as the first instructors of our husbandmen.

Even in our own days this useful spirit had not forsaken them. The best-cultivated fields, the richest peasants, and those the best fed and the least annoyed, the finest teams, the fattest flocks, and the best-regulated farms, were found on the possessions of the abbeys. This, in our opinion, could not be a just subject of reproach to the clergy.

CHAPTER VIII.

TOWNS AND VILLAGES, BRIDGES, HIGH-ROADS, ETC.

But, if the clergy brought the wilds of Europe under cultivation, it was they, too, that multiplied our hamlets and enlarged and embellished our towns. Different quarters of Paris—for instance, those of St. Genevieve and St. Germain l'Auxerrois—were partly built at the expense of the abbeys after which they were named.[1] In general, wherever a monastery was founded there also arose a village. *Chaise-Dieu*, *Abbeville*, and many other places, still indicate their origin by their name.[2] The town of St. Saviour, at the foot of Monte Cassino in Italy, and the surrounding villages, are the work of the monks of St. Benedict. Fulda and Mentz also originated with monastic establishments; and in all the ecclesiastical districts of Germany, as in Prussia, Poland, Switzerland, Spain, and England, a great number of towns and cities were founded by the monastic or military orders. The places which first emerged from barbarism were those that were subject to ecclesiastical princes. Europe owes half of its monuments and useful foundations to the munificence of cardinals, abbots, and bishops.

But it will perhaps be said that these works attest only the

---

1 *Hist. de la ville de Paris.*

2 With respect to Great Britain, it may be observed that the words *God, Christ, Cross, Bishop, Abbot, Monk, Church, Kirk,* &c. enter into the composition of the names of many places, and confirm the justness of our author's remark. S

immense wealth of the Church. We all know how universal is the inclination to depreciate services; man is averse to gratitude. The clergy found the soil uncultivated; they covered it with luxuriant harvests. Having acquired opulence by their industry, they expended their revenues in the erection of public buildings. If you reproach them with wealth so honorable both in its application and its source, you accuse them of no other crime than that of having conferred a twofold benefit.[1]

All Europe was without either roads or inns; her woods were infested by robbers and assassins; her laws were impotent, or rather, there were no laws; religion alone, like a massive column rising from the midst of Gothic ruins, afforded shelter and a point of communication to mankind.

France, under the second race of her kings, having fallen into the most deplorable anarchy, travellers were detained, plundered, and murdered, chiefly at the passages of rivers. A number of bold and skilful monks undertook to put a stop to these enormities. They formed themselves into a company by the appellation of Hospitallers *Pontifes*, or bridge-builders.[2] They bound themselves by their institute to assist travellers, to repair the public roads, to construct bridges, and to entertain strangers in the houses which they erected on the banks of the rivers. They first settled on the Durance, at a dangerous place called *Maupas* or *Mauvais-pas*, (*bad passage*,) but, thanks to these generous monks, it soon acquired the name of *Bon-pas*, (*good passage*,) which it still retains. It was this order that built the bridge over the Rhone at Avignon. Everybody knows that the post-houses and the system of posts in general, improved by Louis XI., were originally established by the University of Paris.

On a rugged and lofty mountain of Rouergue, covered with snow and fogs during eight months of the year, is seen a monastery erected about the year 1120 by Alard, Viscount of Flan-

---

[1] Maitland, in his work on the *Dark Ages*, p. 394, thus speaks of the monks:— . . . "The extraordinary benefit which they conferred on mankind by this clearing and cultivating, was small in comparison with the advantages derived from them by society *after they had become large proprietors—landlords with more benevolence, and farmers with more intelligence and capital, than any others.*" Such is the testimony of a Protestant clergyman in regard to the influence of the monastic wealth. T.

[2] In the twelfth century. T.

ders. That nobleman, returning from a pilgrimage, was attacked on this spot by robbers; he made a vow, if he escaped from their hands, to found a hotel for travellers in this desert and to drive the banditti from the mountain. He fulfilled his engagements; and the house of Albrac or Aubrac rose *in loco horroris et vastæ sotitudinis*,[1] as it is expressed in the charter of foundation. Here Alard stationed priests for the service of the Church, knights Hospitallers to escort travellers, and ladies of quality to wash the feet of pilgrims, to make their beds, and to take care of their garments.

In the ages of barbarism, pilgrimages were of great utility; that religious principle which drew all ranks of people from their homes powerfully contributed to the progress of civilization and letters. In 1600, the year of the great jubilee, not less than four hundred and forty thousand five hundred strangers were received into the Hospital of St. Philip Neri at Rome; each of them was boarded, lodged, and wholly maintained, for three days.

There was not a pilgrim that returned to his native village but left behind him some prejudice and brought back some new idea. One age has always something to balance against another; at present, perhaps, persons belonging to the higher classes of society travel more than they formerly did; but, on the other hand, the peasant is more stationary. War summoned him to the banner of his lord, and religion into distant countries. If we could recall to life one of those ancient vassals whom we are accustomed to represent to ourselves as stupid slaves, we should, perhaps, be surprised to find him possessed of more intelligence and information than the free rustic of the present day.

Previously to his departure for foreign countries, the traveller applied to his bishop, who gave him an apostolic letter, with which he passed in safety throughout all Christendom. The form of these letters varied according to the rank and profession of the bearer; whence they were called *formatæ*. Thus it was the whole study of religion to knit again those social ties which barbarism was incessantly breaking.

The monasteries, in general, were inns at which strangers found lodging and entertainment by the way. That hospitality

[1] "In a place of horror and a vast wilderness."—Deut. xxxii. 10.

55

which we admire in the ancients, and traces of which we still meet with in the East, flourished among the religious, many of whom, by the name of *Hospitallers*, were especially devoted to the exercise of that engaging virtue. In the washing of feet, the blazing fire, the refreshing repast, and the comfortable couch, hospitality appeared, as in the days of Abraham, in all its beauty. If the traveller was poor, he was supplied with food, raiment, and money sufficient till he should reach another monastery, where he received the same treatment. Ladies mounted on their palfreys, knights in quest of adventure, kings bewildered in the chase, knocked at midnight at the gates of ancient abbeys, and shared the hospitality that was given to the obscure pilgrim. Sometimes two hostile knights met in one of these convents and made merry together till sunrise, when, sword in hand, they vindicated the superiority of their ladies and of their respective countries. Boucicault, on his return from the Prussian crusade, lodged in a monastery with several English knights, and singly maintained, in defiance of them all, that a Scotch knight, whom they had attacked in the woods, had been treacherously put to death.

In these inns of religion it was considered as doing great honor to a prince, to propose that he should pay some attentions to the poor who happened to be there at the same time. Cardinal de Bourbon, having attended the unfortunate Elizabeth into Spain, stopped on his return at the hotel of Roncevaux, in the Pyrenees, where he waited at table upon three hundred pilgrims and gave each of them three reals to help them on their journey. Poussin was one of the last travellers that availed himself of this Christian custom. He went from monastery to monastery at Rome, painting altar-pieces in return for the hospitality which he received, and thus renewed in his own profession the adventures of Homer.[1]

[1] There is a place—probably the only one remaining in this island—that retains some traces of this ancient monastic bounty; that is, St. Croix, commonly called St. Cross, near Winchester. To the traveller who knocks at the gate of this hospital and asks for refreshment the porter gives bread and beer—a faint image of what was the hospitality of the convents abroad. S.

CHAPTER IX.

ARTS, MANUFACTURES, COMMERCE.

NOTHING is more at variance with historical truth than to represent the first monks as indolent people who lived in affluence at the expense of human superstition. In the first place, this affluence was very far from being real The order, by its industry, might have acquired wealth, but it is certain that the life of the monks individually was one of great self-denial. All those delicacies of the convent, so exceedingly exaggerated, were confined, even in our time, to a narrow cell, austere practices, and the simplest diet, to say nothing more. In the next place, it is a gross falsehood that the monks were but pious sluggards; if their numerous hospitals, their colleges, their libraries, their religious duties, and all the other services of which we have spoken, had not been sufficient to employ all their time, they would have found out other ways of being useful. They applied themselves to the mechanical arts, and extended the commerce of Europe, both internal and external.

The congregation of the third order of St. Francis, called *Bons Fieux,* manufactured cloth and lace at the same time that they taught the children of the poor to read and took care of the sick. The company of *Poor Brethren, Shoemakers, and Tailors,* was instituted in the same spirit. In the Convent of Hieronymites in Spain, several manufactures were carried on. Most of the first monks were masons as well as husbandmen. The Benedictines built their houses with their own hands, as appears from the history of Monte Cassino, Fontevrault, and several others

With respect to internal trade, many fairs and markets belonged to the abbeys and were established by them. The celebrated fair of Landyt à St. Denis owed its origin to the University of Paris The nuns supplied great part of the linens of Europe; the beer of Flanders, and most of the finer wines of the Archi pelago, Hungary, Italy, and Spain, were made by religious congregations. The exportation and importation of corn, either for foreign countries or for the armies, also depended in part on the great ecclesiastical proprietors. The churches promoted the trade in parchment, wax, linen, silks, jewelry, marbles, and the manufactures of wool, tapestry, and gold and silver plate. They alone in the barbarous ages afforded some employment to artists, whom they brought for the purpose from Italy and the remotest corners of Greece. The monks themselves cultivated the fine arts, and were the painters, sculptors, and architects of the Gothic age. If their works now appear rude to us, let us not forget that they form the connecting link between ancient and modern times, that but for them the chain of letters and the arts would have been irreparably broken; and let not the refinement of our taste involve us in the guilt of ingratitude.

With the exception of that small portion of the North comprehended in the line of the Hanseatic towns, all foreign commerce was formerly carried on by the Mediterranean. The Greeks and Arabs brought us the commodities of the East, which they shipped at Alexandria; but the Crusades transferred this source of wealth into the hands of the Franks. "The conquests of the Crusaders," says Fleury, "secured to them freedom of trade in the merchandise of Greece, Syria, and Egypt, and consequently in the productions of the East, which had not yet found their way to Europe by other channels."[1]

Robertson, in his excellent work on the commerce of the ancients and moderns with the East Indies, confirms, by the most curious details, what Fleury has here advanced. Genoa, Venice, Pisa, Florence, and Marseilles, owed their opulence and their power to these enterprises of an extravagant zeal which the genuine spirit of Christianity has long condemned.[2] It cannot,

---

[1] *Hist. Eccles.*, tome xviii. p. 20.

[2] Fleury, *loc. cit.* Our author is here misled by Fleury, whose Ecclesiastical History, with its discourses, abounds with inaccuracies of statement and opinion, which have been exposed by Marchetti and several other critics. The chief motives that prompted the Crusades were those of religion and humanity,—to check and diminish the Mohammedan power in the East and afford the Christians of that region a sufficient protection. It is not, then, true that they were "enterprises of an extravagant zeal." It is equally incorrect to assert that they have been condemned by "the genuine spirit of Christianity;" for the results of the Crusades were to arrest the ambition and rapacity of the

however, be denied that modern navigation and commerce sprang from those celebrated expeditions. Whatever was good in them belongs to religion, and all the rest to human passions. If the Crusaders were wrong in attempting to wrest Egypt and Syria from the Saracens, let us not sigh in beholding those fine countries a prey to the Turks, who seem to have naturalized pestilence and barbarism in the native land of Phidias and Euripides. What harm would there be if Egypt had been a colony of France since the days of St. Louis, and if the descendants of French knights were reigning at Constantinople, Athens, Damascus, Tripoli, Carthage, Tyre, and Jerusalem?

Whenever Christianity has proceeded *alone* upon distant expeditions, she has afforded abundant evidence that the mischiefs of the Crusades did not proceed from her, but from the inordinate passions of men. Our missionaries have opened to us sources of trade, for which they spilled no blood but their own, and of that indeed they have been very lavish. We refer the reader to what we have already said on this subject in the book which treats of the missions.

CHAPTER X.

CIVIL AND CRIMINAL LAWS.

An inquiry into the influence of Christianity upon laws and governments, like that which we have instituted in regard to morals and poetry, would form the subject of a very interesting work. We shall merely point out the way and present a few results, in order to complete the sum of the benefits conferred by religion.

We have only to open at random the councils, the canon law, the bulls and rescripts of the court of Rome, to be convinced that our ancient laws (collected in the capitularies of Charle-

Turks, to save European civilization, and secure the independence of Christian states—effects which true Christianity cannot but approve. See *Universal History*, vol. iv · Alzog, *Hist. de l'Eglise*, vol. ii. pp. 283 and 338; Fredet, *Mod Hist.*, vol. i. p. 80. T.

magne, the formulas of Marculfe, and the ordinances of the kings of France) borrowed numberless regulations from the Church, or, rather, were partly compiled by learned priests or assemblies of ecclesiastics.

From time immemorial, the bishops and metropolitans enjoyed considerable privileges in civil matters. To them was committed the promulgation of imperial decrees relative to the public tranquillity; they were taken for umpires in disputes: they were a kind of natural justices of the peace, that religion gave to mankind. The Christian emperors, finding this custom established, thought it so salutary[1] that they confirmed it by new enactments. Each graduate, from the sub-deacon to the sovereign pontiff, exercised a certain jurisdiction, so that the religious spirit operated at a thousand points and in a thousand ways upon the laws. But was this influence favorable or detrimental to the public welfare? In our opinion it was favorable.

In the first place, in all that is termed *administration* the wisdom of the clergy has been invariably acknowledged, even by writers the most inimical to Christianity.[2] When a country is in a state of peace, men do not indulge in mischief for the mere pleasure of doing it. What interest could a council have in enacting an unjust law respecting the order of succession or the conditions of marriage? or why would a priest, authorized to decide on any point of law, have prevaricated? If it is true that education and the principles imbibed in our youth influence our character, ministers of the gospel must in general have been actuated by a spirit of mildness and impartiality,—at least in those things which did not regard their order or themselves individually. Moreover, the *esprit de corps*, which may be bad in the whole, is always good in part. It is fair to presume that a member of a great religious society will distinguish himself in a civil post rather by his integrity than by his misdemeanor, were it only for the credit of his order and the responsibility which that order imposes upon him.

The councils, moreover, were composed of prelates of all coun-

[1] Eus., *de Vit. Const.*, lib. iv. cap. 27; Sozom., lib. i. cap. 9; *Cod. Just.*, lib. i. tit. iv. l. [illegible] 7.

[2] See Voltaire's *Essai sur les Mœurs.*

tries, and therefore had the immense advantage of being in a manner strangers to the people for whom they enacted laws. Those antipathies, those predilections, those feudatory prejudices which usually accompany the legislator, were unknown to the fathers assembled in council. A French bishop had a sufficient knowledge of his own country to oppose a canon at variance with its customs; but he had not authority enough over the Italian, Spanish, and English prelates, to make them adopt an unjust regulation: he enjoyed the liberty of doing good, but his situation restrained him from mischief. Machiavel, if we recollect right, proposes that the constitution of a state should be modelled by a foreigner; but this foreigner might be seduced by interest, or be ignorant of the genius of the nation whose government he is to fix. From these two great inconveniences the council was exempt, since it was above the influence of bribery by its wealth, and, at the same time, acquainted with the particular character of nations by the different members of whom it was composed.

As the Church invariably based her legislation upon moral principles in preference to political considerations, (as we see in the case of rape, divorce, or adultery,) her ordinances must naturally have had a character of rectitude and universality. Accordingly, most of the canons are not relative to this or that country; they embrace all Christendom. Charity, the forgiveness of injuries, constituting the essence of Christianity, and being particularly required in the priesthood, the influence of this sacred character on morals must partake of those virtues. History is incessantly exhibiting to us the priest praying for the unfortunate, imploring mercy for the guilty, and interceding for the innocent. The right of sanctuary in churches, liable as it was to abuse, is nevertheless a strong proof of the forbearance which the spirit of religion introduced into criminal jurisprudence. It was this evangelical compassion that animated the Dominicans when they denounced with so much energy the cruelties of the Spaniards in the New World. In short, as our civil code was framed in a barbarous age, and the priest was then the only individual who possessed any learning, he could not fail to exert a happy influence upon the laws and impart a knowledge which was wanting in those around him.

We have a beautiful illustration of that spirit of justice which

Christianity tended to introduce into our tribunals. St. Ambrose observes that, if the bishops are obliged by their character to implore the clemency of the magistrate in criminal matters, they ought never to interfere in civil causes, which are not submitted to their own cognizance. "For," says he, "you cannot solicit for one of the parties without injuring the other, and perhaps incurring the guilt of a great injustice."[1] Admirable spirit of religion!

The moderation of St. Chrysostom is not less remarkable. "God," says this great saint, "has permitted a man to put away his wife for adultery, but not for *idolatry*."[2] According to the Roman law, persons noted with infamy could not act as judges.[3] St. Ambrose and St. Gregory improve upon this excellent law; for they would not have those who have committed great faults to retain the situation of judges, lest they should condemn themselves in condemning others.[4]

In criminal matters the prelate kept aloof, because religion abhors blood. St. Augustin, by his entreaties, obtained the life of the Circumcelliones, convicted of the assassination of Catholic priests.[5] The Council of Sardis even made a law enjoining bishops to interpose their mediation in sentences of exile and banishment.[6] Thus the unfortunate culprit owed not only his life to this Christian charity, but, what is of still greater value, the privilege of breathing his native air.

The following regulations of our criminal jurisprudence are extracted from the canon law:—1. You must not condemn an absent person who may possess lawful means of vindicating himself. 2. The accuser and the judge cannot be admitted as wit-

---

[1] Ambros., *de Offic.*, lib. iii. cap. 3. [2] *In Cap. Isai.* iii.

[3] Infamy, in the civil law, is that total loss of character or public disgrace which a convict incurs, and by which a person is rendered incapable of being a witness or juror. T.

[4] Hericourt, *Lois Eccl.*, p. 760, Quest. 8.

[5] The Circumcelliones were a band of fanatics, in the fourth century, belonging to the heretical sect of Donatists, and were so called from their roving about in towns and villages under pretence of redressing injuries, but in reality perpetrating innumerable outrages, among which was that of setting slaves free without the permission of their masters. In this last respect they have many imitators in our times. T.

[6] Conc. Sard., can. 17.

nesses. 3. Great criminals cannot be accusers.[1] 4. Let the dignity of a person be ever so exalted, his single deposition cannot suffice for the condemnation of the accused."[2]

The reader is referred to Hericourt for the remainder of these laws, which confirm our assertion that we are indebted to the canon law for the best regulations of our civil and criminal code. The canon law is in general much milder than the civil law, and we have in several points rejected its Christian spirit: for instance, the seventh council of Carthage decides that when there are several counts in an indictment, if the accuser fail to prove the first count, he shall not be allowed to produce evidence in regard to the others; but among us a different custom prevails.

This great indebtedness of our civil system to the regulations of Christianity is a point of considerable importance, which, however, has attracted very little notice, although it is well worthy of observation.[3]

Finally, the manorial jurisdictions in the feudal times were necessarily less oppressive to the dependents of abbeys and prelacies than to the vassals of a count or baron. The ecclesiastical lord was bound to have certain virtues which the warrior did not think himself obliged to practise. The abbots soon discontinued following the army, and their dependants became peaceful husbandmen. St. Benedict of Aniane, the reformer of the Benedictines in France, accepted the lands that were offered to him, but not the *serfs*, whom he immediately set at liberty.[4] This example of generosity in the middle of the tenth century is very striking, and it was a *monk* that displayed it.

[1] This admirable canon was not adhered to in our laws.

[2] Hericourt, *loc. cit. et seq.*

[3] Montesquieu and Robertson have bestowed a few words upon it.

[4] Helyot.

CHAPTER XI.

POLITICS AND GOVERNMENT.

THE custom which assigned to the clergy the first place in the assemblies of modern nations, was the offspring of that great religious principle which all antiquity considered as the foundation of political existence. "I know not," says Cicero, "whether the destruction of piety toward the gods would not be the destruction, also, of good faith, of human society, and of the most excellent of virtues, justice." *Haud scio an pietate adversus deos sublata, fides, etiam, et societas humani generis, et una excellentissima virtus, justitia, tollatur.*[1]

Since religion was considered, down to our own days, as the basis of civil society, let us not deem it a crime in our ancestors to have thought like Plato, Aristotle, Cicero, and Plutarch, and to have placed the altar and its ministers in the highest position of social life.

But, though no one may dispute the influence of the Church on the body politic, yet it may perhaps be alleged that this influence has been injurious to liberty and the public weal. We shall make but one reflection on this vast and profound subject. Let us go back for a moment to general principles, which must always be the starting-point in endeavoring to reach any particular truth.

Nature seems to have but one mode of creating, both in the moral and in the physical order. To be productive, she blends strength with mildness. Her energy appears to reside in the general law of contrasts. If she were to join violence to violence, or weakness to weakness, instead of producing any positive result she would only destroy by excess or by defect. All the legislations of antiquity exhibit this system of opposition which gives birth to the body politic.

This truth once admitted, we must look for the points of opposition. The two principal, in our opinion, consist, the one in the

[1] *De Nat. Deor.*, i. 2.

manners of the people, the other in the institutions that are to be given to this people. If they are of a weak and timid character, let their constitution be energetic and vigorous; if bold, impetuous, and inconstant, let their government be mild, moderate, invariable. Thus, theocracy was not adapted to the Egyptians. It enslaved them without imparting the virtues which they needed. They were a pacific nation, and consequently required military institutions.

The sacerdotal influence, on the contrary, produced admirable effects at Rome. That queen of the world owed her greatness to Numa, who understood the necessity of giving religion the first rank among a nation of soldiers He who has no fear of men ought to fear the gods.

The observation which we have just made respecting the Romans is equally applicable to the French. They need no excitement, but restraint. People talk of the danger of theocracy; but in what warlike nation did a priest ever lead men into slavery?

We must therefore bear in mind this grand general principle, and not confine ourselves to certain particular local and accidental circumstances, if we wish rightly to estimate the influence of the clergy upon our old constitution. All the outcries against the wealth of the Church and against its ambition result from narrow views of an immense subject. Those who raise them scarcely take a superficial view of objects, and never attempt to fathom their profound nature. In our body politic Christianity was like those religious instruments which the Spartans used in time of battle, and which were intended not so much to animate the soldier as to moderate his ardor.

If we consult the history of our states-general, we shall find that the clergy always acted the admirable part of moderators. They pacified, they soothed the minds of men, and prevented their rushing to extremities. The Church alone possessed information and experience when haughty barons and ignorant commoners knew nothing but factions and absolute obedience. She alone, from the habit of holding synods and councils, understood the art of public speaking and debate She alone had dignity when it was wanting in all around her We behold her alternately opposing the excesses of the people, remonstrating freely with the sovereign, and defying the anger of the nobles Her superior knowledge, her conciliatory spirit, her mission of peace, the very nature of her interests, could not fail to inspire her with generous ideas in politics, which were not to be found in the two other orders. Placed between these, she had every thing to fear from the nobility and nothing from the commons, of whom, for this very reason, she became the natural protector. Accordingly, we see her in times of disturbance voting in preference with the latter. The most dignified spectacle which our old states-general exhibited was that bench of aged prelates who, with the mitre on their heads and the crosier in their hands, alternately pleaded the cause of the people against the great, and of the sovereign against his factious nobility.

These prelates frequently fell victims to their devotedness. At the beginning of the thirteenth century, such was the hatred of the nobles against the clergy, that St. Dominic was necessitated to preach a kind of crusade to wrest the possessions of the Church from the barons, by whom they had been seized. Several bishops were murdered by the nobles or imprisoned by the court. They experienced by turns the vengeance of the monarch, of the aristocracy, and of the people.

If you take a more extensive view of the influence of Christianity on the political existence of the nations of Europe, you will see that it prevented famines, and saved our ancestors from their own fury, by proclaiming those intervals of peace denominated the *peace of God*, during which they secured the harvest and the vintage. In popular commotions the popes often appeared in public like the greatest princes. By rousing sovereigns, sounding the alarm, and forming leagues, they prevented the West from falling a prey to the Turks. This service alone rendered to the world by the Church would entitle her to a religious veneration.

Men unworthy of the name of Christians slaughtered the people of the New World, and the Court of Rome fulminated its bulls to prevent these atrocities.[1] Slavery was authorized by law, and the Church acknowledged no slaves among her children.[2]

---

[1] The celebrated bull of Paul III.

[2] The decree of Constantine declares that every slave who embraces Christianity shall be free, that is, the Christian slave was civilly free; but, as we have before observed, the Church respected the rights of masters, while she used every prudent means to abolish slavery. T.

The very excesses of the Court of Rome have served to diffuse the general principles of the law of nations. When the popes laid kingdoms under an interdict,—when they made emperors account for their conduct to the Holy See,—they arrogated a power of which they were not possessed;[1] but in humbling the majesty of the throne they perhaps conferred a benefit on mankind. Kings became more circumspect. They felt that they had a curb, and the people a protector. The papal rescripts never failed to mingle the voice of nations and the general interests of humanity with particular complaints. *We have been informed that Philip, Ferdinand, or Henry, oppresses his people, &c.* Such was the exordium of almost all those decrees of the Court of Rome.

If there existed in Europe a tribunal to judge nations and monarchs in the name of God, and to prevent wars and revolutions, this tribunal would doubtless be the master-piece of policy and the highest degree of social perfection. The popes, by the influence which they exercised over the Christian world, were on the point of effecting this object.

Montesquieu has ably proved that Christianity is hostile, both in spirit and counsel, to arbitrary power; and that *its principles are more efficacious than honor in monarchies, virtue in republics, and fear in despotic states.* Are there not, moreover, Christian republics which appear to be more strongly attached to their religion than the monarchies? Was it not, also, under the gospel dispensation that that constitution was formed which Tacitus considered as a dream, so excellent did it seem to him? "In all nations," says that profound historian, "either the people, or the nobility, or a single individual, governs; for a form of government composed at once of all three is but a brilliant chimera."[2]

---

[1] Here, again, our author is not exact in his statements To place a Catholic kingdom under interdict was merely an act of spiritual authority by which the pope, as supreme pastor, exercised his jurisdiction over a portion of his flock. For the same reason, he could admonish emperors or kings who belonged to his flock of the crimes which they had committed. If the sovereign pontiff sometimes deposed the civil ruler, he acted on such occasions only in accordance with the jurisprudence of the age, in deference to the national will, and in defence of civil and religious freedom, as the author intimates in the same paragraph See *Miscellanea* of Bishop Spalding, art. *Age of Gregory VII*, p. 151, &c. T

[2] Tacitus, *Annal.*, lib. iv.

Tacitus could not foresee that this brilliant chimera would one day be realized among the barbarians whose history he has left us.[1] The passions under polytheism would soon have overturned a government which is preserved only by the accuracy of its counterpoises. The phenomenon of its existence was reserved for a religion which, by maintaining the most perfect moral equilibrium, admits of the establishment of the most perfect political balance.

Montesquieu discovered the principle of the English constitution in the forests of Germany. It would perhaps have been more simple to trace it in the division of the three orders—a division known to all the great monarchies of modern Europe. England began, like France and Spain, with its states-general. Spain became an absolute monarchy, France a temperate monarchy, and England a mixed monarchy. It is remarkable that the *Cortes* of the first enjoyed several privileges not possessed either by the *states-general* of the second, or by the *parliaments* of the third; and that the nation which was once the most free sank under the most absolute government. On the other hand, the English, who were nearly reduced to slavery, gradually raised themselves to independence; while the French, who were neither very free nor very much enslaved, continued nearly in the same state as they were at first.

Lastly, the division of the three orders was a grand and fertile political idea. Wholly unknown to the ancients, it has produced among the moderns the system of representation, which may be classed among the three or four discoveries that have created another universe. To the glory of our religion be it also said that the system of representation partly originated in the ecclesiastical institutions; for the Church exhibited the first model of it in her councils, composed of the *sovereign pontiff*, the *prelates*, and the *deputies of the inferior clergy;* and then the Christian priests, not having separated themselves from the state, gave rise to that new order of citizens which, by its union with the two others, completed the representation of the political body.

We must not omit a remark which tends to support the preceding facts, and proves that the spirit of the gospel is eminently

[1] *In Vitæ Agric.*

favorable to liberty. The Christian religion adopts as a tenet the doctrine of moral equality,—the only kind of equality that it is possible to preach without convulsing the world. Did polytheism at Rome endeavor to persuade the patrician that he was not of nobler dust than the plebeian? What pontiff would have been bold enough to hold such uncourtly language in the hearing of a Nero and a Tiberius? Soon would the body of the unfortunate priest have been thrown into the *gemoniæ*.[1] Such lessons, however, Christian potentates daily receive from that pulpit which has been so justly termed the chair of truth.

Upon the whole, Christianity is peculiarly admirable for having transformed the *physical man* into the *moral man*. All the great principles of Greece and Rome, such as equality and liberty, are to be found in our religion, but applied to the mind and considered with reference to the most sublime objects.

The counsels of the gospel form the genuine philosopher and its precepts the genuine citizen. There is not a petty Christian state under which a person may not live more agreeably, than he could have done among the most renowned people of antiquity, excepting Athens, which was attractive, but horridly unjust. Among modern nations there is an internal tranquillity, a continual exercise of the most peaceful virtues, which never prevailed on the banks of the Ilissus and the Tiber. If the republic of Brutus or the monarchy of Augustus were all at once to rise from the dust of ages, we should be shocked at the life of the Romans. Picture to yourself the games of the goddess Flora and the continual slaughter of gladiators, and you will be convinced of the prodigious difference which the gospel has made between us and the Pagans. The meanest of Christians, if a virtuous man, is more moral than was the most eminent of the philosophers of antiquity.

"Finally," says Montesquieu, "we are indebted to Christianity for a certain political law in government, and a certain law of nations in war, for which mankind cannot be sufficiently grateful. It is owing to this law that among us victory leaves

[1] A place at Rome where the carcasses of criminals were thrown. T.

the conquered in possession of those great blessings,—life, liberty, laws, property, and always religion,—when the conqueror is not blind to his own interests.[1]

Let us add to all these benefits one which ought to be inscribed in letters of gold in the annals of philosophy:—

THE ABOLITION OF SLAVERY.

CHAPTER XII.

GENERAL RECAPITULATION.

It is not without a certain degree of fear that we approach the conclusion of our work. The serious reflections which induced us to undertake it, the hazardous ambition which has led us to decide, as far as lay in our power, the question respecting Christianity,—all these considerations alarm us. It is difficult to discover how far it is pleasing to the Almighty that men should presume to take into their feeble hands the vindication of his eternity, should make themselves advocates of the Creator at the tribunal of the creature, and attempt to defend by human arguments those counsels which gave birth to the universe. Not without extreme diffidence, therefore, convinced as we are of the incompetency of our talents, do we here present the general recapitulation of this work.

Every religion has its mysteries. All nature is a secret.

The Christian mysteries are the most sublime that can be; they are the archetypes of the system of man and of the world.

The sacraments are moral laws, and present pictures of a highly poetical character.

Faith is a force, charity a love, hope complete happiness, or, as religion expresses it, a complete virtue.

The laws of God constitute the most perfect code of natural justice.

[1] *Spirit of Laws*, book xxiv. chap. 5.

The fall of our first parents is a universal tradition.

A new proof of it may be found in the constitution of the moral man, which is contrary to the general constitution of beings.

The prohibition to touch the fruit of knowledge was a sublime command, and the only one worthy of the Almighty.

All the arguments which pretend to demonstrate the antiquity of the earth may be contested.

The doctrine of the existence of a God is demonstrated by the wonders of the universe. A design of Providence is evident in the instincts of animals and in the beauty of nature.

Morality of itself proves the immortality of the soul. Man feels a desire of happiness, and is the only creature who cannot attain it; there is consequently a felicity beyond the present life; for we cannot wish for what does not exist.

The system of atheism is founded solely on exceptions. It is not the body that acts upon the soul, but the soul that acts upon the body. Man is not subject to the general laws of matter; he diminishes where the animal increases.

Atheism can benefit no class of people:—neither the unfortunate, whom it bereaves of hope, nor the prosperous, whose joys it renders insipid, nor the soldier, of whom it makes a coward, nor the woman, whose beauty and sensibility it mars, nor the mother who has a son to lose, nor the rulers of men, who have no surer pledge of the fidelity of their subjects than religion.

The punishments and rewards which Christianity holds out in another life are consistent with reason and the nature of the soul.

In literature, characters appear more interesting and the passions more energetic under the Christian dispensation than they were under polytheism. The latter exhibited no dramatic feature, no struggles between natural desire and virtue.

Mythology contracted nature, and for this reason the ancients had no descriptive poetry. Christianity restores to the wilderness both its pictures and its solitudes.

The Christian marvellous may sustain a comparison with the marvellous of fable. The ancients founded their poetry on Homer, while the Christians found theirs on the Bible: and the beauties of the Bible surpass the beauties of Homer.

To Christianity the fine arts owe their revival and their perfection.

In philosophy it is not hostile to any natural truth. If it has sometimes opposed the sciences, it followed the spirit of the age and the opinions of the greatest legislators of antiquity.[1]

In history we should have been inferior to the ancients but for the new character of images, reflections, and thoughts, to which Christianity has given birth. Modern eloquence furnishes the same observation.

The relics of the fine arts, the solitude of monasteries, the charms of ruins, the pleasing superstitions of the common people, the harmonies of the heart, religion, and the desert, lead to the examination of the Christian worship.

This worship everywhere exhibits a union of pomp and majesty with a moral design and with a prayer either affecting or sublime. Religion gives life and animation to the sepulchre. From the laborer who reposes in a rural cemetery to the king who is interred at St. Dennis, the grave of the Christian is full of poetry. Job and David, reclining upon the Christian tomb, sing in their turn the sleep of death by which man awakes to eternity.

We have seen how much the world is indebted to the clergy and to the institutions and spirit of Christianity. If Schoonbeck, Bonnani, Giustiniani, and Helyot, had followed a better order in their laborious researches, we might have presented here a complete catalogue of the services rendered by religion to humanity. We would have commenced with a list of all the calamities incident to the soul or the body of man, and mentioned under each affliction the Christian order devoted to its relief. It is no exaggeration to assert that, whatever distress or suffering we may think of, religion has, in all probability, anticipated us and provided a remedy for it. From as accurate a calculation as we were able to make, we have obtained the following results :—

There are computed to be on the surface of Christian Europe about four thousand three hundred towns and villages. Of

---

[1] We are at a loss to know what sciences were ever opposed by Christianity. T.

these four thousand three hundred towns and villages, three thousand two hundred and ninety-four are of the first, second, third, and fourth rank. Allowing one hospital to each of these three thousand two hundred and ninety-four places, (which is far below the truth,) you will have three thousand two hundred and ninety-four hospitals, almost all founded by the spirit of Christianity, endowed by the Church, and attended by religious orders. Supposing that, upon an average, each of these hospitals contains one hundred beds, or, if you please, fifty beds for two patients each, you will find that religion, exclusively of the immense number of poor which she supports, has afforded daily relief and subsistence for more than a thousand years to about three hundred and twenty-nine thousand four hundred persons.

On summing up the colleges and universities, we find nearly the same results; and we may safely assert that they afford instruction to at least three hundred thousand youths in the different states of Europe.[1]

In this statement we have not included either the Christian hospitals and colleges in the other three quarters of the globe, or the female youth educated by nuns.

To these results must be added the catalogue of the celebrated men produced by the Church, who form nearly two-thirds of the distinguished characters of modern times. We must repeat, as we have shown, that to the Church we owe the revival of the arts and sciences and of letters; that to her are due most of the great modern discoveries, as gunpowder, clocks, the mariner's compass, and, in government, the representative system; that agriculture and commerce, the laws and political science, are under innumerable obligations to her; that her missions introduced the arts and sciences among civilized nations and laws among savage tribes; that her institution of chivalry powerfully contributed to save Europe from an invasion of new barbarians; that to her mankind is indebted for

The worship of one only God;

The more firm establishment of the belief in the existence of that Supreme Being;

---

[1] See note WW, where the reader will find the basis of this calculation, although the figures are expressly set down much lower than the reality.

A clearer idea of the immortality of the soul, and also of a future state of rewards and punishments;

A more enlarged and active humanity;

A perfect virtue, which alone is equivalent to all the others—Charity.

A political law and the law of nations, unknown to the ancients, and, above all, the abolition of slavery.

Who is there but must be convinced of the beauty and the grandeur of Christianity? Who but must be overwhelmed with this stupendous mass of benefits?

CHAPTER XIII.

WHAT WOULD THE PRESENT STATE OF SOCIETY BE IF CHRISTIANITY HAD NOT APPEARED IN THE WORLD?—CONJECTURES—CONCLUSION.

We shall conclude this work with a discussion of the important question which forms the title of this last chapter. By endeavoring to discover what we should probably be at present if Christianity had not existed, we shall learn to appreciate more fully the advantages which we owe to it.

Augustus attained imperial power by the commission of crime, and reigned under the garb of virtue. He succeeded a conqueror, and to distinguish himself he cultivated peace. Incapable of being a great man, he determined to acquire the character of a fortunate prince. He gave a long repose to his subjects. An immense focus of corruption became stagnant, and the prevailing calm was called prosperity. Augustus possessed the genius of circumstances, which knew how to gather the fruits which true genius had produced. It follows true genius, but does not always accompany it.

Tiberius had too great a contempt for mankind, and but too plainly manifested this contempt. The only sentiment which he frankly displayed was the only one that he ought to have dissembled; but he could not repress a burst of joy on finding the Roman people and senate sunk even below the baseness of his own heart.

When we behold this sovereign people falling prostrate before Claudius and adoring the son of Ænobarbus, we may naturally suppose that it had been honored with some marks of indulgence. Rome loved Nero. Long after the death of that tyrant, his phantoms thrilled the empire with joy and hope. Here we must pause to contemplate the manners of the Romans. Neither Titus, nor Antoninus, nor Marcus Aurelius, could change the groundwork of them; by nothing less than a God could this be accomplished.

The Roman people was always an odious people; it is impossible to fall into the vices which it displayed under its imperial rulers, without a certain natural perverseness and some innate defect in the heart. Corrupted Athens never was an object of execration; when in chains, she thought only of enjoying herself. She found that her conquerors had not deprived her of every thing, since they had left her the temple of the Muses.

When Rome had virtues, they were of an unnatural kind. The first Brutus butchered his sons, and the second assassinated his father. There are virtues of situation, which are too easily mistaken for general virtues, and which are but mere local results. Rome, while free, was at first frugal, because she was poor; courageous, because her institutions put the sword into her hand, and because she sprang from a cavern of banditti. She was, besides, ferocious, unjust, avaricious, luxurious; she had nothing admirable but her genius; her character was detestable.

The decemvirs trampled her under foot. Marius spilt at pleasure the blood of the nobles, and Sylla that of the people; as the height of insult, he publicly abdicated the dictatorship. Catiline's accomplices engaged to murder their own fathers,[1] and made a sport of overthrowing that majesty of Rome which Jugurtha proposed to purchase.[2] Next come the triumvirs and their proscriptions. Augustus commands a father and son to

---

[1] *Sed filii familiarum, quorum ex nobilitate maxuma pars erat parentes interficerent.* Sallust, *in Catil.* xliii.

[2] Sallust, *in Bell. Jugurth.*

kill each other,[1] and the father and son obey. The senate proves itself too debased even for Tiberius.[2] The god Nero has his temples. Without mentioning those informers belonging to the most distinguished patrician families; without showing the leaders of one and the same conspiracy denouncing and butchering one another;[3] without pointing to philosophers discoursing on virtue amid the debaucheries of Nero, Seneca excusing a parricide, Burrhus[4] at once praising and deploring it; without seeking under Galba, Vitellius, Domitian, and Commodus, for those acts of meanness which, though you have read them a hundred times, will never cease to astonish,—one single fact will fully portray Roman infamy. Plautian, the minister of Severus, on the marriage of his daughter with the eldest son of the emperor, caused one hundred freemen of Rome, some of whom were husbands and fathers of families, to be mutilated, "in order," says the historian, "that his daughter might have a retinue of eunuchs worthy of an Eastern queen.[5]

To this baseness of character must be added a frightful corruption of manners. The grave Cato made no scruple to assist at the prostitutions of the Floral games. He resigns his wife Marcia, pregnant as she was, to Hortensius; some time afterward Hortensius dies, and, having left Marcia heir to all his fortune, Cato takes her back again, to the prejudice of the son of Hortensius. Cicero repudiates Terentia for the purpose of marrying Publia, his ward. Seneca informs us that there were women who no longer counted their years by consuls, but by the number of their husbands;[6] Tiberius invents the *scellarii* and the *spintriæ;* Nero publicly weds his freedman Pythagoras,[7] and Heliogabalus celebrates his marriage with Hierocles.[8]

It was this same Nero, already so often mentioned, that instituted the Juvenalian feasts. Knights, senators, and ladies of the highest rank, were obliged to appear on the stage, after the example of the emperor, and to sing obscene songs, at the same

[1] Suet., *in Aug.*, and Amm. Alex. [2] Tacit., *An.* [3] *Id. ibid.*, lib. xv.

[4] Tacit., *An.*, lib. xvi. Papinianus, a lawyer and prefect of the *prætorium*, who made no pretensions to the character of a philosopher, being commanded by Caracalla to justify the murder of his brother Geta, replied, "It is easier to commit fratricide than to justify it." *Hist. Aug.*

[5] Dion., lib. lxxvi. [6] *De Benefic.* iii. 16. [7] Tacit., *An.*, 15.

[8] Dion., lib. lxxix ; *Hist. Aug.*

time imitating the gestures of the clowns.[1] For the banquet of Tigellinus, on the lake of Agrippa, houses were erected on the shore, where the most illustrious females of Rome were placed opposite to courtesans perfectly naked! At the approach of night all was illuminated,[2] that, the veil of darkness being removed, the debauchees might gratify an additional sense.

Death formed an essential part of these festivities of the ancients. It was introduced as a contrast, and for the purpose of giving a zest to the pleasures of life. Gladiators, courtesans, and musicians, were all introduced to enliven the entertainment A Roman, on quitting the arms of a strumpet, went to enjoy the spectacle of a wild beast quaffing human blood; after witnessing a prostitution, he amused himself with the convulsions of an expiring fellow-creature. What sort of a people must that have been who stationed disgrace both at the entrance and at the exit of life, and exhibited upon a stage the two great mysteries of nature, to dishonor at once the whole work of God?

The slaves who cultivated the earth were constantly chained by the foot, and the only nourishment allowed them consisted of a little bread, with salt and water. At night they were confined in subterraneous dungeons, which had no air but what they received through an aperture in the roof. There was a law that prohibited the killing of African lions, which were reserved for the Roman shows. A peasant who would have defended his life against one of those animals would have been severely punished.[3] When an unfortunate wretch perished in the arena, torn by a panther or gored by the horns of a stag, persons afflicted with certain diseases ran to bathe themselves in his blood and to lick it with their eager lips.[4] Caligula wished that the whole Roman people had but one head, that he might strike it off with a single blow.[5] The same emperor fed the lions intended for the games of the circus with human flesh; and Nero was on the point of compelling an Egyptian remarkable for his voracity to devour living people.[6] Titus, by way of celebrating his father's birthday, delivered up three thousand Jews to be devoured by wild beasts.[7] Tiberius was advised to put to death one of his old

[1] Tacit, *An*, 14. [2] Tacit, *loc. cit.* [3] *Cod. Theod*, tome vi. p. 92.
[4] Tert, *Apologet.* [5] Suet., in *Vit. Cal.*
[6] Suet, *in Caligula et Nero.* [7] Joseph, *de Bell. Jud*, lib. vii.

friends who was languishing in prison. "I am not yet reconciled to him," replied the tyrant,—an expression which breathes the true spirit of Rome. It was a common thing to slaughter five, six, ten, twenty thousand persons of all ranks, of both sexes, of every age, on the mere suspicion of the emperor;[1] and the relatives of the victims adorned their houses with garlands, kissed the hands of the *god*, and assisted at his entertainments. The daughter of Sejanus, only nine years old, who said that she would do so no more, and who requested to be scourged, when on her way to prison was violated by the executioner before he strangled her—so great was the respect paid by these virtuous Romans to the laws. During the reign of Claudius was exhibited the spectacle (and Tacitus mentions it as a fine sight[2]) of nineteen thousand men slaughtering one another on the lake Fucinus for the amusement of the Roman populace. The combatants, before engaging in the bloody work, saluted the emperor with these words, *Ave imperator, morituri te salutant!* "Hail, Cæsar! those who are about to die salute thee!"—an expression not less base than impressive.

It was the total extinction of all moral feeling which inspired the Romans with that indifference in regard to death which has been so foolishly admired. Suicide is always common among a people of corrupt morals. Man, reduced to the instinct of the brute, dies with the same unconcern. We shall say nothing of the other vices of the Romans: of infanticide, authorized by a law of Romulus and confirmed by the Twelve Tables, or of the sordid avarice of that renowned people. Scaptius lent a sum of money to the senate of Salamis, which being unable to repay it at the stipulated time, he kept the assembly besieged by armed men till several of the members died with hunger. Brutus, the Stoic, being connected in some way with this extortioner, interested himself in his behalf with Cicero, who could not restrain his indignation at the circumstance.[3]

If therefore the Romans sank into slavery, their morals were the cause of it. It is baseness that first produces tyranny, and by a natural reaction tyranny afterward prolongs that baseness.

---

[1] Tacit., lib. xv.; Dion., lib. lxxvii.; Herodian., lib. iv. [2] *An.*, lib. xii.

[3] The interest of the sum was four per cent. a month. See Cic., *Epist. ad Attic.*, lib. v., epist. 2

Let us no more complain of the present state of society; the most corrupt people of modern times is a people of sages in comparison with the pagan nations.

If we could for a moment suppose that the political order of the ancients was more excellent than ours, still their *moral* order could not be compared to that which Christianity has produced among us; and, as morality is after all the basis of every social institution, never while we are Christians shall we sink into such depths of depravity as the ancients.

When at Rome and in Greece the political ties were broken, what restraint was left for men? Could the worship of so many infamous divinities preserve those morals which were no longer supported by the laws? So far from checking the corruption, this worship became one of its most powerful agents. By an excess of evil which makes us shudder, the idea of the existence of the Deity, which tends to the maintenance of virtue among men, encouraged vice among the pagans, and seemed to eternize guilt by imparting to it a principle of everlasting duration.

We have traditions of the wickedness of men and of the dreadful catastrophes which have never failed to follow the corruption of manners May we not suppose that God has so combined the physical and moral order of the universe that a subversion of the latter necessarily occasions a change in the former, and that great crimes naturally produce great revolutions? The mind acts upon the body in an inexplicable manner, and man is perhaps the mind of the great body of the universe. How much this would simplify nature, and how prodigiously it would enlarge the sphere of man! It would also be a key to the explanation of miracles, which would then fall into the ordinary course of things.[1] Let deluges, conflagrations, the overthrow of states, have their secret causes in the vices and virtues of man; let guilt and its punishment be the weights

[1] If the author here means that in the given hypothesis all events or facts would be of the natural order, and that there would no longer be any thing of the miraculous or preternatural order, his remark is manifestly incorrect, because, although crime were always, as it now frequently is, followed by a visible temporal punishment, all the occasions or reasons for the intervention of miraculous power would not on that account necessarily cease. T.

placed in the two scales of the moral and physical balance of the world the correspondence would be admirable, and would make but one whole of a creation which at the first view appears to be double.[1]

It may be, then, that the corruption of the Roman empire drew forth from the recesses of their deserts the barbarians, who, unconscious of the secret commission that was given them to destroy, instinctively denominated themselves *the scourge of God*. What would have become of the world if the great ark of Christianity had not saved the remnant of the human race from this new deluge? What chance would have been left for posterity? Where would the light of knowledge have been preserved?

The priests of polytheism did not form a body of learned men, except in Persia and Egypt; but the magi and the Egyptian priests, who, be it remarked, never communicated their knowledge to the vulgar, no longer existed as bodies at the time of the invasion of the barbarians. As for the philosophic sects of Athens and Alexandria, they were confined almost entirely to those two cities, and consisted at the utmost of a few hundred rhetoricians who might have been massacred with the rest of the inhabitants.

Among the ancients we find no zeal for making converts, no ardor for diffusing instruction, no retirement to the desert, there to live with God and to cultivate and preserve the sciences. What priest of Jupiter would have gone forth to arrest Attila in his way? What pagan pontiff would have persuaded an Alaric to withdraw his troops from Rome? The barbarians who overran the empire were already half-christianized; but, marching as they were under the bloody banner of the Scandinavian or Tartar god,—meeting in their way no force of religious sentiment which would compel them to respect existing institutions, nor any solidly-established morals, which had only begun to be formed

---

[1] This view of the correspondence between sin and its punishment in this world is not inconsistent with faith, to a certain extent. Sin, so far as it demands only a temporal punishment, may be expiated by the sufferings of this life; but mortal sin, unrepented of, calls for an eternal punishment, which, consequently, must be reserved for a future state. T.

among the Romans under the influence of Christianity,—it cannot be doubted that they would have destroyed all before them. Such, indeed, was the design of Alaric. "I feel within me," says that barbarous monarch, "something that impels me to burn the city of Rome." We behold here a man elevated upon ruins and exhibiting the proportions of a giant.

Of the different nations that invaded the empire, the Goths seem to have been the least tinctured with the spirit of devastation. Theodoric, the conqueror of Odoacer, was a great prince, but then he was a Christian. Boetius, his prime minister, was also a Christian and a scholar. This baffles all conjectures. What would the Goths have done had they been *idolaters?* They would doubtless have overthrown every thing, like the other barbarians. They indeed sank very rapidly into a state of corruption; and if, instead of adoring Christ, they had worshipped Flora, Venus, and Bacchus, what a horrid medley would have resulted from the sanguinary religion of Odin and the obscure fables of Greece!

Polytheism was so little calculated for the work of conservation that it could not sustain itself, and, on falling into ruins on every side, Maximinus wished to invest it with the Christian forms by way of propping up the tottering fabric. He placed in each province a priest who corresponded to the bishop, a high-pontiff who represented the metropolitan.[1] Julian founded pagan convents, and made the ministers of Baal preach in their temples. This arrangement, copied from Christianity, soon disappeared, because it was not upheld by the spirit of virtue nor founded on morality.

The only class amid the conquered nations whom the barbarians respected was that of the priests and monks. The monasteries became so many asylums where the sacred flame of science was preserved together with the Greek and Latin languages. The most illustrious citizens of Rome and Athens, having sought a refuge in the Christian priesthood, thus escaped death or slavery, to which they would have been doomed with the rest of the people.

We may form some conception of the abyss into which we

[1] Eus., lib. viii. cap. 14; lib. ix. cap. 2–8.

should at this day be plunged, if the barbarians had overrun the world during the prevalence of polytheism, by the present state of those nations in which Christianity is extinguished. We should all be Turkish slaves, or something still worse; for Mohammedanism has at least a tincture of morality borrowed from the Christian religion, of which it is, after all, but a very wretched excrescence.[1] But, as the first Ismael was an enemy of Jacob of old, so the second is the persecutor of the modern Israel.

It is, therefore, highly probable that, but for Christianity, the wreck of society and of learning would have been complete. It is impossible to calculate how many ages would have been necessary for mankind to emerge from the ignorance and gross barbarism in which they would have been ingulfed. Nothing less than an immense body of recluses scattered over three quarters of the globe, and laboring in concert for the promotion of the same object, was requisite to preserve those sparks which have rekindled the torch of science among the moderns. Once more, we repeat it, no order of paganism, either political, philosophical, or religious, could have rendered this inestimable service in the absence of Christianity. The writings of the ancients, by being dispersed in the monasteries, partly escaped the ravages of the Goths. Finally, polytheism was not, like Christianity, a kind of *lettered* religion, if we may be allowed the expression; because it did not, like the latter, combine metaphysics and ethics with religious dogmas. The necessity which the Christian clergy were under of publishing books themselves, either to propagate the faith or to confute heresy, powerfully contributed to the preservation and the revival of learning.

Under every imaginable hypothesis we shall invariably find that the gospel has been a barrier to the destruction of society; for, supposing that it had never appeared upon earth, and, on the other hand, that the barbarians had continued in their forests, the Roman world, sinking more and more in its corruption, would have been menaced with a frightful dissolution

[1] In the original, *une secte très-éloignée*—an expression entirely too mild for the designation of Mohammedanism in its relation to Christianity. T.

Would the slaves have revolted? The slaves were as depraved as their masters; they shared the same pleasures and the same disgrace; they had the same religion,—a religion of the passions,—which destroyed every hope of a change in the principles of morality. Science made no further progress; its movement was retrograde; the arts declined. Philosophy served but to propagate a species of impiety, which, without leading to a destruction of the idols, produced the crimes and calamities of atheism among the great, while it left to the vulgar those of superstition. Did mankind improve because Nero ceased to believe in the deities of the Capitol and contemptuously defiled the statues of the gods?[1]

Tacitus asserts that a regard for morality still existed in the remote provinces;[2] but these provinces were beginning to be indoctrinated in the Christian faith,[3] and we are reasoning in the supposition that Christianity was not known, and that the barbarians had not quitted their deserts. As for the Roman armies, which would probably have dismembered the empire, the soldiers were as corrupt as the rest of the citizens, and would have been much more depraved had they not been recruited by Goths and Germans. All that we can possibly conjecture is that, after protracted civil wars and a general commotion which might have lasted several centuries, the human race would have been reduced to a few individuals wandering among ruins. But what a length of time would have been requisite for this new stock to put forth its branches! What a series of ages must have revolved before the sciences, lost or forgotten, could have revived, and in what an infant state would society be at the present day!

As Christianity preserved society from total destruction by converting the barbarians and by collecting the wrecks of civilization and the arts, so it would have saved the Roman world

[1] Tacit., *An.*, lib. xiv.; Suet., *in Neron.*

[2] *Id.*, *ibid.*, lib. xvi 5.

[3] Dionys. et Ignat., *Epist. ap. Eus.*, iv. 23; Chrys., *Op.*, tome vii. pp. 658 and 810, edit. Savil; Plin., *Epist.* x.; Lucian, *in Alex.*, c. 25. Pliny, in his celebrated letter here quoted, complains that the temples are forsaken, and that purchasers are no longer to be found for the sacred victims

from its own corruption, had not the latter fallen beneath foreign arms. Religion alone can renew the original energy of a nation. That of the Saviour had already laid the moral foundation. The ancients permitted infanticide, and the dissolution of the marriage tie, which is, in fact, the first bond of society; their probity and justice were relative things; they extended not beyond the limits of their native land; the people collectively had different principles from the individual citizen; modesty and humanity were not ranked among the virtues; the most numerous class of the community was composed of slaves; and the state was incessantly fluctuating between popular anarchy and despotism. Such were the mischiefs to which Christianity applied an infallible remedy, as she has proved, by delivering modern societies from the same evils. The very excess of Christian austerity in the first ages was necessary. It was requisite that there should be martyrs of chastity when there were public prostitutions,—penitents covered with sackcloth and ashes when the law authorized the grossest violations of morality,—heroes of charity when there were monsters of barbarity; finally, to wean a whole degenerate people from the disgraceful combats of the circus and the arena, it was requisite that religion should have her champions and her exhibitions, if we may so express it, in the deserts of Thebais.

JESUS CHRIST may therefore, with strict truth, be denominated, in a material sense, that SAVIOUR OF THE WORLD which he is in a spiritual sense. His career on earth was, even humanly speaking, the most important event that ever occurred among men, since the regeneration of society commenced only with the proclamation of the gospel. The precise time of his advent is truly remarkable. A little earlier, his morality would not have been absolutely necessary, for the nations were still upheld by their ancient laws; a little later, that divine Messiah would have appeared after the general wreck of society.[1] We boast of our philosophy at the present day; but, most assuredly, the levity with which we treat the institutions of Christianity

[1] These remarks very happily illustrate the declaration of an inspired apostle. St. Paul says, *When the fulness of time* (the πληρωμα τυ καιρυ—the accomplishment of the destined period) *was come, God sent his Son into the world.* S.

is any thing but philosophical. The gospel has changed mankind in every respect and enabled it to take an immense step toward perfection. If you consider it as a grand religious institution, which has regenerated the human race, then all the petty objections, all the cavils of impiety, fall to the ground. It is certain that the pagan nations were in a kind of moral infancy in comparison to what we are at the present day. A few striking acts of justice, exhibited by a few of the ancients. are not sufficient to shake this truth or to change the general aspect of the case.

Christianity has unquestionably shed a new light upon mankind. It is the religion that is adapted to a nation matured by time It is, if we may venture to use the expression, the religion congenial to the present age of the world, as the reign of types and emblems was suited to the cradle of Israel. In heaven it has placed one only God; on earth it has abolished slavery. On the other hand, if you consider its mysteries (as we have done) as the archetype of the laws of nature, you will find nothing in them revolting to a great mind. The truths of Christianity, so far from requiring the submission of reason,[1] command, on the contrary, the most sublime exercise of that faculty.

This remark is so just, and Christianity, which has been characterized as the religion of barbarians, is so truly the religion of philosophers, that Plato may be said to have almost anticipated it. Not only the morality, but also the doctrine, of the disciple of Socrates bears a striking resemblance to that of the gospel. Dacier, his translator, sums them up in the following manner:—

"Plato proves that the *Word* arranged this universe and rendered it visible; that the knowledge of this Word leads to a happy life here below and procures felicity after death; that the soul is immortal; that the dead will rise again; that there will be a last judgment of the righteous and the wicked, where each will appear only with his virtues or his vices, which will be the cause of everlasting happiness or misery.

"Finally," says the learned translator, "Plato had so grand

---

[1] That is, the suppression of reason. T

and so true a conception of supreme justice, and was so thoroughly acquainted with the depravity of men, that, according to him, if a man supremely just were to appear upon earth, he would be imprisoned, calumniated, scourged, and at length CRUCIFIED, by those who, though fraught with injustice, would nevertheless pass for righteous.[1]

The detractors of Christianity place themselves in a false position, which it is scarcely possible for them not to perceive. If they assert that this religion originated among the Goths and Vandals, it is an easy matter to prove that the schools of Greece had very clear notions of the Christian tenets. If they maintain, on the contrary, that the doctrine of the gospel is but the *philosophical* teaching of the ancients, why then do our *philosophers* reject it? Even they who discover in Christianity nothing more than ancient allegories of the heavens, the planets, and the signs of the zodiac, by no means divest that religion of all its grandeur. It would still appear profound and magnificent in its mysteries, ancient and sacred in its traditions, which in this way would be traceable to the infancy of the world. How extraordinary that all the researches of infidels cannot discover in Christianity any thing stamped with the character of littleness or mediocrity!

With respect to the *morality* of the gospel, its beauty is universally admitted: the more it is known and practised, the more will the eyes of men be opened to their real happiness and their true interest. Political science is extremely circumscribed. The highest degree of perfection which it can attain is the representative system,—the offspring, as we have shown, of Christianity. But a religion whose precepts form a code of morality and virtue is an institution capable of supplying every want, and of becoming, in the hands of saints and sages, a universal means of felicity. The time may perhaps come when the mere form of government, excepting despotism, will be a matter of indifference among men, who will attach themselves more particularly to those simple, moral, and religious laws which constitute the permanent basis of society and of all good government.

Those who reason about the excellence of antiquity, and would fain persuade us to revive its institutions, forget that social order

---

[1] Dacier, *Discours sur Platon*, p. 22.

is not, neither can it be, what it formerly was. In the absence of a great moral power, a great coercive power is at least necessary among men. In the ancient republics, the greater part of the population, as is well known, were slaves; the man who cultivated the earth belonged to another man: there were *people*, but there were no *nations*

Polytheism, which is defective in every respect as a religious system, might therefore have been adapted to that imperfect state of society, because each master was a kind of absolute magistrate, whose rigid despotism kept the slave within the bounds of duty and compensated by chains for the deficiency of the moral religious force. Paganism, not possessing sufficient excellence to render the poor man virtuous, was obliged to let him be treated as a malefactor.

But, in the present order of things, how could you restrain an immense multitude of free peasants, far removed from the vigilance of the magistrate? how could you prevent the crimes of an independent populace, congregated in the suburbs of an extensive capital, if they did not believe in a religion which enjoins the practice of duty and virtue upon all the conditions of life? Destroy the influence of the gospel, and you must give to every village its police, its prisons, its executioners. If, by an impossibility, the impure altars of paganism were ever re-established among modern nations,—if, in a society where slavery is abolished, the worship of *Mercury the robber* and *Venus the prostitute* were to be introduced,—there would soon be a total extinction of the human race.[1]

Here lies the error of those who commend polytheism for having separated the moral from the religious force, and at the same time censure Christianity for having adopted a contrary system. They perceive not that paganism, having to deal with an immense nation of slaves, was consequently afraid of enlightening the human race; that it gave every encouragement to the sensual part of man, and entirely neglected the cultivation of the soul. Christianity, on the contrary, meditating the destruction of slavery, held up to man the dignity of his nature, and inculcated

---

[1] A frightful illustration of these remarks was witnessed during the French revolution. T.

the precepts of reason and virtue. It may be affirmed that the doctrine of the gospel is the doctrine of a free people, from this single circumstance:—that it combines morality with religion.

It is high time to be alarmed at the state in which we have been living for some years past. Think of the generation now springing up in our towns and provinces; of all those children who, born during the revolution, have never heard any thing of God, nor of the immortality of their souls, nor of the punishments or rewards that await them in a future life: think what may one day become of such a generation if a remedy be not speedily applied to the evil. The most alarming symptoms already manifest themselves: we see the age of innocence sullied with many crimes.[1] Let philosophy, which, after all, cannot penetrate among the poor, be content to dwell in the mansions of the rich, and leave the people in general to the care of religion; or, rather, let philosophy, with a more enlightened zeal and with a spirit more worthy of her name, remove those barriers which she proposed to place between man and his Creator.

Let us support our last conclusions with authorities which philosophy will not be inclined to suspect.

"A little philosophy," says Bacon, "withdraws us from religion, but a good deal of philosophy brings us back to it again: nobody denies the existence of God, excepting the man who has reason to wish that there were none."

"To say that religion is not a restraint," observes Montesquieu, "because it does not always restrain, is equally absurd as to say that the civil laws also are not a deterring agent. . . . The question is not to ascertain whether it would be better for a certain individual or a certain nation to have no religion than to abuse that which they have; but to know which is the least evil, —that religion should be sometimes abused, or that there should be none at all among mankind.[2]

"The history of Sabbaco," says that eminent writer, whom we continue to quote, "is admirable. The god of Thebes appeared to him in a dream, and ordered him to put to death all the priests

[1] The public papers teem with details of the crimes committed by little malefactors, eleven or twelve years old. The danger must be highly alarming, since the peasants themselves complain of the vices of their children.

[2] *Spirit of Laws*, book xxiv. chap. 2.

of Egypt. He conceived that it was not pleasing to the gods that he should reign any longer, since they enjoined things so contrary to their ordinary pleasures, and accordingly he retired into Ethiopia."[1]

Finally, Rousseau exclaims, "Avoid those who, under the pretence of explaining nature, sow mischievous doctrines in the hearts of men, and whose apparent skepticism is a hundred times more positive and dogmatic than the decided tone of their adversaries. Under the arrogant pretext that they alone are enlightened, true, and sincere, they imperiously subject us to their peremptory decisions, and presume to give us, as the general principles of things, the unintelligible systems which they have erected in their imaginations. Overthrowing, destroying, trampling under foot all that is respected by men, they bereave the afflicted of the last consolation in their misery; they take from the rich and powerful the only curb of their passions; they eradicate from the heart the remorse consequent on guilt, the hopes inspired by virtue; and still they boast of being the benefactors of the human race. Never, say they, can truth be hurtful to men. I think so too; and this, in my opinion, is a strong proof that what they teach is not the truth.

"One of the most common sophisms with the philosophic party is to contrast a supposed nation of good philosophers with one of bad Christians; as if it were easier to form a people of genuine philosophers than a people of genuine Christians. I know not if, among individuals, one of these characters is more easy to be found than the other; but this I know, that when we come to talk of nations, we must suppose such as will make a bad use of philosophy without religion, just as ours abuses religion without philosophy; and this seems to me to make a material alteration in the state of the question.

"It is an easy matter to make a parade of fine maxims in books; but the question is whether they agree with, and necessarily flow from, the principles of the writer. So far, this has not been the case It also remains to be seen whether philosophy, at its ease and upon the throne, would be capable of controlling the love of glory, the selfishness, the ambition, the

[1] *Spirit of Laws*, book xxiv. chap. 4.

little passions of men, and *whether it would practise that engaging humanity which, with pen in hand, it so highly commends.*

"ACCORDING TO PRINCIPLES, PHILOSOPHY CAN DO NO GOOD WHICH RELIGION WOULD NOT FAR SURPASS; AND RELIGION DOES MUCH THAT PHILOSOPHY CANNOT ACCOMPLISH.

"Our modern governments are unquestionably indebted to Christianity for a better-established authority and for less frequent revolutions. It has made them less sanguinary, as is proved by comparing them with the governments of antiquity. Religion, becoming better known and discarding fanaticism, imparted a greater mildness to Christian manners. This change was not the effect of letters; for the spirit of humanity has not been the more respected in those countries which could boast of their superior knowledge. The cruelties of the Athenians, the Egyptians, the Roman emperors, the Chinese, attest this truth. What numberless works of mercy have been produced by the gospel!"

As for us, we are convinced that Christianity will rise triumphant from the dreadful trial by which it has just been purified. What gives us this assurance is that it stands the test of reason perfectly, and the more we examine it the more we discover its profound truth. Its mysteries explain man and nature; its works corroborate its precepts; its charity in a thousand forms has replaced the cruelty of the ancients. Without losing any thing of the pomp of antiquity, its ceremonies give greater satisfaction to the heart and the imagination. We are indebted to it for every thing,—letters, sciences, agriculture, and the fine arts; it connects morality with religion, and man with God; Jesus Christ, the saviour of moral man, is also the saviour of physical man. His coming may be considered as an advent the most important and most felicitous, designed to counterbalance the deluge of barbarism and the total corruption of manners. Did we even reject the supernatural evidences of Christianity, there would still remain in its sublime morality, in the immensity of its benefits, and in the beauty of its worship, sufficient proof of its being the most divine and the purest religion ever practised by men.

"With those who have an aversion for religion," says *Pascal*, "you must begin with demonstrating that it is not contradictory to reason; next show that it is venerable, and inspire them with respect for it; afterward exhibit it in an amiable light, and excite a wish that it were true; then let it appear by incontestable proofs that it is true; and, lastly, prove its antiquity and holiness by its grandeur and sublimity."

Such is the plan which that great man marked out, and which we have endeavored to pursue. Though we have not employed the arguments usually advanced by the apologists of Christianity, we have arrived by a different chain of reasoning at the same conclusion, which we present as the result of this work.

Christianity is perfect; men are imperfect.

Now, a perfect consequence cannot spring from an imperfect principle.

Christianity, therefore, is not the work of men.

If Christianity is not the work of men, it can have come from none but God.

If it came from God, men cannot have acquired a knowledge of it but by revelation.

Therefore, Christianity is a revealed religion.

NOTES.

NOTE A, (p. 47.)

THE *Encyclopedie* is a wretched work, according to the opinion of Voltaire himself. "I have accidentally seen," says he, writing to D'Alembert, "some articles by those who, with me, perform the tasks of journeymen in that great shop. Most of them are written without method. The article *Femme* (Woman) has just been copied into one of the literary journals, and is most severely ridiculed. I could not suppose that you would have admitted such an article into so grave a work Any one would imagine that it was composed for a lackey of Gil Blas."—*Corresp. between Voltaire and D'Alembert,* vol i. p. 19, letter 13, Nov. 1756.

"You encourage me to tell you that people in general complain of the tiresome, vague, and desultory articles which various persons furnish you in order to show off. They should think of the work, and not of themselves. Why have you not recommended a certain plan to your assistants, such as derivations, definitions, examples, reasons, clearness, brevity? I have met with none of these in the dozen articles—the only ones I have seen." (Letter 22d Dec., 1756; see also 29th Dec., 1757.)

D'Alembert, in the *Discourse* prefixed to the third volume of the *Encyclopedie,* and Diderot, in the fifth, (article *Encyclopedie,*) have themselves written the keenest of satires on their performances.—See the *Correspondence between Voltaire and D'Alembert,* vol. i. p. 19.

NOTE B, (p. 79.)

In conjunction with this passage from the *Apology* of St. Justin, the reader will be interested by the account which Pliny the younger has given of the manners of the early Christians. His letter to Trajan on this subject, as well as the answer of the emperor, shows that the innocence of the Christians was fully admitted, and that their religious faith was their only crime. We learn also from this source the wonderful diffusion of the gospel; for at that time, in a portion of the empire, *the temples were almost deserted* This letter of Pliny was written one or two years after the death of St. John the Evangelist, and about forty prior to the appearance of St. Justin's *Apology*. Though well known, its insertion here may not be devoid of utility:—

"*Pliny, Proconsul in Bithynia and Pontus, to the Emperor Trajan.*

"I make it a solemn duty, sire, to acquaint you with all my difficulties; for who can enlighten or direct me in my doubts better than yourself? I have never assisted at the indictment and trial of any Christian; so that I know not on what grounds they are accused, nor to what extent they ought to be punished I am much influenced by the difference of age. Should all be made to suffer without distinguishing between the young and those more advanced in years? Should they who repent be pardoned, or is it useless to renounce Christianity after having once embraced it? Is it the mere profession that we punish, or the crimes imputed to that profession? In the cases that have come under my notice, I have observed the following mode of proceeding: I inquired of them whether they were Christians; and, if they acknowledged it, I subjected them to a second and a third interrogatory, threatening them with punishment. If they persisted, I put them to the torture; because, whatever might be the nature of the principles to which they adhered, I judged that they deserved to suffer on account of their disobedience and invincible obstinacy. Others, given to the same folly, I propose to send to Rome, as they are citizens of the empire. The crime of these people having spread, as it generally happens, a variety of cases presented themselves. A memorial, without any signature, was placed in my hands, which charged different persons with being Christians who deny that they are, or ever were, members of that profession. They invoked the gods in my presence, and in such language as I prescribed, and also offered incense and wine to your image, which I had brought expressly with the statues of our divinities. They also vented their imprecations against Christ, which, it is said, no true Christian can ever be compelled to do. I concluded, therefore, to discharge them. Others, accused by an informer, acknowledged at first that they were Christians, and immediately after denied it; saying that, although formerly attached to that belief, they had renounced it,—some more than three years before, others a longer time, and others again more than twenty years. All these people adored your image and the statues of the gods, and uttered maledictions against Christ. They declared that they had committed no other fault than what is implied in their observances, namely:—they assembled on an appointed day before sunrise and sang alternately the praises of Christ as a Divine Being. They bound themselves by oath not to commit any crime, but to abstain from theft and adultery, to fulfil their promises, and not to deny the trust confided to them. Afterward they separated, and again came together to partake of an innocent repast; but this they discontinued after the publication of my edict, by which, agreeably to your commands, I prohibited all kinds of meetings. I have deemed it necessary to apply the torture in order to extort the truth from certain unmarried women (slaves) who were admitted to be employed in the Christian administrations. It led, however, to no disclosure beyond the fact that they were guilty of a foolish and excessive superstition; which has caused me to suspend all further proceedings until after the reception of your commands. This matter appears to me deserving of your attention from the great number of persons involved; for an immense multitude of both sexes, and of every age and condition, are daily implicated in these charges, and will continue to be so. The contagion has not only infected the cities, but it has spread into the towns and provinces. It seems to me, however, that it may be remedied and arrested. I can say with certainty that the temples, which had been almost deserted, are now frequented; and the sacrifices, for a long time disregarded, begin to attract attention. Victims are sold in every direction, while some time ago they found few purchasers. We may judge from this what a number of persons may be reclaimed from their errors if pardon be promised to the repentant."

"*Trajan to Pliny.*

"My dear Pliny:—You have acted right in regard to the Christians who were cited before you; for it is impossible, in this kind of affair, to have any certain and general form of proceeding. The Christians should not be pursued. If they are accused and convicted, let them be punished. If the party deny that he is a Christian, and prove it by his actions,—that is, by an invocation of the gods,—he should be pardoned, no matter what suspicion may have previously existed against him. But in no case whatever should any anonymous informations be admitted; for that would be a dangerous precedent, and quite foreign to our principles."

NOTE C, (p. 81)

An illustration of the frightful consequences of an excessive population is exhibited among the Chinese, who annually destroy an immense number of children. The more we examine the question the more convinced do we become that Jesus Christ acted in a manner worthy of the universal legislator, when he encouraged a number of men to follow his example by leading a life of celibacy. Libertinism may no doubt have availed itself of the counsel of St. Paul to palliate excesses injurious to society; and superficial minds may have been led by such abuse to declaim against the counsel itself; but what is there that human corruption will not abuse? What institution is not liable to be assailed by those short-sighted people who are incapable of embracing in one view its various parts? Moreover, without those Christian recluses who appeared three hundred years after the Messiah, what would have become of letters, of the arts and sciences? Finally, the opinion we have expressed is confirmed by modern economists, and among them Arthur Young, who contend that large domains are more favorable than smaller ones to every kind of culture except that of the vine. Now, in any country that has little commerce, and is essentially given to agriculture, if the population is too great there must necessarily be a very extensive division of property, or this country will be exposed to everlasting revolutions; unless, indeed, the peasant be a slave, as among the ancients, or a serf, as in Russia and in a part of Germany.

NOTE D, (p. 97.)

Mr. Ramsay, a Scotchman, passed from Anglicanism to Socinianism, thence to pure Deism, and finally to a universal Pyrrhonism. Having consulted Fénélon, he was reconverted to Christianity and became a Catholic. Mr. Ramsay has himself left us the interesting conversation which resulted in his conversion. We shall quote that part of it which points out the limits of reason and of faith. He had proved to Mr. Ramsay the authenticity of the Sacred Writings and the excellent morality which they contain "But, monseigneur," asked Mr. R., "how is it that the Bible presents so strange a contrast of luminous truths and obscure dogmas? I should like to see those sublime notions of which you have just spoken, apart from what the priests denominate *mysteries*." Fénélon answered:—"Why should we reject that light which consoles the heart because it is mingled with obscurity which humbles the intellect? Should not the true religion elevate and lower man by showing him at once his greatness and his weakness? You have not, as yet, a sufficiently enlarged view of Christianity.

It is not only a holy law that purifies the heart; it is also a mysterious wisdom that subdues the understanding. It is a continual sacrifice, by which our whole being pays homage to the Supreme Reason. By practising its morality, we renounce pleasures through love for Infinite Beauty. By believing its mysteries, we sacrifice our ideas through respect for Eternal Truth. Without this twofold sacrifice of our thoughts and our passions, the holocaust would be imperfect—the victim would be defective. It is thus that man entirely disappears in presence of the Being of beings. We are not to examine whether it is necessary for God to reveal to us mysteries in order to humble our understanding. The question is whether or not he has revealed them. If he has spoken, obedience and love cannot be separated. Christianity is a fact. As you admit the evidences of this fact, you can no longer examine what you are to believe or not to believe. All the difficulties which you have suggested vanish at once when the mind is cured of its presumption. It is easy then to believe that the Divine Nature and the order of Divine Providence are wrapped in mystery impenetrable to our weak reason. The Infinite Being must be incomprehensible to his creatures. On the one hand, we behold a Legislator whose law is altogether divine, who proves his mission by miraculous facts, the evidence of which it is impossible to reject; on the other hand, we find mysteries that baffle our understanding. What are we to do between these two embarrassing extremes of a clear revelation and an impenetrable obscurity? Our only resource is to make the sacrifice of our intellect—a sacrifice which forms a part of the worship which we owe to the Supreme Being. Does not God possess an infinite knowledge which we have not? If he makes known some part of it by supernatural means, we are no longer to examine into the nature of what is revealed, but into the certainty of the revelation. Mysteries appear to us to be inconsistent without in reality being so. This apparent inconsistency proceeds from the narrowness of our mind, which does not embrace a sufficiently extensive knowledge to see the accord between our natural ideas and supernatural truths."

NOTE E, (p. 103.)

In the polyglott of Anthony Vitré, we read:—

Vulgate—Ego sum Dominus Deus tuus.

Septuagint—Ἐγω εἰμὶ κύριος ὁ Θεός σοῦ.

Latin of Chaldaic text—Ego Dominus tuus.

Walton's polyglott has the same reading as above for the Vulgate and Septuagint.

Latin of Syriac version—Ego sum Dominus Deus tuus.

Latin interlinear version in the Hebrew—Et e terra Ægypti eduxi te, qui tuus Dominus Deus ego.

Latin of the Samaritan Hebrew—Ego sum Dominus Deus tuus.

Latin of the Arabic version—Ego sum Deus Dominus tuus.

NOTE F, (p. 107.)

The truths of the Scripture may be traced even among the savages of the New World.

"You may have perceived," says Charlevoix, "in the fable of Atahensic driven from heaven, some vestiges of the history of the first woman banished from the terrestrial paradise in punishment of her disobedience, and the tradition of the deluge as well as the ark in which Noah was saved with his family This circumstance leads me to reject the opinion of Father Acosta, who pretends that this tradition relates to some particular deluge in America. In fact, the Algonquins, and almost all the tribes that speak their language, supposing the creation of the first man, say that his posterity having almost entirely perished by a general inundation, *Messon*, or, as others call him, *Saket-chack*, who saw the whole earth buried under the water, despatched a crow to the bottom of the abyss in order to bring him some earth; but the crow having failed in its mission, he sent a musk-rat, which was more successful, that with the earth brought him by this animal he restored the world to its former state, that he pierced the trees that could be seen with arrows, which were changed into branches; that he accomplished many other wonders, that, in acknowledgment of the services rendered by the musk-rat, he married a female of that species of animal, and repeopled the earth; that he communicated his immortality to a certain savage, in a small package, which he forbade him to open under pain of losing the precious gift."

Father Bouchet, in his letter to the Bishop of Avranches, gives the most curious particulars respecting the resemblance between the Indian fables and the principal truths of our religion and the traditions of Scripture; and the Asiatic Researches confirm the account of that learned French missionary.

"Most of the Indians," says Bouchet, "assert that the numerous deities whom they now adore are but inferior gods, subordinate to the Supreme Being, who is alike the Lord of gods and men. This idea which they have of a being infinitely superior to other divinities, shows at least that their ancestors adored only one God, and that polytheism was introduced among them in the same way in which it was among all idolatrous nations.

"I do not pretend that this primitive knowledge is a clear proof of any intercourse having existed between the Indians and the Egyptians or Jews. I know, indeed, that the Author of nature, without any such aid, has engraved this fundamental truth upon the minds of all men, and that it cannot be altered except by the inordinacy and corruption of their hearts. For the same reason, I shall say nothing of their belief respecting the immortality of the soul and other similar truths

"They maintain that Bruma, one of the three inferior gods, has received the power of creating, and that he created the first man from the slime of the earth, and placed him in *Choream*—a delightful garden, abounding in every kind of fruit, and having a tree the product of which would impart immortality if it were permitted to eat it. It would be strange that people should have formed so exact an idea of the terrestrial paradise if they had never heard of it from others. In their desire to obtain immortality, they had recourse to the tree of life, and succeeded in their design. But the famous serpent, called *Cheiem*, who had been appointed to guard the tree, was enraged upon discovering that it had been used by the inferior gods; and he poured forth a great quantity of poison, which was felt over the whole earth, and would have proved fatal to all men, had not the god *Chiven* interposed, and, taking compassion upon mankind, swallowed the poison which the wicked serpent has spread abroad.

"Here is another fable. The god *Routren*, who had the power of destroying created beings, formed one day the resolution to drown them; but *Vishnou*, the preserver of creatures, being aware of his design, appeared to *Sattiavarti*, his chief confidant, informed him of what *Routren* contemplated, and told him that he would provide a large vessel as the means of saving him, and of preserving what would be requisite for repeopling the world, all which really happened.

"These Indians also honor the memory of one of their penitents, who, like the patriarch Abraham, was on the point of sacrificing his son to one of the gods, as he had been required to do; but whose good will was accepted by the divinity, and dispensed him from the execution of the act.

"Thus, as we find the history of the creation, of the tempter, of the flood, of Abraham, you will likewise discover in the Indian mythology the notion of a great chief who was exposed in a river, but, having been withdrawn from this danger, grew up, became the leader of his companions, defeated their enemies, and conducted them safely through the waters of the sea. You will also find some resemblances to the Hebrew customs and ceremonies, especially such as relate to purifications and that inviolable law which forbids persons to marry out of their own tribe or caste. Here we trace Moses and the book of Leviticus. The sacred book of the Indians is called *Vedam*, for which they have a profound veneration, and which I believe to be an imitation of the Pentateuch. What is still more extraordinary, they retain a confused notion of the adorable Trinity, formerly preached to them. Their three principal gods are Bruma, Vishnu, and Routren. 'You must,' said one of the Brahmins, 'represent to yourself God and his three different names, which correspond to his three principal attributes, very much as those triangular pyramids which stand before the gate of some temples.'"

This mythology alludes still more plainly to the mystery of the Incarnation. It is universally admitted among the Indians that the Deity has several times become incarnate, and almost all believe that on these occasions it was Vishnu, the second of their gods, who assumed the form of man and appeared thus in the character of a Saviour. These people have also notions and practices which recall very forcibly the sacraments of baptism and penance, and even the holy Eucharist.

NOTE G, (p. 121.)

"Chronology is nothing more than a heap of bladders full of wind; it has sunk under all those who, while walking upon it, imagined that they were treading upon solid ground. We have at the present day *eighty* systems, not one of which is true.

"We reckon, said the Babylonians, 473,600 years of celestial observations. A Parisian comes to them: Your account, says he, is correct; your years were days of the solar year; they make 1297 of our years, from Atlas, King of Africa, a great astronomer, to the arrival of Alexander at Babylon.

"This new-comer from Paris needed only to have said to the Chaldeans, You are exaggerators, and our ancestors were ignorant fellows; nations are subject to too many revolutions to preserve astronomical calculations for 4736 centuries; and as to Atlas, King of the Moors, nobody knows at what time he lived. Pythagoras had just as much reason to pretend that he had been a cock, as you to boast of the art of observation."—Voltaire, *Quest. Encyclop.* tome 3, p. 59, art. *Chronol.*

NOTE H, (p. 126.)

It is plain, for many reasons, that the Indians who now inhabit North America could not have constructed the works which are seen on the banks of the Scioto. Moreover, they all agree in saying that when their ancestors came to those western wilds they found these ruins in the same state in which we behold them. Are they remains of the Mexican civilization? Nothing of the kind, however, is to be met with either in Mexico or Peru. These monuments also indicate a knowledge of iron, and a more advanced state of the arts than existed in the New World. Add to this that the empire of Montezuma did not extend so far to the east, since the Natches and Chickasaws, when they left New Mexico, about the beginning of the sixteenth century, discovered on the banks of the *Meschacebé*[1] only wandering hordes.

These fortifications have been attributed to Ferdinand de Soto; but how can we suppose that that Spaniard, who, with his few adventurers, remained only three years in the Floridas, had the force or leisure to raise those enormous works? Moreover, the form of the tombs, and of other parts of the ruins, has no correspondence with the customs and arts of the Europeans. It is certain, too, that the conqueror of Florida did not penetrate beyond Chattafallai, a village of the Chickasaws, situated on a branch of the Mobile River. In short, these monuments are traceable to a period much more remote than the discovery of America. We noticed among these ruins an old decayed oak, which had grown over the ruins of another oak which had fallen at its base, and nothing of which remained but the bark. The latter had also risen upon its predecessor, and this one again had sprung up in the same way. The locality of the two last was discerned by the intersection of two circles of red and petrified sap, which could be seen even with the ground, by removing a thick covering consisting of leaves and moss. Now, if we allow only three centuries to each of these oaks, we shall have a period of twelve hundred years that has passed over those ruins.

If we continue this historical investigation, (which, however, affords no argument in favor of the antiquity of men,) we shall find that there is no rational theory respecting the people who raised these ancient works. The Welch chronicles tell us of a certain Madoc, son of a prince of Wales, who, being discontented in his own country, embarked in 1170, directed his course to the west, discovered a fertile land, returned to England, and then, with twelve vessels, went back to the new region which he had found. It is said that there are still to be found, near the sources of the Missouri, white Indians, who are Christians and speak the Celtic language. Even supposing Madoc and his party to have landed in America, it seems to us plain enough that they could not have constructed the immense works to which we have alluded.

About the middle of the ninth century, the Danes, who were then very skilful in navigation, discovered Iceland, whence they passed to a region farther

---

[1] This is the true name of the Mississippi or Meschusippi, and signifies the *bearded father of waters* See Duprat, Charlevoix, and other travellers. We speak here from our own investigations also

west, called *Vinland*, on account of the numerous vines which they found there.[1] There can scarcely be a doubt that this continent was America, and that the Esquimaux of Labrador are the descendants of the Danes. It is pretended also that the Gauls found their way to America; but neither the Scandinavians, nor the Celts of America or Neustria, have left any monuments similar to those which we are now seeking to authenticate.

It may perhaps be said that the Phœnicians or Carthagenians, in their commercial intercourse with Bœtica, (now Andalusia,) the British or Scilly Islands, (formerly Cassiterides,) or the western coast of Africa,[2] were driven upon the American shore. Some writers pretend that the Carthagenians had regular colonies there, which, from political views, were afterward abandoned. If such had been the case, why was not some vestige of Phœnician manners found among the Caribbeans, among the savages of Guiana, of Paraguay, or even of Florida? Why are the ruins of which we speak in the interior of North America, rather than in some part of South America opposite to the African shore?

There are other writers who are inclined to make the Jews the authors of these monuments, and contend that the Ophir of the Scriptures is located in the West Indies. It was asserted by Columbus that he had seen the remains of Solomon's furnaces in the mines of Cibao. We may add that many customs of the savages appear to be of Jewish origin, such as breaking the bones of the victim at the sacred repast, consuming the whole offering, having places of retirement for the purification of women. The inferences, however, from these facts, amount to very little; for why, if the above-mentioned hypothesis were correct, would we find among the Hurons a language and a deity rather Greek than Jewish? Is it not remarkable that *Ares-Koni* should be the god of war in the Athenian citadel and in the fort of the Iroquois? The most judicious critics are decidedly opposed to the transmigration of the Israelites to Louisiana, proving very clearly that Ophir was on the African coast.[3]

As to the Egyptians, they opened, closed, and resumed again, the commerce of Taprobane (now Ceylon) by the Persian Gulf; but were they acquainted with the fourth continent? We answer that the ruins of Ohio exhibit no traces of Egyptian architecture. The bones found there are not embalmed, and the skeletons are in a recumbent, not vertical, position. Moreover, how is it that none of these ancient works are met with from the sea-coast to the Alleghenies? Why are they all concealed beyond this chain of mountains? Whatever people may be supposed to have established a colony in America, they must have first inhabited the plain between the mountains and the Atlantic coast, before they penetrated a distance of four hundred leagues to the region where the ruins in question are found; unless it be said (what is not devoid of probability) that the former shore of the ocean was at the base of the Apalachian and Allegheny ridges, and that the waters subsequently receded from Pennsylvania, Maryland, Virginia, Carolina, Georgia, and Florida.[4]

---

[1] Mall., *Intr. à l'hist. du Dan.*

[2] *Vide* Strabo. Ptol., Hann., *Perip.* d'Anvill., &c.

[3] *Vide* Saur. d'Anvill.

[4] We say nothing of the Greeks, and particularly the people of Rhodes, because they rarely went beyond the Mediterranean, although they were well skilled in navigation.

NOTE I, (p. 132.)

Freret has done the same thing for the Chinese, and Bailly has in like manner reduced their chronology, as well as that of the Egyptians and Chaldeans, to the computation of the Septuagint. These authors cannot be suspected of partiality to our opinion. (See Bailly, tome i.)

NOTE K, (p. 136.)

Buffon, who was so anxious to reconcile his system with the book of Genesis, made the origin of the world more remote, by considering each of the six days mentioned by Moses as a long series of ages; but it must be admitted that his arguments are not calculated to give much weight to his conjectures. It would be useless to say more concerning this system, which is wholly overthrown by the first principles of natural philosophy and chemistry; or to make any remarks on the formation of the earth, detached from the mass of the sun by the oblique collision of a comet, and suddenly subjected to the laws of gravitation which govern the celestial bodies: or the gradual cooling of the earth, which presupposes the same homogeneousness in the globe as in the cannon-ball which was used for an experiment, or the formation of mountains of the first order, which implies the transmutation of argillaceous into siliceous earth, &c.

We might swell this list of systems, which, after all, are nothing but systems. They have destroyed each other, and, to the unbiassed mind, they have never proved any thing against the truth of the Holy Scriptures. (See the admirable Commentary on Genesis, by Monsr. De Luc, and the *Letters* of the learned Euler.)

NOTE L, (p. 138.)

To complete what we have said on the existence of God and the immortality of the soul, we shall here present the metaphysical proofs of these truths They are all derived from *matter, motion, and thought.*

1. *Matter.*

FIRST PROPOSITION —Something has existed from all eternity; and it is proved by the fact that something exists.

SECOND PROPOSITION.—Something has existed from all eternity, and must be independent and immutable. Otherwise, there would be an infinite succession of causes and effects without a first cause, which is a contradiction.

THIRD PROPOSITION —Something has existed from all eternity, independent and immutable, and is not matter.

Proof.—If it were matter, this matter would exist necessarily. But matter could not exist necessarily without its modes being also necessary. These, however, are subject to perpetual change, as experience teaches.

FOURTH PROPOSITION.—Something has existed from all eternity independent and immutable, which is not matter, and which is necessarily one

Proof.—If two independent principles could exist together, we conceive that one might exist alone, since he has no need of the other. But, in this case, neither of these principles would exist necessarily, and, therefore, there can only be one independent or necessary being.

Fifth Proposition.—Something has existed from all eternity, independent and immutable, which is not matter, which is necessarily one, and a free agent.

Proof.—If the Supreme Cause were not a free agent, that which exists actually could never have existed. Therefore, &c.

Sixth Proposition.—Something has existed from all eternity, &c., which is a free agent, and is infinitely powerful, wise, good, and supreme in all perfection.

Proof.—If there were any limit to the perfections of the Eternal Being, such limitation would proceed either from himself or from some other cause. But neither can be supposed; for he is independent of other causes, and there is no incompatibility between his self-existence and the highest degree of perfection. Therefore, &c.

Now, the Being that possesses all these attributes is God.

2. *Motion.*

Motion is either essential to matter or communicated to it. If it were essential, the component parts of matter would be always in motion. But there are many bodies in a state of repose: therefore, motion is not essential to matter, but communicated to it by some being out of the material order.

"Is it not surprising," says Cicero, "to find men who believe that certain solid and indivisible bodies move by their own natural weight, and that the beautiful world around us has been formed by the casual aggregation of these bodies? If any one can believe this possible, why should he not believe that if a number of characters of gold or any other substance, representing the twenty-one letters of the alphabet, were thrown upon the ground, they would fall precisely in that order which would compose the *Annals of Ennius?* I doubt whether a single verse would thus be formed by chance. But how can men assert that corpuscles, which have neither color, quality, or feeling, and which are always floating about at hap-hazard, could have formed the world, or, rather, can produce every moment innumerable worlds to take the place of others? If the concourse of atoms can make a world, why could it not produce something much easier of formation,—for instance, a portico, a temple, a house, a city?"[1]

"As all the sects agree," says Bayle, "that the laws of motion cannot produce—I will not say a mill, a clock, but—the most simple tool in the shop of a locksmith, how could they produce the body of a dog, or even a rose or a pomegranate? To think of explaining these results by the stars or by substantial forms is pitiful. There must be a cause that has an idea of its work and is acquainted with the means of producing it. All this is necessary in him who makes a watch or builds a ship: how much more is it requisite for the organization of living beings!"[2]

"If we suppose," says Crousaz, "the eternal existence and motion of atoms, we might infer that, in coming together, they formed certain masses, and that these masses were adapted to certain effects. But there is an infinite difference between this and supposing that these masses, formed by the fortuitous con-

---

[1] *De Natura Deor.*, ii. 37.

[2] Art. *Serment*, note C.

course of atoms, assumed a regular arrangement, and the properties of some were precisely such as were required by the others.

"If you had ten tickets, numbered 1, 2, 3, &c., and folded up, how many trials would be necessary before you would arrange them in such order that number 1 would come first, number 2 second, and so on as far as number 10? . . . . . The difficulty of arranging many things, without the exercise of any discernment, increases always in proportion to their number and the number of permutations. . . . . As an example of their multiplicity, *a* and *b* may be combined in two ways—*ab, ba; abc* in six different ways, and *abcd* in twenty-four.

"Infinity, arranged two-and-two, would reach infinity. . . . . What sources of confusion! What infinitude of disorder! What endless forms of chaos! . . . . . To say that in the course of time a regular combination took place would be supposing an infinite regularity in the midst of confusion; for it would be to suppose that all the different combinations *ad infinitum* had succeeded each other in order, and, in this way, the regular combination had taken its place in this succession, as if some intelligence had made this arrangement."[1]

This kind of reasoning has great weight, and is well suited to minds that require mathematical evidence. Some infidels have supposed that they alone can produce demonstrations by $a + b$, and that Christians trust altogether to their imagination. . . . . But has not Leibnitz, in his *Théodicée*, proved the existence of God by a geometrical process? Have not Huyghens, Keil, Marcalle, and a hundred others, presented similar theorems? Plato called the Deity the *Eternal Geometrician*, and Archimedes has left us the most beautiful and most striking symbol of the Divinity—a triangle inscribed in a circle. . . . .

The absurdity of those who look upon the world as the result of a fortuitous combination of atoms is thus strikingly presented by Hancock:—

"Suppose all men to be blind, and commanded, while in this state, to report themselves on the plains of Mesopotamia: how many ages would be required before they would make their way to this common rendezvous? Would they ever reach it? This, however, would be much easier of execution for men than for the atoms of Democritus to accomplish what he ascribes to them. But, admitting that so fortunate a combination is not impossible, how happens it that nothing new is produced, and that the same chance that collected the atoms for the formation of the universe has not scattered them for its destruction? Will it be said that they are held together by the principles of attraction and gravitation? But this principle of attraction and gravitation either preceded or followed the formation of the universe. If it preceded it, why was its action suspended? If it followed it, whence did it proceed? Did it not spring from some other source than matter, which, by its very nature, is susceptible of motion in any direction? If it be said that *nature* maintains herself in this permanent state, this nature, according to the system of Democritus, is nothing else than the fortuitous concourse which, as is readily conceived, cannot explain the conservation of the world any more than its formation.[2]

To escape the difficulties arising from the supposition that the world was

[1] *Examen du Pyrronisme*, sect. viii. p. 426.

[2] *On the Existence of God*, sect. v

formed by the motion of matter, Spinosa, after Strabo, maintained that there is only one substance in the world, and that substance is God, combining matter and spirit and the attributes of thought and extension. Thus, my foot, my hand, a stone, all the physical and moral accidents of life, are parts of the Deity. The pagans made gods out of the vilest objects on earth; but it was reserved for an atheist to deify, in one eternal substance, all the crimes and infirmities of the world. When God has retired from a man, his mind becomes the theatre of strange thoughts, which it would be difficult for the most skilful person to explain. The doctrine of Spinosa, which is the most impious and untenable of all systems, has been completely refuted by Bayle, Clarke, Leibnitz, Crouzas, and others.

It would be useless to invoke the contempt of our readers upon the *forms* and *qualities* of matter of Anaximander, or the *plastic forms* of the Stoics, which, according to them, effected the order of the universe. Infidels themselves have refuted these reveries. Nothing remains then but the law of *necessity* for explaining the existence of the universe. But this necessity was either created or uncreated. If the former, who created it? If the latter, that necessity which arranges all things, which produces so admirable an order, which is one, indivisible, and without extension, is no other than God.

3. *Thought.*

Whence proceeds human thought, and what is its nature? It is either matter, motion, or repose;—matter, or its two accidents, as nothing else exists in the universe. That thought is not material is plain enough. That it is not the repose of matter is also manifest, since thought implies movement. But is it a material motion, or an effect of material motion?

If thought is an effect of motion, or motion itself, it must resemble it. Now, the effect of motion is to break, to disunite, to displace, while thought neither separates bodies nor puts them in motion. Motion itself is a change of situation, while thought never leaves its seat, and moves without losing its repose.

Motion has its measure and its degrees; thought, on the contrary, is indivisible. There is no fourth or half of a thought; it is one.

The motion of matter has its bounds, which prevent it from extending beyond a certain space. Thought travels in infinite space. How could we conceive an atom starting from the human brain with the rapidity of lightning, and at the same instant reaching heaven and earth, yet without leaving the brain? If it did leave it, it would exist out of man, and would no longer be man himself.

Motion has only a present action, while thought embraces the past and the future. Hope, for instance, is a future movement; but how could a material movement in the future exist at the present time?

Thought, therefore, is not material motion. Is it an effect of this motion?

Thought cannot be an effect of motion, because an effect cannot be more noble than its cause, or a consequence more powerful than its principle. Now, thought is more noble and powerful than motion, since it has an apprehension of the latter, which does not apprehend it, and in the least moment of time traverses a space which motion could not travel over in a thousand ages.

If you say that thought is neither motion nor the effect of an interior motion of the brain, but an agitation produced by an external cause, you only go over the same ground; for this agitation is motion, and, if motion is thought, it must be a thinking principle; so that the foot that walks, or the stone that falls, is a thinking substance. But, combine such material things as you will, you cannot make them think.

If thought is something different from matter and motion, what is it, or whence does it proceed? As it did not exist in me before I was created, it must have been produced. If produced, it must have originated out of the material order, since matter contains not the principle of thought. The source of thought, out of the material order, must be more excellent than that thought itself; and, as thought is indivisible, and therefore immortal, the cause that produced it must be indivisible and immortal But, as that cause existed prior to my thought, it was either produced or existed from eternity. If produced, where is its principle? and if you indicate this principle, what is the source of his principle itself?

NOTE M, (p. 176.)

But if all we have said concerning the *senses* be not sufficient to convince the unbeliever, let us proceed a little farther, and show that the very limits within which the power of our external senses is confined tend to make us more happy than if the power extended much farther, as it has been enabled to do, in these later ages, by the aid of certain instruments.

Let us suppose that our eyes possessed the faculty of distinguishing objects which they cannot discern without a microscope; they would, it is true, show us a world of new creatures; a drop of water in which pepper has been steeped, or a drop of vinegar, would resemble a lake or a river full of fish; the froth of putrid and offensive liquids would look like a field covered with flowers and plants; cheese would appear to be composed of large hairy spiders; and so on in regard to an infinite multitude of other objects; but it is likewise easy to conceive the disgust which the sight of these insects would produce against many things which otherwise are very good and very useful in themselves. I have seen people burst into a laugh at the sight of the little animals which appear, by means of a microscope, in a piece of cheese, and quickly draw back their hands when any of these insects happened to fall, lest it should drop upon them; but others made more serious reflections on the wisdom of God, who has thought fit to hide these things from the ignorant and the timid, and to manifest them to others by means of microscopes, that those who endeavor to penetrate into these miracles might not want the necessary assistance.

"Would unbelieving philosophers ever wish that their eyes possessed the properties of the best microscopes, supposing them to be acquainted with their nature and principle? And would they think themselves fortunate in beholding objects so diminutive magnified to such a degree, while at the same time their whole field of vision would not occupy a larger space than a grain of sand? They would not be able to see any object distinctly, unless at a very small distance from the eye, for instance, one or two inches. As to more distant objects, as men, beasts, trees, and plants, to say nothing of the sun, the moon, the stars,—those orbs in which the majesty of the Supreme Being shines resplendent,—these would be entirely invisible to them, or they would only see them in a very confused manner, if the naked eye could penetrate as far as when provided with good microscopes. All who have made experiments on the subject admit that by means of these instruments we may discern bodies composed of a thousand small parts; whence it follows that to see every thing distinctly, even to its primitive particles, vision ought to extend infinitely beyond what it does with the aid of the best microscopes.

"On the other hand, let us suppose that our eyes were large telescopes, like those which we employ to observe so many new stars in the heavens, and to make so many discoveries in the sun, the moon, and other celestial bodies; still they would be liable to this inconvenience, that they would be of scarcely any use for seeing the objects which surround us, and they would also deprive us of the view of the other objects upon the earth, because we should see the vapors and exhalations which are continually rising, and which, like thick clouds, would hide from us all other visible things. This is but too well known to those who are in the habit of using those instruments.

"In like manner, if the smell was as nice and delicate in men as it seems to be in certain varieties of the canine species, not a creature could come near us; and it would be impossible for us to pass where others had gone, without perceiving a strong impression from the effluvia emitted by them. A thousand things would, in spite of us, call off our attention; and when we would wish to turn our minds to more important subjects, we would be involuntarily chained down to the vilest trifles.

"If our tongue were of so delicate a texture as to make us perceive as much taste in things which have scarcely any as in those whose savor is as strong as that of ragouts and spices, everybody would admit that this alone would be sufficient to render our victuals highly disagreeable after we had eaten of them only two or three times.

"Could the ear distinguish all the sounds with the same accuracy as at present, when a person speaks softly at the widest end of a speaking-trumpet? or would we be able to pay attention to a great number of things? Certainly we would not, any more than when we are in the midst of a confused noise, the clamor of numberless voices, the din of drums and cannon. Those who have witnessed the inconveniences suffered by the sick, whose hearing is too acute, will have no difficulty to comprehend this truth.

"If our feeling were as delicate in all the parts of the body as in those which possess the greatest sensibility and in the membranes of the eyes, must we not admit that we would be miserable indeed, and would be liable to acute pain even when touched by the lightest feather?

"Finally, can we reflect on all this without acknowledging the goodness of Him who is its Author, who has not only given us such noble organs as our external senses, without which our body would not be superior to a mere log; but who has also, in his adorable wisdom, confined our senses within certain limits without which they would only have been a trouble to us, and have prevented us from examining a thousand objects of the highest importance?" —Nieuwentyt, on the *Exist. of God*, book i. chap. 3.

NOTE N, (p. 230.)

"Genuine philosophers would not have asserted, like the author of the *Système de la Nature*, that Needham, the Jesuit, created eels, and that God was incapable of creating man. To them Needham would not have appeared a philosopher; and the author of the *Système* would have been deemed but a shallow prater by the Emperor Marcus Aurelius."—*Quest. Encyclop.*, tome vi art. *Philosoph.*

In another place, opposing the atheists, and speaking of the savages, who were looked upon as having no idea of a God, Voltaire says, "It may be urged that they live in society and have no notion of a God, consequently, people may live in society without religion. In that case, I reply that wolves live in the same manner, and that an assemblage of barbarian cannibals, as you suppose them to be, is not a society; and I would likewise ask if, when you have lent your money to some one of your society, you would wish that neither your debtor, your lawyer, nor your judge, should believe in God?"—*Ibid.*, tome ii. art. *Atheism.*

The whole of this article on atheism is worthy of perusal. In politics, Voltaire shows the same aversion to all those empty theories which have convulsed the world "I do not like the government of the mob," he repeats a hundred times. (See his *Letters to the King of Prussia.*) His pleasantries on democratic republics, his indignation against popular excesses, in short, the whole tenor of his works, proves that he sincerely hated all quacks in philosophy.

This is the most appropriate place for submitting to the reader a number of passages extracted from Voltaire's works, which prove that I have not gone too far in asserting that he entertained a secret antipathy to sophists. At any rate, if we are not convinced, we cannot do otherwise than conclude that, as Voltaire was eternally supporting both sides of the question, and incessantly changing his sentiments, his opinion in morals, philosophy, and religion must be considered as of very little weight.

In 1766.

"I have nothing in common with the modern philosophers, except their horror of intolerant fanaticism."—*Corresp*, x. 337.

In 1741.

"The superiority which dry and abstract physics have usurped over the *belles-lettres* begins to provoke me Fifty years ago we had much greater men in physics and geometry than at present, and their names were scarcely ever mentioned. Things are wonderfully altered. I was a friend to physics while that science did not aspire to the dominion over poetry; now, that it has crushed all the arts, I shall consider it only as a tyrant to be avoided. I will come to Paris to deposit my protest in your hands. I shall attend in future to no other studies than those which render society more agreeable and smooth the decline of life. It is impossible to converse on physics for a quarter of an hour and understand one another; but we may talk all day long of poetry, music, history, literature, &c."—*Corresp*, iii. 170.

"The mathematics are a very fine science; but take away about a score of theorems useful in mechanics and astronomy, and all the rest is merely a fatiguing curiosity."—*Corresp*, ix 484.

To M. Damilaville.

"By the people I mean the populace who depend on their labor alone for a subsistence I doubt whether this class of citizens ever have the time or the capacity for acquiring knowledge; they would starve before they would become philosophers To me it appears absolutely necessary that some should be poor and ignorant. Had you a farm to cultivate, like me, and ploughs to keep at work, you would not fail to be of my opinion."—*Corresp.* x. 396.

59*

"I have read something in the *Antiquité dévoilée*, or rather *très-voilée*. The author begins with the deluge and ends always with chaos. I prefer one of your stories to all that balderdash."—*Corresp.*, x. 409.

In 1766.

"I would be very sorry to be the author of that work, (*le Christianisme dévoilé*,) not only as an academician, but likewise as a philosopher, and particularly as a citizen. It is diametrically opposed to my principles. This book leads to atheism, which I abhor. I have always considered atheism as the grossest aberration of reason, because it is quite as ridiculous to say that the arrangement of the universe is no demonstration of a Supreme Artisan as it would be impertinent to assert that a watch is no proof of the existence of a watchmaker.

"I find not less fault with that book as a citizen; the author seems too hostile to the existing powers. Were all men of his way of thinking, we would have nothing but universal anarchy.

"I make a practice of writing upon the margin of my books what I think of them. When you condescend to visit Ferney, you will see the margins of the *Christianisme dévoilé* covered with remarks, which prove that the author is mistaken in regard to the most important facts."—*Corresp.*, xi. 143.

In 1762. *To M. Damilaville.*

"Brethren should always show respect for morals and the throne. Morality is too deeply wounded in the work of Helvetius, and the throne is too little respected in the book which is dedicated to him." (*Le Despotisme Oriental.*)

In another place, speaking of the same work, he observes, "You would imagine that the author wishes us to be governed neither by God nor man."—*Corresp.*, viii. 148.

In 1768. *To M. de Villevieille.*

"My dear marquis, there is nothing good in atheism. This system is very bad, both in physics and in morals. A good man may very well inveigh against superstition and fanaticism, and may detest persecution. He renders a service to mankind if he diffuses the principles of toleration; but what good can he do by disseminating those of atheism? Will men be more virtuous for not acknowledging a God who enjoins the practice of virtue? Assuredly not. I would have princes and their ministers to acknowledge a God,—nay, more,—a God who punishes and who pardons. Without this restraint, I should consider them ferocious animals, who, to-be-sure, would not eat me just after a plentiful meal, but certainly would devour me were I to fall into their clutches when they are hungry, and who, after they had picked my bones, would not have the least idea that they had done any thing wrong."—*Corresp.*, xii. 349.

In 1749.

"I am of a very different way of thinking from Saunderson, who denies the existence of a God because he was born blind. I may perhaps be wrong; but, were I in his place, I would acknowledge an intelligent Being who has furnished me with so many substitutes for sight; and, in perceiving by the mind's eye infinite relations in all things, I would divine the existence of a workman infinitely skilful. It is very impertinent to inquire who and what he is, and why he has made all created beings, but to me it appears extremely bold to deny his existence."—*Corresp.*, iv. 14.

In 1753.

"To me it seems absurd to make the existence of God dependent on $a + b \div z$.

"What would become of mankind were we obliged to study dynamics and astronomy in order to obtain a knowledge of the Supreme Being? He who has created us all should be manifest to all, and the most common proofs are the best, for the very reason that they are the most common. We want but eyes, and no algebra, to see the daylight."—*Corresp.*, iv. 463.

"A thousand principles escape our researches, because all the secrets of the Creator were not framed for us. It has been imagined that Nature always acts by the shortest way,—that she employs the least possible force and the greatest economy; but what would the partisans of this opinion reply to those who would demonstrate that the human arm exerts a force of about fifty pounds to raise the weight of a single one;—that the heart employs an immense power to express a drop of blood,—that a carp spawns thousands of eggs to produce one or two fishes;—that an oak yields an innumerable quantity of acorns, which very often produce not a single oak? I still think, as I long ago told you, that there is more profusion than economy in nature." —*Corresp.*, iv. 463.

NOTE O, (p. 232.)

As the philosophy of the present day extols polytheism precisely because it has made this separation, and censures Christianity for having united the moral with the religious force, I did not conceive that this proposition could be attacked. Nevertheless, a man of great intelligence and taste, and to whom the utmost deference is due, seems to have doubted the correctness of the assertion. He has objected to me the personification of moral beings, as that of wisdom in Minerva, &c.

I may be wrong, but to me personifications seem not to prove that morals were combined with religion in polytheism. Most assuredly, in adoring all the vices deified, people adored also the virtues. But did the priest teach morality in the temples and among the poor? Did his ministry consist in consoling the afflicted with the hope of another life, or inviting the poor to virtue, the rich to charity? If any moral was attached to the worship of the goddess of *Justice*, of *Wisdom*, was not this moral absolutely destroyed, particularly for the people, by the worship of the most infamous divinities? All that can be said is that there were some sentences engraven on the front and on the walls of the temples, and that, in general, the priest and the legislator inculcated to the people the fear of the gods. But this is not sufficient to prove that the profession of morality was essentially connected with polytheism, when every thing, on the contrary, demonstrates that it was totally distinct.

The moral precepts which occur in Homer are almost always independent of the celestial action; they consist merely in a reflection made by the poet on the event which he is relating or the catastrophe which he describes. If he personifies remorse, the divine anger, &c.,—if he portrays the guilty in Tartarus and the just in the Elysian Fields,—these are certainly beautiful fictions, but they constitute not a moral code attached to polytheism, as the gospel is attached to the Christian religion. Take from it the gospel, and Christianity will be no more. Take from the ancients the allegory of Minerva, of Themis, of Nemesis, and polytheism will still continue to exist. It is, moreover, certain that a worship which admits of but one God must be intimately connected with morality, because it is united with truth; whereas a religion which acknowledges a plurality of gods necessarily deviates from morality, by approximating to error.

As to those who make it a crime in Christianity to have added the force of morals to that of religion, they will find my answer in the last chapter of this work, where I show that *the modern nations, for want of the ancient slavery, ought to have a powerful curb in their religion.*

(NOTE P, p. 287.)

Here are some fragments which we recollect, and which might be taken for the production of some Greek poet, so strongly are they tinctured with the style of antiquity:—

"Accours, jeune Chromis, je t'aime, et je suis belle,
Blanche comme Diane et légère comme elle,
Comme elle grande et fière; et les bergers, le soir,
Lorsque, les yeux baissées, je passe sans les voir,
Doutent si je ne suis qu'une simple mortelle,
Et me suivant des yeux disent: Comme elle est belle!
Nééra ne vas point te confier aux flots,
De peur d'être déesse; et que les matelots
N'invoquent, au milieu de la tourmente amère,
La blanche Galathée et la blanche Néère."

Another idyl, called *Le Malade*, and too long for quotation, is replete with the most impressive beauties. The following fragment is of a different kind. From the melancholy which pervades it, you would imagine that Chenier, when he composed it, had a presentiment of his fate:—

"Souvent las d'être esclave et de boire la lie
De ce calice amer que l'on nomme la vie;
Las du mépris des sots qui suit la pauvreté,
Je regarde la tombe, asile souhaité;
Je souris à la mort volontaire et prochaine
Je me prie, en pleurant, d'oser *rompre ma chaine.*
. . . .
Et puis mon cœur s'écoute et s'ouvre à la faiblesse,
Mes parens, mes amis, l'avenir, ma jeunesse,
Mes écrits imparfaits, car à ses propres yeux
L'homme sait se cacher d'un voile spécieux.
À quelque noir destin qu'elle soit asservie,
D'une étreinte invincible il embrasse la vie:
Il va chercher bien loin, plutôt que de mourir,
Quelque prétexte ami pour vivre et pour souffrir.
Il a souffert, il souffre: aveugle d'espérance,
Il se traine au tombeau de souffrance en souffrance:
Et la mort, de nos maux le remède si doux,
Lui semble un nouveau mal, le plus cruel de tous."

The works of this young man, his various accomplishments, his noble proposal to M de Malesherbes, his misfortunes and death, all serve to attach the most lively interest to his memory It is remarkable that about the end of the last century France lost three promising geniuses in their dawn,—Malfilâtre, Gilbert, and André Chenier. The two former perished in misery, and the latter on the scaffold.

NOTE Q, (p 299)

We subjoin an explanation of the word *descriptive*, that it may not be taken in a different sense from that which we assign to it Several persons have been shocked at our assertion, for want of thoroughly comprehending what we meant to say. The poets of antiquity certainly have descriptive passages. This it would be absurd to deny, especially if we give the utmost latitude to the expression, and understand by it descriptions of garments, repasts, armies, ceremonies, &c &c.; but this kind of *description* is totally different from ours. Upon the whole, the ancients have painted *manners*, we portray *things;* Virgil describes the *rustic habitation*, Theocritus the *shepherds*, and Thomson the *woods* and *solitudes*. If the Greeks and Latins said a few words concerning a landscape, it was only for the purpose of introducing characters in it and rapidly forming a ground for the picture; but they never distinctly represented, like us, rivers, mountains, and forests. It may, perhaps. be objected that the ancients were right in considering descriptive poetry as an *accessary*, and not as the *principal* subject of the piece. and I am myself of this opinion. A strange abuse has been made in our time of the descriptive kind; but it is not the less true that it is an additional instrument in our hands, and that it has extended the sphere of poetic images, without depriving us of the delineation of manners and passions such as it existed for the ancients.

(NOTE R, p. 305.)

INDIAN POETRY.

Extract from the drama of *Sacontala* —"Hear, O ye trees of this hallowed forest, hear and lament the departure of Sacontala for the palace of her wedded lord,—of Sacontala, who drank not, though thirsty, before you were watered; who cropped not, through affection for you, one of your fresh leaves, though she would have been pleased with such an ornament for her locks; whose chief delight was in the season when your branches are spangled with flowers."

Chorus of Wood-Nymphs.—"May her way be attended with prosperity! May propitious breezes sprinkle for her delight the odoriferous dust of rich blossoms! May pools of clear water, green with the leaves of the lotos, refresh her as she walks! and may shady branches be her defence from the scorching sunbeams!"—Robertson's *India*, 8vo., p. 237.

ERSE POETRY.

Song of the Bards.—First Bard.

"Night is dull and dark: the clouds rest on the hills: no star with green trembling beam, no moon, looks from the sky. I hear the blast in the wood, but I hear it distant far. The stream of the valley murmurs, but its murmur is sullen and sad. From the tree at the grave of the dead the long-howling owl is heard. I see a dim form on the plain! It is a ghost! It fades, it flies! Some funeral shall pass this way. The meteor marks the path.

"The distant dog is howling from the hut of the hill; the stag lies on the mountain moss; the hind is at his side. She hears the wind in her branchy horns. She starts, but lies again.

"The roe is in the cleft of the rock. The heath-cock's head is beneath his wing. No beast, no bird, is abroad, but the owl and the howling fox,—she on a leafless tree, he in a cloud on the hill.

"Dark, panting, trembling, sad, the traveller has lost his way. Through shrubs, through thorns, he goes along the gurgling rill; he fears the rocks and the fen. He fears the ghosts of night. The old tree groans to the blast. The falling branch resounds. The wind drives the withered burs, clung together, along the grass. It is the light tread of a ghost! he trembles amid the night.

"Dark, dusky, howling, is night; cloudy, windy, and full of ghosts. The dead are abroad, my friends; receive me from the night."—*Ossian.*

NOTE S, (p. 322.)

Imitation by Voltaire.

"Toi sur qui mon tyran prodigue ses bienfaits,
Soleil! astre de feu, jour heureux que je haïs,
Jour qui fais mon supplice, et dont mes yeux s'étonnent;
Toi, qui sembles le dieu des cieux qui t'environnent,
Devant qui tout éclat disparoit et s'enfuit,
Qui fais pâlir le front des astres de la nuit;
Image du Très-Haut qui régla ta carrière,
Hélas! j'eusse autrefois eclipsé ta lumière!
Sur la voûte des cieux élevé plus que toi,
Le trône où tu t'assieds s'abaissoit devant moi;
Je suis tombé; l'orgueil m'a plongé dans l'abîme.
Hélas! je fus ingrat, c'est là mon plus grand crime.
J'osai me révolter contre mon Créateur:
C'est peu de me créer, il fut mon bienfaiteur;
Il m'aimoit: j'ai forcé sa justice éternelle
D'appesantir son bras sur ma tête rebelle;
Je l'ai rendu barbare en sa sévérité;
Il punit à jamais, et je l'ai mérité.
Mais si le repentir pouvoit obtenir grace--
Non, rien ne fléchira ma haine et mon audace;
Non, je déteste un maître, et sans doute il vaut mieux
Régner dans les enfers qu'obéir dans les cieux."

NOTE T, (p. 338.)

Dante has some fine passages in his *Purgatory*, but his imagination, so inventive in the description of hell, has no longer the same fecundity in depicting sufferings mingled with consolations. The dawn, however, which he be holds on leaving Tartarus, that light which he sees passing rapidly over the sea, have some freshness and beauty :—

"Sweet hue of eastern sapphire, that was spread
O'er the serene aspect of the pure air,
High up as the first circle, to mine eyes
Unwonted joy renewed, soon as I 'scaped
Forth from the atmosphere of deadly gloom,
That had mine eyes and bosom filled with grief.
The radiant planet, that to love invites,
Made all the Orient laugh, and veiled beneath
The Pisces' light, that in his escort came.
To the right hand I turned, and fixed my mind
On the other pole attentive, where I saw
Four stars ne'er seen before save by the ken
Of our first parents. Heaven of their rays
Seemed joyous. O thou northern site! bereft
Indeed, and widowed, since of these deprived.
  As from this view I had desisted, straight
Turning a little toward the other pole,
There from whence now the wain had disappeared,
I saw an old man standing by my side
Alone, so worthy of reverence in his look
That ne'er from son to father more was owed.
Low down his beard, and mixed with hoary white,
Descended, like his locks, which, parting, fell
Upon his breast in double fold. The beams
Of those four luminaries on his face
So brightly shone, and with such radiance clear
Decked it, that I beheld him as the sun.

. . . .

Then on the solitary shore arrived,
That never sailing on its waters saw
Man that could after measure back his course.

. . . .

  Now had the sun to that horizon reach'd,
That covers, with the most exalted point
Of its meridian circle, Salem's walls;
And night, that opposite to him her orb
Rounds, from the stream of Ganges issued forth,
Holding the scales that from her hands are dropped
When she reigns highest; so that where I was,
Aurora's white and vermeil-tinctured cheek
To orange turned as she in age increased.
  Meanwhile we lingered by the water's brink,
Like men who, musing on their road, in thought
Journey, while motionless the body rests.
When lo! as near upon the hour of dawn,
Through the thick vapors Mars, with fiery beam,
Glares down in west, over the ocean floor;

So seemed, what once again I hope to view,
A light, so swiftly coming through the sea,
No wingéd course might equal its career,
From which, when for a space I had withdrawn
Mine eyes, to make inquiry of my guide,
Again I looked, and saw it grown in size
And brightness."

Dante's Purgatory, Cary's Trans., cantos 1, 2.

NOTE U, (p. 352.)

The reader will be pleased to find here the exquisite passage of Bossuet on St. Paul:—

"That you may understand, then, who that preacher is, destined by Providence to confound human wisdom, hear the description which I have borrowed from himself in the First Epistle to the Corinthians.

"Three things usually contribute to render a speaker pleasing and impressive:—the person of the orator, the beauty of the subjects which he treats, and the ingenious manner in which he illustrates them. The reason of this is evident; for the esteem in which the speaker is held procures a favorable hearing; excellent things nourish the mind, and the talent of explaining them in a pleasing manner obtains for them an easy access to the heart; but, from the way in which the preacher of whom I am speaking represents himself, it is easy to judge that he possesses none of these advantages.

"In the first place, Christians, if you look at his person, he acknowledges himself that his figure is not commanding—*his bodily presence is weak;*[1] and if you consider his condition, he is contemptible, and necessitated to earn a subsistence by the exercise of a mechanical art. Hence he says to the Corinthians,[2] 'I was with you in weakness and in fear, and in much trembling,' from which it is easy to conclude how contemptible his person must have been. What a preacher, Christians, to convert so many nations!

"But, perhaps, the doctrine was so plausible and attractive as to give weight to this man who was so exceedingly despised. This is not the case. 'I judged not myself,' says he,[3] 'to know any thing among you but Jesus Christ and him crucified;' that is to say, he knows nothing but what shocks, but what scandalizes, but what appears to be folly and extravagance. How then can he hope his auditors to be persuaded? But, great Paul! if the doctrine which thou proclaimest is so strange and difficult, employ at least polished terms; cover with the flowers of rhetoric the hideous face of thy gospel, and soften its austerity by the charms of thy eloquence. 'God forbid,' replies this great man, 'that I should mingle human wisdom with the wisdom of the Son of God; 'tis the will of my Master that my words be not less harsh than my doctrine appears incredible:—*not in the persuasive words of human wisdom.*'[4] St. Paul rejects all the artifices of rhetoric. His speech, instead of flowing with that agreeable smoothness, with that attempered equality which we admire in orators, appears uneven and unconnected to those who have not studied its import; and the refined of the earth, who pretend to have an acute ear, are

[1] 2 Cor. x. 10.
[2] 1 Cor. ii. 3.
[3] 1 Cor. ii 2.
[4] 1 Cor. ii. 4

offended by the harshness of his irregular style. But, my brethren, let us not be ashamed of this. The discourse of the apostle is simple, but his thoughts are quite divine. If he is ignorant of rhetoric, if he despises philosophy, Jesus Christ stands him instead of all things; and his name, which is continually upon his lips, his mysteries, which he treats so divinely, will render his simplicity omnipotent. He will go:—this man so ignorant in the art of speaking well, with his harsh address, with his diction which betrays the foreigner, will go to polished Greece, the mother of philosophers and orators; and, in spite of the opposition of the world, he will there establish more churches than Plato gained disciples by that eloquence which was accounted divine. He will preach Jesus in Athens, and the most learned of its senators will quit the Areopagus for the school of this barbarian. He will push his conquests still farther: he will humble at the feet of the Saviour the majesty of the Roman fasces in the person of a pro-consul, and he will cause the judges before whom he is summoned to tremble in their tribunals. Rome herself shall hear his voice; and that imperial city shall one day esteem herself more highly honored by an epistle addressed to her citizens by Paul than by all the celebrated orations delivered by her own Cicero.

' And how, Christians, how happens all this? It is because Paul possessed means of persuasion which Greece never taught and which Rome never acquired. A supernatural power which delights in exalting what the proud despise accompanied the august simplicity of his words. Hence it is that we admire in his glowing epistles a certain virtue more than human, which convinces against all common rules, or, rather, which convinces less than it captivates the understanding; which does not charm the ear, but strikes home to the heart As a mighty river in its course through the plain still retains the impetuosity acquired in the mountains among which it rises, so that celestial virtue contained in the writings of St. Paul retains, in conjunction with simplicity of style, all the vigor which it derived from heaven, whence it descended.

"It was by this divine virtue that the simplicity of the apostle vanquished all things. It overthrew idols, established the cross of Jesus, and persuaded multitudes of men to die in defence of its glory; finally, in his admirable epistles, it has explained such grand secrets, that the most sublime geniuses, after having been long engaged in the loftiest speculations of which philosophy is capable, have descended from the vain height to which they imagined themselves raised, that they might learn to lisp in the school of Jesus Christ, under the instruction of St. Paul."

NOTE V, (p. 378

Pliny's catalogue is as follows:—

Painters of the three great Schools, Ionian, Sicyonian, and Attic.

Polynotus of Thasos painted a warrior with his buckler. He also painted the temple of Delphi, and the portico of Athens, in competition with Milo.

Apollodorus of Athens. A priest in the act of adoration. Ajax set on fire by lightning.

Zeuxis Alcmene, Pan; Penelope, Jupiter seated on a throne and surrounded by the other gods standing, the infant Hercules strangling two sepents in the presence of Amphytrion and Alcmene, who turns pale with fright, the Sacinian Juno; the grapes; Helen; Marsias.

Parrhasius. The curtain; the people of Athens personified; Theseus; Meleager; Hercules and Perseus; the high-priest of Cybele; a Cretan nurse with her child; Philoctetes; the god Bacchus; two children, accompanied by Virtue; a pontiff, attended by a boy holding a box of incense and crowned with flowers; a racer, armed, running in the lists; another armed runner laying aside his arms after the race; Æneas; Achilles; Agamemnon; Ulysses contending with Ajax for the armor of Achilles.

Timanthes. Sacrifice of Iphigenia; a sleeping Polyphemus, whose thumb little satyrs are measuring with a thyrsus.

Pamphylus. A battle before the city of Phlius; a victory of the Athenians; Ulysses in his ship.

Echion. Bacchus; tragedy and comedy personified; Semiramis; an old woman carrying a lamp before a new-married female.

Apelles. Campaspe naked, represented as Venus Anadiomene; King Antigonus; Alexander brandishing a thunderbolt; Megabysus, priest of Diana; Clytus preparing for battle and receiving his helmet from his attendant; a Habron, or effeminate man; Menander, King of Caria; Anceus; Gorgosthenes, the tragedian; the Dioscuri; Alexander and Victory; Bellona chained to the car of Alexander; a hero naked; a horse; Neoptolemus on horseback fighting the Persians; Archelous with his wife and daughter; Antigonus armed; Diana dancing with a number of young females; the three pieces known by the appellations of lightning, thunder, and thunderbolt.

Aristides of Thebes. A city taken by assault; representing a mother wounded and dying; battle with the Persians; quadrigæ racing; a supplicant; hunters with game; portrait of Leontio, the painter; Biblis; Bacchus and Ariadne; a tragedian, accompanied by a boy; an old man instructing a child to play on the lyre; a sick man.

Protogenes. The Lialyssus; a satyr dying for love; Cydippus; Tlepolemus; a contemplative Philiscus; a wrestler; King Antigonus; Aristotle's mother; Alexander; Pan.

Asclepiodorus. The twelve great gods.

Nicomachus. The rape of Proserpine; Victory on a car soaring in the air; Ulysses; Apollo; Diana; Cybele seated on a lion; female Bacchanals and Satyrs; Scylla.

Philoxenes of Eretria. The battle between Alexander and Darius; three Sileni.

Grotesque and Fresco Paintings.

Under this head Pliny mentions Pyreicus, who painted in great perfection the shops of barbers and cobblers, asses, &c. This is precisely the Flemish school. He then says that Augustus caused landscapes and sea-views to be painted on the walls of the palaces and temples. The most celebrated pieces of this kind represented peasants at the entrance of a village, bargaining with some women to carry them on their shoulders across a marsh. These are the only landscapes ascribed to antiquity, and even these were only painted in fresco. We shall recur to this subject in another note.

Encaustic Painting.

Pausanias of Sicyone. The Hemeresios, or child; Glycera seated and crowned with flowers, a hecatomb.

Euphranor. An equestrian combat; the twelve gods; Theseus; Ulysses feigning madness, a warrior sheathing his sword.

Cydias. The Argonauts.

Antidotas. A champion armed with a buckler; the wrestler and flute-player.

Nicias the Athenian. A Forest; Nemæa personified; Bacchus; Hyacinthus, Diana, the tomb of Megabysus; the necromancy of Homer; Calypso; Io and Andromeda; Alexander; Calypso sitting.

Athenion. Phylarcus; Syngenico, Achilles disguised as a female, a groom with a horse.

Lamonachus of Byzantium. Ajax; Medea; Iphigenia in Taurus; a Lecythion, or tumbler; a noble family, a Gorgon

Aristolaus. Epaminondas; Pericles; Medea; Virtue; Theseus; the people of Athens personified; a hecatomb.

Socrates. The daughters of Æsculapius, Hygeia, Egle, Panacea, Laso; Œnos, or the indolent rope-maker.

Antiphilus. A child blowing the fire; females spinning; King Ptolemy hunting; the satyr in ambush.

Aristophon. Anceus wounded by the boar of Calydon; an allegorical picture of Priam and Ulysses.

Artemon. Danaë and the pirates; Queen Stratonice; Hercules and Dejanire; Hercules on Mount Œta; Laomedon.

Pliny proceeds to name about forty inferior painters, but mentions very few performances by them (*Plin.*, lib. xxxv)

Against this catalogue we have only to set that which may be obtained at the *Museum.* We shall merely observe that most of these antique paintings are portraits or historical pieces; and that, if we would be quite impartial, we should oppose only mythological subjects to Christian subjects.

NOTE W, (p 380)

The catalogue of ancient paintings left us by Pliny contains not one single landscape, if we except the paintings in fresco. Some of the pieces of the great masters may possibly have had a tree, a rock, a corner of a valley, or of a forest, or a stream, in the background, but this is not sufficient to constitute a landscape properly so called, such as the pencil of a Lorrain and a Berghem has produced.

Among the antiquities of Herculaneum, nothing has been discovered to induce an opinion that the ancient school of art had painters of landscape. We merely find in the *Telephus* a woman sitting, crowned with garlands, and leaning upon a basket filled with ears of corn, fruit, and flowers. Hercules stands before her with his back turned toward the spectator, and a doe is suckling an infant at his feet. A faun is playing on his pipe in the distance, and a winged female forms the background to the figure of Hercules This composition is beautiful, but it is not the genuine landscape, the naked landscape, the representation of an accident of nature alone.

Though Vitruvius asserts that Anaxagoras and Democritus said something concerning perspective in treating of the Greek stage, still there is reason to doubt whether the ancients were acquainted with this department of the art, without which there can be no such thing as landscape-painting The design of the subjects found at Herculaneum is dry, and greatly resembles sculpture and bas-relief. The shadows, composed of a mixture of red and black, are equally thick from the top to the bottom of the figure, and consequently do not make objects appear at a certain distance. Even fruits, flowers, and vases, are deficient in perspective, and the upper contour of these last does not correspond with the same horizon as their base: in a word, all those subjects borrowed from *fable* that are found in the ruins of Herculaneum prove that mythology blinded painters to the genuine landscape, as it did poets to genuine nature.

The ceilings of the baths of Titus, which Raphael studied, contained only representations of the human form. Some of the iconoclast emperors permitted flowers and birds to be painted on the walls of the churches in Constantinople The Egyptians, who united to the Greek and Latin mythology many other divinities of their own, had not the art of representing nature. Some of their paintings still to be seen on the walls of their temples do not rise higher, in point of composition, than the Chinese daubs.

Father Sicard, speaking of a small temple situated among the grottos of Thebais, says, "The ceiling, the walls, the interior, the exterior, all is painted, and with colors so vivid, yet so soft, that one would not credit it without having seen it. . . . On the right you see a man standing, with a rod in each hand, leaning upon a crocodile, and a maiden near him with a rod in her hand. On the left of the gate you also see a man standing and leaning upon a crocodile, holding a sword in the right hand and a burning torch in the left. In the interior of the temple are represented flowers of every color, instruments of various construction, and other grotesque and emblematical figures. On one side you meet with a hunting-piece, where all the birds that frequent the Nile are caught by one fall of a trap, and on another is a fishing-scene, where the fishes of that river are taken in a single net," &c.—*Lettr. Edif.*, tome v. p. 144.

To find landscape among the ancients, you must examine their mosaics, though even these are historical subjects. The famous mosaic in the palace of the Barberini princes at Palestrina represents in its upper part a mountainous country with hunters and animals. In the lower part is the river Nile, winding around a number of small islands. Egyptian men are seen pursuing the crocodile, Egyptian women lying beneath their cradles, a woman presenting a palm to a warrior, &c. All this is vastly different from the landscape of Claude le Lorrain.

NOTE X, (p. 390.)

The abbé Barthelemi found the prelate Baiardi engaged in a reply to the monks of Calabria, who had consulted him on the subject of the Copernican system. "He returned a very long and learned answer to their questions, explained the laws of gravitation, cautioned them against the delusions of the senses, and concluded with exhorting them not to disturb the ashes of Copernicus."—*Voy. en Ital.*

NOTE Y, (p. 412.)

We can scarcely persuade ourselves that some of these notes were by Voltaire, so unworthy are they of his pen. But it is absolutely impossible to overcome the disgust excited every moment by the dishonesty of the editors and the praises which they lavish on each other. Who would believe, unless he had seen it in print, that, in a note upon a note, the commentator is styled the

Secretary of Marcus Aurelius, and Pascal the *Secretary of Port Royal?* In a hundred other passages Pascal's ideas are distorted, that he may be considered as an atheist. When he says, for example, that *human reason alone cannot arrive at a perfect demonstration of the existence of God*, how they triumph, how they exclaim, What a curious spectacle to see M. de Voltaire espouse the cause of God against Pascal! This is in truth making game of common sense, and presuming rather too much on the good-nature of the reader.

Is it not evident that Pascal reasons as a Christian who would press the argument of the *necessity of revelation?* But there is something worse even than that in this commented edition. It is not clear to us that the *New Thoughts* which have been added to it are not at least perverted, to say no more. What authorizes us to think so is the liberty that has been taken to retrench several of the old ones, and frequently to divide the others, (under the pretext that the former arrangement was arbitrary,) so that they no longer have the same meaning as before Every person knows how easy it is to alter a passage by breaking the concatenation of ideas, and by separating two members of a sentence so as to produce two complete sentences. There is an address, an artifice, a secret design in this edition which would have rendered it dangerous, had not the notes fortunately destroyed all the effect that was expected from it.

NOTE Z, (p. 414.)

Besides the plans of reform and improvement which have come to the knowledge of the public, a multitude of projects proposed in the council of Louis XIV are said to have been found since the revolution among the old papers in the office of the ministry; among the rest, one for the *extension of the frontiers of France to the Rhine*, and another *for the seizure of Egypt*. As to the edifices and works for the embellishment of Paris, they appear to have been all discussed. It was in contemplation to finish the Louvre, to convey water to the city, to lay open the quays, &c. &c. Reasons of economy, or some other motive probably, prevented the execution of these plans. That age had done so much that it was necessary for it to leave something to be done by posterity.

NOTE AA, (p. 427.)

I shall advance but one single fact in reply to all the objections which may be alleged against the old establishment of the censorship. Was it not in France that all works against religion were composed, sold, published,—nay, even frequently printed? and were not the great themselves the first to recommend and to protect them? In this case the censorship was a mere bugbear, since it was never able to prevent a book from appearing, or an author from writing his sentiments with freedom on any subject whatever; and, after all, the greatest hardship that could befall a writer was to be obliged to spend a few months in the Bastile, whence he was soon released with the honors of a persecution, which afterward constituted his *only* title to celebrity.

NOTE BB, (p. 443.)

Extracts from St. Chrysostom.

Amid the inconsistent and disgraceful acts which blurred the reign of the weak Arcadius, the following is not the least . . . . Eutropius, by birth obscure, by nature cruel, vindictive, and ambitious, was raised to the highest dignities of the state, and was styled Consul and Father of the Emperor. In the zenith of his greatness, he exercised his power with the most excessive tyranny, and enacted the severest laws against the Christian church. At length the day of retribution came. He was stripped of all his grandeur, his titles and his wealth, and was reduced to the order of the meanest citizen. Thus conditioned, he fled for refuge to the altar of the cathedral. Chrysostom received him with the charity of a Christian and the tenderness of a parent. On the succeeding day, when the news of his disgrace and flight had been published through the city, the people flocked in crowds to the cathedral, that they might exult in the distress of their once dreaded tyrant and drag him forth to punishment. The time was critical. There was no leisure for premeditation. . . . . The orator ascended the pulpit, and in a rich stream of extemporaneous eloquence, which, as Suidas observes, no other man in any age possessed, he addressed his impassioned auditors to this effect:—

"In every season of our lives, but most especially in the present, we may exclaim, 'Vanity of vanities! all is vanity!' Where now are the costly insignia of the consulship, and where the blaze of torches? Where now is the enthusiasm of applause, and the crowded hall, and the sumptuous banquet, and the midnight revelry? Where is the tumult that echoed through the city, the acclamations which resounded in the hippodromes, and the flattery of the spectators? All these are fled. The first tempestuous gale hath scattered the rich foliage on the ground, presenting to our eyes the naked tree, reft of its blooming honors and bowed inglorious to the earth. So wild hath been the storm, so infuriate the blast, that it threatened to tear up the very roots from their proud foundation and to rend the nerves and vitals of the tree. Where now are the fictitious friends?—where is the swarm of parasites, the streaming goblets of exhaustless wine, the arts which administered to luxury, the worshippers of the imperial purple, whose words and actions were the slaves of interest? . . . . They were the vision of a night and the illusion of a dream, but when the day returned they were blotted from existence; they were flowers of the spring, but when the spring departed they were all withered; they were a shadow, and it passed away: they were a smoke, and it was dissolved; they were bubbles of water, and they were broken; they were a spider's web, and it was torn. Wherefore, let us proclaim this spiritual saying, incessantly repeating, 'Vanity of vanities! all is vanity!' This is a saying which should be inscribed on our garments, in the Forum, in the houses, in the highways, on the doors, and on the thresholds; but far more should it be engraven on each man's conscience and be made the theme of ceaseless meditation. Since fraud, and dissimulation, and hypocrisy, are sanctioned in the commerce of the world, it behooves each man, on each passing day, at supper and at dinner and in the public meetings, to repeat unto his neighbor, and to hear his neighbor repeating unto him, 'Vanity of vanities! all things are vanity!'

"Did I not continually say to you that wealth is a fugitive slave, but my words were not endured? Did I not perpetually remind you that it is a servant void of gratitude, but you were not willing to be convinced? Lo! experience hath proved to thee that it is not only a fugitive slave, not only an ungrateful servant, but likewise a destroyer of man. It is this which hath undone thee, which hath abased thee in the dust.

'Did I not frequently observe that the wound inflicted by a friend is more worthy of regard than the kisses of an enemy? If thou hadst endured the wounds my hands inflicted, perchance their kisses had not engendered this death to thee. For my wounds are the ministers of health, but their kisses are the harbingers of disease. . . . . Where now are thy slaves and cup-bearers? Where are they who walked insolently through the Forum, obtruding upon all their encomiums on thee? They have taken the alarm; they have renounced thy friendship; they have made thy downfall the foundation of their security.

"Far different our practice In the full climax of thy enormities we braved thy fury, and now that thou art fallen, we cover thee with our mantle and tender thee our service. The Church, unrelentingly besieged, hath spread wide her arms and pressed thee to her bosom, while the theatres, those idols of thy soul, which so oft have drawn down thy vengeance upon us, have betrayed thee, have abandoned thee. And yet how often did I exclaim, 'Impotent is thy rage against the Church; thou seekest to overturn her from her lofty eminence, and thy incautious steps will be hurried down the precipice;' but all was disregarded! The Hippodromes, having consumed thy riches, sharpen their swords against thee, while the Church—poor suffering victim of thy wrath!—traverses the mountains, valleys, woods, panting to rescue thee from the snare.

"I speak not these things to trample on a prostrate foe, but more firmly to establish the upright. I am not to lacerate a wound yet bleeding, but to insure sweet health to those who are unwounded I wish not to bury in an abyss of waters him who is half-drowned already, but to caution those whose bark glides smoothly on the ocean, lest they should be wrecked at last. And how shall they be preserved? Let them meditate on the vicissitudes of mortals. This very man, had he but feared a change, had not experienced a change. But, since neither foreign nor domestic examples could reclaim him, ye at least, who are enshrined in wealth, from his calamity should derive instruction. Nothing is more imbecile or more empty than the affairs of men; therefore, whatever terms I might employ to denote their vileness, my illustration would be insufficient. To call them a blade of grass, a smoke, a dream, a flower, would be to stamp a dignity upon them; for they are less than nothing!

"That they are not only visionary and unsubstantial, but likewise pregnant with disaster, is manifest from hence Was ever man more elevated, more august, than he? Did he not surpass the universe in wealth? Did he not ascend the meridian of dignities? Did not all men tremble and bend before him? Lo! he is become more necessitous than the slave, more miserable than the captive, more indigent than the beggar wasted with excess of hunger, each day doth he behold swords waving, gulfs yawning, the lictors, and the passage to the grave. Were this moment to be his last, he would be utterly unconscious; he regards not the sun's fair beam, but, standing in meridian day, as though he were enveloped in tenfold darkness, his sight and feelings are extinct. But wherefore do I attempt to delineate those sufferings, which he himself, in glowing colors, depicts unto us? Even yesterday, when soldiers from the imperial palace came to drag him to his fate, with what a speed, with what an agitation, did he rush unto the altar? Pale was his countenance, as though he were an inmate of the tomb, his teeth chattered, his whole frame trembled, his speech was broken, his tongue was motionless; ye would have thought his very heart had been congealed to stone.

"Believe me, I relate not this to insult and triumph in his fall, but that I may soften your hearts' rough surface, may infuse one drop of pity, and persuade you to rest satisfied with his present anguish. Since there are persons in this assembly who even reproach my conduct in admitting him to the altar, to smooth the asperity of their hearts I unfold the history of his woes. Wherefore, O my friend, art thou offended? Because, thou wilt reply, that man is sheltered by the Church who waged an incessant war against it. This is the especial reason for which we should glorify our God, because he hath permitted him to stand in so awful a necessity as to experience both the power and the clemency of the Church:—the power of the Church, because his continued persecutions have drawn down this thunderbolt on his head; and her clemency, because, still bleeding from her wounds, she extends her shield as a protection, she covers him with her wings, she places him in an impregnable security, and, forgetting every past circumstance of ill, she makes her bosom his asylum and repose. No illustrious conquest, no high-raised trophy, could reflect so pure a splendor; this is a triumph which might cover the infidel with shame and raise even the blushes of the Jew! It is this which irradiates her face with smiles and lights up her eye with exultation. She hath received, she hath cherished, a fallen enemy; and, when all besides abandoned him to his fate, she alone, like a tender mother, hath covered him with her garment, and withstood at once the indignation of the prince, the fury of the people, and a spirit of inextinguishable hatred! This is the glory, the pride of our religion! What glory is there, you will exclaim, in receiving an iniquitous wretch unto the altar? Ah! speak not thus, since even a harlot took hold of the feet of Christ,—a harlot utterly impure; yet no reproach proceeded from Jesus' lips. He approved, he praised her. The impious did not contaminate the holy, but the pure and spotless Jesus rendered by his touch the impure harlot pure. O man, remember not thine injuries Are we not the servants of a crucified Redeemer, who said, as he was expiring, 'Forgive them, for they know not what they do'? But he interdicted this asylum, you will say, by his decrees and laws. Lo! he now perceives the nature of what he did, and is himself the first to dissolve the laws which he enacted. He is become a spectacle to the world, and, though silent, from hence he admonisheth the nations, Do not such things as I have, lest ye should suffer what I suffer. Illustrated by this event, the altar darts forth an unprecedented splendor, and shines, a warning beacon to the earth. How tremendous, how august, doth it appear, since it holds this lion in chains and crouching at your feet!

"Thus, too, the victorious monarch is illustrious, not because he is seated on a throne, invested with purple and adorned with jewels, but because he treads beneath his feet captive barbarians, who crouch at his footstool and grovel in the dust. . . . .

"That he used not his power to conciliate your love ye yourselves attest in your tumultous concourse.

"This day, a most brilliant spectacle, a most venerable assembly, is presented to my eyes; the church is thronged as on the festival of Easter, and this culprit, with a silence more eloquent than the trumpet's voice, summoneth the city hither. Ye virgins abandoning your chambers, ye matrons quitting your retirements, ye men leaving the Forum empty, have flocked together here, that ye might behold the nature of man convicted, the frailty of human affairs publicly exposed, and yon meretricious countenance, which yesterday was brightened with the tints of youth, now betraying the grim wrinkles of disease and age,—this reverse of fortune, like a dripping sponge, having wiped off the plastered paint and the fictitious charm . . . . Such is the potency of this hapless day. It hath rendered the proudest of nature's tyrants the meanest, the most abject of her children!

"Doth the rich man enter here? Abundant is his gain. For, beholding the common scourge of nations degraded from such an elevation, tamed of his savage nature, and become more timid than the most timid animal, bound without fetters to that pillar, and girt around with fear as with a chain, he calms his effervescent pride, he represses his swelling spirit, and, making a suitable reflection on sublunary concerns, he retires, learning from experience, and feeling with conviction, that all flesh is grass and all the glory of man as the flower of the field: the grass withereth and the flower fadeth. . . . .

"The poor man, entering here and gazing on yon spectacle of wo, accounteth not himself as vile, nor grieveth that he is poor. Nay, he droppeth a tear of gratitude to his poverty, because it hath been to him a citadel which never can be stormed, a harbor where no billows rage, a wall of adamantine strength." —*Discourse on the Disgrace of Eutropius.*

The object of St. Chrysostom in this address was not only to instruct his people, but to move them by the recital of the reverses which he so forcibly depicted. In this he had the consolation to succeed. Notwithstanding their aversion for Eutropius, who was justly regarded as the author of all they had to suffer, both in public and private, the whole auditory was moved to tears. When the orator perceived this, he continued:—

"Have I calmed your minds? Have I banished anger from your midst? Have I checked the impulses of inhumanity? Have I excited your compassion? Yes; those tears that are flowing from your eyes sufficiently attest it. Now that your hearts are affected and an ardent charity has melted their icy hardness, let us go in a body to cast ourselves at the feet of the emperor, or rather let us pray the God of mercy to appease him, that he may grant an entire pardon."

This appeal had its effect, and St. Chrysostom saved the life of Eutropius. But, some days after, the latter had the imprudence to leave the church, when he was arrested and banished to the island of Cyprus; subsequently, put on trial at Chalcedon, he was there condemned to death.

From the 1st book De Sacerdotio.

St. Chrysostom had an intimate friend, named Basil, who had persuaded him to leave his maternal home and to live with him in a state of retirement. "When my afflicted mother first heard of this," says St. Chrysostom, "she took me by the hand, and, leading me into her chamber, she made me sit down with her at the very bed on which she had brought me forth, and, weeping, she spoke to me words which affected me much more than her tears. 'My son,' said she, 'it was not the will of God that I should enjoy for a long time the virtuous company of your father. Having died soon after the sufferings which gave you birth, he left you an orphan, and me a widow, sooner than was conducive to the welfare of either. I have endured all the pains and troubles of widowhood, which certainly cannot be understood by those who have not experienced them. No language can express the perplexity and excitement of a young woman who has just left the paternal house, who is unacquainted with business matters, and who, plunged in affliction, finds herself implicated in new cares, which, on account of her youth and the weakness of her sex, she is but little fitted to assume. She must supply the deficiency of her servants and guard against the effects of their malice; she must be on the defensive against the evil designs of her relatives, suffer continually from the injustice of partisans and from the insolence and cruelty which they display in the collection of taxes.

"'When a father leaves a daughter after him, this child must be a source of great trouble and solicitude to her mother. Nevertheless, this charge is supportable, as it is not accompanied with apprehension or expense. But, if she has a son, she finds it much more difficult to bring him up, and he becomes a perpetual subject of fear and anxiety, without speaking of what it costs to educate him. All these evils, however, have not induced me to marry again. I have not allowed myself to be overcome by these difficulties, and, trusting in the grace of God, I have resolved to bear up against all the trials of my widowhood.

"'But my only consolation in this state has been to have you always before my eyes, and to behold in you the living image and faithful portrait of my deceased husband; a consolation which began from your infancy, when as yet you could not articulate a word, and when parents derive the greatest joy from their children.

"'Moreover, I have never given you any reason to think that, while I bear with fortitude the evils of my present condition, I have, with a view to escape them, diminished the estate of your father,—a misfortune which I know frequently befalls minors. On the contrary, I have preserved all that was left to you, though I have omitted no expense that was required for your education: this I have drawn from my own resources. But I do not say this with a view to remind you of your obligations to me. For all that I have done I ask of you only one favor: do not begin for me a second widowhood; do not reopen a wound that had begun to heal. Wait at least until my death; it is, perhaps, not far off. They who are young may hope to see old age; but at my time of life I can only look for death. When you will have buried me in your father's tomb, and mingled these bones with his ashes, you may then enter upon any journey or travel over any sea that you wish; no one will prevent you. But, while I still breathe, have some regard for my presence, and do not become tired of your mother. Do not draw upon yourself the divine indignation, by causing so much grief to a mother who has not deserved it. If I seek to involve you in worldly pursuits, if I try to force upon you the management of my affairs, which are also yours, oh, then you may, with my consent, disregard the laws of nature, the trials which I suffered in rearing and educating you, the respect which you owe to a mother, and, indeed, every motive of this kind; but, if I do every thing in my power to insure you a tranquil and happy life, let this consideration at least, if nothing else, influence your mind. Whatever may be the number of your friends, none of them will allow you as much freedom as I will. Moreover, no one feels the same ardent interest as I do in your improvement and welfare.'"

St. Chrysostom could not resist this touching appeal; and, notwithstanding the repeated solicitations of his friend Basil, he could not be induced to leave a mother who loved him so tenderly and who was so worthy of being loved. Is there any thing in pagan antiquity more beautiful thas this,—more feeling, more tender, more eloquent, more characterized by that simple and natural eloquence so infinitely superior to all the studied formality of art? Is there any thing in this discourse which could be considered as an effort of thought or an affectation of sentiment or language? Does it not appear, on the contrary, as the language only of the heart, the promptings of nature herself? But what is most admirable here is the wonderful self-possession of that mother overwhelmed with affliction. Although merged in grief,—though in a state which rendered it almost impossible to command her feelings,—not a word of anger or complaint falls from her lips against the author of her distress and her alarms, either through respect for the virtue of Basil or the fear of irritating her son, whom she wished only to move and to overcome.

NOTE CC, (p. 448.)

"To great talents," says M. de la Harpe, "it is given to animate the cold and to conquer the indifferent, and, when combined with *example*, (an advantage which all our preachers have fortunately enjoyed,) it is certain that the ministry of the word nowhere has such power and such dignity as in the pulpit. Everywhere else it is a man who addresses men here it is a being of a superior order; exalted between heaven and earth, it is a mediator placed by God between himself and his creature. Independent of earthly considerations, he proclaims the oracles of eternity. The very place from which he speaks, and that where he is heard, confounds and eclipses all other species of grandeur that it may fill the mind with its own Kings humble themselves like the lowest of their subjects before his tribunal, and repair thither for instruction alone. Every thing around him adds weight to his words. his voice resounds throughout the sacred edifice amid the silence of universal devotion. If he calls God to witness, God is present on the altars, if he declares the nothingness of life, death is at hand to attest it and to remind those who hear him that they are seated upon tombs.

"It cannot be denied that external objects—the decorations of the temples and the pomp of the ceremonies—have a considerable influence on the minds of men, and operate upon them before the preacher, provided he destroys not their effect. Let us figure to ourselves Massillon in the pulpit ready to pronounce the funeral oration of Louis XIV, first casting his eyes around him, fixing them for some time on that awful and imposing pomp which attends kings even into those abodes of death that contain naught but coffins and ashes, then casting them down for a moment with an air of meditation, finally raising them toward heaven, and in a firm and solemn tone pronouncing these words. '*God alone is great, my brethren!*' What an exordium is comprehended in this single sentence accompanied with that action! how sublime it is rendered by the spectacle which surrounds the preacher! how these few words annihilate whatever is not God!"

NOTE DD, (p. 455)

Lichtenstein.—The encyclopedists are a sect of self-styled philosophers, who have arisen in our times and who imagine themselves superior to all antiquity in point of knowledge. With the effrontery of cynics, they have the impudence to put forth every paradox that enters their heads. Affecting an a.quaintance with geometry, they contend that no one can think rightly who has not studied that science, and, consequently, that they alone possess the art of reasoning well. Their discourse, even on the most common occasions, is filled with scientific words. They will tell you, for instance, that certain laws have been wisely framed in the inverse ratio of the squares of the distances; that one nation, about to form an alliance with another, is drawn to it by the power of attraction, and that both will soon be assimilated. If you propose a walk, they will speak of it as the resolution of a curve. If they have a gravel-colic, they cure themselves by the laws of hydrostatics. If a louse bites them, they are disturbed by an infinitely small animal of the first order. If they fall, it is because they lost their centre of gravity. If some journalist is bold enough to attack them, they drown him in a deluge of ink and vituperation. Such treason against philosophy is considered unpardonable.

Eugene.—But what have those fools to do with our name in the world or with the opinion which men form of us?

Lichtenstein. —Much more than you think, because they vilify all the sciences, except their mathematics. According to them, poetry is but a frivolous sort of writing, the fictions of which should be discarded: a poet should flourish his rhymes only in algebraic equations. As to history, it should be studied inversely, beginning with our times and ascending to the antediluvian period. All governments are reformed by those men. France should be a republic, with a geometrician for its lawgiver, and with other geometricians to govern it by subjecting all its affairs to the infinitesimal calculus. Such a republic would enjoy a constant peace and would have no need of an army. . . . . Those gentlemen affect a holy horror of war. . . . . If they abominate armies and generals who acquire distinction, that does not prevent them from carrying ‹n a paper war against each other and using the weapons of Billingsgate. If they had troops at their disposal, they would soon bring them into action. . . . . The terms they employ in mutual abuse are called philosophical licenses. Thought should be ennunciated; any truth is worth proclaiming; and, as they alone are the depositaries of truth, they think themselves privileged to express all the extravagant ideas that enter their brains, in the expectation of being applauded.

Marlborough.—I suppose there is no longer any lunatic asylum in Europe. If there is, those gentlemen ought certainly to be placed there, in order to legislate for fools like themselves.

Eugene.—My advice would be to confide to them the government of some province that requires punishment. They would find, after having turned every thing topsy-turvy, that they are a set of ignoramuses; that it is easy to criticize, but difficult to execute; and, especially, that people expose themselves to talk nonsense without end when they undertake to speak of what they do not understand.

Lichtenstein.—Men who are self-conceited never acknowledge themselves to be in the wrong. According to them a wise man never makes a mistake he alone is enlightened, and from him must proceed that knowledge which will dissipate the thick gloom in which the blind multitude are enveloped;

but the Lord knows how he enlightens them. At one time he discourses on the origin of prejudices at another, on the mind, then on the system of nature. There is no end to this stuff. They have a set of scamps for their followers, who pretend to imitate them, and set themselves up as sub-preceptors of mankind. and, as it is easier to utter abuse than to allege good reasons, they assail the military on all occasions with their indecent invectives.

Eugene.—One coxcomb will always find another coxcomb to admire him; but do soldiers quietly submit to injuries?

Lichtenstein.—They let the curs bark, and continue their way.

Marlborough.—But why this violent opposition to the noblest of all professions,—a profession which, by extending over others its protection, allows them to go on in peace?

Lichtenstein.—As they are altogether ignorant of the military art, they imagine that they bring it into contempt by decrying it. As I have remarked, they denounce the sciences generally, and hold up geometry alone as worthy of esteem, in order to extinguish all glory that belongs to others and concentrate it upon themselves.

Marlborough.—But we have not neglected philosophy, or geometry, or belles-lettres, and we have been satisfied with having some merit in our line.

Eugene.—Nay, more; at Vienna I was the patron of learned men, and gave them distinction, even when they were little thought of by others.

Lichtenstein.—No doubt; because you were really great men, while these self-dubbed philosophers are but a set of scamps whose vanity would lead them to cut a certain figure. This, however, does not prevent reiterated abuse from injuring the name of men who are truly great. People believe that bold sophistry is the main thing for a philosopher, and that he who advances a paradox carries off the palm How often have I heard persons condemning, in a most ridiculous strain, your very best actions, and qualifying you as men who had usurped a reputation in an age of ignorance, which was incapable of appreciating merit!

Marlborough.—Our age an age of ignorance! That's too much!

Lichtenstein.—The present age is the age of philosophers.

Œuvres de Frederic II.

NOTE EE, (p. 456.)

Portrait of J. J. Rousseau and Voltaire, by La Harpe.

. . . .

Deux surtout, dont le nom, le talent, l'éloquence,
Faisant aimer l'erreur, ont fondé sa puissance,
Préparèrent de loin des maux inattendus,
Dont ils auroient frémis, s'ils les avoient prévus.
Oui, je le crois, témoins de leur affreux ouvrage,
Ils auroient des François desavoué la rage.
Vaine et tardive excuse aux fautes de l'orgueil!
Qui prend le gouvernail doit connoître l'écueil.
La foiblesse réclame un pardon légitime,
Mais de tout grand pouvoir l'abus est un grand crime

Ils ont parlé d'en haut aux peuples ignorans;
Leur voix montait au ciel pour y porter la guerre:
Leur parole hardie a parcouru la terre.
Tous deux ont entrepris d'ôter au genre humain
Le joug sacré qu'un Dieu n'imposa pas en vain;
Et des coups que ce Dieu frappe pour les confondre,
Au monde, leur disciple, ils auront à répondre.
Leur noms toujours chargés de reproches nouveaux,
Commenceront toujours le récit de nos maux.
Ils ont frayé la route à ce peuple rebelle,
De leur triste succès la honte est immortelle.
   L'un qui dès sa jeunesse errant et rebuté,
Nourrit dans les affronts son orgueil révolté,
Sur l'horizon des arts sinistre météore,
Marqua par le scandale une tardive aurore,
Et, pour premier essai d'un talent imposteur,
Calomnia les arts, ses seuls titres d'honneur,
D'un moderne cynique affecta l'arrogance,
Du paradoxe altier orna l'extravagance,
Ennoblit le sophisme, et cria *vérité;*
Mais par quel art honteux s'est-il accrédité?
Courtisan de l'envie, il la sert, la caresse,
Va dans les derniers rangs en flatter la bassesse;
Jusques aux fondemens de la société
Il a porté la faux de son *égalité:*
Il sema, fit germer, chez un peuple volage,
Cet esprit novateur, le monstre de notre age,
Qui couvrira l'Europe et de sang et de deuil.
Rousseau fut parmi nous l'apôtre de l'orgueil;
Il vanta son enfance à Genève nourrie,
Et pour venger un livre, il troubla sa patrie,
Tandis qu'en ses écrits, par un autre travers,
Sur sa ville chétive il régloit l'univers.
J'admire ses talens, j'en déteste l'usage;
Sa parole est un feu, mais un feu qui ravage,
Dont les sombres lueurs brillent sur des débris.
Tout, jusqu'aux vérités, trompe dans ses écrits,
Et du faux et du vrai ce mélange adultère
Est d'un sophiste adroit le premier caractère.
Tour à tour apostat de l'une et l'autre loi,
Admirant l'évangile et réprouvant la foi,
Chrétien, déiste, armé contre Genève et Rome,
Il épuise à lui seul l'inconstance de l'homme,
Demande une statue, implore une prison;
Et l'amour-propre enfin égarant sa raison
Frappe ses derniers ans du plus triste délire;
Il fuit le monde entier qui contre lui conspire,
Il se confesse au monde, et toujours plein de soi,
Dit hautement à Dieu: *nul est meilleur que moi.*

L'autre encore plus fameux, plus éclatant génie,
Fut pour nous soixante ans le dieu de l'harmonie.
Ceint de tous les lauriers, fait pour tous les succès,
Voltaire a de son nom fait un titre aux Francais.
Il nous a vendu cher ce brillant héritage,
Quand libre en son exil, rassuré par son âge,
De son esprit fougueux l'essor independant
Prit sur l'esprit du siécle un si haut ascendant.
Quand son ambition toujours plus indocile
Pretendit detrôner le Dieu de l'évangile,
Voltaire dans Ferney, son bruyant arsenal,
Secouait sur l'Europe un magique fanal,
Que pour embraser tout, trente ans on a vu luire,
Par lui l'impieté puissante pour détruire,
Ebranla d'un effort aveugle et furieux,
Les trônes de la terre appuyées dans les cieux.
Ce flexible Protée etait né pour seduire :
Fort de tous les talens, et de plaire et de nuire,
Il sut multiplier son fertile poison,
Armé du ridicule, eludant la raison,
Prodiguant le mensonge, et le sel, et l'injure,
De cent masques divers il revêt l'imposture,
Impose à l'ignorant, insulte à l'homme instruit;
Il sut jusqu'au vulgaire abaisser son esprit,
Faire du vice un jeu, du scandale une école,
Grace à lui, le blasphème et piquant et frivole
Circulait embelli des traits de la gaité;
Au bon sens il ôta sa vieille autorité,
Repoussa l'examen, fit rougir du scrupule,
Et mit au premier rang le titre d'incredule.

NOTE FF, (p. 457.)

In 1752, M. de Montesquieu, writing to the abbé de Guasco, says, "Huart wants to bring out a new edition of the *Persian Letters;* but there are some *juvenilia* which I should like first to retouch."

In reference to this we find the following note by the editor:—"He told some of his friends that, were he now publishing these letters for the first time, he would omit some in which he had been hurried away by the ardor of youth; that, being obliged by his father to stick close to his desk all day, he was so weary of it at night that to amuse himself he sat down to compose a Persian Letter, and this flowed from his pen without study."—*Œuvres de Montesquieu,* tome 7, p. 233.

NOTE GG, (p. 458.)

Such was the opinion of Voltaire, whom I am fond of quoting to unbelievers, respecting the age of Louis XIV. and ours. This is sufficiently proved by the subjoined passages from his letters, to which we must always look for his real sentiments.

"Racine is truly great, and so much the greater as he never seems t aim at being so. The perfect man is indeed to be seen in the author of Athalia."—*Corresp. gen.*, tome viii. p. 465.

"I once imagined that Racine would be my consolation, but he throws me into despair. 'Tis the height of insolence to write a tragedy after that great man. I know of none but bad plays since his time, and very few good ones before it."—*Ibid.*, viii. 467.

"I have no reason to complain of the kindness with which you speak of *Brutus* and *the Orphan;* I will even acknowledge that there are some beauties in those two performances; but I repeat, Racine forever! The more you read him, the more you discover an unrivalled genius, seconded by all the resources of art. In a word, if any thing on earth approaches perfection, it is Racine."—*Ibid.*, viii. 501.

"The fashion of the present day is to speak contemptuously of Colbert and Louis XIV.; but this fashion will pass away, and those two characters will be transmitted to posterity with Boileau."—*Ibid.*, xv. 108.

"I could easily show that the tolerable productions of the present time are all borrowed from the good works of the age of Louis XIV. Our badly-written books are not so bad as those written in the time of Boileau, Racine, and Molière, because in the insipid publications of our days there are always some passages evidently extracted from authors who lived in the age of good taste. We are like thieves, who change and ridiculously adorn the clothes which they have stolen to prevent their being known. With this knavery is joined a rage for dissertation and paradox, the whole being a compound of impertinence which is inexpressibly disgusting."—*Ibid.*, xiii. 219.

"Accustom yourself to a dearth of talents of every kind; to understanding grown common and to genius become rare; to a deluge of books on war, which will result in our being beaten; on finances, which will leave us without a penny; on population, which will not supply us with recruits and laborers; and on all the arts without our succeeding in any."—*Ibid.*, vi. 391.

Finally, in his excellent letter to Lord Hervey, Voltaire has urged what has been worse said, and a thousand times repeated, respecting the age of Louis XIV. This letter, written 1740, is as follows:—

. . . . "But, above all, my lord, be not so angry with me for styling the last century the age of Louis XIV. Full well I know that Louis XIV. had not the honor of being the master or the benefactor of a Boyle, a Newton, a Halley, an Addison, a Dryden; but, in the age called after Leo X., had that pontiff the merit of every thing? Were there not other princes who contributed to refine and enlighten mankind? A preference has, nevertheless, been given to the name of Leo X., because he encouraged the arts more than any other individual. In this respect, what monarch has rendered greater service to mankind than Louis XIV.? What monarch was more munificent, showed more taste, distinguished himself by more laudable institutions? I admit that he did not accomplish all that he might have done, because he was a man; but he accomplished more than any other, because he was a great man. My strongest reason for estimating him so highly is that, with his well-known faults, he enjoys a greater reputation than any of his contemporaries; that, although he expelled from France a million of men, who were all interested in decrying him, all Europe esteems and ranks him among the greatest and the best of monarchs.

"Name then, my lord, a sovereign who has invited to his country a greater number of eminent foreigners, and who has been a greater patron of merit in his subjects. Sixty scholars of Europe, astonished at being known to him, received gratuities from him at once. 'Though the king is not your sovereign,' said Colbert, in writing to them, 'he is desirous of being your benefactor; he has commanded me to transmit to you the enclosed bill of exchange as a token of his esteem.' A Bohemian, a Dane, received these letters, dated from Versailles. Guillemini erected a house at Florence with the gifts of Louis XIV.; he inscribed the king's name on the front of it; and you will not admit that he is at the head of the age of which I am speaking!

"What he did in his own kingdom ought forever to serve as an example. He committed the education of his son and grandson to the most eloquent and the most learned men in Europe. He provided for three sons of Pierre Corneille, two in the army and one in the church; he fostered the rising genius of Racine by a considerable present for a young man who was both unknown and poor; and, when that genius had acquired maturity, those talents which often shut the door to fortune secured one for him He possessed more than fortune; he enjoyed the favor and sometimes the familiarity of a master whose mere look was a bounty. In 1688 and 1689 he attended the king in his excursions to Marly,—an honor so earnestly solicited by the courtiers; he slept in the king's chamber during his indispositions, and read to him those master-pieces of eloquence and poetry which embellished that illustrious reign.

"'Tis this favor, bestowed with discernment, that produces emulation and excites great geniuses. It is much to found institutions, it is something to support them; but to stop short with these establishments is frequently to provide the same retreats for the useless member of society and for the great man, to receive into the same hive the bee and the drone.

"Louis XIV. extended his care to every thing; he protected the academies and rewarded such persons as distinguished themselves; he did not lavish his favors on one species of merit to the exclusion of the rest, like many princes, who encourage not what is excellent, but what pleases them; natural philosophy and the study of antiquity shared his attention. Nor did it relax during the wars which he waged with Europe; for, while building three hundred citadels, while he had on foot four hundred thousand soldiers, he caused an observatory to be erected, and a meridian to be traced from one end of the kingdom to the other,—an operation unparalleled in the world He had translations of the best Greek and Latin authors printed in his palace; he sent mathematicians and natural philosophers to the recesses of Africa and America, to extend the sphere of knowledge. Consider, my lord, that, but for the voyage and experiments of the persons whom he sent to Cayenne in 1672, and the measures of M. Picard, Newton would never have made his discovery respecting attraction. Consider, I beg of you, a Cassini and a Huygens, both renouncing their native country which they honor, and repairing to France to enjoy the esteem and bounty of Louis XIV. And do you imagine that the English themselves owe him no obligations? Tell me, then, in what court Charles II. acquired such politeness and such a refined taste. Were not the best writers of the age of Louis XIV. your models? Was it not from them that Addison, who of all your countrymen possessed the most correct taste, frequently borrowed the subjects of his excellent observations? Bishop Burnet acknowledges that this taste, acquired in France by the courtiers of Charles II., had introduced among you a reformation even in the pulpit itself, notwithstanding the difference of our religions; such is universally the influence of right reason. Tell me if the well-written books of that time were not employed in the education of all the princes of the empire? In what courts of Germany were not French theatres established? What prince did not strive to imitate Louis XIV.? What nation did not then follow the fashions of France?

"You adduce, my lord, the example of Peter the Great, who introduced the arts into his empire and who was the founder of a new nation; you tell me, nevertheless, that his age will never be called in Europe the age of the Czar Peter, and hence you conclude that I ought not to style the past age the age of Louis XIV. Between these two there seems to me to be a very wide difference. The Czar Peter acquired information among foreign nations, and carried home the arts to his own country; but Louis XIV. instructed other nations; every thing, even to his very faults, was useful to them. The Protestants who quitted his dominions carried with them an industry which had constituted the wealth of France. Do you reckon as nothing so many manufactures of silk and glass? The latter were brought to perfection among you by our refugees, and we have lost what you have gained.

"Finally, the French language, my lord, has become almost the universal language. To whom are we indebted for this? Was it so widely diffused in the time of Henry IV.? Certainly not; the Italian and Spanish were alone studied. Our eminent writers produced this change; but who patronized, employed, encouraged these writers? Colbert, you will perhaps tell me. So it was; and I admit that the minister is entitled to a share of his master's glory. But what would a Colbert have effected under any other prince?—under your William, who was fond of nothing, under Charles II. of Spain, or under many other sovereigns?

"Would you believe, my lord, that Louis XIV. reformed the taste of the court in more than one way? He chose Lulli for his musician, and took the privilege from Lambert, because Lambert was a man of mean abilities and Lulli possessed superior talents. He could discriminate between wit and genius; he gave to Quinault the subjects of his operas; he directed the paintings of Le Brun; he supported Boileau, Racine, and Molière against their enemies; he encouraged the useful as well as the fine arts; he lent money to Van Robais for his manufactures; he advanced millions to the East India Company which he had formed; he conferred pensions on learned men and brave officers. Not only were great things done during his reign, but it was himself who did them. Do not disdain, then, my lord, the efforts which I make to raise to his glory a monument which I consecrate still more to the benefit of the human race.

"I esteem Louis XIV., not merely because he was the benefactor of the French, but because he was the benefactor of mankind; it is as a man, and not as a subject, that I write; my design was to portray the last age, and not simply a prince. I am tired of histories which relate nothing but the adventures of a king, as if he existed alone, or as if nothing existed but in relation to him. In a word, it is rather the history of a great age than that of a great king which I am writing.

"Pelisson would have written more eloquently than I; but he was a courtier and a pensioner. I am neither; to me, therefore, it belongs to speak the truth."—*Corresp. gen.*, iii. 53.

NOTE HH, (p. 460.)

The abbé Fleury, in his work on the *Manners of the Christians*, expresses the opinion that the ancient monasteries were built on the plan of the Roman houses, as described in Vitruvius and Palladio. "The church," says he, "which we come to first, that seculars may have free access to it, seems to occupy the place of the first hall, termed by the Romans *atrium.* From this they passed into a court surrounded by covered galleries, to which was given the name of *peristile.* This corresponds exactly with the cloisters which you enter after passing through the church, and from which you proceed to other parts of the edifice, as the chapter-house, which is the exhædron of the ancients, the refectory, which answers to the *triclinium*, and the garden, which is behind all the rest, as it was in the houses of antiquity."

NOTE II, (p. 476.)

The following is the beautiful hymn alluded to by the author, as translated from the Portuguese by Dr. Leyden:—

Hymn to the B. V. Mary, Star of the Sea.

Star of the wide and pathless sea,
Who lov'st on mariners to shine,
These votive garments wet, to thee
We hang within thy holy shrine.
When o'er us flashed the surging brine,
Amid the warring waters tost,
We called no other name but thine,
And hoped when other hope was lost.
Ave Maris Stella.

Star of the vast and howling main,
When dark and lone is all the sky,
And mountain-waves o'er ocean's plain
Erect their stormy heads on high;
When virgins for their true loves sigh,
They raise their weeping eyes to thee:
The star of ocean heeds their cry,
And saves the foundering bark at sea.
Ave Maris Stella.

Star of the dark and stormy sea,
When wrecking tempests round us rave,
The gentle virgin-form we see
Bright rising o'er the hoary wave;
The howling storms, that seem to crave
Their victims, sink in music sweet;
The surging sea recedes, to pave
The path beneath thy glistening feet.
Ave Maris Stella.

Star of the desert waters wild,
Who, pitying, hear'st the seaman's cry,
The God of mercy, as a child,
On that chaste bosom loves to lie;
While soft the chorus of the sky
Their hymns of tender mercy sing,
And angel-voices name on high
The mother of the heavenly King.
Ave Maris Stella.

Star of the deep! at that blest name
The waves sleep silent round the keel,
The tempests wild their fury tame
That made the deep's foundations reel.
The soft celestial accents steal
So soothing through the realms of wo,
That suffering souls[1] a respite feel
From torture in the depths below.
Ave Maris Stella.

Star of the mild and placid seas,
Whom rainbow-rays of mercy crown,
Whose name thy faithful Portuguese,
O'er all that to the depths go down,
With hymns of grateful transport own;
When gathering clouds obscure their light,
And heav'n assumes an awful frown,
The star of ocean glitters bright.
Ave Maris Stella.

Star of the deep! when angel lyres
To hymn thy holy name essay,
In vain a mortal harp aspires
To mingle in the mighty lay!
Mother of God! one living ray
Of hope our grateful bosom fires,
When storms and tempests pass away,
To join the bright immortal choirs.
Ave Maris Stella.

NOTE KK, (p. 485.)

The different parts of the office derive their names from the periods into which the Romans distributed the day. The first part of the day was called *Prima;* the second, *Tertia;* the third, *Sexta;* the fourth, *Nona;* because they commenced with the first, third, sixth, and ninth hours. The first watch was called *Vespera,* or evening.

[1] We have here omitted the expression, *newly-damned,* which seems inadmissible, even as a poetical license. T.

NOTE LL, (p. 493.)

"Formerly I celebrated mass with a levity which gradually introduces itself into the most solemn acts when they are performed too often. Since my conversion, I celebrate with more reverence. I become penetrated with the majesty of the Supreme Being; I am filled with the idea of his presence and of the insufficiency of the human mind, which has so slight a conception of what relates to its divine Author. Recollecting that I offer to him, according to an established form, the vows of the people, I carefully observe all the ceremonies and recite the prayers with attention, omitting nothing that is prescribed. When I draw near to the moment of consecration, I collect my thoughts, and endeavor to perform this act with all the dispositions which the Church and the grandeur of the sacrament require. I strive to silence reason in the presence of Supreme Intelligence, asking myself, 'Who art thou, to measure infinite power?' I pronounce the sacramental words with respect and with all the faith of which I am capable. Whatever the dignity and excellence of this incomprehensible mystery, I feel assured that on the day of judgment I shall not be punished for the sin of having profaned it in my heart."—Rousseau, *Emile*, tome iii.

NOTE MM, (p. 496.)

"Absurd rigorists in religion have no idea of the influence of ceremonies over the people. They have never witnessed our veneration of the cross on Good-Friday, or the enthusiasm of the multitude at the procession of Corpus-Christi,—an enthusiasm by which I myself am sometimes overcome. I have never beheld that long line of priests in their sacerdotal robes,—those youthful acolythes, in their white surplices tied round with a broad blue cincture, scattering flowers before the Blessed Sacrament,—that crowd going before and following after in religious silence,—that immense number of men with their heads bowed to the earth,—I have never heard that grave and affecting chant, entoned by the clergy and followed up by countless men, women, and children,—without being deeply moved, and even forced to shed tears. In all that there is an impressiveness of melancholy which is indescribable. I was acquainted with a Protestant artist who had resided a long time in Rome, and who acknowledged that he had never assisted at the services in St. Peter's, when the Pope officiated surrounded by the cardinals and all the Roman prelates, without becoming a Catholic. . . . . Take away all external symbols, and what remains will soon be reduced to a metaphysical jumble, that will assume as many strange forms and appearances as there are heads."—Diderot, *Essais sur la Peinture.*

NOTE NN, (p. 510.)

The *Feralia* of the ancient Romans differed from our *Commemoration of the Dead* in being celebrated only in memory of those who had died during the year. They began about the 18th of February and lasted eleven days, during which marriages were prohibited, sacrifices were suspended, the statues of the gods were veiled, and the temples closed. Our anniversary services, and those of the 7th, 9th, and 40th days, are borrowed from the Romans, who themselves derived them from the Greeks.[1] These last had their *ἐναγίσματα*, or offerings for souls to the infernal gods; their *νεκυσια*, or funeral; *ταρχηματα*, or burial; *εννατα*, or novena;—also, triacades or triacontades, the thirtieth day. The Latins had their *justa, exequiæ, inferiæ, parentationes, novendulia, denicalia, februa, feralia.* When the dying man was about to expire, his friend or nearest relative applied his lips to his to catch his last gasp, after which his body was placed in the hands of proper persons, to be washed, embalmed, and carried to the tomb, or funeral pile, with the usual ceremonies. The priests headed the convoy, in which were carried portraits of the deceased's ancestors, with crowns and trophies. The whole pageant was preceded by two bands of vocalists, one singing lively airs, the other engaged in a more solemn chant. It was supposed by the ancient philosophers that the soul (which was a mere harmony, according to them) ascended amid these funeral sounds to Olympus, where it would enjoy the heavenly melody of which it was an emanation. (See Macrobius, *De Somnio Scipionis.*) The body was deposited in a sepulchre or funeral urn, with a last farewell:—*Vale, vale, vale: nos te ordine quo natura permiserit sequemur.*

NOTE OO, (p. 519.)

"Above the town of Brig, the valley is transformed into a narrow and impassable precipice, the bottom of which is occupied by the Rhone. The road crosses the northern mountains and leads into a most frightful solitude. The Alps present nothing more dismal. You travel for two hours, without meeting the least sign of a dwelling, along a dangerous path which is overhung with frowning woods, and on the brink of a precipice the depth of which cannot be reached by the eye. This is a celebrated place for murders; and, when I passed it, I saw several heads mounted on pikes,—a worthy decoration of this terrific region! At length you arrive at the village of Lax, situated in the most desert and retired part of this country. The land on which it is built has a rapid descent toward the precipice, from the bottom of which you hear the dull roar of the Rhone. On the other bank is another village, similarly situated. The two churches stand opposite to each other, and from one of the cemeteries I heard the chant of both parishes, which seemed to answer each other. Let those who are acquainted with the grave and melancholy character of the German hymns imagine them sung in a place like this, accompanied by the distant noise of the river and the roaring of the wind amid the firs!" —*Letters on Switzerland,* by William Coxe, vol. ii., note by Raymond.

NOTE PP, (p. 525.)

The royal tombs destroyed in the abbey of St. Dennis by the Vandals of the French revolution, on the 6th, 7th, and 8th of August, 1793, amounted to fifty-one. Thus, the work of nearly twelve centuries was demolished in three days. The coffins containing the remains of the distinguished dead were broken and scattered on every side, while their bones or ashes were thrown together promiscuously in a common ditch. The valuables discovered in these repositories of departed greatness were sacrilegiously pillaged and turned to profane uses. In 1796, the lead with which the whole church was covered

[1] The author here is inaccurate: the Roman liturgy has no service for the 9th and 40th days. T.

was torn off, melted, and converted into bullets. This venerable monument, the vaults of which once enclosed the remains of the royal houses of France, from Dagobert, in 663, to the son of Louis XVI., in 1789, has since been restored to its ancient splendor.

NOTE QQ, (p. 531.)

Robertson has done justice to Voltaire in saying that that universal writer is not so unfaithful an historian as is commonly supposed. We think with him that Voltaire did not always quote incorrectly; but it is certain that he was guilty of many omissions, which we cannot impute to ignorance on his part. Moreover, his citations are presented in such way as to bear a very different sense from that intended by the authors Thus, he has the appearance of being exact while, at the same time, he is remarkably at fault. He had no need of employing this artifice in his excellent histories of Louis XIV. and Charles XII ; but, in his *Histoire Générale*, which, from beginning to end, is but a slander of the Christian religion, he resorts to every species of weapon to effect his purpose. At one time it is a flat denial, at another, a bold assertion. Then, he mutilates and distorts facts. He confidently affirms that there was no Christian hierarchy for nearly one hundred years. He quotes no authority for this strange assertion, but merely says, "It is admitted," &c. According to him, we have no voucher for the succession immediately after St. Peter but the *fraudulent list contained in an apocryphal work entitled Pontificate of Damascus*.[1] while we possess a treatise of St. Irenæus on heresies, which presents a complete catalogue of the popes from the time of the apostles.[2] He counts twelve to the period when he wrote. Irenæus was born about the year 120 of the Christian era, and was a disciple of Papias and St. Polycarp, who themselves had been disciples of St. John the Evangelist. He was not far, therefore, from being an eye-witness of what he relates. He names St. Linus after St Peter, and informs us that it is this Linus who is referred to in the Epistle of St. Paul to Timothy.[3] How is it that Voltaire, or those who aided him in his work, were not awed by this overwhelming authority, if aware of its existence? How could he assert that no one ever heard of Linus, when this first successor of Peter is mentioned by the apostles themselves?

NOTE RR, (p. 535.)

He even goes so far as to deny the persecution under Nero, and asserts that no Roman emperor, until Domitian, molested the Christians. "It was as unjust," says he, "to impute this accident (the burning of Rome) to the Christian body as to the emperor, (Nero.) Neither he, nor the Christians, nor the Jews, had any interest in the destruction of Rome; but it was necessary to do something by way of appeasing the people, who had become excited against the strangers in the city, obnoxious alike to the Romans and the Jews. Hence, a few unfortunates were sacrificed to public revenge.[4] This temporary violence

[1] *Essai sur les Mœurs des Nations*, ch. viii.
[2] Lib. iii. ch. 3.
[3] Lib iii ch 4
[4] What revenge, if they were not guilty?

does not appear to have been a persecution against their faith. It had nothing to do with their religion, which was unknown to the Romans and was confounded with Judaism, which was as much protected by the laws as it was an object of contempt."[1] Here we have one of the strangest paragraphs that ever fell from the pen of an historian.

Did Voltaire never read Suetonius or Tacitus? He denies the existence or authenticity of certain inscriptions discovered in Spain, which give thanks to Nero for having abolished *a new superstition* in the province. One of these inscriptions, however, is to be seen at Oxford:—*Neroni Claud. Cais. Aug. Max. ob Provinc. latronib. et Tlis qui novam generi hom. superstition inculcab. purgat.* Nor can we see why Voltaire should have any doubt of the superstition here spoken of being the Christian religion. Suetonius, alluding to it, uses the very same language:—*Afflicti suppliciis Christiani, genus hominum superstitionis novæ ac maleficæ.*[2] We shall now learn from Tacitus what was that temporary violence so knowingly exercised, not against *Jews*, but against *Christians*.

"To silence rumor, Nero hunted up some guilty persons, and inflicted the most cruel tortures upon unfortunate people who were abhorred for their crimes and commonly called *Christians*. Christ, from whom they derived their name, was condemned to death, under Tiberius, by Pontius Pilate, which had the effect of checking for a moment this detestable superstition. But the torrent soon overflowed again, not only in Judea, where it had originated, but even in Rome, where every filth of the earth vents itself ultimately and increases. Those who acknowledged themselves Christians were the first arrested, and their testimony led to the seizure of an *immense multitude*, who were less convicted of having fired the city of Rome than of hating their fellow-men. Their punishment was accompanied by the popular derision. Some were enveloped in the skins of beasts, to be devoured by dogs; others were crucified, or their bodies, covered with pitch, served as torches by night. Nero gave the use of his own gardens for this exhibition, and at the same time mingled in the games of the circus, appearing in the dress of a coachman or driving a chariot. Though the victims were guilty and merited capital punishment, they excited the compassion of the spectators, who considered them sacrificed not so much to the public good as to the amusement of a savage."[3]

There is a painful contrast between the sentiment of pity to which Tacitus alludes and the spirit of a certain modern writer. The Roman historian speaks evidently of the Christians, and not of the Jews. The words *hating their fellow-men*, in the passage above quoted, may have led Voltaire to assert that the Romans supposed their victims to be Jews, and not Christians; but he did not perceive that, while endeavoring to rob the latter of a just compassion, he bore an honorable testimony to their merit; for it is highly glorious to the Christians, says Bossuet, to have had for their first persecutor the persecutor of the human race.

NOTE SS, (p. 552.)

Mons. de Clo———, having been compelled to fly from the terrors of the revolution with one of his brothers, joined the army of Condé, where he served with honor until the restoration of peace, when he resolved to retire from the

[1] *Essai*, ch. ii [2] Sueton., *in Nerone*. [3] *Annal.*, lib. xv. 44.

world. He went to Spain and entered a Trappist monastery, where he died a short time after his profession. While travelling in Spain, and during his novitiate at the convent, he wrote several letters to his family and friends, which we give below, just as they came from his pen.[1] The reader will find in them a faithful delineation of the religious life which existed among the Trappists, and which is now but an historical tradition.[2] These letters, written in an unaffected style, often display a considerable elevation of sentiment, and are characterized throughout by that simplicity which is the more agreeable as it is peculiar to the French mind and is daily becoming more rare among us. The subject of the letters recalls all our misfortunes. They place before us a young and gallant Frenchman driven from his country by the revolution, and offering himself as a voluntary victim to the Almighty in expiation of the evils and impieties of his country. Thus did St. Jerom, in the depth of solitude, endeavor, by his tears and prayers, to avert the downfall of the Roman empire. This collection of letters forms a complete history, and would no doubt have met with an extensive sale had it been published as an interesting narrative. But the charm of this correspondence is in its religious tone, which confirms what we have endeavored to show in this work:—

To his fellow-emigrants at Barcelona.

"*March* 13, 1799.

"My last journey, dear friends, was very pleasant. I passed through Aranjuez, where the royal family were. I remained five days at Madrid, and the same at Saragossa, where I had the happiness of visiting Our Lady *del Pilar*. I found the travelling in Spain more agreeable than in any other country, . . . but to speak of such things now is no longer to my taste. I have bid adieu to the mountains and plains, and renounced all travelling projects in this world, in order to begin the journey of the world to come. For the last nine months I have been at the Trappist monastery of Sainte-Susan, where, with the grace of God, I will end my days. I have not as much merit as others in suffering bodily pains, because by my epicureanism they had become habitual. Our life here is not an idle one. We rise at half-past one in the morning, and pass the time until five in prayer and spiritual reading. We then go to work, which continues till about half-past four in the afternoon, when we break our fast. This is the rule for the brothers. The fathers also work much, but at the appointed time they leave the field, to chant the office of the Blessed Virgin, the canonical office, and that of the dead. . . Every half-hour the superior notifies us to raise our thoughts to God, which serves very much to lighten our pains. It reminds us that we are working for a Master who will not delay to reward us at the proper time. I have witnessed the death of one of our fathers. Oh! if you knew what consolation is experienced at the moment of death! Our reverend abbot asked the dying priest if he regretted to have suffered a little during life. I confess to my shame that I have sometimes felt a wish to die, like those cowardly soldiers who wish to be released before the time. Saint

[1] As the same sentiments occur in several letters, we present them somewhat abridged. T.

[2] The reader will remember that this work was published when France was just emerging from the desolating effects of the revolution, which had abolished all religious houses. T.

Mary of Egypt did penance for forty years. She was less guilty than I am, and she has now been enjoying the glory of heaven for a thousand years. Pray for me, my dear friends, that we may meet again on the great day. . . . .

To his brothers and sisters in France.

"*Holy Week*, 1799.

"I have been here at St. Susan's since the first Monday of Lent. It is a Trappist monastery, where I expect to end my days. I have already passed through the most austere season of the year. We never rise later than half-past one, and at the first sound of the bell the community assemble in the church. The brothers (of whom I am one, under the name of Brother J. Climaens) leave the chapel at half-past two, for the reading of the Psalms or some other spiritual book. At four, they return to the church, where they remain until five, when they commence their manual labor. They work in a shop until daylight; then, each one taking a large and a small pickaxe, they proceed in order to the out-door employment, which continues sometimes until half-past three o'clock, P. M., when the work is resumed in the shop, preparatory to dinner, which takes place at half-past four. On leaving the table, the community go in procession to the church, reciting the *Miserere*, and in coming from it they chant the *De profundis*, after which they return to the labor of the shop. Here they card, spin, manufacture cloth and other things, each one according to his knowledge. Every thing used in the house is made by the brothers, as far as practicable. Each one has to eat his bread in the sweat of his brow, professing poverty and striving to give no one any trouble,—on the contrary, offering hospitality to all who come to see us. We possess, however, only two teams of mules, about two hundred sheep, and a few goats that feed on the barren mountains around us. It can only be the effect of a particular providence that seventy persons live together on so little, besides the great number of strangers from every direction, who are always treated to white bread and the best lenten diet that we can prepare with oil or butter—which we never use ourselves. When we use wheat bread, the flour must be unbolted. As I am not very skilful in the shop, I pick beans or lentils for the table. Rice is not picked in the same way. All these things are cooked only with water and salt.

"At a quarter to six we go to prayer or spiritual reading for fifteen minutes. After the reading, which is made aloud, the fathers recite *Complin* in the church. While they are going thither, the prior distributes work among the brothers. Towards the end of *Complin*, the bell rings, summoning all to the *Salve Regina*, which lasts for a quarter of an hour. The chant is beautiful, and suffices of itself to make you forget all the labors of the day. This is followed by fifteen minutes' adoration. At a quarter after seven we recite the *Sub tuum præsidium*, after which all the inmates of the establishment repair to the cloister, and there, prostrating themselves in a row, in that lowly posture recite with David the psalm *Miserere* in perfect silence. This last ceremony appears to me sublime; for man never seems more in his place than when humbled in the presence of the Almighty. At length the reverend father abbot rises, and, standing at the door of the church, he gives holy water to the whole community as they pass out on their way to the dormitory. Here they kneel down at the [illegible] until the signal for retiring, which takes place at half-past se[illegible]

"For some time after entering a house like this, a person is annoyed by the many little trials which come continually in the way of old habits For instance: you are never allowed to lean on any thing when seated, nor to sit down when fatigued, merely for the sake of resting yourself. Man is born to labor in this world, and he ought not to look for repose until he has finished his pilgrimage. In this way you lose all ownership of your body. If you happen to wound yourself a little severely, or break an earthen vessel, you have to acknowledge it immediately on your knees, and in silence. For this purpose you merely show the wound you have received or the fragments of the article that was broken. There is also the confession of one's faults. You must accuse yourself aloud, even of unintentional faults. Moreover, you are often reported by one of the brothers for faults of various kinds that you may have committed. It would be too long to tell you of other things.

"The greatest austerity is practised during the time of Lent. At other seasons we never dine later than two o'clock. It was in Lent that I entered this establishment, like those racers who begin by exercising with leaden shoes. It seems to me now that we lead the life of Sybarites, and we can truly say that we do very little in comparison to the labor and self-denial of the saints. When I think of what is undertaken by men who travel to the South Seas, cross the Isthmus of Panama, penetrating through the thickets that have been forming since the origin of time, suffering the burning heats of the equator or the rigors of the frigid zone, and all this only in search of gold,—when I consider what vain efforts they make to obtain such treacherous objects, and on the other hand that they who labor for God are never disappointed,—we cannot but exclaim, Alas! how little do we do for heaven!

"We are all convinced of this truth; and there are brothers among us who would be willing to embrace every kind of penance; but no austerity can be practised here without an express permission, which is rarely granted, because, being poor, we must husband our strength in order to work. If sometimes I happen to doze, when leaning against a wall, some charitable brother soon rouses me, and methinks I hear him say, 'You will rest when you get to the paternal home,' *in domo æternitatis.* When at work, either in the field or in the shop, the eldest brother now and then gives a signal by clapping his hands, when each one suspends his occupation and for five or six minutes raises his thoughts to heaven amid a profound silence; this suffices to moderate the cold of winter and the heats of summer. You must witness it in order to form an idea of the contentment and joy which reign in the community. The best evidence of the happiness that such a life confers is the reunion of the Trappists after their expulsion from France, and the number of convents of this order that have been founded in different countries In this house there are about seventy members, and applicants for admission are rejected every day. I had some difficulty in being permitted to enter: but fortunately I succeeded, trusting in the protection of the Blessed Virgin, to whom I addressed myself before leaving Cordova. I was not discouraged by the first refusal, knowing very well that the reverend father abbot is not the sovereign master, accordingly, in a few days, he came to my room, and, embracing me, said, 'In future, consider me as your brother; I would have reason to reproach myself if I dismissed one who flies from the world in order to labor for his salvation in this house.'

"This, indeed, by the grace of God, is my only motive in coming hither. I had formed the resolution three months before quitting France. But where or how was I to accomplish my design? I knew not. It is but a short distance from Barcelona to this place; but the shortest way is not always that of Divine Providence. It seemed to be the will of God that I should go first to Cordova, passing through one of the most beautiful regions on earth,—the kingdoms of Valentia, Murcia, and Grenada. I never beheld a more charming country than Andalusia. The more I travelled the more I felt increasing within me the desire of visiting other lands. But, having met in the vicinity of Tarragona a Swiss officer whom I had known in Valais, he took my bundle upon his horse and we travelled together. Our conversation happening to turn upon *Val-Sainte* and upon the trials of the poor monks who had been obliged to seek a refuge in Russia, he told me that they had formed a colony in Aragon. I at once resolved to go thither, and set out upon that long journey, travelling alone day and night, and across mountains which, near Tortosa, became very dense. In this part of the country the traveller often proceeds over fifteen miles without meeting a human being, while here and there he sees a number of crosses, indicating the melancholy end of some one who has passed that way.

"The country through which I journeyed, whether cheerful or gloomy, inspired me with pleasant thoughts, or threw me into that kind of sadness which, by the variety of sentiments it suggests, becomes agreeable. I don't think that I ever made a journey with more confidence or with more pleasure. I met with none but good, respectable, and charitable people on my way. No place is more cheerful than a Spanish inn, from the number of persons assembled there. On arriving, I hung up my sack on a nail, without the slightest concern, and, having agreed upon the fare, a poor traveller like me was in no danger of being cheated. I must observe, also, that I never found a people more disinterested. The servants persisted in declining the little remuneration which I offered them, and oftentimes a coachman would take charge of my wallet for several days, without accepting any compensation. In short, I have a high regard for this nation, which knows how to respect itself, which does not go abroad to engage in foreign service, and which preserves a true originality of character. A great deal is said about the loose morality of this country, but I do not think that it equals that of France. What noble people you find here! Were it possible to destroy religion in Spain, it would not produce fewer martyrs than our own country. I doubt, however, whether this will be attempted. Libertinism must first pass from the mind to the heart; and the Spaniards are yet very far from that degree of perversion. The more elevated as well as the humbler class of society have a practical respect for religion; and, though very high-spirited, they claim no superiority in the church: there you will see the duchess seated next to her servant. The church is generally the handsomest building in the place, and is kept very clean; the pavement is covered with mats, at least in Andalusia. Thousands of lamps burn day and night in the temple of God. You will sometimes see as many as ten or eleven lamps burning in a small chapel of the Blessed Virgin. Though an immense quantity of bee-hives are found here among the mountains, the people procure wax from France, Africa, and America.

"I have written an account of my travels to some of my friends, and requested them to send it to you If you see it, it will amuse you One day, in a desert country, I came to a magnificent gate, the only remains of a vast city constructed by the ancient Romans. I stopped to examine that gate, which has no doubt been there for two thousand years; and it occurred to my mind that that city was once inhabited by people who, when in the flower of their age, imagined that death was far from them, or never gave it a thought; that there were different parties among them, some fiercely at war with others, and now their ashes have been lying for ages in a promiscuous mass. I also saw Murviedro, the site of the ancient Saguntum, and, reflecting upon the vanity of time, I turned my thoughts wholly upon eternity. What will it matter to me, in twenty or thirty years hence, that I have been despoiled of my fortune during an antichristian persecution? St. Paul, the hermit, having been accused by his brother-in-law, retired into the desert, leaving his relative great wealth; but, as St Jerom remarks, who would not now wish rather to have worn the poor tunic of St. Paul, with his virtues, than the royal purple, with its cares and punishment? All these considerations induced me to take refuge here at once and to dismiss all further projects of travel. If I get to heaven, as I hope, after having done penance, I shall then see all the countries of the earth.

"Toward the end of Lent, after a hard day's work, I was seized with a severe hemorrhage in the evening, which continued every morning after, and I felt myself daily growing weaker After Easter, however, as the community dined at half-past eleven and had a good collation in the evening, my health improved. From Easter to Pentecost we are allowed to use the milk of goats. While the rule of the house is rigid, the superiors are charity itself. Our reverend abbot is even accused of being too indulgent; but, if this is a fault, it is one peculiar to the saints. The only privilege he enjoys is that of rising earlier and retiring later than the rest. His bed is like that of his brethren —two boards placed together, with a pillow of straw He has no room but the parlor, where any one who suffers from pain of mind or of body can apply to him for comfort and receive it. I have already experienced what I was told on entering here. Though the brethren never speak together, they have the most friendly feeling for each other. If any one becomes negligent, it gives them pain, they pray for him: he is admonished with the greatest charity, and if it be necessary to dismiss him, or if he wish of his own accord to leave, every thing that he brought to the house is returned to him, and not a penny is retained as a compensation for his board and clothing Every thing is done to make him satisfied at his departure. When the father, mother, or brother, of a religious dies, and the family notify the superior of the event, all the community are directed to pray for the deceased; but no one knows the name of the individual who is the object of these prayers. Let this, my dear brother, be a source of consolation to you in your last moments.

"I desire nothing so much as to die here, and that soon, not to increase the number of my sins. But, should I be obliged to leave this place on account of my shattered health, I will purchase a little homestead and continue to live by the sweat of my brow This is the vocation of all men. I would prefer a residence in Spain to returning to France. In any event, it will have been a great benefit to me to have learned here how to do penance, and to despise my body, which will so soon return to dust, in order to save my soul, which is immortal. We must consider, also, that it is not the dress nor the house that makes one virtuous. The bad angels rebelled in heaven itself, and Adam sinned in the terrestrial paradise; and I know well that I am not personally better for being in this holy community. Theoretically, I am disposed to suffer, since our Divine Saviour has traced for us the path of self-denial as the only road to heaven; but, in practice, when I feel cold I naturally seek the sunshine, and, when too warm, the refreshing shade.

"P. S.—Nearly forty days have elapsed since I commenced this letter, and I become more and more sensible of the great mercy of God in withdrawing me from the high-road of the world and placing me in this house. I now see that so inestimable a grace could have been secured to me only through the precious merits of Him who has redeemed us all and who seeks only the salvation of the sinner. . . . . I have bestowed an alms of three hundred francs upon the house of La Trappe in behalf of my three sisters and three brothers; and, if I persevere, it will afford me great consolation to hear so many excellent prayers offered up here for my family. . . . . Farewell, brothers and sisters! Think of me only in your prayers; for I am civilly dead in regard to you, and expect not to see you again before the day of the resurrection. Be charitable; do good to them who have sought to injure you: for alms-deeds is a kind of second baptism, which effaces sin and is an almost infallible means of securing heaven. Distribute, then, freely to the poor; when you are merciful to them you are so to Jesus Christ himself, who will have pity on you. May you be well convinced of what I say! Farewell!

"*June* 2, 1799."

Extract from a Letter to his Brother.

"Oh! may we have the happiness to get to heaven! What shall we not then see! Let us hope in Him who has taken upon himself the sins of the world and by his death has restored us to life. If any thing remain of my possessions, it is my wish that a chapel be erected to Our Lady of the Seven Dolors, within the limits of our paternal estate, as we once proposed on our way to Munich. You remember what pleasure we experienced, after having passed through a Protestant country, in beholding again the sign of salvation, the only hope of the sinner. As soon as the police will throw no obstacle in the way, have crosses erected on the wayside, for the consolation of travellers, with seats for such as are fatigued, and place there the inscription which we saw in Bavaria:—*Ihr müden ruhen sie aus,*—'Take some rest, you who are weary.'

"*April*, 1800."

The following year, the writer of these letters was admitted to the religious vows, and, nine months after, he was called to the reward of his sacrifices for the love of God. While living in the community he was the edification of all around him, by his profound humility, his prompt obedience, his tender and ardent charity, and his invincible patience. But the spirit of poverty was his distinguishing trait. He witnessed the approach of his last hour with the greatest peace, thanking God continually for having afforded him, in this house of penance, the means of satisfying for his sins and preparing himself for the next world. "How happy I am!" he said, while lying upon the ashes and straw where he died, and taking the reverend abbot by the hand in a most feeling manner, which affected all present. "You are the author of my salvation; for, in opening to me the gates of the monastery, you opened to me those of heaven. You have prevented me from perishing miserably in the world, and I will pray God to reward your great charity toward me." He received the last sacraments in the church, according to the custom of the Trappists, and, some days before he died, he begged pardon of his brethren for the faults they might have witnessed in his conduct, and entreated them to obtain for him, by their prayers, the grace of a happy death.

NOTE TT, (p. 607.)

When, in a preceding part of this work, we alluded to the fine historical subjects of modern times, which would become interesting in the hands of some able writer, the *Histoire des Croisades*, by Michaud, had not yet made its appearance. We have elsewhere expressed our opinion of this excellent production, from which we will here quote a passage in confirmation of what we have said respecting the advantages which Europe derived from the institution of chivalry:—

"Chivalry was known in the West before the Crusades. These wars, which appeared to have the same aim as chivalry,—that of defending the oppressed, serving the cause of God, and combating with infidels,—gave this institution more splendor and consistency—a direction more extended and salutary.

"Religion, which mingled itself with all the institutions and all the passions of the Middle Ages, purified the sentiments of the knights and elevated them to the enthusiasm of virtue. Christianity lent chivalry its ceremonies and its emblems, and tempered, by the mildness of its maxims, the asperities of warlike manners.

"Piety, bravery, and modesty, were the distinctive qualities of chivalry:—'*Serve God, and he will help you; be mild and courteous to every gentleman, by divesting yourself of all pride; be neither a flatterer nor a slanderer, for such people seldom come to great excellence. Be loyal in words and deeds, keep your word; be helpful to the poor and to orphans, and God will reward you.*'[1] Thus said the mother of Bayard to her son: and these instructions of a virtuous mother comprised the whole code of chivalry.

"The most admirable part of this institution was the entire abnegation of self,—that loyalty which made it the duty of every knight to forget his own glory and only publish the lofty deeds of his companions-in-arms. The deeds of valor of a knight were his fortune, his means of living, *and he who was silent upon them was a robber of the property of others.* Nothing appeared more reprehensible than for a knight to praise himself. 'If the squire,' says *Le Code des Preux*, 'be vain-glorious of what he has done, he is not worthy to become a knight.' An historian of the Crusades offers us a singular example of this virtue, which is not entirely humility, and might be called

---

[1] "Servez Dieu, et il vous aidera: soyez doux et courtois à tout gentilhomme en ôtant de vous tout orgueil, ne soyez flatteur ne rapporteur, car telles manières de gens ne viennent pas à grande perfection. Soyez loyal en faits et en dits; tenez votre parole: soyez secourables à pauvres et orphelins, et Dieu vous le guerdonnera."

the false modesty of glory, when he describes Tancred checking his career in the field of battle, to make his squire swear to be forever silent upon his exploits.

"The most cruel insult that could be offered to a knight was to accuse him of falsehood. Want of truth, and perjury, were considered the most shameful of all crimes. If oppressed innocence implored the succor of a knight, wo to him who did not respond to the appeal! Shame followed every offence toward the weak and every aggression toward an unarmed man.

"The spirit of chivalry kept up and strengthened among warriors the generous sentiments which the military spirit of feudalism had given birth to. Devotion to his sovereign was the first virtue, or rather the first duty, of a knight. Thus in every state of Europe grew up a young military power, always ready for fight, and always ready to sacrifice itself for prince or for country, as for the cause of justice and innocence.

"One of the most remarkable characteristics of chivalry, and that which at the present day most strongly excites our surprise and curiosity, was the alliance of religious sentiments with gallantry. *Devotion and love,*—such was the principle of action of a knight; *God and the ladies,*—such was his device.

"To form an idea of the manners of chivalry, we have but to glance at the tournaments, which owed their origin to it, and which were as schools of courtesy and festivals of bravery. At this period, the nobility were dispersed and lived isolated in their castles. Tournaments furnished them with opportunities for assembling; and it was at these brilliant meetings that the memory of ancient gallant knights was revived—that youth took them for models, and imbibed chivalric virtues by receiving rewards from the hands of beauty.

"As the ladies were the judges of the actions and the bravery of the knights, they exercised an absolute empire over the minds of the warriors; and I have no occasion to say that this ascendency of the softer sex threw a charm over the heroism of the *preux* and the *paladins.* Europe began to escape from barbarism from the moment the most weak commanded the most strong,—from the moment when the love of glory, when the noblest feelings of the heart, the tenderest affections of the soul, every thing that constitutes the moral force of society, was able to triumph over every other force.

"Louis IX., a prisoner in Egypt, replies to the Saracens that he will do nothing without Queen Marguerite, 'who is his lady.' The Orientals could not comprehend such deference, that they have remained so far in the rear of the nations of Europe in nobleness of sentiment, purity of morals, and elegance of manners.

"Heroes of antiquity wandered over the world to deliver it from scourges and monsters; but these heroes were not actuated by religion, which elevates the soul, nor by that courtesy which softens the manners. They were acquainted with friendship, as in the cases of Theseus and Pirithous, and Hercules and Lycas; but they knew nothing of the delicacy of love. The ancient poets take delight in representing the misfortunes of certain heroines abandoned by their lovers; but, in their touching pictures, there never escapes from their plaintive muse the least expression of blame against the hero who thus caused the tears of beauty to flow. In the Middle Ages, or according to the manners of chivalry, a warrior who should have imitated the conduct of Theseus to Ariadne, or that of the son of Anchises toward Dido, would not have failed to incur the reproach of treachery.

"Another difference between the spirit of antiquity and the sentiments of the moderns is, that among the ancients love was supposed to enervate the courage of heroes, and that in the days of chivalry, the women, who were the judges of valor, constantly kept alive the love of glory and an enthusiasm for virtue in the hearts of the warriors. We find in *Alain Chartier* a conversation of several ladies, who express their opinions upon the conduct of their knights, who had been present at the battle of Agincourt. One of these knights had sought safety in flight, and the lady of his thoughts exclaims, 'According to the law of love, I should have loved him better dead than alive' In the first Crusade. Adela, Countess of Blois, wrote to her husband, who was gone to the East with Godfrey of Bouillon.—'Beware of meriting the reproaches of the brave.' As the Count of Blois returned to Europe before the taking of Jerusalem, his wife made him blush at his desertion, and forced him to return to Palestine, where he fought bravely and found a glorious death. Thus the spirit and the sentiments of chivalry gave birth to prodigies equally with the most ardent patriotism of ancient Lacedæmon: and these prodigies appeared so simple, so natural, that the chroniclers only repeat them in passing, and without testifying the least surprise at them.

"This institution, so ingeniously called 'Fountain of Courtesy,' which comes from God, is still much more admirable when considered under the all-powerful influence of religious ideas. Christian charity claimed all the affections of the knight, and demanded of him a perpetual devotion for the defence of pilgrims and the care of the sick. It was thus that were established the orders of St. John of the Temple, of the Teutonic Knights, and several others, all instituted to combat the Saracens and solace human miseries. The infidels admired their virtues as much as they dreaded their bravery. Nothing is more touching than the spectacle of these noble warriors who were seen by turns in the field of battle and in the asylum of pain, sometimes the terror of the enemy, and as frequently the consolers of all who suffered. That which the paladins of the West did for beauty the knights of Palestine did for poverty and misfortune. The former devoted their lives to the ladies of their thoughts; the latter devoted theirs to the poor and the infirm. The grand-master of the military order of St. John took the title of 'Guardian of the poor of Jesus Christ,' and the knights called the sick and the poor 'Our lords.' It appears almost an incredible thing, but the grand-master of the order of St. Lazarus, instituted for the cure and the relief of leprosy, was obliged to be chosen from among the lepers[1] Thus the charity of the knights, in order to be the better

[1] Le Père Helyot, in his *Histoire des Ordres Monastiques*, vol. i p 263, expresses himself thus, when speaking of the order of St Lazarus.—"What is very remarkable is, that they could only elect as grand-master a leprous knight of the hospital of Jerusalem, which lasted up to the time of Innocent IV..—that is to say about the year 1253,—when, having been obliged to abandon Syria, they addressed the pontiff and represented to him that always having had, from their foundation a leprous knight for grand-master, they found themselves in the impossibility of electing one, because the infidels had killed all the leprous knights of their hospital at Jerusalem For this reason they prayed the pontiff to allow them to elect for the future, as grand-master, a knight who had not been attacked by leprosy and

acquainted with human miseries, in a manner ennobled that which is most disgusting in the diseases of man. Did not this grand-master of St. Lazarus, who was obliged himself to be afflicted with the infirmities he was called upon to alleviate in others, imitate, as much as is possible on earth, the example of the Son of God, who assumed a human form in order to deliver humanity?

"It may be thought there was ostentation in so great a charity; but Christianity, as we have said, had subdued the pride of the warriors, and that was, without doubt, one of the noblest miracles of the religion of the Middle Ages. All who then visited the Holy Land could but admire in the knights of St. John, the Temple, and St. Lazarus, their resignation in suffering all the pains of life, their submission to all the rigors of discipline, and their docility to the least wish of their leader. During the sojourn of St. Louis in Palestine, the Hospitallers having had a quarrel with some Crusaders who were hunting on Mount Carmel, the latter brought their complaint before the grand-master. The head of the hospital ordered before him the brothers who had outraged the Crusaders, and, to punish them, condemned them to eat their food on the ground upon their mantles. 'It happened,' says the Sieur de Joinville, 'that I was present with the knights who had complained, and we requested the master to allow the brothers to arise from their mantles, which he refused.' Thus the rigor of the cloisters and the austere humility of cenobites had nothing repulsive for these warriors. Such were the heroes that religion and the spirit of the Crusades had formed. I know that this submission and humility in men accustomed to arms may be turned into ridicule; but an enlightened philosophy takes pleasure in recognising the happy influence of religious ideas upon the manners of a society given up to barbarous passions. In an age when all power was derived from the sword, in which passion and anger might have carried warriors to all kinds of excesses, what more agreeable spectacle for humanity could there be than that of valor humbling itself and strength forgetting itself?

"We are aware that the spirit of chivalry was sometimes abused, and that its noble maxims did not govern the conduct of all knights. We have described in the history of the Crusades the lengthened discords which jealousy created between the two orders of St. John and the Temple. We have spoken of the vices with which the Templars were reproached toward the end of the Holy

---

who might be in good health; and the pope referred them to the Bishop of Truscate, that he might accord them this permission after having examined if that could be done according to the will of God. This is reported by Pope Pius IV. in his bull of the year 1565, so extended and so favorable to the order of St. Lazarus, by which he renews all the privileges and all the gifts that his predecessors had granted to it, and gives it fresh ones. Here is what he says of the election these knights ought to make of a leprous grand-master:—"Et Innocentius IV., per eum accepto, quod licet de antiquâ approbatâ et hactenus pacificè observatâ consuetudine obtentum esset, ut miles leprosus domûs Sancti-Lazari Hierosolymitani in ejus magistrum assumeretur; verùm quia ferè omnes milites leprosi dictæ domus ab inimicis fidei miserabiliter interfecti fuerant, et hujusmodi consuetudo nequiebat commodè observari: idcirco tunc episcopo Tusculano per quasdam commiserat, ut, si sibi secundùm Deum visum foret expedire, fratribus ipsis licentiam, aliquem militem sanum et fratribus prædictæ domus Sancti-Lazari in ejus magistrum (non obstante consuetudine hujusmodi de cætero eligendi) auctoritate apostolicâ concederet.

Wars We could speak still more of the absurdities of knight-errantry; but our task is here to write the history of institutions, and not that of human passions. Whatever may be thought of the corruption of men, it will always be true that chivalry, allied with the spirit of courtesy and the spirit of Christianity, awakened in human hearts virtues and sentiments of which the ancients were ignorant.

"That which proves that every thing was not barbarous in the Middle Ages is that the institution of chivalry obtained from its birth the esteem and admiration of all Christendom. There was no gentleman who was not desirous of being a knight. Princes and kings took honor to themselves for belonging to chivalry. In it warriors came to take lessons of politeness, bravery, and humanity. Admirable school! in which victory laid aside its pride and grandeur its haughty disdain; to which those who had riches and power came to learn to make use of them with moderation and generosity.

"As the education of the people was formed upon the example of the higher classes of society, the generous sentiments of chivalry spread themselves by degrees through all ranks, and mingled with the character of the European nations, gradually there arose against those who were wanting in their duties of knighthood, a general opinion, more severe than the laws themselves, which was as the code of honor, as the cry of the public conscience. What might not be hoped from a state of society, in which all the discourses held in camps, in tournaments, in meetings of warriors, were reduced to these words:—'Evil be to him who forgets the promises he has made to religion, to patriotism, to virtuous love, evil be to him who betrays his God, his king, or his lady'?

"When the institution of chivalry fell by the abuse that was made of it, or rather in consequence of the changes in the military system of Europe, there remained still in European society some of the sentiments it had inspired, in the same manner as there remains with those who have forgotten the religion in which they were born, something of its precepts, and particularly of the profound impressions which they received from it in their infancy. In the times of chivalry the reward of good actions was glory and honor. This coin, which is so useful to nations and which costs them nothing, did not fail to have some currency in following ages. Such is the effect of a glorious remembrance, that the marks and distinctions of chivalry serve still in our days to recompense merit and bravery.

"The better to explain and make clear all the good that the Holy Wars brought with them, we have elsewhere examined what would have happened if they had had all the success they might have had. Let us now attempt another hypothesis, and let our minds dwell for a moment upon the state in which Europe would have been without the expeditions which the West so many times repeated against the nations of Asia and Africa. In the eleventh century, several European countries were invaded and others were threatened by the Saracens. What means of defence had the Christian republic then, when most of the states were given up to license, troubled by discords, and plunged in barbarism? If Christendom, as M. de Bonald remarks, had not then gone out by all its gates, and at repeated times, to attack a formidable enemy, have we not a right to believe that this enemy would have profited by the inaction of the Christian nations, and that he would have surprised them amid their divisions, and subdued them one after another? Which of us does not tremble with horror at thinking that France, Germany, England, and Italy might have experienced the fate of Greece and Palestine?"—*Hist. of Crus.*, vol iii. p. 295, Robson's trans.

NOTE UU, (p. 626.)

We request the reader's attention to the following extracts from Robertson's History of America:—

"From the time that ecclesiastics were sent as instructors into America, they perceived that the rigor with which their countrymen treated the nations rendered their ministry altogether fruitless. The missionaries, in conformity to the mild spirit of that religion which they were employed to publish, early remonstrated against the maxims of the planters with respect to the Americans, and condemned the *repartimientos* or *distributions*, by which they were given up as slaves to their conquerors, as no less contrary to natural justice and the precepts of Christianity than to sound policy. The Dominicans, to whom the instruction of the Americans was originally committed, were most vehement in testifying against the *repartimientos*. In the year one thousand five hundred and eleven, Montesino, one of their most eminent preachers, inveighed against this practice, in the great church of St. Domingo, with all the impetuosity of popular eloquence. Don Diego Columbus, the principal officers of the colony, and all the laymen who had been his hearers, complained of the monk to his superiors; but they, instead of condemning, applauded his doctrine as equally pious and seasonable. The Franciscans, influenced by the spirit of opposition and rivalship which subsists between the two orders, discovered some inclination to take part with the laity and to espouse the defence of the *repartimientos*. But, as they could not with decency give their avowed approbation to a system of oppression so repugnant to the spirit of religion, they endeavored to palliate what they could not justify, and alleged, in excuse for the conduct of their countrymen, that it was impossible to carry on any improvement in the colony unless the Spaniards possessed such dominion over the natives that they could compel them to labor.[1]

"The Dominicans, regardless of such political and interested considerations, would not relax in any degree the rigor of their sentiments, and even refused to absolve or admit to the sacrament such of their countrymen as continued to hold the natives in servitude.[2] Both parties applied to the king for his decision in a matter of such importance. Ferdinand empowered a committee of his privy council, assisted by some of the most eminent civilians and divines in Spain, to hear the deputies sent from Hispaniola in support of their respective opinions. After a long discussion, the speculative point in controversy was determined in favor of the Dominicans. The Indians were declared to be a free people, entitled to all the natural rights of men; but, notwithstanding this decision, the *repartimientos* were continued upon their ancient footing.[3] As this determination admitted the principle upon which the Dominicans founded their opinion, they renewed their efforts to obtain relief for the Indians with additional boldness and zeal. At length, in order to quiet the colony, which

[1] Herrera, dec. 1, lib. viii. chap. 11. ... iii. chap. 6, p. 97.
[2] Oviedo, lib. ... chap. 6, p. 97. [3] Herrera, dec. 1, lib. viii. chap. 12, lib. ix. chap. 5.

was alarmed by their remonstrances and censures, Ferdinand issued a decree of his privy council, (1513,) declaring that, after mature consideration of the Apostolic Bull. and other titles by which the crown of Castile claimed a right to its possessions in the New World, the servitude of the Indians was warranted both by the laws of God and of man; that, unless they were subjected to the dominion of the Spaniards and compelled to reside under their inspection, it would be impossible to reclaim them from idolatry or to instruct them in the principles of the Christian faith; that no further scruple ought to be entertained concerning the lawfulness of the *repartimientos*, as the king and council were willing to take the charge of that upon their own consciences; and that therefore the Dominicans and monks of other religious orders should abstain for the future from those invectives which, from an excess of charitable but ill-informed zeal, they had uttered against that practice.[1]

"That his intention of adhering to this decree might be fully understood, Ferdinand conferred new grants of Indians upon several of his courtiers, (25.) But, in order that he might not seem altogether inattentive to the rights of humanity, he published an edict, in which he endeavored to provide for the mild treatment of the Indians under the yoke to which he subjected them; he regulated the nature of the work which they should be required to perform, he prescribed the mode in which they should be clothed and fed, and gave directions with respect to their instructions in the principles of Christianity.[2]

"But the Dominicans, who, from their experience of what was past, judged concerning the future, soon perceived the inefficacy of those provisions, and foretold that, as long as it was the interest of individuals to treat the Indians with rigor, no public regulations could render their servitude mild or tolerable. They considered it as vain to waste their own time and strength in attempting to communicate the sublime truths of religion to men whose spirits were broken and their faculties impaired by oppression. Some of them, in despair, requested the permission of their superiors to remove to the continent, and to pursue the object of their mission among such of the natives as were not hitherto corrupted by the example of the Spaniards or alienated by their cruelty from the Christian faith. Such as remained in Hispaniola continued to remonstrate, with decent firmness, against the servitude of the Indians.[3]

"The violent operations of Albuquerque, the new distributor of Indians, revived the zeal of the Dominicans against the *repartimientos*, and called forth an advocate for that oppressed people who possessed all the courage, the talents, and activity, requisite in supporting such a desperate cause. This was Bartholomew de las Casas, a native of Seville, and one of the clergymen sent out with Columbus in his second voyage to Hispaniola in order to settle in that island. He early adopted the opinion prevalent among ecclesiastics with respect to the unlawfulness of reducing the natives to servitude; and, that he might demonstrate the sincerity of his conviction, he relinquished all the Indians who had fallen to his own share in the division of the inhabitants among their conquerors, declaring that he should ever bewail his own misfortune and guilt in having exercised for a moment this impious dominion over his fellow-creatures.[4]

[1] Herrera, dec. 1, lib. ix. chap. 14.
[2] Ibid., dec. 1, lib. ix. chap. 14.
[3] Id., ibid., Touron. *Histoire Générale de l'Amérique*, tom. i. p. 252.
[4] Fr. Aug. Davila Padilla, *Hist. de la Fund. [illegible] Mexico*, p. 303. 304; Herrera, dec. 1. lib. x. chap. 12.

From that time he became the avowed patron of the Indians, and by his bold interpositions in their behalf, as well as by the respect due to his abilities and character, he had often the merit of setting some bounds to the excesses of his countrymen. He did not fail to remonstrate warmly against the proceedings of Albuquerque; and, though he soon found that attention to his own interest rendered this rapacious officer deaf to admonition, he did not abandon the wretched people whose cause he had espoused. He instantly set out for Spain, with the most sanguine hopes of opening the eyes and softening the heart of Ferdinand by that striking picture of the oppression of his new subjects which he would exhibit to his view.[1]

"He easily obtained admittance to the king, whom he found in a declining state of health. With much freedom, and no less eloquence, he represented to him all the fatal effects of the *repartimientos* in the New World, boldly charging him with the guilt of having authorized this impious measure, which had brought misery and destruction upon a numerous and innocent race of men whom Providence had placed under his protection. Ferdinand, whose mind as well as body was much enfeebled by his distemper, was greatly alarmed at this charge of impiety, which at another juncture he would have despised. He listened with deep compunction to the discourse of Las Casas, and promised to take into serious consideration the means of redressing the evil of which he complained. But death prevented him from executing his resolution. Charles of Austria, to whom all his crowns devolved, resided at that time in his paternal dominions in the Low Countries. Las Casas, with his usual ardor, prepared immediately to set out for Flanders, in order to occupy the ear of the young monarch, when Cardinal Ximenes, who, as regent, assumed the reins of government in Castile, commanded him to desist from the journey and engaged to hear his complaints in person.

"He accordingly weighed the matter with attention equal to its importance; and, as his impetuous mind delighted in schemes bold and uncommon, he soon fixed upon a plan which astonished the ministers trained up under the formal and cautious administration of Ferdinand. Without regarding either the rights of Don Diego Columbus or the regulations established by the late king, he resolved to send three persons to America as superintendents of all the colonies there, with authority, after examining all circumstances on the spot, to decide finally with respect to the point in question. It was a matter of deliberation and delicacy to choose men qualified for such an important station. As all the laymen settled in America, or who had been consulted in the administration of that department, had given their opinion that the Spaniards could not keep possession of their new settlements unless they were allowed to retain their dominion over the Indians, he saw that he could not rely on their impartiality, and determined to commit the trust to ecclesiastics. As the Dominicans and Franciscans had already espoused opposite sides in the controversy, he, from the same principle of impartiality, excluded both these fraternities from the commission. He confined his choice to the monks of St. Jerome—a small but respectable order in Spain. With the assistance of their general, and in concert with Las Casas, he soon pitched upon three persons whom he deemed equal to the charge. To them he joined Zuazo, a private

[1] Herrera, dec. 1, lib. x, chap. 12; dec. 2, lib. i, chap. 11; Davila Padilla, *Hist.*, p. 304.

lawyer of distinguished probity, with unbounded power to regulate all judicial proceedings in the colonies. Las Casas was appointed to accompany them, with the title of protector of the Indians.[1]

"To vest such extraordinary powers, as might at once overturn the system of government established in the New World, in four persons, who, from their humble condition in life, were little entitled to possess this high authority, appeared to Zapata and other ministers of the late king a measure so wild and dangerous that they refused to issue the despatches necessary for carrying it into execution. But Ximenes was not of a temper patiently to brook opposition to any of his schemes. He sent for the refractory ministers and addressed them in such a tone that, in the utmost consternation, they obeyed his orders.[2] The superintendents, with their associates Zuazo and Las Casas, sailed for St. Domingo. Upon their arrival, the first act of their authority was to set at liberty all the Indians who had been granted to the Spanish courtiers or to any person not residing in America. This, together with the information which had been received from Spain concerning the object of the commission, spread a general alarm. The colonists concluded that they were to be deprived at once of the hands with which they carried on their labor, and that, of consequence, ruin was unavoidable. But the fathers of St. Jerom proceeded with such caution and prudence as soon dissipated all their fears. They discovered, in every step of their conduct, a knowledge of the world and of affairs which is seldom acquired in cloister, and displayed a moderation as well as gentleness still more rare among persons trained up in the solitude and austerity of a monastic life. Their ears were open to information from every quarter; they compared the different accounts which they received; and, after a mature consideration of the whole, they were fully satisfied that the state of the colony rendered it impossible to adopt the plan proposed by Las Casas and recommended by the cardinal. They plainly perceived that the Spaniards settled in America were so few in number that they could neither work the mines which had been opened, nor cultivate the country; that they depended, for effecting both, upon the labor of the natives, and, if deprived of it, they must instantly relinquish their conquests or give up all the advantages which they derived from them; that no allurement was so powerful as to surmount the natural aversion of the Indians to any laborious effort, and that nothing but the authority of a master could compel them to work; and, if they were not kept constantly under the eye and discipline of a superior, so great was their natural listlessness and indifference that they would neither attend to religious instruction nor observe those rites of Christianity which they had already been taught. Upon all those accounts, the superintendents found it necessary to tolerate the *repartimientos*, and to suffer the Indians to remain under subjection to their Spanish masters. They used their utmost endeavors, however, to prevent the fatal effects of this establishment, and to secure to the Indians the consolation of the best treatment compatible with a state of servitude. For this purpose they revived former regulations, they prescribed new ones, they neglected no circumstance that tended to mitigate the rigor of the yoke; and by their authority, their example, and their exhortations, they labored to inspire their countrymen with

[1] Herrera, dec. 2, lib. ii. c. 3. [2] Ibid., dec. 2, lib. ii. c. 6.

sentiments of equity and gentleness toward the unhappy people upon whose industry they depended. Zuazo, in his department, seconded the endeavors of the superintendents. He reformed the courts of justice in such a manner as to render their decisions equitable as well as expeditious, and introduced various regulations which greatly improved the interior policy of the colony. The satisfaction which his conduct and that of the superintendents gave was now universal among the Spaniards settled in the New World; and all admired the boldness of Ximenes in having departed from the ordinary path of business in forming his plan, as well as his sagacity in pitching upon persons whose wisdom, moderation, and disinterestedness, rendered them worthy of this high trust.[1] Las Casas alone was dissatisfied. The prudential consideration which influenced the superintendents made no impression upon him. He regarded their idea of accommodating their conduct to the state of the colony as the maxim of an unhallowed, timid policy, which tolerated what was unjust because it was beneficial. He contended that the Indians were by nature free, and, as their protector, he required the superintendents not to bereave them of the common privilege of humanity. They received his most virulent remonstrances without emotion, but adhered firmly to their own system. The Spanish planters did not bear with him so patiently, and were ready to tear him in pieces for insisting on a requisition so odious to them. Las Casas, in order to screen himself from their rage, found it necessary to take shelter in a convent; and, perceiving that all his efforts in America were fruitless, he soon set out for Europe, with a fixed resolution not to abandon the protection of a people whom he deemed to be cruelly oppressed.[2]

"Had Ximenes retained that vigor of mind with which he usually applied to business, Las Casas must have met with no very gracious reception upon his return to Spain. But he found the cardinal languishing under a mortal distemper and preparing to resign his authority to the young king, who was daily expected from the Low Countries. Charles arrived, took possession of the government, and, by the death of Ximenes, lost a minister whose abilities and integrity entitled him to direct his affairs. Many of the Flemish nobility had accompanied their sovereign to Spain. From that warm predilection to his countrymen which was natural at his age, he consulted them with respect to all the transactions in his new kingdom; and they, with an indiscreet eagerness, intruded themselves into every business and seized almost every department of administration.[3] The direction of American affairs was an object too alluring to escape their attention. Las Casas observed their growing influence; and, though projectors are usually too sanguine to conduct their schemes with much dexterity, he possessed a bustling, indefatigable activity, which sometimes accomplishes its purposes with greater success than the most exquisite discernment and address. He courted the Flemish ministers with assiduity. He represented to them the absurdity of all the maxims hitherto adopted with respect to the government of America, particularly during the administration of Ferdinand, and pointed out the defects of those arrangements which Ximenes had introduced. The memory of Ferdinand was odious to the

[1] H[illegible] ii. [illegible] 15; [illegible], *Hist. Gener.* lib. ii. c. 14, 15, 16.
[2] [illegible] 1. [3] [illegible] *Charles V.*

Flemings. The superior virtues and abilities of Ximenes had long been the object of their envy. They fondly wished to have a plausible pretext for condemning the measures both of the monarch and of the minister, and of reflecting some discredit on their political wisdom. The friends of Don Diego Columbus, as well as the Spanish courtiers who had been dissatisfied with the cardinal's administration, joined Las Casas in censuring the scheme of sending superintendents to America. This union of so many interests and passions was irresistible; and, in consequence of it, the fathers of St. Jerom, together with their associate Zuazo, were recalled. Roderigo de Figueroa, a lawyer of some eminence, was appointed chief-judge of the island, and received instructions, in compliance with the request of Las Casas, to examine once more, with the utmost attention, the point in controversy between him and the people of the colony, with respect to the treament of the natives, and, in the mean time, to do every thing in his power to alleviate their sufferings and prevent the extinction of the race.[1]

"This was all that the zeal of Las Casas could procure at that juncture in favor of the Indians. The impossibility of carrying on any improvements in America, unless the Spanish planters could command the labor of the natives, was an insuperable objection to his plan of treating them as free subjects. In order to provide some remedy for this, without which he found it was in vain to mention his scheme, Las Casas proposed to purchase a sufficient number of negroes from the Portuguese settlements on the coast of Africa, and to transport them to America, in order that they might be employed as slaves in working the mines and cultivating the ground. One of the first advantages which the Portuguese had derived from their discoveries in Africa arose from the trade in slaves. Various circumstances concurred in reviving this odious commerce, which had been long abolished in Europe, and which is no less repugnant to the feelings of humanity than to the principles of religion. As early as the year one thousand five hundred and three, a few negro slaves had been sent into the New World.[2] In the year one thousand five hundred and eleven, Ferdinand permitted the importation of them in great numbers.[3] They were found to be a more robust and hardy race than the natives of America. They were more capable of enduring fatigue, more patient under servitude, and the labor of one negro was computed to be equal to that of four Indians.[4] Cardinal Ximenes, however, when solicited to encourage this commerce, peremptorily rejected the proposition, because he perceived the iniquity of reducing one race of men to slavery while he was consulting about the means of restoring liberty to another.[5] But Las Casas, from the inconsistency natural to men who hurry with headlong impetuosity toward a favorite point, was incapable of making this distinction. While he contended earnestly for the liberty of the people born in one quarter of the globe, he labored to enslave the inhabitants of another region; and, in the warmth of his zeal to save the Americans from the yoke, pronounced it to be lawful and expedient to impose one still heavier upon the Africans. Unfortunately for the latter, Las Casas's plan was adopted. Charles granted a patent to one of his Flemish favorites, containing an exclusive right of importing four thousand negroes

[1] Herrera, dec. 2, lib. ii. c. 16, 19, 21: lib. iii. c. 7, 8.
[2] Ibid., dec. 2, lib. v. c. 12.
[3] Ibid., lib. viii. c. 9.
[4] Ibid., lib. ix. c. 5.
[5] Ibid., dec. 2, lib. ii. c. 8.

into America. The favorite sold his patent to some Genoese merchants for twenty-five thousand ducats, and they were the first who brought into a regular form that commerce for slaves between Africa and America which has since been carried on to such an amazing extent.[1]

"But the Genoese merchants, (1518,) conducting their operations at first with the rapacity of monopolists, demanded such a high price for negroes that the number imported into Hispaniola made no great change upon the state of the colony. Las Casas, whose zeal was no less inventive than indefatigable, had recourse to another expedient for the relief of the Indians. He observed that most of the persons who had settled in America hitherto were sailors and soldiers employed in the discovery or conquest of the country—the younger sons of noble families, allured by the prospect of acquiring sudden wealth, or desperate adventurers, whom their indigence or crimes forced to abandon their native land. Instead of such men, who were dissolute, rapacious, and incapable of that sober, persevering industry which is requisite in forming new colonies, he proposed to supply the settlements in Hispaniola and other parts of the New World with a sufficient number of laborers and husbandmen, who should be allured by suitable premiums to remove thither. These, as they were accustomed to fatigue, would be able to perform the work to which the Indians, from the feebleness of their constitutions, were unequal, and might soon become useful and opulent citizens. But, though Hispaniola stood much in need of a recruit of inhabitants, having been visited at this time with the small-pox, which swept off almost all the natives who had survived their long-continued oppression, and though Las Casas had the countenance of the Flemish ministers, this scheme was defeated by the Bishop of Burgos, who thwarted all his projects.[2]

"Las Casas now despaired of procuring any relief for the Indians in those places where the Spaniards were already settled. The evil was become so inveterate there as not to admit of a cure. But such discoveries were daily making in the continent as gave high idea both of its extent and populousness. In all those vast regions there was but one feeble colony planted; and, except a small spot on the Isthmus of Darien, the natives still occupied the whole country. This opened a new and more ample field for the humanity and zeal of Las Casas, who flattered himself that he might prevent a pernicious system from being introduced there, though he had failed of success in his attempts to overturn it where it was already established. Full of this idea, he applied for a grant of the unoccupied country stretching along the seacoast from the Gulf

[1] Herrera, dec. 1, lib. ii. c. 20. It is but just to remark, according to other writers,—1. That the proposal to transport negroes from Africa, on this occasion, did not originate with Las Casas. He merely approved of the measure already suggested. 2. This measure, as he understood it, consisted, not in making slaves of those who were free, but merely in transporting to America those negroes who were already suffering a cruel slavery in their own country. 3. Whence it follows that the plan of Las Casas tended to ameliorate the condition of those unhappy Africans, and, far from being an oppressive or unjust policy, was entirely consistent with the humane and active zeal which he had displayed for the benefit of the American Indians. If his measures afterward degenerated by the cupidity of others into the abuses of the slave-trade, it was not the effect of any design or co-operation on his part. S[illegible] Baluffi. *L'Ameri[illegible] un tempo Spagnuola*, p. 255, &c.; Henrion, *Hist.* [illegible] tome i. p. 350, &c. T.

[2] Ibid., dec [illegible]

of Paria to the western frontier of that province now known by the name of Santa Martha He proposed to settle there with a colony composed of husbandmen, laborers, and ecclesiastics. He engaged, in the space of two years, to civilize ten thousand of the natives, and to instruct them so thoroughly in the arts of social life that from the fruits of their industry an annual revenue of fifteen thousand ducats should arise to the king. In ten years he expected that his improvements would be so far advanced as to yield annually sixty thousand ducats. He stipulated that no soldier or sailor should ever be permitted to settle in this district, and that no Spaniard whatever should enter it without his permission. He even projected to clothe the people whom he took along with him in some distinguishing garb, which did not resemble the Spanish dress, that they might appear to the natives to be a different race of men from those who had brought so many calamities upon their country.[1] From this scheme, of which I have traced only the great lines, it is manifest that Las Casas had formed ideas concerning the method of treating the Indians similar to those by which the Jesuits afterward carried on their great operations in another part of the same continent. He supposed that the Europeans, by availing themselves of that ascendant which they possessed in consequence of their superior progress in science and improvement, might gradually form the minds of the Americans to relish those comforts of which they were destitute, might train them to the arts of civil life, and render them capable of its functions.

"But to the Bishop of Burgos and the Council of the Indies this project appeared not only chimerical, but dangerous in a high degree. They deemed the faculties of the Americans to be naturally so limited, and their indolence so excessive, that every attempt to instruct or to improve them would be fruitless. They contended that it would be extremely imprudent to give the command of a country extending above a thousand miles along the coast to a fanciful presumptuous enthusiast, a stranger to the affairs of the world and unacquainted with the arts of government. Las Casas, far from being discouraged with a repulse, which he had reason to expect, had recourse once more to the Flemish favorites, who zealously patronized his scheme, merely because it had been rejected by the Spanish ministers They prevailed with their master, who had lately been raised to the imperial dignity, to refer the consideration of this measure to a select number of his privy counsellors. Las Casas having excepted against the members of the Council of the Indies as partial and interested, they were all excluded. The decision of men chosen by recommendation of the Flemings was perfectly conformable to their sentiments. They warmly approved of Las Casas's plan, and gave orders for carrying it into execution, but restricted the territory allotted him to three hundred miles along the coast of Cumana, allowing him, however, to extend it as far as he pleased toward the interior part of the country.[2]

"This determination did not pass uncensured. Almost every person who had been in the West Indies exclaimed against it, and supported their opinion so confidently, and with such plausible reasons, as made it advisable to pause and to review the subject more deliberately. Charles himself, though accustomed at this early period of his life to adopt the sentiments of his ministers

[1] Herrera, dec. 2. lib. iv. c. 2.

[2] Gomara, *Hist. Gen r.*, c 77; Herrera, dec. 2, lib iv. c. 3; Oviedo, lib xix. c. 5.

with such submissive deference as did not promise that decisive vigor of mind which distinguished his riper years, could not help suspecting that the eagerness with which the Flemings took part in every affair relating to America flowed from some improper motive, and began to discover an inclination to examine in person into the state of the question concerning the character of the Americans and the proper manner of treating them. An opportunity of making this inquiry with great advantage soon occurred, (June 20.) Quevedo, the Bishop of Darien, who had accompanied Padrarias to the continent in the year one thousand five hundred and thirteen, happened to land at Barcelona, where the court then resided. It was quickly known that his sentiments concerning the talents and disposition of the Indians differed from those of Las Casas; and Charles naturally concluded that, by confronting two respectable persons, who, during their residence in America, had full leisure to observe the manners of the people whom they pretended to describe, he might be able to discover which of them had formed his opinion with the greatest discernment and accuracy.

"A day for this solemn audience was appointed. The emperor appeared with extraordinary pomp, and took his seat on a throne in the great hall of the palace. His principal courtiers attended. Don Diego Columbus, Admiral of the Indies, was summoned to be present. The Bishop of Darien was called upon first to deliver his opinion. He, in a short discourse, lamented the fatal desolation of America by the extinction of so many of its inhabitants; he acknowledged that this must be imputed, in some degree, to the extensive rigor and inconsiderate proceedings of the Spaniards, but declared that all the people of the New World whom he had seen, either in the continent or in the islands, appeared to him to be a race of men marked out by the inferiority of their talents for servitude, and whom it would be impossible to instruct or improve unless they were kept under the continual inspection of a master. Las Casas, at greater length and with more fervor, defended his own system. He rejected with indignation the idea that any race of men was born to servitude as irreligious and inhuman. He asserted that the faculties of the Americans were not naturally despicable, but unimproved; that they were capable of receiving instruction in the principles of religion as well as of acquiring the industry and arts which would qualify them for the various offices of social life; that the wildness and timidity of their nature rendered them so submissive and docile that they might be led and formed with a gentle hand. He professed that his intentions in proposing the scheme now under consideration were pure and disinterested; and, though from the accomplishment of his designs inestimable benefits would result to the crown of Castile, he never had claimed, nor ever would receive, any recompense on that account.

"Charles, after hearing both and consulting with his ministers, did not think himself sufficiently informed to establish any general arrangement with respect to the state of the Indians; but, as he had perfect confidence in the integrity of Las Casas, and as even the Bishop of Darien admitted his scheme to be of such importance that a trial should be made of its effects, he issued a patent, (1522,) granting him the district of Cumana, formerly mentioned, with full power to establish a colony there according to his own plan.[1]

[1] Herrera, dec. [illegible] lib. iv [illegible] 4, 5; [illegible] 74, 97; Remisal, *Hist. Gener.*, lib. ii. [illegible]

"Las Casas pushed on the preparations for his voyage with his usual ardor. But, either from his own inexperience in the conduct of affairs, or from the secret opposition of the Spanish nobility, who universally dreaded the success of an institution that might rob them of the industrious and useful hands which cultivated their estates, his progress in engaging husbandmen and laborers was extremely slow, and he could not prevail on more than two hundred to accompany him to Cumana.

"Nothing, however, could damp his zeal. With this slender train, hardly sufficient to take possession of such a large territory, and altogether unequal to any effectual attempt toward civilizing its inhabitants, he set sail. The first place at which he touched was the island of Puerto Rico. There he received an account of a new obstacle to the execution of his scheme, more insuperable than any he had hitherto encountered. When he left America, in the year one thousand five hundred and sixteen, the Spaniards had little intercourse with any part of the continent except the countries adjacent to the Gulf of Darien. But, as every species of internal industry began to stagnate in Hispaniola when, by the rapid decrease of the natives, the Spaniards were deprived of those hands with which they had hitherto carried on their operations, this prompted them to try various expedients for supplying that loss. Considerable numbers of negroes were imported, but, on account of their exorbitant price, many of the planters could not afford to purchase them In order to procure slaves at an easier rate, some of the Spaniards in Hispaniola fitted out vessels to cruise along the coast of the continent. In places where they found themselves inferior in strength they traded with the natives, and gave European toys in exchange for the plates of gold worn by them as ornaments; but wherever they could surprise or overpower the Indians, they carried them off by force and sold them as slaves.[1] In those predatory excursions such atrocious acts of violence and cruelty had been committed that the Spanish name was held in detestation all over the continent. Whenever any ships appeared, the inhabitants either fled to the woods, or rushed down to the shore in arms to repel those hated disturbers of their tranquillity They forced some parties of the Spaniards to retreat with precipitation; they cut off others, and, in the violence of their resentment against the whole nation, they murdered two Dominican missionaries, whose zeal had prompted them to settle in the province of Cumana.[2] This outrage against persons revered for their sanctity excited such indignation among the people of Hispaniola, who, notwithstanding all their licentious and cruel proceedings, were possessed with a wonderful zeal for religion and a superstitious respect for its ministers, that they determined to inflict exemplary punishment, not only upon the perpetrators of that crime, but upon the whole race. With this view they gave the command of five ships and three hundred men to Diego Ocampo, with orders to lay waste the country of Cumana with fire and sword, and to transport all the inhabitants as slaves to Hispaniola. This armament Las Casas found at Puerto Rico, in its way to the continent; and, as Ocampo refused to defer his voyage, he immediately perceived that it would be impossible to attempt the execution of his pacific plan in a country destined to be the seat of war and desolation.[3]

---

[1] Herrera, dec. 3, lib. ii. c. 3

[2] Oviedo, *Hist.*, lib. xix. p 3.

[3] Herrera, dec. 2, lib. ix. c. 8, 9.

"In order to provide against the effects of this unfortunate incident, he set sail directly for St. Domingo, (April 12,) leaving his followers cantoned out among the planters of Puerto Rico. From many concurring causes, the reception which Las Casas met with in Hispaniola was very unfavorable. In his negotiations for the relief of the Indians, he had censured the conduct of his countrymen settled there with such honest severity as rendered him universally odious to them. They considered their ruin as the inevitable consequence of his success. They were now elated with hope of receiving a large recruit of slaves from Cumana, which must be relinquished if Las Casas were assisted in settling his projected colony there. Figueroa, in consequence of the instructions he had received in Spain, had made an experiment concerning the capacity of the Indians that was represented as decisive against the system of Las Casas. He collected in Hispaniola a good number of the natives, and settled them in two villages, leaving them at perfect liberty and with the uncontrolled direction of their own actions. But that people, accustomed to a mode of life extremely different from that which takes place wherever civilization has made any considerable progress, were incapable of assuming new habits at once. Dejected with their own misfortunes, as well as those of their country, they exerted so little industry in cultivating the ground, appeared so devoid of solicitude or foresight in providing for their own wants, and were such strangers to arrangement in conducting their affairs, that the Spaniards pronounced them incapable of being formed to live like men in social life, and considered them as children, who should be kept under the perpetual tutelage of persons superior to themselves in wisdom and sagacity.[1]

"Notwithstanding all those circumstances, which alienated the persons in Hispaniola to whom Las Casas applied from himself and from his measures, he, by his activity and perseverance, by some concessions and many threats, obtained at length a small body of troops to protect him and his colony at their first landing. But upon his return to Puerto Rico he found that the diseases of the climate had been fatal to several of his people, and that others, having got employment in that island, refused to follow him. With the handful that remained, he set sail and landed in Cumana. Ocampo had executed his commission in that province with such barbarous rage, having massacred many of the inhabitants, sent others in chains to Hispaniola, and forced the rest to fly for shelter to the woods, that the people of a small colony, which he had planted at a place which he named *Toledo*, were ready to perish for want in a desolated country. There, however, Las Casas was obliged to fix his residence, though deserted both by the troops appointed to protect him and by those under the command of Ocampo, who foresaw and dreaded the calamities to which he must be exposed in that wretched station. He made the best provision in his power for the safety and subsistence of his followers; but, as his utmost efforts availed little toward securing either the one or the other, he returned to Hispaniola, in order to solicit more effectual aid for the preservation of men who, from confidence in him, had ventured into a post of so much danger. Soon after his departure, the natives, having discovered the feeble and defenceless state of the Spaniards, assembled secretly, attacked them with

[1] Herrera, dec. 2, lib. x. c. 5.

the fury natural to men exasperated by many injuries, cut off a good number, and compelled the rest to fly in the utmost consternation to the island of Cubagua. The small colony settled there on account of the pearl-fishery, catching the panic with which their countrymen had been seized, abandoned the island, and not a Spaniard remained in any part of the continent, or adjacent islands, from the Gulf of Paria to the borders of Darien. Astonished at such a succession of disasters, Las Casas was ashamed to show his face after this fatal termination of all his splendid schemes. He shut himself up in the convent of the Dominicans at St. Domingo, and soon after assumed the habit of that order.[1]

"Though the expulsion of the colony from Cumana happened in the year one thousand five hundred and twenty-one, I have chosen to trace the progress of Las Casas's negotiations from the first rise to their final issue without interruption. His system was the object of long and attentive discussion; and though his efforts in behalf of the oppressed Americans, partly from his own rashness and imprudence, and partly from the malevolent opposition of his adversaries, were not attended with that success which he promised with too sanguine confidence, great praise is due to his humane activity, which gave rise to various regulations that were of some benefit to that unhappy people." —*History of America*, book iii.

"Cortes, astonished and enraged at their obstinacy, (the Tlascalans,) was going to overturn their altars and cast down their idols with the same violent hand as at Tempoalla, if Father Bartholomew de Olmedo, chaplain to the expedition, had not checked his inconsiderate impetuosity. He represented the imprudence of such an attempt in a large city newly reconciled and filled with people no less superstitious than warlike; he declared that the proceeding at Tempoalla had always appeared to him precipitate and unjust; that religion was not to be propagated by the sword or infidels to be converted by violence; that other weapons were to be employed in this ministry: patient instruction must enlighten the understanding, and pious example captivate the heart, before men could be induced to abandon error and embrace the truth.[2] . . . . At a time when the rights of conscience were little understood in the Christian world and the idea of toleration unknown, one is astonished to find a Spanish monk of the sixteenth century among the first advocates against persecution and in behalf of religious liberty. The remonstrances of an ecclesiastic no less respectable for wisdom than virtue had their proper weight with Cortes." —*Ibid.*, book iv.

Having shown that the depopulation of America could not be attributed to the policy of the Spanish government, Robertson adds the remarks which we have cited in the text, and which declare that destruction still less imputable to any intolerant measures of the Catholic missionaries. He says in another place, "When the zeal of Philip II. established the inquisition in America in the year 1570, the Indians were exempted from the jurisdiction of that severe tribunal, and still continue under the inspection of their diocesans."—*Ibid.*, book viii.

---

[1] Herrera. dec. 2, lib. x. c. 5; dec. 3, lib. ii. c. 3, 4, 5; Oviedo, *Hist.*, lib. xix c. 5; Gomara, c. 77; Davila Padilla, lib. i. c. 97; Remisal, *Hist. Gen.*, lib xi. c. 22, 23.

[2] B. Diaz, c. lxxvii. p. 54 . c. lxxxiii. p. 61.

If we examine attentively and impartially all the facts mentioned by the Presbyterian writer,—if at the same time we consider the number of hospitals established by the American Indians, the admirable missions of Paraguay, &c —we cannot resist the conviction that there never was a fouler calumny than that which attributes to Christianity the destruction of the aboriginal people of the New World.

The Irish Massacre

The Irish massacre, in 1641, was the result of national much more than of religious animosities. Oppressed for a long time by the English, robbed of their possessions, thwarted in their manners, customs, and religion, reduced almost to the condition of slaves by haughty and tyrannical masters, the Irish were at length driven to despair, and resolved upon acts of vengeance. They were not, however, the aggressors in this horrible tragedy, they were objects of violence themselves before they inflicted it upon others. Millon, in his *Recherches sur l'Irlande*, appended to his translation of *Arthur Young*, mentions some interesting facts which it may be useful to lay before the reader.

Some of the Irish having taken up arms in consequence of the oppressive system which weighed upon their unhappy country, a military force was ordered to march against them and to exterminate them "'The officers and soldiers,' says Castlehaven, 'without discriminating rebels from subjects, killed indiscriminately in many places men, women, and children, which exasperated the rebels, and induced them to commit in turn the same cruelties upon the English' It is evident, from the assertion of Lord Castlehaven, that the English were the aggressors by order of their commanders, and that the crime of the Irish was their having followed so barbarous an example[1]

"'I cannot believe,' adds Castlehaven, 'that there were at that time in Ireland, without the walls of the towns, a tenth part of the British subjects whom Temple and others mention to have been killed by the Irish. It is evident that he repeats two or three times, in different places, the names of persons and the same circumstances, and that he puts down some hundreds as having been massacred at that time who lived for several years afterward. It is therefore right that, notwithstanding the unfounded calumnies which some have circulated against the Irish, I should do justice to their nation, and declare that it was never the intention of their chiefs to authorize the cruelties which were practised among them.'

"The example of the Scotch in a great degree caused the Irish Catholics to rebel, who were already dissatisfied at seeing themselves on the eve of either renouncing their religion or quitting their country. A petition to this effect, signed by many thousand Protestants of Ireland and presented to the English parliament, justified their fears It had been already boasted of in public that before the end of the year there would not be a single Papist in Ireland, this produced its effect in England. The king having by a forced condescension surrendered his Irish affairs to the parliament, that tribunal made an ordinance on the 8th December which promised the entire extirpation of the Irish. It was decreed that Popery would not be any longer suffered in either Ireland or any other of his majesty's states. This parliament likewise granted, in Feb

[1] MacGe .h .a ı. p. 574

ruary following, to English adventurers, in consideration of a certain sum of money, two millions five hundred thousand acres of profitable lands in Ireland, without including bogs, woods, or barren mountains, and this at a time when the number of landed proprietors implicated in the insurrection was exceedingly small. To satisfy the engagements entered into with the English, as above, many honest men who never conspired against the king or state were to be dispossessed, &c.

"The Irish, particularly those of Ulster, had not forgotten the unjust confiscation of six whole counties within the forty years immediately preceding. They looked upon the new possessors as unjust possessors of the property of others, and . . . the grief of these old proprietors was changed into revenge; they seized upon the houses, the flocks, and the furniture of the new-comers, whose fine and commodious habitations, erected on the lands of the Irish, were destroyed either by force or by the flames[1]

"Such were the first hostilities committed by the Irish against the English. No blood had yet been spilled. The English were the first aggressors, and, their example having been too closely followed by the Catholics of Ulster, the disorder soon became general throughout the kingdom. It was a national quarrel between the Irish Catholics and the English Protestants, which led, in 1641, to a dreadful scene of bloodshed. MacGeoghegan asserts that six times as many Catholics as Protestants were killed on this occasion:—1. Because the former were scattered through the country and consequently more exposed to the rage of a licentious soldiery, while the latter were for the most part entrenched in fortified towns and castles, which protected them against the violence of a maddened populace. Those who resided in the country retired upon the first alarm to the cities and other places of security, where they remained during the war; some passed over to England or Scotland, so that very few perished, with the exception of those who had been overtaken by the first fury of the rebels. The country-people were put to the sword by the English soldiery without distinction of age or sex. 2. The number of Catholics who suffered death from the Cromwellians on the charge of participating in the massacre was so small that they could not have possibly put to death so great a number of Protestants.[2]

"So soon as the war had ended, courts of justice were held to convict the murderers of the Protestants. The whole who were convicted amounted to one hundred and forty Catholics, who were chiefly of the lower classes: though, their enemies being the judges, witnesses were suborned to prosecute, and several among those found guilty declared themselves innocent of the crimes for which they were sentenced to suffer. If similar investigations had taken place against the Protestants, and witnesses from among the Catholics admitted against them, nine parliamentarians out of every ten would have been inevitably convicted (before a fair tribunal) of murder upon the Catholics."[3]

Thus do we find that those sanguinary results which have been charged

[1] MacGeoghegan, p 575, &c. [2] Ibid, p. 576

[3] Millon, *Recherches sur l'Irlande* See MacGeoghegan *loc. cit.*

upon a religion of peace and humanity were produced by the passions of men, by their animosities and interests, often quite foreign to the question of religion. What would philosophy say if it were accused nowadays of having erected the scaffolds of Robespierre? Was it not in the name of philosophy that so many innocent victims were slaughtered, as the name of religion has been abused for the perpetration of crime? How many acts of cruelty and intolerance may be objected to those very Protestants who boast of being alone in practising the philosophy of Christianity! The penal statutes against the Irish Catholics, called *Laws of Discovery*, equal in oppression and surpass in immorality all the legislation with which Catholic countries have ever been reproached. By these laws,

1. All Roman Catholics were completely disarmed.
2. They were declared incompetent to acquire lands.
3. Entails were made void, and divided equally among the children.
4. If a child abjured the Catholic faith, he inherited the paternal estate, though the youngest of the family.
5. If the son abjured his religion, the father lost all control over his property, receiving only a pension from his estate, which fell to the son.
6. No Catholic could take a lease for more than thirty-one years.
7. Unless two-thirds of the yearly value were reserved, an informant could obtain the benefit of the lease.
8. A priest who celebrated mass was transported, and, if he returned, was hung.
9. If a Catholic owned a horse worth over five pounds sterling, it was confiscated to the benefit of the informer.
10. According to a regulation of Lord Hardwick, Catholics were declared incapable of lending money on mortgage.[1]

It is worthy of remark that this law was not passed till five or six years after the death of King William,—that is, when the disturbances in Ireland had ceased, and England had reached its climax of enlightenment, civilization, and prosperity. It must not be supposed that in those days of excitement, when the best men are sometimes led too far, the true members of the Catholic Church approved the excesses of the party that bore their name. The massacre of St. Bartholomew was a subject of tears even at the Court of Medici and in the chamber of Charles IX.

"I have been informed," says Brantome, "that at the massacre of St. Bartholomew, Queen Isabella, not being aware of what was going on, retired to her chamber as usual, and heard nothing of the event until the next morning. On learning it, she exclaimed, 'Alas! is my husband aware of this?' 'Yes, madam,' it was answered her, 'he directs the whole affair!' 'Oh! how is that?' she rejoined. 'What counsellors could have inspired him with such a design? O, my God, I beseech thee to forgive him; for, if thou dost not take pity on him, I fear much that this error will not be pardoned him;' and, immediately taking her book of devotions, she began to pray God with tears in her eyes."[2]

---

[1] *Travels of Arthur Young.*

[2] *Mémoires*, tome ii.

NOTE VV, (p. 632.)

"The summit of Mount St. Gothard," says Ramond,[1] "is a granite level, bare, and surrounded with rocks of moderate height and very irregular form, which bound the view on every side and confine it within the most frightful solitude. Three small lakes, and the gloomy asylum of the capuchin monks, are the only objects that break the monotony of this desert region, which presents not the slightest appearance of vegetation. The profound silence which reigns there is something new and surprising to those who come from the plains below. Not the least murmur is to be heard in the place. The wind in its course meets with no foliage; but, when violent, it makes a plaintive sound along the pointed rocks. In vain would the traveller hope, by ascending these cliffs, to obtain a view of some inhabited country. Below is seen but a confusion of rocks and torrents, while in the distance are discerned only barren peaks covered with eternal snows, piercing the clouds which float over the valleys and often conceal them under an impenetrable veil. Nothing beyond this reaches the eye, except a dark-blue sky, which, sinking far below the horizon, completes the picture on all sides, and appears like an immense sea enveloping this mass of mountains.

"The poor capuchins who reside at the asylum are during nine months of the year buried under the snow, which often accumulates, in one night, as high as the roof of their house and closes every entrance into the convent. In this case, they form an egress from the upper windows, which serve as doors. It is easy to conceive that they must frequently suffer from hunger and cold, and that, if any cenobites are entitled to assistance, *they* are assuredly of the number."[2]

Military hospitals trace their origin to the Benedictine monks. Every convent of that order supported a veteran soldier, and afforded him a retreat for the remainder of his life. By uniting these different benefactions in one, Louis XIV. established the *Hôtel des Invalides*.[3] Thus has the religion of peace opened an asylum also for our old warriors.

NOTE WW, (p. 667.)

It is very difficult to present an exact account of the colleges and hospitals, owing to the incompleteness of statistical and geographical works. Some give the population of a state, without mentioning the number of cities; others mention the number of parishes, omitting that of cities. The maps are covered with the names of towns, castles, and villages. The histories of particular provinces generally disregard statistical information, telling us only of the ancient wars of barons and of municipal rights. Ecclesiastical historians, also, are too circumscribed in their subjects, and dwell but little on facts of a gene-

---

[1] *Traduct. des Lettres de Coxe sur la Suisse.*

[2] Such is the dictate of humanity, which, however, seems to have been little understood by the radical government of Switzerland, when, a few years ago, it robbed the heroic monks of Mount St. Bernard of their revenues. T.

[3] A magnificent institution, among the principal monuments of Paris, where veteran and infirm soldiers are provided with every comfort. See Part 3, b. 1, ch. 6. T.

ral interest. The following are the results which we have been able to gather from our imperfect sources of information :—[1]

Extract from the Ecclesiastical portion of M. de Beaufort's Statistics.

France.—18 archbishoprics, 117 bishoprics, 34,498 parishes, 366,000 ecclesiastics, 36 academies, 24 universities.

Austria, (Hered.)—3 archbishoprics, 15 bishoprics, 6 universities, 6 colleges.

Tuscany.—3 archbishoprics, 2 bishoprics, 2 universities.

Russia.—30 archbishoprics and bishoprics, (Greek,) 18,319 parishes, 68,000 ecclesiastics, 4 universities.

Spain.—8 archbishoprics, 51 bishoprics, 19,683 parishes, 27 universities.

England.—2 archbishoprics, 25 bishoprics, 9684 parishes.

Ireland.—4 archbishoprics, 19 bishoprics, 2293 parishes.

Scotland.—13 synods, 98 presbyteries, 938 parishes, 4 universities.

Prussia.—1 Catholic bishop, 6 universities.

Portugal.—1 patriarch, 5 archbishoprics, 19 bishoprics, 3343 parishes, 2 universities.

Naples.—23 archbishoprics, 145 bishoprics, 1 university, and several colleges.

Sicily.—3 archbishoprics, 10 bishoprics, 4 universities.

Sardinia.—3 archbishoprics, 26 bishoprics, 3 universities.

Papal States.—3 archbishoprics, 5 bishoprics, 8 universities, and several colleges.

Sweden.—1 archbishopric, 14 bishoprics, 2538 parishes, 3 universities, 10 colleges.

Denmark.—12 bishoprics, 2 universities.

Poland.—2 archbishoprics, 6 bishoprics, 4 universities.

Venice.—1 patriarch, 4 archbishoprics, 31 bishoprics, 1 university.

Holland.—6 universities.

Switzerland.—4 bishoprics, 1 university.

Palatinate of Bavaria.—1 archbishopric, 4 bishoprics, 2 universities, 1 academy of sciences.

Saxony.—3 universities, 5 presbyterian colleges, 1 academy of sciences.

Hanover.—750 parishes, 1 university.

Wirtemberg.—Lutheran Consistory, 14 abbeys, 1 university, and several colleges.

Hesse-Cassel.—2 universities, 1 academy of sciences.

The word college in this enumeration is used in rather a vague sense.

---

[1] The statistics here given are far from being correct at the present day; but the vast increase which has taken place in the number of educational and charitable institutions corroborates the remarks of the author. T.

From the work of Helyot we have collected the following summary of the principal hospitals in Europe:—

Religious of St. Anthony Viennois.	
In France	
Italy	4
Germany	4
Hospitals unknown	
Canons, Regular, of Roncevaux.	
Roncevaux	1
Ostie	1
Several unknown.	
Order of the Holy Ghost.	
Rome	2
Bergerac	1
Troyes	1
Several unknown.	
Religious called Porte-Croix, Monasteries with Hospitals.	
Italy	200
France	7
Germany	9
Bohemia	15
Canons and Canonesses of St. James-of-the-Sword.	
Spain	20
Religious Women, Hospitalers of the Order of St. Augustin.	
Hôtel-Dieu, at Paris	1
Saint-Louis	1
Moulins	1
Brothers of Charity of St. John-of-God.	
Spain and Italy	18
France	24
Religious Women, Hospitalers of Charity of Our Lady.	
France	12
Religious Women, Hospitalers of Loche.	
France	18
Italy	12
Religious Women, Hospitalers of St. John of Jerusalem.	
France	2
	359

Brought forward	359
Daughters of Charity, founded by St. Vincent of Paul. France, Poland, and the Netherlands	286
Sisters Hospitalers of St. Martha. France	4
Canonesses Hospitalers. France	2
Filles-Dieu	2
Sisters Hospitalers. France	9
Third Order of St. Francis. France	5
Gray Sisters	23
Brugelettes and *Brothers Infirmarians.* Spain, Portugal, and Flanders	14
Sisters Hospitalers of St. Thomas of Villanova. France	14
Sisters of St. Joseph. France	8
Sisters of Miramion. Paris	3
Total of principal hospitals	729

It is obvious that Helyot refers only to the principal establishments served by the different religious orders, as no capital city is mentioned in this enumeration, except Paris, though it is certain that others contain from twenty to thirty hospitals. These central houses have their branches, which are indicated in most authors only by *etceteras.*

It is scarcely possible to state with certainty the number of colleges in Europe, as they are not mentioned by writers. We may observe that the religious of St. Basil, in Spain, have at least four in each province,—that all the Benedictine congregations applied themselves to the instruction of youth,—that the Jesuit provinces embraced all Europe,—that the universities had a great number of schools and colleges dependent on them,—and that we have undoubtedly made a very low estimate in computing the number of scholars under Christian instruction at three hundred thousand.

By an examination of the different geographies, particularly that of Guthrie, we reckon the number of cities in Europe at 3294, assigning one hospital to each:—

	Cities.
Norway	20
Denmark	31
Sweden	75
Russia	83
Scotland	103
England	552
Ireland	39
Spain	208
Portugal	51
Piedmont	37
Italian Republic	43
San Marino	1
Venetian States and Parma	23
Ligurian Republic	15
Republic of	2
Tuscany	22
Papal States	36
Naples	60
Sicily	17
Corsica and other islands	21
France, with its new territory	960
Prussia	30
Poland	40
Hungary	67
Transylvania	8
Gallicia	16
Swiss Republic	91
Germany	643
Total	3294

THE END.

CPSIA information can be obtained
at www.ICGtesting.com
Printed in the USA
LVOW03s2307130117
520954LV00023B/338/P